READER'S DELIGHT

200 plus World Famous PERSONALITIES

READER'S DELIGHT

AN IMPRINT OF RAMESH PUBLISHING HOUSE

NEW DELHI

Published by Alok Gupta for Reader's Delight
(An Imprint of Ramesh Publishing House)

Admin. Office:
12-H, New Daryaganj Road, Opp. Officers' Mess,
New Delhi-110002 ✆ 23275224, 23245124
E-mail: info@rameshpublishinghouse.com
Website: www.rameshpublishinghouse.com

Showroom:
- Balaji Market, New Delhi-6 ✆ 23253720, 23282525
- 4457, Nai Sarak, Delhi-6, ✆ 23918938

INDEMNIFICATION CLAUSE

- This book is being sold/distributed on the condition and understanding that the information given herein are merely for guidance and reference and must not be taken as authority, and neither the author nor the publishers individually or collectively, shall be responsible to indemnify the buyer/user/possessor of this book beyond the selling price of this book for any reason under any circumstances. If you do not agree to it, please do not buy/accept/use/possess this book.
- Though every care has been taken in printing this book, errors or ommissions might have crept inadvertently. The publishers shall be obliged if such error or ommission is brought to their notice.
- Subject to Delhi jurisdiction.

Book Code: A-35

ISBN: 978-93-86845-04-7

10th Revised Edition: June 2025

Price: ₹ 360/-

Printed at: Deepak Offset, Delhi

Preface

In this book, "200 plus World's Famous Personalities" we have presented biographies of more than 200 Great Personalities in alphabetical order and in great details with their memorable quotes. We have covered world's famous people from every walk of life, from politicians to entertainers, to scientists to artists. Reading these biographies can be inspiring for anybody, regardless of his or her field. Often, reading a book about someone who succeeded against the odds is all it takes to inspire your own feats of greatness.

As opposed to a profile or curriculum vitae, a biography develops a complex analysis of personality, highlighting different aspects of it and including intimate details of experiences. A biography is more than a list of impersonal facts like birth, education, work, relationships and death.

Biographies may be about other people, but readers will learn a lot about themselves in the subject matter. Because the nature of a biography is to give a person's complete story, very few started at the top. Their stories of achievement will often mirror a reader's own journey to their station in life.

From politics to playwrights, royals to republicans, find a life worth reading about the biographies of these great people. You can read about US Presidents from George Washington to Abraham Lincoln, or bring Shakespeare and Lata Mangesker back to life. Find out more about the men and women of science. The well-lived life is worth examining. You can simply impress your friends and family with your knowledge about these great people.

— Publisher

Contents

★★★

(Dr.) A.P.J. Abdul Kalam

(1931–2015)

Scientist & Ex-President of India

"Let us sacrifice our today so that our children can have a better tomorrow."

A. P. J. Abdul Kalam served the nation as President of India (July 2002 to July 2007). A notable scientist and an engineer, he is often referred to as the 'Missile Man of India'.

Born on October 15, 1931 at Rameshwaram in Tamil Nadu, Dr. Avul Pakir Jainulabdeen Abdul Kalam, specialized in Aeronautical Engineering from Madras Institute of Technology. Dr. Kalam made significant contribution as Project Director to develop India's first indigenous Satellite Launch Vehicle (SLV-III), which successfully injected the Rohini satellite in the near earth orbit in July 1980 and made India an exclusive member of the Space Club. He was responsible for the evolution of the Indian Space Research Organisation's (ISRO) launch vehicle programme, particularly, the Polar Satellite Launch Vehicle (PSLV) configuration.

After working for two decades in ISRO and mastering launch vehicle technologies, Dr. Kalam took up the responsibility of developing Indigenous Guided Missiles at Defence Research and Development Organisation as the Chief Executive of Integrated Guided Missile Development Programme (IGMDP). He developed and operationalised AGNI and PRITHVI missiles and for building indigenous capability in critical technologies through networking of multiple institutions. He worked as the Scientific Adviser to Defence Minister and Secretary, Department of Defence Research & Development from July 1992 to December 1999. During this period, he led to the weaponisation of strategic missile systems and the Pokhran-II nuclear tests in collaboration with the Department of Atomic Energy, which made India a nuclear weapon state. He also gave thrust to self-reliance in defence systems by progressing multiple development tasks and mission projects such as Light Combat Aircraft.

As Chairman of Technology Information, Forecasting and Assessment Council (TIFAC), and as an eminent scientist, he led the country with the help of 500 experts to arrive at Technology Vision 2020 giving a road map for transforming India from the present developing status to a developed nation. Dr. Kalam has served as the Principal Scientific Advisor to the Government of India, in the rank of Cabinet Minister, from November 1999 to November 2001 and evolved policies, strategies and missions for many development applications.

Dr. Abdul Kalam was also the Chairman, Ex-officio, of the Scientific Advisory Committee to the Cabinet (SAC-C). He piloted India Millennium Mission 2020. He took up academic pursuit as Professor, Technology and Societal Transformation at Anna University, Chennai in November 2001, and was involved in teaching and research tasks. Above all, he took up a mission to ignite the young minds for national development by meeting high school students across the country.

Dr. Kalam was one of the most distinguished scientists of India with the unique honour of receiving doctorates from 30 universities and institutions. He had been awarded the coveted civilian awards -

Padma Bhushan (1981) and Padma Vibhushan (1990) and the highest civilian award, Bharat Ratna (1997). He was a recipient of several other awards and fellow of many professional institutions. Dr. Abdul Kalam served as the 11th President of India from July 25, 2002 to 2007. His focus was on transforming India into a developed nation by 2020.

On April 29, 2009, he became the first Asian to be bestowed with the Hoover Medal, America's top engineering prize, for his outstanding contribution to public service. In 2011, he was honoured Doctor of Science by S. Gujarati University and IEEE honourship.

In May 2011, Kalam launched his mission for the youth of the nation called the What Can I Give Movement with a central theme to defeat corruption. A.P.J. Abdul Kalam's 79th birthday was recognised as World Students' Day by United Nations. He had also received honorary doctorates from 40 universities.

In his literary pursuit four of his books - "India 2020 - A Vision for the New Millennium" (1998), "Wings of Fire" (1999), "Ignited Minds - Unleashing the power within India" (2002) and "My journey: Transforming Dreams into Actions (2013)" have become household names in India and among the Indian nationals abroad. These books have been translated in many Indian languages.

Dr. Kalam died in Shillong on July 27, 2015 while delivering a lecture. We will never forget his contribution in the making of modern India.

❑❑❑

A.R. Rahman

(1966)

Musical Maestro

"What cannot be put into words can be expressed through music."

Allah Rakha Rahman, is an Oscar, Padma Bhushan and Grammy Award winner Indian film composer, record producer, musician and singer. This genius with his exceptional talent has reached heights of success that people of his age can only dream of. Even then this small man remains humble and credits all his inspiration and success to Allah.

Rahman made his debut in 1992 with Mani Ratnam's Tamil movie, *Roja* (Rose), which was subsequently dubbed into many languages including Hindi. He is a recipient of the Padma Shri, which is one of India's highest civilian national honours.

The musical maestro of Indian Cinema was born on January 6, 1966 in Madras, to a musically affluent family. He was born as A. S. Dileep Kumar to parents K. A. Sekhar, a music composer and mother Kasturi. He came to be known as A. R. Rahman later when the family converted to Islam. Rahman started learning piano at the tender age of four. He lost his father during his childhood. As a result, the pressure of supporting the family fell on young Rahman.

At the age of 11, he joined Illaiyaraja's troupe as a keyboardist. He also played on the orchestra of M. S.Vishwanathan and Ramesh Naidu and accompanied Zakir Hussain and Kunnakudi Vaidyanathan on world tours. The experience allowed him to obtain a scholarship at Trinity College of Music at Oxford University, where he received a degree in Western Classical Music.

He has done jingles for popular ads like Parry's, Leo Coffee, Boost, Titan, Premier Pressure Cooker, Asian Paints, etc. Rahman went on to compose more than 300 jingles and received awards and recognition for his work and he continued in advertising for five years.

In 1989, he started a small studio of his own, called Panchathan Record Inn, attached to his house, where he began experimenting in sound engineering, design and production. At first he was, hesitant about composing music for the Indian film industry, primarily because most film makers at the time used songs as "fillers" - a means by which the audience was given a break from the movie's plot.

In 1991, director Mani Ratnam, approached him and offered job as composer of music for his upcoming film *Roja*, at a price of ₹ 25,000. Rahman got the national award for the best music director that year. From then, there was no looking back for him. He got offers from a lot of directors of south and the Hindi film industry. *Rangeela* and later *Mumbai* established his popularity in the north too. Rahman's music wave arrived with a big bang in the tinsel world with sales of more than 40 million albums over a period of 3 years. He has also dabbled in playback singing with songs like 'Hamma Hamma' in *Mumbai*, 'Dil Se Re' in *Dil Se* etc.

Apart from films, Rahman has also done compositions for patriotic albums like 'Vande Mataram' a tribute to the motherland released simultaneously in 28 countries across the world. He received the Padmashree from the government of India in 2000. He has received many honorary awards for his contributions to global music. In 2009, for his score of many Oscar winning movie 'Slumdog Millionaire', Rahman won the Critics' Choice Award, the Golden Globe Award for Best Original Score, the BAFTA Award for Best Film Music, and two Academy Awards for Best Original Music, Score and Best Original Song for 'Jai Ho'. He is the first Indian to win two Oscars in one year.

He received the Padma Bhushan Award in 2010. Rahman won Lifetime Achievement Award in Dubai International Film Festival in December 2011. He is the first musician to win this award. On 7 May 2012, he was conferred Honorary Doctorate from the Miami University, Ohio. He also received a Christmas card from the US President's family and an invitation for the dinner at White House.

In 2013, Rahman had two releases: *Raanjhanaa* and *Maryan.* Both were successful, with the former nominated for a number of awards and the latter the iTunes India Tamil Album of 2013. In 2014, his first release for the year was the Imtiaz Ali's road movie *Highway* which garnered positive reviews. His next were the scores for the two back to back Hollywood films, *Million Dollar Arm* and *The Hundred Foot Journey,* both of which got into the contended list for the original score category nomination at the Oscars.

On 15 August, 2018, Rahman appeared as the host in the 5-episode series of Amazon Prime Video titled "Harmony". On 16 January, 2019, Maruti Suzuki India Limited launched NEXA Music, a platform where 24 artists will be picked and mentored by Rahman and Clinton Cerejo to create international music in India. Rahman also appeared as a judge on The Voice. The show began airing on 3 February, 2019 on StarPlus.

A.R. Rahman won the Best Music Direction - Background Score at the 70th National Film Awards (announced on 16 August 2024) for his work on "Ponniyin Selvan: Part I". This marks his seventh National Award, making him the music director with the most wins in India.

❑❑❑

Abraham Lincoln

(1809–1865)

Politician

"Every blade of grass is a study; and to produce two, where there was but one, is both a profit and a pleasure."

Abraham Lincoln often called Abe Lincoln, was an American politician who served as the 16th President of the United States (1861–1865), and as the first President from the Republican Party. He is best known for ending slavery and preserving the Union by overseeing the war effort during the American Civil War.

Lincoln was born in Hardin (now Larue) on February 12, 1809. His father, Thomas Lincoln, was a migratory carpenter and farmer, nearly always poverty-stricken. His mother, Nancy Hanks, is less known to the world, who died in 1818, after the family had settled in the Spencer County. Abraham had almost no formal schooling—the scattered weeks of school attendance in Kentucky and Indiana amounted to less than a year; but he taught himself, reading and rereading a small stock of books.

In the year 1831, he began by working in a store and managing a mill in the village of New Salem. He won much popularity among the inhabitants of the frontier town by his great strength and his flair for storytelling, but most of all by his strength of character. His sincerity and capability won respect that was strengthened by his ability to hold his own in the roughest society. He was chosen the captain of a volunteer company gathered for the Black Hawk War (1832), but the company did not see any battle.

When Lincoln returned to New Salem, he became a partner in a grocery store but its business failed, leaving him with a heavy burden of debt. He became a surveyor for a time, and was even a village postmaster. He did various odd jobs, including rail splitting. All the while he sought to improve his education and studied law.

Finally, in 1834, Lincoln achieved success when he was elected to the state legislature, in which he served four successive terms and achieved prominence as a Whig. In 1836, he obtained his licence as an attorney, and the next year, he moved to Springfield, where he became a law partner of John T. Stuart. Lincoln's practice steadily increased. That first partnership was succeeded by many others.

On November 4, 1842, at the age of 33, Lincoln married Mary Todd, who was from a prominent family from Kentucky. The couple had four sons.

Abraham continued his interest in politics and entered on the national scene by serving one term in Congress (1847–49). He remained obscure, however, and his attacks as a Whig on the motives behind the Mexican War (though he voted for war supplies) seemed unpatriotic to his constituents. So he lost popularity at home. Lincoln worked hard for the election of the Whig candidate, Zachary Taylor, in 1848, but when he was not rewarded with the office he desired (Commissioner of the General Land Office), he decided to retire from politics and return to the practice of law.

Lincoln emerged again into politics in 1854, when he was caught up in the rising quarrel over slavery. He firmly opposed the policy of Stephen A. Douglas and particularly, the Kansas-Nebraska Act. He became a Republican in 1856. He quickly came to the fore in the party as a moderate opponent of slavery who could win both the abolitionists and the conservative free-staters, and at the Republican National Convention of 1856, he was prominent as a possible vice presidential candidate. Two years later, he was nominated by the Republican Party to oppose Douglas in the Illinois senatorial race.

As time passed, Lincoln became more and more the object of adulation; a full-blown "Lincoln legend" appeared. He stands out as a statesman of noble vision, great humanity, and remarkable political skill.

On the night of April 14, 1865, came the shocking news that Lincoln had been shot by actor John Wilkes Booth when he was attending a performance at Ford's Theatre. The next morning, Lincoln died. His death was turned into a worldwide grief even among those who had been his opponents, and many considered him a martyr.

❑❑❑

Arvind Kejriwal

(1968)

Politician

"Education cannot be a matter of charity,
Education has to be a matter of Right."

That was the year 1968, 16th day of the month of August, that happiness and cheer spread in the household of Mr. Govind Ram Kejrwal in Siwan, Haryana on the arrival of a boy.

That he would live not only for his own family and its welfare but for the happiness and welfare of the people of the state (Delhi) of which, he would be appointed the Chief Minister of and the boy, who would rise to democratic heights in quick time and would create an indelible mark for his family and would create a name for himself across the world in just 3 years of time (i.e. from 2012 through 2015) because of his unique and wholesale electoral gains and how he won hearts and favours among the masses.

Learning genius as he used to be since early age, with mind and senses pretty sharp to grasp topics and chapters quickly and had always stood meritorious. The trend or say habit to outperform others, continued till graduation and till post graduation, when he got enrolment into IIT Kharagpur and got into the stream of mechanical engineering.

Following his mechanical course completion, he got a breakthrough in Tata Steel, in 1989 and he was posted at Jamshedpur. In 1992, he quit job to take a dip into social work by joining hands with Missionaries of charity in Kolkata, Ramakrishna mission in Northeast and the Nehru Yuva Sangathan. In 1995, he managed to get into the payroll of IRS, Indian Revenue Service. In December 1999, while still in IRS service, he laid the foundation of an NGO named as Parivartan and Manish Sisodiya was also a part of this massive move. The objectives were to take grievances about public works social welfare schemes income tax, electricity etc. In 1991, when RTI act was unveiled, he helped solving people's problems with this.

By the year 2006, he had been well settled in IRS department and had excelled to become joint Commissioner of Income Tax, in New Delhi, but he relinquished this job as well. In the same year, he was bestowed with Raman Magsaysay Award for Emergent Leadership, as he helped people in a large number and also contributed to the massive spread of RTI movement in the most energetic manner. In 2011, he got into the Anna Hazare group and had been a front-face of movement and social awareness campaign about Jan Lok Pal Bill and the effort soon got popular pan India. In 2012, the political party AAP (Aam Admi Party) was formally unveiled. In 2013, AAP fights Delhi Assembly elections and bags 28 seats but still managed government formation with the seat-help extended from Congress party. In 2014, he stepped down from seat as he was sad that Jan Lok Pal Bill couldn't be tabled in assembly. In 2014 Lok Sabha elections, he decided to stand against PM candidate of BJP Narender Damodar Das Modi from Varanasi, but was beaten heavily, though AAP won 4 seats in Punjab.

In 2015, AAP registered a massive win in state polls of Delhi and got 67 seats out of 70. From there on, they started initiating new programes for public welfare. In February of 2017, AAP fought election in Punjab and Goa and bagged 20 seats in Punjab but 0 in

Goa. In April 2017, BJP defeated AAP in civic elections. In 2019, Lok Sabha elections were held whereby AAP could not win at any of 7 seats. On February 11, 2020, AAP again came to power in Delhi state in assembly polls by winning 62 seats out of 70.

Mohalla Clinics that are primary health centres in Delhi was first set up by the Aam Aadmi Party government in 2015, and as of 2018, 187 such clinics have been set up across the state and served more than 2 million residents. Mohalla Clinics offer a basic package of essential health services including medicines, diagnostics, and consultation free of cost. These clinics serve as the first point of contact for the population, offer timely services, and reduce the load of referrals to secondary and tertiary health facilities in the state. Beginning in October 2019, New Delhi began rolling out free bus transit for women on the Delhi Transport Corporation, with women travelling for free when using pink tickets carrying a message from Kejriwal. He has been criticised for his controversial remarks over Biharis and "outsiders". Shunglu Committee submitted a report to LG of Delhi raising questions over decisions of Government of Delhi.

Outside Delhi, his party registered another major victory in 2022 Punjab Legislative Assembly election. His party was defeated in the 2025 Delhi Legislative Assembly election, and he even lost his seat against Parvesh Verma by a margin of over 4,000 votes from the New Delhi Assembly constituency.

❑❑❑

Adolf Hitler

(1889–1945)

Dictator

"If freedom is short of weapons,
we must compensate with willpower."

Adolf Hitler, a charismatic, Austrian-born demagogue, rose to power in Germany during the 1920s and early 1930s at a time of social, political, and economic upheaval. When he failed to take power by force in 1923, he eventually won it by democratic means. When he came into power, he eliminated all opposition and launched an ambitious programme of world domination and elimination of the Jews.

Adolf Hitler was born on April 20, 1889, as the fourth child of Alois Schickelgruber and Klara Hitler in the Austrian town of Braunau, near German border. His father was fifty-one when Hitler was born. He was short-tempered, strict and brutal. He frequently hit the young Hitler. Alois had an elder son from a previous marriage but he had ended up in jail for theft. Alois was determined that Hitler was not going to go down the same way, and hence, he brought up Hitler in a brutal way. Hitler quit school at the age of 16, partially as a result of ill health and partially because of his poor school work.

He spent six years in Vienna, living on a small legacy from his father and an orphan's pension. In May 1913, Hitler, seeking to avoid military service, left Vienna for Munich, the capital of Bavaria. In January, a notice for his arrest came from the Austrian government. Hitler was arrested from his home and taken to the Austrian Consulate. Upon reporting to Salzburg for duty, he was found unfit and too weak to bear arms.

When World War I was about to begin, Hitler submitted a petition to get enlisted in the Bavarian army. Many a times, Hitler escaped death, and was awarded two Iron Crosses for bravery, and he rose to the rank of lance corporal.

Hitler was recruited to join a military intelligence unit after the World War I. He was assigned to keep tabs on the German Worker's Party. Hitler saw this party as a vehicle to reach his political ends. His blossoming hatred of the Jews became part of the organisation's political platform. Advertising for the party's meetings appeared in anti-Semitic newspapers. The turning point of Hitler's mesmerising oratorical career occurred at one such meeting held on October 16, 1919.

Hitler drafted a party programme consisting of twenty-five points, with the assistance of party staff. This platform was presented at a public meeting on February 24, 1920, with over 2,000 eager participants. Versailles Treaty was among the 25 points which were: confiscating war profits, expropriating land without compensation for use by the state, revoking civil rights for the Jews, and expelling those Jews who had immigrated into Germany after the war began.

Hitler held a rally in Munich on November 8, 1923, and announced a revolution. He was arrested for the crime of conspiracy to commit treason, and was imprisoned for five years at Landsberg. Hitler served only nine months of his five-year term and was released on December 20, 1924.

After his release in 1924, Hitler gained popular support by attacking the Treaty of Versailles and prom...ng Pan-Germanism, antisemitism, and anti-communism with charismatic oratory and Nazi propaganda. After his appointment as chancellor in 1933, he transformed the Weimar Republic into the Third Reich, a single-party dictatorship based on the totalitarian and autocratic ideology of Nazism.

Hitler's aim was to establish a new order of absolute Nazi German hegemony in continental Europe. To this end, his foreign and domestic policies had the aim of seizing Lebensraum ("living space") for the Germanic people. He directed the rearmament of Germany and the invasion of Poland by the Wehrmacht in September 1939, resulting in the outbreak of World War II in Europe. Under Hitler's rule, in 1941 German forces and their European allies occupied most of Europe and North Africa. In 1943, Germany was forced onto the defensive and suffered a series of escalating defeats. By late 1944, both the Red Army and the Western Allies were advancing into Germany. Recognising the strength and determination of the Red Army, Hitler decided to use his remaining mobile reserves against the American and British troops, which he perceived as far weaker, but the offensive failed. In the final days of the war, during the losing Battle of Berlin in 1945, after midnight of 29 April, Hitler married his long-time partner, Eva Braun, but on 30 April 1945, the two committed suicide to avoid capture by the Red Army which was closing in, and their corpses were burned. Berlin surrendered on May 2, 1945.

Hitler's aggressive foreign policy is considered to be the primary cause of the outbreak of World War II in Europe. His antisemitic policies and racially motivated ideology resulted in the death of at least 5.5 million Jews, and millions of other people whom he and his followers deemed racially inferior. Hitler left Germany devastated; his legacy is the memory of one of the most dreadful tyrannies of modern times.

Agatha Christie

(1890–1976)

Author

"Invention, in my opinion, arises directly from idleness, possibly also from laziness to save oneself trouble."

Agatha Christie is known throughout the world as the 'queen of crime'. Her books have sold over a billion copies in the English language with another billion in 44 other foreign languages. She is the most widely published author of all times in any language, out-sold by only the Bible and Shakespeare. Agatha Christie is the author of 79 crime novels and a short story collection, 19 plays, and 6 novels written under the name of Mary Westmacott.

She was born on September 15, 1890 as Agatha Mary Clarissa Miller in Torquay, Devon, to an American father and a British mother. Agatha was the youngest of three children in a conservative, well-to-do family. Taught at home by a governess and tutor, as a child, Agatha Christie never attended school. However, at the age of sixteen, she was sent to school in Paris where she studied singing and playing the piano. Christie was an accomplished pianist but her stage fright and shyness prevented her from pursuing a career in music.

In 1914, when Agatha turned 24, she married Colonel Archibald Christie, an aviator in the Royal Flying Corps. The marriage turned out to be an unsuccessful one. The couple had one daughter, Rosalind Hicks, and she got divorced in 1928.

During World War I, Agatha worked at a hospital as a nurse, a job that also influenced her work. It was while working there that Agatha Christie first came up with the idea of writing a detective novel. Although it was completed in a year, it was not published until 1920, five years later.

Christie wrote more than 30 novels featuring Poirot. Among the most popular were *The Murder of Roger Ackroyd* (1926), *Murder on the Orient Express* (1934), and *Death on the Nile* (1937).

In December 1926, she disappeared for several days, causing quite a storm in the press. Her car was found in a chalk pit. She was eventually found staying at a hotel in Harrogate, where she claimed to have suffered amnesia due to a nervous breakdown following the death of her mother and her husband's infidelity.

In 1930, Christie married a Roman Catholic (despite her divorce), Sir Max Mallowan, a young archaeologist whom she met on a trip to Mesopotamia. Mallowan was 14 years younger than Agatha, and her travels with him contributed the background to several of her novels set in the Middle East. Their marriage was happy in the early years, and endured despite Mallowan's many affairs in later life, notably with Barbara Parker, whom he married in 1977, the year after Agatha's death. In 1971, she was awarded the high honour of becoming a Dame of the British Empire.

At the height of her career, Christie wrote two novels that she intended to be published after her death. They were the last cases of her two great detectives, Hercule Poirot and Jane Marple - respectively, *Curtain* and *Sleeping Murder*. When she wrote the novels, Christie had not thought that she would live so long. Following the success of the film version of *Murder on the Orient Express* in 1974, Christie authorised the release of *Curtain*, in which Poirot is killed. As Margery Allingham said: Christie has "entertained more people for more hours at a time than any other writer of her generation."

Agatha Christie breathed her last on January 12, 1976, at the age of 85 from natural causes, at Winterbrook House, Cholsey near Wallingford, Oxford shire. She was buried at St. Mary's Churchyard in Cholsey, Oxon. Mallowan died two years later.

Christie's only child, Rosalind Hicks, died on October 28, 2004, also aged 85, from natural causes. Christie's grandson, Mathew Prichard, now owns the royalties of his grandmother's works.

❑❑❑

Allu Arjun

(1982)

Actor

"If we give something positive to others, it will return to us. If we give negative, that negativity will be returned."

Allu Arjun, born on April 8, 1982, in Chennai, Tamil Nadu, is one of the most celebrated actors in Telugu cinema. He hails from a prominent film family; his father, Allu Aravind, is a renowned film producer, and his grandfather, Allu Ramalingaiah, was a legendary comedian in Telugu cinema. His uncle is megastar Chiranjeevi, and his cousins Ram Charan and Varun Tej are also prominent actors in the Telugu film industry. Arjun grew up in Chennai before moving to Hyderabad, where he completed his schooling at St. Patrick's School. He later earned a degree in Business Administration from MSR College, Hyderabad.

From a young age, Allu Arjun showed a deep passion for dance and acting. His talent was evident early on, and he made his first screen appearance as a child artist in the 1985 film *Vijetha*. He later appeared in a minor role in *Daddy* (2001), starring Chiranjeevi. His official debut as a lead actor came in 2003 with *Gangotri*, directed by K. Raghavendra Rao. Though the film received mixed reviews, Arjun's performance was praised, and he won the CineMAA Award for Best Male Debut.

Arjun's breakthrough came in 2004 with *Arya*, directed by Sukumar. His role as a carefree and selfless lover won hearts, making him an overnight sensation. The film was a blockbuster, and he received his first Nandi Special Jury Award. Following this, he continued to deliver box-office hits, including *Bunny* (2005), *Desamuduru* (2007), and *Parugu* (2008), the last of which won him his first Filmfare Award for Best Actor – Telugu.

Between 2010 and 2020, Allu Arjun cemented his position as one of the top actors in Tollywood. He showcased his versatility in films like *Vedam* (2010), where he played a slum dweller, earning widespread acclaim. His high-energy performances in *Julayi* (2012), *Race Gurram* (2014), and *Sarrainodu* (2016) further solidified his stardom. He became known for his exceptional dance skills, stylish looks, and ability to portray a wide range of characters. In 2020, he starred in *Ala Vaikunthapurramuloo*, which became one of the highest-grossing Telugu films of all time. His performance, combined with the film's chartbuster songs, earned him another Filmfare Award for Best Actor.

Arjun's most defining moment came with *Pushpa : The Rise* (2021), directed by Sukumar. Playing the role of Pushpa Raj, a red sandalwood smuggler, he transformed himself physically and delivered one of his career-best performances. The film became a pan-Indian blockbuster, breaking box-office records and earning him the National Film Award for Best Actor in 2023, making him the first Telugu actor to win this honor. His dialogues, mannerisms, and the famous "Thaggede Le" gesture became a cultural phenomenon across India.

Beyond acting, Allu Arjun is known for his philanthropy and entrepreneurial ventures. He has been involved in numerous charitable activities, including blood donation drives and supporting underprivileged children. During the COVID-19 pandemic, he contributed generously to relief efforts. He also ventured into business by launching *800 Jubilee*, a luxury nightclub in Hyderabad.

Allu Arjun married Sneha Reddy on March 6, 2011, in a grand ceremony attended by celebrities and politicians. The couple has two children, Allu Ayaan (born in 2014) and Allu Arha (born in 2016). Arjun often shares glimpses of his family life on social media,. and his daughter, Arha, made her acting debut in *Shaakuntalam* (2023).

❑❑❑

Alexander Graham Bell

(1847–1922)

Scientist and Inventor

"What this power is I cannot say.
All I know is that it exists."

Alexander Graham Bell was a Scottish-born American scientist and inventor, most famous for his pioneering work on the development of the telephone.

Bell was born on 3 March 1847 in Edinburgh and educated there and in London. His father and grandfather were both authorities on elocution and at the age of 16, Bell himself began researching the mechanics of speech. In 1870, Bell emigrated with his family to Canada, and the following year he moved to the United States to teach. There he pioneered a system called visible speech, developed by his father, to teach deaf-mute children. In 1872, Bell founded a school in Boston to train teachers of the deaf. The school subsequently became part of Boston University, where Bell was appointed professor of vocal physiology in 1873. He became a naturalised U.S. citizen in 1882.

Bell had long been fascinated by the idea of transmitting speech, and by 1875 had come up with a simple receiver that could turn electricity into sound. Others were working along the same lines, including an Italian-American Antonio Meucci. However, Bell was granted a patent for the telephone on 7 March 1876 and it developed quickly. Within a year the first telephone exchange was built in Connecticut and the Bell Telephone Company was created in 1877, with Bell the owner of a third of the shares, quickly making him a wealthy man.

Bell might easily have been content with the success of his telephone invention. His many laboratory notebooks demonstrate, however, that he was driven by a genuine and rare intellectual curiosity that kept him regularly searching, striving, and wanting always to learn and to create. He would continue to test out new ideas through a long and productive life. He would explore the realm of communications as well as engage in a great variety of scientific activities involving kites, airplanes, tetrahedral structures, sheep-breeding, artificial respiration, desalinization and water distillation, and hydrofoils.

With the enormous technical and later financial success of his telephone invention, Bell's future was secure, and he was able to arrange his life so that he could devote himself to his scientific interests. Toward this end, in 1881, he used the $10,000 award for winning France's Volta Prize to set up the Volta Laboratory in Washington, D.C. A believer in scientific teamwork, Bell worked with two associates, his cousin Chichester Bell and Charles Sumner Tainter, at the Volta Laboratory. Their experiments soon produced such major improvements in Thomas Edison's phonograph that it became commercially viable. After 1885, when he first visited Nova Scotia, Bell set up another laboratory there at his estate, Beinn Bhreagh, near Baddeck, where he would assemble other teams of bright young engineers to pursue new and exciting ideas.

Among one of his first innovations after the telephone was the "photophone," a device that enabled sound to be transmitted on a beam of light. Bell and his assistant, Charles Sumner Tainter, developed the photophone using a sensitive selenium crystal and a mirror that would vibrate in response to a sound. In 1881, they successfully sent a photophone message over 200 yards from one building to another. Bell regarded the photophone as "the greatest invention I have ever made; greater than the telephone." Bell's invention reveals the principle upon which today's laser and fiber optic communication systems are founded, though it would take the development of several modern technologies to realize it fully.

Alexander Graham Bell died peacefully, with his wife Mabel by his side, in Cape Breton Island, Nova Scotia, Canada, on August 2, 1922. The entire telephone system was shut down for one minute in tribute to his life. Within a few months, Mabel also passed away. Bell's contribution to the modern world and its technologies was enormous.

Months before he died, Bell told a reporter, "There cannot be mental atrophy in any person who continues to observe, to remember what he observes, and to seek answers for his unceasing hows and whys about things."

❑❑❑

Alfred Nobel

(1833–1896)

Scientist

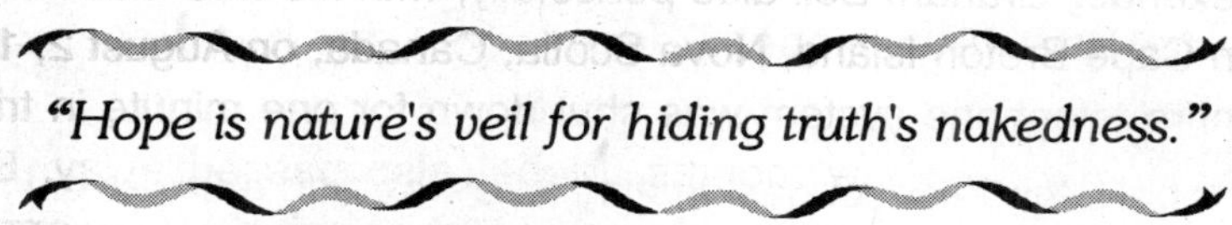

Alfred Bernhard Nobel was a Swedish chemist, engineer, innovator, and armaments manufacturer. He is the inventor of dynamite. Nobel also owned Bofors, which he had redirected from its previous role as primarily an iron and steel producer to a major manufacturer of cannon and other armaments. He held more than 350 different patents, dynamite being the most famous.

He was the third son of Immanuel Nobel and Andriette Ahlsell Nobel. Through his father he was a descendant of the famous Swedish scientist Olaus Rudbeck. Born in Stockholm on 21 October 1833, he went with his family to Saint Petersburg in 1842, where his father (who had invented modern plywood) started a "torpedo" works. Alfred studied chemistry with Professor Nikolai Nikolaevich Zinin. When Alfred was 18, he went to the United States to study chemistry for four years and worked for a short period under John Ericsson, who designed the American Civil War ironclad USS Monitor.

Though he remained unmarried, he had at least three loves. His first love was in Russia with a girl named Alexandra, who rejected his proposal. In 1876 Austro-Bohemian Countess Bertha Kinsky became Alfred Nobel's secretary. But after only a brief stay she left him to marry her previous lover, Baron Arthur Gundaccar von Suttner. Though her personal contact with Alfred Nobel had been brief, she corresponded with him until his death in 1896, and it is believed that she was a major influence in his decision to include a peace prize among those prizes provided in his will. Bertha von Suttner was awarded the 1905 Nobel Peace prize, 'for her sincere peace activities'.

Nobel's third and longest-lasting love was with a flower girl named Sofie Hess from Vienna. This liaison lasted for 18 years and in many of the exchanged letters, Nobel addressed his love as 'Madame Sofie Nobel'.

He had not only a scientific temperament but he gained proficiency in six languages: Swedish, French, Russian, English, German and Italian. He also developed literary skills to write poetry in English. His *Nemesis*, a prose tragedy in four acts about Beatrice Cenci, partly inspired by Percy Bysshe Shelley's *The Cenci*, was printed while he was dying.

During his research Nobel found that when nitroglycerin was incorporated in an absorbent inert substance like *kieselguhr* (diatomaceous earth) it became safer and more convenient to handle, and this mixture he patented in 1867 as 'dynamite'.

Nobel later on combined nitroglycerin with various nitrocellulose compounds, similar to collodion, but settled on a more efficient recipe combining another nitrate explosive, and obtained a transparent, jelly-like substance, which was a more powerful explosive than dynamite. 'Gelignite', or blasting gelatin, as it was named, was patented in 1876; and was followed by a host of similar combinations, modified by the addition of potassium nitrate and various other substances. Gelignite was more stable, transportable and conveniently formed to fit into bored holes, like those used in drilling and mining, than the previously used compounds and was adopted as the standard technology for mining in the Age of Engineering bringing Nobel a great amount of financial success.

In 1888, Alfred's brother Ludvig died while visiting Cannes and a French newspaper erroneously published Alfred's obituary. It condemned him for his invention of dynamite and is said to have brought about his decision to leave a better legacy after his death. The obituary stated *Le marchand de la mort est mort* ("The merchant of death is dead") and went on to say, "Dr. Alfred Nobel, who became rich by finding ways to kill more people faster than ever before, died yesterday." Alfred was disappointed with what he read and concerned with how he would be remembered. On 27 November 1895, at the Swedish-Norwegian Club in Paris, Nobel signed his last will and testament and set aside the bulk of his estate to establish the Nobel Prizes, to be awarded annually without distinction of nationality. He died of a stroke on 10 December 1896 at Sanremo, Italy. After taxes and bequests to individuals, Nobel's gave 31,225,000 Swedish kronor (equivalent to about 1.8 billion kronor or 250 million US dollars in 2008) to fund the prizes.

The first three of these prizes are awarded for eminence in physical science, in chemistry and in medical science or physiology; the fourth is for literary work "in an ideal direction"and the fifth prize is to be given to the person or society that renders the greatest service to the cause of international fraternity, in the suppression or reduction of standing armies, or in the establishment or furtherance of peace congresses.

Alfred Nobel was buried in Norra begravningsplatsen in Stockholm.

Albert Einstein

(1879–1955)

Physicist

"The secret to creativity is knowing how to hide your sources."

Albert Einstein is a world renowned German-American physicist. He developed the Special and General Theories of Relativity which along with Quantum Mechanics is the foundation of modern physics.

Albert Einstein was born at Ulm, in Wurttemberg, Germany, on March 14, 1879. Six weeks later, the family moved to Munich and he began his schooling there at the Luitpold Gymnasium. Later, they moved to Italy and Albert continued his education at Aarau, Switzerland. In 1896, he entered the Swiss Federal Polytechnic School in Zurich to be trained as a teacher in physics and mathematics. In 1901, the year he gained his diploma, he acquired Swiss citizenship and, as he was unable to find a teaching post, he accepted a position as technical assistant in the Swiss Patent Office. In 1905, he obtained his doctorate degree.

During his stay at the Patent Office, and in his spare time, he produced much of his remarkable work and in 1908, he was appointed as the Privatdozent in Berne. In 1909, Einstein became Professor Extraordinary at Zurich, and in 1911, Professor of Theoretical Physics at Prague, returning to Zurich in the following year to fill a similar post. In 1914, he was appointed Director of the Kaiser Wilhelm Physical Institute and Professor in the University of Berlin. He became a German citizen in 1914 and remained in Berlin until 1933 when he renounced his citizenship for political reasons and emigrated to America to take the position of Professor of Theoretical Physics at Princeton. He became a United States citizen in 1940 and retired from his post in 1945.

After World War II, Einstein was a leading figure in the World Government Movement, and was offered the Presidency of the State of Israel, which he declined. He collaborated with Dr. Chaim Weizmann in establishing the Hebrew University of Jerusalem.

At the start of his scientific work, Einstein realised the inadequacies of Newtonian mechanics and his special theory of relativity stemmed from an attempt to reconcile the laws of mechanics with the laws of the electromagnetic field. He dealt with classical problems of statistical mechanics in which they were merged with quantum theory, which led to an explanation of the Brownian movement of molecules. He investigated the thermal properties of light with a low radiation density and his observations laid the foundation of the photon theory of light.

In his early days in Berlin, Einstein postulated that the correct interpretation of the Special Theory of Relativity must also furnish a theory of gravitation and in 1916, he published his paper on the General Theory of Relativity. During this time, he also contributed to the problems of the theory of radiation and statistical mechanics.

In the 1920's, Einstein embarked on the construction of unified field theories, although he continued to work on the probabilistic interpretation of quantum theory, and he persevered with this work in America. He contributed to the statistical mechanics by his development of the Quantum Theory of a Monatomic Gas and has also accomplished valuable work in connection with atomic transition probabilities and relativistic cosmology.

After his retirement, he continued to work towards the unification of the basic concepts of physics, taking the opposite approach, and geometrisation, to the majority of physicists.

Einstein's researches are, of course, well chronicled and his more important works include *Special Theory of Relativity* (1905), *General Theory of Relativity* (1916), *Investigations on Theory of Brownian Movement* (1926), and *The Evolution of Physics* (1938). Among his non-scientific works, *About Zionism* (1930), *Why War?* (1933), *My Philosophy* (1934), and *Out of My Later Years* (1950) are perhaps the most important.

Albert Einstein received honorary doctorate degrees in science, medicine and philosophy from many European and American universities. During the 1920's, he lectured in Europe, America and the Far East and was awarded Fellowships or Memberships of all the leading scientific academies throughout the world. He gained numerous awards in recognition of his work, including the Copley Medal of the Royal Society of London in 1925, and the Franklin Medal of the Franklin Institute in 1935.

Einstein's gifts inevitably resulted in his dwelling much in intellectual solitude and, for relaxation, music played an important part in his life. He married Mileva Maric in 1903 and they had a daughter and two sons. This marriage was dissolved in 1919 and in the same year, he married his cousin, Elsa Lowenthal, who died in 1936. He died on April 18, 1955 at Princeton, New Jersey.

Alexander Fleming

(1881–1955)

Biologist and Pharmacologist

"Nature makes penicillin. I just found it."

Sir Alexander Fleming was a Scottish biologist and pharmacologist. Fleming published many articles on bacteriology, immunology, and chemotherapy. His best-known achievements are the discovery of the enzyme, *lysozyme* in 1922 and isolation of the antibiotic substance, penicillin from the fungus, *Penicillium notatum* in 1928, for which he shared a Nobel Prize with Florey and Chain.

On a farm in Scotland on August 6, 1881, an amazing person was born. This person was Alexander Fleming. He attended Louden Moor School, Darvel School, and Kilmarnock Academy before moving to London where he attended the Polytechnic. He spent four years in a shipping office before entering St. Mary's Medical School, London University. He qualified with distinction in 1906 and began research at St. Mary's under Sir Almroth Wright, a pioneer in vaccine therapy.

Alexander Fleming completed his M.B.B.S. from London and awarded, with Gold Medal in 1908. He became a lecturer at St. Mary's

Hospital in 1914. In World War I, he served as a captain in the Army Medical Corps, being mentioned in dispatches, and in 1918, he returned to St. Mary's Hospital. He was elected Professor of Bacteriology, University of London in 1948. He was also elected Fellow of the Royal Society in 1943 and knighted in 1944.

Fleming became interested in the natural bacterial action of the blood and in antiseptics from the very beginning of his medicine career. He was able to continue his studies throughout his military career and on demobilisation, he settled to work on antibacterial substances which would not be toxic to animal tissues.

In 1921, he discovered an important bacteriolytic substance in tissues and secretions which he named *Lysozyme*. About this time, he devised sensitivity titration methods and assays in human blood and other body fluids, which he subsequently used for the titration of penicillin. In 1928, while working on influenza virus, he observed that mould had developed accidentally on a staphylococcus culture plate and that the mould had created a bacteria-free circle around itself. He was inspired to further experiment and he found that a mould culture prevented growth of staphylococci, even when diluted 800 times. He named the active substance as penicillin.

Fleming has gained many awards and recognitions, which include Hunterian Professor (1919), Arris and Gale Lecturer (1929) and Honorary Gold Medal (1946) of the Royal College of Surgeons; Williams Julius Mickle Fellowship, University of London (1942); Charles Mickle Fellowship, University of Toronto (1944); John Scott Medal, City Guild of Philadelphia (1944); Cameron Prize, University of Edinburgh (1945); Moxon Medal, Royal College of Physicians (1945); Cutter Lecturer, Harvard University (1945); Albert Gold Medal, Royal Society of Arts (1946); Gold Medal, Royal Society of Medicine (1947); Medal for Merit, USA (1947); and the Grand Cross of Alphonse X the Wise, Spain (1948).

He served as President of the Society for General Microbiology. He was a Member of the Pontifical Academy of Science and

Honorary Member of almost all the medical and scientific societies of the world. He was the Rector of Edinburgh University during 1951-1954, Freeman of many boroughs and cities and Honorary Chief Doy-gei-tau of the Kiowa tribe. He was also awarded doctorate, Honoris Causa, degrees of almost thirty European and American Universities.

In 1915, Fleming married Sarah Marion Mc Elroy of Killala, Ireland, who died in 1949. Their son is a general medical practitioner. Fleming remarried in 1953; his bride was Dr. Amalia Koutsouri-Voureka, a Greek colleague at St. Mary's.

In his younger days, he was a keen member of the Territorial Army, and served from 1900 to 1914 as a private doctor in the London Scottish Regiment. Dr. Fleming died on March 11, 1955 and is buried in St. Paul's Cathedral.

❑❑❑

Alexander 'The Great'

(356–323 BC)
World Conqueror

"There is nothing impossible to him who will try."

Alexand III Philippou Makedonon, most popularly known as Alexander 'The Great' is considered as the most powerful military leader and conqueror of the ancient world. He was an inspiration for later conquerors such as Hannibal the Carthaginian, the Romans Pompey and Caesar, and Napoleon. Alexander conquered much of what was then the civilized world and driven by his divine ambition of the world conquest.

Alexander was born in 356 BC in Pella, the ancient capital of Macedonia. He was the son of Philip II, King of Macedonia, and Olympias, the princess of neighbouring Epirus. He spent his childhood watching his father transforming Macedonia into a great military power, winning victory after victory on the battlefields throughout the Balkans.

Even as a young boy, Alexander was fearless and strong. At the age of twelve, he tamed the beautiful and spirited Bucephalus ("ox-head" in Greek), a horse that no one else could ride. Alexander knew the Iliad by heart. He loved Homer, and always slept with a copy of the Iliad under his pillow. His first teacher was Leonidas, a relative of Olympias.

He had a tremendous desire to secure for himself a place in the pantheon of Gods. The cost of his successes all over the world was tremendous but he did not seem to mind as long as his goals were being achieved.

When he was 13, Philip hired the Greek philosopher, Aristotle to be Alexander's personal tutor. During the next three years, Aristotle gave training to Alexander in rhetoric and literature and stimulated his interest in science, medicine, and philosophy, all of which became of importance in Alexander's later life.

Alexander's first brush with combat came during Philip's expedition against Byzantium in 340 BC. He was then sixteen years old and was left in Macedonia in the charge of the royal seal. But the constantly restless Alexander perceived this as an opportunity to show his battle skills. Alexander managed to subjugate the rebellious Maedi, a Thracian tribe. Defeating a tribe is admirable but it cannot be compared to a full-fledged warfare.

When he was only 18, he commanded part of Philip's cavalry at the battle of Chaeronea. Alexander also acted as his father's ambassador to Athens. In 336 BC, Philip was suddenly assassinated, before he was able to depart, during the marriage celebration of his daughter at Aegae. The death of Philip is shrouded in mystery. There is a hint of suspicion that Alexander could have been one of the perpetrators.

Soon after his father's death, Alexander ascended on the Macedonian throne. Alexander quickly disposed of all of his domestic enemies by ordering their execution. But soon, he had to act outside Macedonia. Philip's death caused series of rebellions among the conquered nations and the Illyrians, Thracians, and Greeks saw a chance for independence. Alexander acted swiftly.

In seven days, Alexander reached Thessaly and then reached Boeotia, five days later. By a forced march, he took the Thebans completely by surprise, and in a few days, he captured the city. The march for glory was well and truly on. Alexander started with blitz campaigns against the Triballi and Ilyrians, which took him across the Danube. His army comprised of 30,000 foot soldiers and over 5,000 cavalry.

Another positive outcome of Alexander's hegemonistic tendencies was that it created an economically and culturally, a single market extending from Gibraltar to Punjab, open to trade, social and cultural exchange.

Alexander had vast plans, including his governmental reorganisation and an expedition to Arabia. But he was taken seriously ill with malaria at Babylon. On an afternoon of June 10, 323 BC, Alexander died of a mysterious illness in the palace of Nebuchadrezzar II of Babylon. He was just one month shy of attaining 33 years of age. Various theories have been proposed for the cause of his death which includes poisoning by the sons of Antipater or others, sickness that followed a drinking party, or a relapse of the malaria he had contracted in 336 BC.

Alexander did not have the luxury of living for a long time. It is difficult to even imagine the kind of conquering that he would have managed, had he lived longer. His body was placed in a gold coffin and taken to Memphis, in Egypt. Later, it was carried to Alexandria, and placed in a beautiful tomb.

❑❑❑

Amartya Sen

(1933)

Economist

"Freedoms are not only the primary ends of development, they are also among its principal means."

Prof. Amartya Kumar Sen is one of the greatest intellectuals and economists of modern India. Amartya Sen is a philosopher, economist and a social thinker. At a time when the world was talking of globalization, liberalization and free market economy, Prof. Sen dared to differ. No wonder, he was awarded the Nobel Prize for welfare economics in the face of market oriented economics. Instead of the growth oriented economic path to prosperity, Amartya Sen has emphasized the need for giving a human face to development.

Amartya Kumar Sen was born on November 3, 1933 at Shantiniketan, West Bengal. His ancestral home was in Wari, Dhaka in modern-day Bangladesh. Tagore is said to have given Amartya Sen his name ("Amartya" meaning "immortal").

Sen began his high-school education at St Gregory's School in Dhaka in 1941, in modern-day Bangladesh. In his early childhood, he was exposed to the plight of the poor. The sight of people dying during famine shocked him. It was, perhaps, this shocking experience that made him study the economic mechanism underlying famines and poverty.

His family migrated to India following the partition in 1947. Sen studied in India at the school system of Vishwa-Bharati University, Presidency College, Kolkata (formerly Calcutta) and at the Delhi School of Economics before moving to Trinity College, Cambridge, where he earned a First Class BA in 1956 and then a PhD in 1959. He was also allowed four years to immerse himself in philosophical issues during his stay at Trinity College.

Sen's first wife was Nabaneeta Dev Sen, a much loved Indian writer and scholar, with whom he had two children: Antara and Nandana. His marriage broke up shortly after they moved to London in 1971. His second wife was Eva Colorni, with whom he lived from 1973 onwards. She died from stomach cancer quite suddenly in 1985. They had two children, Indrani and Kabir. His present wife is Emma Georgina Rothschild, an economic historian, and an expert in Adam Smith and Fellow of King's College, Cambridge.

Dr. Sen's Collective Choice and Social Welfare (1970) helped to renew interest in welfare issues. He received the Nobel Memorial Prize in Economics for his work in welfare economics in 1998. He also received the Bharat Ratna, the highest civilian award in India in 1999. In 1999, he also received an honorary citizenship of Bangladesh from Prime Minister Sheikh Hasina in recognition of his achievements in winning the Nobel Prize, given that his family origins were in what has become the modern state of Bangladesh. In 2002, he received the International Humanist Award from the International Humanist and Ethical Union. *Eisenhower Medal*, for Leadership and Service USA, was conferred upon him in 2000. In 2003, he was conferred the Lifetime Achievement Award by the Indian Chamber of Commerce.

In January 2004, Prof. Amartya Sen returned to Harvard, where he currently teaches. With the Nobel Prize, Prof. Sen became more determined about his old obsessions like literacy, basic health care and gender equity, specifically in India and Bangladesh. He set up the Pratichi Trust, with a part of the prize money, to take forward his work.

In May 2007, he was appointed as Chairman of Nalanda Mentor Group to steer the execution of Nalanda University project, which seeks to revive the ancient seat of learning at Nalanda, Bihar, India into an international university.

As a writer, Sen has many books to his credit, which include 'The Argumentative Indian' and 'The Idea of Justice'.

In 2010, Time Magazine listed him in their 100 most influential persons in the world and New Statesman listed him in their 2010 edition of "World's 50 Most Influential People who matter." In 2011 the National Humanities Medal was given to Sen and in 2013 he was conferred with a Commander of the French Legion of Honour.

On 19 July 2012, Sen was named the first chancellor of the proposed Nalanda University (NU). On 20 February 2015, Amartya Sen withdrew his candidature for second term.

The German Publishers and Booksellers Association awarded him the 2020 Peace Prize of the German Book Trade for his pioneering scholarship addressing issues of global justice and combating social inequality in education and healthcare. On May 26, 2021, Sen was awarded Spain's top Princess of Asturias Award in the Social Sciences category, the Spanish Prize Foundation.

In 2021, Amartya Sen was awarded the prestigious Gold Medal from The National Institute of Social Sciences for his distinguished service to humanity.

Ambani Dhirubhai

(1932–2002)

Business Tycoon

"Our dreams have to be bigger. Our ambitions higher. Our commitment deeper. And our efforts greater. This is my dream for Reliance and for India."

Dhirubhai Ambani was an Indian business tycoon and founder of Reliance Industries Limited. Dhirajlal Hirachand Ambani is not just the usual rags-to-riches story or a Reliance patriarch but will be remembered as the one who rewrote Indian corporate history placing the ordinary investor on the perch and building a truly global corporate group in the country.

Dhirajlal Hirachand Ambani, known as Dhirubhai, was born on December 28, 1932, in Gujarat, into a Modh family of very moderate means. He was the second son of a school teacher, Hirachand Ambani.

Armed with a Matriculation certificate, he moved to Aden as a teenager in order to seek his fortune. He started to work as a petrol station attendant before taking up a clerical position for an oil company that was the sole distributor of Shell products there.

While in Aden, home to many Gujarati expatriates, he realised that a discrepancy between the rial-sterling exchange rate and the intrinsic value of the silver content in Aden's coinage afforded an excellent opportunity to make money. This arbitrage generated some $3,000 in seed money for the modest trading enterprise that Ambani set up when he returned to Bombay in 1958 with Rs 50,000.

Sensing good opportunity in the business of textiles, Dhirubhai started his first textile mill at Naroda, near Ahmedabad in 1966. Textiles were manufactured using polyester fibre yarn. He began the brand 'Vimal', which was named after his elder brother, Ramaniklal Ambani's son, Vimal Ambani. Extensive marketing of the brand, "Vimal" in the interiors of India made it a household name. Franchise retail outlets were started that used to sell only 'Vimal' brand of textiles. In the year 1975, a technical team from the World Bank visited Reliance Textile's Manufacturing unit at Naroda. This unit had the rare distinction of being certified as 'excellent even by developed country standards' in that period.

Asia Week magazine voted Ambani amongst the 50 most powerful men in Asia - not once but three times, in 1996, 1998 and 2000. The Federation of Indian Chambers of Commerce and Industry (FICCI), conferred on him the Indian entrepreneur of the 20th Century award.

Dhirubhai Ambani expired on Saturday, July 6, 2002, roughly ten minutes before midnight, at Mumbai's Breach Candy Hospital where he had been admitted after he suffered a vascular stroke on the evening of June 24, the same year. This was his second stroke – the first had occurred more than sixteen years earlier, in February 1986, leaving the right side of his body paralysed.

He is survived by Kokilaben Ambani, his wife, two sons, Mukesh Ambani and Anil Ambani, and two daughters, Nina Kothari and Deepti Salgaocar.

❑❑❑

Amitabh Bachchan

(1942)

Actor

"No one can go through life without their share of knocks. I am no different from any other."

Amitabh Bachchan can be categorized as India's most popular and successful actor of Hindi films. He is popularly known as BIG B. Amitabh Bachchan is extremely popular in the Indian sub-continent and the Middle East and many other parts of the world.

Bachchan's acting career began in 1969, reaching heights in the mid 70–80s. After withdrawing from the acting career in the early 90s, Bachchan returned in 1997 and became the host of the television show, *Kaun Banega Crorepati?* on Star Plus. He is presently once again active in the Indian film industry. Bachchan was also a member of the Indian Parliament (MP), being elected in 1984 from Allahabad. His political career was short lived as he resigned from this post after only 3 years.

'Amitabh Bachchan — the 'Shahenshah' of Bollywood was born to a well-known poet, Harivansh Rai Bachchan and Teji Bachchan in Allahabad on October 11, 1942. He has a brother named Ajitabh.

Amitabh attended Allahabad's Boys' High School, followed by Nainital's Sherwood College, where he gained a degree in Arts. He later went on to study at Kirori Mal College in Delhi University earning a degree in science.

Before entering Bollywood, he was working as an executive in a shipping firm at Kolkata. Bachchan was also a former stage actor and a radio announcer. His career graph in acting took an upward swing with the release of *Zanjeer* in 1973. He monopolised the Hindi cinema after proving his worth as an accomplished actor when casted against Rajesh Khanna in *Anand* and Dilip Kumar in *Shakti* (1982).

At the beginning of his career in Bollywood, he had to struggle a lot because of his unconventional looks and his height.

Some of his successful films include *Anand* (1970), *Namak Haram* (1973), *Abhiman* (1973), *Milli* (1975), *Deewar, Sholay* (1975), *Mukaddar ka Sikandar* (1978), *Trishul* (1978), *Silsila* (1981), *Agni-path* (1990). Amitabh features best in song and dance sequences. His rendering of *Khai Ke Paan Banaraswala* (Don) and *Jumma Chumma dede* (Hum), became a craze with the younger generation. He has won many Filmfare Awards, National Awards and has been conferred *Padma Shri* for his histrionic achievements.

After a pause for some time, he came back to the silver screen to perform some selective roles. He also established his own company, Amitabh Bachchan Corporation Ltd (ABCL).

Amitabh married Jaya Bhaduri, a well-known actress. It was on the sets of *Ek Nazar* (1972) that Amitabh and Jaya Bhaduri fell in love. The couple has two children, Shweta and Abhishek.

In July of 1999, Amitabh Bachchan was named the Superstar of the Millennium by the BBC Online poll where he defeated many Hollywood legends such as Alec Guinness, Marlon Brando, Sir Laurence Olivier and Charlie Chaplin.

Amitabh Bachchan is the first Indian actor to have been immortalised in wax at Madame Tussauds Wax Museum in London. On

Amitabh Bachchan's 64th birthday, the French Government honoured him with its highest civilian award, the Legion d'honneur Honour.

After receiving accolades and encomiums for putting the Indian movie industry on the world map, Amitabh Bachchan was conferred an honorary doctorate degree on November 4, 2006 by his Alma Mater; Delhi University.

In the years that followed, Amitabh featured in films such as *Nishabd* (2006), *Cheeni Kum* (2007), *Bhootnath* (2008) and *Paa* (2009). *Paa* won him his third National Film Award for Best Actor and fifth Filmfare Best Actor Award. In 2010 he dubbed in Malayalam film *Kandahar* and acted in *Teen Patti* along with Hollywood legend Ben Kingsley. The Lifetime Achievement Award was conferred upon him at the 2010 Asian Film Awards. In 2011, he was honoured with an Honorary Doctorate by the Queensland University of Technology in Brisbane, Australia. He made his Hollywood debut in 2013 with *The Great Gatsby.*

In 2014, he played the role of the friendly ghost in the sequel *Bhoothnath Returns.* The next year, he played the role of a grumpy father suffering from chronic constipation in *Piku.* It won him his fourth National Film Award for Best Actor and his third Filmfare Critics Award for Best Actor.

In 2016, he appeared in the women-centric courtroom drama film *Pink* which was highly praised by critics and with an increasingly good word of mouth, was a resounding success at the domestic and overseas box office. In 2017, he appeared in the third instalment of the Sarkar film series: Ram Gopal Varma's *Sarkar 3.*

He received the Lifetime Achievement Award at the 2023 Joy Awards in Saudi Arabia. This award honours his remarkable career and his impact on the film industry.

Ankit Tiwari

(1986)

Singer

"Music is a very sensitive thing. We get musically attached to a project and it has the power to affect your mood."

People, on this planet, resort to different ways to worship and to please Almighty God just to seek His favour and blessing so as to be successful in life. Among the various ways of worshipping God, singing devotional songs and bhajans, just like we hear Christian carols in churches and hymns and it appears that such worship and devotion was answered by God in case of Mr. Rajendra Kumar Tiwari, as he was blessed with a son in the year 1986 on 06th of March, who was filled with devotion too and his melodious passion and singing dedication would take him higher on career graph, with a humble beginning in Kanpur, Uttar Pradesh.

His parents managed music band which was called "Raju Suman & Party" and both were devotional singers who have gathered a fame in the city. This won't be wrong to say that music and melody runs in Ankit's blood and since early age, he got introduced to classical music, musical instruments and singing and their nuances. He did his schooling from Jugal Devi Saraswati Vidya Mandir, Kanpur.

On picking up basics of singing or say classical singing, as he witnessed at home, right from the beginning, he started developing jingles and also contributed with background music to some TV soaps. Gradually, his towering musical readiness fetched sweet fruit as he got a breakthrough in 2010 with the movie "Do Dooni Chaar", which was soon followed by "Saheb Biwi Aur Gangster" in the year that followed. All such projects fell by his way, as film-makers instantly detected his hidden talent for singing and musical devotion and how he would cut a dash for himself in the field, in the years to come.

He was born in a family of singing and music artists, and thus had (and still has) knack for music. At home, musical instruments galore and when we, as kids, played with toys, he tried his hands on dholak, sitar, harmonium, table etc. Truly, to his family, music is a way of worship Almighty.

He was sent to Dada Sen and Shankar Lal Bhat to pick-up singing at the very tender age of 5 years. In field of classical music, he got his training from Vinod Kumar Dwidi and passion got him practice hard, say upto 12 hours a day.

Later, in city of Gwalior, at the radio station, he became "Production Head" and took care of music there. Later in 2008, he moved for Mumbai and composed music for commercials, but his dream of registering it big on silver screen came true in 2010 when he composed music for the movie "Do Dooni Chaar".

As his interest and passion was deeply rooted in music, he was all set to be a music composer and the idea of singing never crossed his mind. Film-maker Tigmanshu Dhulia identified a singer in him and goaded him towards singing. Initially, his dream and hopes of being a singer were dashed on several counts, when his voice and command over "surs" was found weak during voice auditions and he got a rejection at the hands of many music directors.

As the proverb goes, "slow and steady wins the race" his destiny got the sheen when his voice and singing left a great influence on the mind of Mahesh Bhatt and the latter immediately offered him a contract to sing for his movie "Aashiqui-2" and there was no turning back from there.

In various successful bollywood flicks, he has been a music director such as PK (2014), Khamoshiyan (2015), Tum Bin-2 (2016) and Sadak-2 (2020). Other than being a perfected and celebrated singer, he is also a seasoned piano and dhrupad player and is also skilled in other western musical instruments too. He is also a partner in company "Brotherhood Entertainment Private Limited" which is into movie production business. His soul-mate is Pallavi Shukla who is his paternal grand-mother's selection for him. He has made his grand appearance in a handful of music videos too, i.e. Badtameez (2016), Mehbooba (2018) and Tere Do Naina (2019). In 2019, he got one of the biggest honours of his life, as he bagged a doctorate degree by the Victoria Global University, based in US, when its 18th convocation was organized at Russian Cultural Centre.

Ankit Tiwari, on the back of his sheer hard-work and dedication, has become a widely popular and super successful artist in just a few years' time. He has won awards for his singing and music and recognition on various platforms over the years.

As a golden outcome, awards, fame and recognition started to rain on him, sooner, such as: Best Musical Director award (2014) for movie *Aashiqui-2,* Upcoming Male Vocalist of the Year (2013) for movie *Aashiqui-2,* Upcoming Music Composer of the Year (2013) for movie *Aashiqui-2,* Album of the Year (2013) for movie *Aashiqui-2.*

Ankit Tiwari received the Best Male Singer award at the Indian Music Awards 2024 for his romantic track “Tum Kya Mile” from the film “Rocky aur Rani Kii Prem Kahaani” featuring Alia Bhatt and Ranveer Singh.

❑❑❑

Annie Besant

(1847–1933)

Women's Rights Activist, Writer

"Better remain silent, better not even think, if you are not prepared to act."

In the field of education, social reforms and political struggle, Dr. Annie Besant was the foremost woman leader, India had seen in the pre-Independence era. She earned fame early, due to her eloquence, social work and radical views. She was hailed as Europe's best orator by George Bernard Shaw.

Annie Wood was born in 1847, in London to a middle-class family of Irish origin. Annie was always proud of being Irish and supported the cause of Irish self-rule throughout her adult life. Annie's father, a doctor, died when she was only five years old. Without any savings, Annie's mother found work looking after boarders at Harrow School. Mrs. Wood was unable to care for Annie and she persuaded a friend, Ellen Marryat, to take the responsibility for her upbringing.

In 1866, Annie met Frank Besant. Although only nineteen, Annie agreed to marry the young clergyman. By the time, she was twenty-three, she had two children. However, Annie was very unhappy because her independent spirit clashed with the traditional views of her husband. Annie also began to question her religious beliefs.

In 1877, Annie Besant and Charles Bradlaugh decided to publish *The Fruits of Philosophy*, Charles Knowlton's book advocating birth control. Besant and Bradlaugh were charged with publishing material that was 'likely to deprave or corrupt those whose minds are open to immoral influences'. Besant and Bradlaugh were both found guilty of publishing an 'obscene libel' and sentenced to six months in prison. At the Court of Appeal, the sentence was quashed.

In 1880, Charles Bradlaugh was elected the MP for Northampton, but as he was not a Christian, he refused to take the oath, and was expelled from the House of Commons. While working with Bradlaugh, Besant also became friends with socialists such as Walter Crane, Edward Aveling and George Bernard Shaw.

After joining the Social Democratic Federation, Annie started her own campaigning newspaper called *The Link*. Like Catherine Booth of the Salvation Army, Annie was concerned about the health of young women workers at the Bryant & May match factory.

Besant also joined the socialist group, the Fabian Society, and in 1889, contributed to the influential book, *Fabian Essays*. The book included articles by George Bernard Shaw, Sydney Webb, Sydney Olivier, Graham Wallas, William Clarke and Hubert Bland. Edited by Shaw, the book sold 27,000 copies in two years.

In 1889, Annie Besant was elected to the London School Board. After heading the poll with a fifteen thousand majority over the next candidate, Besant argued that she had been given a mandate for large-scale reform of local schools. Some of her many achievements included a programme of free meals for undernourished children and free medical examinations for all those in elementary schools.

In the 1890s, Annie Besant became a supporter of Theosophy, a religious movement founded by Madame Blavatsky in 1875. Theosophy was based on the Hindu ideas of *karma* and reincarnation with *nirvana* as the eventual aim. Annie Besant went to live in India but she remained interested in the subject of women's rights.

She founded the Central Hindu College at Varanasi in 1898, and received a degree in Sanskrit literature, English literature and Indian history from the same institution.

She continued to write letters to the British newspapers arguing the case for women's suffrage (voting rights) and in 1911, Annie Besant was one of the main speakers at an important suffrage rally in London.

While in India, Annie joined the struggle for Indian Home Rule, and in 1916, she established the Indian Home Rule League becoming its first president. She was also the president of the Indian National Congress in 1917, but later, the congress splitted with Gandhi. At times, during the First World War, she was interned by the British authorities.

After being president of the Theosophical Society in 1907, Annie Besant wrote enormous books and pamphlets on theosophy. She travelled (1926–27) in England and the United States with Jiddu Krishnamurti, whom she announced as the new *Messiah*. However, by 1929, the young man himself denounced all claims about himself as the World Teacher. Annie Besant died in India in 1933 at an age of 86.

❑❑❑

Archimedies

(287–212 BC)

Mathematician, Physicist, Inventor

"Give me a lever long enough and a fulcrum on which to place it, and I shall move the world."

Archimedes was a great mathematician, physicist, engineer, inventor, and astronomer. His outstanding contributions in the field of science brought about significant changes to the scientific world. Some of his notable contributions to the field of maths and science include the finding and development of the laws and principles of mechanics, buoyancy, hydrostatics, specific gravity, the lever, and the pulley; in addition, he discovered ways to measure a circle and the volume of a solid.

Archimedes was born in 287 BC in the Greek city-state of Syracuse on the island of Sicily. His father, Phidias was an astronomer. Archimedes is said to be a relative of Hiero II, the then king of Syracuse and presumably lived a royal life. He spent most of his life in Syracuse except for the time he went to Alexandria, Egypt to get his education. Belonging to a Greek family young Archimedes was always encouraged to get education and be knowledgeable. Besides maths and science his other major interests included: poetry, politics, astronomy, music, art and military tactics.

Opportunity came when he got the chance to continue his studies in a famous school of mathematics founded by Euclid. Here he got the pleasure to study astronomy, physics and mathematics with other geniuses and big minds of that era. Under the guidance of two great mathematicians and scholars: Conon of Samos, and Eratosthenes of Cyrene, Archimedes grew up to be a great scientist.

There are many stories about how Archimedes made his discoveries. A famous one tells how he uncovered an attempt to cheat King Hieron. The king ordered a golden crown and gave the crown's maker the exact amount of gold needed. The maker delivered a crown of the required weight, but Hieron suspected that some silver had been used instead of gold. He asked Archimedes to find about the matter. One day, Archimedes was considering it while he was getting into a bathtub. He noticed that the amount of water overflowing the tub was proportional (related consistently) to the amount of his body that was being immersed (covered by water). This gave him an idea for solving the problem of the crown. He was so thrilled that he ran naked through the streets shouting, "Eureka!" "Eureka!" (Greek for "I have discovered it!").

Archimedes also studied aspects of the lever and pulley. A lever is a kind of basic machine in which a bar is used to raise or move a weight, while a pulley uses a wheel and a rope or chain to lift loads. Such mechanical investigations would help Archimedes assist in defending Syracuse when it came under attack.

Another great discovery by Archimedes is his famous 'Archimedes Screw'. This is still a famous tool in Egypt used for irrigation. This screw was mainly invented to remove water from the hold of large ship; however it is also helpful for handling light, loose materials such as ash, grain, sand etc. Also known as 'the ship shaker', The Claw of Archimedes is a great weapon designed by Archimedes for the purpose of defending his home city Syracuse.

Archimedes is also famous for his contributions to the filed of mathematics. These include: the use infinitesimals in a way that is similar to modern integral calculus, the mathematical proof of the formula for area of a circle, the solution to the problem as an infinite geometric series etc.

During the Roman conquest of Sicily in 214 BC Archimedes worked for the state, and several of his mechanical devices were employed in the defence of Syracuse. Among the war machines attributed to him are the catapult and - perhaps legendary - a mirror system for focusing the sun's rays on the invaders' boats and igniting them.

Archimedes died in 212 B.C. during the Second Punic war, when Syracuse was captured by the Roman forces after a two year siege. According to Plutarch, Archimedes was researching a mathematical diagram, when a Roman soldier ordered him to meet General Marcus (who was engaged in the siege of Syracuse). But Archimedes declined saying that he had to finish his diagram so he should not be disturbed. Furious, the Roman soldier killed Archimedes. General Marcus was angered by the death of Archimedes, because he didn't wish him any harm. Another popular theory regarding Archimedes' death is that he was killed while actually surrendering to the Romans.

This great scientist and mathematician passed away but his contributions led the world towards scientific development and betterment of the human race.

❑❑❑

Aristotle

(384 BC–322 BC)

Philosopher

"In the arena of human life,
the honours and rewards fall to
those who show their good qualities in action."

Aristotle is one of the "big three" in ancient Greek philosophy, along with Plato and Socrates. Aristotle is known for his carefully detailed observations about nature and the physical world, which laid the groundwork for the modern study of biology. Among his works are the texts, Physics, Metaphysics, Rhetoric and Ethics.

Aristotle was born in 384 BC, in Stagira, near Macedonia at the northern end of the Aegean Sea. His father, Nicomachus, was the family physician of King Amyntas of Macedonia. It is believed that Aristotle's ancestors had been the physicians of the Macedonian royal family for several generations. Coming from a long line of physicians, Aristotle received training and education that inclined his mind towards the study of natural phenomenon. This education had long-lasting influences, and was probably the root cause of his less idealistic stand on philosophy as opposed to Plato. Aristotle's father died when he was a boy, and Aristotle was left under the care of his guardian, Proxenus.

When he was seventeen, Proxenus sent him to study at Plato's Academy in Athens, the heart of the intellectual world at that time. Aristotle remained at the academy for twenty years, until Plato's death in 347 BC. Although Aristotle was Plato's most promising student, Aristotle did not succeed Plato as the head of the academy because of their opposing views on several fundamental philosophical issues, specifically regarding Plato's theory of ideas. Aristotle was more concerned than Plato with the actual material world, and did not believe that the only thing that mattered is the realm of ideas and perfect forms.

After leaving the academy, Aristotle was invited to live in the court of his friend, Hermeas, ruler of Atarneus and Assos in Mysia. Aristotle remained there for three years, where he married Pythias, his niece and adopted the daughter of the king.

Later in life, he married Herpyllis, with whom he had a son, named Nicomachus. When Hermeas' kingdom was taken over by the Persians, Aristotle moved to Mytilene. King Amyntas invited Aristotle to tutor his thirteen-year old son, Alexander. Aristotle taught Alexander for five years until King Amyntas died and Alexander came to power.

In gratitude for Aristotle's services, Alexander provided him generously with means for the acquisition of books and for the pursuit of scientific inquiry. While the extent to which Aristotle's teaching influenced Alexander's successes in conquering an empire is disputable, Alexander did try to organise much of his empire along the model of the Greek city-state.

In 335 BC, he went back to Athens, where he found the academy flourishing under Xenocrates. Aristotle founded his own school, the Lyceum, and operate it for twelve years, where he wrote extensively on a wide range of subjects such as politics, metaphysics, ethics, logic and science.

He agreed with Plato that the cosmos is rationally designed and that philosophy can come to know absolute truths by studying universal forms. Their ideas diverged, however, Aristotle thought that one finds the Universal in particular things, while Plato believed the Universal exists apart from particular things, and that material things are only a shadow of true reality, which exists in the realm of ideas and forms. Aristotle's philosophy involved both inductive and deductive reasoning, observing the workings of the world around him and then reasoning from the particular to a knowledge of essences and universal laws. In a sense, Aristotle was the first major proponent of the modern scientific method.

In 322 BC, Aristotle died unexpectedly and the government of Athens was overthrown by the anti-Macedonian forces.

❑❑❑

Arnold Schwarzenegger

(1947)

Bodybuilder, Actor, and Politician

"You can't climb the ladder of success with your hands in your pockets."

One of the world's leading bodybuilder, Arnold Schwarzenegger went on to become one of Hollywood's biggest stars and then the governor of California. He was nicknamed, 'The Austrian Oak', in 1965, when he won the 'Mr. Europe Junior' title. He went on to win five Mr. Universe titles and was named, "Mr. Olympia", seven times. He also appeared in the documentary Pumping Iron (1977).

Schwarzenegger was born on July 30, 1947 in Thal, Austria, a town bordering the Styrian capital, Graz, and christened Arnold Alois Schwarzenegger. His father was a local police Chief Gustav Schwarzenegger. Arnold had a good relationship with his mother and kept in touch with her until her death.

Gustav was a strict and demanding father, who generally favoured the elder of his two sons, Meinhard. Meinhard died in a car accident in 1971, and Gustav died the following year.

In 1965, when he joined the Austrian Army, his commanding officer withheld the pass to leave the base to take part in some bodybuilding contest. Arnold felt deserted, and won the trophy. He was thrown into military jail when he returned from the contest. It was only then, that the senior officers took a closer look at the trophy, which happened to be the top position of 'Mr. Universe junior' After that, he was officially allowed to train during his year of service.

In 1968, he won the International Power Lifting Championship and decided to move to the United States of America.

His body was his success. Even today, people often refer to him as the "Austrian Oak". But Arnold Schwarzenegger is not an example for all muscles and no brains. He also holds an academic Business degree and is known for his smartness concerning business and money matters.

In 1982, he got the lead role in *Conan the Barbarian* and *Terminator*, starting his career as a convincing actor in action movies. Obsessed with money, Schwarzenegger obtained a business degree from the University of Wisconsin and began investing his earnings. He invested his money in real estate, making a fortune and married Maria Shriver in 1986. She was from an influential American family, the Kennedy family. In 1991, he acted in *Terminator 2: Judgement Day*, his most successful movie ever. His trademark is the frequent movie line "I'll be back". With films like *Twins* or *Total Recall* Schwarzenegger gained acclaim for his acting, too.

In 2003, he not only starred in *Terminator 3: Rise of the Machines*, but also announced his intention to run for the elections for the office of Californian Governor. On October 7, 2003, Arnold won elections for Governor becoming one more successful actor turned politician of the American history. He was reelected on November 7, 2006 to serve a full term as Governor and again on January 5, 2007. During his term he continued to act in films.

In January 2011, just weeks after leaving office in California, he announced that he was returning to acting. He appeared in *The Expendables 2* (2012), and starred in *The Last Stand* (2013), his first leading role in 10 years.

He is also an example that you do not have to speak English with a flawless accent to relive the American dream and rise from a dishwasher to a millionaire.

He starred in Sabotage, released in March 2014, and appeared in *The Expendables 3,* released in August 2014. He starred in the fifth Terminator movie *Terminator Genisys* in 2015.

In August 2016, his filming of action-comedy *Why We're Killing Gunther* was temporarily interrupted by bank robbers near the filming location in Surrey, British Columbia. He was announced to star and produce in a film about the ruins of Sanxingdui called *The Guest of Sanxingdui* as an ambassador. Schwarzenegger returned to the Terminator franchise with *Terminator: Dark Fate,* which was released on November 1, 2019.

In 2023, Schwarzenegger published "Be Useful: Seven Tools for Life," offering insights from his diverse experiences. The following year, he received an honorary doctorate from the Berlin Hertie School for his climate protection efforts. In January 2025, he pledged $1 million to Los Angeles wildfire relief, underscoring his commitment to philanthropy.

Arthur Conan Doyle

(1859–1930)

Author

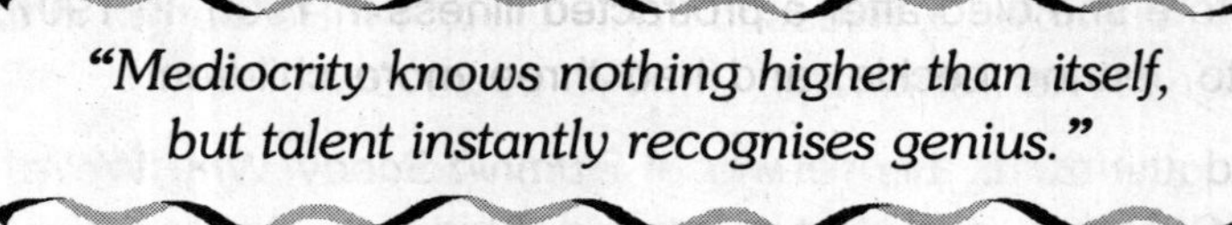

"Mediocrity knows nothing higher than itself, but talent instantly recognises genius."

Arthur Conan Doyle was a Scottish author most noted for his stories about the detective Sherlock Holmes, which are generally considered a major innovation in the field of crime fiction, and the adventures of Professor Challenger. He was a prolific writer whose other works include science fiction stories, historical novels, plays and romances, poetry, and non-fiction.

Arthur Conan Doyle was born in Edinburgh, Scotland, in 1859. Doyle's family (Conan was his middle name, and it was only later in life that he began to use it as his surname) sent him to Jesuit boarding schools to be educated, and he later entered the University of Edinburgh Medical School in 1881.

One of his professors at the university was Dr. Joseph Bell, who became the model for Doyle's Sherlock Holmes. It was Bell who drummed into Doyle's head the importance of using his innate powers of observation to help him deduce the nature of a patient's affliction.

While in school, Conan Doyle began writing to earn a little extra money. His first story, *The Mystery of the Sasassa Valley* was published in the *Chambers* Journal in 1879.

Shortly after, his father fell ill, and Doyle was forced to become the breadwinner for the family. He worked for a while as a ship's doctor, and then opened his own medical practice near Portsmouth. In his spare time, Doyle did more of writing.

In 1885, Conan Doyle married Louise Hawkins, and had two children before she died after a protracted illness in 1900. In 1907, he remarried to Jeanne Leckie, and had three more children.

His third attempt at a novel was *A Study in Scarlet*, the story which introduced Sherlock Holmes to the world. This was published in Mrs. Beeton's Christmas annual, in 1887. Encouraged by publishers to keep writing, Conan Doyle wrote his second Holmes mystery, *The Sign of the Four*, in 1890. These novels were successful and stories followed that Conan Doyle could afford to give up his medical practice and devote himself to writing, full time.

The first Sherlock Holmes short story, *A Scandal in Bohemia*, appeared in *The Strand Magazine* in 1891, to be followed by two dozen more stories over the next several years. The stories proved enormously successful, but Conan Doyle tired of his own creations, killed Holmes in 1894 in *The Final Problem*.

He underestimated the popularity of his creation. So great was the hold that the character of Sherlock Holmes had taken on the public imagination that Conan Doyle found himself at the centre of a storm of controversy.

He was inundated with letters of protest from readers. He bowed to the inevitable, and revived the character of Holmes, who appeared in numerous short stories over the next 23 years.

But Conan Doyle did not confine himself to Sherlock Holmes. He wrote several popular works of historic fiction, including *Micah Clarke*

(1888), *The White Company* (1890), *Rodney Stone* (1896), and *Sir Nigel* (1906).

Conan Doyle served as a doctor in the Boer War, and on his return, he wrote two books defending England's participation in that conflict. It was for these books that he received his knighthood in 1902.

After the death of his son in World War I, Conan Doyle became interested in spiritualism. He was convinced that it was possible to communicate with the dead, and his views led to a certain amount of ridicule from the mainstream society.

Sir Arthur Conan Doyle died on July 7, 1930, and is buried in the churchyard at Minstead Hampshire. He can rightly be credited with helping create the literary genre of the detective story. Though Edgar Allen Poe's Dupin predates Sherlock Holmes, it was the Holmes' stories that solidified in the public mind what a good detective should be.

❑❑❑

Arundhati Roy

(1961)

Author

"When a symbol unmoors itself from what it symbolizes, it loses meaning. It becomes ineffective."

Susanna Arundhati Roy is the first Indian woman to have won Britain's prestigious, 'Booker Prize'. She is a well-known author not only in India but abroad as well.

Arundhati was born on November 24, 1961, in Bengal and grew up in Aymanam village, Kottayam, Kerala. She is the daughter of Mary Roy, a popular social activist, and her father is a Bengali Hindu tea planter. Her parents separated when she was very young and she did her formal education in Corpus Christi School, run by her mother in Kottayam District, Kerala. She was just 16 when she left her home and settled in Delhi. Arundhati did her degree in Architecture at the Delhi School of Architecture. She met Gerard Da Cunha , a fellow architecture student during this period and married him. But sadly, their marriage lasted only for four years.

After a brief stint in the field of architecture, she realised that it was not her cup of tea. Then she left for Goa, making a life out at the beach, but in a few months, she got tired of it and returned back to Delhi. Then Arundhati took a job at the National Institute of Urban Affairs where she met Pradeep Krishen, a film director, and now her husband. He offered her a small role in *Massey Saab*. She went to Italy on a scholarship for eight months to study the restoration of monuments. During those months in Italy, she realised that she was a writer.

When Arundhati returned from Italy, she worked with Pradeep Krishen and they planned an episode television for the Doordarshan called the *Banyan Tree* which did not materialise and was shelved by the producers after shooting 2–3 episodes. She wrote and starred in *In Which Annie Gives it Those Ones*, a film on college life in India, based on her experiences in the University of Delhi, and wrote the screenplay for Pradeep Krishen's film, *Electric Moon* (1992).

Arundhati Roy quickly came to the limelight for her work as a screenwriter. She wrote a series of essays called *The Great Indian Rope Trick* which attracted media attention, in defence of former dacoit Phoolan Devi, who she felt had been exploited by Shekhar Kapur's film, 'Bandit Queen'. Her debut novel, *The God of Small Things* shot her into prominence in 1997, by winning the prestigious British Booker prize in London and becoming an international bestseller. The book won £20,000 as prize and sold nearly 400,000 copies globally by October that year.

With *The Cost of Living*, a book comprising two essays, *The Greater Common Good* (1999), and *The End of Imagination* (1998), she turned into activism.

She has been an active participant in public demonstrations against the construction of the Sardar Sarovar Dam on the Narmada River in Western India and has donated a substantial amount around 1.5 million rupees, equivalent to her Booker Prize money, for the cause. She was even arrested along with other protestors campaigning for the cause.

Her published book is *We Are One : A Celebration of Tribal Peoples*. She has also spoken on and published several articles such as *Promotion of equal rights* supporting equal rights for the lower castes in India, *War on Terrorism* (2001) against the Iraq war, and commented on War in Sri Lanka (2009) and US policy in Afghanistan.

With her publications, Arundhati has carved a niche for herself as a political journalist. This unusual woman who has been on several lists of 'the 50 most beautiful women in the world' is not intimated by her success and fame but is an inspiration to all those who seek to speak up against the powers in support of the poor and the oppressed. She now lives in Delhi with her husband, Pradeep Krishen and her two daughters, Pia and Mithva from her previous marriage.

She was awarded the Sydney Peace Prize in May 2004 for her work in social campaigns and advocacy of non-violence. In June 2005, she took part in World Tribunal on Iraq. In January 2006, she was awarded the Sahitya Academy award for her collection of Essays, 'The Algebra of Infinite Justice', but declined to accept it. In November 2011, she was awarded the Norman Mailer Prize for distinguished writing.

Her another novel titled The Ministry of Utmost Happiness was published in 2017. The novel was chosen for the Man Booker Prize 2017 Long List. The Ministry of Utmost Happiness was also nominated as a finalist for the National Book Critics Circle Award for fiction in January 2018.

Arundhati Roy was named one of the Financial Times' 25 Most Influential Women of 2024. She received the prestigious PEN Pinter Prize 2024, awarded to writers who demonstrate "fierce intellectual determination" and address social issues.

❑❑❑

Ashoka 'The Great'

(304 BC–232 BC)

Emperor

"I have enforced the law against killing certain animals but the greatest progress of righteousness among men comes from the exhortation in favour of non-injury to life."

Ashoka, the third emperor of the Maurya dynasty, is considered the greatest ruler of ancient India. He combined the piety of a saint with the practical qualities of a king, and in the history of Buddhism, he ranks second only to Buddha. In his edicts, he is referred to as "Devanampriya" or "The Beloved of the Gods of heaven".

Ashoka was born in 304 BC as the son of the Maurya Emperor, Bindusara by a relatively lower ranked queen named Dharma. Dharma was said to be the daughter of a poor Brahmin who introduced her into the harem of the emperor as it was predicted that her son would be a great ruler.

Ashoka had several elder half-brothers and just one younger sibling, Vitthashoka, another son of Dharma. The princes were extremely competitive, but young Ashoka excelled in the military and academic disciplines in which the boys were tutored. There was a great deal of sibling rivalry, especially between Ashoka and his brother Susima, both as warriors and as administrators.

After the death of his father, his elder brother, Suman was to take over the reins of the kingdom. But as most of the ministers found Ashoka more efficient, they helped him attain power.

Ashoka was a good administrator and at first, set about restoring peace in his kingdom. This took about 3 years, after which he formally accepted the throne and was crowned the king in 273 BC. During his reign, the country made progress in terms of science and technology as well as advanced in medicine and surgery. Religion was emphasised and so the people were honest and straightforward and truthful.

Ashoka, himself was a great philanthropist and worked day and night for the welfare of his people. He knew exactly what was going on in each part of his vast territory. He would not partake any of his meals until and unless he had fed a thousand Brahmins.

Kalinga was the first and the last battle that Ashoka ever fought and serves as a watermark in his life as it changed the course of his life forever. It was during this war that he earned the title, 'Ashoka the Great'.

Kalinga was a prosperous little kingdom lying between the river Godavari and Mahanadi, close to the Bay of Bengal. Ashoka wanted to capture this fertile land, and so had it surrounded by his army men. But the brave and loyal people of Kalinga did not want to lose their independence.

A fierce battle followed, in which there were too many casualties. There were more than a lakh prisoners of war. In the midst of the battlefield, Ashoka stood with the wounded, crippled and the dead all around him. This was the consequence of his greed. A new light dawned on him, and he swore that he would never wage a war again.

Ashoka was initiated into Buddhism, after which his life was completely transformed. He religiously followed the principles of Buddhism - that of truth, charity, kindness, purity and goodness.

He did his bit towards the propagation of this religion by engraving its principles on pillars throughout his kingdom. The Ashoka pillars, as they are now called, were over 40 feet high and extremely heavy. He also attempted to spread this religion to Syria, Egypt and Macedonia, and sent his son, Mahendra and daughter, Sanghamitra to Sri Lanka for this purpose.

Ashoka opened charitable hospitals and dispensaries for the welfare of the poor. He planted trees to provide shade and opened inns for the shelter of travellers. He also laid out green parks and gardens to beautify his kingdom. Wells and tanks were also constructed for the benefit of his people. Ashoka believed in non-violence and so he banned the sacrifice of animals. Besides this, he opened clinics for birds and animals too. His good works earned him the name of "Devanampriya Priyadarshi".

He died in 232 BC after doing a great deal of good for his kingdom and the world at large. Ashoka's fame had spread far and wide. To commemorate his rule and its implications, the Government of India has adopted the *Ashoka Chakra* as its national symbol, which can be seen till today on the national flag.

❑❑❑

Audrey Hepburn

(1929–1993)

Actress

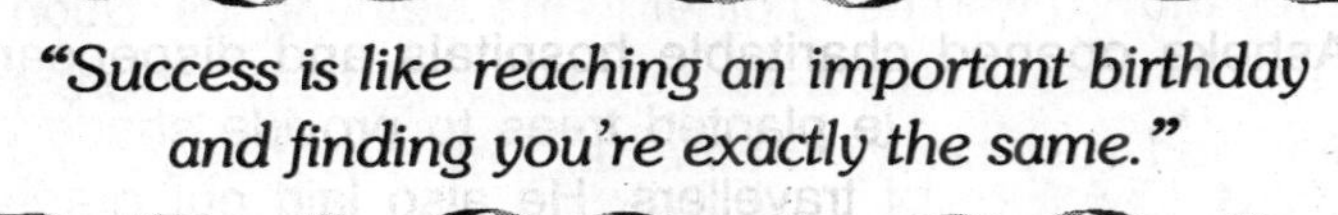

"Success is like reaching an important birthday and finding you're exactly the same."

Audrey Hepburn was an Academy Award-winning actress, fashion model, and humanitarian. Hepburn trained extensively to be a ballerina, instead becoming a leading Hollywood actress during the 1950s and 1960s. In 1999, she was ranked as the third greatest female star of all time by the American Film Institute in their list of AFI's 100 Years, 100 Stars.

Audrey Hepurn was born on May 4, 1929 to a Dutch Baroness and a wealthy English banker. She was the only child of Joseph Victor Anthony Ruston, an Englishman, and Baroness Ella van Heemstra van Ufford Ruston, a Dutch aristocrat descended from the French nobility. Her father later appended the surname of his grandmother, Kathleen Hepburn to the family's surname, and her surname became Hepburn-Ruston. She had two half-brothers, Arnoud Robert Alexander "Alex" Quarles van Ufford and Ian Edgar Bruce Quarles van Ufford, by her mother's first marriage to the Dutch nobleman, Hendrik

Gustaaf Adolf Quarles van Ufford. She was a descendant of King Edward III of England and James Hepburn, 4th Earl of Bothwell, from whom Katharine Hepburn may have also been descended.

Hepburn's father's job required the family to travel often between Brussels, England, and The Netherlands. From 1935 to 1938, Hepburn attended private academy for girls in Kent. In 1935, her parents divorced and her father, who was a Nazi sympathiser, left the family. She later called this the most traumatic moment of her life.

Audrey moved with her mother to the Netherlands. Soon after, the Nazi army invaded Holland, Audrey suffered from severe starvation, anaemia, and respiratory problems. The occupation ended when Audrey was sixteen. Her mother moved to London where Audrey attended the Arnhem Conservatory from 1939 to 1945. There she was trained in ballet, in addition to learning a standard school curriculum.

Audrey was finally discovered by Collette, a French novelist who insisted that she should be casted as the lead role in *Gigi*, a Broadway adaptation of her novel. Despite her lack of acting experiences, Audrey impressed audiences with her performance and was asked to be given the role as Princess Anne in William Wyler's, *Roman Holiday* starring opposite Gregory Peck.

Audrey's film debut gave her the *Oscar* that year for the best actress. From 1953–1967, Audrey starred in several more successful films, and was nominated four more times for an *Oscar* for her work in *Sabrina*, *The Nun's Story*, *Breakfast at Tiffany's*, and *Wait Until Dark*.

In 1954, Audrey married Mel Ferrer and with him achieved one of her lifelong goals, to have a child. Sean, her son was born on July 17, 1960. Audrey took time off from film making to raise her son. But in 1968, she and Mel divorced. A year later, Audrey married an Italian psychologist, Dr. Andrea Mario Dotti and gave birth to another son,

Luca. However, two years later, Audrey and the doctor separated and finally divorced in 1980.

In 1987, Audrey was officially appointed to succeed Danny Kaye (who died that year) as the Goodwill Ambassador for UNICEF. Accompanied by her companion, Robert Wolders, she visited such places as Ethiopia, Sudan, Bangladesh, and Vietnam.

After returning from Somalia in 1991, Audrey was diagnosed with colon cancer. On January 20, 1993, Audrey Hepburn died at the age of 63 in Tolchenaz, Switzerland.

In 2006, the Sustainable Style Foundation inaugurated the "Style & Substance Award in Honour of Audrey Hepburn" to recognise the high profile individuals that work to improve the quality of life for children around the world. The first award was given to Hepburn posthumously and received by the Audrey Hepburn Children's Fund.

❑❑❑

Aung San Suu Kyi

(1945)

Political Figure

"The only real prison is fear, and the only real freedom is freedom from fear."

Aung San Suu Kyi is the Nobel Prize-winning peace activist who was long detained by the military dictatorship of Myanmar. She is one of the world's most renowned freedom fighters and advocates of non-violence, having served as the figurehead for Burma's struggle for democracy since 1988.

A devout Buddhist, Suu Kyi won the *Rafto Prize* and the *Sakharov Prize* for Freedom of Thought in 1990 and in 1991, was awarded the *Nobel Peace Prize* for her peaceful and non-violent struggle under a repressive military dictatorship.

Aung San Suu Kyi was born on June 19, 1945 in the city of Rangoon, Burma. She is the daughter of General Aung San Kyi and Daw Khin Kyi. Her father, General Aung San was a popular hero, who helped to establish the national independence (1948). Aung San was assassinated in July 1947. She lived with her mother, Khin Kyi, and two brothers. Suu Kyi left Burma with her family and lived and studied in India and the United Kingdom since early childhood.

During the next several years, she worked abroad and met her future husband, Dr. Michael Aris. The couple soon married and had two children. In 1988, she returned to Burma at a time of political upheaval and ended up leading the National League for Democracy (NLD) in opposition to the ruling military regime to take care of her ailing mother.

Inspired by the non-violent practices of Mahatma Gandhi and Martin Luther King, Jr., Suu Kyi entered politics to work for democratisation. She also helped to establish the National League for Democracy on September 27, 1988, and was put under house arrest on July 20, 1989. Aung San Suu Kyi was offered freedom if she would leave the country, but she refused.

The authorities arrested her again in 2002, during the time when the NLD was having secret negotiations with the Junta (or the ruling military) in an effort to break the political deadlock.

In May 2003, she was again detained, taken into "protective custody" as confrontations between the NLD and the government supporters increased. Despite diplomatic pressure and international pleas for her release, she continues to be held in Myanmar. In May 2006, the ruling military Junta announced an extension of her house arrest for an indefinite period.

Burma was renamed Myanmar in 1989, by the ruling military party, the State Law and Order Restoration Council (now called the State Peace and Development Council).

She has won numerous international awards, including the Nobel Peace Prize, Sakharov Prize from the European Parliament, United States Presidential Medal of Freedom, Jawaharlal Nehru Award from India and Rafto Human Rights Prize. She has called upon people around the world to join the struggle for freedom in Burma, saying "Please use your liberty to promote ours."

Aung San Suu Kyi featured prominently in the music video for Rice's collaboration with Lisa Hannigan, "Unplayed Piano", which was apparently written for Suu Kyi.

In 2003's MTV Europe Music Awards, she was given the "Free Your Mind" award. In a list compiled by the magazine, *New Statesman* in 2006, Suu Kyi was voted as the number one "Hero of our time". International pressures led to her release on November 13, 2010, after 15 years of housearrest.

In 2011, she was awarded the Wallenberg Medal. On 19 September, 2012, she was presented with the Congressional Gold Medal, which is, along with the Presidential Medal of Freedom, the highest civilian honour in the United States.

On 1 April, 2012, her party, the National League for Democracy, announced that she was elected to the lower house of the Burmese parliament, representing the constituency of Kawhmu; her party also won 43 of the 45 vacant seats in the lower house. The election results were confirmed by the official electoral commission the following day.

In 2015 elections her party NLD won a sweeping victory, winning at least 255 seats in the House of Representatives and 135 seats in the House of Nationalities. In addition, Suu Kyi won re-election to the House of Representatives. On 30 March, 2016 she took over the roles of Foreign Affairs Minister, President's Office Minister, Education Minister and Electric Power and Energy Minister in President Htin Kyaw's government; later she relinquished the Ministries of Education and Electric Power and Energy. Moreover, President Htin Kyaw created a position called State Counsellor (de facto Prime Minister) for her. The position of State Counsellor was approved by the House of Nationalities on 1 April, 2016 and the House of Representatives on 5 April, 2016. The next day, her role as State Counsellor was established.

In 2019 she appeared in the International Court of Justice where she defended the Burmese military against allegations of genocide against the Rohingya. On 1 February, 2021 she was arrested and deposed by the military during the 2021 Myanmar coup d'état after it declared the November 2020 Myanmar general election results, which the NLD won, fraudulent. The coup sparked protests across the country.

❑❑❑

Aurobindo Ghosh

(1872–1950)

Scholar and Poet

"Spirituality is indeed the master key of the Indian mind; the sense of the infinitive is native to it."

Sri Aurobindo Ghosh was a revolutionary, poet, writer, and spiritual master. Despite his fascinating life, he was sceptical of any biographies. Sri Aurobindo paved a new approach to yoga, which he termed as "Integral Yoga". His writings and outer life give a profound glimpse into the life of this unique spiritual master. He felt yoga and spirituality need not involve retreating from the world. Sri Aurobindo wished to bring the Divine into all aspects of life. For the last 40 years of his life, he worked tirelessly for this goal of bringing down a new spiritual consciousness.

Sri Aurobindo Ghosh was born on of August 15, 1872. He spent his formative years in England studying at St Paul's and Trinity College where he excelled in the study of literature and the classics. In 1892, he returned to India where he became heavily involved in the Indian independence movement. Aurobindo was a natural leader and one of the most radical nationalist politicians.

Because of his radicalism, in 1908, Sri Aurobindo was arrested on suspicion of being involved in a bomb plot and was remanded in Alipore jail. It was in jail that Sri Aurobindo had significant spiritual experiences, and became aware of a divine inner guidance. He also realised the omnipresence of God even in a darkened prison cell.

Due to the commitment of Sri Aurobindo's lawyer, C. R. Das, he was released without charge. However, this experience had changed Sri Aurobindo's outlook. Henceforth, he retired from politics and focussed his energies on spirituality.

Sri Aurobindo travelled to Pondicherry, South India where he could practise yoga undisturbed. In 1914, he was later joined by a French woman, Mira Richards, who later became known as the Mother of the Sri Aurobindo Ashram. Together, they founded the Sri Aurobindo Ashram, which began to attract disciples with their dynamic reinterpretation of yoga.

In addition to being a spiritual Guru to many of his disciples, Sri Aurobindo was a noted poet, philosopher and writer. His main works were *The Life Divine*, *The Synthesis of Yoga*, *Essays on the Gita* and *Savitri*. Savitri was an epic work of poetry that he worked on for over 20 years.

Sri Aurobindo did not negate the world like Indian *yogis* of the past. Instead, Sri Aurobindo affirmed that our entire life is Yoga; through a conscious aspiration, and it is possible for man to evolve into a higher consciousness – a consciousness of truth and inner harmony. Sri Aurobindo called this new consciousness as super mental.

A significant event occurred in 1947, when India attained full independence. This was a goal Sri Aurobindo had continued to aspire for, despite his retreat from politics. Independence was achieved on his birthday, i.e., August 15 in the year, 1947.

For over 40 years, Sri Aurobindo worked tirelessly for his vision of a divine life on earth. Through his writings and poetry, he left a legacy which reflected his hopes of a golden future for humanity. Sri Aurobindo entered into *mahasamadhi* on December 5, 1950.

Although Sri Aurobindo wrote most of his works in English, his major works were later translated into a number of languages, including several Indian languages such as, Hindi, Bengali, Oriya, Gujarati, Marathi, Sanskrit, Tamil, Telugu, Kannada, and Malayalam. These were also translated in French, German, Italian, Dutch, Spanish, Chinese, Portuguese, Slovene and Russian. A large amount of his work in Russian translation is also available.

❑❑❑

Ayn Rand

(1905–1982)

Writer and Philosopher

"A desire presupposes the possibility of action to achieve it; action presupposes a goal which is worth achieving."

Ayn Rand was a novelist and philosopher, best known for developing objectivism and for writing the novels *We the Living*, *The Fountainhead*, *Atlas Shrugged*, and *The Novella Anthem*.

Ayn Rand was born in St. Petersburg, in the year 1905 in Russia as Alissa Rosenbaum. During her younger years, she lived a comfortable, affluent, middle-class existence. Her father had become a chemist despite quotas on Jews studying at the university. Her mother subscribed her to children's literary magazines, which inspired her to write her own stories. (According to the Rand mythology, she decided to become a writer at tender age of nine). In 1917, she and her family witnessed the Russian Revolution as the Communist Party took over the government. The financial condition of the family became very low.

In 1921, when she was 16 years old, she enrolled at Petrograd State University. During her second year, she was expelled as anti-proletariat, but thanks to protests by foreign governments, she was reinstated. After Ayn Rand finished her degree, she enrolled at the State Technicum for Screen Arts, where she studied screenwriting.

At this point, Rosenbaum (Rand) knew that her philosophy did not fit with the Communist agenda, and she probably realised that she needed to leave Russia. In January 1926, she got a passport to visit her relatives for a short time in Chicago. But she never returned and, soon after, her arrival in Chicago, Ayn left for Hollywood, hoping to get a job as a screenwriter. Around this time, she changed her name. In addition to the usual reasons that people change their names upon entering Hollywood, Rand may have intended to protect her relatives in Russia, who could be punished for the ideas and arguments she was planning to express through films.

Ayn claimed that she arrived in Hollywood with only fifty dollars in her pocket and that the day after she arrived in Hollywood; she was given a car ride and a job as a movie extra by film director, Cecil B. DeMille. While this account is probably at least partially untrue, Rand did work as an extra in several of DeMille's films. In fact, it was on the set of DeMille's film, *King of Kings* that she met her future husband, actor Frank O'Connor.

Rand's career as a writer was launched in 1932, when she successfully sold a screenplay to Universal Studios. While the film was never produced, she then wrote the play, *The Night of January 16th*, which was produced on Broadway in 1934. Her first novel, *We the Living* (1936), portrays life in post-communist Russia. This novel was followed by *Anthem* (1938), a science fiction novel about a future dystopia where the world has been corrupted by communism. Rand did not enjoy real success until the publication of *The Fountainhead* in 1943. Rand's last novel, which is mostly considered as her masterpiece, *Atlas Shrugged*, was published in 1957.

Rand also proposed a theory of aesthetics which she publicised in a series of essays published between 1965 and 1971. According to

Louis Torres and Michelle Kamhi, "Rand's esthetic theory forms an integral part of her total philosophic system. Rand usually named Aristotle as her most important philosophical influence, though Nietzsche also had a clear influence on her. She also claimed to have been inspired by John Locke's ideas about property.

In 1949, Rand began corresponding with a young man named Nathan Blumenthal. By the late 1950's, Nathan Blumenthal, and his then wife Barbara were at the centre of a group of young intellectuals who were devoted to Ayn Rand- both to her works and to Rand personally. Nathan formed an institute with the intent of sponsoring lectures and publications on her philosophy. At some point during this time, Nathan stated, their relationship moved beyond friendship. For almost a decade Nathan was Rand's biggest supporter, advocate, and colleague. In 1962, he and Rand started the Objectivist Newsletter, which became a small magazine called *The Objectivist* by 1965.

According to Branden, Rand ended their relationship in 1968, when she discovered he was having another affair with a woman he would later marry. Rand expelled Branden from the movement, announcing their break in an article in *The Objectivist* without mentioning their relationship. They never reconciled.

Rand's life grew more complicated over the next years. She developed lung cancer, the Nathaniel Branden Institute fell apart, and the Collective slowly disintegrated. Rand's husband died in 1979, and she began to reduce her activities. She died from heart failure in 1982.

❑❑❑

Azim Hashim Premji

(1945)

Business Magnate

"Character is one factor that will guide all our actions and decisions."

Azim Hashim Premji, the founder, Chairman and Managing Director of Wipro Technologies, is one of the world's most successful businessman. He is regarded as The Bill Gates of India after transforming his father's vegetable-products company, Wipro, into a multi-national computer giant.

Azim Hashim Premji was born on July 24, 1945 in Bombay, India. He was studying Electrical Engineering from Stanford University, USA when due to the sudden demise of his father M.H. Premji in 1966, he was called upon to handle the family business. At the age of 21 when Premji took over the reins of family business, he inherited ₹ 7 crore worth Western India Vegetable Products Company. The Amalner-based vanaspathi manufacturing company later became Wipro Products,Wipro Ltd and Wipro Corp. He has since after a gap of thirty years completed his degree in Electrical Engineering.

Under Premji's leadership Wipro embarked on an ambitious phase of expansion and diversification. The Company began manufacturing light bulbs with General Electric and other consumer products including soaps, baby care products, shampoos, powder etc. In 1975, Wipro Fluid Power business unit manufacturing hydraulic cylinders and truck tippers was started. But Premji's ambitions did not stop there.

In the 1980s Wipro entered the IT field, taking advantage of the removal of IBM from the Indian market in 1975. Thus, Wipro became involved in developing computer hardware, software development and related items, under a special license from Sentinel. As a result, the $1.5 million company in hydrogenated cooking fats grew within a few years to a $662 million diversified, integrated corporation in services, medical systems, technology products and consumer items with offices worldwide.

Wipro's IT division became the world's first to win SEI CMM level 5 and PCMM Level 5 (People Capability Maturity Model) certification, the latest in quality standards. Wipro works with leading global companies, such as Alcatel, Nokia, Cisco and Nortel and has a joint venture in Medical Systems with General Electric company. A growing number of European firms and US rely on the Banglore-based Wipro to handle their software needs, keep their databases and computer networks up and running, and answer calls from customers.

In the year 2001, Premji established Azim Premji Foundation, a not-for-profit organization with a vision of influencing the lives of millions of children in India by facilitating the universalisation of elementary education.

In 2001, he was voted among the 20 most powerful men in the world by Asiaweek. He was named by Fortune (August 2003) as one of the 25 most powerful business leaders outside the US, Forbes (March 2003) listed him as one of ten people globally, Business Week featured (October 2003) him on their cover with the sobriquet 'India's tech king'. In April 2004, Times Magazine rated him among the 100 most influential people in the world. The Indian Institute of Technology, Roorkee and the Manipal Academy of Higher Education have both conferred honorary doctorates on him. He is also a member of the Prime Minister's Advisory Committee for Information Technology in India.

In January 2006, he was the 10th richest man in the world. Premji was awarded the Padma Bhushan in 2005 and Padma Vibhushan in 2011 by the Government of India. He was placed in 41st position with a wealth of $6.4 billion in the Forbes Billionaire List 2000.

Premji's story of success and prominence clearly shows how determination and perseverance, when coupled with knowledge, clear vision and proper planning, enable one to reach the peak of success and leadership. A straight forward person, he is an absolute workaholic and according to him work is the only way to success and survival in a competitive environment.

He topped the EdelGive Hurun India Philanthropy List for 2020. In 2019, he dropped from the 2nd position in the Forbes India Rich list to 17th position after giving away a huge amount to charity.

Azim Premji topped the list of "India's most generous" released by Hurun India and EdelGive on 10 November 2020. He donated ₹ 7,904 crore in financial year 2019-20 which is a 17-fold jump from the ₹ 453 crore donated in FY2019. Education is the primary cause for his donations.

In December 2024, Premji was ranked 19th on the Forbes list of India's 100 richest tycoons, with a net worth of $32.2 billion.

❑❑❑

Baba Amte

(1914–2008)

Social Leader

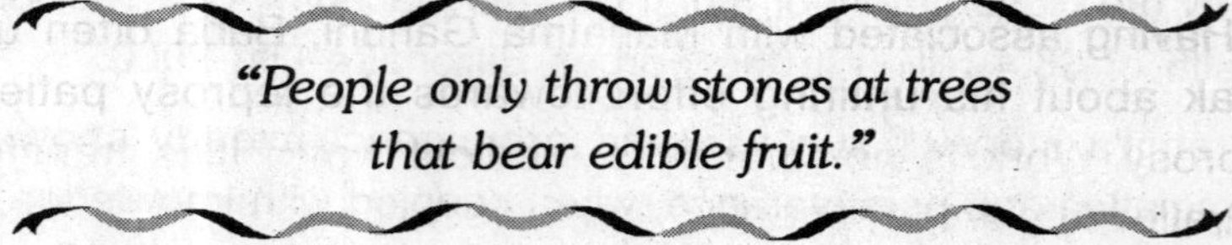

One of India's most revered social and moral leaders, Baba Amte had devoted his life to the care and rehabilitation of leprosy patients, even allowing his body to be used for experiments to grow leprosy germs. His community development project at Anandwan is recognised and respected around the world.

Murlidhar Devidas Amte, fondly called as Baba Amte - the patron of Anandwan, was born a day after Christmas in 1914, to a wealthy landowner. His father had every possible luxury, money could buy.

By the time he was fourteen, Baba owned his own gun and hunted boar and deer. He developed a special interest in cinema, wrote reviews for the film magazine, *The Picture Goer* and even corresponded with Greta Garbo and Norma Shearer.

Baba Amte's tryst with the sorrow, pain and diseases began in the tiny village of Warora,in Central India. All around him were the leprosy patients in utter squalor and neglect. Diseases in those days were like flashing Neon billboards of *Times Square,* for which there were no definite remedy. Leprosy, tuberculosis, cholera, etc. were the foremost in raising the mortality rate.

Baba firmly believed the importance of Human rights. He used to say "A person can live without fingers, but he cannot live without self respect". In order to cater to the larger segment of the society, Baba formed the Maharogi Sewa Samiti in 1951.

Having associated with Mahatma Gandhi, Baba often used to speak about his untiring effort towards the leprosy patients as "Leprosy Work is not merely a medical work; It is transforming frustration into the joy of dedication, personal ambition to self service". His ideas are crystal clear when it comes to the upliftment of the lepers and weaker strata of the society.

Soon the news spread like a bushfire and lepers from near and far started pouring into Anandwan. Around 1951, with the discovery of the wonder drug DDS, the face of Leprosy treatment changed forever. With excellent cure rate and sincere nursing, soon the patients were on path to fall recovery.

During those times, the social scenario was not conducive for the lepers to get back into the social bandwagon. The rejected lepers finally found solace in Anandwan, the one which guarded their dignity and pride. They proved once again by contributing to the successful small scale industry that indeed they are talented and gifted. The inmates with words of encouragement from Baba soon began manufacturing things needed for the nearby markets. Handicrafts, machines, footwear, clothes and many other products slowly started trickling out of the small scale industries of Anandwan.

Deeply disturbed by the communal and separatist strife, he plunged into his maiden effort of curbing the sad scenario by launching the "Knit India Movement". His rendezvous with the oppressed people continued inspite of the poor response from the government. His lonely crusade brought him to the banks of river, Narmada. The protest was against the huge World Bank funded dam, in Gujarat which in due course of time, was to bring a sizeable area of land under water and displace the local tribal community who have been residing in the areas for generations.

He was a recipient of many national and international awards. The notable amongst which are Damien – Dutton Award USA in 1983 , The Ramon Magsaysay Award in 1985, The United Nations Human Rights Prize in 1988, International Giraffe Award in 1989 , The Templeton Award in 1990 , The Padmashree, The Padma Vibhushan, The Gandhi Peace Prize, Dr Ambedkar International Award and many more.

Baba Amte passed away on February 9, 2008. The end came at his own commune for leprosy patients 'Anandvan' at Warora village in Chandrapur district of Maharashtra.

❑❑❑

Baba Ramdev

(1965)

Yoga Guru

"Yog se yeh Aaryavrat desh punah Vishva guru ke garimamay pad par pratishthit hoga."
(India will again become world leader through Yoga).

Baba Ramdev, also known as Swami Ramdev is a renowned Yoga teacher. Through his Yoga Pranayama educational show, which is broadcast on numerous TV channels, he has taken the art of Yoga to each and every household far and wide. He is responsible for a revolution in Yoga and Health.

Ramdev was born as 'Ramkishan Yadav' in 1965 in Alipur, in the Mahendragarh district of Indian state of Haryana. He studied in his Narnaul village school till fifth and upto eight class in nearby village Shahjadpur. Thereafter, he joined a yogic monastery (gurukul) in Khanpur village to study Sanskrit and Yoga. Eventually, he renounced worldly life and entered into Sanyas (monastic living)-taking the name Swami Ramdev.

Then he went to Jind district and joined the Kalva gurukul under Acharya Baldevji Maharaj and offered free Yoga training to villagers across Haryana. It is said that he travelled the Himalayas for several years before he settled in Haridwar. He claims to have discovered several medicinal plants in the Himalayas which he uses in treating his patients. Ramdev started relentless efforts to popularise Yoga in 1995 with the establishment of D Y M Trust along with Acharya Karamveer.

In 1995, Ramdev joined the order of Swamis after being initiated into the ascetic order by Swami Shankerdevji Maharaj. While training to be a Swami, Ramdev spent many years undertaking an intense and thorough study of ancient Indian scriptures. At the same time, he also practiced intense self-discipline and meditation.

As a promotional vehicle for Yoga, Baba Ramdev established the Divya Yoga Mandir Trust in 1995. In this project, he was accompanied by Acharya Karamveer and Acharya Balkrishna. The headquarters of the trust are at the Kripalu Bagh Ashram of Haridwar.

Patanjali Yog Peeth was Baba Ramdev's ₹ 100-crore dream project at Bahadrabad in Haryana. It is the first Yoga University with a naturopathy department, a patients' residential complex, a hall for 5,000 people to practice yoga. In addition to helping people learn about Yoga and spirituality, these institutions also provide a comprehensive facility that promotes the practice of Ayurveda - the traditional system of holistic medicine developed in India.

Baba Ramdev teaches Pranayama, a series of techniques for breath control that were developed as a part of the ancient Indian System of Yoga. He has worked diligently to help make the practice of Pranayama achievable by the ordinary layperson. Ths six Pranayamas are—Bhastrika, Kapal Bhati, Bhaya, Anulom Vilom, Bhramri and Udgeeth. He has been conducting Yog science camp regularly all over the country, and sometimes abroad as well. In 2006, Baba Ramdev spent almost a month in London teaching Pranayam and Yoga.

Baba Ramdev teaches that God resides in every human being and that the body is God's temple. He is a firm believer in the of Vasudhaiva Kutumbakam (the whole World is one family) and decries practices that discriminate on the basis of caste, creed or gender.

In January 2007, KIIT University in Odisha awarded Swami Ramdev with an Honorary Doctorate degree in recognition of his efforts at popularizing the Vedic science of Yoga. The degree was presented to him in a ceremony presided over by the respected scientist and Nobel laureate Richard Ernst. In 2010, he was honoured by Doctrate of Sciences by Amity University and Doctor of Science by Dr. D.Y. Patil Deemed University. In January 2011 he was honoured with Sri Chandrashekharendra Saraswati National Eminence Award.

In 2010, Ramdev announced plans to form a political party called *Bharat Swabhiman* (India Pride). He said that it would contest every seat in the next national elections. A year later, he stated that, instead of forming a political party, he would influence politics by encouraging a grounds well of popular reaction. In January 2015, he was considered for Padma Vibushan, second highest civillian award but day before 66th Republic Day, he humbly refrained from taking it by putting the fact he is an ascetic.

In May 2016, American business magazine Fast Company ranked Ramdev 27th in its Most Creative Business People of 2016 list. In April 2017, Magazine India Today Ranked #5th in India's 50 Most powerful people of 2017 list.

Baba Ramdev was ranked 78th in the list of 100 Most Powerful Indians in 2022 by The Indian Express. His influence in the fields of Yoga, Ayurveda, and business through Patanjali Ayurved has certainly made him a prominent figure in India.

Bachendri Pal

(1954)

Mountaineer

"Will power, self belief and transparency
– It's important"

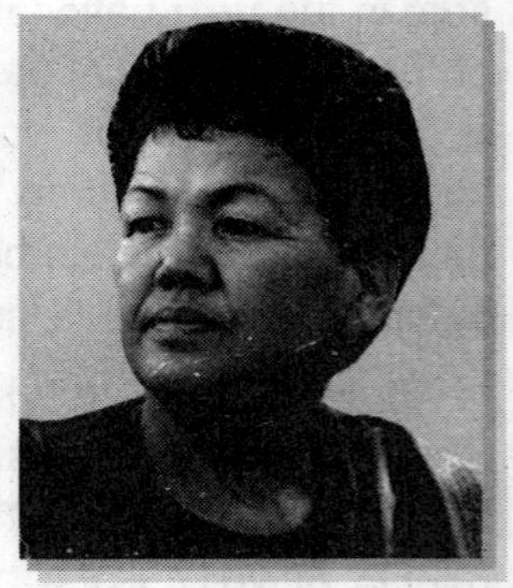

She is the first Indian woman (and the fifth in the world), to scale the Mt. Everest, the highest peak in the world.

Bachendri Pal was born, into a family of very moderate means, in 1954 in a village named Nakuri in Garhwal. Her father, Kishan Singh Pal, was a small trader. Eventually, he had settled in Uttarkashi, where he married. Bachendri was an active child, and did well in her school. She excelled in sports too.

Her first exposure to mountaineering was at the age of 12 years, when during a picnic with her classmates, she along with her several schoolmates climbed to a 13,123 ft. high peak. They could not climb down as it had already become dark, and had to spend the night at the peak without any food or cover. The experience remained ingrained into her memory, heightening her love for adventure and the mountains. Despite many constraints, she continued her schooling, and completed it successfully. While in college, she also secured the first position in a rifle shooting event, beating other boys and girls. She also completed university courses leading to securing an MA and a Bachelor's degree in education.

The family was facing financial crunch, and she wanted a job desperately. However, the offers coming to her were not of her choice. When she shared with her parents her desire to become a professional mountaineer, the family felt "devastated". For her parents, relatives and the local people, the most suitable job for a woman was teaching, and mountaineering was certainly not something appropriate for a woman.

However, Bachendri did not budge from her determination. She joined the Nehru Institute of Mountaineering (NIM). She was declared the best student and was considered as "Everest material". In 1982, while at NIM, she climbed Gangotri I (21,900 ft) and Rudugaria (19,091 ft).

In 1984, India had scheduled its fourth expedition, christened "Everest, 84", to the Mount Everest. Bachendri was selected as one of the members of the elite group of six Indian women and eleven men who were privileged to attempt an ascent to the Mount Everest. The news made her filled with a sense of ecstasy and excitement. The elite team was flown to Kathmandu, the capital of Nepal in March 1984; and from there the team moved onwards. Recalling her first glimpse of the Mount Everest, Bachendri once reminisced: "We the hill people have always worshipped the mountains ... my overpowering emotion at this awe-inspiring spectacle was, therefore, devotional."

On May 22, 1984, some other climbers joined the team to ascent the summit of the Mount Everest. Bachendri was the only woman in this group. They continued the ascent climbing the "vertical sheets of frozen ice", cold winds sometimes blowing at the speed of about 100 kms per hour, temperatures touching below up to –30 to 40°C. On May 23, 1984, Bachendri reached the summit of Mount Everest, and at 1:07 pm (IST), she was standing at the peak (29,084 ft) along with one other climber. The peak was small to accommodate two persons; and there was a vertical drop of thousands of feet all around the peak. So they first made themselves secured by anchoring themselves by digging their ice axes into the snow.

Bachendri then sat on her knees, touched the summit with her head in the Hindu gesture of thanksgiving to the Almighty. She remained on the summit for about 43 minutes, and took some photographs too.

She climbed down and reached the base camp safely. Her achievement brought her felicitation from many quarters across the world. In India, the President, the Prime Minister, and J. R. D. Tata congratulated her in person.

In 1985, Bachendri Pal led an Indo-Nepalese Everest Expedition team comprising of only women. The expedition created seven world records and set benchmarks for Indian mountaineering. Nine years later, in 1994, she led an all women team of rafters, covering 2,500 km from Haridwar to Kolkata.

She is the first recipient of Virangana Lakshmibai Rashtriya Samman 2013-14, which was given by the Government of Madhya Pradesh on 18 June 2013 for her personal achievement in Adventure sports and women's upliftment in the country.

She was awarded the third highest civilian award Padma Bhushan by Government of India in 2019.

In 2021, she led the 'FIT@50+ Women's Trans Himalayan Expedition', a five-month journey covering approximately 4,500 kilometers across 40 mountain passes, inspiring women over 50 to embrace physical activity. In 2021, she was honoured with the Uttarakhand Gaurav Samman by the Government of Uttarakhand.

❑❑❑

Bal Gangadhar Tilak

(1856–1920)

Social Reformer and Freedom Fighter

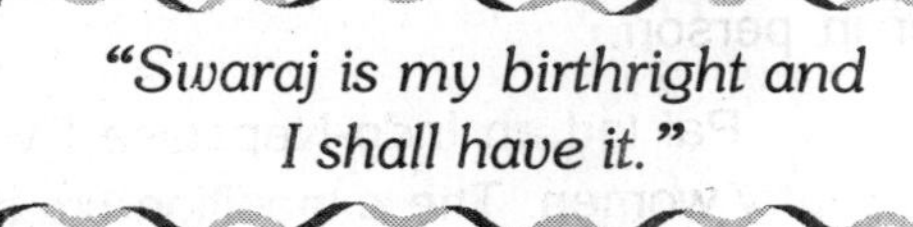

"Swaraj is my birthright and I shall have it."

Bal Gangadhar Tilak is recognised as the Father of Indian Unrest. He was one of the prime architects of modern India and heralded the Asian nationalism. Tilak was a scholar of Indian history, Sanskrit, Hinduism, Mathematics and Astronomy.

Bal Gangadhar Tilak was born on 1856, in a village, Chikhali, near Ratnagiri, Maharashtra, into a middle class Chitpavan Brahmin family. Tilak was an avid student with a special aptitude for mathematics. He received Bachelor of Arts degree from 'The Deccan College', Pune in 1879 and LLB from the Elphinston College, Mumbai in 1882. He was among the founders of the New English School, Pune (1881) of which Prof. Chiplunkar became the Principal. He was among India's first generation of youth to receive a modern, college education.

After graduation Tilak began teaching mathematics in a private school in Pune and later became a journalist. He became a strong critic of the western education system, feeling it demeaning to Indian students and disrespectful to India's heritage. He organised the Deccan Education Society to improve the quality of education for India's youth. He taught Mathematics at Fergusson College in Pune.

Tilak is often misinterpreted. Perhaps, it is so because of his style of operation which raised bitter controversies and still more bitter opponents even outside the bureaucracy. Violent arguements characterised his relationship with social reformists such as Agarkar, Ranade and moderates like Ferozshah Mehta. Many blame him for opposing the Age of Consent Bill which raised the age limit for marriage of girls to 12 (from 10). He educated all of his daughters and did not marry them till they were over 16. There are instances when he privately paid for the education of women.

Tilak had a genius for organisation and with Agarkar, started the newspapers, *Kesari* and *The Maratha* in 1881, and in 1890's, began the annual celebration of 'Shivaji Festival' and 'Ganapati Festival' which served a platform for people to join in the nationalist movement against the British. Soon he came to be regarded as the undisputed leader of Maharashtra and was honoured with the title, 'Lokmanya' in 1893, which became synonymous with him in the 1900.

As the nation fumed over the partition of Bengal (1905), Tilak assumed the national leadership with his extremist attitude and stated his position unequivocally as "Swarajya (self rule) is my birth right and I shall have it."

The next three years saw meteoric rise in his stature and the British power which had long since considered him their chief concern and had sent him to prison twice already, decided on a firmer measure. Much has been said of his trial of 1908. He utilised his time in prison in scholarly pursuits and wrote '*Gita Rahasya*', a commentary on the Gita. He returned to the Indian political scene in 1915. The political situation was fast changing under the shadow of World War I. Mahatma Gandhi's star was on the rise with Satyagraha at Sabarmati in 1914.

The British charged Tilak in 1918. He fought those charges both in India and England, and was judged guilty. Amidst rumours of yet another sentence, he headed the Home-Rule Commission in England to debate India's constitutional demands. By that time, Gandhi had made preparations of the first nationwide Non-cooperation Movement and, perhaps, it was to make way for Gandhi that Tilak left for England. Tilak was, probably, the only leader who could have put brakes on Gandhi.

In the 20's, many of Tilak's followers, Dadasaheb Khaparde and N.C. Kelkar being the most prominent among them, supported Gandhi but none could have his say in the new order. Aurobindo Ghosh had retired to an ascetic life and Savarkar was serving two life sentences in Andaman.

Tilak's health continued to deteriorate rapidly by the end of July 1920, he was unconscious for three days. His last words in the final momentary recovery were, "This happened in 1818 (End of Peshwa) and this in 1918. A hundred years' history— what a life of servitude...Unless Swaraj is obtained, India shall not prosper. It is necessary for our very own existence."

On August 1, 1920, Bal Gangadhar Tilak was declared dead. It is said that the British made an extraordinary request that his brain be handed over to them so that it could be studied, preserved and exhibited. However it was not complied with.

❑❑❑

Barack Hussain Obama

(1961)

Politician

"My job is not to represent Washington to you, but to represent you to Washington."

Barack Hussain Obama was born on August 04, 1961, in Hawaii, to parents from different ethnicities who met during their studies at the University of Hawaii and were united by deep and mutual respect. His Mother Ann Dunham hailed from US state of Kansas and was a white American, while his Dad was from Kenya, Africa who had come to American state of Hawaii to pursue higher studies in its university. As his father soon returned to Kenya, divorce occurred between his parents and later his mother married with Lolo Soetoro, a native of Indonesia. He received his elementary education in Indonesia for 4 years. Before fifth grade, he returned to Honolulu to live with his maternal grandparents and attend Punahou School on scholarship.

His mom had a deep leaning towards the civil rights movement of 1950s and 60s and always discussed its nuances with young Obama which had a deep impact upon him. He once mentioned, "To be black was to be the beneficiary of a great inheritance, a special destiny, glorious burdens that only we were strong enough to bear".

In his memoir *Dreams from My Father* (1995), Obama describes the complexities of discovering his identity in adolescence. After two years at Occidental College in Los Angeles, he transferred to Columbia University, where he studied political science and international relations. Following graduation in 1983, Obama worked in New York City, then became a community organizer on the South Side of Chicago, coordinating with churches to improve housing conditions and set up job-training programs in a community hit hard by steel mill closures. In 1988, he went to Harvard Law School, where he attracted national attention as the first African American president of the Harvard Law Review. Returning to Chicago, he joined a small law firm specializing in civil rights.

In 1992, Obama married Michelle Robinson, a lawyer who had also excelled at Harvard Law. Their daughters, Malia and Sasha, were born in 1998 and 2001, respectively. Obama was elected to the Illinois Senate in 1996, and then to the U.S. Senate in 2004. At the Democratic National Convention that summer, he delivered a much acclaimed keynote address. Some pundits instantly pronounced him a future president, but most did not expect it to happen for some time. Nevertheless, in 2008 he was elected over Arizona Senator John McCain by 365 to 173 electoral votes.

When Barack Obama was elected president in 2008, he became the first African American to hold the office. As an incoming president, Obama faced many challenges-an economic collapse, wars in Iraq and Afghanistan, and the continuing menace of terrorism. Inaugurated before an estimated crowd of 1.8 million people, Obama proposed unprecedented federal spending to revive the economy and also hoped to renew America's stature in the world. During his first term he signed three signature bills: an omnibus bill to stimulate the economy, legislation making health care more accessible and affordable, and legislation reforming the nation's financial institutions. Obama also pressed for a fair pay act for women, financial reform legislation, and efforts for consumer protection. In 2009, Obama became the fourth president to receive the Nobel Peace Prize.

In 2012, he was reelected over former Massachusetts Governor Mitt Romney by 332 to 206 electoral votes. The Middle East remained a key foreign policy challenge. Obama had overseen the killing of Osama bin Laden, but a new self-proclaimed Islamic State arose during a civil war in Syria and began inciting terrorist attacks. Obama sought to manage a hostile Iran with a treaty that hindered its development of nuclear weapons. The Obama administration also adopted a climate change agreement signed by 195 nations to reduce greenhouse gas emissions and slow global warming.

In the last year of his second term, Obama spoke at two events that clearly moved him-the 50th anniversary of the civil rights march from Selma to Montgomery, and the dedication of the National Museum of African American History and Culture. "Our union is not yet perfect, but we are getting closer," he said in Selma. "And that's why we celebrate," he told those attending the museum opening in Washington, "mindful that our work is not yet done."

Since leaving office, Obama has remained active in Democratic politics, including campaigning for candidates in the 2018 midterm elections, appearing at the 2020 Democratic National Convention and campaigning for Biden during the 2020 presidential election. Outside of politics, Obama has published three bestselling books: Dreams from My Father (1995), The Audacity of Hope (2006) and A Promised Land (2020).

In 2021, he co-hosted the podcast *Renegades: Born in the USA* with Bruce Springsteen. He won a Grammy (2022) for *A Promised Land* and an Emmy for *Our Great National Parks*. In 2024, he endorsed Kamalá Harris for president and actively campaigned for her, continuing his advocacy for democracy and human rights.

❑❑❑

Benito Mussolini

(1883–1945)

Dictator

"Fascism is a religion. The twentieth century will be known in history as the century of Fascism."

Benito Mussolini was a Fascist dictator of Italy from 1922 to 1943. He centralised all power in himself as the leader of the Fascist party and attempted to create an Italian empire, ultimately in alliance with Hitler's Germany.

Mussolini was born in the village of Dovia di Predappio in the province of Forli, in Emilia-Romagna on July 29, 1883 to Rosa and Alessandro Mussolini. He was named Benito after Mexican reformist President Benito Juarez. His mother, Rosa Maltoni, was a teacher. His father, Alessandro, was a blacksmith who often encouraged Benito to disobey authority (other than his own). He adored his father, but his love was never reciprocated. Like his father, who was a member of the first Socialist International, Benito became a socialist. He was not baptised as a child.

He was sent to a boarding school later that year and at the age 11 was expelled for stabbing a fellow student in the hand, throwing an inkpot at a teacher, and using a stick to poke out his classmate's eyes.

Benito qualified as an elementary schoolmaster in 1901. In 1902, he immigrated to Switzerland, but was arrested for vagrancy. He returned to Italy to do military service.

Later, in 1908, he joined a newspaper in the Austrian town of Trento. Benito wrote a novel named The Cardinal's Mistress. He was later expelled by the Austrians. Benito became the editor at Forli of a socialist newspaper, La Lotta di Classe, (The Class Struggle).

By 1910, Mussolini became secretary of the local Socialist party. When Italy declared war on Turkey in 1911, he was imprisoned for pacifist propaganda. Mussolini became editor of the official Socialist newspaper, Avanti. He then moved to Milan.

As World War I broke out, and Mussolini stated that Italy should not join. However, several months later, he unexpectedly changed his position. He left the Socialist party. In 1914, Mussolini founded a new newspaper, *Il Popolo d'Italia*, and group, *Fasci d'Azione Rivoluzionaria*. Later, he was called up for military service, where he was wounded in grenade practice in 1917.

Fascism became an organised political movement in March 1919, when Mussolini founded the *Fasci de Combattimento*. He entered parliament in 1921. When the governments of Giovanni Giolitti, Ivanoe Bonomi, and Luigi Facta failed, Mussolini was invited by the king in October 1922, to form the government.

Mussolini introduced strict censorship. He assumed dictatorial powers and dissolved all other political parties. In 1929, a concordat with the Vatican was signed, by which the Italian state was recognised by the Roman Catholic Church.

In foreign policy, Mussolini shifted to a form of aggressive nationalism. He bombed Corfu in 1923, and set up a puppet regime in Albania, forming an alliance with the Nazi Germany.

He made the "Pact of Steel" with Hitler in May, 1939. In April 1939, he occupied Albania. After the fall of France, Mussolini declared war. His army was of poor quality, and soon suffered defeats. His colleagues turned against him. The king too dismissed and arrested him.

In April 1945, just before the Allied armies reached Milan, Mussolini, along with his mistress, Clara Petacci, was caught by The Italian partisans as Nussolini tried to take refuge in Switzerland. Mussolini was abruptly executed. The duke was survived by his wife, Rachele, their two sons, Vittorio and Romano, and daughter Edda, the widow of Count Ciano. A third son, Bruno, had been killed in an air accident.

❑❑❑

Bertrand Russell

(1872–1970)

Philosopher

"Fear is the main source of superstition, and one of the main sources of cruelty. To conquer fear is the beginning of wisdom."

Bertrand Arthur William Russell was a British philosopher, logician, essayist, and social critic, best known for his work in mathematical logic and analytic philosophy. His most influential contributions include his defence of logicism, and his theories of definite descriptions and logical atomism. Along with G. E. Moore, Russell is generally recognised as one of the founders of analytic philosophy.

Bertrand Arthur William Russell was born at Trelleck on May 18, 1872. His parents were Viscount Amberley and Katherine, daughter of the 2nd Baron Stanley of Alderley. At the age of three, he was left an orphan. His father had wished him to be brought up as an agnostic. To avoid this, he was made a ward of court, and brought up by his grandmother. Instead of being sent to school, Russell was taught by governesses and tutors, and thus, acquired a perfect knowledge of French and German.

In 1890, he went into residence at Trinity College, Cambridge, and after being a very high Wrangler, and obtaining a first class with distinction in philosophy, he was elected a fellow of his college in 1895. But Russell had already left Cambridge in the summer of 1894 and for some months was delegate at the British embassy at Paris.

In December 1894, he married Miss Alys Pearsall Smith. After spending some months in Berlin studying social democracy, they went to live near Haslemere, where he devoted his time to the study of philosophy. In 1900, he visited the Mathematical Congress at Paris. Russell was impressed with the ability of the Italian mathematician, Peano and his pupils, and immediately studied Peano's works.

In 1903, he wrote his first important book, *The Principles of Mathematics*, and with his friend, Dr. Alfred Whitehead, proceeded to develop and extend the mathematical logic of Peano and Frege. From time to time, he abandoned philosophy for politics. In 1910, Russell was appointed lecturer at Trinity College.

After the First World War broke out, he took an active part in the No Conscription fellowship and was fined £100 as the author of a leaflet criticising a sentence of two years on a conscientious objector. His college deprived him of his lectureship in 1916. Russell was offered a post at the Harvard University, but was refused a passport. He intended to give a course of lectures (afterwards published in America as *Political Ideals*, 1918) but was prevented by the military authorities. In 1918, he was sentenced to six months' imprisonment for a pacifistic article he had written in the *Tribunal*. Russell's *Introduction to Mathematical Philosophy* (1919) was written in prison. His *Analysis of Mind* (1921), was the outcome of some lectures he gave in London, which were organised by a few friends who got up a subscription for the purpose.

In 1920, Russell had paid a short visit to Russia to study the conditions of Bolshevism on the spot. In the autumn of the same year, he went to China to lecture on philosophy at the Peking University. On his return in September 1921, having been divorced by his first wife, he married Miss Dora Black. They lived for six years in Chelsea during the winter months and spent the summers near Lands End.

In 1927, he and his wife started a school for young children, which they carried on until 1932. He succeeded to the earldom in 1931. Russell was divorced by his second wife in 1935 and the following year married Patricia Helen Spence. In 1938, he went to the United States and during the next years taught at many of the country's leading universities. In 1940, he was involved in legal proceedings when his right to teach philosophy at the College of the City of New York was questioned because of his views on morality. When his appointment to the college faculty was cancelled, he accepted a five-year contract as a lecturer, but the cancellation of this contract was announced in January 1943 by Albert C. Barnes, director of the foundation.

Russell was elected a fellow of the Royal Society in 1908, and re-elected a fellow of Trinity College in 1944. He was awarded the Sylvester medal of the Royal Society, 1934, the 'de Morgan medal' of the London Mathematical Society in the same year, the Nobel Prize for Literature, 1950.

After a life marked by controversy (including dismissals from Trinity College, Cambridge, and City College, New York), Russell was awarded the 'Order of Merit' in 1949 and the Nobel Prize for Literature in 1950. Also noted for his many spirited anti-war and anti-nuclear protests, Russell remained a prominent public figure until his death at the age of 97 in 1970.

❑❑❑

Benjamin Franklin

(1706–1790)

Diplomat, Writer and Sciencist

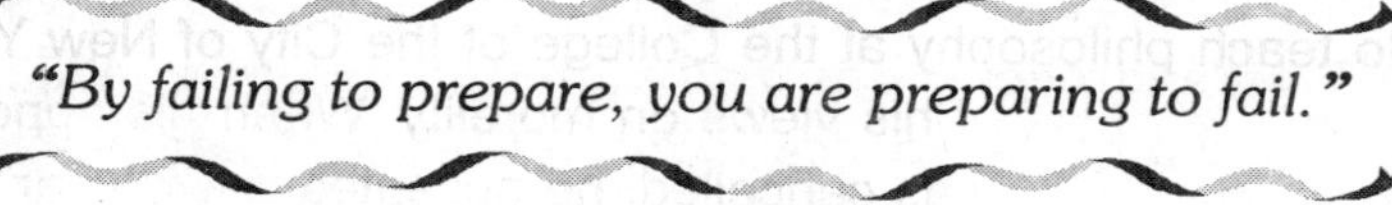

"By failing to prepare, you are preparing to fail."

Benjamin Franklin was a statesman, diplomat, writer, scientist and inventor. He was one of the most versatile and talented men in colonial America and a leading figure in the American struggle for independence.

Franklin organized the United States' first lending library and volunteer fire department. His scientific pursuits included investigations into electricity, mathematics and mapmaking. He helped draft the Declaration of Independence and the U.S Constitution, and negotiated the 1783 Treaty of Paris, which marked the end of the Revolutionary War.

Benjamin Franklin was born in Boston on 17 January 1706. He attended school only briefly, and then helped his father, who was a candle and soap maker. He apprenticed to his brother, a printer, and began writing anonymously for his brother's newspaper. Franklin and his brother quarrelled, and in 1723 Franklin ran away to Philadelphia. After 18 months in London, Franklin settled in Philadelphia, establishing himself as a printer. He bought the 'Pennsylvania Gazette', which he edited and which became one of the American colonies' major newspapers. He also wrote and published 'Poor Richard's Almanack', an astronomy journal.

By 1748, Franklin had made enough money to retire from business and concentrate on science and inventing. His inventions included the Franklin stove and the lightning rod. He demonstrated with his famous kite experiment that lightning and electricity are identical. Franklin also became more active in politics. He was clerk of the Pennsylvania Assembly (1736-1751), a member of the Assembly (1750-1764), and deputy postmaster for the Colonies (1753-1774), reorganising the postal service to make it efficient and profitable.

Franklin was also involved in many public projects, including founding the American Philosophical Society, a subscription library and, in 1751, an academy which later became the University of Pennsylvania.

From 1757 to 1774, Franklin lived mainly in London where he was the colonial representative for Pennsylvania, Georgia, New Jersey and Massachusetts. His attempts to reconcile the British government with the colonies proved fruitless. On his return to America, the war of independence had already broken out and he threw himself into the struggle. In 1776, he helped to draft, and was then a signatory to, the Declaration of Independence. His illegitimate son William, royal governor of New Jersey between 1762 and 1776, remained loyal to Britain, causing a rift that lasted for the rest of Franklin's life.

Later that year, Franklin and two others were appointed to represent America in France. Franklin negotiated the Franco-American Alliance which provided for military cooperation between the two countries against Britain and ensured significant French subsidies to America. In 1783, as American ambassador to France, Franklin signed the Treaty of Paris, ending the American War of Independence. He was extremely popular and well known in France, but in 1785 he returned to America. He continued to be deeply involved in politics, helping to draft the Constitution.

Back in the United States, in 1785 Franklin became president of the Supreme Executive Council of Pennsylvania. At the Constitutional Convention, though he did not approve of many aspects of the finished document and was hampered by his age and ill-health, he missed few if any sessions, lent his prestige, soothed passions, and compromised disputes.

In his twilight years, working on his *Autobiography*, Franklin could look back on a fruitful life as the toast of two continents. Energetic nearly to the last, in 1787 he was elected as first president of the Pennsylvania Society for Promoting the Abolition of Slavery - a cause to which he had committed himself as early as the 1730s. His final public act was signing a memorial to Congress recommending dissolution of the slavery system. Shortly thereafter, in 1790 at the age of 84, Franklin passed away in Philadelphia and was laid to rest in Christ Church Burial Ground.

Franklin mapped the Gulf Stream, invented swim fins, the lightning rod and musical instruments, established colleges, and amassed scores of other accomplishments. His self-education earned him honorary degrees from Harvard, Yale, Oxford University in England, and the University of St. Andrews in Scotland.

Franklin's voracious capacity for knowledge, investigation and finding practical solutions to problems was his primary focus, as was his commitment to "doing good," which led to the concept of paying it forward.

❑❑❑

Beyonce Knowles

(1981)

Singer and Actress

"Whatever I do. It has to be something that's gonna teach me something about life."

Beyoncé Giselle Knowles-Carter, simply known as Beyoncé is an American singer, songwriter and actress. She performed in various singing and dancing competitions as a child, and rose to fame in the late 1990s as lead singer of R&B girl-group Destiny's Child. Managed by her father Mathew Knowles, the group became one of the world's best-selling girl groups of all time. Their hiatus saw the release of Knowles' debut album *Dangerously in Love* (2003), which established the singer as a viable solo artist worldwide; it sold 11 million copies, earned five Grammy Awards and featured the *Billboard* number one singles "Crazy in Love" and "Baby Boy".

Beyoncé was born on September 4, 1981, in Houston, Texas. She started singing at an early age.

Teaming up with her cousin, Kelly Rowland, and two classmates, Beyoncé formed an all-female singing group. Her father, Matthew

Knowles, served as the band's manager. The group went through some name and line-up changes before landing a record deal in 1997 with Columbia Records. Destiny's Child soon became one of the most popular R&B acts, with the release of their first, self-titled album. Gaining momentum, the group scored its first No. 1 single on the pop charts with "Bills, Bills, Bills," off their second album. The recording also featured another smash hit, "Say My Name."

While enjoying her group's success, Beyoncé began exploring other projects. She made her acting debut in 2001 with a starring role in MTV's *Carmen: A Hip Hopera*. She then co-starred with Mike Myers in the spy parody *Goldmember* the following year. On the musical front, Beyoncé took center stage as a solo artist, releasing her first album, *Dangerously in Love*, in 2003. It sold millions of copies and won five Grammy Awards. On the album, Beyoncé worked with a number of different artists, including Missy Elliott, Sean Paul and Jay-Z.

Destiny's child released their last studio album, *Destiny Fulfilled*, in 2004 and officially broke the following year.

Beyoncé on her own, continued to enjoy great success. Her second studio album, 2006's *B'Day* featured such hits as "Irreplaceable" and "Beautiful Liar." On the big screen, she starred opposite Jennifer Hudson, Jaime Foxx and Eddie Murphy in *Dreamgirls*. The film was adapted from the hit Broadway musical of the same name.

In 2008, Beyoncé married rapper and music mogul Jay-Z in a small, private ceremony in New York City. The newly-wed continued to work as hard as ever, promoting her latest effort, *I am ... Sasha Fierce* (2008). Beyoncé scored two big hits off the album—"Single Ladies (Put a Ring On It)" and "If I Were a Boy." She also returned to the big screen that year, starring as R&B legend Etta James in *Cadillac Records*.

The following January, Beyoncé sang James' trademark song, "At Last," for President Barack Obama and First Lady Michelle Obama at his inaugural ball. Beyoncé found herself under fire for performing a private concert for Libyan leader Muammar Qaddafi on New Year's Eve in 2010. She later donated her fee from the event to help victims of the Haitian earthquake. Later that year, Beyoncé reached the top of the album charts with her latest solo release, *4*.

At the 2010 Grammy Awards, Beyoncé walked away with six honors—the most wins in a single night by a female artist. Her record was matched two years later by pop/soul artist Adele. In 2010, she also tied the record for most No. 1 hits on Billboard's Pop Songs chart, which is based on radio airplay. In 2011, she made the Forbes Top 10 list of entertainment's highest-earning women. By 2013, Beyoncé had won 16 Grammys.

Beyoncé and Jay-Z welcomed a baby daughter, Blue Ivy Carter, on January 7, 2012. On February 6, 2016, Beyoncé released "Formation" and its accompanying music video exclusively on the music streaming platform Tidal. On April 16, 2016, Beyoncé released a teaser clip for a project called *Lemonade*. It turned out to be a one-hour film which aired on HBO. At the 59th Grammy Awards, *Lemonade* led with nine nominations including Album of the Year, and Record of the Year and Song of the Year for "Formation" and ultimately won two, Best Urban Contemporary Album for *Lemonade* and Best Music Video for "Formation". Beyoncé occupied the sixth place for *Time magazine's* 2016 Person of the Year. In January 2017, it was announced that Beyoncé would headline the Coachella Music and Arts Festival. This would make Beyoncé only the second female headliner of the festival since it was founded in 1999.

In December 2024, Beyonce was crowned the Greatest Pop Star of the Century by Billboard. Beyonce's win for Album of the Year with "Cowboy Carter" at the 2025 Grammy Awards is indeed historic. She became the first Black woman to win the Best Country Album Grammy, and her win for Album of the Year marks a significant milestone in her career.

Bhagat Singh

(1907-1931)

Revolutionary Leader

"Zindagi to Apne hi Dum par jee jati hai....
Dusro ke kandho pe to Janaze utha karte hain...."

Bhagat Singh was an Indian revolutionary, considered to be one of the most famous martyrs of the Indian freedom struggle. He is also believed by many to be one of the earliest Marxists in India and has been labelled so by the Communist Party of India (Marxist). He was one of the leaders and founders of the Hindustan Socialist Republican Association.

Bhagat Singh was born on September 28, 1907 in a Sikh family in village Banga in Layalpur district of Punjab. He was the third son of Sardar Kishan Singh and Vidyavati. Bhagat Singh's family was actively involved in freedom struggle. His father Kishan Singh and uncle Ajit Singh were members of Ghadr Party founded in the United States to oust British rule from India. Family atmosphere had a great effect on the mind of young Bhagat Singh and patriotism flowed in his veins from childhood.

While studying at the local DAV School in Lahore, in 1916, young Bhagat Singh came into contact with some well-known political leaders like Lala Lajpat Rai and Rash Bihari Bose. Punjab was politically very charged in those days. In 1919, when the Jallianwala Bagh massacre took place, Bhagat Singh was only 12 years old. The massacre deeply disturbed him. On the next day of the massacre, Bhagat Singh went to the Jallianwala Bagh and collected soil from the spot. He kept it as a memento for the rest of his life. The massacre strengthened his resolve to drive the British out from India.

In response to Mahatma Gandhi's call for the non-cooperation against the British rule in 1921, Bhagat Singh left his school and actively participated in the movement. In 1922, when Mahatma Gandhi suspended the Non-cooperation Movement against the violence at Chauri-chaura in Gorakhpur, Bhagat was greatly disappointed. His faith in non violence weakened and he came to the conclusion that armed revolution was the only practical way of winning freedom.

To continue his studies, Bhagat Singh joined the National College in Lahore, founded by Lala Lajpat Rai. At this college, which was a centre of revolutionary activities, he came into contact with revolutionaries such as Bhagwati Charan, Sukhdev and others.

In 1928, he attended a meeting of revolutionaries in Delhi and came into contact with Chandrasekhar Azad. The two formed the 'Hindustan Samajvadi Prajatantra Sangha'.

In February 1928, a committee from England, called Simon Commission visited India. The purpose of its visit was to decide how much freedom and responsibility could be given to the people of India. But there was no Indian on the committee. This angered the Indians and they decided to boycott the Simon Commission.

While protesting against the Simon Commission in Lahore, Lala Lajpat Rai succumbed to injuries. Bhagat Singh was determined to avenge Lajpat Rai's death by shooting the British official responsible for killing Deputy Inspector General Scott. He shot down Assistant Superintendent Saunders instead, mistaking him for Scott. Bhagat Singh had to flee from Lahore to escape death punishment.

The British government took repressive measures. Under the Defence of India Act, it gave more power to the police to arrest persons to stop processions with suspicious movements and actions. Bhagat Singh who was in hiding all this while, volunteered to throw a bomb in the Central Legislative Assembly where the meeting to pass the ordinance was being held.

On April 8, 1929, Bhagat Singh and Batukeshwar Dutt threw bombs in the Central Assembly Hall while the assembly was in session. The bombs did not hurt anyone. Bhagat Singh and Batukeshwar Dutt deliberately courted arrest by refusing to run away from the scene. Meanwhile, the killers of Saunders were identified by the treachery of Bhagat Singh's friends who became "Approvers".

In jail, he went on hunger strike to protest the inhuman treatment of fellow-political prisoners by jail authorities. On October 7, 1930, Bhagat Singh, Sukh Dev and Raj Guru were awarded death sentence by a special tribunal for terrorist activities.

Despite great popular pressure and numerous appeals by political leaders of India, Bhagat Singh and his associates were hanged in the early hours of March 23, 1931. His supporters, who had been protesting against the hanging, immediately declared him as a *shaheed* (martyr). Singh was cremated at Hussainiwala on the banks of the Sutlej River in Lahore.

❑❑❑

Bhim Rao Ambedkar

(1891–1956)

Scholar, Political Leader

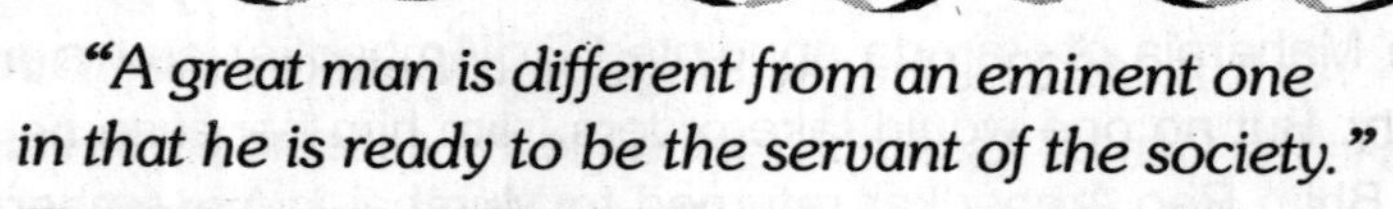

"A great man is different from an eminent one in that he is ready to be the servant of the society."

Bhim Rao Ambedkar was a Buddhist revivalist, an Indian jurist, scholar and Bahujan political leader who is the chief architect of the Indian constitution. He spent his life fighting against the system of Hindu untouchability and the Indian Caste System. He has been honoured with Bharat Ratna.

Dr. Bhim Rao Ambedkar was born on April 14, 1891 in Madhya Pradesh. He was the fourteenth child of Ramji and Bhimabai Sakpal Ambedkar. Dr. B.R. Ambedkar belonged to the "untouchable" *Mahar* caste. His father and grandfather served in the British Army.

Ambedkar passed his matriculation examination from Mumbai University with flying colours in 1908. Ambedkar joined the Elphinstone College for further education. In 1912, he graduated in Political Science and Economics from Mumbai University and got a job in Baroda.

In 1913, Bhim Rao Ambedkar lost his father. In the same year, Maharaja of Baroda awarded scholarship to Bhim Rao Ambedkar and sent him to America for further studies. He immersed himself in the studies and attained a degree in Master of Arts and a Doctorate in Philosophy from the Columbia University in 1916 for his thesis, "National Dividend for India: A Historical and Analytical Study". From America, Dr. Ambedkar proceeded to London to study economics and political science. But the Baroda government terminated his scholarship and called him back.

The Maharaja of Baroda appointed Dr. Ambedkar as his political secretary. But no one would take orders from him because he was a *Mahar*. Bhim Rao Ambedkar returned to Mumbai in November 1917.

In July 1924, he founded the *Bahishkrit Hitkaraini Sabha* (Outcastes Welfare Association). The aim of the Sabha was to uplift the downtrodden, socially and politically and bring them to the level of others in the society.

In 1927, he led the Mahad March at the Chowdar Tank at Colaba, near Mumbai, to give the untouchables the right to draw water from the public tank where he burnt copies of the *Manusmriti* publicly.

In 1929, Ambedkar made the controversial decision to co-operate with the All-British Simon Commission which was to look into setting up a responsible Indian Government in India. The Congress decided to boycott the Commission and drafted its own version of a constitution for free India. The Congress version had no provisions for the depressed classes. Ambedkar became more skeptical of the Congress's commitment to safeguard the rights of the depressed classes.

When a separate electorate was announced for the depressed classes under Ramsay McDonald 'Communal Award', Gandhiji went on a fast unto death against this decision. Leaders rushed to Dr. Ambedkar to drop his demand. On September 24, 1932, Dr.

Ambedkar and Gandhiji reached an understanding, which became the famous Poona Pact. According to the pact, the separate electorate demand was replaced with special concessions like reserved seats in the regional legislative assemblies and Central Council of States.

In 1937, Dr. Ambedkar introduced a Bill to abolish the "khoti" system of land tenure in the Konkan region, the serfdom of agricultural tenants and the *Mahar* "watan" system of working for the government as slaves. A clause of an agrarian bill referred to the depressed classes as 'Harijans,' or people of God. Bhim Rao was strongly opposed to this title for the untouchables. He was against any such reference. But the Indian National Congress succeeded in introducing the term, 'Harijan'. Ambedkar felt bitter that they could not have any say in what they were called for.

In 1947, when India became independent, the first Prime Minister, Pt. Jawaharlal Nehru, invited Dr. Bhim Rao Ambedkar, who had been elected as a member of the constituent assembly from Bengal, to join his cabinet as a Law Minister. The Constituent Assembly entrusted the job of drafting the Constitution to a committee and Dr. Ambedkar was elected as Chairman of this Drafting Committee. In February 1948, Dr. Ambedkar presented the Draft Constitution before the people of India, and it was adopted on November 26, 1949.

In October 1948, Dr. Ambedkar submitted the Hindu Code Bill to the Constituent Assembly in an attempt to codify the Hindu law. The Bill caused great divisions even in the Congress party.

On May 24, 1956, on the occasion of Buddha Jayanti, he declared in Mumbai, that he would adopt Buddhism in October. On October 14, 1956, he embraced Buddhism along with many of his followers. On December 6, 1956, Dr. B.R. Ambedkar died peacefully in his sleep.

Bill Gates

(1955)

Software Pioneer

"Capitalism is this wonderful thing that motivates people; it causes wonderful inventions to be done. But in this area of diseases of the world at large, it's really let us down."

Bill Gates, the co-founder, chairman, former chief software architect, and former CEO of Microsoft, is also the founder of Corbis. He is consistently ranked in the Forbes list of the world's wealthiest people and was the wealthiest overall from 1995 to 2009—excluding 2008, when he was ranked third; in 2011 he was the wealthiest American and the world's second wealthiest person. As of October 2021, Gates had an estimated net worth of US$129 billion, making him the fourth-richest person in the world.

Gates is one of the best-known entrepreneurs of the personal computer revolution.

William Henry Gates III was born in Seattle, Washington to William H. Gates, Sr. and Mary Maxwell Gates on October 28, 1955. He belonged to a wealthy family. His father was a prominent lawyer, his mother served on the board of directors for the First Interstate Bank and The United Way, and her father, J. W. Maxwell, was a national bank president. Gates has one elder sister, Kristi (Kristianne), and one younger sister, Libby.

Gates excelled in elementary school, particularly in mathematics and the science. At thirteen, he enrolled in the Lakeside School, Seattle's most exclusive preparatory school where tuition fee in 1967 was $5,000 (Harvard tuition fee that year was $1760). When he was in the eighth grade, Lakeside obtained an ASR-33 teletype terminal and a donation of computer time on a general electric computer from a *Mothers Club* rummage sale.

Gates took an interest in programming the GE system in BASIC and was excused from math classes to pursue his interest. After the Mothers Club donation was exhausted, he and other students sought time on other systems, including DEC PDP minicomputers. One of these systems was a PDP-10 belonging to Computer Centre Corporation, which banned the Lakeside students after it caught them exploiting bugs in the operating system to obtain free computer time. After that experience, Gates swore off computers for a year and a half.

In 1968, CCC (Computer Centre Corporation) approached the Lakeside computing students (Gates, Paul Allen, Ric Weiland, and Kent Evans) with an offer of free computer time in exchange for fixing the bugs in the system software. Rather than using the system via teletype, he went to CCC's offices and studied source code for various programmes that ran on the system, not only in BASIC but FORTRAN, LISP, and machine language as well. The arrangement with CCC continued until 1970, when it went out of business. The following year, Information Sciences Inc. hired the Lakeside students to write a payroll programme in COBOL, providing them not only computer time but royalties as well. Gates also formed a venture with Allen, called Traf-O-Data, to make traffic counters based on the Intel 8008 processor.

Gates enrolled at Harvard University in the fall of 1973 without a definite study plan. While at Harvard, he met his future business partner, Steve Ballmer. Gates left Harvard to devote his energies to Microsoft, a company he had begun in 1975 with his childhood friend Paul Allen.

Gates was married on January 1, 1994, to Melinda French Gates. The couple has two children: a daughter, Jennifer Katharine Gates, born in 1996; and a son, Rory John Gates, born in 1999.

On May 3, 2021, the Gates announced they had decided to divorce after 27 years of marriage and 34 years as a couple. The divorce was finalized on August 2, 2021.

In 1999, Gates wrote the book *Business @ the Speed of Thought*, which received wide critical acclaim, and was listed on the bestseller lists of the *New York Times*, *USA Today*, *The Wall Street Journal* and *Amazon.com*. Gates' previous book, *The Road Ahead*, published in 1995, held the No. 1 spot on the *New York Times*' bestseller list for seven weeks.

Philanthropy is also important to Gates. He and his wife, Melinda, have endowed a foundation—Bill & Melinda Gates Foundation, with more than $21 billion to support philanthropic initiatives in the areas of global health and learning. In November 2006, he and his wife were awarded the Order of the Aztec Eagle for their philanthropic work. Gates stepped down from his post on June, 2008 to devote himself totally to the work of the foundation.

Gates has received honorary doctorates. He was also made an honorary trustee of Peking University in 2007. Gates was also made an honorary Knight Commander of the Order of the British Empire (KBE) by Queen Elizabeth II in 2005, in addition to having entomologists name the Bill Gates flower fly, *Eristalis gatesi*, in his honour. He was awarded the 2010 Bower Award for Business Leadership of The Franklin Institute for his achievements in business and for his philanthropic work and 2010 Silver Buffalo Award by the Boy Scouts of America for his service to youth.

On February 4, 2014, Gates stepped down as chairman of Microsoft to become Technology Advisor alongside Satya Nadella. In March 2020, Gates left his board positions at Microsoft and Berkshire Hathaway to focus on his philanthropic efforts including climate change, global health and development, and education.

Birju Maharaj

(1937-2022)

Kathak Dancer

"Beauty lies in an individual's heart. I have found even some very ugly girls to be beautiful within."

Pandit Birju Maharaj is one of the foremost exponents of the country's Kathak dancers. He is a direct descendant of a line of dancers who have been intimately linked with the city and culture of Lucknow for two centuries. Son of well-known Achchan Maharaj and nephew and student of Shambhu Maharaj, Birju Maharaj made his mark in the arena when he received the coveted Sangeet Natak Akademi award at the age of 28.

Pandit Birju Maharaj alias Brij Mohan Nath Mishra was born on February 4, 1937. He took training in Kathak under the guidance of his father, Achchan Maharaj and uncles, Lacchu Maharaj and Shambhu Maharaj. He studied with his father until the latter's death in 1947. Thereafter, he continued his training with his uncles, and not surprisingly, Birju Maharaj draws together in his own dance style, the strengths of each: from his father he claims to have inherited the suppleness of the torso and chest, the play of the neck, head, and face, the precision of the footwork, and the fullness of movement; from Lacchu Maharaj he learned the stylised *chals* of the *gat* and the fluidity of movement; from Shambhu Maharaj, he adopted the power of movement and the force needed to dance paran. In his own words, Birju Maharaj has likened Lacchu Maharaj and Shambhu Maharaj to the moon and the sun, and Acchan Maharaj, the sky. Combined, they form his universe.

Birju Maharaj gave his first performance at the young age of seven at Lucknow and after that there was no looking back. This exponent of the Lucknow *gharana* has a suitably old-world charm and his personal simplicity endear him to everyone. But the magic comes from within, filtered through an astounding talent and decades of hard work. Birju Maharaj has many faces— he is a shy gopi, waiting for her lover; he is a naughty child, stealing butter; he is a valiant warrior-king, vanquishing his enemies in battle; he is God himself, omnipresent, omnipotent and omniscient.

Not only in India, he is familiarly known abroad, nearly all over the world. He has extensively toured across the globe, which includes USSR, USA, Japan, UAE, UK, France, Germany, Italy, Austria, Czechoslovakia, Burma (Myanmar), Sri Lanka, etc. for performances as well as lecture-demonstrations. Besides being a superb dancer, he is also gifted with a number of other qualities which add to his artistic career.

Birju Maharaj is a wonderful singer having command over, *Thumri*, *Dadra*, *Bhajan* and *Ghazals* and is also a superb drummer, playing nearly all drums with ease and precision. He has given a new dimension to Kathak by experimenting this technique in the application of dance-dramas, which has become a very successful medium for mass propagation. As a choreographer, he is the finest in the country today. His bold and intellectual compositions in traditional themes are brilliant, whereas his contemporary works are also refreshing in concept, crisp and entertaining.

Birju Maharaj directed and composed music and sung playback for two classical dance sequences in the film, *'Shatranj ke Khiladi'* directed by Satyajit Ray. A measure of his genius is the fact that at the age of 28, he received the Sangeet Natak Akademy Award. He is also a recipient of the country's second highest civilian award-Padma Vibhushan, besides several other prestigious awards such as, Kalidas Samman, Lata Mangeshkar Puraskar, Nritya Choodamani, Andhra Ratna, Nritya Vilas, Adharshila Shikhar Samman, Soviet Land Nehru Award, Shiromani Samman and the Rajiv Gandhi Peace Award.

He has been conferred with the Honorary Doctorate degrees from Banaras Hindu University, as well as Khairagarh University. He is widely acclaimed not only as a performer but also as an inspiring 'Guru' - teacher, having successfully trained numerous students in India and abroad.

Birju Maharaj taught at Sangeet Bharati, Bharatiya Kala Kendra and headed the teaching faculty, Kathak Kendra in Delhi till his retirement in 1998.

Maharaj also choreographed and composed music for many Indian movies. Some of the performances that he choreographed included for Saswati Sen in Satyajit Ray's *Shatranj ke Khiladi* (1977), Madhuri Dixit in *Dil To Pagal Hai* (1997) and *Devdas* (2002), Kamal Haasan in *Vishwaroopam* (2012), Deepika Padukone in *Bajirao Mastani* (2015) and Alia Bhatt in *Kalank* (2019). His choreography for Kamal Hassan in *Vishwaroopam* won him the National Film Award for Best Choreography in 2012, while his choreography for Deepika Padukone in *Bajirao Mastani* won him a Filmfare Award for Best Choreography in 2016.

He died from a heart attack at his residence in Delhi, on 16 January 2022, less than a month before his 85th birthday.

❑❑❑

Bob Dylan

(1941)

Singer

"Behind every beautiful thing, there is a some kind of pain."

Bob Dylan is one of the most influential singer-songwriters of the 20th century whose career began in the early 1960s with songs that chronicled social and political issues.

Bob Dylan was born Robert Allen Zimmerman on May 24, 1941, in Duluth, Minnesota, to parents Abram and Beatrice Zimmerman. He and his younger brother David were raised in the community of Hibbing, where he graduated from Hibbing High School in 1959. Driven by the influences of early rock stars like Elvis Presley, Jerry Lee Lewis and Little Richard (whom he used to imitate on the piano at high school dances), the young Dylan formed his own bands, including the Golden Chords, as well as a group he fronted under the pseudonym Elston Gunn.

While attending the University of Minnesota in Minneapolis, he began performing folk and country songs at local cafés, taking the name "Bob Dillon."

In the fall of 1961, after one of his performances received a rave review in The New York Times, he signed a recording contract with Columbia Records, at which point he legally changed his surname to Dylan. Released early in 1962, Bob Dylan contained only two original songs, but showcased Dylan's gravelly-voiced singing style in a number of traditional folk songs and covers of blues songs.

By 1964 Dylan was playing 200 concerts annually, but had become tired of his role as "the" folk singer-songwriter of the protest movement. Another Side of Bob Dylan, recorded in 1964, was a much more personal, introspective collection of songs, far less politically charged than Dylan's previous efforts.

Beginning in the 1980s, Dylan began touring full time, sometimes with fellow legends Tom Petty and the Heartbreakers and the Grateful Dead. Notable albums during this period included Infidels (1983); the five-disc retrospective Biograph (1985); Knocked Out Loaded (1986); and Oh Mercy(1989), which became his best-received album in years. He recorded two albums with the all-star band the Traveling Wilburys, also featuringGeorge Harrison, Roy Orbison, Tom Petty and Jeff Lynne.

In 2006, Dylan released the studio album Modern Times. After hitting stores in late August, it reached the top of the album charts the next month. A mixture of blues, country, and folk, the album was praised for its rich sound and imagery. Several critics also remarked the album had a playful, knowing quality. Showing no signs of slowing down, Dylan continued to tour throughout the first decade of the 21st century, and released the studio album Together Through Life in April 2009.

In 2010, he released a bootleg album called The Witmark Demos, followed by a new boxed set entitled Bob Dylan: The Original Mono Recordings. In addition, he exhibited 40 of his original paintings for a solo show at the National Gallery of Denmark. In 2011, he released yet another live album, Bob Dylan in Concert - Brandeis University 1963, and in September 2012, released his newest studio album, Tempest. Shadows in the Night, a cover album of American standards, followed in 2015. A year later, Dylan released Fallen Angels, his thirty-seventh studio album which features more classic songs from the Great American Songbook. In 2017, he continued to celebrate the classics with his three-disc studio album Triplicate, which features 30 American standards including "Stormy Weather," "As Time Goes By" and "The Best Is Yet To Come."

As a musician, Dylan has sold more than 100 million records, making him one of the best-selling artists of all time. He has also received numerous awards including eleven Grammy Awards, a Golden Globe Award, and an Academy Award. Dylan has been inducted into the Rock and Roll Hall of Fame, Minnesota Music Hall of Fame, Nashville Songwriters Hall of Fame, and Songwriters Hall of Fame. The Pulitzer Prize jury in 2008 awarded him a special citation for "his profound impact on popular music and American culture, marked by lyrical compositions of extraordinary poetic power." In May 2012, Dylan received the Presidential Medal of Freedom from President Barack Obama. In 2016, he was awarded the Nobel Prize in Literature "for having created new poetic expressions within the great American song tradition".

In 2018, Dylan was one of the artists featured on the six-track EP Universal Love: Wedding Songs Reimagined, a collection of classics from various eras revised with same-sex pronouns.

Dylan gave fans a pleasant surprise with the March 2020 release of a 17-minute song, "Murder Most Foul," about the assassination of John F. Kennedy.

In 2023, the biopic *A Complete Unknown*, starring Timothée Chalamet, depicted his early career, introducing his legacy to a younger audience.

❑❑❑

Britney Spears

(1981)

Singer

"Onstage I'm the happiest person in the world."

Britney Jean Spears is an American pop music singer. Her career encompasses chart-topping records, high-profile advertising and a foray into both acting and reality television.

Britney Jean Spears was born on December 2, 1981, in Kentwood, Louisiana. Her pursuit of a musical career had begun at an early age. At the age of 8, Britney auditioned for the popular children's variety show, 'The New Mickey Mouse Club', but was refused because of her young age. Britney spent the next three summers in New York, where she studied at the famous Off Broadway Dance Centre and at the Professional Performing Arts School. She began appearing in various broadway productions.

It was on her third attempt with the Mickey Mouse Club that she was accepted as one of the Mouseketeers along with future pop contemporaries Christina Aguilera, Justin Timberlake and J.C. Chasez.

Later, Britney signed with Jive Records, and her debut album was released when she was 17 years old. "...Baby One More Time" is her biggest hit till date. The album was a rage with the pre-teenage and teenage crowd. By the time she had released her second album, she had already co-authored a book titled, *Heart to Heart* with her mother, Lynne Spears.

She co-hosted the American Music Awards with L.L. Cool J., and performed at the Rock in Rio festival. Spears performed with Aerosmith,' N Sync, Nelly, and Mary J. Blige at the Super Bowl.

She became a brand ambassador for Pepsi in 2001. She also co-authored another book with her mother called *A Mother's Gift*. She even entered the restaurant industry with her own establishment, 'Nyla' but it was a commercial failure and has shut down. Spears' ambitions of becoming a movie star took a jolt when her film, "Crossroads" bombed badly and she was awarded with the Razzie Awards for Worst Actress.

Her luck with the Grammy awards has not been very good either. In 2000, Spears was nominated for two Grammy awards; Best Female Pop Vocal Performance for the single "...Baby One More Time", and the 'Best New Artist'. She did not receive either award. Spears was again nominated twice in 2003 but lost out on both occasions. She finally struck gold with "Toxic" in the category of Best Dance Recording.

Britney Spears shocked audiences in a remix rendition of Madonna's "Like A Virgin" and "Hollywood." Britney released her first fragrance, "Curious." It is a floral scent with vanilla and musk. The fragrance had the biggest debut in sales in the history of Elizabeth Arden. "Curious" was honoured by the Fragrance Foundation, naming it ' the Best Women's Fragrance'.

Britney's penchant for the bizarre took a new twist when she married childhood friend Jason Alexander in an impromptu ceremony in the Little White Wedding Chapel on the Las Vegas Strip on January 3, 2004. The couple agreed to an annulment later the same day. On

September 18, 2004, Britney Spears legally married Kevin Federline, a professional dancer; it was a marriage that ended in 2007.

In November 2005, Britney released her first remix album *B in The Mix : The Remixes* which sold over 1 lakh copies. In 2007 she released her fifth album *Blackout* which debuted at number two on the UK Albums Chart and the US Billboard. In 2008 she won two Awards at the MTV Europe Music Awards 2008, 'Album of the Year' for *Blackout* and 'Act of 2008'. In February 2009, she achieved further success with her 2008 comback album *Circus*. Same year, she released a new fragrance entitled "*Hidden Fantasy*". Her compilation album *The Singles Collection* was released in 2009.

In June 2010 she was ranked sixth on Forbes list of the 100 most powerful and influential celebrities in the world.

In May 2016, Spears launched a casualrole-play gaming application titled *Britney Spears: American Dream.* The app, created by Glu Mobile, was made available through both iOS and Google Play. On May 22, 2016, Spears performed a medley of her past singles at the 2016 Billboard Music Awards. In addition to opening the show, Spears was honored with the Billboard Millennium Award.

As of 2017, according to the BBC, she has sold over 100 million records worldwide, making her one of the best-selling music artists of all time; and more than 70 million records in United States, including 36.9 million digital singles and 33.6 million digital albums.

In 2024, Britney Spears was prominently featured at the MTV Video Music Awards (VMAs). Britney Spears received multiple nominations at the 2025 Billboard Music Awards, acknowledging her enduring influence in the music industry.

Bruce Lee

(1940–1973)

Actor

"Notice that the stiffest tree is most easily cracked, while the bamboo or willow survives by bending with the wind."

Bruce Lee was an American-born Chinese martial artist, instructor, actor and founder of the *Jeet Kune Do* martial arts system. He is widely regarded as one of the most influential and famous martial artists of all time. He is also widely known as the greatest icon of martial arts cinema and a key figure of modern popular culture.

Bruce Lee was born in San Francisco in November 1940. He was the son of a famous Chinese opera singer. At birth, he was given the English name, "Bruce" by Dr. Mary Glover. Interestingly, the name "Bruce" was never used within his family until he enrolled in La Salle College, a Hong Kong high school, at 12 years of age, and then again at another Catholic boys' school, St Francis Xavier's College.

Bruce moved to Hong Kong where he soon became a child star in the growing Eastern film industry. His first film was called *The birth of mankind*, his last film which was uncompleted at the time of his death in 1973 was called, *Game of Death*. Bruce was a loner and was constantly getting himself into fights. With this in mind, he looked towards Kung Fu as a way of disciplining himself. The famous Yip Men taught Bruce his basic skills, but it was not long before he was mastering the master. Yip Men was acknowledged to be one of the greatest authorities on the subject of Wing Chun, a branch of the Chinese Martial Arts. Bruce mastered this before progressing to his own style of *Jeet Kune Do*.

At the age of 19, Bruce left Hong Kong to study for a degree in philosophy at the University of Washington, in America. It was at this time that he took on a waiter's job and also began to teach some of his skills to students who would pay. Some of the Japanese schools in the Seattle area tried to force Bruce out, and there were many confrontations and duels fought for Bruce to remain.

He met his wife Linda at the University, where he was studying. His martial arts school flourished and he soon graduated. Bruce Lee gained some small roles in Hollywood films - *Marlowe,* etc, and some major stars were begging to be students of the *Little Dragon*. He regularly gave displays at exhibitions, and it was during one of these exhibitions that he was spotted by a producer and signed up to do *The Green Hornet* series. The series was quite successful in the States - but was a huge hit in Hong Kong. Bruce visited Hong Kong in 1968 and he was overwhelmed by the attention he received from the people he had left.

Bruce Lee once said on a radio programme that if the price was right he would do a movie for the Chinese audiences. He returned to the States and completed some episodes of Longstreet. He began writing his book on *Jeet Kune Do* at roughly the same time.

Back in Hong Kong, producers were desperate to sign Bruce for a martial arts film, and it was Raymond Chow, the head of Golden Harvest who produced *The Big Boss*.

On July 20, 1973, just one month before the premiere of *Enter the Dragon*, Bruce Lee died in Hong Kong at the age of 32. The official cause of his sudden and utterly unexpected death was a brain oedema, found in an autopsy to have been caused by a strange reaction to a prescription painkiller he was reportedly taking for a back injury. Controversy surrounded Lee's death from the beginning, as some claimed he had been murdered.

❑❑❑

C.V. Raman

(1888–1970)

Scientist

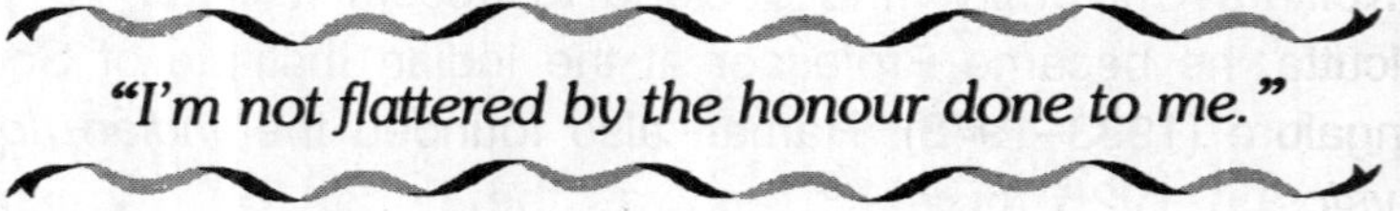

"I'm not flattered by the honour done to me."

C.V. Raman is one of the most renowned scientists produced by India. His full name was Chandrasekhara Venkata Raman. For his pioneering work on scattering of light, C.V. Raman won the Nobel Prize for Physics in 1930.

Chandrasekhara Venkata Raman was born at Trichinopoly in Southern India on November 7, 1888. His father was a lecturer in mathematics and physics so that from the very beginning, he was immersed in an academic atmosphere. C.V. Raman entered the Presidency College, Madras, in 1902, and in 1904 passed his BA examination, winning the first place and the gold medal in Physics. In 1907, he gained his MA degree, obtaining the highest distinctions.

His earliest researches in optics and acoustics - the two fields of investigation to which he has dedicated his entire career - were carried out while he was a student.

Since at that time, a scientific career did not appear to present the best possibilities, Raman joined the Indian Finance Department in 1907. Though the duties of his office took most of his time, Raman found opportunities for carrying on experimental research in the laboratory of the Indian Association for the Cultivation of Science at Calcutta (Kolkata) of which he became the Honorary Secretary in 1919.

In 1917, he was offered the newly endowed Palit Chair of Physics at Kolkata University, and decided to accept it. After 15 years at Calcutta, he became Professor at the Indian Institute of Science at Bangalore (1933–1948). Raman also founded the *Indian Journal of Physics* in 1926, of which he was the Editor. He sponsored the establishment of the Indian Academy of Sciences and served as president since its inception. He also initiated the proceedings of that academy, in which much of his work has been published.

Some of Raman's early memoirs appeared as bulletins of the Indian Association for the Cultivation of Science dealing with the "Maintenance of Vibrations"; dealing with the theory of the musical instruments of the violin family. He contributed an article on the theory of musical instruments to the 8th Volume of the *Handbuch der Physik*, 1928.

In 1922, Raman published his work on the "Molecular Diffraction of Light", the first of a series of investigations with his collaborators which ultimately led to his discovery of the radiation effect on February 28, 1928 and gained him the 1930 Nobel Prize in Physics.

Other investigations carried out by Raman were his experimental and theoretical studies on the diffraction of light by acoustic waves of ultrasonic and hypersonic frequencies (published in 1934-1942), and those on the effects produced by X-rays on infrared vibrations in crystals exposed to ordinary light.

In 1948 Raman, through studying the spectroscopic behaviour of crystals, approached in a new manner the fundamental problems of crystal dynamics. His laboratory has been dealing with the structure and properties of diamond, the structure and optical behaviour of numerous iridescent substances. Among his other interests have been the optics of colloids, electrical and magnetic anisotropy, and the physiology of human vision.

Raman has been honoured with a large number of honorary doctorates and memberships of scientific societies. He was elected a Fellow of the Royal Society early in his career (1924), and was knighted in 1929. C.V. Raman died on November 21, 1970, at the age of eighty two.

❑❑❑

C.N.R. Rao

(1934)

Chemist

*"We will accept only whatever is good for India ...
The deal cannot be forced on us.
The country's interest will be protected."*

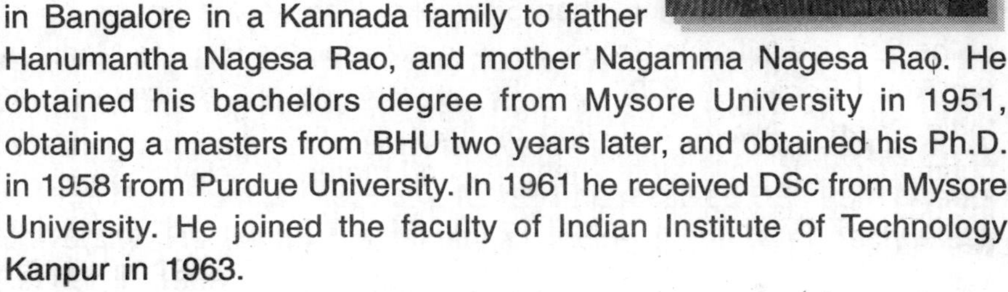

Chintamani Nagesa Ramachandra Rao, also known as C.N.R. Rao, is an Indian chemist who has worked mainly in solid-state and structural chemistry. He currently serves as the Head of the Scientific Advisory Council to the Prime Minister of India.

C.N.R. Rao was born on 30 June, 1934 in Bangalore in a Kannada family to father Hanumantha Nagesa Rao, and mother Nagamma Nagesa Rao. He obtained his bachelors degree from Mysore University in 1951, obtaining a masters from BHU two years later, and obtained his Ph.D. in 1958 from Purdue University. In 1961 he received DSc from Mysore University. He joined the faculty of Indian Institute of Technology Kanpur in 1963.

Rao is currently the National Research Professor, Linus Pauling Research Professor and Honorary President of Jawaharlal Nehru Centre for Advanced Scientific Research,Bangalore which he founded in 1989. He was appointed Chair of the Scientific Advisory Council to the Indian Prime Minister in January 2005, a position which he had occupied earlier during 1985–89. He is also the director of the International Centre for Materials Science (ICMS).

Earlier, he served as a faculty member in the Department of Chemistry at the Indian Institute of Technology Kanpur from 1963 to 1976 and as the Director of the Indian Institute of Science from 1984 to 1994. He has also been a visiting professor at Purdue University, the University of Oxford, the University of Cambridge and University of California, Santa Barbara. He was the Jawaharlal Nehru Professor at the University of Cambridge and Professorial Fellow at the King's College, Cambridge during 1983-1984.

Rao is one of the world's foremost solid state and materials chemists. He has contributed to the development of the field over five decades. His work on transition metal oxides has led to basic understanding of novel phenomena and the relationship between materials properties and the structural chemistry of these materials.

Rao was one of the earliest to synthesize two-dimensional oxide materials such as La_2CuO_4. His work has led to a systematic study of compositionally controlled metal-insulator transitions. He has made immense contributions to nanomaterials over the last two decades, besides his work on hybrid materials.

He is the author of around 1800 research papers. He has authored and edited more than 58 books. Rao serves on the board of the Science Initiative Group. He was awarded the Hughes Medal by the Royal Society in 2000, and he became the first recipient of the India Science Award, instituted by the Government of India, for his contributions to solid state chemistry and materials science, awarded in 2004. He has won several other international prizes and awards. He was awarded Dan David Prize in 2005, by the Dan David Foundation, Tel Aviv University, which he shared with George Whitesides and Robert Langer. In 2005, he was conferred the title Chevalier de la Légion d'honneur (Knight of the Legion of Honour) by France, awarded by the French Government. He was also awarded an honorary Doctor of Science by the University of Calcutta in 2004.

Dr. Rao has also been conferred with China's top science award for his important contributions in boosting Sino-India scientific cooperation. The award was given by Chinese Academy of Sciences (CAS) in January 2013, which is China's top academic and research institution for natural sciences. He received 'Distinguished academician award' from IIT Patna in 2013.

He is a member of many of the world's scientific associations, including the U.S. National Academy of Sciences, American Academy of Arts and Sciences, the Royal Society (London; FRS, 1982), French Academy, Japanese Academy, Serbian Academy of Sciences and Arts and the Pontifical Academy.

Dr. Rao has Honorary Doctorates from 86 Universities worldwide. On 16 November 2013, The Government of India decided to confer upon him Bharat Ratna, the highest civilian award in India making him the third Scientist after C.V.Raman and A P J Abdul Kalam to get the award.

Earlier, he was also conferred with Padma Shri and Padma Vibhushan by Government of India and Karnataka Ratna by the Karnataka State Government.

He was honoured with the Order of the Rising Sun of Japan in 2015.

2017: The Von Hippel Award by the Materials Research Society.

2021: International ENI award 2020 for research in renewable energy sources and energy storage, also called the Energy Frontier award.

Additionally, the Karnataka Science and Technology Academy established the “Prof. C.N.R. Rao Lifetime Achievement Award in STEAM” to recognise outstanding contributions in science, technology, engineering, arts, and mathematics.

❑❑❑

Chandrashekhar Azad

(1906–1931)

Revolutionary Leader

"Dushman ki goliyon ka hum samna karenge.
Azad hee rahe hain Azad hee rahenge."

(We will face the bullets of enemy;
We have been independent, will remain independent.)

Chandrashekhar Azad was an Indian revolutionary and the mentor of Bhagat Singh. Azad is considered one of the most famous Indian revolutionaries, along with Bhagat Singh, Sukhdev, Rajguru, Ram Prasad Bismil, and Ashfaqullah Khan.

Pandit Sita Ram Tiwari, father of Chandrasekhar Azad, was a poor, orthodox Brahmin, who had to leave his home village Badarka in Uttar Pradesh in search of a livelihood. He served as a watchman in a state garden in Bhavra, a village formerly in Alirajpur state and now in the Jhabua district of Madhya Pradesh. It was here, in a bamboo hut plastered with mud, that Jagrani Devi gave birth to Chandrashekhar Azad on July 23, 1906.

Azad received his early schooling in Bhavra. He was fond of wandering and hunting with Bhil boys of his neighbourhood, with bows and arrows. This was very much disliked by his orthodox father. When Chandrashekhar Azad was about 14 years old, he somehow reached

Varanasi. There he entered a Sanskrit *pathshala*, where he was provided free boarding and lodging. Till his death, he was unmarried and lived the austere life of a 'Brahmachari', which he began in this *pathshala*.

Those were the days of the great national upsurge of non-violence, non-cooperation movement of 1920–21 under the leadership of Mahatma Gandhi. Young Chandrashekhar Azad, along with other students, was fascinated and drawn into it. By nature, he loved energetic activities more than passive studies. Very soon, he became a favourite of the local leaders like Shiva Prasad Gupta. When arrested, Azad was so young that his handcuffs were too big for his wrists. He was put on trial before a magistrate who was notorious for his brutality towards freedom- fighters. Chandrashekhar Azad's attitude in the court was defiant. He gave his name as 'Azad', his father's name as 'Swatantra' and his residence as 'prison'. The magistrate was provoked. He sentenced him to fifteen lashes of flogging. Azad's body was stripped and tied to the flogging triangle. As lash after lash tore his skin, he shouted slogans: 'Mahatma Gandhi Ki Jai', 'Vande mataram', etc. His amazing endurance, courage and fortitude were highly appreciated and he was publicly honoured as 'Azad'. The name stuck thereafter.

When the Non-Cooperation Movement was withdrawn, the revolutionary movement again flared up. Chandrashekhar Azad's natural aptitudes led him to contact Manmath Nath Gupta. Through him, he joined the Hindustan Socialist Republican Army where he soon gained the admiration of its leaders. They lovingly called him "quick-silver" for his restless energy. He took an active part in every armed action of the party under the leadership of Ramprasad Bismil. He was involved in the 'Kakori Conspiracy' (1926), the attempt to blow up the Viceroy's train (1926), the Assembly Bomb Incident, the Delhi Conspiracy, the shooting of Saunders at Lahore (1928) and the Second Lahore Conspiracy.

The parent contributor attended a secret meeting with Chandrashekhar Azad and Sukhdev Raj in the Alfred Park, Allahabad, in February 1931. Azad was of the opinion that the Hindustan Socialist Republican Army had moved far ahead and that no purpose would be served by asking individuals to take to armed action. The time had come to pass on to mass revolutionary actions culminating in a socialist revolution. To achieve this, it was necessary to make a thorough study of the methods that were so successfully used by the Bolsheviks in Russia. For this purpose, as a regular member of the HSR Army, the present contributor was asked to proceed to Russia on his own resources. The only help, the party would give him was an automatic pistol with a magazine of eleven cartridges. The assignment was fulfilled in letter and spirits, but alas, Azad was no more there to guide and instruct the group further.

As is believed by most of the knowledgeable revolutionary comrades of the time, Azad was betrayed by an associate who turned a traitor. On February 27, 1931, in the Alfred Park, Allahabad, Azad was surrounded by a well- armed police party. For quite some time, he held them at bay, single- handed, with a small pistol and a few cartridges. Even the enemy was all praise for his sharp shooting skill and courageous composure, as he could hit quite a few of the assailants who were firing at him from behind covers. Left with only one bullet, he fired it at his own temple and lived up to his resolve that he would never be arrested and dragged to the gallows to be hanged.

❑❑❑

Charles De Gaulle

(1890–1970)

French General and Statesman

"In order to become the master, the politician poses as the servant."

Famed French leader, Charles de Gaulle rose from French soldier in World War I to exiled leader and, eventually, president of the Fifth Republic, a position he held until 1969.

The son of a philosophy and literature professor, Charles de Gaulle was born on 22 November, 1890, into a patriotic and devoutly Catholic family. De Gaulle was a well-educated and well-read child. Early on, he dreamed of being a military leader. He enrolled at the country's top military academy, Saint-Cyr, in 1909. In 1912, he completed his studies and joined an infantry regiment that was commanded by Colonel Philippe Pétain, serving as a lieutenant.

During World War I, de Gaulle distinguished himself on the battlefield. He was wounded twice early on, and received a medal for his service. Promoted to captain, de Gaulle fought in one of the war's most deadly confrontations—the Battle of Verdun—in 1916. During the fight, he was injured and, subsequently, taken prisoner. After several failed escape attempts, de Gaulle was freed at the end of the war.

A bright and skilled soldier, de Gaulle enrolled in a special training program at the École Supérieure de Guerre after the war. He later worked with Pétain and served on France's Supreme War Council. Gaining some international experience, de Gaulle spent time in Germany and the Middle East.

Also an insightful writer, de Gaulle explored a number of military issues in his books. He published his examination of Germany, *La Discorde chez l'ennemi*, in 1924. Another important book was *Vers l'armée de métier* (1932), in which he made suggestions for creating a better army. This critical work was largely ignored by French military officials, but not by the Germans. The German military followed some of de Gaulle's recommendations in World War II. He and his mentor, Petain, had a fall out over another book, a military history piece entitled *La France et son armée* (1938).

At the time fighting broke out between Germany and France, de Gaulle was leading a tank brigade. He was temporarily appointed the brigadier general of the 4th Armoured Division in May of 1940. Continuing to rise up professionally, de Gaulle became the undersecretary for defense and war for French leader Paul Reynaud that June. A short while later, Reynaud was replaced by Pétain. Pétain's new government, sometimes called the Vichy government, worked out a deal with Germany to avoid further bloodshed. The Vichy regime became infamous for collaborating with the Nazis.

A dedicated nationalist, de Gaulle did not accept France's surrender to Germany in 1940. He instead fled to England, where he became a leader of the Free French movement, with the support of British prime minister Winston Churchill.

From London, de Gaulle broadcast a message across the English Channel to his countrymen, calling for them to resist the German occupation. He also organized soldiers from French colonies to fight alongside the allied troops.

De Gaulle sometimes irritated other allied leaders with his demands and perceived arrogance. American President Franklin D.

Roosevelt reportedly could not stand him. In fact, at the war's end, de Gaulle was purposely left out of the Yalta Conference, as Germany negotiated its surrender. He did, however, secure his nation an occupation zone in Germany and a seat on the United Nation's Security Council. De Gaulle enjoyed wide support at home and, in 1945, became president of France's provisional government. In a dispute over greater power for the country's executive branch, de Gaulle resigned this post.

For several years, de Gaulle led his own political movement, "Rally for the French People," which did not gain much momentum. He them retired from politics in 1953.

But the French government, known as the Fourth Republic, began to crumble in the late 1950s, and de Gaulle once again returned to public service to help his country. He helped form the country's next government, becoming its president in January 1959. Establishing France's Fifth Republic, de Gaulle dedicated himself to improving the country's economic situation and maintaining its independence. He sought to keep France separate from the two superpowers—the United States and the Soviet Union. To show France's military relevance, de Gaulle successfully campaigned for the country to press on with its nuclear weapons program.

Sometimes inflexible and intractable, de Gaulle nearly saw his government toppled by student and worker protests in 1968. He managed to restore order to the country, but left power soon after, following a battle over political and economic reforms. In April 1969, de Gaulle resigned from the presidency.

After his resignation, de Gaulle retired to his home in Colombey-les-Deux-Eglises. But he had little time to enjoy the quiet life of this village, as he died of a heart attack on November 9, 1970.

France mourned the loss of its famous statesman and military leader; the country had lost one of its greatest heroes—a hero who had seen his people through war, and proved to be instrumental in his country's recovery. ❑❑❑

Charles Darwin

(1809–1882)

Naturalist and Author

"A man who dares to waste one hour of time has not discovered the value of life."

Darwin is the first of the evolutionary biologists. He is the originator of the concept of natural selection. His principal works, *The Origin of Species by Means of Natural Selection* (1859) and *The Descent of Man* (1871), marked a new epoch. His works were violently attacked and energetically defended, then; and, it seems, yet today.

He was born at Shrewsbury on the February 12, 1809. He was the younger of the two sons and the fourth child of Dr Robert Waring Darwin. His mother died when Charles Darwin was eight years old.

Darwin's early education was conducted at Shrewsbury, first for a year at a day-school, then for seven years at Shrewsbury School under Dr Samuel Butler (1774—1839). He gained little from the narrow system which was then universal.

In 1825, he went to Edinburgh to prepare for the medical profession, for which he was unfitted by nature. After two sessions his father realised this, and in 1828 sent him to Cambridge with the idea that he should become a clergyman. Darwin matriculated at Christ's College, and took his degree in 1831, tenth in the list of those who do not seek honours.

Till this time, he had been keenly interested in sport, and in entomology, especially the collecting of beetles. Both at Edinburgh, where in 1826, he read his first scientific paper, and at Cambridge he gained the friendship of much older scientific men—Robert Edmond Grant and William Macgillivray at the former, John Stevens Henslow and Adam Sedgwick at the latter. He had two terms' residence to keep after passing his last examination, and studied Geology with Sedgwick.

From 1831 to 1836, Darwin served as naturalist aboard, on a British science expedition around the world. In South America, Darwin found fossils of extinct animals that were similar to modern species. On the Galapagos Islands in the Pacific Ocean, he noticed many variations among plants and animals of the same general type as those in South America. The expedition visited places around the world, and Darwin studied plants and animals everywhere he went, collecting specimens for further study.

Upon his return to London, he conducted a thorough research of his notes and specimens. Out of this study, several related theories grew: one, evolution did occur; two, evolutionary change was gradual, requiring thousands to millions of years; three, the primary mechanism for evolution was a process called natural selection; and four, the millions of species alive today arose from a single original life form through a branching process called "speciation."

On January 29, 1839, Darwin married his cousin Emma Wedgwood at Maer in an Anglican ceremony arranged to suit the Unitarians. After first living in Gower Street, London, the couple moved to Down House in Downe on September 17, 1842. The Darwins had ten children, three of whom died early.

Darwin's theory of evolutionary selection holds that variation within species occurs randomly and that the survival or extinction of each organism is determined by that organism's ability to adapt to its environment. He set forth these theories in his book called, *On the Origin of Species by Means of Natural Selection*, or the *Preservation of Favoured Races in the Struggle for Life* (1859) or *The Origin of Species* in short.

Darwin's work had a tremendous impact on religious thought. Many people strongly opposed the idea of evolution because it conflicted with their religious convictions. Darwin avoided talking about the theological and sociological aspects of his work, but other writers used his theories to support their own theories about society. Darwin was a reserved, thorough, hard working scholar who concerned himself with the feelings and emotions not only of his family, but friends and peers as well.

After the publication of the *Origin of Species*, Darwin continued to write on Botany, Geology, and Zoology until his death. It has been supposed that Darwin renounced evolution on his deathbed. He died in the year, 1882. Darwin is buried in Westminster Abbey.

Charles Dickens

(1812–1870)

Novelist

"No one is useless in this world who lightens the burden of it to anyone else."

Charles John Huffam Dickens, pen-name "Boz", was a cherished English novelist of the Victorian era. The popularity of his novels and short stories during his lifetime and to the present is demonstrated by the fact that none of his novels has ever gone out of print.

Charles Dickens born on February 7, 1812, was the son of John and Elizabeth Dickens. John Dickens was a clerk in the Naval Pay Office. He had a poor head for finances, and in 1824, found himself imprisoned for debt. His wife and children, with the exception of Charles, who was put to work at Warren's Blacking Factory, joined him in the Marshalsea Prison. When the family finances were put at least partly to rights and his father was released, the twelve-year-old Dickens, already scarred psychologically by the experience, was further wounded by his mother's insistence that he continue to work at the factory. His father, however, rescued him from that fate, and between 1824 and 1827, Dickens was a day pupil at a school in London.

In 1829, he became a freelance reporter at Doctor's Commons Courts, and in 1830, he met and fell in love with Maria Beadnell, the daughter of a banker. By 1832, Dickens had become a very successful shorthand reporter of Parliamentary debates in the House of Commons, and began work as a reporter for a newspaper. In 1834, still a newspaper reporter, adopted the soon to be famous pseudonym, "Boz."

The first series of sketches by Boz was published in 1836, and that same year Dickens was hired to write short texts to accompany a series of humorous sporting illustrations by Robert Seymour, a popular artist. Seymour committed suicide after the second number, however, and under these peculiar circumstances, Dickens altered the initial conception of *The Pickwick Papers*, which became a novel (illustrated by Hablot K. Browne, *Phiz*, whose association with Dickens would continue for many years). *The Pickwick Papers* continued in monthly parts through November 1837, and, to everyone's surprise, it became an enormous popular success.

After the success of *Pickwick*, he embarked on a full-time career as a novelist, producing work of increasing complexity at an incredible rate, although he continued, as well, his journalistic and editorial activities. *Oliver Twist* was begun in 1837, and continued in monthly parts until April 1839. It was in 1837, too, that Catherine's younger sister Mary, whom Dickens idolised, died. She too would appear, in various guises, in Dickens's later fiction. A son, Charles, the first of ten children, was born in the same year.

In 1847, in Switzerland, Dickens began *Dombey* and *Son*, which ran until April 1848. *The Battle of Life* appeared in December of that year. In 1848, Dickens also wrote an autobiographical fragment, directed and acted in a number of amateur theatricals, and published what would be his last Christmas book, *The Haunted Man*, in December 1849 saw the birth of David Copperfield, which would run through November 1850.

In 1853, he toured Italy with Augustus Egg and Wilkie Collins, and gave, upon his return to England, the first of many public readings from his own works. *Hard Times* began to appear weekly in *Household Words* in 1854, and continued until August. Dickens's family spent the summer and the fall in Boulogne. In October 1855, they arrived in Paris in October, and Dickens began *Little Dorrit*, which continued in monthly parts until June 1857. In 1856, Dickens and Wilkie Collins collaborated on a play, *The Frozen Deep*, and Dickens purchased *Gad's Hill*, an estate he had admired since childhood.

In 1865, an incident occurred which disturbed Dickens greatly, both psychologically and physically: Dickens and Ellen Ternan, returning from a Paris holiday, were badly shaken up in a railway accident in which a number of people were injured.

Dickens's final public readings took place in London in 1870. He suffered another stroke on June 8 at Gad's Hill, after a full day's work on Edwin Drood, and died the next day. He was buried at Westminster Abbey on June 14, and the last episode of the unfinished *Mystery of Edwin Drood* appeared in September.

❑❑❑

Charlie Chaplin

(1889–1977)

Actor

"Nothing is permanent in this wicked world - not even our troubles."

Sir Charles Spencer Chaplin was the most famous actor in early to mid Hollywood cinema, and later also a notable director. His principal character was *The Tramp*: a vagrant with the refined manners and dignity of a gentleman who wears a tight coat, oversized pants and shoes, a derby or bowler hat, a bamboo cane, and his signature square moustache.

Charlie Chaplin was born in London on April 16, 1889. Both his parents were music hall entertainers and Charlie started appearing on the stage while still a child. His father, Charles Chaplin, deserted the family and eventually died of alcoholism. His mother, Hannah Chaplin, found it increasingly difficult to find work on the stage and in 1895, the family entered the Lambeth Workhouse. Later, Charlie's mother had a mental breakdown and was sent to the Cane Hill Lunatic Asylum.

Chaplin's career as an entertainer seemed destined. He claimed that his first appearance before an audience was at the age of five, when he stepped on the stage at Aldershot Canteen theatre to take over from his mother whose voice suddenly failed her. At the age of eight, he joined Jacksons Eight Lancashire Lads, one of the juvenile variety troupes which were popular then. He later obtained favourable press notices as a child in the legitimate theatre, and played the West End and lengthy provincial tours as Billy, the page boy in Sherlock Holmes.

His first film, *Making a Living* (1914), in which he was dressed as a dubious dandy was indifferent, though well received by the trade press. For his second film, a five minute improvisation shot during the event which gave it its title, *Kid Auto Races at Venice* (1914), he adopted the costume that became world famous. According to legend, it was made up from various items borrowed from other Sennett comedians: Fatty Arbuckle's huge trousers; Charles Avery's tiny jacket; a derby hat belonging to Arbuckle's father-in-law; Ford Sterling's boots, so oversized that they had to be worn on the wrong feet; and Mack Swain's moustache, sharply pruned.

In 1919, he co-founded the United Artists film distribution company with Mary Pickford, Douglas Fairbanks and D. W. Griffith, all of whom were seeking to escape the growing power consolidation of film distributors and financiers in the developing Hollywood studio system. This move, along with complete control of his film production through his studio, assured Chaplin's independence as a filmmaker. He served on the board of UA until the early 1950s.

Chaplin's last American film was a nostalgic tribute to his youth in the backstreets and variety theatres of London. Full of autobiographical references, *Limelight* (1952), narrates of the friendship and mutual support of an old, failed, alcoholic comedian and a dancer struck with psychosomatic paralysis.

At 77, Chaplin made one last film, a pleasant romantic comedy, *A Countess from Hong Kong* (1967). It might have been more successful and more kindly received if he had not made the mistake of using international stars - Marlon Brando and Sophia Loren - unsuited to his style of working. He never wholly retired, however. Almost until the end of his life, he continued to work on the preparations of a film called, *The Freak*. Having composed the music for his sound films, he continued to create new scores for reissues of his silent pictures.

Chaplin died on Christmas Day, in 1977, in Vevey, Switzerland, following a stroke at the age of 88, and was interred in Corsier-Sur-Vevey Cemetery in Corsier-Sur-Vevey, Vaud. A year later, his body was stolen in an attempt to extort money from his family. The plot failed, the robbers were captured, and the body was recovered 11 weeks later near Lake Geneva. After that event, the body was again buried under six feet of concrete to prevent another such attempt.

❑❑❑

Chiranjeevi

(1955)

Actor, Politician and Philanthropist

"In India, there are lots of places that I love, but my favourite is Kashmir."

Chiranjeevi, born as Konidela Siva Sankara Vara Prasad on August 22, 1955, in Mogalthur, West Godavari district of Andhra Pradesh, India, is a luminary in Indian cinema and politics. His father, Konidela Venkata Rao, was a police constable, and his mother, Anjana Devi, was a homemaker. Growing up in a modest household, Chiranjeevi imbibed values of discipline and hard work from an early age.

He completed his schooling in his native village and pursued his intermediate education at CSR Sharma College in Ongole. Subsequently, he graduated with a Bachelor of Commerce degree from Sri Y N College in Narsapur. During his college years, Chiranjeevi actively participated in cultural activities, particularly theater, which ignited his passion for acting. This fervour led him to enrol at the Madras Film Institute to hone his acting skills.

Chiranjeevi made his acting debut in 1978 with the film "Pranam Khareedu". Initially, he played minor and supporting roles, but his dedication and talent soon earned him recognition. His breakthrough came with the 1983 film "Khaidi", directed by A. Kodandarami Reddy, where he portrayed a rugged protagonist seeking justice. The film's success catapulted him to stardom, establishing him as a leading actor in Telugu cinema.

Throughout the 1980s and 1990s, Chiranjeevi delivered a series of blockbuster hits, showcasing his versatility across various genres. Films like "Rudraveena" (1988), where he played a classical musician advocating social change, and "Jagadeka Veerudu Athiloka Sundari" (1990), a fantasy film co-starring Sridevi, highlighted his acting prowess. His role in "Gharana Mogudu" (1992) made him the highest-paid actor in India at the time, reflecting his immense popularity.

Chiranjeevi's contributions to cinema have been recognised with numerous accolades. He has received three Nandi Awards, the highest honour for Telugu cinema, and nine Filmfare Awards South. In 2006, the Government of India honoured him with the Padma Bhushan for his contributions to Indian cinema. Further cementing his legacy, he was awarded the Padma Vibhushan in 2024. In 2024, he also achieved a Guinness World Record as the most prolific actor-dancer in the Indian film industry, having performed in 537 songs with over 24,000 dance moves.

Beyond his cinematic achievements, Chiranjeevi ventured into politics to serve the public. In 2008, he founded the Praja Rajyam Party in Andhra Pradesh, focusing on social justice and the upliftment of marginalised communities. Although the party garnered significant attention, it faced challenges in the political arena. In 2011, the Praja Rajyam Party merged with the Indian National Congress, and Chiranjeevi was appointed as the Minister of Tourism in 2012, a position he held until 2014.

Chiranjeevi's personal life has been anchored by his family. He married Surekha, the daughter of veteran actor Allu Ramalingaiah, on February 20, 1980. The couple has three children: son Ram Charan, who has established himself as a leading actor in Telugu cinema; and daughters Sushmita and Srija. Despite his fame, Chiranjeevi has maintained a grounded and private family life, often crediting his family's support for his success.

Demonstrating a commitment to social causes, Chiranjeevi established the Chiranjeevi Charitable Trust (CCT) in 1998, comprising a blood bank and eye bank. The trust has been lauded for its services, having assisted thousands in need of blood and eye donations. The Government of Andhra Pradesh recognised the trust as the 'Best Voluntary Blood Bank' for five consecutive years from 2002 to 2007, underscoring its impact on public health.

After a brief hiatus from acting, Chiranjeevi made a triumphant return to the silver screen with his 150th film, "Khaidi No. 150", in 2017. The film, a remake of the Tamil hit "Kaththi", was both a critical and commercial success, reaffirming his enduring appeal. He continued to captivate audiences with projects like "Sye Raa Narasimha Reddy" (2019), a historical biopic about a freedom fighter, and "Acharya" (2022), where he shared screen space with his son, Ram Charan.

Chiranjeevi's journey from a small village in Andhra Pradesh to becoming a megastar and respected politician is a testament to his talent, resilience, and dedication. His ability to adapt and reinvent himself across different domains has ensured his relevance over the decades.

❑❑❑

Christopher Columbus

(1451–1506)

Navigator

"Following the light of the sun,
we left the Old World."

Christopher Columbus was an Italian Spanish navigator who sailed west across the Atlantic Ocean in search of a route to Asia but achieved fame by making landfall in the Americas instead.

Christopher Columbus was the eldest of five sons of Domenico Colombo and Susanna Fontanarossa. Christopher was born between August and October 1451, in Genoa, Italy. He had two younger brothers, Bartholomew and Diego. Christopher received little formal education and was largely a self-taught man, later learning to read Latin and write Castilian.

Columbus began on the sea early, making his first voyage, to the Aegean Island of Chios, in 1475. One year later, he survived a shipwreck off cape St. Vincent in which he had to swim ashore. In 1477, Columbus sailed to England and Ireland with Portuguese marine, and also bought sugar in Madeira for a Genoese firm.

In 1479, Christopher married Felipa Perestello Moniz from a impoverished noble Portuguese family. Their son, Diego was born in 1480. Felipa died in 1485, and Columbus later began a relationship with Beatriz Enriquez de Harana of Cordabo, with whom Christopher had his second son, Ferdinand. Columbus and Enriquez never married, but Columbus supported her.

In the mid-1480's, Christopher focussed on his plans of discovery. His biggest dream was to find a westward route to Asia. In 1484, he had asked King John II of Portugal to back his voyage west, but was refused. The next year, he set out to Spain with his son, Diego to seek aid of Queen Elizabeth of Castile and her husband, King Ferdinand of Aragon. Even though the Spanish monarchs first rejected Christopher's request, they gave him a small annuity to live on, and he remained determined to convince them. In January of 1492, Christopher obtained the support of Elizabeth and Ferdinand, after being rejected twice.

On August 3, 1492 the fleet of three ships-Nina, Pinta, and the Santa Maria-set forth from Palos, on the Tinto river in southern Spain. The first sight of land came at dawn on October 12 from the Pinta Ship. The place of the first Caribbean landfall was most likely modern, San Salvador, or Waitling Island, in the Bahamas.

Thinking he has reached the East Indies, Columbus referred to the native inhabitants of the island as "Indians," a term often used to identify indigenous people of the New World. The three ships sailed along other Bahama Islands and landed in Cuba, which Columbus falsely called Mainland of Cathay (China). There was little gold there and his exploration continued by sea to Ayti on December 6, which Columbus renamed La Isla Espanola, or Hispaniola. He seemed to have thought Hispaniola was Japan, but in any case, the land was rich in gold and other natural resources, and allowed Columbus to return to Spain in the spring of 1493 with riches enough to convince his sovereigns of his success.

After a difficult journey back to Europe, Columbus paid a visit to King John II of Portugal, which bought up suspicion that he had connections with Spain's enemy. After displaying all of his treasures to the queen and the king, they were easily pursued to fund another journey. This time there were at least 17 ships and 1,300 men set sail on September 25, 1493. A route to Hispaniola and Navidad, the settlement he had founded there, Columbus and his fleet entered the West Indies near Dominica and proceeded past Guadeloupe and other, lesser Antilles before reaching Borinquen.

Upon reaching Navidad, Columbus found the settlement destroyed and the Spanish settlers dead, victims of a strong native attack. Columbus declared himself Governor of Hispaniola, intending it to become a trading post for European settlers. After searching the Cuban coastline and the Jamaican for gold Columbus declared Hispaniola, the richest source for gold and other spoils.

In February 1492, 12 ships returned to Spain from La Isebela commanded by Columbus associate, Antonio de Torres. Under the command of Columbus, two associates led a campaign of violence against the native inhabitance of Hispaniola, in revenge of their murdered comrades Navidad, they killed and captured many natives, taking them as slaves.

He set sail on May 9, from Cadiz on four ships, arriving at Santo Domingo on Hispaniola on June 29. He was searching for the strait to India, but did not find it and was forced to turn back. By the end of his voyage back, Columbus was not too healthy. He was suffering from Arthritis as well as other effects from a bout with Malaria. With a small portion of gold from Hispaniola, he lived comfortably for his last years. Columbus died in Vallodid on May 20, 1506.

❑❑❑

Clint Eastwood

(1930)

Actor, Producer and Director

"The less secure a man is, the more likely he is to have extreme prejudice."

Clint Eastwood is an iconic American actor, film producer, composer, and Academy Award-winning film director. Eastwood is famous for his tough anti-hero roles, including the Inspector *Dirty Harry Callahan* in the *Dirty Harry* series and the *Man with No Name* in Sergio Leone's *Spaghetti Westerns*.

He was born on May 31, in 1930 in San Francisco. The son of a steel worker, Eastwood was a college dropout from Los Angeles College, attempting a business related degree. He found work in such B-films as *Tarantula* (1955), and Francis in the *Navy* (1955) until he got his first breakthrough with the long-running TV series *Rawhide* (1959). As *Rowdy Yates*, he made his own show and became a household name around the country.

But Eastwood found even bigger and better things with Per un pugno di dollari (1964) ("A Fistful of Dollars"), and Peŕ qualche dollaro in piu (1965) *For a Few Dollars More*. But it was the third sequel to

A Fistful of Dollars where he found one of his trademark roles: Buono, il brutto, il cattivo, Il (1966) *The Good, The Bad and The Ugly*. The movie was a big hit and he became an instant international star. Eastwood got some excellent roles thereafter, such as, *Where Eagles Dare* (1968) found him second fiddle to Richard Burton but to the tune of $ 800,000 in this classic World War II movie.

The year 1971 proved to be his best year in films, or at least one of his best. It was his role as the hard edge police inspector in *Dirty Harry* (1971) that gave Eastwood one of his signature roles and invented the loose-cannon cop genre that has been imitated even to this day. Eastwood had constant quality films with *Thunderbolt and Lightfoot* (1974) and *Magnum Force* (1973), a sequel to *Dirty Harry* (1971). But 1976 found Eastwood with even more legendary films.

As the late seventies approached, Eastwood found more solid work in comedies like *Every Which Way But Loose* (1978) and in thrillers like *'Escape from Alcatraz'* (1979), but he seemed to have lost his edge in making great films. But it was the fourth sequel to *Dirty Harry*, *Sudden Impact* (1983), that made him a viable star for the eighties. In 1988, he did his fifth and up to this point final *Dirty Harry* movie, *The Dead Pool* (1988). About this time, with outright bombs like *The Rookie* (1990) and *Pink Cadillac* (1989), it was fairly obvious that Eastwood's star was declining as it never had before.

But Eastwood surprised yet again. First with his western, *Unforgiven* (1992), which garnered him an Oscar for director, and nomination for best actor. Then he took on the secret service in *In the Line of Fire* (1993), which was a big hit, followed by the interesting but poorly received drama, *A Perfect World* (1993).

In 2005, Eastwood found critical and commercial success when he directed, produced, scored, and starred in the boxing drama *Million Dollar Baby*. The film won the Academy Award for Best Picture, as well as earning Eastwood a best Actor nomination and a win for Best Director. Eastwood also received a *Grammy* nomination for the score he composed for the film which grossed more than $216 million at the box office and was his highest-grossing film at the time.

In 2008, Eastwood directed the Oscar-nominated drama *Changeling*, which starred *Angelina Jolie*. Later that year, he ended his "self-imposed acting hiatus" with *Gran Torino.* It grossed close to $30 million during its wide-release opening weekend in January 2009, making Eastwood, at age 78, the oldest leading man to reach # 1 at the box office. In 2009, Eastwood directed the movie *Invictus*.

Clint Eastwood received the AFI Life Achievement Award in 1996 and received an honorary degree from AFI in 2009.

In February 2010, Eastwood was recognized by President Barack Obama with an arts and humanities award. Obama described Eastwood's films as "essays in individuality, hard truths and the essence of what it means to be American." Eastwood starred in the baseball drama Trouble with the Curve (2012), as a veteran baseball scout. In August 2013, the Eastwoods separated after 17 years of marriage.

In October 2020, it was announced that Eastwood would direct, produce, and star in Cry Macho, an adaptation of the 1975 novel of the same name, for Warner Bros. Pictures. Production of the film took place in New Mexico between November and December 2020. It was released on September 17, 2021, to mixed reviews.

Clint Eastwood was honoured with the Modern Master Award at the Santa Barbara Film Festival on January 29, 2025. The award was presented by actor Sean Penn, recognizing Eastwood's outstanding contributions to cinema over the decades.

❑❑❑

Dadabhai Naoroji

(1825–1917)

Political Leader

"The chief cause of India's poverty, misery, and all material evils is the exhaustion of its previous wealth."

Dadabhai Naoroji was a Parsi intellectual and an educator, and an early Indian political leader. He was a member of Parliament in the Parliament of the United Kingdom between 1892 and 1895, and the first Asian to be a British MP.

Dadabhai was born on September 4, 1825 to a poor Parsi family in Mumbai. His father, Naoroji Palanji Dordi, died when Dadabhai was only four years old. He was brought up by his illiterate mother, Maneckbai who gave Dadabhai the best possible English education. As a student, he had a knack for mental Mathematics and went on to distinguish himself in Mathematics and English at the Elphinstone Institution (now a college) in Mumbai. So impressed were his peers that one professor called him the "promise of India." Another offered to pay half the expenses for Dadabhai to study abroad. His Parsi elders refused to pay the other half of the expenses out of fear that Dadabhai would convert to Christianity and marry an English woman.

On completion of his education, Dadabhai was appointed the Head Native Assistant Master at the Elphinstone Institution and went on to become the first Indian professor of Mathematics and Natural Philosophy.

Dadabhai entered the political fray in 1852. The East India Company acquired a 20-year lease to "manage" India from the British Government in 1833. The company applied for renewal of the lease in 1853. Dadabhai strongly opposed the renewal of the lease and organised large meetings and sent petitions to the British government in England to deny the company a renewal. Even though the British Government did renew the company's lease, his petitions dispelled a lot of ignorance regarding India.

Dadabhai felt that the British misrule of India was because of ignorance of the way of life and needs of the Indian people. To remedy this, he felt that he must educate the Indian masses of their rights. Dadabhai began free literacy classes for girls in Marathi and Gujarati. He set up the *Dnyan Prasarak Mandali* (Society for Promotion of Knowledge) for the education of adult menfolk. Topics of general awareness were discussed before large gatherings. Then he believed that the British bureaucracy in India must be made aware of the problems of India. He wrote several petitions to governors and viceroys regarding India's problems.

Finally, he felt that the British people and the British parliament must be made aware of India's plight. He yearned to go to England to put forward India's case there. Dadabhai got this opportunity when the rich Cama family invited him to join in a business venture in England. He did not think twice, and set sail for England on June 27, 1855.

Dadabhai was elected to the British parliament in 1892 from Central Finsbury as the Liberal Party candidate. This made it possible for him to work for India from within! He got a resolution passed for holding preliminary examinations for the I.C.S. in India and England simultaneously and also got the Wiley Commission, the royal commission on Indian expenditure, to acknowledge the need for even distribution of administrative and military expenditure between India and England.

Dadabhai's efforts were rewarded in 1896 when the Secretary of State for India agreed to appoint nine Indians out of 60 to the Indian Civil Service (I.C.S.) by nomination.

As the years passed, he grew more and more disillusioned with the "fair-minded" British. After spending years collecting statistics, Dadabhai propounded the drain theory: "The inevitable consequence of foreign domination is the drain of wealth of the subject nation to the country of the rulers." Dadabhai proved that the average annual income of an Indian was barely Rs. 20. Examining the import and export figures for 37 years, he proved that India's exports exceeded its imports by Rs. 50 crore annually.

He was key to the establishment of the Indian National Congress (I.N.C.) founded by A.O. Hume. More importantly, he averted a split in the Congress between the extremists like B.G. Tilak, B.C. Pal, and A. Ghosh and the moderates. The extremists advocated the boycott of British goods and asked for *swaraj* (self-government).

He died at the ripe age of 92 on June 30, 1917. Two months later, the Minto Morley reforms were passed in the British parliament granting much of what Dadabhai had been fighting for.

The "Grand Old Man of India," as Dadabhai was fondly known, can be viewed as the architect that laid the foundation of the Indian freedom struggle. He sacrificed his career and his family for India. He resigned his professorship to go to England to increase the awareness of India in Britain. His only son and his mother died while he was in England. Dadabhai's methods of justice for India were always non-violent and constitutional.

❑❑❑

Dalai Lama

(1935)

Spiritual Leader

"The True value of existence is revelead through compassion."

His Holiness the XIVth Dalai Lama, Tenzin Gyatso, is the spiritual and temporal leader of the Tibetan people. His Holiness was recognized at the age of two, in accordance with Tibetan tradition, as the reincarnation of his predecessor the 13th Dalai Lama. The Dalai Lamas are the manifestations of the Bodhisattva of Compassion, who chose to reincarnate to serve the people. Dalai Lama means Ocean of Wisdom.

Lhamo Thondup was born on July 6, 1935 in Taktser, China, northeast of Tibet, to a peasant family. Lhamo Thondup was the fifth of 16 children-seven of whom died at a young age. After several months of searching for a successor to the 13th Dalai Lama and following many significant spiritual signs, religious officials located Lhamo Thondup, at age 2, and identified him as the reincarnation of the 13th Dalai Lama, Thubten Gyatso. Young Lhamo was renamed Tenzin Gyatso and proclaimed the 14th Dalai Lama.

Tenzin began his religious education at age 6. His schooling consisted of logic, Tibetan art and culture, Sanskrit, medicine and Buddhist philosophy, which is divided into five other categories dealing with the perfection of wisdom, monastic discipline, metaphysics, logic and epistemology-the study of knowledge. At age 11, Tenzin met Heinrich Harrer, an Austrian mountaineer, who became one of his tutors, teaching him about the outside world. The two remained friends until Harrer's death in 2006.

In 1950, at 16, His Holiness was called upon to assume full political power as Head of State and Government when Tibet was threatened by the might of China. In 1954 he went to Peking to talk with Mao Tse-Tung and other Chinese leaders, including Chou En-Lai and Deng Xiaoping. In 1956, while visiting India to attend the 2500th Buddha Jayanti, he had a series of meetings with Prime Minister Nehru and Premier Chou about deteriorating conditions in Tibet. In 1959 he was forced into exile in India after the Chinese military occupation of Tibet. Since 1960 he has resided in Dharamsala, aptly known as "Little Lhasa", the seat of the Tibetan Government-in-Exile.

His Holiness continues to present new initiatives to resolve the Tibetan issues. At the Congressional Human Rights Caucus in 1987 he proposed a Five-Point Peace Plan as a first step towards resolving the future status of Tibet. This plan calls for the designation of Tibet as a zone of peace, an end to the massive transfer of ethnic Chinese into Tibet, restoration of fundamental human rights and democratic freedoms and the abandonment of China's use of Tibet for nuclear weapons production and the dumping of nuclear waste, as well as urging "earnest negotiations" on the future of Tibet and relations between the Tibetan and Chinese people.

In 1989, the Dalai Lama was awarded the Nobel Peace Prize for his nonviolent efforts for the liberation of Tibet and his concern for global environmental problems. The Committee's citation stated, "The Committee wants to emphasize the fact that the Dalai Lama in his struggle for the liberation of Tibet consistently has opposed the use of violence. He has instead advocated peaceful solutions based upon tolerance and mutual respect in order to preserve the historical and cultural heritage of his people." In recent years, a number of Western universities and institutions have conferred peace awards and honorary doctorate degrees upon the Dalai Lama in recognition of his distinguished writings in Buddhist philosophy, as well as his outstanding leadership in the service of freedom and peace.

On 29 May 2011 His Holiness signed the document formally transferring his temporal authority to the democratically elected leader. In so doing he formally put an end to the 368-year old tradition of the Dalai Lamas functioning as both the spiritual and temporal head of Tibet.

In 2019, the Dalai Lama fully-sponsored the first-ever 'Celebrating Diversity in the Muslim World' conference in New Delhi on behalf of the Muslims of Ladakh.

A biographical graphic novel, Man of Peace, also envisaging the Dalai Lama's return to Tibet, was published by Tibet House US. The Extraordinary Life of His Holiness the Fourteenth Dalai Lama: An Illuminated Journey, illustrations and text by artist Rima Fujita, narrated by the Dalai Lama, was published by Simon and Schuster in 2021.

❑❑❑

Dhyan Chand

(1905–1979)

Hockey Player

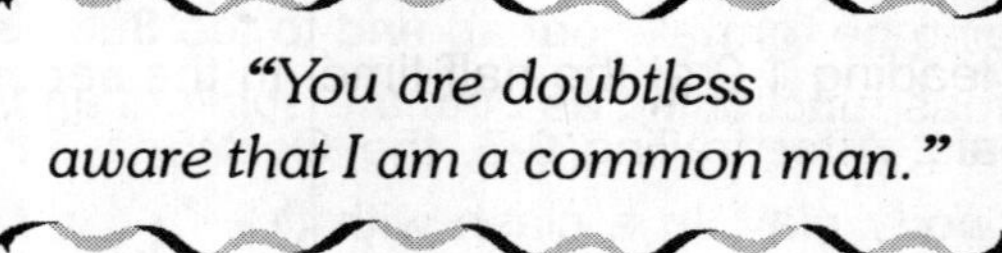

"You are doubtless aware that I am a common man."

Major Dhyan Chand Singh was a former Indian hockey player and Olympian. He got the title, "Chand" or (moon) from his first coach, Pankaj Gupta, who had predicted that he would one day shine like a *chand* or moon. Dhyan Chand was affectionately called *Dadda*.

Dhyan Chand was born on August 29, 1905 to a Rajput family in Prayag in Uttar Pradesh. His father was an army Subedar. Soon afterwards, he moved to Jhansi where he spent his formative years. After an early education, he joined the Indian Army at the age of 16, in 1922. Dhyan Chand was a Sepoy of the 14 Punjab Regiment. Subedar-Major Bhole Tiwari of Brhamin regiment noticed his excellent dribbling skills and knack for scoring goals.

On the field he was named the "Wizard of Hockey" for he exerted complete control on the ball. It appeared that the ball used to stick to his hockey stick while playing. So great was the magic of Dhyan

Chand that the Tokyo officials broke his hockey stick to search for a magnet inside. On one occasion, a lady from the audience asked Dhyan Chand to play with her walking stick instead. He scored goals even with that.

In 1936, Dhyan Chand got the opportunity to participate in the Summer Olympics at Berlin. He captained the Indian hockey team in game. In a patriotic note, they raised the Indian tricolour in the dressing room and sang *Vande Mataram,* an Indian nationalist song, rather than the British national anthem, which they were obliged to sing.

Indians were leading 1-0 at the half time. In the second half, they scored seven goals. After trailing 0-6, the Germans are reported to have resorted to body play. In a clash with the German goalkeeper, Dhyan Chand broke one of his teeth, but was soon back in action.

The match was attended by Nazi dictator Adolf Hitler who left the game midway as he could not bear to see his "racially superior" team being demolished. Sensing something amiss, Dhyan Chand was ordered to change his stick, but the flow of goals continued. India won the match 8-1, with Dhyan Chand scoring 6 goals.

Adolf Hitler is said to have left his special box in a huff, after Germany's rout. Next day, he invited him for a meeting the following day. There are various accounts of the meeting. One is that Hitler asked Dhyan Chand what post did he hold in India. On learning that the hockey wizard was a mere Naik in the Indian army, Hitler offered to make Dhyan Chand a Field Marshal, should he decide to live in Germany. He politely refused, saying that he had a large family to look after, in India. Another version is that Hitler called him up at the end of the match and asked him the question, "What will you take to play for Germany?" To this, Dhyan Chand replied, "Nothing sir, India is my India".

After World War II, he continued to play till the age 42. Dhyan Chand hit a total of 61 goals in 22 matches against East Africa. In 1948, he retired from the sports.

After his retirement, Dhyan Chand earned a diploma in coaching from the National Institute of Sports, Patiala, Punjab. However, he found it difficult to coach something that was innate to him.

In 1956, he retired from the army with the rank of Major. The Government of India honoured him by conferring the Padma Bhushan (India's third highest civilian honour) in that year. However, the Arjuna Award for sports excellence was never awarded to him.

Dhyan Chand was very sad to see India finish seventh at the Montreal Olympics, 1976. The Indian team included his son, Ashok Kumar. When he was on his deathbed at All India Institute of Medical Sciences, he reportedly told a doctor that Indian hockey was dying. He then went into a coma and died on December 3, 1979.

Exactly a year after his death, the Indian Postal Service issued a commemorative stamp in his honour.

29th August, his birthday is celebrated as the National Sports Day in India. The President gives away sport-related awards such as the Rajiv Gandhi Khel Ratna Award, Arjuna Award and Dronacharya Award on this day at the Rashtrapati Bhavan.

In 2002, the union sports ministry of India introduced a Lifetime Achievement Award in sports in the name of Dhyan Chand.

Residents of Vienna, Austria honoured him by setting up his statue with four hands and four sticks, depicting his control and mastery over the ball. One of his statues is near the India Gate, New Delhi while another has been erected in 2005 at Medak in Andhra Pradesh.

In honour to Major Dhyan Chand, PM Narendra Modi on 6 August, 2021 announced to change the name of Rajiv Gandhi Khel Ratna Award and now this award would be known as Major Dhyan Chand Khel Ratna Award.

❑❑❑

Diego Maradona

(1960-2020)

Football Player

"God makes me play well. That is why I always make the sign of a cross when I walk out on to the pitch. I feel I would be betraying him if I didn't."

Diego Maradona was quite possibly the greatest football player the world has ever seen. Certainly, in the age that Maradona played football, it was a higher tempo sport than the one enjoyed by the Brazilian Pele, so the skill that the Argentinean showed can be regarded as extra brilliant.

Born in a slum area on the outskirts of Buenos Aires in 1960, Diego Armando Maradona was blessed with unique skill. As a youngster, he would often entertain the crowds at football matches at half time, with demonstrations of ball juggling, at which he was extremely adept. It was due to these amazing feats that he would acquire the nickname 'El pibe de oro', (the golden boy).

Local Argentinean clubs were quick to take note of the youngster's skill. His first club was Argentinios Juniors, but he had soon moved on to the world recognised Boca Juniors. He made his full international debut in 1977, at the age of 17. A year later, Argentina won the World Cup, but the young Maradona was not in the squad. Although he had a supreme talent, the International side was very strong that year anyway, so instead he was nurtured gently. This meant him leading the Argentina youth team to win the Youth Team World Cup in 1979.

By the time the next World Cup came along (Spain 1982), Maradona was an established member of the National team. Although many people reckoned that he performed poorly in that tournament, massive clubs all around the world became aware of the unparalleled skill he possessed. He showed excellent balance and strength, and his skill and ball control were second to none. Subsequently, he moved to the great Spanish club, Barcelona.

This move meant worldwide fame and a huge fortune. Maradona found it difficult to cope and it was whilst in Spain that he first took cocaine. In 1984, he moved to Naples in Italy where he was very successful (league champions twice, UEFA Cup, Italian Cup, Italian Supercup).

In 1986, he was at the peak of his footballing powers and led Argentina to win the World Cup. On the way, he scored a fantastic goal against England, dribbling the ball half the length of the pitch before coolly sliding it into the net. Maradona also scored the infamous 'Hand of God' goal, where he claimed his illegal handball was an act of God. Rumours persisted, however, about his activities off the field. In 1991, he failed a dope test and was banned. On his return, he played for a variety of clubs, including a return to Boca Juniors.

Disaster struck for Maradona after the Nigeria game at the 1994 World Cup. He tested positive for the banned substance, ephedrine, and was banned from playing football for a year. Without him, Argentina were soon eliminated from that particular World Cup. By this stage in his career, years of drug abuse were beginning to take their toll. He returned from his ban to play for his home club, Boca Juniors, until his retirement from football in 1997.

He increasingly suffered ill health and weight gain. After his recovery and overcoming his cocaine addiction, he became a popular TV host in Argentina. He became head coach of the Argentina national football team in November 2008. His contract expired after the 2010 World Cup.

In 2000 Maradona published his autobiography Yo Soy El Diego ("I am "The Diego") which became an instant bestseller in his home country. He was FIFA best football player of the country (2000). He became head coach of the Argentina national team in November 2008. On March 22, 2010 Maradona was chosen number 1 in the Greatest 10 World Cup players of all time by *The Times*.

But for his terrible addiction to cocaine, Maradona would have definitely become the greatest football player the world has ever seen. He still came pretty close though; nobody since has quite matched up to him at his best. He will be always remembered for the superb football that he played, rather than his well-documented private life.

On 1 September 2014, Maradona, along with many current and former footballing stars, took part in the "Match for Peace", which was played at the Stadio Olimpico in Rome, with the proceeds being donated entirely to charity. On 17 August 2015, Maradona visited Ali Bin Nasser, the Tunisian referee of the Argentina–England quarter-final match at the 1986 World Cup where Maradona scored his Hand of God, and paid tribute to him by giving him a signed Argentine Jersey.

In May 2018, Maradona was announced as the new chairman of Belarusian club Dynamo Brest. He arrived in Brest and was presented by the club to start his duties in July. From September 2018 to June 2019, Maradona was coach of Mexican club Dorados. He was the coach of Argentine Primera División club Gimnasia de La Plata from September 2019 until his death on November 25, 2020.

❑❑❑

Edmund Hillary

(1919–2008)
Mountaineer

"People do not decide to become extraordinary. They decide to accomplish extraordinary things."

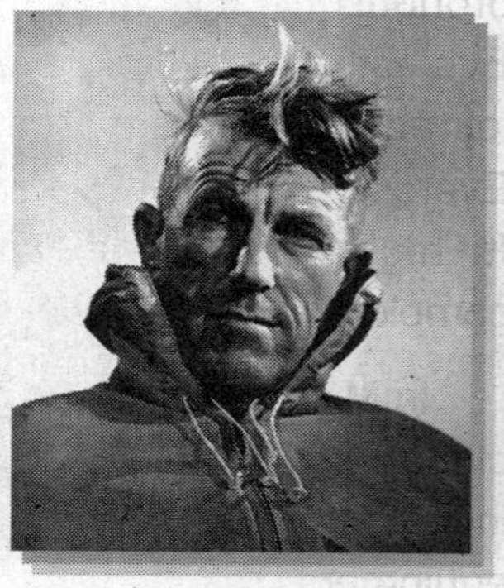

Edmund Hillary and his Sherpa guide, Tenzing Norgay were the first humans to reach the Earth's highest point: the summit of Mount Everest in the Himalayas. Hillary was knighted for his feat and in later years led expeditions to the South Pole and to the source of the Yangtze River. He also committed himself to humanitarian work among the Sherpas through his Himalayan Trust.

Edmund Hillary was born in Auckland, New Zealand, on July 20, 1919. He spent his childhood in Tuakau, a rural area just south of Auckland where he went to the local primary school. Hillary was gifted with an active imagination and had a passion for reading adventure stories. Later, he travelled daily to the city for secondary schooling, where he was a shy and awkward boy. As a child, he helped in his father's beekeeping business and eventually had to quit school to work with his father full-time.

In 1935, during a ski weekend on a school trip to Mount Ruapehu, Hillary discovered his joy in the mountains and it never left him. He would often escape to the mountains to enjoy skiing and hiking, and he developed a love of climbing. A few years later, Hillary climbed his first mountain, the 7,500 ft. Mount Oliver in New Zealand.

Hillary enlisted with the Royal New Zealand Air Force in World War II (1939–45), where New Zealand aided the Allied powers of America, England, and Russia in their war against the Axis powers of Germany, Italy, and Japan. While serving as a navigator in the South Pacific, he was wounded in battle. Despite the physical setback, Hillary was determined to make a full recovery and resume mountain climbing.

During the 1940s, Hillary made many climbs in New Zealand, particularly in the Southern Alps. He quickly became recognised for his daring, strength, and reliability. Then came climbs in Europe that brought the invitation to join Sir John Hunt's expedition to Mount Everest, in the Himalaya Mountains in Nepal. For two years, Hillary joined Hunt in the Scottish Highlands to prepare themselves for Everest. The highest point on Earth, Mount Everest measures 29,028 ft. high, roughly six miles. No one in history had successfully completed the climb, and many lives were lost during attempts.

In March 1953, Hillary and Hunt, along with twenty other of the best climbers in the world, gathered at Everest. Their company also included 350 Nepalese workers carrying 10,000 pounds of food and equipments, as well as thirty-six Sherpas, people who are familiar with the rugged terrain and are invaluable guides for climbers.

With the party's base camp just 1,100 ft. from the summit, Hunt sent a two-man team, the rest of the way. They failed but returned to the camp with valuable information about how to attack the summit. Next, Hunt chose Hillary and Sherpa guide Tenzing Norgay (1914–1986) to make an attempt. After a heroic and death-defying climb, the two reached the summit on May 29, 1953, becoming the first two people to reach the top of the world.

Hillary wanted to use the sophisticated snow-Cats available to Fuchs, but he had to settle for Ferguson farm tractors for transport and hauling. When the last dump was established, Hillary made his own decision to head for the pole, which he reached with his three tractors on January 4, 1958. He was the first person to travel there by land in forty-six years.

Hillary's achievements were recognised internationally with the award of numerous decorations and honorary degrees, beginning with his knighthood in 1953. They reflect the rare warmth and respect in which he was held. Later on, he was appointed New Zealand's high commissioner to India. He was also the honorary president for New York's Explorers Club. In 1975, Hillary's wife and teenage daughter were killed in an airplane crash. He later remarried, and after leading one last expedition in 1977, he retired to his bee farm outside of Auckland.

Hillary had also remained active in the region where he made his famous climb. The Sir Edmund Hillary Himalayan Trust provides funds and expertise to support reforestation, build schools and hospitals, and use technology such as solar power. He personally raised funds for the Nepalese people throughout the 1990s through public speaking engagements and lectures in the United States.

In a 1995 interview with James Clash, Hillary said, "I think the most worthwhile things I've done have not been on the mountains or in the Antarctic, but doing projects with my friends, the Sherpa people. The twenty-seven schools we've now established, the hospitals—those are the things I would like to be remembered for." He died in Auckland on January 11, 2008. Indian Government awarded him Padma Vibhushan posthumously.

Edwin Hubble

(1889–1953)

Astronomer

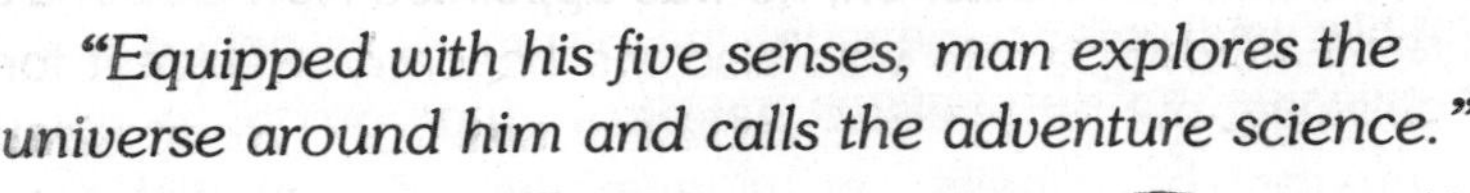

"Equipped with his five senses, man explores the universe around him and calls the adventure science."

Edwin Hubble was a man who changed our view of the universe. In 1929, he showed that galaxies are moving away from us with a speed proportional to their distance. The explanation is simple, but revolutionary: the universe is expanding.

Hubble was born in Missouri in 1889. His family moved to Chicago in 1898, where at High School he was a promising, though not exceptional, pupil. He was more remarkable for his athletic ability, breaking the Illinois State high jump record. At university too, Edwin was an accomplished sportsman playing for the University of Chicago basketball team. He won a Rhodes scholarship to Oxford where he studied law. It was only some time after he returned to the US that he decided his future lay in astronomy.

In the early 1920s, Hubble played a key role in establishing just what galaxies are. It was known that some spiral nebulae (fuzzy clouds of light on the night sky) contained individual stars, but there was no consensus as to whether these were relatively small collections of stars within our own galaxy, the 'Milky Way' that stretches right across the sky, or whether these could be separate galaxies, or 'Island universes', as big as our own galaxy but much further away. In 1924, Hubble measured the distance to the Andromeda nebula, a faint patch of light with about the same apparent diametre as the moon, and showed it was about a hundred thousand times as far away as the nearest stars. It had to be a separate galaxy, comparable in size to our own Milky Way but much further away.

Hubble was able to measure the distances to only a handful of other galaxies, but he realised that as a rough guide, he could take their apparent brightness as an indication of their distance. The speed with which a galaxy was moving towards or away from us was relatively easy to measure due to the Doppler shift of their light. Just as a sound of a racing car becomes lower as it speeds away from us, so the light from a galaxy becomes redder. Though our ears can hear the change of pitch of the racing car engine, our eyes cannot detect the tiny red-shift of the light, but with a sensitive spectrograph, Hubble could determine the redshift of light from distant galaxies.

The observational data available to Hubble by 1929 was sketchy, but whether guided by inspired instinct or outrageous good fortune, he correctly divined a straight line fit between the data points showing that the redshift was proportional to the distance. Since then, much improved data has shown the conclusion to be a sound one. Galaxies are receding from us, and one another, as the universe expands. Within General Relativity, the theory of gravity proposed by Albert Einstein in 1915, the inescapable conclusion was that all the galaxies, and the whole Universe, had originated in a Big Bang, thousands of millions of years in the past. And so the modern science of cosmology was born.

Hubble made his great discoveries on the best telescope in the world at that time — the 100-inch telescope on Mount Wilson in southern California. Today his name is carried by the best telescope we have, not on Earth, but a satellite observatory orbiting our planet. The Hubble Space Telescope is continuing the work begun by Hubble himself to map our universe, and producing the most remarkable images of distant galaxies ever seen, many of which are available via the World Wide Web.

He died of a cerebral thrombosis on September 28, 1953, in San Marino, California. His wife, Grace, did not have a funeral for him and never revealed what was done with his body. It was apparently Hubble's wish to have no funeral service and be buried in an unmarked grave, or that he wanted to be cremated.

❑❑❑

Eiji Toyoda

(1913–2013)

Industrialist

"A person's life is an accumulation of time – just one hour is equivalent to a person's life. Employees provide their precious hours of life to the company, so we have to use it effectively, otherwise, we are wasting their life."

Eiji Toyoda is a prominent Japanese industrialist, and is largely responsible for the success of the car manufacturer, Toyota.

He studied engineering at Tokyo Imperial University from 1933 to 1936. During this time, Toyoda's cousin, Kiichiro established an automobile plant at the Toyoda Automatic Loom Works.

He joined his cousin in the plant at the conclusion of his degree and throughout their lives, shared a deep friendship. In 1936, the company changed its name from Toyoda Automatic Loom Works to Toyota, and its first cars rolled off the production line that year, built from General Motors parts and components.

Eiji Toyoda was born on September 12, 1913, in Kinjo, Nishi Kasugai, Aichi, Japan, the son of Heikichi and Nao Toyoda. Toyoda's uncle, Sakichi, founded the original family business, Toyoda Automatic Loom Works, in 1926 in Nagoya, about 200 miles west of Tokyo,

Japan. The family was so involved in the business that Eiji's father Heikichi (younger brother of Sakichi) even made his home inside the spinning factory. Such an early exposure to machines and business would have a significant effect on Toyoda's life.

Sakichi ultimately sold the patents (documents that give a person the legal right to control the production of an invention for a specific period of time) for his design to an English firm for two hundred fifty thousand dollars, at a time when textiles was Japan's top industry and used the money to pay for his eldest son, Kiichiro's venture into auto making in the early 1930s.

After graduating in 1936 with a mechanical engineering degree from the University of Tokyo—training ground for most of Japan's future top executives—the twenty-three-year-old Toyoda joined the family spinning business as an engineering trainee and transferred a year later to the newly formed Toyota Motor Company. The company was a relative newcomer to the auto business in Japan. Eiji worked on the A1 prototype, the forerunner of the company's first production model, a six-cylinder sedan that borrowed heavily from Detroit automotive technology and resembled the radically styled Chrysler Airflow model of that period. During those early years, Toyoda gained lots of hands-on experience.

In 1967, Toyoda was named president of Toyota Motor Company—the first family member to assume that post since Kiichiro resigned in 1950. A year later, the two branches of the company were unified in the new Toyota Motor Corporation, with Eiji Toyoda as chairman and Shoichiro Toyoda as president and chief executive officer.

The Toyodas led their company to a record in 1984. Toyota sold an all-time high 1.7 million vehicles in Japan and the same number overseas and profits peaked at $2.1 billion in 1985. While that performance would certainly earn Toyota a mention in automotive history books, Eiji Toyoda and his company may be better remembered for a unique management style that has been copied by hundreds of Japanese companies and is gaining acceptance in the United States.

The Toyota approach, adopted at its ten Japanese factories and twenty-four plants in seventeen countries, has three main objectives: keeping inventory to an absolute minimum through a system called *kanban*, or "just in time;" insuring that each step of the assembly process is performed correctly the first time; and cutting the amount of human labour that goes into each car.

What Toyoda accomplished for Toyota Motor was a dazzling success at a time when Detroit automakers were struggling to stay profitable. Toyota, Japan's number one automaker, spearheaded the tidal wave of small, low-priced cars that swept the United States after successive energy crises in the mid and late-1970s.

In addition to running the largest corporation in Japan—and the world's third largest automaker, behind General Motors (GM) and Ford—Toyoda has overseen the development of a highly efficient manufacturing system that is being copied worldwide. Although Eiji Toyoda gave up his post as chairman in 1994, he continued to hold the title of honorary chair of the company.

In his later years, Toyoda was hospitalised for hip problems, and was wheelchair-bound for a time, undergoing treatment at the Toyota Memorial Hospital in Toyota City, Japan, close to company headquarters.

Five days after his 100th birthday, Toyoda died of heart failure in the same hospital on 17 September 2013. He was a real visionary and inspirational leader who is described as the Japanese equivalent of Henry Ford.

❑❑❑

Emily Jane Brontë

(1818–1848)

Novelist and Poet

"Whatever our souls are made of, his and mine are the same"

Emily Brontë was an English novelist and poet, best remembered for her only novel, *Wuthering Heights*, now considered a classic of English literature. Emily was the third eldest of the four surviving Brontë siblings, between the youngest Anne and her brother Branwell. She published under the pen name Ellis Bell.

Emily Brontë was born on 30 July 1818 in Thornton, near Bradford in Yorkshire, to Maria Branwell and Patrick Brontë. She was the younger sister of Charlotte Brontë and the fifth of six children. In 1824, the family moved to Haworth, where Emily's father was perpetual curate, and it was in these surroundings that their literary gifts flourished.

After the death of their mother in 1821, when Emily was three years old, the older sisters Maria, Elizabeth and Charlotte were sent to the Clergy Daughters' School at Cowan Bridge, where they encountered abuse and privations later described by Charlotte in

Jane Eyre. Emily joined the school for a brief period. When a typhus epidemic swept the school, Maria and Elizabeth caught it. Maria, who may actually have had tuberculosis, was sent home, where she died. Emily was subsequently removed from the school along with Charlotte and Elizabeth. Elizabeth died soon after their returning home.

At home in Haworth, Brontë enjoyed her quiet life. She read extensively and began to make up stories with her siblings. The surviving Brontë children, which included brother Branwell, had strong imaginations. They created tales inspired by toy soldiers given to Branwell by their father. In 1835, the shy Emily tried leaving home for school. She went with Charlotte to Miss Wooler's school in Roe Head where Charlotte worked as a teacher. But she stayed only a few months before heading back to Haworth.

Coming from a poor family, Brontë tried to find work. She became a teacher at the Law Hill School in September 1837, but she left her position the following March. Brontë and his sister Charlotte went to study in Brussels in 1842, but the death of their aunt Elizabeth forced them to return home.

In 1844, Emily began going through all the poems she had written, copying them neatly into two notebooks. One was labelled "Gondal Poems", the other was unlabelled. The first one involved a fictional world called Gondal, which she created with her sister Anne. She wrote both prose and poems about this imaginary place and its inhabitants. Emily also wrote other poems as well. Her sister Charlotte discovered some of Emily's poems and sought to publish them along with her own work and some by Anne. The three sisters used male pen names for their collection—*Poems by Currer, Ellis, and Acton Bell.*

Published in 1846, the book sold only a few copies and garnered little attention.

In 1847, Emily published her novel, *Wuthering Heights*, as two volumes of a three-volume set (the last volume being *Agnes Grey* by her sister Anne). Its innovative structure somewhat puzzled critics.

Although it received mixed reviews when it first came out, and was often condemned for its portrayal of amoral passion, the book subsequently became an English literary classic. In 1850, Charlotte edited and published *Wuthering Heights* as a stand-alone novel and under Emily's real name. Although a letter from her publisher indicates that Emily was finalizing a second novel, the manuscript has never been found.

At first, reviewers did not know what to make of *Wuthering Heights*. It was only after Brontë's death that the book developed its reputation as a literary masterwork. She died of tuberculosis on December 19, 1848, nearly two months after her brother, Branwell, succumbed to the same disease. Her sister Anne also fell ill and died of tuberculosis the following May.

Interest in Brontë's work and life remains strong today. The parsonage where Brontë spent much of her life is now a museum.The Brontë Society operates the museum and works to preserve and honour the work of the Brontë sisters.

❑❑❑

Enid Blyton

(1897–1968)

Writer

"I don't care for thrillers that frighten
Or tomes that are meant to enlighten."

Enid Blyton was a British writer who published over 600 children's or juvenile books during her 40-year career. Blyton's most famous series was *The Famous Five*. Her works celebrated good food, spirit of comradeship, and honesty. By the 1980s, Blyton's books had sold some 60 million copies and had been translated into nearly seventy languages.

Enid Blyton was born on August 11, 1897, in London, in a small flat above a shop in East Dulwich. She was the eldest of three children. Her father, Thomas Carey Blyton, had many talents: he painted in water colours, wrote poetry, learnt to play piano, taught himself foreign languages, and was a photographer. He took care of his children's private school fees and sent regularly money to support his family.

From her earliest childhood, Blyton had been schooled in the belief that she would eventually be a musician. However, she had also started to write and send stories, articles, and poems to various periodicals. Although her family thought, that most of her writing was a waste of time, she remained undaunted. Her first published poem, entitled *Have You-?* - appeared in *Nash's Magazine* (1917). Blyton's first book, *Child Whispers* (1922), was a collection of verse. This twenty-four-page work was followed by *Real Fairies: Poems* (1923), *Responsive Singing Games* (1923), *The Enid Blyton Book of Fairies* (1924), *Songs of Gladness* (1924), *The Zoo Book* (1924), and other books published by J. Saville and Newnes.

In 1924, Blyton married Hugh Pollock, an editor of the book department of George Newnes.

Blyton's first full-length children's adventure book, *The Secret Island,* was published in 1938. This fast-moving story, woven around familiar characters, led to such series as *The Famous Five, The Secret Seven,* the *Adventure* series, the *Mystery* series, and the *'Barney' Mystery* books.

During World War II, when publishing was restricted, Blyton managed to get her works printed. During the following decades, she ruled the field of juvenile literature. Blyton could write 10,000 words a day, which enabled her to keep up her prodigious output. In 1940, eleven books were published under her name, including *The Secret of Spiggy Holes*, which had appeared earlier in serial form in *Sunny Stories, Twenty-Minute Tales* and *Tales of Betsy May,* both collections of short stories, *The Children of Cherry Tree Farm,* and a story book annual for the *News Chronicle*. The remainder were brought out by George Newnes, who continued as Blyton's main publisher. Under the pseudonym Mary Pollock, she wrote *Three Boys and a Circus* and *Children of Kidillin*.

Blyton's marriage ended in 1942. Next year, she married Kenneth Darrell Waters, a middle-aged surgeon. An exploding shell at the 'Battle of Jutland' during the First World War had permanently impaired his hearing, but helped with a hearing aid, he could pick up Blyton's speech. He was also genuinely interested in her work and they shared many interests in common, including gardening.

In 1945, Blyton decided to wind up her column for the *Teachers' World*. Seven years later, she withdrew from *Sunny Stories*. In 1953, appeared the first edition of *Enid Blyton Magazine*. Regular news was given for sponsored clubs. The Famous Five Club originated through a series of books about the 'Famous Five'. After the publication of the first story in 1942, a new title followed each year.

In 1949, appeared *Little Noddy Goes to Toyland*, a story of a little toy man, who always ends up in trouble and has to seek help from his Toyland friends. Its sales exceeded expectations.

At the end of the 1990s, well over 300 Blyton titles were still in print, including editions of the *Famous Five* stories linked to the popular television serialisation (1995) and modern adventure games, also based on the '*Famous Five*' series.

Enid Blyton Magazine was closed in 1959. In the early sixties, the author found it increasingly difficult to concentrate to writing. Her husband died in 1967. During the months that followed, her own illness grew progressively worse. Blyton died in her sleep on November 28, 1968, in a Hampsted nursing home. Although her books have been criticised for racism, sexism, and snobbishness, they have always found new readers from new generations. "She was a child, she thought as a child and she wrote as a child," as the psychologist, Michael Woods summarised the secret of her writing.

❑❑❑

Ernest Hemingway

(1899–1961)

Novelist

"All my life I've looked at words as though I were seeing them for the first time."

One of the most famous American novelist, short-story writer and essayist, whose deceptively simple prose style have influenced wide range of writers.

Ernest Hemingway was born on July 21, 1899 in Oak Park, 10 miles from Chicago. Ernest was the second of Clarence Edmonds Hemingway and Grace Hall's six children. Both his grandfathers had fought in the American Civil War, although Grace's father was born in Sheffield. His mother was a music teacher and his father, a doctor. Hemingway was enthusiastic about his work but, after seven months, he volunteered as a Red Cross driver and sailed for Europe in 1918.

His affair with an American nurse, Agnes Von Kurowsky, gave basis for the novel, *A farewell to arms* (1929). The tragic love story and study of an American ambulance officer's disillusionment in the war and his role as a deserter was filmed first time in 1932, starring Gary Cooper, Helen Hayes, and Adolphe Menjou.

After the World War I, Hemingway worked for a short time as a journalist in Chicago. He moved in 1921 to Paris, where he married the first of his four wives, Hadley Richardson. In 1922, he went to Greece and Turkey to report on the war between those countries. In 1923, Hemingway made two trips to Spain, on the second to see bullfights at Pamplona's annual festival.

He divorced his wife in 1927 and married Pauline Pfeiffer who was a Catholic, so he converted into a Catholic. They moved to Key West in Florida in 1928, the same year that his father, tormented by illness and financial problems, committed suicide.

The novel *Farewell to Arms* was published in 1929. During the Second World War, he was a war correspondent for seven months. In 1954, he won the Nobel Prize for Literature.

Because of his strong action plots and spare, visually exact prose, many screen adaptations of his work have been made, including: *A Farewell to Arms* (1933); *To Have and Have Not* (1944) and *The Old Man and the Sea* (1958). Hemingway disliked almost all of the films of his books and was only involved with the production of the *Old Man and the Sea*. *Across the River and Into the Trees* was Hemingway's first novel in a decade and poorly received.

The Old Man and the Sea, published first in *Life* magazine in 1952, restored again his fame. It told a story of an old Cuban fisherman named Santiago who finally catches a giant marlin after weeks of not catching anything. As he returns to the harbour, the sharks eat the fish, lashed to his boat. The model for Santiago was a Cuban fisherman, Gregorio Fuentes, who died in January 2002, at the age of 104. Fuentes had served as the captain of Hemingway's boat, Pilar in the late 1930s and was occasionally his tapster.

Hemingway - himself a great sportsman - liked to portray soldiers, hunters, bullfighters - tough, at times primitive people whose courage and honesty are set against the brutal ways of modern society, and who in this confrontation lose hope and faith. His straightforward prose, his spare dialogue, and his predilection for understatement are particularly effective in his short stories, some of which are collected in *Men Without Women* (1927) and *The Fifth Column* and *The First Forty-Nine Stories* (1938).

During 1960–61, he disintegrated physically. Hemingway had high blood pressure, diabetes, kidney and liver disease. The drugs he was put on had the side effects of making him depressed. He was taken into the Mayo Clinic where he was treated with electric shock treatment that exacerbated his mental illness.

On release from hospital on July 2, 1961, he committed suicide by shooting himself with his favourite shotgun in the head one morning in the hallway of his home in Ketchum, Idaho.

Several of Hemingway's novels have been published posthumously. *True at First Light*, depiction of a safari in Kenya, appeared in July 1999. Its staggering language and self-pity reveal mostly the downfall of his famous style.

❑❑❑

Fidel Castro

(1926–2016)

Political Leader

"It does not matter how small you are if you have faith and plan of action."

Fidel Castro was the former President of Cuba. After commanding the revolution that overthrew Fulgencio Batista in 1959, he held the title of Prime Minister until 1976, when he became president of the Council of State as well as the Council of Ministers.

Fidel Castro was born on August 13, 1926 in Mayari, Cuba. During his childhood, he attended private Catholic School and graduated to attend the University of Havana in 1945. His teachers immediately noticed Fidel's amazing memory, which he used to memorise his books.

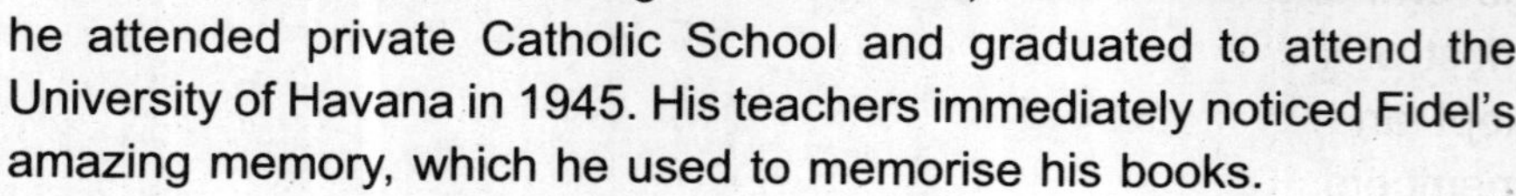

He graduated with his degree in law in 1950 and had seen the power of political movements. He became a full-fledged member of the Orthodoxo Party and campaigned for a seat in the Cuban Congress. However, his plans were disrupted when Fulgencio Batista seized control of the Cuban government in order to prevent the rise of the Orthodoxos. Under Batista, thousands of political opponents were murdered and the people were held under massive oppression.

Fidel began plotting militant action against the Batista regime. On July 26, 1953, he led them in a guerilla attack on the Moncada army barracks in Santiage de Cuba. The militia seized weapons and other supplies and their success caused the citizens there to rally to his flag. Unfortunately, the government sent in reinforcements, which managed to kill nearly all of the revolutionaries and send Fidel to prison for fifteen years.

After a year, Batista granted amnesty to all political prisoners, including Fidel, and they were released. He had not lost his revolutionary attitude and moved to Mexico to form a new army of guerillas to overthrow the Cuban government. There he met Che Guevara, who was serving as a medical intern in Mexico City. They quickly joined forces and assembled a group of eighty-two guerillas, training them in the art of war. The group was called the 26th of July, in memory of the attack on the barracks in 1953.

On December 2, 1956, the group returned to Cuba using a boat. When a man fell overboard, Fidel refused to continue until he was found. They landed, but the group was quickly destroyed by the Cuban army.

The few survivors, including Fidel and Che, went into the mountains to hide. There they were able to conduct small hit-and-run operations as well as initiate a propaganda campaign. He promised a government free of corruption and honest to the people, and kept most of the Cuban Constitution of 1940. However, his word was not kept and over the years, he executed thousands of Batista Party members.

In 1959, Fidel toured many countries, including the United States, to encourage unity among nations. Although President Eisenhower refused to meet him, Vice President Nixon met with Fidel, later calling him a communist dictator that should be overthrown. He travelled again to the United States to speak before the United Nations general council. When they threatened to refuse him an audience, he stayed in a hotel nearby. During his stay, he met many leaders of the time, including Malcolm X and Khrushchev.

He continued supporting revolutionaries in other countries, including Che, who had left Cuba to lead a revolutionary effort in Bolivia. Despite Che's death in 1967, Fidel continued sending Cuban soldiers to unstable countries in Central and South America to encourage the Communist revolution.

Following intestinal surgery from an undisclosed digestive illness, Castro transferred his responsibilities to the First Vice-President, his younger brother Raúl Castro, on July 31, 2006. On February 24, 2008, five days before his mandate was to expire, he announced he would neither seek nor accept a new term as either president or commander-in-chief. On February 24, 2008, the National Assembly elected Raúl Castro to succeed him as the President of Cuba.

In October 2009, Castro was named "World Hero of Solidarity" by the United Nations General Assembly. In August 2010, he gave his first speech to the Cuban National Assembly in four years. Former Cuban President Fidel Castro resigned his role as secretary of Cuba's Communist Party in April 2011.

He died on November 25, 2016.

Florence Nightingale

(1820–1910)

Humanitarian & Social Worker

"To understand God's thoughts we must study statistics, for these are the measure of His purpose."

Florence Nightingale is known as the founder of modern nursing and one of the most famous women in history, few people know that she spent the last half of her life confined to her home and often bedridden, suffering from an illness similar to what we now call ME/CFS (Myalgic Encephalomyelitis/ Chronic Fatigue Syndrome).

She was born on May 12, 1820 to wealthy British parents travelling in Italy. Named for the city in which she was born, young Florence never quite fit the mould of a Victorian lady. She was well educated in literature, music, drawing and the domestic arts. A women of her social standing was expected to marry and devote her life to her family, entertaining, and cultural pursuits. However, she felt an early calling to serve, and refused to marry.

When she attempted to go to work as a nurse, her horrified family repeatedly opposed her. In those days, hospitals were often dirty and dark and nurses were untrained, sometimes drunken women. Finally, at the age of 33, she was able to obtain some minimal training and begin her career.

In 1854, the British press began reporting that soldiers wounded in the Crimean War were being poorly cared for in deplorable conditions. Nightingale recruited and equipped a group of nurses and went off to Turkey to help. Her arrival was not celebrated by the surgeons there, who resented the interference of a woman.

Undaunted, she worked tirelessly to improve conditions in the hospital. Her changes revolutionised British military medical care, increasing standards for sanitation and nutrition and dramatically lowering mortality rates. While visiting the front lines, she became ill and never really recovered.

Although an invalid for the rest of her life, Nightingale continued to have an influence on standards of nursing care and training. In 1859, she helped to establish the first Visiting Nurse Association and in 1860, she established a school that became a model for modern nurses training.

She was considered an expert on the scientific care of the sick and was asked by the United States for her advice on caring for the wounded soldiers of the Civil War. Through correspondence and reports, she continued her influence throughout her last years. She was the first woman to receive the British Order of Merit.

God had always led her. She remembered no particular sermon or circumstances whichever made any great impression upon her. But the first idea she could recollect when she was a child was a desire to nurse the sick. Her day dreams were all of hospitals and she visited them whenever she could. She never communicated about it to any one, as she knew it would have been laughed at. She thought that God had called her to serve Him in that way.

In 1907, the International Conference of Red Cross Societies listed her as a pioneer of the Red Cross Movement.

Florence Nightingale died at her home, 10 South Street, in London, on Saturday, August 13, 1910. News of her death spread quickly throughout England and across the oceans to the other countries of the world. Her courage and devotion had not been forgotten.

Florence Nightingale was known by the British soldiers in the Crimea as the "lady with the lamp" because of the late hours that she worked tending to the sick and wounded. Today, she is remembered as a symbol of selfless caring and tireless service.

❑❑❑

Franklin Delano Roosevelt

(1882–1945)

Politician

"Happiness lies in the joy of achievement and the thrill of creative effort."

Franklin Delano Roosevelt was the 32nd president of the United States. As a president, he was elected to the office four times. He led the United States through two of the greatest crises of the 20th century - the Great Depression and World War II.

Franklin D. Roosevelt was born in Hyde Park, New York on January 30, 1882, as the son of James Roosevelt and Sara Delano Roosevelt. His parents and private tutors provided him with almost all his formative education. He attended Groton (1896–1900), a prestigious preparatory school in Massachusetts, and received a BA degree in history from Harvard in only three years (1900–03). Roosevelt next studied law at New York's Columbia University where he passed the bar examination in 1907.

In the meantime, in 1905, he had married a distant cousin, Anna Eleanor Roosevelt, who was the niece of President Theodore Roosevelt. The couple had six children, five of whom survived.

Roosevelt was reelected to the State Senate in 1912, and supported Woodrow Wilson's candidacy at the Democratic National Convention. As a reward for his support, Wilson appointed him Assistant Secretary of the Navy in 1913, a position he held until 1920.

While vacationing at Campobello Island, New Brunswick in the summer of 1921, Roosevelt contracted poliomylitis (infantile paralysis). Despite courageous efforts to overcome his crippling illness, he never regained the use of his legs.

Following his reelection as governor in 1930, Roosevelt began to campaign for the presidency. While the economic depression damaged Hoover and the Republicans, Roosevelt's bold efforts to combat it in New York enhanced his reputation.

In Chicago, in 1932, Roosevelt won the nomination as the Democratic Party candidate for president. He broke with tradition and flew to Chicago to accept the nomination in person. He then campaigned energetically calling for government intervention in the economy to provide relief, recovery, and reform. His activist approach and personal charm helped to defeat Hoover in November 1932 by seven million votes.

The depression worsened in the months preceding Roosevelt's inauguration, March 4, 1933. Factory closings, farm foreclosures, and bank failures increased, while unemployment soared. Roosevelt faced the greatest crisis in American history since the Civil War. He undertook immediate actions to initiate his New Deal. To halt depositor panics, he closed the banks temporarily. Then he worked with a special session of Congress during the first "100 days" to pass recovery legislation which set up alphabet agencies such as the AAA (Agricultural Adjustment Administration) to support farm prices and the CCC (Civilian Conservation Corps) to employ young men.

Roosevelt easily defeated Alfred M. Landon in 1936 and went on to defeat by lesser margins, Wendell Willkie in 1940 and Thomas E. Dewey in 1944. He thus became the only American president to serve more than two terms.

By 1939, Roosevelt was concentrating increasingly on foreign affairs with the outbreak of war in Europe. New Deal reform legislation diminished, and the ills of the Depression would not fully abate until the nation mobilised for war.

The Japanese surprise attack on Pearl Harbour, December 7, 1941, followed four days later by Germany's and Italy's declarations of war against the United States, brought the nation irrevocably into the war. Roosevelt exercised his powers as Commander-in-Chief of the Armed Forces, a role he actively carried out. He worked with and through his military advisers, overriding them when necessary, and took an active role in choosing the principal field commanders and in making decisions regarding wartime strategy.

He moved to create a "grand alliance" against the Axis powers through "The Declaration of the United Nations," January 1, 1942, in which all nations fighting the Axis agreed not to make a separate peace and pledged themselves to a peacekeeping organisation (now the United Nations) on victory.

He gave priority to the western European front and with the help of General George Marshall, Chief of Staff of US army, duirng World War II, he plan a holding operation in the Pacific and organise an expeditionary force for an invasion of Europe. The United States and its allies invaded North Africa in November 1942 and Sicily and Italy in 1943. The D-Day landings on the Normandy beaches in France, on June 6, 1944, were followed by the allied invasion of Germany, six months later. By April 1945, victory in Europe was certain.

The unending stress and strain of the war literally wore Roosevelt out. By early 1944, a full medical examination disclosed serious heart and circulatory problems; and although his physicians placed him on a strict regime of diet and medication, the pressures of war and domestic politics weighed heavily on him.

During a vacation at Warm Springs, Georgia, on April 12, 1945, he suffered a massive stroke and died two and one-half hours later without regaining consciousness. He was 63 years old. His death came on the eve of complete military victory in Europe and within months of victory over Japan in the Pacific. President Roosevelt was buried in the Rose Garden of his estate at Hyde Park, New York.

❑❑❑

Gabriel Garcia Marquez

(1928–2014)

Novelist, Journalist and Political Activist

"Nobody deserves your tears, but whoever deserves them will not make you cry."

Gabriel Jose Garcia Marquez, also known as Gabo, was a Colombian novelist, journalist, publisher, and political activist. In 1982, he also received Nobel Prize in Literature. Widely credited with introducing the global public to magical realism, he had secured both significant critical acclaim and widespread commercial success.

Gabriel Jose Garcia Marquez was born on March 6, 1928 in Aracataca, a banana town in Colombia. The predominant banana industry and the massacre of striking banana workers in 1928 were the events that influenced his work. He was raised by his maternal grandparents for eight years. Several of his superstitious aunts lived with him, and later, he credited much of his storytelling style - telling fantasy stories as if they were the implacable truth, to his grandmother. In 1936, because of his grandfather's death and his grandmother's increasing blindness, Garcia Marquez returned to his parents' home in Sucre, a site of many non-Macondo stories.

Between 1936–1946, he studied in Barranquilla. In 1947, he entered the National University of Colombia in Bogota as a Law student. However, three years later, Garcia Marquez abandoned the law for journalism at the University of Cartagena. His fifteen stories were published in the newspaper *El Espectador* between 1950–1955.

During this period, he began to admire modernists such as Woolf, Joyce, and Faulkner. In Faulkner's mythical Yoknaputawpha, Garcia Marquez found the seeds for Macondo, and he began to grow dissatisfied with his earlier stories, believing them to be too abstracted.

Upon graduation, Garcia Marquez returned to Bogot as a reporter for *El Espectador*. His first novel, *Leaf Storm* was published in 1955. In the same year, he travelled to Europe as correspondent for *El Espectador*, and finally settled in Paris where he found that he was out of job.

After a brief stay in London, Garcia Marquez returned to Caracas to work as a journalist in 1957. His novel *No One Writes to the Colonel* was published in 1958, but he felt it was too far away from his imagined goal — a picture he had been developing for years. He knew his ultimate work would take place in the mythical town of Macondo, the name of a banana plantation near Aracataca, yet he still had to find the right tone for his tale.

In the same year, Garcia Marquez witnessed the fall of the Venezuela's dictator, which rooted the seed for *The Autumn of the Patriarch*. He also married Mercedes Barcha in Barranquilla. From 1959–1961, he worked for the Cuban news agency *La Prensa* in Cuba and New York. Afterwards, he resided in Mexico and worked as a screen writer, journalist, and publicist. *The Evil Hour* and *Big Mama's Funeral* were published in 1962, however, none of his works had sold over 700 copies.

On January 1965, an inspiration suddenly arose in his mind. He had found his tone — a natural tone expressed with an "unperturbed face". After eighteen months of seclusion, his masterpiece *One Hundred Years of Solitude* was published in June 1967. Within a week, 5,000 copies were sold, and half a million copies in 3 years. Success had come at last: the novel won the Chianchiano Prize in Italy, and was named the Best Foreign Book in France in 1969.

In 1970, the book was published in English and was chosen as one of the best twelve books of the year by *Time*. Two years later, Garcia Marquez was awarded the Romulo Gallegos Prize and the Neustadt Prize. In 1973, after the assassination of the president of Chile, he decided to take a more active political role.

In 1974, he founded *Alternativa* in Bogota and participated in the Russell Tribunal to publicise human rights abuses in Latin America. A year later, *Autumn of the Patriarch,* a novel of an archetypical South American tyrant, was published.

In 1981, the year in which Garcia Marquez received the French Legion of Honour medal and *Chronicle of a Death Foretold* was published, the Colombian military accused him of conspiring with the M-19 guerrillas, and he seeked asylum in Mexico. Colombia soon regretted after he was awarded the Nobel Prize for Literature in 1982 - for his wonderful work in combining fantasy elements and mythology with realistic fiction, the style so-called magic realism.

By 1986, his other famous novel, *Love in the Time of Cholera* was born, which suggested undoubtly the universal appeal of Garcia Marquez as a writer. His other remarkable novels— *The General in his Labyrinth, Strange Pilgrims,* and *Love and Other Demons* were published respectively in 1989, 1992, and 1994. By now one of the most world-known writers, he eased into a lifestyle of writing, teaching and political activism in Mexico City.

In 2002, Garcia Marquez published the memoir, *Vivir para contarla*, the first of a projected three-volume autobiography. The book was a bestseller in the Spanish-speaking world. Edith

Grossman's English translation, *Living to Tell the Tale*, was published in November 2003 and has become another bestseller. On September 10, 2004, the Bogota daily *El Tiempo* announced a new novel, *Memoria de mis putas tristes*, a love story that was published the following October with a first print run of one million copies.

In May 2008, despite the fact that Garcia Marquez had earlier declared that he "had finished with writing", it was announced that the author was now finishing a new novel, "novel of love" that had yet to be given a title, to be published by the end of the year. However, in April 2009 his agent, Carmen Balcells, told the Chilean Newspaper Tercera that Marquez was unlikely to write again.

His novel *Of Love and Other Demons* has been adapted and directed by a Costa Rican film maker, Hilda Hidalgo. Hidalgo's film was released in April 2010.

He died on April 17, 2014.

❑❑❑

Galileo Galilei

(1564–1642)

Scientist

"All truths are easy to understand once they are discovered; the point is to discover them."

Galileo Galilei was an Italian scientist who formulated the basic law of falling bodies, which he verified by careful measurements. He constructed a telescope with which he studied lunar craters, and discovered four moons revolving around Jupiter and espoused the Copernican cause.

Galileo was born in 1564, in Pisa. Galilei's parents were Vincenzo Galilei and Guilia Ammannati. Galileo was their first child and spent his early years with his family in Pisa. In 1572, when Galileo was eight years old, his family returned to Florence, his father's hometown. However, Galileo remained in Pisa and lived for two years with Muzio Tedaldi who was related to Galileo's mother by marriage. When he reached the age of ten, he left Pisa to join his family in Florence and there he was educated by Jacopo Borghini. Once he was old enough to be educated in a monastery, his parents sent him to the Camaldolese

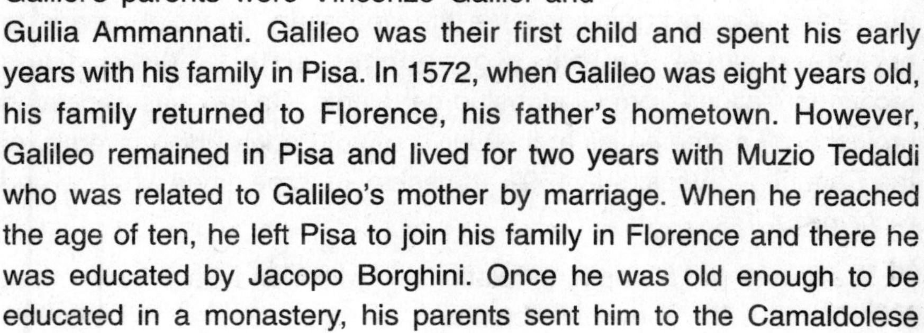

Monastery at Vallombrosa which was situated on a magnificent forested hillside 33 km southeast of Florence.

Galileo did continue his schooling in Florence, however, in a school run by the Camaldolese monks. In 1581, Vincenzo sent him back to Pisa to live again with Muzio Tedaldi and now to enrol for a medical degree at the University of Pisa. Galileo returned to Florence for the summer vacations and there, he continued to study mathematics.

He began teaching mathematics, first privately in Florence, and then during 1585–86 at Siena where he held a public appointment. During the summer of 1586, he taught at Vallombrosa, and in the same year he wrote his first scientific book *The little balance*. In the following year, he travelled to Rome to visit Clavius who was professor of mathematics at the Jesuit Collegio Romano there. A topic which was very popular with the Jesuit Mathematicians at that time was centres of gravity.

After leaving Rome, Galileo remained in contact with Clavius by correspondence and Guidobaldo del Monte was also a regular correspondent. In 1588, Galileo received a prestigious invitation to lecture on the dimensions and location of hell in Dante's *Inferno* at the Academy in Florence.

In 1591, Vincenzo Galilei, Galileo's father, died and since Galileo was the eldest son, he had to provide financial support to the rest of the family and in particular have the necessary financial means to provide dowries for his two younger sisters. With strong recommendations from Guidobaldo del Monte, Galileo was appointed professor of mathematics at the University of Padua (the University of the Republic of Venice) in 1592 at a salary of three times what he had received at Pisa.

Galileo began a long term relationship with Maria Gamba, who was from Venice, but they did not marry, perhaps Galileo felt that his financial situation was not good. In 1600, their first child Virginia was born, followed by a second daughter, Livia in the following year. In 1606, their son, Vincenzo was born.

Galileo began to make a series of telescopes whose optical performance was much better than that of the Dutch instrument. His first telescope was made from available lenses and gave a magnification of about four times. To improve on this, Galileo learnt how to grind and polish his own lenses and by August 1609, he had an instrument with a magnification of around eight or nine. Galileo immediately saw the commercial and military applications of his telescope for ships at sea.

By the end of 1609, he had turned his telescope on the night sky and began to make remarkable discoveries. The astronomical discoveries he made with his telescopes were described in a short book called the *Starry Messenger* published in Venice in May 1610. He had also sent Cosimo de Medici, the Grand Duke of Tuscany, an excellent telescope for himself.

The Venetian Senate, perhaps realising that the rights to manufacture telescopes that Galileo had given them were worthless, froze his salary. However, he had succeeded in impressing Cosimo and, in June 1610, only a month after his famous little book was published, Galileo resigned from his post at Padua and became Chief Mathematician at the University of Pisa (without any teaching duties) and 'Mathematician and Philosopher' to the Grand Duke of Tuscany.

In 1611, he visited Rome where he was treated as a leading celebrity; the Collegio Romano put on a grand dinner with speeches to honour Galileo's remarkable discoveries. He was also made a member of the Accademia dei Lincei. While in Rome, and after his return to Florence, Galileo continued to make observations with his telescope. Already in the *Starry Messenger,* he had given rough periods of the four moons of Jupiter.

Galileo first turned his telescope on Saturn on July 25, 1610 and it appeared as three bodies. Continued observations were indeed very puzzling for him as the bodies on either side of Saturn vanished when the ring system was edge on. Also in 1610, he discovered that, when seen in the telescope, the planet, Venus showed phases like those of the Moon, and therefore, must orbit the Sun not the Earth.

Other observations made by Galileo included the observation of sunspots. He reported these in *Discourse on floating bodies* which he published in 1612 and more fully in *Letters on the sunspots* which appeared in 1613. In 1616, Galileo wrote the *Letter to the Grand Duchess* which vigorously attacked the followers of Aristotle.

In February 1632, he published *Dialogue Concerning the Two Chief Systems of the World - Ptolemaic and Copernican.*

In 1634, he suffered a severe blow when his daughter, Virginia, Sister Maria Celeste, died. She had been a great support to her father through his illnesses and Galileo was shattered and could not work for many months. When he did manage to restart work, he began to write Discourses and Mathematical demonstrations concerning the two new sciences. In 1642, Galileo died at his home outside Florence.

❑❑❑

Greta Thunberg

(2003)

Environmental Activist

"We deserve a safe future. And we demand a safe future. Is that really too much to ask?"

She has been a very young and zestful environmental activist who is courageous enough to rebuke the whole world on an international forum for going lenient on massive industrialization without check and to contribute to carbon release and to have allowed to activities that have caused damage to our environment and have resulted in climate change.

She laid the foundation of a movement known as Fridays for Future in 2018, which is also referred to as School Strike for Climate.

As for her life, her mother used to sing in Opera while her father was an actor. She suffered from Asperger Syndrome, which is an autism spectrum disorder (ASD) and is characterized by abnormalities in social interactions but one develops intelligence and language normally.

It is said that people with Asperger syndrome, focus on an idea or interest very deeply and Thunberg's picked up climate change as the topic of her focus. At first, she came to know about the issue when she was eight years old and under the influence, she altered her own ways of living and turned vegan and ruled out boarding an airplane. (Both livestock and aeroplanes emit gases in a great amount, that contribute to global warming)

To put a greater impact, she encouraged lawmakers to address climate change and in September 2018, before the Swedish election, she did not attend school for almost three weeks as she had to sit outside the parliament of her country, with a sign that stated "Skolstrejk för Klimatet" (School Strike for Climate). She was alone on the first day but more and more people joined her on other days and her efforts attracted global attention. After the election, Thunberg returned to school but still skipped classes on Fridays to strike and these days got the reference of Fridays For Future.

Her action ad devotion put inspiration in hundreds of thousands of students across the world who would participate in their own Fridays for Future. The countries like Belgium, Canada, the United States, the United Kingdom, Finland, Denmark, France and the Netherlands were gripped by strikes.

As a result, world had started acknowledging her devotion and great knowledge on the environment and she was invited to address gathering about climate change. She gave speeches at the World Economic Forum in Davos, Switzerland and the European Parliament and also just outside the parliament of Italy, France, the United Kingdom, and the United States. In September of 2019, in New York City, her appearance at a UN climate event garnered widespread interest as she travelled to the US, on a yacht that emitted zero-emission and she stunned all and sundry with her epic speech, "You have stolen my dreams and my childhood with your empty words...We are in the beginning of a mass extinction, and all you can talk about is money, and fairy tales of eternal economic growth. How dare you!"

In that month, millions of protesters participated in climate strikes in more than 163 countries and Thunberg is also credited for shifting the views of many people as well as their habits regarding climate change. Her influence is termed as "Greta effect" and she has had many critics as well. She was called a "brat" in 2019 by Brazilian Pres. Jair Bolsonaro.

Other than her devotion to environment, she also worked to raise awareness about Asperger and has inspired those who confronted a similar problem. She does admit that Asperger prevented her growth in some ways but she manages to count its advantages too as she tweeted, "I have Aspergers and that means I'm sometimes a bit different from the norm. And-given the right circumstances-being different is a superpower."

Her speeches are an eye-opener which are available in form of a collection under the title, "No One Is Too Small to Make a Difference (2019). On her work and life, a documentary is also being made in 2020 with the title, "I am Greta".

In 2021, she was nominated for the Nobel Peace Prize. In 2022, her foundation donated €100,000 to support youth climate activists from the Most Affected People and Areas (MAPA) attending COP27 in Egypt.

George Bernard Shaw

(1856–1950)

Writer

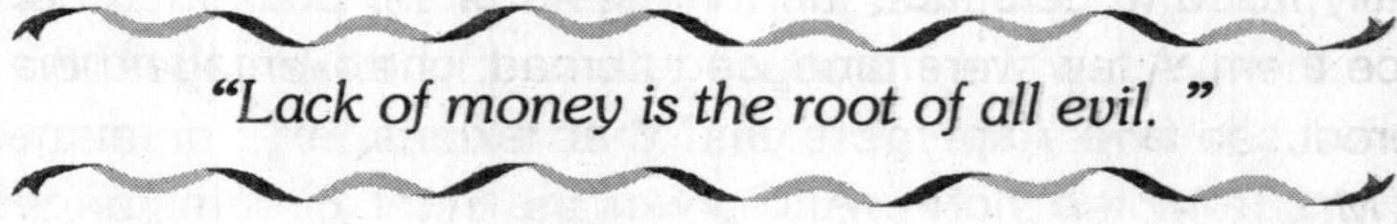

"Lack of money is the root of all evil."

George Bernard Shaw was an Irish protestant playwright based in the United Kingdom. He was uniquely the winner of the Nobel Prize in Literature and an Academy Award for writing adapted screenplay.

George Bernard Shaw was born on 1856 in Dublin, in a lowermiddle-class family of Scottish-Protestant ancestry. His father was a failed corn-merchant, with a drinking problem and a squint, and his mother was a professional singer, the disciple of Vandeleur Lee, a voice teacher claiming to have a unique and original approach to singing.

When Shaw was just short of his sixteenth birthday, his mother left her husband and son, and moved with Vandeleur Lee to London, where the two set up a household, along with Shaw's elder sister, Lucy. There, Shaw's mother worked as a clerk for an estate office.

In 1876, Shaw left Dublin and his father, and moved to London. He went with his mother's *menage*. There he lived with his mother and sister while pursuing a career in journalism and writing. The first medium he tried as a creative writer was prose, completing five novels before any of them were published. He read voraciously, in public libraries and in the British Museum reading room.

In 1891, at the invitation of J.T. Grein, a merchant, theatre critic, and director of a progressive private new-play society, The Independent Theatre, Shaw wrote his first play, *Widower's Houses*. For the next twelve years, he wrote close to a dozen plays, though he generally failed to persuade the managers of the London Theatres to produce them. A few were produced abroad; one (*Arms and the Man*) was produced under the auspices of an experimental management; one (*Mrs Warren's Profession*) was censored by the Lord Chamberlain's Examiner of Plays and several were presented in single performances by private societies.

In 1898, after a serious illness, Shaw resigned as theatre critic, and moved out of his mother's house where he was still living to marry Charlotte Payne-Townsend, an Irish woman of independent means. Their marriage lasted until Charlotte's death in 1943.

In 1904, Harley Granville Barker, an actor, director and playwright, twenty years younger than Shaw who had appeared in a private theatre society's production of Shaw's *Candida*, took over the management of the Court Theatre on Sloane Square in Chelsea and set it up as an experimental theatre specializing in new and progressive drama. Over the next three seasons, Barker produced ten plays by Shaw, and he began writing new plays with Barker's management specifically in mind.

Over the next ten years, all but one of Shaw's plays, (*Pygmalion* in 1914) was produced either by Barker or by Barker's friends and colleagues in the other experimental theatre managements around England. With royalties from his plays, Shaw, who had become financially independent on marrying, now became quite wealthy. Throughout the decade, he remained active in the Fabian Society, in city government , and on committees dedicated to ending dramatic censorship, and to establishing a subsidised National Theatre.

The outbreak of war in 1914 changed Shaw's life. For Shaw, the war represented the bankruptcy of the capitalist system, the last desperate gasps of the nineteenth-century empires, and a tragic waste of young lives, all under the guise of patriotism. He expressed his opinions in a series of newspaper articles under the title, *Common Sense About the War*.

After the war, Shaw found his dramatic voice again and rebuilt his reputation, first with a series of five plays about "creative evolution," *Back to Methuselah*, and then, in 1923, with *Saint Joan*. In 1925, he was awarded the Nobel Prize for Literature. He donated the cash award towards an English edition of the Swedish playwright, August Strindberg, who had never been recognised with a Nobel prize by the Swedish Academy. Shaw's plays were regularly produced and revived in London. He lived the rest of his life as an international celebrity, travelling the world, continually involved in local and international politics. And he continued to write thousands of letters and over a dozen more plays.

In 1950, Shaw fell off a ladder while trimming a tree on his property at Ayot St. Lawrence in Hertfordshire, outside London, and died a few days later of complications from the injury, at the age of 94. He had been at work on yet another play (*Why She Would Not*). In his will, he left a large part of his estate to a project to revamp the English alphabet. After that, the project failed, the estate was divided among the other beneficiaries in his will: the National Gallery of Ireland, the British Museum, and the Royal Academy of Dramatic Art.

❑❑❑

George Washington

(1732–1799)

Ist President of United States

"Every post is honorable in which a man can serve his country."

George Washington served as a general and commander-in-chief of the colonial armies during the American Revolution, and later became the first president of the United States, serving from 1789 to 1797.

George Washington was born on February 22, 1732 in westermoreland county, Vinginia. He lost his father at age 11 and his half brother, Lawrence, took over that role. Washington's mother was protective and demanding, keeping him from joining the British navy as Lawrence wanted. Lawrence owned Mount Vernon, and George lived with him from the age of 16. He was schooled entirely in Colonial Virginia and never went to college. He was good at math which suited his chosen profession of surveying.

In 1749, Washington was appointed as surveyor for Culpepper County, Virginia after a trek for Lord Fairfax into the Blue Ridge Mountains. He was in the military from 1752-58 before being elected to the Virginia House of Burgesses in 1759. He spoke against Britain's policies and became a leader in the Association. From 1774-75 he attended both Continental Congresses. He led the Continental Army from 1775-1783 during the American Revolution. He then became the president of the Constitutional Convention in 1787.

Despite being a member of the Federalist Party, in 1789, Washington was immensely popular as a war hero and was an obvious choice as the first president for both federalists and anti-federalists. He was unanimously elected by the 69 electors. His runner up, John Adams, was named Vice President.

In 1792, George Washington was able to rise above the politics of the day and carry every electoral vote - 132 from 15 states - to win a second term. John Adams, as runner-up, remained the Vice President.

Washington could have been a king. Instead, he chose to be a citizen. He set many precedents for the national government and the presidency: The two-term limit in office, only broken once by Franklin Roosevelt, and then later ensconced in the Constitution's 22nd Amendment. He crystallized the power of the presidency as a part of the government's three branches, able to exercise authority when necessary, but also accept the balance of power inherent in the system.

He was not only considered a military and revolutionary hero, but a man of great personal integrity, with a deep sense of duty, honor, and patriotism. For over 200 years, Washington has been acclaimed as indispensible to the success of the Revolution and the birth of the nation. But his most important legacy may be that he insisted he was dispensable, asserting that the cause of liberty was larger than any single individual.

Washington's significance cannot be overstated. He led the Continental Army to victory over the British. He believed in a strong federal government which greatly influenced the nation during his eight years in office. He did not allow others to trap him as royalty. He worked on the principle of merit. His warning against foreign entanglements was heeded by future presidents. By declining a third term, he set up the precedent of a two-term limit.

Washington's administration was one of precedents with many standards that are still followed. He always relied on his cabinet for advice. Since his cabinet appointments went unchallenged, presidents are generally able to choose their own cabinets.

Domestically, Washington was able to stop the first real challenge to federal authority with the suppression of the Whiskey Rebellion in 1794. Pennsylvania farmers were refusing to pay a tax and he sent troops to ensure compliance.

In foreign affairs, Washington was a huge proponent of neutrality. He declared the Proclamation of Neutrality in 1793 which stated that the US would be impartial toward belligerent powers currently in a war. This upset some who felt US owed a greater allegiance to France. His belief in neutrality was reiterated during his Farewell Address in 1796 where he warned against foreign entanglements. This warning became part of the American political landscape.

Washington did not want to run a third time. He retired to Mount Vernon. He was again asked to be the American commander if the US went to war with France over the XYZ affair. However, fighting never occurred on land and he did not have to serve. He died on December 14, 1799 possibly from a streptococcal infection of his throat made worse from being bled four times.

The news of his death spread throughout the country, plunging the nation into a deep mourning. Many towns and cities held mock funerals and presented hundreds of eulogies to honor their fallen hero. When the news of this death reached Europe, the British fleet paid tribute to his memory, and Napoleon ordered ten days of mourning. George Washington is considered one of the most important and influential president of America of all time whose legacy still lives on today.

❑❑❑

Gianni Versace

(1946–1997)

Fashion Designer

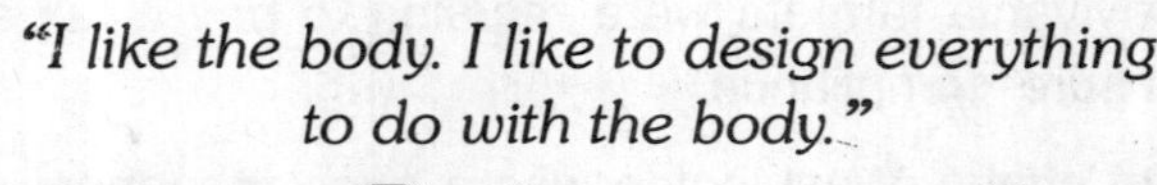

"I like the body. I like to design everything to do with the body."

Gianni Versace was a charismatic and accomplished Italian designer of clothing and theatre costumes. He was influenced by Andy Warhol and modern abstract art; and considered one of the most colourful and talented designers of the late 20th century.

Although years of designing for the theatre earned him a respectable reputation in the fashion industry, it was his collaborations with American photographer, Richard Avedon that helped Versace become one of the world's elite designers. His 1982 collection introduced metallic garments that would become his trademark, and his elaborate stage costumes for Elton John in the late '80s helped cement his reputation as one of the beautiful people. Gianni with his brother Santo and sister Donatella Versace were brought up in Reggio Calabria, by their father and dressmaker mother, Francesca.

He began his apprenticeship at a young age, helping his mother find precious stones and gold braid with which to embroider dresses. He studied architecture before moving to Milan at the age of 25 to work in fashion design. In the mid-seventies, his knits drew the attention of head-hunters at Genny and Callaghan. Complice hired him to design their leather and suede collections, and a few years later, encouraged by his success, Versace presented his first signature collection for women at the *Palazzo della Permanente Art Museum* of Milan. His first menswear collection followed in September of the 1978.

Versace considered himself a tailor, rather than a designer. He knew how to cut and sew the clothes he made. He tried on the men's collections personally and had his sister, Donatella try on the women's clothing. The Versace look of the young, aggressive and sexy woman is well-known. He liked to create sexy clothes for his women, skin-tight with low cuts and high slits on the skirts. Versace was among the first to revive the cat suit, to bring back the mini skirt, to show tights worn as trousers, to bring the bustier out at night and bead it. In 1982, his dresses made with fine metal mesh first appeared and were a hit.

In less than 10 years, Versace built an empire worth $808 million. He used celebrities, including Madonna, Jon Bon Jovi, Naomi Campbell, Tina Turner, and even Tupac Shakur as models for both the runway and print ads. He was one of the first Italian designers to hire world-class photographers such as Richard Avedon to photograph his advertising campaigns, also using the top fashion models for these ads.

In 1982, Versace opened a new chapter in his career, making costumes for the theatre, opera and ballet. He began a close collaboration with choreographer Maurice Bejart. He went on to design accessories, jewellery, furnishings, and china. He was also hired as a costume designer on the TV series, 'Miami Vice'. This led to his relocation to Miami Beach.

The designer battled with a rare cancer of the inner ear. He was presumed to be in remission when, one July morning in the summer of 1997, returning from his customary walk on Ocean Drive, he was gunned down outside his ocean-front mansion in Miami Beach, Florida. He was murdered by spree killer Andrew Cunanan, who committed suicide shortly after the murder. Police reported that Andrew Cunanan had committed suicide using the same handgun that had been used to murder Gianni Versace.

In September 1997, Versace's brother, Santo Versace was announced as the new CEO of the Versace holding. Versace's sister Donatella Versace is the new head of his designs. Elton John dedicated his 1997 album, *The Big Picture* to Versace.

❑❑❑

Gopal Krishna Gokhale

(1866–1915)

Freedom Fighter

"I am not a democrat. I don't believe in democracy. I believe in liberty and rights"

Gopal Krishna Gokhale was one of the pioneers of the Indian National Movement. He was a senior leader of the Indian National Congress. Gokhale gave voice to the aspirations of millions of Indians who were looking for freedom from the British rule. Gandhiji considered him as his political guru. He founded the "Servants of India Society"– an organisation dedicated to the cause of common people. Gokhale's contribution to the making of Indian nation is invaluable.

Gopal Krishna Gokhale was born on May 9, 1866 in Kothapur, Maharashtra. His father Krishna Rao was a farmer who was forced to work as clerk, as the soil of the region was not conducive for agriculture. Gokhale received his early education at the Rajaram High School in Kothapur with the help of financial assistance from his elder brother. Later on, he moved on to Bombay (now Mumbai) and graduated from Elphinstone College, Bombay (now Mumbai) in 1884 at the age of 18.

He was one of the first generations of Indians to receive college education. Gokhale was respected widely in the nascent Indian intellectual community and across India. Education influenced Gokhale greatly. His understanding of the English language allowed him to express himself without hesitation and with utmost clarity. His appreciation and knowledge of history instilled in him a respect for liberty, democracy, and the parliamentary system. After graduation, he moved on to teaching, and took a position as an Assistant Master in the New English School in Pune.

In 1885, Gokhale moved on to Pune and became one of the founding members of Fergusson College, along with his colleagues in Deccan Education Society. Gopal Krishna Gokhale gave nearly two decades of his life to Fergusson College and rose to become the principal of the college. During this time, he came in contact with Mahadev Govind Ranade. Ranade was a judge, scholar, and social reformer, whom Gokhale called his *guru*. Gokhale worked with Ranade in *Puna Sarvajanik Sabha* of which he became the secretary.

Gopal Krishna Gokhale entered public life in 1886 at the age of 20. He delivered a public address on “India under the British Rule”, which was highly appreciated. He regularly contributed articles to Bal Gangadhar Tilak's weekly, *Mahratta*. Through his articles, he tried to awaken the latent patriotism of Indian people. Soon, Gokhale was promoted as secretary of the Deccan Education Society.

When the Indian National Congress held its session in Pune in 1895, he was the secretary of the Reception Committee. From this session, Gokhale became a prominent member of the Indian National Congress. He was twice elected as president of Pune Municipality. For a while, Gokhale was also a member of the Mumbai Legislative Council, where he spoke strongly against the then Government.

In 1902, he left the Fergusson College and became a member of the Imperial Legislative Council in Delhi. There he spoke for the people of the country in an able manner. Gokhale had an excellent grasp of the economic problems of India, which he ably presented during the debates.

In 1905, Gokhale started a new society called "Servants of India Society". This society trained workers for the service of the country. In the same year, he went to England to voice his concerns relating to the unfair treatment of the Indian people by the British government. In a span of 49 days, he spoke in front of 47 different audiences, captivating everyone of them. Gokhale pleaded for gradual reforms to ultimately attain Swaraj, or self-government, in India. He was instrumental in the introduction of the Morley-Minto Reforms of 1909, which eventually became law. Though the reforms sowed the seeds of communal division in India, nevertheless, they gave Indian access to the seats of the highest authority within the government, and their voices were more audible in matters of public interest.

Gopal Krishna Gokhale was a diabetic and asthmatic. Excessive exertion took its toll on Gokhale's health and ultimately, he died on February 19, 1915.

❑❑❑

Guglielmo Marconi

(1874–1937)

Physicist

"Everyday sees humanity more victorious in the struggle with space and time."

Guglielmo Marconi was an Italian physicist and inventor of a successful wireless telegraph. In 1909, he received the Nobel Prize for Physics, which he shared with German physicist Ferdinand Braun. He later worked on the development of shortwave wireless communication, which constitutes the basis of nearly all modern long-distance radio.

Guglielmo Marconi was born at Bologna, Italy, on April 25, 1874, the second son of Giuseppe Marconi, an Italian country gentleman, and Annie Jameson, daughter of Andrew Jameson of Daphne Castle in the County Wexford, Ireland. He was educated privately at Bologna, Florence and Leghorn. Even as a boy, he took a keen interest in physical and electrical science and studied the works of Maxwell, Hertz, Righi, Lodge and others. In 1895, he began laboratory experiments at his father's country estate at Pontecchio where he succeeded in sending wireless signals over a distance of one and a half mile.

In 1896, Marconi took his apparatus to England where he was introduced to Mr. (later Sir) William Preece, Engineer-in-Chief of the post office, and later that year was granted the world's first patent for a system of wireless telegraphy. He demonstrated his system successfully in London, on Salisbury Plain and across the Bristol Channel, and in July 1897 formed The Wireless Telegraph & Signal Company Limited (in 1900 re-named Marconi's Wireless Telegraph Company Limited). In the same year, he gave a demonstration to the Italian Government at Spezia where wireless signals were sent over a distance of twelve miles. In 1899, he established wireless communication between France and England across the English Channel. He erected permanent wireless stations at The Needles, Isle of Wight, at Bournemouth and later at the Haven Hotel, Poole, Dorset.

In 1900, he took out his famous patent No. 7777 for "tuned or syntonic telegraphy" and, on an historic day in December 1901, determined to prove that wireless waves were not affected by the curvature of the Earth, he used his system for transmitting the first wireless signals across the Atlantic between Poldhu, Cornwall, and St. John's, Newfoundland, a distance of 2100 miles.

Between 1902 and 1912, he patented several new inventions. In 1902, during a voyage in the American liner, *Philadelphia*, he first demonstrated *daylight effect* relative to wireless communication and in the same year patented his magnetic detector which then became the standard wireless receiver for many years. In December 1902, he transmitted the first complete messages to Poldhu from stations at Glace Bay, Nova Scotia, and later Cape Cod, Massachusetts, these early tests culminating in 1907 in the opening of the first transatlantic commercial service between Glace Bay and Clifden, Ireland, after the first shorter-distance public service of wireless telegraphy had been established between Bari in Italy and Avidari in Montenegro. In 1905, he patented his horizontal directional aerial and in 1912, a "timed spark" system for generating continuous waves.

In 1914, Guglielmo was commissioned in the Italian Army as a Lieutenant being later promoted to Captain, and in 1916 transferred to the Navy in the rank of Commander. He was a member of the Italian Government mission to the United States in 1917 and in 1919 was appointed Italian plenipotentiary delegate to the Paris Peace Conference. He was awarded the Italian Military Medal in 1919 in recognition of his war service.

During his war service in Italy, he returned to his investigation of short waves, which he had used in his first experiments. After further tests by his collaborators in England, an intensive series of trials was conducted in 1923 between experimental installations at the Poldhu Station and in Marconi's yacht, *Elettra* cruising in the Atlantic and Mediterranean, and this led to the establishment of the beam system for long distance communication. Proposals to use this system as a means of Imperial communications were accepted by the British Government and the first beam station, linking England and Canada, was opened in 1926, other stations being added the following year.

In 1931, Marconi began research into the propagation characteristics of still shorter waves, resulting in the opening in 1932 of the world's first microwave radiotelephone link between the Vatican City and the Pope's summer residence at Castel Gandolfo. Two years later at Sestri Levante, he demonstrated his microwave radio beacon for ship navigation and in 1935, again in Italy, gave a practical demonstration of the principles of radar, the coming of which he had first foretold in a lecture to the American Institute of Radio Engineers in New York in 1922.

He has been the recipient of honorary doctorates of several universities and many other international honours and awards, among them the Nobel Prize for Physics, which in 1909 he shared with

Professor Karl Braun, the Albert Medal of the Royal Society of Arts, the John Fritz Medal and the Kelvin Medal. He was decorated by the Tsar of Russia with the Order of St. Anne, the King of Italy created him Commander of the Order of St. Maurice and St. Lazarus, and awarded him the Grand Cross of the Order of the Crown of Italy in 1902. Marconi also received the freedom of the City of Rome (1903), and was created Chevalier of the Civil Order of Savoy in 1905. Many other distinctions of this kind followed. In 1914, he was both created a Senatore in the Italian Senate and appointed Honorary Knight Grand Cross of the Royal Victorian Order in England. He received the hereditary title of Marchese in 1929.

In 1905, Marconi married the Hon. Beatrice O'Brien, daughter of the 14th Baron Inchiquin. The marriage being annulled in 1927, he married the Countess Bezzi-Scali of Rome, the same year. He had one son and two daughters by his first and one daughter by his second wife. His recreations were hunting, cycling and motoring. Marconi died in Rome on July 20, 1937.

❑❑❑

Henry Ford

(1863–1947)

Philanthropist, Inventor and Businessman

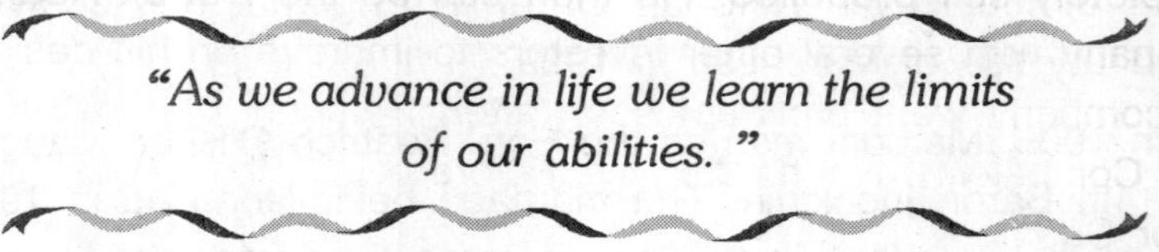

"As we advance in life we learn the limits of our abilities."

Henry Ford was an inventor, philanthropist and a successful American businessman. Ford was the founder of the still popular Ford Motor Company which had its first success with the Model T Ford car that was released in 1908. Henry Ford revolutionised the way cars were designed and built, introducing assembly line factories for producing mass amounts of vehicles that led to lower prices for consumers.

Henry Ford was born on July 30, 1863 in Dearborn, Michigan, United States, in what was then known as Springwells Township. Ford's parents were Irish immigrants and the family lived on a farm, with Henry Ford being the eldest of six children. The family had a comfortable upbringing on the farm with a decent income, but even as a young person, Ford believed there was too much work and not enough income living from the land.

He began his career as an apprentice machinist in 1879, then returned to his family farm in 1882 before starting work with the Westinghouse company to service their steam engines. Ford then went to work at the Edison Illuminating Company where he became chief engineer in 1893.

Henry Ford had always enjoyed mechanical things and was always trying to improve or create more useful machinery. In 1893, he created his first gasoline driven buggy or Quadricycle that was completely self propelled. He then started the Detroit Automobile Company with several other investors to improve on his design, but the company went bankrupt soon after. He then started the Henry Ford Company, which he also left, before eventually starting the Ford Motor Company in 1903.

The Ford Motor Company released the successful Model T car in 1908. Generally cars were built one at a time and were only accessible to the very wealthy, but Ford continued to improve the way the cars were manufactured. In 1913, the cars were being mass produced by one of the first moving assembly lines. In 1918, half of the total amount of cars in the United States were Model T's, 15 million cars were sold, and production of the Model T was finally stopped in 1927.

He also had interests in politics but was never successful as a politician, and unsuccessfully ran for Senate as a Democrat. He also had strong views on labour and how the workforce should be treated. He paid his workers more money for less working days and made the 5 day – 40 hour working week a normal part of working life. Henry Ford created the Ford Foundation in 1936 to promote human welfare through research grants, educational grants and development.

Ford suffered an initial stroke in 1938, after which he turned over the running of his company to Edsel. Edsel's 1943 death brought Henry Ford out of retirement. In ill health, he ceded the presidency to his grandson, Henry Ford II in September 1945, and went into retirement. He died in 1947 of a cerebral haemorrhage at the age of 83 in Fair Lane, his Dearborn estate, and is buried in the Ford Cemetery in Detroit. He took that last ride to Ford Cemetery in a Packard.

On the night of his death, the River Rouge had flooded the local power station and had left Ford's house without electricity. Before going to sleep, Henry and his wife lit candles and oil lamps to light the house. Later that evening, just before dawn, Henry Ford, father of mass production and creator of the modern era, died in the same atmosphere as he had been born 83 years earlier, surrounded by candlelight.

❑❑❑

Henry Kissinger

(1923-2023)

Politician, Professor and Author

"If you don't know where you are going, every road will get you nowhere."

Henry Kissinger was a Harvard professor before assuming leadership in U.S. foreign policy. He was appointed secretary of state in 1973 by President Richard Nixon and co-won the Nobel Peace Prize for his work in the Vietnam War's Paris accords. Kissinger is also a prolific author.

Henry Kissinger was born Heinz Alfred Kissinger on May 27, 1923, in Fürth, a city in the Bavaria region of Germany. Kissinger grew up in an Orthodox Jewish household.

As a child, Kissinger encountered anti-Semitism daily. He and his friends were also regularly abused by local gangs of Nazi youth. These experiences understandably made a lasting impression on Kissinger.

Kissinger was a shy, introverted and bookish child. Kissinger excelled at the local Jewish school and dreamed of attending the

Gymnasium, a prestigious state-run high school. However, by the time he was old enough to apply, the school had stopped accepting Jews. Sensing the impending tragedy of the Holocaust, his family decided to flee Germany for United States in 1938, when Kissinger was 15 years old.

On August 20, 1938, the Kissingers set sail for New York City by way of London. His family was extremely poor upon arrival in the United States, and Kissinger immediately went to work in a shaving brush factory to supplement his family's income. At the same time, Kissinger enrolled at New York's George Washington High School, where he learned English with remarkable speed and excelled in all of his classes. Kissinger graduated from high school in 1940 and continued on to the City College of New York, where he studied to become an accountant.

In 1943, Kissinger became a naturalized American citizen and, soon after, he was drafted into the army to fight in World War II. Thus, just five years after he left, Kissinger found himself back in his homeland of Germany, fighting the very Nazi regime from which he had once fled.

He served first as a rifleman in France and then as a G-2 intelligence officer in Germany. In 1947, upon his return to the United States, he was admitted to Harvard University to complete his undergraduate coursework.

Upon graduating summa cum laude in 1950, Kissinger decided to remain at Harvard to pursue a Ph.D. in the Department of Government.

After receiving his doctorate in 1954, Kissinger accepted an offer to stay at Harvard as a member of the faculty in the Department of Government. Kissinger first achieved widespread fame in academic circles with his 1957 book *Nuclear Weapons and Foreign Policy*. He served as a member of the Harvard faculty from 1954-69, earning tenure in 1959.

However, Kissinger always kept one eye outside academia on policymaking in Washington, D.C. From 1961-68, in addition to teaching at Harvard, he served as a special advisor to Presidents Kennedy and Johnson on matters of foreign policy. Then in 1969, Kissinger finally left Harvard when incoming President Richard Nixon appointed him to serve as his National Security Advisor. As National Security Advisor from 1969-75, and then as Secretary of State from 1973-77, Kissinger would prove one of the most dominant, influential and controversial statesmen in American history.

The great foreign policy trial of Kissinger's career was the Vietnam War. By the time Kissinger became National Security Advisor in 1969, the Vietnam War had become enormously costly, deadly and unpopular. Seeking to achieve "peace with honour," Kissinger combined diplomatic initiatives and troop withdrawals with devastating bombing campaigns on North Vietnam designed to improve the American bargaining position and maintain American credibility with its international allies and enemies.

Henry Kissinger stands out as the dominant American statesman and foreign policymaker of the late 20th century. With his intellectual prowess and tough, skillful negotiating style, Kissinger ended the Vietnam War and greatly improved American relations with its two primary Cold War enemies, China and the Soviet Union. Nevertheless, Kissinger's ruthlessly pragmatic, sometimes Machiavellian tactics have earned him as many critics as admirers.

Henry Kissinger, the renowned American diplomat and political scientist, passed away on November 29, 2023, at the age of 100.

❑❑❑

Hiram Maxim

(1840–1916)

Inventor

"I have created a beautiful machine that is going to encourage our fellow citizens to share my vision of the future! Can you dig it? "

Hiram Maxim, the inventor of machine gun, changed the way of wars when he developed a recoil mechanism that made it possible to load and eject cartridges from a machine gun without using a hand crank. The fully automatic magazine discharged up to 600 rounds of ammunition per minute.

Maxim was born in Sangersville, Maine on Novembr 4, 1840. He became a coach builder in an engineering works in Fitchburg, Massachusetts. During the next few years, he took out several patents including those for gas appliances and electric lamps.

In 1881, Maxim visited the Paris Electrical Exhibition. While he was at the exhibition, he met a man who told him: "If you wanted to make a lot of money, invent something that will enable these Europeans to cut each other's throats with greater facility." Maxim moved to London and over the n few years worked on producing an effective machine-gun.

In 1885, he demonstrated the world's first automatic portable machine-gun to the British Army. Maxim used the energy of each bullet's recoil force to eject the spent cartridge and insert the next bullet. The Maxim Machine-gun would therefore, fire until the entire belt of bullets was used up. Trials showed that the machine-gun could fire 500 rounds per minute and therefore, had the firepower of about 100 rifles.

The Maxim Machine-gun was adopted by the British Army in 1889. The following year, the Austrian, German, Italian, Swiss and Russian armies also purchased Maxim's gun. The gun was first used by Britain`s colonial forces in the Matabele war in 1893–94. In one engagement, fifty soldiers fought off 5,000 Matabele warriors with just four Maxim guns.

Maxim emigrated to England in 1881 and became a naturalised Briton in 1899. Maxim was knighted by Queen Victoria in 1901 for his inventions, many of which had military applications. Maxim founded an armaments company to produce his machine gun in Crayford, Kent, which was later bought out by the Vickers Corporation in 1896, becoming 'Vickers, Son & Maxim'. Their updated version of the design, referred to as the Vickers gun, was the standard British machine-gun for many years. Variants of the Maxim gun were used extensively by all sides during the Great War. His brother, Hudson Maxim was also a military inventor, specialising in explosives.

The success of the Maxim Machine-gun inspired other inventors. The German Army's Maschinengewehr and the Russian Pulemyot Maxima were both based on Maxim's invention.

After the success of his machine-gun, Maxim continued with his experiments. Before his death in 1916, Hiram Maxim also invented a pneumatic gun, the gun silencer (subsequently adapted for car exhausts), a smokeless gunpowder, a mousetrap, carbon filaments for light bulbs and a flying machine.

Maxim is also credited with inventing the common mousetrap and, as a long-time sufferer from bronchitis, he also patented and manufactured the "Pipe of Peace", a menthol amodium inhaler. Over the years, he was involved in several patent disputes with Thomas Edison.

He died in London in 1916 and was buried in West Norwood Cemetery. His son, Hiram Percy Maxim followed in his father and uncle's footsteps and became a mechanical engineer and weapons designer as well, but he is perhaps, best known for his early amateur radio experiments and for founding the American Radio Relay League.

❑❑❑

Ho Chi Minh

(1890–1969)

Political Leader

"Love other human beings as you would love yourself."

Ho Chi Minh, real name Nguyen Tat Thanh was a Vietnamese Communist leader and the principal force behind the Vietnamese struggle against the French colonial rule. Ho was fluent in English, several dialects of Chinese, French, German and Russian besides his native Vietnamese. The city of Ho Chi Minh was named after him.

His army was victorious in the French Indochina War (1946–1954). He led North Vietnam's struggle to defeat the US-supported government in South Vietnam. In 1954, he became the first president of North Vietnam.

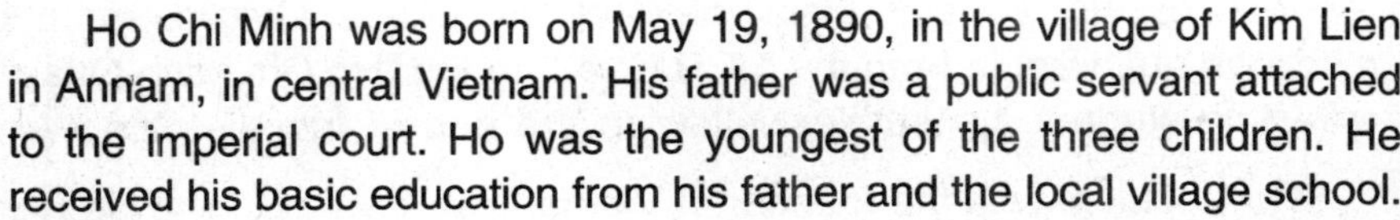

Ho Chi Minh was born on May 19, 1890, in the village of Kim Lien in Annam, in central Vietnam. His father was a public servant attached to the imperial court. Ho was the youngest of the three children. He received his basic education from his father and the local village school.

Ho Chi Minh attended the prestigious National Academy School in Hue, but did not complete his graduation. For a short time, he worked as a teacher in a South Annam fishing town before travelling to

Saigon, where he got training as a kitchen boy and pastry cook's assistant and took a course in navigation.

He moved to Europe in 1911. After the World War I, he moved to Paris and was active in socialist organisations into the 1920s. He visited the Soviet Union to study revolutionary tactics and was sent to China to spread communism throughout Asia. In 1930, Ho Chi Minh founded the Indochinese Communist Party, and spent almost a decade living in China and the Soviet Union. Ho was in Vietnam during World War II, where he organised the league for the Independence of Vietnam, called the Viet Minh.

From the period (1942–43), he was jailed by the anti-communist Nationalist Chinese, during which time he took the name, Ho Chi Minh ("He Who Enlightens"). After World War II, Ho Chi Minh proclaimed the independence of the Democratic Republic of Vietnam declaring himself as the President. He led the Viet Minh through eight years of underground resistance against French colonial forces (1946-54), and then turned to guerilla warfare against the anti-communist government in South Vietnam.

"Uncle Ho," is the symbol of the communists' willingness to sacrifice and to endure a war of attrition. He died in 1969, six years before the US withdrew from South Vietnam and the war ended. Many across the country tearfully mourned his death.His death day was initially reported to be September 3. The death day was actually September 2, but was changed since it coincided with the National Day as celebrated in Vietnam. Recently, the government changed his official death day to September 2. His embalmed body was put on display in a granite mausoleum modelled after Lenin's Tomb in Moscow.

In 1975, the Students' Union of Wadham College, Oxford renamed a college quadrangle from the "JCR Quad" to the "Ho Chi Minh Quad", reflecting student sympathies following the end of the Vietnam War.

Ho Chi Minh was the founder of Vietnamese Communism. He was the very soul of the revolution and of Vietnam's struggle for independence. His successors rely heavily on his memory to keep alive the spirit of revolution in Vietnam. ❑❑❑

Homi Jahangir Bhabha

(1909–1966)

Nuclear Scientist

"My success will be what I make of my work"

Homi Jahangir Bhabha was a pioneer of nuclear physics in his time and is considered the father of nuclear sciences in India. With the help of J. R. D. Tata, he established the Tata Institute of Fundamental Research at Mumbai.

Bhabha was born on October 30, 1909, into a wealthy Parsi family. He had a good library of science books at home and even as a child was interested in science. He used to spend his spare time in painting and writing poetry. He was also fond of music, particularly the Western classics. His father's ambition was to train Bhabha as an engineer and he was sent abroad for higher studies. However, his interest shifted to physics. During his studies abroad, he won many medals and fellowships. He also got the opportunity to work with eminent physicists like Enrico Fermi and Wolfgang Pauli.

He came into highlights in 1937, after his work in the area of cosmic rays. He later joined the Indian Institute of Science, Bangalore, and began to do research on cosmic rays, with huge retrievable plastic balloons carrying instruments high up in the sky. Cosmic rays revealed some revolutionary facts about the nature of matter and research. He thought, he might reveal still more on this subject. And, if research in cosmic rays could be taken up in the country, Indian scientists could, within a short time, be in the forefront in physics. Modern techniques in nuclear, high energy and elementary particle physics could also be developed in the country. He wanted to have an institute exclusively developed to research in this field.

Meanwhile, Bhabha was elected fellow of the Royal Society for his contributions relating to cosmic rays, elementary particles and quantum mechanics. His voice commanded attention and all scientists supported his idea of building a research institute. Bhabha was related to the Tatas, the country's pioneering industrialists.

In 1944, he wrote a letter to the Tata Trustees urging them to build an institute. He argued that the country would not then have to look abroad for experts when nuclear plants for electric power generation came to be built. While other scientists were trying to tap energy from the atom for destructive purposes, he was thinking of its peaceful uses.

In 1945, the Tata Institute of Fundamental Research was set up. Two years later, when the country gained independence, his ideas gained more significance. Jawaharlal Nehru, the first Prime Minister, also wanted to make the country self-sufficient in science and technology and he gave Bhabha a free hand to do what he wanted.

In 1948, the Atomic Energy Commission was set up and Bhabha was made its Chairman. From then on, nuclear energy research has steadily gathered momentum in the country. Under the expert guidance of Bhabha, three atomic reactors, Apsara, Cirus and Zerlina, were built. Survey for uranium ore continued and plants to purify the required materials were also built. Construction of the country's first atomic power station began at *Tarapur* in 1963. Two years later, a plutonium plant was installed, which was hailed as a "great step". In short, Bhabha showed his countrymen and the world that Indians were second to none in gaining scientific knowhow. The climax came on May 18, 1974, when Indian scientists exploded a nuclear device for peaceful purpose at Pokhran in Rajasthan. India became the sixth country to join the nuclear club.

Bhabha also encouraged research in electronics, space science, radio astronomy and microbiology. The telescope at Ootacamund is one of his creations. He was also one of the eminent members of the "atom for peace" conference.

He was killed in an air-crash near the famous Mont Blanc peak of the Alps on January 24, 1966, while he was on his way to Vienna to attend a meeting of the Scientific Advisory Committee of the International Atomic Energy Agency. In 1967, the Atomic Energy Establishment, Trombay, was renamed the Bhabha Atomic Research Centre as a tribute to his dedication and work.

Bhabha was a bachelor. He used to say that he was "married to creativity". He was a first class painter. His pencil sketches are well known and some of his paintings are preserved in British art galleries. He was a man of refined taste and this was very evident whether it was in the choice of design for the building of the Tata Institute of Fundamental Research or the site for the Ooty radio telescope.

❑❑❑

Indira Gandhi

(1917–1984)

Political Leader

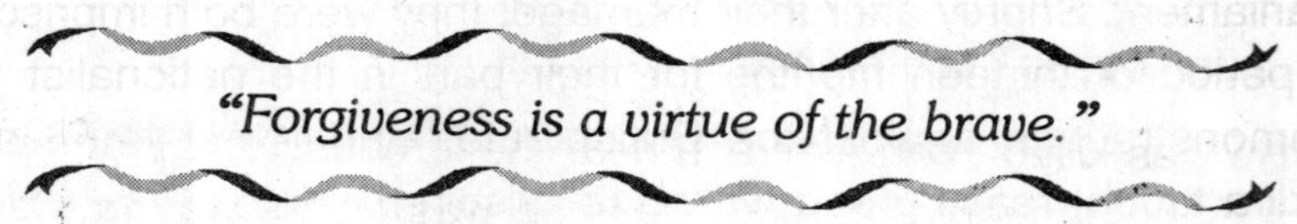

"Forgiveness is a virtue of the brave."

Indira Gandhi, first woman Prime Minister of India, was the most effective and powerful politician of her time in India. Considered a hero by her supporters and cursed by her enemies, Indira Gandhi paved the way for democracy in India during the twentieth century.

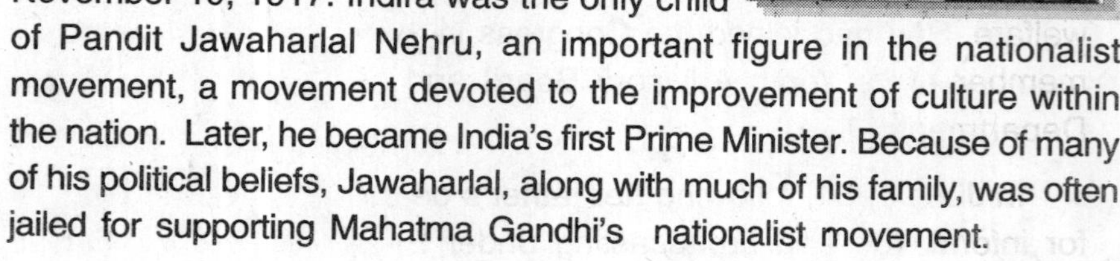

She was born in the city of Allahabad on November 19, 1917. Indira was the only child of Pandit Jawaharlal Nehru, an important figure in the nationalist movement, a movement devoted to the improvement of culture within the nation. Later, he became India's first Prime Minister. Because of many of his political beliefs, Jawaharlal, along with much of his family, was often jailed for supporting Mahatma Gandhi's nationalist movement.

Her family's fight for freedom made Indira's upbringing shaky. Her father was often absent from being jailed, and her mother was bed-ridden from tuberculosis, a terrible disease affecting the lungs and bones. Because of her father's stand against institutions run by the

British government, Indira's early schooling was not consistent. For a while, she was taught at home. Later, she attended an academy run by a poet-philosopher.

Shortly after her mother's death in 1936, Indira enrolled at the Shantiniketan University and later, at the Somerville College, Oxford University, in England. She married Feroze Gandhi in March 1942, despite both the family's objections. Feroze Gandhi became a lawyer and newspaper executive as well as an independent member of the Parliament. Shortly after their marriage, they were both imprisoned for a period of thirteen months for their part in the nationalist political demonstrations against the British rule. During her imprisonment, Indira taught reading and writing to prisoners. Feroze Gandhi died in 1960. They had two sons, Rajiv and Sanjay.

On August 15, 1947, Great Britain released their control over India and the Indian Empire was quickly divided into two countries, today known as India and Pakistan. During this time, Indira served as her father's hostess and housekeeper. Since her father had never remarried after his wife's death in 1936, Indira took charge of her father's large mansion and began helping him in political matters. Together they worked towards peace, arranging a meeting of the Hindu and Muslim religious leaders in New Delhi, India.

Throughout the period of Indira Gandhi's political association with her father, she focused on social welfare work, particularly children's welfare. She had joined the Congress in 1938, and later served as a member of its Youth Advisory Board and chairman of its Woman's Department.

In June 1964, following her father's death, Indira became minister for information and broadcasting under Prime Minister Lal Bahadur Shastri (1904–1966), where she helped to start an Indian television system. In January 1966, when Shastri died, she was elected leader of the Congress Party in Parliament (the governing body of India) and became the third Prime Minister of independent India.

She assumed office at a critical time in the history of the country. A truce had ended the 1965 war between India and Pakistan only a week earlier. The nation was in the midst of a two-year drought, resulting in severe food shortages and a deepening economic crisis with rising prices and rising unemployment. The political situation in India was equally as effected. In the fourth general elections of 1967, the Congress retained majority control , but lost control in half the state legislatures. After twenty years of political dominance, the Congress Party was experiencing serious difficulty.

Indira immediately set about reorganising the party to make it a more effective instrument of administration and national development. Her goal was to achieve a wider measure of social and economic justice for all Indians. As her left-of-centre policies became clear, the Congress Party split, with the younger, more liberal elements rallying around Indira and the older, more conservative party leaders opposing her. This division came to a head in July 1969, when she nationalised the country's fourteen leading banks in a highly popular move meant to make credit more available to agriculture and to small-scale industries.

The split was formalised when Indira's candidate for the presidency of India, V. V. Giri, won over the party's official nominee. Although she took 228 members of Parliament with her into the New Congress, this was not a majority in the 521-member house, and she held power only with support from more liberal parties.

In December 1970, when Indira failed to get the necessary support to abolish, or end, the privileges of the former Indian princes, she called on the President to dissolve the Parliament. Midterm elections were set for March 1971.

A coalition of three parties of the right and an anti-Congress socialist party opposed Indira, who made alliances with liberal parties as well as with some regional parties. Her platform was essentially one of achieving social and economic change more rapidly in an effort to improve the quality of life of the India's people. Her party won a massive victory with over a two-thirds majority in the Parliament.

However, she faced major problems in the areas of food production, population control, land reforms, unemployment, and industrial production. The problems were increased by the arrival in India of almost ten million refugees, who were uprooted as a result of the civil unrest in East Pakistan. In November 1971, Indian troops crossed into East Pakistan to fight the Pakistani forces. A month later, Indira announced recognition of the Bangladesh government set up by East Pakistani rebel leaders. On December 16, Pakistan's commander in East Pakistan surrendered to India.

In the state elections held in India in March 1972, Indira's New Congress Party scored the most overwhelming victory in the history of independent India.

The following year, Indira headed the Congress Party as she returned to Parliament. In 1979, she again became the Prime Minister. In efforts to prove India's non-alliance in the global community, she visited both the United States and the USSR, the former Soviet Union, which consisted of Russia and several smaller states. Internally, riots broke out among Muslim, Hindu, and Sikh religious sects, or groups. Sikhs, looking to separate themselves from India, secured weapons within their sacred Golden Temple in Amritsar, and assumed religious protection.

Indira ordered government troops to storm the temple, leading to many deaths. This led to her assassination at her residence on October 31, 1984, by her own security guards. She was posthumously honoured with Bangladesh Freedom Award for her outstanding contribution to the country's 1971 Liberation War.

❑❑❑

Indra Nooyi

(1955)

Business Woman

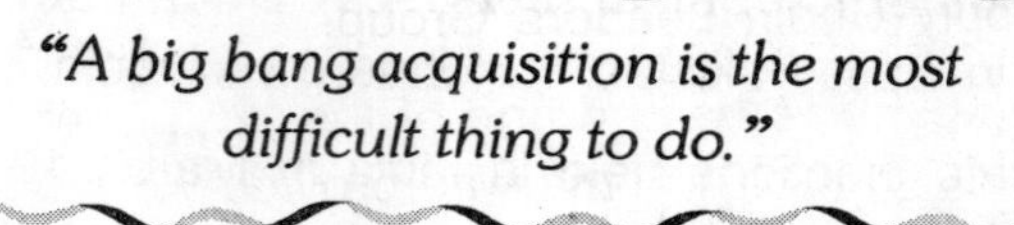

Indra Krishnamurthy Nooyi is the Chairman and Chief Executive Officer of PepsiCo, the world's fourth-largest food and beverage company.

Indra Nooyi was born on October 8, 1955 in Chennai, Tamil Nadu in India. She received a Bachelor's degree in Chemistry from Madras Christian College in 1974, and immediately entered the PGDBA (Post-Graduate Diploma in Business Administration) program at the Indian Institute of Management, Calcutta. After graduating from IIM-C in 1976, she worked in India for several years (including a stretch at Madura Coats). She was admitted to Yale School of Management in 1978 for a master's degree in Management. After Getting her master's degree from Yale in 1980, Nooyi started at The Boston Consulting Group (BCG), from where she moved on to strategy positions of Motorola and ABB.

Indra Nooyi joined PepsiCo in 1994, was named president and Chief Finance Officer (CFO) in 2001. On August 14, 2006, she was named the CEO of PepsiCo, becoming the fifth CEO in PepsiCo's 42-year history. Effective May 2, 2007 she took over the role of chairman. Nooyi also took the lead in the acquisition of Tropicana in 1998, and merger with Quaker Oats Co. She was named the Number 1 Most Powerful Woman in Business in 2006 and 2007 by Fortune Magazine. In 2007, she was awarded Padma Bhushan by Government of India. In 2008, she was elected to the fellowship of the American Academy of Arts and Sciences. She was named 2009 CEO of the Year by Global Supply Chain Leaders Group.

In 2013, Nooyi was named one of the "25 Greatest Global Living Legends" by NDTV. In 2015, she was provided Honorary Doctorate of Humane letters by State University of New York. In December 2016, Nooyi joined a business forum assembled by President-Elect Trump to provide strategic and policy advice on economic issues.

On August 6, 2018, Nooyi stepped down as CEO. However, Nooyi continued to serve as the chairman of the company until early 2019. During her tenure, the company's sales grew 80%. Nooyi served as CEO for 12 years. She serves on the boards of Amazon. Philips has proposed that Nooyi join their board in May 2021.

In 2019, Nooyi became the co-director of the newly created Connecticut Economic Resource Center, a public-private partnership with the Connecticut Department of Economic and Community Development. She will help draft the state's new economic development strategy. In 2021, Nooyi was inducted into the National Women's Hall of Fame.

Nooyi continues to be recognized for her contributions to business and leadership. She was ranked #97 on Forbes' list of America's Self-Made Women in 2024.

❑❑❑

Isaac Newton

(1643–1727)

Physicist, Mathematician and Scientist

"I can calculate the motion of heavenly bodies, but not the madness of people."

Isaac Newton was an established British physicist and mathematician, and is credited as one of the great minds of the 17th century Scientific Revolution. With discoveries in optics, motion and mathematics, Newton developed the principles of modern physics. In 1687, he published his most acclaimed work, *Philosophiae, Natrualis, Principia Mathematica* (*Mathematical Principles of Natural Philosophy*), which has been called the single-most influential book on physics.

Isaac Newton was born on 4 January 1643 in Woolsthorpe, Lincolnshire. His father was a prosperous farmer, who died three months before Newton was born. His mother remarried and Newton was left in the care of his grandparents. In 1661, he went to Cambridge University where he became interested in mathematics, optics, physics and astronomy. In October 1665, a plague epidemic forced the university to close and Newton returned to Woolsthorpe.

The two years he spent there were an extremely fruitful time during which he began to think about gravity. He also devoted time to optics and mathematics, working out his ideas about 'fluxions' (calculus).

In 1667, Newton returned to Cambridge, where he became a fellow of Trinity College. Two years later he was appointed second Lucasian professor of mathematics. It was Newton's reflecting telescope, made in 1668, that finally brought him to the attention of the scientific community and in 1672 he was made a fellow of the Royal Society. From the mid-1660s, Newton conducted a series of experiments on the composition of light, discovering that white light is composed of the same system of colours that can be seen in a rainbow and establishing the modern study of optics (or the behaviour of light).

In 1687, with the support of his friend the astronomer Edmond Halley, Newton published his single greatest work, the '*Philosophiae Naturalis Principia Mathematica*' ('Mathematical Principles of Natural Philosophy'). This showed how a universal force, gravity, applied to all objects in all parts of the universe.

In 1689, Newton was elected member of parliament for Cambridge University (1689–1690 and 1701–1702). In 1696, Newton was appointed warden of the Royal Mint, settling in London. He took his duties at the Mint very seriously and campaigned against corruption and inefficiency within the organisation. In 1703, he was elected president of the Royal Society, an office he held until his death. In 1704, Newton published '*The Opticks*' which dealt with light and colour. He also studied and published works on history, theology and alchemy. He was knighted in 1705.

Toward the end of this life, Newton lived at Cranbury Park, near Winchester, England, with his niece, Catherine (Bancroft) Conduitt, and her husband, John Conduitt. By this time, Newton had become one of the most famous men in Europe. His scientific discoveries were unchallenged. He also had become wealthy, investing his sizeable income wisely and bestowing sizeable gifts to charity. Despite his fame, Newton's life was far from perfect: He never married or made many friends.

By the time he reached 80 years of age, Newton had to drastically change his diet and mobility. Then, in March 1727, Newton experienced severe pain in his abdomen and blacked out, never to regain consciousness.

He died the next day, on March 31, 1727, at the age of 85.

Isaac Newton's fame grew even more after his death, as many of his contemporaries proclaimed him the greatest genius that ever lived. May be a slight exaggeration, but his discoveries had a large impact on Western thought, leading to comparisons to the likes of Plato, Although his discoveries were among many made during the Scientific Revolution, Isaac Newton's universal principles of gravity found no parallels in science at the time.

Newton once, when asked for an assessment of his achievements, replied, "I do not know what I may appear to the world; but to myself I seem to have been only like a boy playing on the seashore, and diverting myself now and then in finding a smoother pebble or prettier shell than ordinary, while the great ocean of truth lay all undiscovered before me."

❑❑❑

Ishwar Chandra Vidyasagar

(1820–1891)

Social Reformer

"The country, whose male population is unaware of the distinction between the good and the evil should not give birth to girls."

Pandit Ishwar Chandra Vidyasagar, a Sanskrit pandit, was an educator, reformer, writer, and a philanthropist. He was considered to be one of the greatest intellectuals and activists of the nineteenth century.

Ishwar Chandra Vidyasagar was born in 1820 in a Brahmin family at Birsingha in Midnapore district. His parents, though poor, managed to send him to Calcutta (now Kolkata) for studies after he finished his early education at the village *pathshala*. Ishwar studied at the Sanskrit College, Calcutta (now Kolkata) from 1829 to 1841. He bagged all the prizes and scholarships for the best performance. Evaluating his performance in various courses - poetry, rhetoric, Vendanta, *Smrti*, astrology and logic, the College Committee endowed Ishwar Chandra with the title of *Vidyasagar* (sea of knowledge) in 1839.

At the age of 21, Ishwar Chandra Vidyasagar started his career as the head pandit of the Fort William College, Calcutta (now Kolkata).

He joined the Sanskrit College as a professor in 1850. In the following year, he became the principal of the college. Concurrently, with his Sanskrit College position, the government entrusted him in 1855 with the added responsibility of the Special Inspector of Schools for the districts of Hooghli, Burdwan, Midnapore and Nadia. He was also an honorary office bearer of several organisations including Asiatic Society and Bethune Society. In 1858, he was made one of the first fellows of the Calcutta University. Ishwar received a certificate of Honour at the Imperial Assemblage in January 1877 and in January 1880, was made a CIE. He also received honours and felicitations from many social, cultural and scientific organisations.

Ishwar Chandra Vidyasagar was not truly a writer in the sense that Bankimchandra and others of his time were. His writings were instructive, reformative and utilitarian, not creative. His earliest works including *Mahabharata Upakramanika* (serialised in the *Tattvabodhini Patrika* (1843–44) and *Vetalapanchavinshati* (1847), were translations.

In fact, the majority of his works, 32 in all, were directly or indirectly translations from Sanskrit, Hindi and English. These were mainly textbooks addressed to school students. His only independent scholarly study, but which remains obscure among the generality, is *Sanskrit Bhasa O Sanskrit Sahitya Shastra Bisyak Prastab* (Propositions on Sanskrit Language and Literature, 1853). But though a textbook writer essentially, Vidyasagar is rated by the established writers of his own time as an artistic writer and inspiring educator. In his hands, Bangla prose style took a new turn. According to critics, Vidyasagar inaugurated a new era in the Bangla prose literature.

A reformer of Bangla prose style, Vidyasagar as a writer had consciously avoided the new but affected prosody pursued by the orientalists at Fort William College, the pedantic and obscurantist style of Rammohan Roy and his followers, and the unrefined linguistic structure of the contemporary newspapers and periodicals. Instead, he charted out for himself a new course which soon laid the foundation of the modern Bangla prose. Here lies the uniqueness of Vidyasagar's contributions.

Since his style found expression in his textbooks essentially and since his books were prescribed commonly in all government and vernacular schools until the early years of the twentieth century, several generations of writers, officers and professionals were very directly and permanently influenced by the Vidyasagarian prose style, the hallmark of which was a grand synthesis of past and present techniques of Bangla language and literature.

Vidyasagar was a great reformer and thinker. In his *Bangalar Itihas*, he has aptly shown, contrary to Marshman's theory, the marked syncretic and synthetic trends of Bengal's social and cultural developments. Though personally an orthodox Hindu, Ishwar Chandra perceived other religionists entirely secularly.

Vidyasagar's reforming mind has found most concrete expression in his socio-religious thoughts. He raised questions about early marriage, polygamy, widow remarriage, and many other ills stifling social developments. Most of his reform thoughts were embodied in his two famous works: *Bidhababibaha Prachalita Haoya Uchit Kina Etadvisayak Prastab*, 2 vols. Polygamy, widow remarriage, child marriage were sensitive issues, because these were supported by the Hindu religion.

Vidyasagar did not mean to hurt the religious sentiments of the common people by directly attacking the evils. In defence of his arguments, he profusely drew instances from the *shastras* and other classical texts, a strategem which had a tremendous impact on the people. His sastra-based and humorous arguments made the defenders of those social evils largely defenceless, though many of the conservatives maligned him savagely. The enactment of the Act of 1856, legalising widow remarriage and the Civil Marriage Act of

1872, restricting bigamy and child marriage and encouraging widow remarriage, owed a great deal to Vidyasagar, whose writings and activities had helped to create public opinion in favour of these issues.

As Special Inspector of Schools, Vidyasagar used his position to encourage landholders and other solvent people to establish educational institutions. Within his inspection zone, he was instrumental in founding dozens of schools, several of which were for girls. Some schools were established at his own initiative and with his financial support.

Vidyasagar's monumental contribution to educational institution building was his Calcutta Metropolitan Institution, a model college with attached schools, which he established in 1864 at his own cost. He also funded the erection of the magnificent building housing the Metropolitan Institution. Vidyasagar's philanthropy was proverbial. It is said that half the money that he got from his salary and his royalties was kept reserved for helping the distressed.

His stature as an educator, reformer, writer and philanthropist grew to such a height that, at his death on July 29, 1891, the whole nation, irrespective of race, religion and caste, mourned. The newspapers and magazines published obituaries and features applauding his deeds and achievements; poets and writers, including Rabindranath Tagore, wrote poems and features in his memory. In these remembrances and recollections, Vidyasagar was rated as the greatest man of the century. The evaluation remains unchanged even today.

❑❑❑

Ismail Merchant

(1935–2005)

Producer, Director, Writer

"If we depended on the judgement of the studios or critics, we never would have made more than one movie."

Ismail Merchant is one half of the prolific Merchant Ivory team which has been responsible for scores of literate, beautifully shot, languid, and sometimes erotic films since the mid-'60s. He is a director and producer of international repute.

Ismail Merchant was born on December 25, 1935 in Bombay, Maharashtra, as Ismail Noormohamed Abdul Reh. He graduated from St. Xavier's College, Bombay and earned his Master's degree in Business Administration from New York University, USA.

In 1961 Ismail Merchant found the perfect collaborators, to put his skills to work in the creative arts, in the form of German/Indian novelist Ruth Prawar Jhabvala and California-born director James Ivory. Merchant and Ivory formed Merchant Ivory Productions. Merchant's financial and marketing expertise as a producer greatly contributed to the team's success and enhanced their international profile. Their first film, "The Householder" (1963) was based on a novel by Prawer

Jabvala. As their partnership developed, Merchant and Ivory moved away from Indian subjects and developed a reputation for intelligent, tasteful adaptations of modern literary classics, especially those of E.M. Forster and Henry James. Among their successful efforts were *Shakespeare Wallah (1965), Roseland (1977), The Europeans (1979), The Bostonians (1984), Heat and Dust (1983), A Room with a View (1985), Maurice (1987), Howards End (1992), Remains of the Day (1993),* and *Surviving Picasso (1996).*

The due offered their take on French farce in 2003 with "Le Divorce". Before his death they also were at work on "The Goddess," a musical about the Hindu goddess Shakti, starring a singing, dancing Tina Turner and "The White Countess," a period drama set in China. Ismail Merchant has directed the short *Mahatma and the Mad Boy (1973)* and the features *In Custody (1994)* and *La Proprietaire (1996)*. For television, he directed and wrote the documentary *The Courtesans of Bombay (1983),* produced the drama *Noon Wine (1985),* and worked on several other productions sans Ivory.

Merchant and Ivory, working together for 40 years made some 46 films and won six Oscars. The team finds its name in the Guinness Book of World Records for the longest partnership in independent cinema. Ismail Merchant is also an Honorary Doctor of Arts at Bard's College, New York. Merchant was also honored by the Mayor of New York and received the Marie des Paris for his outstanding contribution to cinema in France. Merchant Ivory's autobiographical book is entitled, *My Passage from India: A Filmmaker's Journey from Bombay to Hollywood and beyond.* In 2002 Merchant was conferred the Padma Bhusan by the government of India.

Ismail Merchant also carved a niche in the culinary world. He has authored a number of books on cookery. Some of them are Ismail Merchant's Indian Cuisine; Ismail Merchant's Florence; Ismail Merchant's Passionate meals, Ismail Merchant's Paris, Filming and Feasting in France. Besides, he has also authored several books on filmmaking.

He died on May 25, 2005.

❑❑❑

J.K. Rowling

(1965)

Writer

"Anything's possible if you've got enough nerve."

J. K. Rowling is a British novelist best known as the author of the *Harry Potter* fantasy series.

Joanne Kathleen Rowling was born on 31 July 1965, in the quaint village of Chipping Sodbury, in Gloucestershire, England. Her father was Peter James Rowling, and her mother, Anne. Two years after Rowling was born, her mother gave birth to a sister, called Diana. Rowling first began making up stories in order to keep her younger sibling entertained.

Rowling attended school at nearby St. Michael's village school. Quiet and studious, she did well at school, and went on to graduate with a Bachelor's degree in French and Classics at the University of Exeter. Her student days were happy ones by all accounts, and she was also lucky enough to spend a year studying in Paris.

After graduating, Rowling moved to London, where she initially began training to become a bilingual secretary but her attention would wander during meetings as ideas for stories would come to her while she was meant to be taking dictation. But her daydreaming was to prove far more rewarding in the long run, for in early 1990, during the course of a long train journey from Manchester to London, she first had the idea for a story about a young boy who goes to study at a school for wizards.

Shortly afterwards, she decided to retrain as an English teacher, and moved to Portugal, where she met and married a native journalist, called Jorge Arantes, in 1992. She gave birth to their daughter, Jessica Isabel, on 27 July the following year. Sadly, the marriage was short-lived, and the couple separated only four short months later. A year later, Rowling moved back to Britain, and went to live in Edinburgh, Scotland. Life as a single mother living on social security in the bleak Scottish winter was dismal.

However, like all true writers, she channelled her worst experiences to creative ends, and used her experience of depression as the basis for the happiness-sucking wraiths in the Harry Potter books, the Dementors. It was here in this Edinburgh café that she first began to set down on paper her ideas - and the rest, as they say, is history.

Creating the character of Harry Potter did not bring overnight fame and fortune for the struggling single mum; and there were to be many twists and turns along the way before Rowling's quality as an author were fully recognised. In 1995, she finished typing out 'Harry Potter and the Philosopher's Stone' on an old manual typewriter, and sent it out to various literary agents. A reader called Bryony Evans, at Christopher Little literary agents, was quick to recognise the potential of her work, and the firm promptly agreed to represent her, sending the book out to no less than twelve publishers.

It was to be a full year before she received the exciting news that her book had found a publisher: the lucky firm was the small publishing house of Bloomsbury. Rowling was paid an advance of £1,500 for her first novel, which was published in June 1997, with an initial print run of one thousand copies, 500 of which were sold to libraries. Incidentally, these first Harry Potter books are now regarded as collector's items, and are estimated to be worth up to £25,000 apiece.

As her books gained more exposure, Rowling's talent and ability as a children's writer was soon recognised. One of the first awards she won was the much-coveted Nestle Smarties award – indeed, she went on to win the award three consecutive times. A grant of £8,000 from the Scottish Arts Council enabled her to carry on writing full-time – but within a relatively short time, she had sold enough books to guarantee her financial security.

In 1998, one short year after her first book had seen print, she sold the film rights for her first two books to Warner Brothers, for an undisclosed seven-figure sum, making her a millionaire overnight. When her fourth book, *'Harry Potter and the Goblet of Fire'* was published, the book broke all previous publishing records, selling over 372,000 copies in the UK on the first day, and over three million copies in the United States within the first 48 hours. Unsurprisingly, Rowling was named Author of The Year at the British Book Awards in 2000.

Life was going well for Rowling on the personal front too: in December 2001, she married Neil Michael Murray, an anaesthetist, in a private ceremony at her home in Aberfeldy, Scotland. Rowling and Murray's son, David Gordon Rowling Murray, was born in March 2003, and she went on to give birth to a daughter, Mackenzie Jean, in January 2005. Rowling has completed the final installment in the seven-book Harry Potter series, which was published in July 2007. *'The Tales of Beedle The Bard'* was published in December 2008 to raise money for the Children's High Level Group, now called Lumos.

Harry Potter is now a global brand worth an estimated $15 billion, and the last four *Harry Potter* books have consecutively set records as the fastest-selling books in history. The series has been translated into 65 languages.

She released The Casual Vacancy (2012) and-under the pseudonym Robert Galbraith-the crime fiction Cormoran Strike series. Titled Career of Evil, was released on 20 October, 2015 in the United States, and on 22 October, 2015 in the United Kingdom. In 2020, her "political fairytale" for children, The Ickabog, was released in instalments in an online version.

The fifth novel in the series, titled Troubled Blood, was published in September 2020. In May 2021, Troubled Blood won the Crime and Thriller Book of the Year at the British Book Awards.

J.R.D. Tata

(1904–1993)

Businessman

"The effective execution of a plan is what counts and not mere planning on paper."

Jehangir Ratanji Dadabhoy Tata was a pioneer aviator and important businessman of India. He had the honour of being India's first pilot. Tata was also the Chairman of Tata & Sons for 50 years. He launched the Indian International as India's first international airline. He received the Bharat Ratna in the year 1992.

Tata was born on July 29, 1904 in Paris. He was the second child of Mr Ratanji Dadabhoy Tata. He spent much of his childhood in France since his mother was French while his father was a Parsi. He was educated in France, Japan and England before being drafted into the French Army for a mandatory one year period. JRD wanted to extend his service in the force, but destiny had something else in store for him. By leaving the French Army, JRD's life was saved, because shortly thereafter, the regiment in which he served was totally wiped out during an expedition to Morocco.

In 1922, Tata returned to India to join the family business. He inherited most of his grandfather Jamshedji's industrial empire but first became a pioneer in aviation. He had a great personality with a charm and style of his own.

After his father's death in 1926, Tata became the director of the Board of Tata Sons Ltd. Eventually in 1938, he became the chairman of the company. Under his leadership, Tata Sons expanded into one of the largest industrial empire in the country— from ironworks and steelworks into chemicals, hotels, engineering and lots of other industries.

In 1945, Tata Steel promoted the Tata Engineering and Locomotive Company (TELCO) with an objective to produce locomotives for the Indian Railways. Today Telco has emerged as the country's largest commercial vehicle producer.

JRD was the trustee of Sir Dorabji Tata Trust from its inception in 1932, which remained under his wings for over half a century. Under his guidance, this Trust established Asia's first cancer hospital, the Tata Memorial Center for Cancer, Research and Treatment, Bombay (now Mumbai) in1941. It also founded the Tata Institute of Social Sciences, 1936 (TISS), the Tata Institute of Fundamental Research, 1945 (TIFR), and the National Center for Performing Arts.

JRD Tata was the first Indian pilot to qualify for a British private licence. He founded the Tata Airlines in 1932 and by 1953, it developed and came to be known as the Indian Airlines. Till 1978, Tata was the Chairman of the Indian Airlines and Air India. His innovations in India's fledgling hotel and tourist industry as well as his contributions to scientific and technical research and corporate management gained public recognition from the Indian Government. JRD Tata received a number of awards. He received the Padma Vibhushan in 1957 on the eve of the silver jubilee of Air India. He also received the Guggenheim Medal for aviation in 1988.

In 1992, because of his selfless humanitarian endeavours, JRD Tata was awarded India's highest civilian honour, the Bharat Ratna—one of the rarest instances in which this award was granted during a person's lifetime. In the same year, JRD Tata was also bestowed with the United Nations Population Award for his crusading endeavours towards initiating and successfully implementing the family planning movement in India, much before it became an official government policy.

JRD Tata died in Geneva, Switzerland on November 29, 1993 at the age of 89.

Jagjit Singh

(1941–2011)

Singer

"His body may have departed, but his voice lives. His presence will always be felt by those in love, looking for love, and hurt by love."

(A Tribute)

Jagjit Singh was a prominent Indian Ghazal singer, composer, music director and activist. Known as The Ghazal King, he gained acclaim together with his wife Chitra Singh in 1970's and 80's as the first successful husband-wife duo act in the history of recorded Indian music. Together, they are considered to be the pioneers of modern Ghazal singing and regarded as most successful recording artist outside the realm of Indian film music. Their album on HMV comprising music from films, Arth and *Saath Saath* is India's largest selling album of all time. *Sajda*, Jagjit Singh's magnum opus double album with Lata Mangeshkar holds the same record in non-film category. He had sung in Punjabi, Hindi, Urdu, Bengali, Gujarati, Sindhi and Nepali languages.

Jagjit Singh was born on February 8, 1941 in Sri Ganganagar, Rajasthan to Amar Singh Dhiman, a native of Dalla village in Punjab and his mother, Bachan Kaur from Ottallan village, Samrala. He had four sisters and two brothers and he was known as Jeet by his family. He was raised as a Sikh by religion.

He went to Khalsa High School in Sri Ganganagar and then studied science after matriculation at Government College Sri Ganganagar and went onto graduate in Arts at DAV College, Jalandhar. He was a post-graduate in history from Kurukshetra University in Haryana.

Since his childhood he was inclined to music. He learnt music under Pandit Chagganlal Sharma, and later devoted to learning Khayal, Thumri and Dhrupad forms of Indian Classical Music from Ustad Jamaal Khan.

He arrived in Mumbai in 1961 in search of better opportunities for being a musician and singer. He lived as a paying guest and his earlier assignments were singing advertisement jingles. Singh was first offered to sing in a Gujarati film, *Dharati Na Chhoru* produced by Suresh Amin. In 1976, his album *The Unforgetables* hit music stores. Essentially a ghazal album, its emphasis on melody and Jagjit's fresh voice was a departure from the prevalent style of ghazal rendition, which was heavily based on classical and semi-classical Indian music.

Jagjit met Chitra in 1967. At the time, Chitra was married and had a daughter. The marriage ended in divorce, although Chitra's ex-husband remained a family friend, and Jagjit and Chitra married in December 1969. They epitomize the first successful husband-wife singing team. Successful releases of the duo include *Ecstasies*, *A Sound Affair* and *Passions*.

Jagjit Singh was the first Indian composer, and together with his wife Chitra Singh the first recording artist in the history of Indian music to use digital multi-track recording for their (India's first digitally recorded) album, *Beyond Time* (1987).

Their only son, Vivek (19), died in a road accident in 1990. The couple's subsequent album *Someone Somewhere* was the last album with ghazals sung by both. After that Chitra Singh quit singing.

His later albums, including *Hope*, *In Search*, *Insight*, *Mirage*, *Visions*, *Kahkashan*, *Love Is Blind*, *Chirag* also achieved success. *Sajda* had ghazals sung by Jagjit and Lata Mangeshkar.

Jagjit Singh also sang (as playback singer) for various songs in Bollywood films including *Arth*, *Saath Saath*, and *Premgeet*. All the songs of film *Premgeet* were composed by Jagjit Singh himself. His compositions for the TV serial *Mirza Ghalib* (based on the life of the poet Mirza Ghalib), remain extremely popular among ghazal aficionados.

His later ghazals have acquired a more soulful and poignant demeanour, as in albums such as *Marasim*, *Face To Face*, *Aaeena*, *Cry For Cry*. His ghazals have been used in more recent Bollywood films like *Dushman*, *Sarfarosh*, *Tum Bin* and *Tarkieb*.

Besides ghazals, Jagjit Singh has also sung bhajans and Gurbani (Hindu and Sikh devotional hymns respectively). Albums such as *Maa*, *Hare Krishna*, *Hey Ram...Hey Ram*, *Ichhabal* and also *Man Jeetai Jagjeet* in Punjabi, put him in the league of Bhajan singers such as Mukesh, Hari Om Sharan, Yesudas, Anup Jalota and Purushottam Das Jalota.

He was honoured by many awards including India's third highest civilian award, Padma Bhushan (2003), Ghalib Academy Award (2005), Sahitya Kala Academy Award (1998, Rajasthan govt.), Sangeet Natak Academy Award, Dayavati Modi Award and D. Litt by Kurukshetra University (2003).

Jagjit Singh died of illness on October 10, 2011. It is a great loss to Indian cinema and music.

Jawaharlal Nehru

(1889–1964)

Political Leader

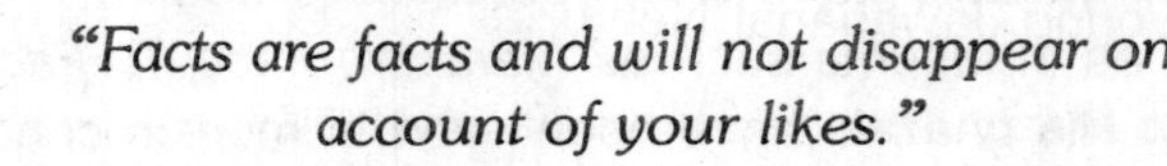

"Facts are facts and will not disappear on account of your likes."

Jawaharlal Nehru, also known as Pandit Jawaharlal Nehru, was one of the foremost leaders of Indian freedom struggle. He was the favourite disciple of Mahatma Gandhi and later on went on to become the first Prime Minister of India. He was very fond of children and children used to affectionately call him *Chacha Nehru.*

Jawaharlal Nehru was born on November 14, 1889. His father Motilal Nehru was a famous Allahabad based barrister. His mother's name was Swaroop Rani. He was the only son of Motilal Nehru. However, he had three sisters. The Nehrus were Saraswat Brahmin of the Kashmiri lineage.

Nehru received education in some of the finest schools and universities of the world. He did his schooling from Harrow and completed his Law degree from Trinity College, Cambridge. The seven years he spent in England widened his horizons and he acquired a rational and skeptical outlook. He sampled the Fabian socialism and Irish nationalism, which added to his own patriotic dedication.

Nehru returned to India in 1912 and started legal practice. He married Kamala Nehru in 1916. Jawaharlal Nehru joined the Home Rule League in 1917. His real initiation into politics came two years later when he came in contact with Mahatma Gandhi in 1919. At that time, Gandhiji had launched a campaign against the Rowlatt Act. Nehru was instantly attracted to Gandhi's commitment for active but peaceful, 'civil disobedience'. Gandhi himself saw promise and India's future in the young Jawaharlal Nehru.

The Nehru family changed their life style according to Mahatma Gandhi's teachings. Jawaharlal and Motilal Nehru abandoned western clothes and tastes for expensive possessions and pastimes. They now wore a *Khadi Kurta* and a *Gandhi* cap. Jawaharlal Nehru took active part in the Non- Cooperation Movement (1920–1922) and was arrested for the first time during the movement. He was released after few months.

Nehru was elected President of the Allahabad Municipal Corporation in 1924, and served for two years as the city's chief executive. This proved to be a valuable administrative experience which stood him in good stead later on when he became the prime minister of the country. He used his tenure to expand public education, health care and sanitation. He resigned in 1926 citing lack of cooperation from civil servants and obstruction from British authorities.

From 1926 to 1928, he served as the general secretary of the All India Congress Committee. In 1928–29, the Congress's annual session under President Motilal Nehru was held. During that session Jawaharlal Nehru and Subhash Chandra Bose backed a call for full political independence, while Motilal Nehru and others wanted dominion status within the British Empire. To resolve the point, Gandhi said that the British would be given two years to grant India, a dominion status. If they did not, the Congress would launch a national struggle for full, political independence. Nehru and Bose reduced the time of opportunity to one year. The British did not respond.

In December 1929, Congress's annual session was held in Lahore and Jawaharlal Nehru was elected as the President of the Congress Party. During that sessions a resolution demanding India's independence was passed and on January 26, 1930 in Lahore, Jawaharlal Nehru unfurled free India's flag. Gandhiji gave a call for the Civil Disobedience Movement in 1930.

When the British promulgated the Government of India Act 1935, the Congress Party decided to contest elections. Nehru stayed out of the elections, but campaigned vigorously nationwide for the party. The Congress formed governments in almost every province, and won the largest number of seats in the Central Assembly. Nehru was elected to the Congress presidency in 1936, 1937, and 1946, and came to occupy a position in the nationalist movement second only to that of Gandhi. Jawaharlal Nehru was arrested in 1942 during the Quit India Movement. Released in 1945, he took a leading part in the negotiations that culminated in the emergence of the dominions of India and Pakistan in August 1947.

In 1947, he became the first Prime Minister of independent India. He effectively coped with the formidable challenges of those times: the disorders and mass exodus of minorities across the new border with Pakistan, the integration of 500-odd princely states into the Indian Union, the framing of a new Constitution, and the establishment of the political and administrative infrastructure for a *parliamentary democracy*.

Jawaharlal Nehru played a key role in building modern India. He set up a Planning Commission, encouraged development of science and technology, and launched three successive *five-year plans*. His policies led to a sizable growth in agricultural and industrial production. Nehru also played a major role in developing independent India's foreign policy. He called for liquidation of colonialism in Asia and Africa and along with Tito and Nasser, was one of the chief architects of the Non-aligned Movement. He played a constructive, mediatory role in bringing the Korean War to an end and in resolving other international crises, such as those over the Suez Canal and the Congo, offering India's services for conciliation and international policing. He contributed behind the scenes towards the solution of several other explosive issues, such as those of West Berlin, Austria, and Laos.

But Nehru could not improve India's relations with Pakistan and China. The Kashmir issue proved a stumbling block in reaching an accord with Pakistan, and the border dispute prevented a resolution with China. The Chinese invasion in 1962, which Nehru failed to anticipate, came as a great blow to him and probably, hastened his death. He died of a heart attack on May 27, 1964.

❑❑❑

Jhumpa Lahiri

(1967)

Author

"When I sit down to write, I don't think about writing, about an idea or a given message. I just try to write a story which is hard enough."

Jhumpa Lahiri is a contemporary American author of Bengali descent. Her given name is Nilanjana Sudeshna. She is well-known for her novel, *Namesake*.

Jhumpa Lahiri was born on July 11, 1967 in London, England and brought up in South Kingstown, Rhode Island. Her parents, a teacher and a librarian, taught her about her Bengali heritage from an early age. Lahiri received her BA in English literature from Barnard College in 1989. She then received multiple degrees from the Boston University: an MA in English, an MA in Creative Writing, and an MA in Comparative Literature with a PhD in Renaissance Studies. She took up a fellowship at Provincetown's Fine Arts Work Centre, which lasted for the next two years (1997–1998).

In 2001, she married Alberto Vourvoulias-Bush, a journalist who was then Deputy Editor of *Time Latin America*. Lahiri currently lives in

Brooklyn with her husband and two children. Jhumpa Lahiri taught creative writing at the Boston University and Rhode Island School of Design. Much of her short fiction concerns the lives of Indian-Americans, particularly Bengalis.

As a collection of nine distinct short stories, *Interpreter of Maladies*, Lahiri's debut, addresses sensitive dilemmas in the lives of Indians or Indian immigrants. The stories' themes include marital difficulties, miscarriages, and the disconnection between first and second generation immigrants in the United States. The stories are set in the northeastern United States, and in India, particularly Kolkata.

The *Namesake*, her second book and first novel, was published in 2003. An anecdote published in the *USA Today* mentions a schoolteacher who found her given name too long and used her nickname, Jhumpa instead. Lahiri adapted this incident in her book, which spans more than thirty years in the life of a fictional family, the Gangulis.

The parents, each born in Kolkata, immigrated to the United States as young adults. Their children, Gogol and Sonali, grew up in the United States and much of the tension of the novel is dependent upon the generation and cultural gap between the parents and the children.

Furthermore, as the title suggests, one of the issues of the novel is the confusion caused by the misunderstanding which occurred when Gogol was very young: his pet name (Gogol) becomes mistaken for his real name. Thus, Gogol's unusual name serves as a symbol of his own unclear cultural identity (further complicated by the fact that Gogol is the last name of a noted Russian author).

Adopted from her first novel, a movie, *Namesake* has also released in 2006 in the United States and United Kingdom. It is directed by Mira Nair and a screenplay adapted from Lahiri's novel by

Sooni Taraporevala. The film stars Kal Penn as the young Gogol. Lahiri, herself, makes a cameo appearance in the film as Aunt Jhumpa.

Her debut collection, *Interpreter of Maladies*, won the 2000 *Pulitzer Prize* for fiction. It was translated into twenty-nine languages and became a bestseller both in the United States and abroad. In addition to the Pulitzer, it received the *PEN/Hemingway Award*, the *New Yorker Debut of the Year award*, an *American Academy of Arts* and *Letters Addison Metcalf Award*, and a nomination for the *Los Angeles Times Book Prize*. Lahiri was awarded a *Guggenheim Fellowship* too, in 2002.

Lahiri also had a distinguished relationship with The New Yorker publishing many short stories. Since 2005, Lahiri has been a Vice President of the PEN American Centre, an organisation designed to promote friendship and intellectual cooperation among writers.

In February 2010, she was appointed a member of the committee on the Arts and Humanities. Lahiri is a member of the President's Committee on the Arts and Humanities appointed by U.S. President Barack Obama.

In September 2013, her novel *The Lowland* was placed on the shortlist for the Man Booker Prize, which ultimately went to *The Luminaries* by Eleanor Catton. The following month it was also long-listed for the National Book Award for Fiction, and revealed to be a finalist on October 16, 2013.

In 2014 She was awarded DSC prize for South Asian Literature for The Lowlands and also won National Humanities Medal in the same year.

2017 : Pen/Malamud Award

In 2023, Jhumpa Lahiri was awarded an Honorary Doctorate from The American University of Rome in recognition of her extraordinary contribution to literature in English and Italian.

❑❑❑

Jimmy Wales

(1966)

Co-founder of Wikipedia

"I'm a big advocate of freedom: freedom of expression, freedom of thought. "

Jimmy Donal Jimbo Wales is an American Internet entrepreneur best known as the co-founder and promoter of the online non-profit encyclopedia Wikipedia and the for-profit Wikia web-hosting company.

Jimmy Wales was born in Huntsville, Alabama on August 7, 1966. He attended a one-room school run by his mother and grandmother through the eighth grade. An intellectually curious child whose education proceeded according to the Montessori system, Wales spent considerable amounts of time reading encyclopedias. He credits this self-directed upbringing with his ability to think creatively.

Wales attended the Randolph preparatory school and studied finance at Auburn University. After graduating, he began a doctoral program in finance at the University of Alabama. He transferred to Indiana University before dropping out of school to take a job in a financial services firm.

While in graduate school, he taught at two universities, but left before completing a PhD in order to take a job in finance and later worked as the research director of a Chicago futures and options firm.

Wales had been interested in the internet from its earliest days. In 1996, he left his job at the firm to cofound a startup called Bomis. Although the venture was not successful, it motivated Wales to pursue his vision of creating an online encyclopedia. In March 2000, he launched Nupedia—an open-content, peer-moderated reference site. He hired an academic, Larry Sanger, to serve as editor-in-chief.

Sanger learned about wikis in 2001 and Wales agreed to adopt the model. On January 15, 2001, with Larry Sanger and others, Wales launched Wikipedia, a free, open content encyclopedia that enjoyed rapid growth and popularity, and as Wikipedia's public profile grew, he became the project's promoter and spokesman. He is historically cited as a co-founder of Wikipedia, though he has disputed the "co-" designation, declaring himself the sole founder. Wikipedia and Nupedia co-existed for a short time, with Wikipedia attracting much more traffic and participation. Without the funding to continue his position, Sanger resigned from both organizations in 2002.

The non-profit Wikimedia Foundation, founded by Wales, has overseen the development of Wikipedia since 2003. Wales serves on the board of trustees of the Wikimedia Foundation, the non-profit charitable organization he helped establish to operate Wikipedia, holding its board-appointed "community founder" seat.

In 2004, Wales and colleague Angela Beesley founded a for-profit internet company called Wikia. His role in creating Wikipedia, which has become the world's largest encyclopedia, prompted *Time* magazine to name him in its 2006 list of "The 100 Most Influential People in the World". He stepped down from his position as CEO in 2009.

Wales began advising the British government on potential open access initiatives in 2012. The goal of the project was to make government-funded research available to taxpayers at no cost. In addition to his paid positions, Wales serves on the advisory boards of a number of academic foundations and research centers.

On May 26, 2014, Google appointed Wales to serve on a seven-member committee on privacy in response to *Google v. Gonzalez,* which led to Google's being inundated with requests to remove websites from their search results.

In 2017, Wales announced that he is launching an online publication called Wikitribune, with a goal to fight fake news through a combination of professional journalists and volunteer contributors.

Wales has been married three times and has two daughters. He has received a number of major awards and honorary degrees from institutions, including Amherst College.

Wales is an outspoken atheist and an adherent of Objectivism, a philosophy popularized by author Ayn Rand. Objectivism privileges individualism, capitalism and reason. He identifies as a libertarian though he is not a supporter of the Libertarian Party.

In October 2019, Wales launched an ad-free social network, WT : Social.

In 2021, on The Tim Ferriss Show podcast, he revealed that he secretly lived in Buenos Aires, Argentina, for one month after reading Ferriss's book The 4-hour Workweek.

❑❑❑

Jeff Bezos

(1964)
Entrepreneur

"We are comfortable planting seeds and waiting for them to grow into trees."

When we visit the e-commerce website Amazon or when we want to grab the most authentic news stories on a variety of subjects, we click over to "The Washington Post" but we seldom think about the effort behind these blooming business ventures. He has recently launched a space exploration company 'Blue Origin'. The mind is Jeff Bezos, an American entrepreneur who founded these and is their CEO which has made him stand in the line of the richest people in the world.

He was born on January 12, 1964, in Albuquerque, New Mexico. His mother was Jacklyn Gise Jorgensen and father was Ted Jorgensen. From an early age, he developed a penchant for computers and got enrolled on Computer Science and electrical engineering at Princeton University. Completing his graduation and as his potential was sighted, he did many jobs on Wall Street such as Fitel, Bankers' Trust and by the time it was 1990, he was promoted to the rank of vice president at the investment firm D.E. Shaw. After four years, Bezos relinquished his job to set up Amazon.com, which was a virtual bookstore online and gathered immense fame on the internet in a short time. In 2013, he bought 'The Washington Post' and in 2017 Amazon also bagged Whole Foods. In February 2021, there was a declaration that Bezos would quit from CEO post in the third quarter of the present year.

His inclination towards the nascent world of e-commerce was well-calculated. He left his job in 1994 and came to Seattle with his intention and efforts focussed upon the untapped potential of the internet market as he established an online bookstore.

That was on July 16th, 1995 that Amazon.com was opened by him and the name of the website was borrowed from the meandering river in South America and he asked 300 of his friends for its beta test.

The company met a great success and sans any press promotion, Amazon.com was relied upon for books across the United States while demand from foreign countries increased too. In just a couple of weeks from its launch, sales reached the figure of $20,000 a week and its progress was rapid enough to startle Bezos and his teammates.

Amazon.com turned public in 1997 and there were questions raised for its sustenance if traditional retailers launched their bookstores online. After two years, the start-up not only sustained but also overshadowed its competitors to grab the No. 1 position in the e-commerce field.

Bezos continued to give way to new offerings with the sale of CDs and videos in 1998 and later clothes, electronics, toys and more stuff emerged on Amazon with the strengthening of partnerships.

There were many other start-ups that had to cease operations but Amazon went ahead registering annual sales which went up from $510,000 in 1995 to over $17 billion by the time it was 2011.

In a letter that Bezos wrote to shareholders in 2018, he was boastful of over 100 million paid subscribers for Amazon Prime. By the month of September that year, the value of Amazon was over $1 trillion which is claimed to be the second company ever to touch that record after Apple. By the closing months of 2018, an announcement was made from Amazon where the minimum wage for its workers was raised to $15 per hour. The company faces heat and criticism as workers protested during Prime Day in July 2019.

In 2006, there was launched a video-on-demand service on Amazon.com. Earlier it was known as Amazon Unbox on TiVo and was rebranded as Amazon Instant Video.

In 2013, numerous original programs are said to have been streamed by Bezos with the launch of Amazon Studios while the company got on everyone's nerves with "Transparent" and "Mozart in the Jungle" which are critically acclaimed.

As for its first feature film, the company produced and unveiled Spike Lee's *Chi-Raq* in 2015. In the following year 2016, Bezos appeared in the cameo role of an alien in Star Trek *Beyond.*

This was in 2007, that Kindle, a handy digital book reader was offered by Amazon, allowing users to buy, download, read and store their selected books. Bezos grabbed the headlines in December 2013 when he declared an innovative initiative from Amazon termed "Amazon Prime Air" and drones were included as part of service offering to customers. Fire Phone was launched by Amazon in 2014 which was a pretty miscalculated step and much criticism was heaped upon him for being too gimmicky. The product was discarded the following year. Market segment of food delivery was under his sight and in 2017 announcement was made from Amazon about the acquisition of Whole Foods grocery chain against a whopping cash payment of $13.7 billion.

He is the second wealthiest person in the world, with a net worth of US$251 billion as of December 17, 2024, according to Forbes and the Bloomberg Billionaires Index.

❑❑❑

John F. Kennedy

(1917–1963)

Political Leader

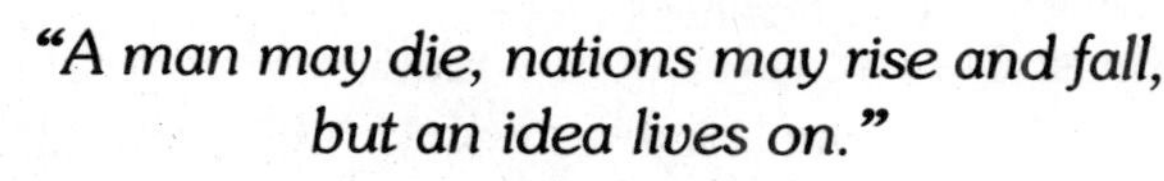

"A man may die, nations may rise and fall, but an idea lives on."

John F. Kennedy was the president of USA from 1961 until his assassination in 1963. He was killed by an assassin's bullets as his motorcade wound through Dallas, Texas. Kennedy was the youngest man elected as a President; and the youngest to die.

John Fitzgerald Kennedy was born on May 29, 1917 at Brookline (Massachusetts). His father Joseph Kennedy was an ambitious politician, who became from son of a pubkeeper to a millionaire. He married the daughter of the mayor of Boston, Rose Fitzgerald. John F. Kennedy was their second son. During World War II their eldest son lost his life, when his aeroplane exploded above the Canal.

Kennedy studied at Harvard and after he had finished, he also had to serve in the war. As lieutenant of the PT 109 he once was shipwrecked, but he survived and because of his heroism he saved the lives of his crew.

In 1952, he became senator of Massachusetts. In 1956, he almost became running mate of Adlai Stevenson, but lost to Estes Kefauver of Tennessee: anyway, they lost the elections. In 1958, he won reelection in Massachusetts by 875,000 votes, the largest majority in the state's history. He was elected for president in November 1960, after a less than easy election contest. He defeated Richard Nixon and became the youngest (43) to be elected to the White House in American history 'till then. In contrast to Al Smith in 1928 (first Catholic presidential candidate), Kennedy was elected despite of being Catholic.

The 35th, first Catholic, president ended his inaugural address on January 20, in 1961 with the following words: "My fellow citizens of the world: ask not what America will do for you, but what together we can do for the freedom of man".

During his presidency, he passed two crises which had to do with Cuba. The first in April 1961, at the Bay of Pigs, was an assault on Cuba. It was a plan developed by the CIA under the Eisenhower Administration. Castro's troops quickly defeated the landing attempt. It was a failure for the Kennedy Administration, which can be explained by poor advice he had received from the military, the CIA, and from many liberals.

The Cuba crisis in 1962 is a much more complicated crisis, caused by placing of intermediate range missiles in Cuba by the Russians.

When Kennedy found out, the world was close to nuclear war in October 1962, because Kennedy's military consultants recommended an immediate air strike. But Kennedy's brother, the military and attorney general Robert Kennedy disagreed, because the US would act like Japan with Pearl Harbour and loose its faith. The president instituted a naval blockade against Russian ships and demanded removal of the missiles. After about a week, the Russians agreed and Kennedy promised not to invade Cuba.

In 1961, Kennedy passed the Berlin Crisis. The problem of West and East Berlin was not solved and it became even worse in August 1961 because of the construction of the Berlin Wall.

The Cold War had its downs when Kennedy was the president of USA, but also its ups. A 'hotline' insured instantaneous communication between the Kremlin and White House for times of crisis threatening the peace. Both governments became more peaceful and in 1963 they signed the Test Ban Treaty, which outlawed atmospheric testing of nuclear weapons.

During his presidency, the internal policy existed for an important part of policy for equal rights for all citizens. Kennedy had to deal with a lot of resistance and most of his bills were rejected. He had plans to improve the social policy, but only under his successor Johnson most of Kennedy's ideas were accepted by Congress.

On November 22, 1963 Kennedy visited Dallas with his wife Jackie. He was shot during a riding tour in an open limousine and died after about half an hour. According to the official Warren-report, Lee Harvey Oswald killed the president, but there is serious doubt about this because of many strange things. For example, the dying of many witnesses, the killing of Oswald and the problem of how one bullet could have killed the President and also hit the Governor of Texas.

The sad fact is that John F. Kennedy was just forty six years old, when he died and left a wife and two children.

John Lennon

(1940–1980)

Musician

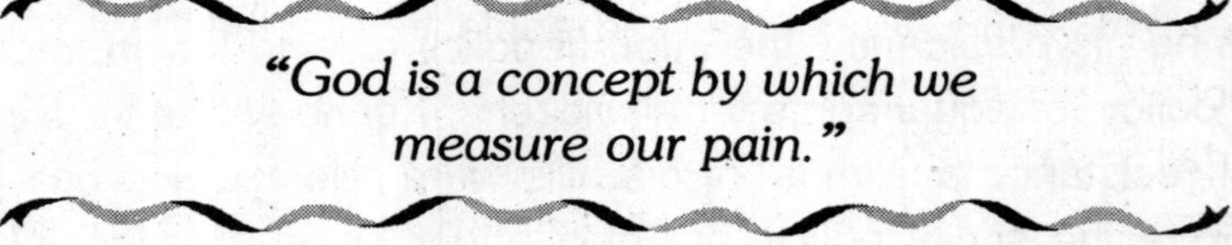

John Winston Lennon, later John Ono Lennon, was best known as a singer, songwriter, and guitarist for *The Beatles*. His creative career also included the roles of solo musician, political activist, artist, actor and author. As half of the legendary Lennon-McCartney songwriting team, he heavily influenced the development of rock music, leading it towards more serious and political messages.

John Lennon was born on October 9, 1940 in Liverpool, England. When he was four years old, his parents separated and he moved to his aunt Mimi. As a child, John was a prankster and he enjoyed getting in trouble. As a boy and young adult, he enjoyed drawing grotesque figures and cripples. One of the reasons for his obsession with cripples and deformities was because of the Death of his Mother Julia. John's school master thought that John could go to an art school for college, since he did not get good grades in school, but had artistic talent. He made it to art school, but was not allowed to play *Rock and Roll*.

During his college days, John met a woman by the name of Cynthia Powell, who became his first wife. As a child, he lived a life of uninterrupted calm. He did not recall feeling desperately sad or unusually happy. Unfortunately that calm was suddenly shattered when his mother died before his 18th birthday. John considered his aunt, the greatest person. They lived in a little house, with frilly curtains at the windows, and an old apple tree in the front garden. When John was away from home, he thought about aunt, Mimi and her frilly curtains and her apple tree, and he realised how fortunate he was. Because, though his mother was taken away from him, he was given something precious in return.

At the age of sixteen, he created the group called the *Quarry Man*. They performed at school. One day, Paul McCartney was introduced to him. At this point, John asked Paul if he could join the group, and he accepted the next day. Paul McCartney introduced George Harrison to John Lennon. The first recording they made was called *That will be the day* by Buddy Holly.

John came up with the name *Beatles* for the group. He had a vision when he was 12 years old - a man appeared on a Flaming pie and said unto them, 'From this day on you are *Beatles* with an 'A'. The *Beatles* were discovered by Brian Epstein in the Cavern, where they were performing. After Brian discovered the *Beatles*, he became their manager. The *Beatles* released their first single *Love me Do*, with George Martin as their producer. This song went up the charts the second day it was released. *Love Me Do* got up to 17. *The Beatles,* first number one chart was *Please Please Me* written by John Lennon. This song was inspired primarily by Roy Orbison but also fed by John's infatuation with the pun in Bing Crosby's famous *Please, lend your little ears to my please.*

John married Cynthia Powell in August 1962 and they had a son together who they called Julian.Cynthia described John as "Rough, ready and not her type at all, but had an irresistible character". Since the *Beatles* were becoming very popular at that time, Cynthia had to keep a very low profile. John Lennon divorced Cynthia and re-married with Yoko Ono, whom he met at the Indica Gallery in November 1966. In 1970, the *Beatles* broke up, after Paul McCartney announced that he was leaving the *Beatles*. After the *Beatles* broke up, John Lennon went his way. He started doing this by releasing his first solo album, *Imagine*.

In 1972, John Lennon gave a charity concert. The concert was held in Madison Square Garden on August 30, 1972, to help improve the living conditions of the mentally handicapped children. Beginning with the Toronto Peace Festival in 1969, John with Yoko did a series of rock concerts as their statement of Peace and Love, and to spotlight various social issues effectively. All proceeds from the concerts were given to the needy. This concert in Madison Square garden turned out to be the last concert John did with the Plastic Ono Band. In 1972, the Vietnam War protest was at its height. The Feminist Movement was in a stage of awakening. The concert was filled with love of brotherhood and sisterhood. Everybody joined in on the stage at the end when they sang, *Give Peace a chance*. People could not contain themselves and marched down Fifth Avenue after the performance, singing *Give Peace a Chance.* John Lennon performed with his new band called the *Plastic Ono Band*.

In 1973, John and Yoko separated for 14 months, because of all the public pressure and problems they were going through. John went to Los Angeles and he was single again after a long time. He became a drunk and was only partying . May Pang became John's companion during this time as a guidance. During this time, people began seeing more of John. He recorded different records like *Mind Games*, *Rock and Roll*, *Walls and Bridges* etc. He worked with Ringo on his album,

David Bowie with his "Fame" album and also with Elton John during this time. After going through all this, John realised that there was not really anybody that loves him, besides Yoko. So he returned back to Yoko. He realised that he really loved her and could not live without her.

On October 9, 1975, Yoko gave birth to John's other son Sean. As a devoted father, he left his music career for the next five years. But then he realised that there is no life without music. He started writing to songs with ease since there were no pressure. John wrote all the songs on *Double Fantasy* in a period of 3 weeks. This album was written, recorded, and released in 1980. When John was singing and writing this album, he was visualising everybody in his age group. Unfortunately, John was shot in front of his apartment complex in New York while he was in the process of releasing another album, *Milk and Honey*. John died at the age of 40 in Roosevelt Hospital on December 8, 1980, after receiving multiple gun shots in the back.

The *Double Fantasy* is a great album, which contain one ironic title song, *Just like starting over*. John was just starting over again, when he was killed. John was not a follower, but a leader and was always fighting for people's rights. He was a person who cared for other people and expressed himself by making different political statements. He was not only a great music writer, but also an excellent pop artist and did a lot in the Rock and Roll music world. John cannot and will never be replaced by anybody. His songs will live forever in all our hearts and minds.

❑❑❑

John Von Neumann

(1903–1957)

Mathematician

"There's no sense in being precise when you don't even know what you're talking about."

John von Neumann was one of the pre-eminent scientists, along with being a great mathematician and physicist. He was an early pioneer in fields such as game theory, nuclear deterrence, and modern computing. He made contributions to quantum physics, functional analysis, set theory, economics, computer science, topology, hydrodynamics, etc. Von Neumann's intellect was dizzying.

He was born on December 28, 1903 as Neumann Janos Lajos (Hungarian names have the family name first) in Budapest, Hungary to Neumann Miksa, a lawyer who worked in a bank, and Kann Margit.

John was an extraordinary prodigy. At the age of six, he could divide two 8-digit numbers in his head and converse with his father in ancient Greek. John Von was already very interested in maths, the nature of numbers and the logic of the world around him. By eight, he had mastered calculus and by twelve, he was at the graduate level in mathematics. In 1911, Von Neumann entered the Lutheran Gymnasium. The school had a strong academic tradition which seemed to count for more than the religious affiliation both in Neumann's eyes and in those of the school.

Von Neumann completed his education at the Lutheran Gymnasium in 1921. However, his father did not want his son to take up a subject that would not bring him wealth. Max Neumann asked Theodore von Karman to speak to his son and persuade him to follow a career in business. Finally, all agreed on the compromise subject of chemistry for Von Neumann's university studies.

He received his PhD in mathematics (with minors in experimental physics and chemistry) from the University of Budapest at the age of 23. He published a definition of ordinal numbers when he was 20, the definition is the one used today. Von Neumann received his diploma in chemical engineering from the Technische Hochschule in Zürich in 1926.

By the age of 25, Von Neumann had published ten major papers; and by the age of 30, nearly three dozen. He became the co-editor of the *Annals of Mathematics* in 1933 and, two years later, he became the co-editor of *Compositio Mathematica*. He held both these editorships until his death.

John Von Neumann was married twice. His first wife was Mariette Kovesi, whom he married in 1930. He agreed to convert to Catholicism to placate her family. Von Neumann and Marietta had a daughter Marina in 1936, but their marriage ended in divorce, in 1937. The following year, he married Klara Dan, also from Budapest, whom he met on one of his European visits. After marrying, they sailed to the United States and made their home in Princeton.

During and after World War II, Von Neumann served as a consultant to the armed forces. From 1940, he was a member of the Scientific Advisory Committee at the Ballistic Research Laboratories at the Aberdeen Proving Ground in Maryland. Von Neumann also helped develop the first electronic computer, the ENIAC, at the University of Pennsylvania.

He received two Presidential Awards, the Medal for Merit in 1947 and the Medal for Freedom in 1956. He had also received the Albert Einstein Commemorative Award and the Enrico Fermi Award in 1956. In 1938, he was awarded the Bôcher Memorial Prize for his work in analysis.

Perhaps, all deaths can be considered to come too early. John Von Neumann's own death came far too early. He died on February 8, 1957. He was diagnosed with bone cancer or pancreatic cancer, possibly caused by exposure to radioactivity while observing A-bomb tests in the Pacific, and possibly in later work on nuclear weapons at Los Alamos, New Mexico. He died within a few months of the initial diagnosis, in excruciating pain. When he died, he was developing a theory of the structure of the human brain.

It is often said that modern mathematics is so vast that no one can know more than a tiny fraction of it. Someone once asked Von Neumann how much of mathematics he himself knew. He went into one of his characteristic thinking trances. After a moment, he had an answer, "Twenty-eight percent."

❑❑❑

Joseph Stalin

(1878–1953)

Socialist Leader

"Education is a weapon whose effects depend on who holds it in his hands and at whom it is aimed."

The Soviet statesman, Joseph Stalin was the supreme ruler of the Soviet Union. He led his country alongside America and England through World War II (1939–45) in their fight against Germany, Italy and Japan. As ruler of Russia, Stalin was the leader of world communism for almost thirty years.

Joseph Stalin was born of Iosif Vissarion Ivanovich Dzhugashvili on December 18, 1878, in Gori, Georgia. He was the only surviving son of Vissarion Dzhugashvili, a cobbler who first practised his craft in a village shop but later in a shoe factory in the city. Stalin's father died in 1891. Stalin's mother, Ekaterina, a religious and illiterate (unable to read or write) peasant woman, sent her teenage son to the theological seminary in Tpilisi (Tiflis), Georgia, where Stalin prepared for the ministry. Shortly before his graduation, however, he was expelled in 1899 for spreading subversive views (ideas that went against those of the government).

Stalin joined the underground revolutionary Marxist movement in Tpilisi, a movement devoted to the views of Karl Marx (1818–1883) and Frederich Engels (1821–1896). The following year he was arrested, imprisoned, and later exiled (forced to move) to Siberia, a cold and remote region of Russia. Stalin escaped from Siberia in 1904 and rejoined the Marxist underground in Tpilisi. When the Russian Marxist movement split into two factions (rival groups), Stalin identified himself with the Bolsheviks.

During the time of the 1904–1905 revolution, Stalin made a name for himself as the organiser of daring bank robberies and raids on money transports, an activity that Marxist leader, V. I. Lenin (1870–1924) considered important due to the party's need for funds. Many other Marxists considered this type of highway robbery unworthy of a revolutionary socialist.

Stalin participated in congresses (governing parties) of the Russian Social Democratic Workers Party at Tampere, London, and Stockholm, Sweden, in 1905 and 1906, meeting Lenin for the first time at these congresses. In 1912, Lenin recruited Stalin into the Central Committee of the Bolshevik Party. He adopted the name, Stalin ("man of steel") around 1913.

After the fall of czarism, Stalin made his way at once to Petrograd, Russia, where until the arrival of Lenin from Switzerland, he was the senior Bolshevik and the editor of *Pravda,* the party newspaper. In 1927, Stalin succeeded in defeating the entire opposition and in eliminating its leaders from the party.

About Stalin's private life, little is known beyond the fact that he seems always to have been a lonely man. His first wife, a Georgian girl named Ekaterina Svanidze, died of tuberculosis, a terrible disease that attacks the lungs and bones. His second wife, Nadezhda Alleluyeva, killed herself in 1932, apparently over Stalin's dictatorial rule of the party. The only child from his first marriage, Jacob, fell into

German hands during World War I. The two children from his second marriage outlived their father, but they were not always on good terms with him. The son, Vasili, an officer in the Soviet Air Force, drank himself to death in 1962. The daughter, Svetlana, fled to the United States in the 1960s.

The price the Soviet Union paid for this great achievement remains staggering. It included the destruction of all free enterprise (business organisations) in both town and country. The transformation of Soviet agriculture in the early 1930s into collectives (groups of managed farms) tremendously damaged the country's food production. Living standards were drastically lowered at first, and more than a million people died of starvation. Meanwhile, Stalin jailed and executed vast numbers of party members, especially the old revolutionaries and the leading figures in many other areas. Stalin created a new kind of political system characterised by severe police control, strengthening of the government, and personal dictatorship. Historians consider his government one of history's worst examples of totalitarianism, or having complete political control with no opposition.

From the middle of the 1930s onwards, Stalin personally managed the vast political and economic system he had established. Formally, he took charge of it in May 1941, when he assumed the office of chairman of the Council of Ministers. After Germany invaded the Soviet Union, Stalin also assumed formal command of the entire military establishment.

Stalin died of a brain haemorrhage (an abnormal bleeding of the brain) on March 5, 1953. His body was placed in a tomb next to Lenin's in Red Square in Moscow. After his death, Stalin became a controversial figure in the communist world, where appreciation for his great achievements was offset by harsh criticism of his methods.

Kailash Satyarthi

(1954)

Child Right Activist

"There is no greater violence than to deny the dreams of our childrens."

Kailash Satyarthi is an Indian children's rights and education advocate and an activist against child labour. He founded the *Bachpan Bachao Andolan* in 1980 and has acted to protect the rights of more than 83,000 children from 144 countries. It is largely because of Satyarthi's work and activism that the International Labour Organization adopted Convention No. 182 on the worst forms of child labour, which is now a principal guideline for governments around the world.

Originally named Kailash Sharma, Satyarthi was born on 11 January 1954 in the Vidisha district of central Indian state Madhya Pradesh.

He attended Government Boys Higher Secondary School in town, and completed his degree in electrical engineering at Samrat Ashok Technological Institute, Vidisha and a post-graduate degree in high-voltage engineering. He then joined a college inBhopal as a lecturer for a few years.

In 1980, he gave up his career as an engineer and became secretary general for the Bonded Labor Liberation Front. He has also been involved with the Global March Against Child Labor and its international advocacy body, the International Center on Child Labor and Education (ICCLE), which are worldwide coalitions of NGOs, teachers and trades unionists. He has also served as the President of the Global Campaign for Education, from its inception in 1999 to 2011, having been one of its four founders alongside ActionAid, Oxfam andEducation International.

In addition, he established Good Weave International (formerly known as Rugmark) as the first voluntary labelling, monitoring and certification system of rugs manufactured without the use of child-labour in South Asia. This latter organisation operated a campaign in Europe and the United States in the late 1980s and early 1990s with the intent of raising consumer awareness of the issues relating to the accountability of global corporations with regard to socially responsible consumerism and trade. Satyarthi has highlighted child labor as a human rights issue as well as a welfare matter and charitable cause. He has argued that it perpetuates poverty, unemployment, illiteracy, population growth, and other social problems, and his claims have been supported by several studies. He has also had a role in linking the movement against child labour with efforts for achieving "Education for All". He has been a member of a UNESCO body established to examine this and has been on the board of the Fast Track Initiative (now known as the Global Partnership for Education). Satyarthi serves on the board and committee of several international organisations including the Center for Victims of Torture (USA), the International Labor Rights Fund (USA), and the International Cocoa Foundation. He is now reportedly working on bringing child labour and slavery into the post-2015 development agenda for the United Nation's Millennium Development Goals.

Satyarthi, along with Pakistani activist Malala Yousafzai, was awarded the Nobel Peace Prize in 2014 "for their struggle against the suppression of children and young people and for the right of all children to education". Satyarthi is the fifth Nobel Prize winner for India and only the second Indian winner of the Nobel Peace Prize after Mother Teresa in 1979.

He lives in New Delhi, India. Satyarthi has been the subject of a number of documentaries, television series, talk shows, advocacy and awareness films. Satyarthi has been awarded the following national and international honours:

- **1994** : The Aachener International Peace Award (Germany).
- **1995** : Robert F. Kennedy Human Rights Award (USA).
- **1999** : Friedrich Ebert Stiftung Award (Germany).
- **2002** : Wallenberg Medal, awarded by the University of Michigan.
- **2006** : Freedom Award (USA).
- **2008** : Alfonso Comin International Award (Spain).
- **2009** : Defenders of Democracy Award (US).
- **2014** : Nobel Peace Prize.
- **2014** : Honorary Doctor of Philosophy Degree by Alliance University.
- **2015** : Harvard's University Award "Humanitarian of the Year".
- **2016** : Doctor of Humane Letters, Lynchburg College (USA).
- **2016** : Doctor of Law (LLD), West Bengal University of Juridical Sciences (India).
- **2017** : Guinness World Record for Largest Child Safe Guarding Lesson.
- **2017** : Doctor Honoris Causa, EL Rector Magnífico de la Universidad Pablo de Olavide.
- **2018** : Honoris Causa in Science, Amity University (India).
- **2018** : Santokhba Humanitarian Award.
- **2019** : Wockhardt Foundation, Lifetime Achievement Award India TV.
- **2019** : Mother Teresa Memorial Award for Social Justice Asia News.
- **2022** : The Rotary Award of Honour from Rotary International.

❑❑❑

Kalpana Chawla

(1961–2003)

Astronaut

"When you look at the stars and the galaxy, you feel that you are not just from any particular piece of land, but from the solar system."

Kalpana Chawla was the first Indian women astronaut. She held a Certificated Flight Instructor's licence with airplane and glider ratings, commercial pilot's licences for single and multi-engine land and seaplanes, and gliders, and instrument rating for airplanes. She enjoyed flying aerobatics and tail-wheeled airplanes.

Kalpana Chawla was born in Karnal, Haryana on July 1, 1961. Kalpana was the daughter of Banarsi Lal Chawla, a businessman and Sanyogita, a simple housewife. Kalpana's parents originally came to Karnal from the Multan district of West Punjab, which is now known as Pakistan.

Fascinated by flying, Kalpana Chawla was a daring child since childhood. Though she decided to become an astronaut only after completing her bachelor's degree in aeronautical engineering, she expressed her desire to learn flying when she was barely 13. Her childhood was totally different from other girls. Sketching and painting airplanes were more her forte than dressing up Barbie dolls.

Kalpana completed her Graduation from Tagore School, Karnal, India, in 1976. She did bachelor of science degree in aeronautical engineering from the Punjab Engineering College, in 1982. A master of science in aerospace engineering from the University of Texas, 1984, Kalpana Chawla completed her Doctorate of philosophy in aerospace engineering from the University of Colorado, 1988.

In 1982, she landed in the American university. Kalpana met Jean Pierre Harrison, a freelance-flying instructor. Inspired by Jean Pierre, she took up scuba diving, hiking and went on long flying expeditions. She kept her brother informed about her inclination towards Pierre. Kalpana's brother prevailed upon his parents when Kalpana said she wanted to marry Jean Pierre. They were married in 1984.

In 1988, Kalpana Chawla started work at NASA Ames Research Centre in the area of powered-lift computational fluid dynamics. Her research concentrated on simulation of complex air flows encountered around aircraft such as the Harrier in "ground-effect." In 1993, Kalpana Chawla joined Overset Methods Inc., Los Altos, California, as Vice President and Research Scientist to form a team with other researchers specialising in simulation of moving multiple body problems. She was responsible for development and implementation of efficient techniques to perform aerodynamic optimisation.

In December 1994, she was selected by NASA and reported to the Johnson Space Centre in March 1995 as an astronaut candidate in the 15th Group of Astronauts. After completing a year of training and evaluation, she was assigned as a crew representative to work technical issues for the Astronaut Office EVA/Robotics and Computer branches.

On November 20, 1997, Kalpana Chawla was the first Indian woman to go into space, when the US space shuttle Columbia blasted off from the Kennedy Space Centre at Cape Canaveral in Florida. She flew on STS-87 (1997) and STS-107 (2003), logging more than 30 days in space. Chawla was part of the six members crew on a 16-day research mission (January 16 to February 1, 2003) aimed at releasing a free flying satellite to study the Sun's outer atmospheric layers. The experimental carrier, mounted in Columbia's cargo bay, had a variety of high-tech devices designed to study how weightless environment of space affects various physical processes. The STS-107 mission ended abruptly on February 1, 2003 when Space Shuttle Columbia and her crew perished during entry, 16 minutes prior to scheduled landing.

Posthumously awarded the Congressional Space Medal of Honour, the NASA Space Flight Medal, and the NASA Distinguished Service Medal.

On February 5, 2003, India's Prime Minister announced that the meteorological series of satellites, "METSAT", will be renamed as "KALPANA". The first satellite of the series, "METSAT-1", launched by India on September 12, 2002 will be now known as "KALPANA-1".

The 74th Street in the "Little India" section of Jackson Heights, Queens, New York City has been renamed the 74th Street Kalpana Chawla Way in her honour.

Based on her will, a $3,00,000 fund was established on environmental conservation projects around the world. The "Kalpana Chawla Fund for Environmental Stewardship" has also been set up with the National Audubon Society.

❑❑❑

Karl Marx

(1818–1883)

Philosopher and Social Scientist

"Experience praises the most happy, the one who made the most people happy."

The philosopher, social scientist, historian and revolutionary, Karl Marx, is without a doubt the most influential socialist thinker to emerge in the 19th century.

Karl Heinrich Marx was born into a comfortable middle-class home in Trier on the river Moselle in Germany on May 5, 1818. He came from a long line of rabbis on both sides of his family and his father, a man who knew Voltaire and Lessing by heart, had agreed to baptism as a Protestant so that he would not lose his job as one of the most respected lawyers in Trier. At the age of seventeen, Marx enrolled in the Faculty of Law at the University of Bonn. At Bonn, he became engaged to Jenny Von Westphalen, the daughter of Baron Von Westphalen, a prominent member of the Trier society, and the man responsible for initiating Marx in Romantic literature and Saint-Simonian politics.

In October 1842, he became the editor, in Cologne, of the influential *Rheinische Zeitung*, a liberal newspaper backed by industrialists. Marx's articles, particularly those on economic questions, forced the Prussian government to close the paper. Marx then immigrated to France.

Marx was expelled from Paris at the end of 1844 and with Engels, moved to Brussels where he remained for the next three years, visiting England where Engels' family had cotton spinning interests in Manchester. While in Brussels, Marx devoted himself to an intensive study of history and elaborated what came to be known as the materialist conception of history.

Early in 1848, he moved back to Paris when a revolution first broke out and onto Germany where he founded, again in Cologne, the *Neue Rheinische Zeitung*. The paper supported a radical democratic line against the Prussian autocracy and Marx devoted his main energies to its editorship since the Communist League had been virtually disbanded. Marx's paper was suppressed and he sought refuge in London in May 1849 to begin the "long, sleepless night of exile" that was to last for the rest of his life.

During the first half of the 1850s, the Marx family lived in poverty in a three room flat in the Soho quarter of London. Marx and Jenny already had four children and two more were to follow. Of these, only three survived. His major source of income at this time was Engels who was trying a steadily increasing income from the family business in Manchester. This was supplemented by weekly articles written as a foreign correspondent for the *New York Daily Tribune*.

Marx's major work on political economy made slow progress. By 1857, he had produced a gigantic 800 page manuscript on capital, landed property, wage labour, the state, foreign trade and the world market. The *Grundrisse* (or *Outlines*) was not published until 1941. In the early 1860s, he broke off his work to compose three large volumes, *Theories of Surplus Value*, which discussed the theoreticians of political economy, particularly, Adam Smith and David

Ricardo. It was not until 1867 that Marx was able to publish the first results of his work in volume I of *Capital,* a work which analysed the capitalist process of production. In *Capital,* Marx elaborated his version of the 'labour theory' value and his conception of surplus value and exploitation which would ultimately lead to a falling rate of profit in the collapse of industrial capitalism. Volumes II and III were finished during the 1860s but Marx worked on the manuscripts for the rest of his life and they were published posthumously by Engels.

During the last decade of his life, his health declined and he was incapable of sustained effort that had so characterised his previous work. He did manage to comment substantially on contemporary politics, particularly in Germany and Russia. In Germany, he opposed in his *Critique of the Gotha Programme,* the tendency of his followers, Karl Liebknecht (1826-1900) and August Bebel (1840–1913) to compromise with state socialism of Lasalle in the interests of a United Socialist Party. In his correspondence with Vera Zasulich, Marx contemplated the possibility of Russia's bypassing the capitalist stage of development and building communism on the basis of the common ownership of land characteristic of the village, *mir*.

Marx's health did not improve. He travelled to European spas and even to Algeria in search of recuperation. The deaths of his eldest daughter and his wife clouded the last years of his life. Marx died on March 14, 1883 and was buried at Highgate Cemetery in North London.

❑❑❑

Khalil Gibran

(1883–1931)

Poet, Philosopher and Artist

"Doubt is a pain too lonely to know that faith is his twin brother."

Gibran Khalil Gibran was a Lebanese author, philosopher, poet and artist. His poetry is notable for its use of formal language and insights on topics of life using spiritual terms.

Gibran Khalil Gibran was born on January 6, 1883, to the Maronite family of Gibran in Bsharri, a mountainous area in Northern Lebanon. His mother Kamila Rahmeh was thirty when she begot Gibran from her third husband, Khalil Gibran, who proved to be an irresponsible husband leading the family to poverty. Gibran had a half-brother six years older than him called Peter and two younger sisters, Mariana and Sultana, whom he was deeply attached to throughout his life, along with his mother.

Gibran proved to be a solitary and pensive child who relished the natural surroundings of the cascading falls, the rugged cliffs and the neighbouring green cedars, the beauty of which emerged as a dramatic and symbolic influence to his drawings and writings. Being laden with poverty, he did not receive any formal education or learning, which was limited to regular visits to a village priest who doctrine him with the essentials of religion and the Bible, alongside Syriac and Arabic languages. Recognising Gibran's inquisitive and alert nature, the priest began teaching him the rudiments of alphabet and language, opening up to Gibran the world of history, science, and language.

At the age of eight, Khalil Gibran, Gibran's father, was accused of tax evasion and was sent to prison as the Ottoman authorities confiscated Gibran's' property and left them homeless. The family went to live with relatives for a while; however, the strong-willed mother decided that the family should immigrate to the US, seeking a better life and following in suit to Gibran's uncle who immigrated earlier. The father was released in 1894, but being an irresponsible head of the family, he was undecided about immigration and remained behind in Lebanon.

At the age of ten, Gibran fell off a cliff, wounding his left shoulder, which remained weak for the rest of his life ever since this incident. To relocate the shoulder, his family strapped it to a cross and wrapped it up for forty days, a symbolic incident reminiscent of Christ's wanderings in the wilderness which remained etched in Gibran's memory.

On June 25, 1895, the Gibrans embarked on a voyage to the American shores of New York. They settled in Boston's South End, which at the time hosted the second largest Syrian community in the US following New York. The culturally diverse area felt familiar to Kamila, who was comforted by the familiar spoken Arabic, and the widespread Arab customs. Kamila, now the breadwinner of the family, began to work as a peddler on the impoverished streets of South End Boston.

In the school, a registration mistake altered his name forever by shortening it to Khalil Gibran, which remained unchanged till the rest of his life despite repeated attempts at restoring his full name. Gibran entered school on September 30, 1895, merely two months after his arrival in the US. Having no formal education, he was placed in an ungraded class reserved for immigrant children, who had to learn English from scratch. Gibran caught the eye of his teachers with his sketches and drawings, a hobby he had started during his childhood in Lebanon.

Gibran's curiosity led him to the cultural side of Boston, which exposed him to the rich world of theatre, opera and artistic galleries. Prodded by the cultural scenes around him and through his artistic drawings, Gibran caught the attention of his teachers at the public school, who saw an artistic future for the boy. They contacted Fred Holland Day, an artist and a supporter of artists who opened up Gibran's cultural world and set him on the road to artistic fame.

Gibran's works were especially influential in the American popular culture in the 1960s. In 1904, Gibran had his first art exhibition in Boston. From 1908 to 1910, he studied art in Paris with August Rodin. In 1912, he settled in New York, where he devoted himself to writing and painting. Gibran's early works were written in Arabic, and from 1918, he published mostly in English. In 1920, he founded a society for Arab writers, Mahgar (al-Mahgar).

Among his best-known works are, 'The Prophet', a book of 26 poetic essays, which has been translated into over 20 languages. Gibran died in New York City on April 10, 1931: the cause was determined to be cirrhosis of the liver, and tuberculosis. Before his death, Gibran expressed the wish that he be buried in Lebanon and this wish was fulfilled in 1932, when Mary Haskell and his sister, Mariana purchased the Mar Sarkis Monastery in Lebanon.

❑❑❑

Kapil Dev

(1959)

Cricketer

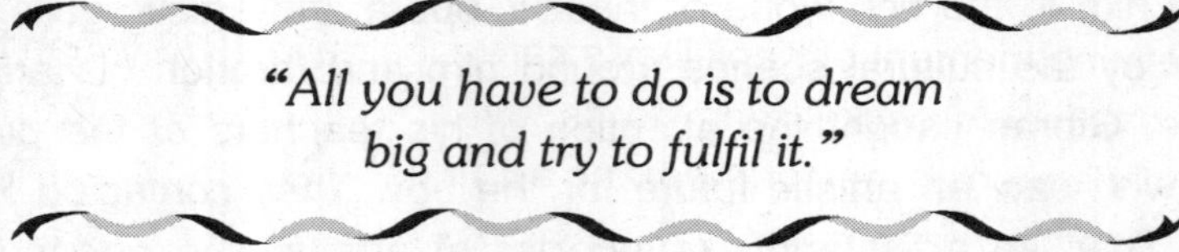

"All you have to do is to dream big and try to fulfil it."

Kapil Dev Nikhanj, born on January 6, 1959, in Chandigarh, India, is one of the most celebrated cricketers in the history of Indian sport. He was born into a Punjabi family that had migrated from Pakistan to India after the Partition in 1947. His father, Ram Lal Nikhanj, was a building contractor, and his mother, Raj Kumari, was a homemaker. Kapil was one of seven siblings and grew up in a modest household, developing a strong sense of discipline and resilience from an early age.

As a child, Kapil showed a keen interest in sports, especially cricket. He studied at DAV School in Chandigarh and began playing cricket in school, showing a natural flair for fast bowling. He joined Desh Prem Azad's cricket coaching camp, where his talent was honed under expert guidance. By the age of 16, he had earned a place in the Haryana cricket team and made his first-class debut in 1975. His consistent performances in the domestic circuit caught the attention of national selectors.

Kapil made his international debut for India in 1978 in a Test match against Pakistan. His aggressive bowling, athleticism, and ability to bat with power made him a unique asset to the Indian team, which had traditionally relied more on spin bowling. Within a few years, he had established himself as India's premier fast bowler and a dependable lower-order batsman. His fearless approach, especially in foreign conditions, made him a standout performer.

The defining moment of Kapil Dev's career came in 1983, when he captained the Indian cricket team to its first-ever Cricket World Cup victory. India entered the tournament as underdogs but surprised everyone with their performance. Kapil's iconic innings of 175 not out against Zimbabwe in a must-win game is considered one of the greatest in the history of One Day Internationals. Under his leadership, India defeated the mighty West Indies in the final at Lord's, which sparked a cricketing revolution in India. The victory not only changed the face of Indian cricket but also inspired a new generation of cricketers.

Over the course of his career, Kapil Dev played 131 Test matches and scored 5,248 runs, including eight centuries. As a bowler, he took 434 Test wickets, which was a world record at the time of his retirement in 1994. He also played 225 One Day Internationals (ODIs), scoring over 3,700 runs and taking 253 wickets. Kapil became the first cricketer in the world to achieve the all-rounder double of 4,000 runs and 400 wickets in Test cricket.

Kapil married Romi Bhatia in 1980, and the couple has a daughter named Amiya Dev, born in 1996. Despite his fame and achievements, Kapil has always remained humble and grounded. His personal life has been free of controversy, and he is admired not only for his cricketing achievements but also for his character and integrity.

After retiring from active cricket, Kapil briefly served as the coach of the Indian national team between 1999 and 2000. He also turned to commentary and television, becoming a popular face in the media. Kapil has authored books, been involved in various business ventures, and taken part in charitable activities related to health and sports. He founded the Khushii foundation, which works to improve the lives of underprivileged children.

For his services to Indian cricket, Kapil Dev has received numerous honours. He was awarded the Arjuna Award in 1979, the Padma Shri in 1982, and the Padma Bhushan in 1991. In 2002, Wisden named him the Indian Cricketer of the Century. In 2010, he was inducted into the ICC Cricket Hall of Fame.

Kapil Dev remains one of the greatest all-rounders the game has ever seen. His legacy is not just built on records, but on the transformation he brought to Indian cricket. He gave the team belief, led them to the pinnacle of success, and inspired a sporting culture that would later produce legends. Even decades after his retirement, his name continues to be associated with courage, leadership, and excellence.

❑❑❑

Khushwant Singh

(1915–2014)

Novelist and Journalist

*"You ask me about the signs of a man of faith?
When death comes to him he has a smile on his lips."*

Khushwant Singh was one of the most prominent Indian novelists and journalists. He is known for his humour and love of poetry. His comparisons of social and behavioural characteristics of Westerners and Indians was laced with his inimitable wit.

Khushwant Singh was born on February 2, 1915 in Punjab. His father was Sir Sobha Singh, a prominent civil contractor in Lutyen's Delhi. He received his bachelor's degree from a Government College in Lahore and was later qualified as a barrister from King's College, London.

Singh's weekly column, "With Malice towards One and All", published in *The Telegraph* and several other newspapers in India, has been one of the most widely read columns in the country. Bold and brazen, endearingly enigmatic, the weekly column was like a breath of fresh air in an otherwise moribund world of *desi* english journalism.

In August 1947, days before the independence of India and Pakistan, Khushwant Singh, then a lawyer practising in the High Court in Lahore, drove to his family's summer cottage in the foothills of the Himalayas.

From there he went on to Delhi, along 200 miles of strangely vacant road, until he came upon a jeep full of armed Sikhs who boasted that they had just massacred a village of Muslims. The same killing was occurring in what was about to become Pakistan, with Sikhs and Hindus among the million victims.

Khushwant Singh had been the editor of *Yojana,* a government journal for two years; *The Illustrated Weekly of India,* a society journal; *The National Herald,* a newspaper; and *Hindustan Times,* one of the most popular English newspapers in India. During his time as the editor, *The Illustrated Weekly of India* became hugely popular, and after him, it suffered a huge drop in readership. He was also a member of Rajya Sabha, the upper house of the Indian parliament until 1986.

Khushwant Singh was awarded the *Padma Bhushan* by the President of India for his services to the country and society in 1974. He returned the honour in 1984 in protest to the siege on Golden Temple by The Indian Army.

In 2006, Roli Books in New Delhi published a new edition of Singh's 1956 novel, *Train to Pakistan,* about the India-Pakistan partition. The new edition is illustrated with 66 of photojournalist Margaret Bourke-White's pictures of the aftermath of the violence. In late 2006, Roli was hoping to find an international distributor for the edition at the Frankfurt Book Fair.

In July 2000, Sulabh International Social Service Organisation awarded him, "Honest Man of the Year Award" for his courage and honesty in his "brilliant incisive writing."

At the award ceremony, Chandrababu Naidu, the then Chief minister of Andhra Pradesh described him as a "humorous writer and incorrigible believer in human goodness with a devil-may-care attitude and a courageous mind." The then Indian External Affairs Minister Jaswant Singh of BJP said that the secret of Khushwant Singh's success lay in his learning and discipline behind the "veneer of superficiality."

On February 20, 2006, the Canadian High Commission in Delhi gave a rare felicitation to Khushwant Singh on his long and eventful writing career which had its inception in the years, he spent in Canada as a young diplomat at the Indian High Commission.

In 2007, he was conferred with Padma Vibhushan by the Government of India, and in 2010, he was awarded Sahitya Academy fellowship by Sahitya Academy of India. His new release was *The Sunset Club*, 2010.

He was honoured with Lifetime Achievement Award by Tata Literature live at Mumbai Litfest in 2013. He had been fellow of King's College London.

He died of natural causes on 20 March 2014 at his Delhi based residence, at the age of 99. He is sruvived by his son and daughter.

❑❑❑

Kiran Bedi

(1949)

Former Police Officer & Social Activist

"You need a better organised society. It's in the end a question of working together to meet the needs of the society, which also includes the needs of women"

Kiran Bedi is a former Indian police officer and is the first woman to join the Indian Police Service (IPS) in 1972. She was one of the most celebrated and widely known police officers who had served the Indian Police Force.

She was born on June 9, 1949 in Amritsar, Punjab. Kiran Bedi is the second of the four daughters of her parents, Prakash Lal Peshawaria and Prem Lata Peshawaria. She completed her schooling from the Sacred Heart Convent School, Amritsar, and obtained her BA degree (1964–68) in English from the Government College for Women, Amritsar. She then earned a Master's degree (1968–70) in Political Science from Punjab University, Chandigarh.

Even while in active service in the Indian Police, she continued her educational pursuits, and obtained a Law degree (LLB) in 1988 from the Delhi University. She was also awarded a Ph.D. in 1993 in Social Sciences by the Department of Social Sciences, the Indian Institute of

Technology, New Delhi. The topic of her thesis was 'Drug Abuse and Domestic Violence'. Her interest in sports revealed her self-discipline and determination as she won many titles including the Junior National Lawn Tennis Championship in 1966, the Asian Lawn Tennis Championship in 1972, and the All-India Interstate Women's Lawn Tennis Championship in 1976. She also won three golds, as well as two silver medals at the Women's Festival Sports held in 1976 in Delhi.

Kiran Bedi began her career as a lecturer in Political Science (1970–72) at the Khalsa College for Women, Amritsar. In July 1972, she became the first female police officer in India when she joined the Indian Police Service (IPS). Her honesty drew attention, although it was not always appreciated. Such was the case when, as a traffic cop on duty at a government function, she ticketed automobiles belonging to high government officials. Despite this, she rose through the ranks, proving herself a capable law enforcement officer who was tough when she felt it was warranted, but always fair. The greatest challenge to her philosophy came in 1994 when she was promoted to the rank of Inspector General of Prisons and given the responsibility of managing the largest and most notorious prison in Asia Pacific area. This was the Tihar Jail which held approximately 8,500 prisoners, mostly male.

Rife with corruption, where prisoners were denied basic human rights and lived in fear of prison officials, Tihar's unofficial title of "hellhole" was well deserved. Bedi's approach was, in her typical fashion, she personally visited the prisoners. She talked to them and learned of the horrible living conditions they endured at the hands of callous and cruel guards. She also learned that the drug trade was alive and well inside the prison. One of her first official acts was to maintain a complaint box. Bedi introduced drug treatment programmes and created an atmosphere that encouraged prayer and meditation.

Navajyoti, set up in 1988, and India Vision Foundation, set up in 1994, are the two major voluntary organisations established by her with the objectives of improving the condition of the drug addicts and the poor people. Her efforts have won national and international recognition, and her organisations was awarded the Serge Soitiroff Memorial Award for drug abuse prevention by the United Nations.

Dr. Kiran Bedi's achievements and hard work have not gone unnoticed. She received the Police Medal for Gallantry as well as the Asia Region Award for her works in the prevention of drug abuse. In 1994, she was awarded the Ramon Magsaysay Award, also known as the Asian Nobel Prize. In 1997, Bedi was the recipient of the Swiss-German Joseph Beuys Award for Holistic and Innovative Management. Yet her greatest achievement may be the effect her achievements have had on Indian women who see Kiran Bedi as a role model and a hero. She was also a police advisor in the United Nations peacekeeping department, and has also been honoured with the UN medal for outstanding service.

In 2005, Kiran Bedi was awarded an honorary degree of Doctor of Law by the City University of New York, in recognition of her "humanitarian approach to prison reforms."

In 2007 Kiran Bedi took voluntary retirement from Indian Police Service. Currently she is involved in many social activities. In October 2010, Arvind Kejriwal invited Bedi to join him in exposing the CWG scam. Bedi accepted the invitation, and by 2011, the two had allied with other activists, including Anna Hazare, to form India Against Corruption (IAC) group.

Their campaign evolved into the 2011 Indian anti-corruption movement. Bedi split from IAC after a faction led by Arvind Kejriwal formed the Aam Aadmi Party (AAP) in 2012. She joined BJP in 2015. She was BJP's Chief Minister (CM) candidate for the 2015 Delhi Assembly elections, but lost the election from Krishna Nagar constituency to AAP candidate SK Bagga by a margin of 2277 votes, and AAP came to power again with an absolute majority after one year. Later, she served as the 24th Lieutenant Governor of Puducherry from 28 May, 2016 to 16 February, 2021.

Kishori Amonkar

(1932–2017)

Singer

"To me it (Music) is a dialogue with the divine, this intense focused communication with the ultimate other."

Kishori Amonkar was a leading Indian classical vocalist. She is considered to have been one of the foremost singers in the Hindustani tradition and is an innovator of the Jaipur gharana, or a community of musicians sharing a distinctive musical style.

Kishori Amonkar née Kurdikar was born in Bombay on 10 April 1932. Her father died when she was 6 years old, leaving Amonkar and her two siblings to be raised primarily by their mother, the classical vocalist Mogubai Kurdikar.

Kishori was married to Ravindra Amonkar, a school teacher, who died in 1992. The couple had two sons.

In the early 1940s, young Kishori began to receive vocal lessons in Hindustani classical music from Anjanibai Malpekar (of the Bhendi Bazar Gharana) and later received training from tutors of several gharanas. Her tutors included Anwar Hussain Khan of Agra

Gharana,Sharadchandra Arolkar of Gwalior Gharana, and Balkrishnabuwa Parwatkar. Amonkar has credited Malpekar, in particular, with teaching her the technique of meend, or gliding, between notes.

Amonkar's later work in light music reformed her classical singing and she modified her Jaipur gharana performance style by applying features from other *gharanas.* She has been both praised and criticized for pushing the boundaries of the Jaipur tradition. Her approach prioritized emotional expression over tradition, so she often departed from gharana's rhythmic, melodic, and structural traditions. Amonkar has criticised the idea that schools, or gharanas, of music determinate or constrain a singer's technique. Amonkar, therefore, has stated that while the Jaipur gharana's technique and methods form the base of her style, she performs several variations on it, including an adoption of alapachaari, or a relaxing of the link between the rhythm and note.

She created many compositions for a number of ragas. Amonkar is also a popular speaker and has traveled throughout India, best known for lectures on the role of rasa (feelings or emotions) in music.

Amonkar received several of India's national awards and civilian honours, including the Padma Bhushan, in 1987, and Padma Vibhushan in 2002. She was awarded the Sangeet Natak Akademi Award for 1985 and the Sangeet Natak Akademi Fellowship for 2009. She was awarded the prestigious Dr. T. M. A. Pai Outstanding Konkani Award in 1991. In 2016, she was one of seven recipients of the M.S. Subbulakshmi Award for classical music.

Amonkar was recognised by several of her contemporaries and fellow musicians for her skill and technique in classical music. The tabla musician, Ustad Zakir Hussain, has said that Amonkar's performances of several ragas, such as Raga Bhoop, are "...landmark performances that take place over hundreds of years and you will talk about them for the rest of your life and rest of the many centuries to come."

Amonkar is the subject of a documentary titled Bhinna Shadja, which was directed by Amol Palekar and Sandhya Gokhale. Several of Amonkar's students have become classical musicians of their own repute, including Nandini Bedekar, Raghunandan Panshikar, Suhasini Mulgaonkar, Mira Panshikar, and Meena Joshi. Amonkar's granddaughter, Tejashree Amonkar, is also a classical musician and was trained by Amonkar.

Amonkar lived in the suburb of Prabhadevi, in Mumbai. She died on 3 April 2017, a week before her 85th birthday, at her residence in Mumbai. She is reported to have died after a brief illness and in her sleep.

❑❑❑

Kumar Mangalam Birla

(1967)

Business Tycoon

"It is a vision which makes the Indian entrepreneur dare and may be even dream."

Kumar Mangalam Biral is the Chairman of the Aditya Biral Group, which is among India's largest business houses.

Born on June 14, 1967, Kumar Mangalam spent the early of his life in Calcutta and Mumbai. He is a Chartered Accountant and did his MBA (Masters in Business Administration) from the London Business School, London. He took over as Chairman in 1995, at the age of 28, after sudden demise of his father, noted industrialist Aditya Birla, after whom the group is named.

When Kumar Mangalam assumed the mantle at the Aditya Birla Group, Doubts were raised about his ability to handle a giant business house with interests spanning viscose, textiles and garments on the one hand and cement, aluminium and fertilisers on the other. But he proved his skeptics wrong. He brought in radical changes, changed business strategies, professionalised the entire group and replaced internal systems. Kumar Mangalam reduced his group's dependence on the cyclic commodities sectors by entering consumer products.

Under his leadership, the Aditya Birla Group, apart from consolidating its position in existing businesses, also ventured into sunrise sectors like cellular telephony, asset management, software and BPO.

The Aditya Birla Group is among India's largest business houses. Among its major Companies in India are Grasim, Hindalco, UltraTech Cement, Aditya Birla Nuvo and Idea Cellular and globally—Novelis, Minacs, Aditya Birla Minerals, Aditya Birla Chemicals. Its joint ventures include Birla Sun Life (Financial Services) and Birla NGK (Insulators). While Kumar Mangalam is the Chairman of all of the Group's blue-chip Companies in India, he serves as Chairman/Director on the Board of the Group's International Companies spanning Thailand, Indonesia, Philippines and Egypt, USA and Canada. The Group's operations extend to Canada, China, USA, U.K., Germany, Hungary, Australia, Laos, Brazil, Italy, France, Luxembourg, Switzerland, Malaysia and Korea.

Additionally, he is on the Board of the G.D.Birla Medical Research & Education Foundation, and a Member of the Board of Governors of the Birla Institute of Technology & Science (BITS), Pilani. He is a Member of the London Business School's Asia Pacific Advisory Board, which provides counsel on the School's strategy and curriculum. He is "Honorary Fellow" of the London Business School (LBS), a title conferred upon him by the Governing Board of the LBS.

Kumar Mangalam Birla held several key positions on various regulatory and professional boards, including chairmanship of the advisory committee constituted by the ministry of company affairs for 2006 and 2007, membership of the prime minister of India's advisory council on trade and industry, chairmanship of the board of trade reconstituted by the union minister of commerce and industry, and membership of the Central Board of Directors of the Reserve Bank of India.

In 1998, Kumar Mangalam was the first and only industrialist to have been appointed as a public nominee on the Governing Board of the Securities and Exchange Board of India (SEBI) by the Finance Ministry. He served as the Chairman of SEBI's 17-Member committee on Corporate Governance constituted in mid-1999, and as Chairman of SEBI's Committee on Insider Trading.

Even since, every year he has been honoured with honours and awards, to name a few—Management Man of the Year-2000, Golden Peacock Award for Business Leadership-2001, Rajiv Gandhi Award for Business Excellence and his contribution to the Country-2001, ranked among first five Asian Business Leaders of CNBC/INSEAD sponsored "Asian Business Leader Award 2002". In 2003, he won the "Business Leader of the Year Award" by Economic Times and "Business Man of the Year 2003" by Business India, becoming the only Chairman/CEO to have won both these prestigious awards in a single year.

He has received several accolades, including the International Advertising Association's "CEO of the Year Award" in 2016; the US India Business Council's "Global Leadership Award" in 2014; Economic Times "Business Leader Award" in 2003 and 2013; Forbes India Leadership Award–Flagship Award "Entrepreneur of the Year 2012; NDTV Profit Business Leadership Awards 2012, "Most Inspiring Leader"; CNBCTV18 IBLA "Business Leader for Taking India Abroad 2012"; CNN-IBN "Indian of the Year Award 2010"; JRD Tata "Leadership Award 2008"; NDTV's "Global Indian Leader of the Year 2007".

In 2023, Birla received the Padma Bhushan, the third highest civilian honour in India. Birla received the Business Leader of the Decade Award at the All India Management Association's (AIMA) 13th Managing India Awards ceremony on April 11, 2023.

❑❑❑

K.V. Kamath

(1947)

Banker & Business Leader

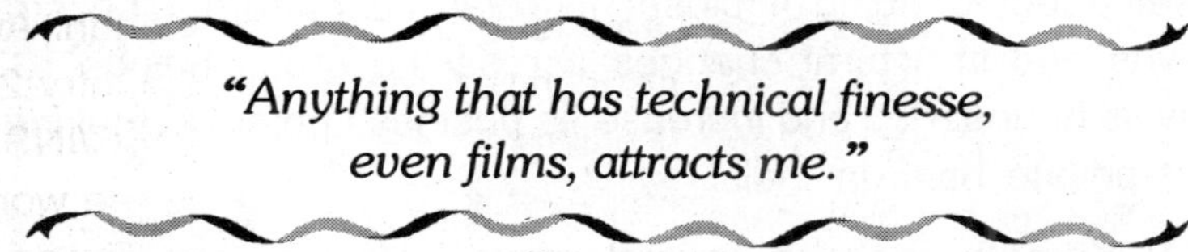

"Anything that has technical finesse, even films, attracts me."

Kundapur Vaman Kamath, commonly referred to as K.V. Kamath, has served as the Chairman of Infosys Limited, the second-largest Indian IT services company, and as the Non-Executive Chairman of ICICI Bank, India's largest private bank. Kamath also served as ICICI Bank's Managing Director and CEO from May 1, 1996 until his retirement from executive responsibilities on April 30, 2009.

Kamath was born on December 2, 1947 in Mangalore, Karnataka in India. In 1969 he graduated with a Bachelor's Degree in Mechanical Engineering from Karnataka Regional Educational College (KREC) and in 1971 obtained his Master's in Business Administration from the Indian Institute of Management, Ahmedabad (IIM-A), Gujarat.

Kamath started his career with ICICI in the Project Finance division in 1971. He moved on to gather a rich and varied experience, which included the setting up of new businesses such as leasing, venture capital, credit rating as well as handling general management positions. As a part of his responsibilities he initiated and implemented ICICI's computerization program.

In 1988, Kamath left ICICI to join the Asian Development Bank (Manila) in their Private Sector Department and was incharge of handling various social projects in South-East Asia. This gave him crucial international exposure. In 1996, he returned to ICICI as its Managing Director and CEO. He immediately instituted major changes and set about bringing it closer to retail customers. The strategic initiatives and structural changes across the group helped ICICI to redraw its boundaries and increase its business potential making it the largest private bank in India.

K.V. Kamath has won several awards. He was named Business Standard's "Banker of the Year" in 2001. "Businessman of the Year" by Forbes Asia and The Economic Times' "Business Leader of the Year" in 2007, the Asian Banker's Leadership Achievement Award for the Asia Pacific & Gulf region for 2007. He has been conferred with an honorary Ph.D. by the Banaras Hindu University. He has been the Vice President of the Confederation of Indian Industry and a Member of the boards of the Indian Institute of Management, Ahmedabad, National Institute of Bank Management and the Manipal University. He was awarded Padma Bhushan in 2008. After his retirement from executive responsibilities of ICICI in April 2009, he has been elected new head of Infosys Ltd. after N. R. Naryanamurthy, in 2011.

After being appointed as the first chief of the New Development Bank set up by the BRICS, he went on to step down from post of Chairman and Independent Director at Infosys effective 5 June, 2015.

❑❑❑

L.N. Mittal

(1950)

Steel Magnate

"When people can see which direction the leaders are going in, it becomes easier to motivate them."

The steel tycoon, Laxmi Niwas Mittal is a London based industrialist and a Forbes 100 billionaire. Mittal holds steel assets in South Africa, Poland, Indonesia, and Kazakhstan.

Lakshmi Niwas Mittal was born on June 15, 1950 at Sadulpur, in Churu district of Rajasthan, in a poor family. The extended family of 20 lived on bare concrete floors, slept on rope beds and cooked on an open fire in the brickyard in a house built by his grandfather. Laxmi Mittal belongs to the Marwari Aggarwal caste and his grandfather worked for the Tarachand Ghanshyam Das firm, one of the leading Marwari industrial firms of pre-independent India. The Mittal family later on moved to Calcutta (now Kolkata) where his father, Mohan Mittal became a partner in a steel company.

Lakshmi Mittal graduated from St. Xaviers in Calcutta (now Kolkata) with a commerce degree in 1969. He began his career working in the family's steelmaking business in India and in 1976, he founded the Mittal Steel Company. He split from his father and two younger brothers in 1994 and took the international arm, with interests in Indonesia, Trinidad and Tobago, while the rest of the family kept the domestic Indian business. In the last few years, Mittal Steel has made a number of acquisitions, buying up a network of steel producers in former communist countries including Kazakhstan, Romania and Ukraine, and pushing into the US in 2004 with the $4.5 billion purchase of International Steel Group. Today, Mittal Steel is the only truly global steel producer in the world with operations on 14 countries, spanning four continents.

His residence at 18-19 Kensington Palace Gardens was bought from Formula One car racing boss, Bernie Ecclestone in 2004 for £57.1 million ($105.7 million), the highest price ever paid for a house. Formerly, this house was the residence of Paul Reuter, the founder of the Reuters news service.

Mittal has two children. He paid over £30 million/$65 million to host his daughter, Vanisha's wedding celebration in Vaux le Vicomte on June 22, 2004 and an engagement ceremony at the Palace of Versailles on June 20, 2004. His son, Aditya is a director of Mittal Steel.

Mittal was awarded the Eighth Honorary Willy Korf Steel Vision Award, the highest recognition for worldwide achievement in the steel industry. The award was presented by the *American Metal Market*, a specialised publication, and Paine Weber's *World Steel Dynamics* in New York.

In 2008 he was awarded Padma Vibhushan by the Government of India. The Mittal family owns 39.87% of Arcelor Mittal, the world's second largest steel company.

The Republic of Kazakhastan has honoured him with *Dostyk* Award in 2010.

Despite being the eighth wealthiest man in Britain in 2002, he does not hold British citizenship. He is also the 47th "most powerful person" of the 70 individuals named in *Forbes'* "Most Powerful People" list for 2012.

In 2019, Forbes named him in the list of India's Richest 2019.

Lakshmi Mittal transitioned from CEO to Executive Chairman of ArcelorMittal, appointing his son, Aditya Mittal, as CEO in February 2021. As of October 2024, his net worth is estimated at $16.7 billion, ranking him 15th among India's 100 richest individuals.

Lal Bahadur Shastri

(1904–1966)

Political Leader

"Jai Jawan, Jai Kisan."

Lal Bahadur Shastri was the second Prime Minister of independent India. He succeeded Jawaharlal Nehru as Prime Minister of India in 1964. He was a significant figure in the struggle for independence.

Lal Bahadur was born in Moghalsarai, which is also spelt as Mughalsarai, on October 2, 1904. His parents were Sharada Prasad and Ramdulari Devi. Though his parents were Srivastavas, Shastri dropped his caste identity in his early years. His father died when he was only a year old. His mother with the help of her father took care of the children.

He acquired virtues like boldness, love of adventure, patience, self-control, courtesy, and selflessness in his childhood.

He abandoned his studies to take part in the Non-Cooperation movement started by Gandhi in 1921. He was given the title 'Shastri' at Kashi Vidya peeth in 1926. During his four years' stay there, he was very much influenced by the lectures of Dr. Bhagawandas on philosophy. In his later life, Shastri displayed poise in the midst of conflict and confusion which he learnt from his teacher, Bhagawandas.

After coming out from Kashi Vidyapeeth, he became the life-member of 'The Servants of the People Society' which was started by Lala Lajpat Rai in 1921. The aim of the society was to train youth who were prepared to dedicate their lives to the service of the country. Shastri earned the love and affection of Lajpat Rai by his earnestness and hard work. Later, he became the President of the society. In 1927, he married Lalitha Devi who was from Mirzapur.

Lal Bahadur Shastri took a leading role in 'Salt Satyagraha' which was intensified by 1930. He also advised people not to pay land revenue and taxes to the British government. He was sent to prison for two and half years for doing so. From this time onwards, prison became his second home. He was sent to prison seven times and was forced to spend nine long years in various prisons on different occasions.

Going to prison became a blessing in disguise for him. He spent time reading a number of books. He became familiar with the works of western philosophers, revolutionaries, and social reformers. Shastri translated the autobiography of Madam Curie, a French scientist who discovered Radium, into Hindi. He was an ideal prisoner. The greatness of Shastri was that he maintained his self-respect even in prison.

After Independence, he became the Minister of Police in the ministry of Govind Vallabh Panth. In 1951, he was appointed as the General Secretary of Lok Sabha before regaining a ministerial post as Railways Minister. He resigned following a rail disaster near Ariyalur. He returned to the Cabinet following the general elections, first as Minister of Transport, and then in 1961, he became the Home Minister.

Nehru died in office on May 27, 1964, and left something of a vacuum.Though eclipsed by such stalwarts of the Congress Party as Kamaraj, and Morarji Desai, the Finance Minister in Nehru's government, Shastri emerged as the concensus candidate in the midst of the party warfare. The ruling Congress Party unanimously elected Shastri as its leader. He became the Prime Minister on June 9, 1964 at a very crucial time in the Indian history.

The first problem he had to face after becoming the Prime Minister was the one caused by Pakistan. After the Chinese aggression, when India's confidence in her strength had been shaken, Pakistan was creating trouble along the borders. But Shastriji would not yield to the wickedness of Pakistan. He first tried to earn the goodwill and support from the other nations for India. He attended a meeting of the non-aligned nations and explained India's position.

Pakistan was awaiting to swallow Kashmir into its territory. She pushed her forces across the eastern border into the Rann of Kutch in Gujarat in 1965. Shastri faced the problem with great tact. But later there was a large scale invasion of the territory by Pakistani soldiers which led to the break out of war along the ceasefire line on the Kashmir border. Addressing the nation on August 13, 1965, Shastri referred to Pakistan's threats and said, "Force will be met with force".

Some big nations feared that if India won a total victory over Pakistan, it would lower their prestige. The Security Council of the United Nations Organisation called on India and Pakistan to stop fighting. On the invitation of Kosygin, the Premier of Soviet Russia, Shastri and Ayub Khan met in Tashkent on January 4, 1966. Shastri wished to give one more chance to Pakistan to live in peace and friendship with India. So he signed the treaty of friendship.

Shastriji had suffered heart attacks twice before and during the period of Pakistan war and the following days, his body had to bear a very heavy strain. He signed the Joint Declaration on January 10, 1966, and died the same night. Gone was the war hero and the messenger of peace, gone was the great statesman who restored to India her honour and self-respect in the assembly of nations. A tiny, tidy figure. A soul that had lived in perfect purity of thought, word, and deed. Such was this man who had lived in our midst. He belonged to the race of heroes of India.

He was posthumously awarded the Bharat Ratna and a memorial was built for him in Delhi. The slogan, *'Jai jawan, Jai kisan'* is attributed to Shastri. He was a star of great brightness in the history of India.

❑❑❑

Lala Lajpat Rai

(1865–1928)

Freedom Fighter

"Every blow on our bodies this afternoon is like a nail driven into the coffin of British imperialism."

Lala Lajpat Rai was an Indian politician who is chiefly remembered as a great leader in the Indian fight for freedom from the British Raj. He was popularly known as *Punjab Kesari.*

Lala Lajpat Rai was born on January 28, 1865 in village, Dhudike, in the present day Moga district of Punjab. He was the eldest son of Munshi Radha Kishan Azad and Gulab Devi. His father was an Aggarwal Bania by caste. His mother inculcated strong moral values in him.

Lala Lajpat Rai joined the Government College at Lahore in 1880 to study Law. While in college, he came in contact with patriots and future freedom fighters like Lala Hans Raj and Pandit Guru Dutt. The three became fast friends and joined the Arya Samaj founded by Swami Dayanand Saraswati. He passed his Vakaalat Examination in Second Division from the Government College in 1885.

Lalaji was proud of the ancient values and rich heritage of India. The session of the Indian National Congress at Allahabad in December 1888 marked the beginning of his political career. At the next session of Congress at Mumbai in 1889, he spoke in support of Tilak's amendment. Bipin Chandra Pal and Gokhale too supported Tilak. Though his name was linked with Tilak and Pal as the leaders of the extremists, he always made efforts to reconcile the differing elements.

The year 1905 was important for the emergence of a new leadership in the Indian National Congress of 'Lal-Bal-Pal', as they were popularly known. The partition of Bengal in 1905 aroused their robust nationalism. The repressive measures of the government against the growing nationalist movement inspired them to infuse national pride and self-respect among people. Lalaji emerged as the undisputed leader of this new spirit.

He left for Britain in April 1914 for this purpose. At this time, the First World War broke out and he was unable to return to India. He went to USA to galvanise support for India. He founded the Indian Home League Society of America and wrote a book called, *Young India*. The book severely indicted British rule in India and was banned in Britain and India even before it was published. He was able to return to India in 1920 after the end of World War.

Lalaji presided over the first session of the All India Trade Union Congress in 1920. He also went to Geneva to attend the Eighth International Labour Conference in 1926 as a representative of Indian labour. He had an opportunity to watch the labour movement in USA and England where he was required to prolong his stay for political reasons.

He was not only a good orator but also a prolific and versatile writer. His journal, *Arya Gazette* concentrated mainly on the subjects related to the Arya Samaj. *Bande Mataram* and *People,* full of fiery essays mirrored the unrest and zeal in him to free his country from the clutches of the foreign rule. He founded the Servants of the People Society, which worked for the freedom movement as well as for social reform movement in the country.

In 1928, the British Government decided to send the Simon Commission to India to discuss constitutional reforms. The Commission had no Indian member. This greatly angered Indians. In 1929, when the Commission came to India, there were protests all over India. Lala Lajpat Rai himself led one such procession against the Simon Commission. While the procession was peaceful, the British Government brutally lathicharged the procession. Lala Lajpat Rai received severe head injuries and died on November 17, 1928.

Larry Page

(1973)

Computer Scientist

"If you're changing the world, you're working on important things. You're excited to get up in the morning."

Lawrence Larry Page is an American computer scientist and Internet entrepreneur who is the co-founder of Google, alongside Sergey Brin.

Page is the inventor of PageRank, the foundation of Google's search ranking algorithm, and he and Brin own approximately 16 percent of Google's stock.

Larry Page was born on 26th March 1973 in East Lansing, Michigan. Both his parents were experts in computers and following his parents line of interest, Page graduated from the University of Michigan with Bachelor of Science in computer engineering and Master of Science from Stanford University. He was interested in computers from an early age and he wanted to start his own company from age 12. He was the first child in his school to do an assignment on word processor. It was during his time in Stanford when the first seeds of this brilliant thought were planted.

After he entered the PhD program, he had to decide on a dissertation theme. This was when he came up with the idea that would link together web pages, like a citation links to a reference. He was joined with college friend and fellow PhD student Sergey Brin, who found this topic to be very appealing. The project was initially named 'Backrub'. Both started working on this huge task of building a crawler that would convert backlink data into a degree of how important a web page was. Consequently, PageRank algorithm was created that made the duo realize that they could make a search engine far greater to the ones that were currently in use. The first version of Google came out in 1996 and it is still available on the Stanford University's website.

Google Inc. was founded in 1998 with Larry Page and Sergey Brin as co-presidents. Its initial domain name was 'Googol' which was derived from a number that is 'one followed by hundred zeros.' This represented the vast amount of data that the search engine was intended to explore. They stated their mission as 'to organize the world's information and make it universally accessible and useful'. With a humble beginning from Page's garage the company expanded to own few offices in California in 1999 and then an entire complex called 'Googleplex', that is of the most extraordinary workplaces of the world comprising of amazing recreational and exercising facilities. By 2001 Google was growing with a fiery speediness and making big profits. The company's first public offering was $1.67 billion which gave it a market capitalization of $23 billion. Page became a multi billionaire at just 27. As a favorite of shareholders, Google's stock prices rose immensely. Page received the Academy of Achievement's 'Golden Plate Award' in 2004.

By 2006, Google consisted of more than 10,000 employees with annual incomes of over ten billion dollars. Google bought several hardware and software companies out of which the most profitable was the purchase of YouTube for 1.65 billion dollars. Today, Google is one of the most used website with over a million servers worldwide. It processes more than a billion search requests every day.

Larry Page is one of the most successful entrepreneurs who laid the foundation for a venture that has changed the way, internet was used.

In 2009, Page received an honorary doctorate from the University of Michigan during graduation commencement ceremonies.

Page married Lucinda Southworth in 2007. Southworth is a research scientist, and the sister of actress and model Carrie Southworth.

In 2011, he was ranked 24th on the Forbes list of billionaires and as the 11th richest person in the United States.

As of October 2012, the Bloomberg Billionaires Index lists Page as the 27th richest man in the world with an estimated net worth of $ 21.1 billion.

On December 3, 2019, Page and Brin announced that they were stepping down from their roles as CEO and president of Alphabet, handing the reins to Pichai. However, the duo were expected to retain their influence over the company's direction as Alphabet's largest individual shareholders.

Page has an estimated net worth of $175 billion as of December 2024, according to the Bloomberg Billionaires Index, and $162.2 billion according to Forbes, making him the sixth-richest person in the world.

❑❑❑

Lata Mangeshkar

(1929-2022)

Singer

"I have been singing for the last 50 years, you know, so I deserve a break. Besides, there are talented singers around who can do justice to their work."

Lata Mangeshkar, born on September 28, 1929, in Indore, Madhya Pradesh, was one of India's most celebrated playback singers. She was the eldest of five siblings in a family deeply rooted in music. Her father, Pandit Deenanath Mangeshkar, was a classical musician and theater actor who introduced her to music at an early age. After his untimely death in 1942, Lata took on the responsibility of supporting her family and began her career as a playback singer in Marathi cinema.

Her breakthrough came in 1949 with the song *Aayega Aanewala* from "Mahal", which cemented her place in the Hindi film industry.

Over a career spanning more than seven decades, Lata lent her voice to over a thousand Hindi films and recorded songs in more than 36 Indian languages, including Marathi, Bengali, and Tamil. Her versatility and emotive singing style made her the preferred choice for generations of music composers and filmmakers. She collaborated with notable composers like S.D. Burman, R.D. Burman, Naushad, and Laxmikant-Pyarelal, delivering timeless classics such as "Pyar Kiya To Darna Kya," "Ajeeb Dastan Hai Yeh," and "Lag Ja Gale."

Lata's contribution to Indian music earned her numerous accolades. She was the recipient of three National Film Awards and multiple Filmfare Awards. In 1989, she was honoured with the Dadasaheb Phalke Award, India's highest award in cinema. The Government of India bestowed upon her the Padma Bhushan in 1969, the Padma Vibhushan in 1999, and the Bharat Ratna, India's highest civilian award, in 2001, making her the second vocalist, after M.S. Subbulakshmi, to receive this honour.

Despite her immense popularity and the adoration of millions, Lata remained unmarried throughout her life. She dedicated herself entirely to her craft and family, often stating that music was her first love. Her personal life was marked by simplicity and humility, qualities that endeared her to fans and colleagues alike.

Beyond playback singing, Lata ventured into music direction and film production. Under the pseudonym "Anand Ghan," she composed music for several Marathi films, including "Ram Ram Pavhane" (1955) and "Sadhi Manase" (1965). She also produced films like "Vaadal" (1953) and "Lekin..." (1990), the latter receiving critical acclaim for its music and storytelling.

Lata's influence extended beyond the realm of music. She was nominated as a member of the Rajya Sabha, the upper house of India's Parliament, in 1999, where she served until 2005. Her tenure was marked by her commitment to cultural and social issues, reflecting her deep connection to India's artistic heritage.

On January 8, 2022, Lata Mangeshkar was admitted to Mumbai's Breach Candy Hospital after testing positive for COVID-19. Despite medical efforts, she passed away on February 6, 2022, at the age of 92. Her death marked the end of an era in Indian music, and she was accorded a state funeral, with two days of national mourning declared in her honour. Lata Mangeshkar's legacy as the "Nightingale of India" remains unparalleled.

❑❑❑

Leander Paes

(1973)

Tennis Player

"Life is a lot like tennis. You need to put your goals on the sidelines and focus on how to deal with what's at hand."

Leander Adrian Paes is one of the most successful Indian tennis players on the men's doubles and mixed doubles circuits. Partnering with Martin Damm, he won US Open Men's Doubles championship in September 2006.

Leander Paes was born in Goa on June 17, 1973 and brought up in Kolkata (then Calcutta). His mother, Jennifer Paes, was a renowned basketball player and captain of the Indian team in the 1980 Asian Basketball Championships. His father, Vece Paes, was a hockey midfielder representing the Indian team in the 1972 Munich Olympics that won the Bronze medal.That medal had always inspired him, and he had dreamed that he would win an Olympic medal for himself one day. As he stood on the podium at the Stone Mountain Park in Atlanta, having won a Bronze in the Tennis singles event of the 1996 Olympics, his eyes went moist, thinking of his father's medal. An Indian had won an individual medal at the Olympics after 44 years.

He joined the Britannia Tennis Academy in Madras (now known as Chennai) in 1985 where he was coached by Dave O'Meara. Leander shot into international fame when he won the 1990 Wimbledon Junior title and rose to No.1 in the junior world-rankings.

Paes' was a wild card entry in the men's singles at Atlanta.

He teamed up with Mahesh Bhupathi to form the Indian doubles team and the duo in 1999, showed their class by winning the French Open and Wimbledon, and entering the finals of the two other Grand Slam Tournaments; the Australian and US Open. But the dream team separated soon after, due to mutual misunderstanding.

They came together again in time for the Sydney Olympics and started regaining their lost prestige at the end of 2000, winning the Men's Double title in Japan Open 2000 followed by World's Doubles Championship in Bangalore, Verizon Atlanta Challenge, US Clay court Championship in Houston. He ranked no. 2 in the world. In 15th Asian Games, 2006 at Doha the duo won a gold.

Paes has maintained his doubles ranking in the top 20 in the world between 2005 and 2007. With wins in the Rotterdam and ATP Masters Series in Indian Wells, he has taken his doubles tally to 38, as of May 2007. In 2007, Leander has 3 wins (2 Doubles 1 singles) and no losses in the Davis Cup. Later in 2008, with Cara Black, he won the 2008 US Open Mixed Doubles title. In 2009, he won the French Open and US Open Men's Doubles titles with Lukas Dlouhy, and was the runner-up in the Mixed Doubles final of the US Open. In 2010 he won the Australian Open Mixed doubles title with Cara Black.

Paes was a joint winner of India's highest sporting honour, the Rajiv Gandhi Khel Ratna Award in the year 1996–1997 along with Nameirakpam Kunjarani. In 2001, he was awarded the Padmashree.

The duo of Leander Paes and Mahesh Bhupati reunited to play a Grand Slam tournament after 9 years and claimed runners-up in the 2011 Australian Open. Paes completed the career Grand Slam in men's doubles after winning the Australian Open in 2012. He also won the 2013 US Open men's doubles with Radek Stepanek defeating Alexander Peya and Bruno Soares 6-1, 6-3. This is Paes' 3rd US Open men's doubles title and 14th Grand Slam title.

Leander Paes has proved to be a genius in the world of sports and it has been proved time and again. Having chalked out a name for himself and also being a multi millionaire, he has many things in store to look forward to. Paes won the 2014 Malaysian Open Men's doubles with Marcin Matkowski. On 1 February, Paes captured his seventh Grand Slam mixed doubles crown at the 2015 Australian Open with Martina Hingis. It was his 15th major crown overall and his third mixed doubles triumph at Melbourne Park. At Wimbledon 2015, Paes teamed up with Martina Hingis to win the mixed doubles championship.

On September 12, 2015, Paes won the mixed doubles at the 2015 US Open partnering Martina Hingis, defeating Sam Querrey and Bethanie Mattek-Sands in three sets. On June 3, 2016, Paes completed his Career Grand Slam in mixed doubles tennis by winning the 2016 French Open with Martina Hingis, thus joining an elite league of players to do so. He also broke Owen Davidson's record for most such titles in gentlemen's section. In 2017, Paes with Scott Lipsky won the Tallahassee challenger title.

Paes retired from professional tennis in 2020, following his last Davis Cup tie in Croatia, with a world record 1295 weeks spent ranked in the Top 100 in men's doubles. On July 20, 2024, he was inducted into the International Tennis Hall of Fame in Newport, Rhode Island.

Leo Tolstoy

(1828–1910)

Philosopher & Author

"Art is not a handicraft, it is the transmission of feeling, the artist has experienced."

Leo Tolstoy, whose full name was the most unwieldy Count Lev Nikolayevich, was a Russian author, novelist, philosopher, Christian anarchist, pacifist, educational reformer, moral thinker and an influential member of the Tolstoy family.

Tolstoy is widely regarded as one of the greatest of all novelists, particularly noted for his masterpieces, *War and Peace* and *Anna Karenina*; in their scope, breadth and realistic depiction of Russian life, the two books stand at the peak of realistic fiction. As a moral philosopher, he was notable for his ideas on non-violent resistance through his work, *The Kingdom of God is Within You*, which in turn influenced such twentieth-century figures as Mahatma Gandhi and Martin Luther King, Jr.

Lev Nikolaevich Tolstoy was born at Yasnaya Polyana, the Tolstoy family estate, a hundred miles south of Moscow on August 28, 1828.

He was the fourth of five children. The Tolstoys were a well-known family of the old Russian nobility. His mother was born a Princess Volkonsky, while his grandmothers came from the Troubetzkoy and Gorchakov princely families. Tolstoy was connected to the grandest families of Russian aristocracy; Alexander Pushkin was his fourth cousin. His parents died when he was a child, and he was brought up by relatives.

His childhood and boyhood were passed between Moscow and Yasnaya Polyana, in a large family of three brothers and a sister. Leo Tolstoy studied languages and law at Kazan University for three years. But he never took a degree. Dissatisfied with the standard of education, he returned in the middle of his studies back to Yasnaya Polyana, and then spent much of his time in Moscow and St. Petersburg.

In 1847, Tolstoy was treated for venereal disease. After contracting heavy gambling debts, he accompanied in 1851 his elder brother Nikolay to the Caucasus, and joined an artillery regiment. In the 1850s Tolstoy also began his literary career, publishing the autobiographical trilogy, *Childhood* (1852), *Boyhood* (1854), and *Youth* (1857).

During the Crimean War, he commanded a battery, witnessing the siege of Sebastopol (1854–55). In 1857, he visited France, Switzerland, and Germany. After his travels, Tolstoy settled in Yasnaja Polyana, where he started a school for peasant children. He investigated during 1860-61, further travels to Europe, the educational theory and practice, and published magazines and textbooks on the subject. In 1862, he married Sonya Andreyevna Bers (or Behrs).

Between the years, 1865 and 1869 appeared Tolstoy's major work, *War and Peace*, an epic tale depicting the story of five families against the background of Napoleon's invasion of Russia. Tolstoy's other masterpiece, *Anna Karenina* (1873–77), told a tragical story of a married woman, who follows her lover, but finally at a train station, throws herself in front of an incoming train.

In the 1880s, Tolstoy wrote such philosophical works as *A Confession*, and *What I Believe*, which was banned in 1884. He gave up his estate to his family, and attempted to live as a poor, celibate peasant. Attracted by Tolstoy's writings, Yasnaya Polyana was visited by hundreds of people from all over the world. In 1901, the Russian Orthodox Church excommunicated him.

Tolstoy died of pneumonia on November 7, 1910 at a remote railway junction after leaving his estate on the urge to live as a wandering ascetic. His collected works, which were published in Soviet Union, consists of 90 volumes.

A letter Tolstoy wrote in 1908 to an Indian newspaper entitled *Letter to a Hindu* resulted in intense correspondence with Mahatma Gandhi, who was in South Africa at the time and was beginning to become an activist. Reading *The Kingdom of God is Within You* had convinced Gandhi to abandon violence and espouse non-violent resistance, a debt Gandhi acknowledged in his autobiography, calling Tolstoy, "the greatest apostle of non-violence that the present age has produced". The correspondence between Tolstoy and Gandhi lasted only for a year, from October 1909 until Tolstoy's death in November 1910, but led Gandhi to give the name, the Tolstoy Colony to his second *ashram* in South Africa. Besides non-violent resistance, the two men shared a common belief in the merits of vegetarianism, the subject of several of Tolstoy's essays.

Leonardo Da Vinci

(1452–1519)

Artist

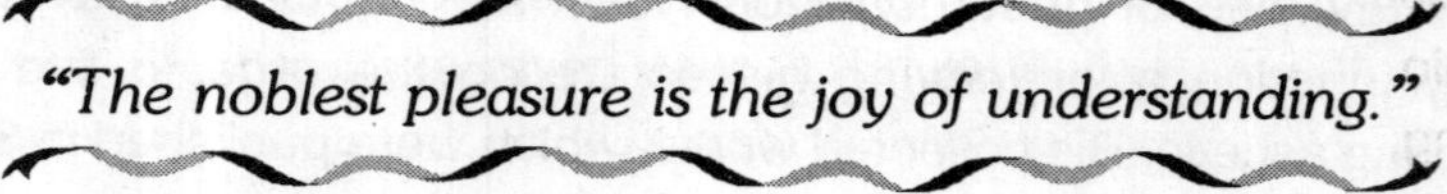

"The noblest pleasure is the joy of understanding."

Leonardo Da Vinci was an Italian Renaissance architect, musician, anatomist, inventor, engineer, sculptor, geometre, and painter. Leonardo is famous for his masterly paintings, such as *The Last Supper* and *Mona Lisa*. He is also known for designing many inventions that anticipated modern technology but were rarely constructed in his lifetime.

Leonardo was born on April 15, 1452, in the small town of Vinci, near Florence, in Tuscany. He was the son of a wealthy Florentine notary and a peasant woman. In the mid-1460s, the family settled in Florence, where Leonardo was given the best education that Florence, a major intellectual and artistic centre of Italy, could offer. He rapidly advanced socially and intellectually. He was handsome, persuasive in conversation, and a fine musician and improviser.

In about 1466, he was apprenticed as a garzone (studio boy) to Andrea del Verrocchio, the leading Florentine painter and sculptor of his days. In Verrocchio's workshop, Leonardo was introduced to many activities, from the painting of altarpieces and panel pictures to the creation of large sculptural projects in marble and bronze.

In 1472, he was admitted to the painters' guild of Florence, and in 1476, he was still considered Verrocchio's assistant. In Verrocchio's Baptism of Christ (c. 1470, Uffizi, Florence), the kneeling angel in the left of the painting is by Leonardo.

In 1478, Leonardo became an independent master. His first commission, to paint an altarpiece for the chapel of the Palazzo Vecchio, the Florentine town hall, was never executed. His first large painting, *The Adoration of the Magi* (Uffizi), begun in 1481 and left unfinished, was ordered for the monastery of San Donato a Scopeto, Florence. Other works ascribed to his youth are the so-called – *Benois Madonna* (c. 1478, Hermitage, St Petersburg), the portrait, *Ginevra de' Benci* (c. 1474, National Gallery, Washington, D.C.), and the unfinished, *St Jerome* (c. 1481, Pinacoteca, Vatican).

In about 1482, Leonardo entered the service of Ludovico Sforza, Duke of Milan, having written the duke an astonishing letter in which he stated that he could build portable bridges; that he knew the techniques of constructing bombardments and of making cannons; that he could build ships as well as armoured vehicles, catapults, and other war machines; and that he could execute sculpture in marble, bronze, and clay. He served as the principal engineer in the duke's numerous military enterprises and was also active as an architect. During his long stay in Milan, Leonardo produced various paintings and drawings most of which are now lost, theatre designs, architectural drawings, and models for the dome of Milan Cathedral. His largest commission was for a colossal bronze equestrian statue of Francesco Sforza, father of Ludovico, for the courtyard of Castello Sforzesco. In December 1499, however, the Sforza family was driven from Milan by French forces. Leonardo had made the clay model but contingency dictated that the metal intended for the statue be used for cannon instead. The model was destroyed by French archers, who used it as a target. Leonardo returned to Florence in 1500.

In 1502, he entered the service of Cesare Borgia, Duke of Romagna and son and chief general of Pope Alexander VI. In his capacity as the duke's chief architect and engineer, Leonardo supervised work on the fortresses of the papal territories in central Italy. In 1503, he was a member of a commission of artists who were to decide on the proper location for Michelangelo's statue of David (1501-1504, Accademia, Florence), and he also served as an engineer in the war against Pisa. Towards the end of the year, Leonardo began to design a decoration for the great hall of the Palazzo Vecchio. The subject was the Battle of Anghiari, a Florentine victory in the war with Pisa. He made many drawings for it and completed a full-size cartoon, in 1505, but he never finished the wall painting. The cartoon itself was destroyed in the 17th century, and the composition survives only in copies, of which the most famous (c. 1615, Louvre) is the one by Peter Paul Rubens.

During this second Florentine period, Leonardo painted several portraits, but the only one that survives is the famous Mona Lisa (1503–1506, Louvre), one of the most celebrated portraits ever painted. It is also known as La Gioconda, after the presumed name of the woman's husband. Leonardo seems to have had a special affection for the picture, for he took it with him on all his subsequent travels.

Leonardo's stylistic innovations are even more apparent in *The Last Supper*, in which he re-created a traditional theme in an entirely new way. Instead of showing the 12 apostles as individual figures, he grouped them in dynamic compositional units of three, framing the figure of Christ, who is isolated in the centre of the picture. Seated before a pale, distant landscape seen through a rectangular opening in the wall, Christ—who is about to announce that one of those present will betray him—represents a calm nucleus while the others respond with animated gestures. In the monumentality of the scene and the weightiness of the figures, Leonardo reintroduced a style pioneered more than a generation earlier by Masaccio.

The Mona Lisa, Leonardo's most famous work, is as well-known for its mastery of technical innovations as for the mysteriousness of its legendary smiling subject. This work is a consummate example of two techniques—*sfumato* and *chiaroscuro*—of which Leonardo was one of the first great masters. *Sfumato* (smoked) is a delicately atmospheric haze or smoky effect produced by subtle, almost infinitesimal transitions between areas of colour, especially evident in the delicate gauzy robes worn by the sitter and in her enigmatic smile. Chiaroscuro (light and dark) is the technique of modelling and defining forms by means of contrasts between light and shadow; the sensitive hands of the sitter are portrayed with a luminous modulation of light and shade, while colour contrast is used only sparingly.

Leonardo actually anticipated many discoveries of modern times. In anatomy, he studied the circulation of the blood and the action of the eye. He made discoveries in meteorology and geology, understood the effect of the Moon on the tides, foreshadowed modern conceptions of continent formation, and surmised the origin of fossilised shells. He was among the originators of the science of hydraulics and probably, devised the hydrometer. His scheme for the canalisation of rivers still has practical value. Leonardo invented a large number of ingenious machines, many potentially useful, such as an underwater diving suit and a model of flying devices.

❑❑❑

Lionel Messi

(1987)

Football Player

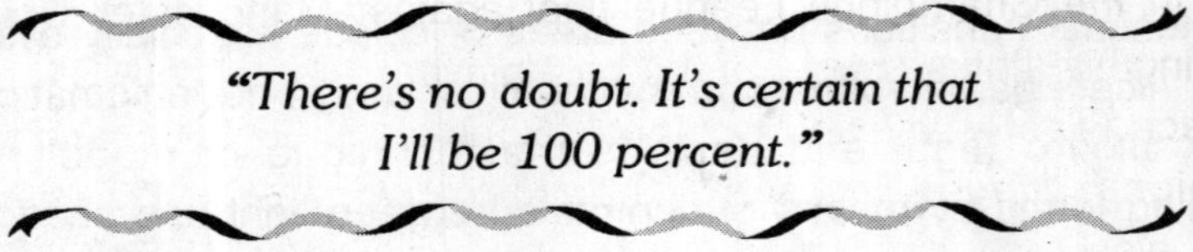

"There's no doubt. It's certain that I'll be 100 percent."

Lionel Andrés Messi was born on June 24, 1987, in Rosario, Argentina. From a young age, his love for football was evident. He played for his local club, Grandoli, coached by his father, before joining Newell's Old Boys, where he became part of the famous "Machine of '87," a youth team known for its dominance. However, at the age of eleven, Messi was diagnosed with growth hormone deficiency, a condition that threatened his football career. Treatment was expensive, and while several Argentine clubs recognised his talent, none were willing to cover the costs.

In 2000, FC Barcelona offered Messi a trial, and after seeing his exceptional skills, the club agreed to pay for his medical treatment. At thirteen, Messi moved to Spain and joined La Masia, Barcelona's renowned youth academy. His technical ability and dribbling made him stand out despite his small stature. In 2003, at just sixteen, he made his first-team debut in a friendly match against Porto. The following year, he played his first official La Liga match, and in 2005, he scored his first goal for the club, assisted by Ronaldinho.

Messi's rise to superstardom accelerated under coach Pep Guardiola in 2008. He inherited the number 10 jersey from Ronaldinho and led Barcelona to an era of dominance. In the 2008-09 season, Messi played a crucial role in Barcelona's historic treble, winning La Liga, Copa del Rey, and the UEFA Champions League. He scored in the Champions League final against Manchester United, confirming his status as one of the best players in the world. Over the next decade, Messi led Barcelona to ten La Liga titles and four Champions League victories, breaking numerous goal-scoring records along the way.

Individually, Messi won a record eight Ballon d'Or awards, making him the most decorated player in history. He became Barcelona's all-time top scorer and the highest goal-scorer in La Liga history. His dribbling, goal-scoring, and playmaking abilities made him one of the greatest footballers ever. However, despite his club success, international glory eluded him for years.

Messi suffered heartbreak in the 2014 FIFA World Cup final against Germany and lost three Copa América finals. Many doubted whether he could ever win a major trophy with Argentina. That changed in 2021 when Argentina won the Copa América, defeating Brazil in the final. Messi was the best player of the tournament, finishing as the top scorer and assist provider. It was a defining moment in his career.

In 2021, Messi left Barcelona due to financial constraints and joined Paris Saint-Germain, where he won two Ligue 1 titles. However, his greatest achievement came in 2022 when he led Argentina to FIFA World Cup victory. In an unforgettable final against France, Messi scored twice and converted his penalty in the shootout. Argentina won, and Messi lifted the World Cup trophy, completing his legacy as the greatest footballer of all time.

In 2023, Messi moved to Inter Miami in Major League Soccer, winning the Leagues Cup and earning the MLS MVP award. As of 2025, he remains active in football, preparing for Copa América 2024. His journey from a small boy in Rosario to the world's greatest footballer is one of resilience and determination. His impact on football is unmatched, and he will always be remembered as a true legend of the game.

❑❑❑

Leonardo DiCaprio

(1974)

Actor, Producer, and Environmental Activist

"If you can do what you do best and be happy, you're further along in life than most people."

Leonardo Wilhelm DiCaprio, born on November 11, 1974, in Los Angeles, California, is an iconic American actor, producer, and environmental activist who has been a fixture in the entertainment industry for decades. The only child of Irmelin, a legal secretary of German descent, and George DiCaprio, a writer, publisher, and distributor of comic books, DiCaprio was exposed to a wide range of creative influences from a young age. His parents' unconventional and artistic lifestyle played a significant role in shaping his worldview and career.

Raised in a modest household, DiCaprio's early years were marked by frequent moves. His parents separated when he was only a year old, and he was raised primarily by his mother in the Los Angeles area. Despite their modest means, Irmelin worked hard to support him and provided him with a strong foundation that encouraged intellectual curiosity and a love for the arts. DiCaprio was passionate about acting from a young age and often participated in school plays, but his path to stardom was not straightforward. Initially, DiCaprio's interests were focused on other areas, including a brief passion for skateboarding and later for soccer and basketball.

By the time DiCaprio was a teenager, he had decided to pursue acting seriously. He attended the Los Angeles Center for Enriched Studies and later enrolled in the prestigious Hollywood High School, where he took part in numerous school plays. Eventually, he joined the LA Youth Theater, where he honed his craft. His first major break came when he was cast in the television series Parenthood in 1990. Although it was a small role, it proved to be a significant stepping stone that helped him land further roles in television. He appeared in several other series, including *The Outsiders* and *Santa Barbara*, but it was his performance in *This Boy's Life* (1993) that garnered him major attention.

Directed by Michael Caton-Jones, *This Boy's Life* was a breakout film for DiCaprio, in which he starred alongside Robert De Niro. His portrayal of a troubled teen facing emotional abuse from his stepfather showcased his immense talent and depth. However, it was his role in *What's Eating Gilbert Grape* (1993) that earned him his first major award nominations. Playing Arnie Grape, a mentally challenged young man, DiCaprio's performance was widely praised, and he received an Academy Award nomination for Best Supporting Actor at the age of 19, cementing his reputation as a gifted actor.

Following his success in *Gilbert Grape*, DiCaprio became one of Hollywood's most sought-after young actors. He continued to prove his versatility with roles in *Romeo + Juliet* (1996), where he played the iconic Shakespearean character in Baz Luhrmann's modernized version of the classic, and *Titanic* (1997), directed by James Cameron. DiCaprio's portrayal of Jack Dawson in *Titanic* turned him into a global superstar. The film was a massive commercial success, becoming the highest-grossing film of all time at the time, and

DiCaprio's character became a beloved figure. His chemistry with co-star Kate Winslet, combined with his raw charm and emotional depth, made the film an unforgettable cultural phenomenon.

Following the success of *Titanic*, DiCaprio took a step back from leading roles in romantic dramas, choosing to focus on more challenging and diverse roles. He worked with renowned directors such as Martin Scorsese, with whom he would form a longstanding collaboration. In films like *Gangs of New York* (2002), *The Aviator* (2004), and *The Departed* (2006), DiCaprio exhibited his range by playing complex, multifaceted characters. His portrayal of Howard Hughes in *The Aviator* earned him his second Academy Award nomination, this time for Best Actor, and his work in *The Departed* helped the film win Best Picture at the Oscars.

DiCaprio continued to challenge himself with roles in films like *Blood Diamond* (2006), where he portrayed a mercenary in war-torn Africa, and *Shutter Island* (2010), a psychological thriller directed by Scorsese. Both films earned him praise for his performances, though he was still pursuing that elusive Academy Award for Best Actor.

Finally, in 2016, DiCaprio won the Academy Award for Best Actor for his gripping portrayal of frontiersman Hugh Glass in *The Revenant*, directed by Alejandro González Iñárritu. The film was noted for its brutal portrayal of survival and DiCaprio's commitment to the physically demanding role, which involved extensive outdoor work in harsh conditions. His victory at the 88th Academy Awards was celebrated by his fans, who had long felt he deserved the recognition for his work. The win solidified his place as one of the finest actors of his generation.

Beyond acting, DiCaprio has used his platform to advocate for environmental causes. In 1998, he founded the Leonardo DiCaprio Foundation, which is dedicated to environmental issues, including climate change, biodiversity, and ocean conservation. He has produced several environmental documentaries, including *The 11th Hour* (2007) and *Before the Flood* (2016), both of which highlight the urgency of addressing climate change. In 2014, DiCaprio was appointed as a United Nations Messenger of Peace for Climate Change.

In his personal life, DiCaprio has been the subject of much media attention, particularly for his relationships with various supermodels. Despite being linked to several high-profile women, he has never been married and has often spoken about his focus on his career and activism. DiCaprio remains one of the highest-paid actors in Hollywood, consistently working with top directors and producing critically acclaimed films.

Throughout his career, DiCaprio has been nominated for and received countless awards. He has won multiple Golden Globe Awards, a BAFTA Award, and the coveted Academy Award for Best Actor. His films have grossed billions of dollars worldwide, making him one of the most commercially successful actors in history.

❑❑❑

Louis Pasteur

(1822–1895)

Chemist and Microbiologist

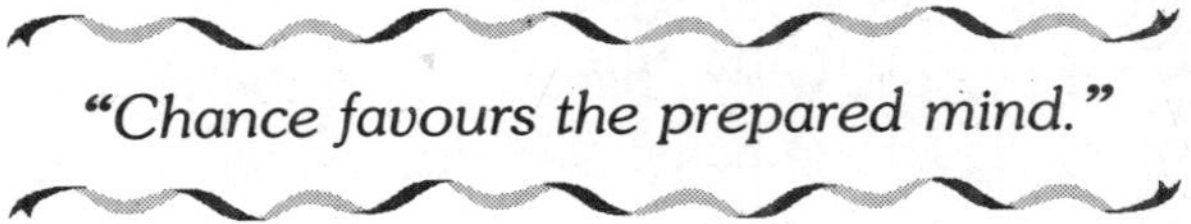

"Chance favours the prepared mind."

French Chemist and Microbiologist Dr. Louis Pasteur discovered that microbes were responsible for souring alcohol and came up with the process of pasteurization, where bacteria is destroyed by heating beverages and then allowing them to cool. His work in germ theory also led him and his team to create vaccinations for anthrax and rabies.

Louis Pasteur was born on December 27, 1822, in Dole, located in the Jura region of France. He grew up in the town of Arbois and his father, Jean-Joseph Pasteur, was a tanner and a sergeant major decorated with the Legion of Honour during the Napoleonic Wars. An average student, Pasteur was skilled at drawing and painting. He earned his Bachelor of Arts degree (1840), Bachelor of Science degree (1842) and a doctorate (1847) at the École Normale in Paris.

Pasteur then spent several years researching and teaching at Dijon Lycée. In 1848, he became a professor of chemistry at the

University of Strasbourg, where he met Marie Laurent, the daughter of the university's rector. They wed on May 29, 1849, and had five children, though only two survived childhood.

In 1854, Pasteur was appointed professor of chemistry and dean of the science faculty at the University of Lille. Here, he worked on finding solutions to the problems with the manufacture of alcoholic drinks. Working with the germ theory, which Pasteur did not invent, but further developed through experiments and eventually convinced most of Europe of its truth, he demonstrated that organisms such as bacteria were responsible for souring wine, beer and even milk. He then invented a process where bacteria could be removed by boiling and then cooling liquid. He completed the first test on April 20, 1862. Today the process is known as pasteurization.

In 1865, Pasteur helped save the silk industry. He proved that microbes were attacking healthy silkworm eggs, causing the disease and that the disease would be eliminated if the microbes were eliminated.

Pasteur's first vaccine discovery was in 1879, with a disease called chicken cholera. After accidentally exposing chickens to the attenuated form of a culture, he demonstrated that they became resistant to the actual virus. Pasteur went on to extend his germ theory to develop causes and vaccinations for diseases such as anthrax, cholera, TB and smallpox.

In 1873, Pasteur was elected as an associate member of the Académie de Médecine. In 1882, the year of his acceptance into the Académie Franaise, he decided to focus his efforts on the problem of rabies. On July 6, 1885, Pasteur vaccinated Joseph Meister, a 9-year-old boy who had been bitten by a rabid dog. The success of Pasteur's vaccine brought him immediate fame. This began an international fundraising campaign to build the Pasteur Institute in Paris, which was inaugurated on November 14, 1888.

Pasteur had been partially paralyzed since 1868, due to a severe brain stroke, but he was able to continue his research. He celebrated his 70th birthday at the Sorbonne, which was attended by several prominent scientists, including British surgeon Joseph Lister. At that time, his paralysis worsened, and he died on September 28, 1895. Pasteur's remains were transferred to a Neo-Byzantine crypt at the Pasteur Institute in 1896.

Louis Pasteur was a great believer in hard work, never content to rest on his laurels he continued to work very hard in his laboratory to develop more cures. He said in advice to other scientists.

"An individual who gets used to hard work can thereafter never live without it. Work is the foundation of everything in this world."

Louis Pasteur had great faith in the good nature of humans. He worked tirelessly to deliver real benefits for the treatment of infectious diseases. More than any other person, Louis Pasteur helped to increase the life expectancy of man in the late nineteenth and early twentieth Century.

❑❑❑

Ludwig Van Beethoven

(1770–1827)

Composer, Pisnist

"Nothing is more intolerable than to have to admit to yourself your own errors."

Ludwig Van Beethoven is considered to be one of the best classical composers in history. He is known for creating his huge symphonies. He created 9 symphonies, not as prolific as Mozart or Haydn, but the quality of these symphonies are beyond belief.

Beethoven was born on December 17, 1770 in Bonn, Germany to Johann Van Beethoven, of Flemish origins, and Magdalena Keverich Van Beethoven. Until recently, December 16, was shown in many reference works as Beethoven's 'date of birth', since we know that he was baptised on December 17, and children at that time were generally baptised the day after their birth. However, modern scholarship declines to rely on such assumptions.

Beethoven's first music teacher was his father, who worked as a musician in the Electoral court at Bonn, but was also an alcoholic who beat him and unsuccessfully attempted to exhibit him as a child prodigy. However, Beethoven's talent was soon noticed by others. He was given instruction and employment by Christian Gottlob Neefe, as well as financial sponsorship by the Prince-Elector. Beethoven's mother died when he was 17, and for several years, he was responsible for raising his two younger brothers.

Beethoven moved to Vienna in 1792, where he studied with Joseph Haydn and other teachers. He quickly established a reputation as a piano virtuoso, and more slowly as a composer. He settled into the career pattern, he would follow for the remainder of his life: rather than working for the church or a noble court (as most composers before him had done). He was a freelancer, supporting himself with public performances, sales of his works, and stipends from noblemen who recognised his ability.

Beethoven's career as a composer is usually divided into Early, Middle, and Late periods.

In the Early period, he is seen as emulating his great predecessors Haydn and Mozart, at the same time exploring new directions and gradually expanding the scope and ambition of his work. Some important pieces from the Early period are the first and second symphonies, the first six string quartets, the first two piano concertos, and about a dozen piano sonatas, including the famous, *Pathetique*.

The Middle period began shortly after Beethoven's personal crisis centreing around deafness, and is noted for large-scale works expressing heroism and struggle which include many of the most famous works of classical music. The Middle period works include six symphonies (Nos. 3 – 8), the last three piano concertos and his only violin concerto, six string quartets (Nos. 7 – 11), many piano sonatas (including the *Moonlight*, *Waldstein*, and *Appassionata*), and Beethoven's only opera, *Fidelio*.

Beethoven's Late period began around 1816 and lasted until he ceased to compose in 1826. The late works are greatly admired for their intellectual depth and their intense, highly personal expression. They include the Ninth Symphony (the *Choral*), the *Missa Solemnis*, the last six string quartets and the last five piano sonatas.

Beethoven's personal life was troubled. Around the age of 28, he started to become deaf, a calamity which led him for some time to contemplate suicide. He was attracted to unattainable (married or aristocratic) women, whom he idealised but never married. A period of low productivity from about 1812 to 1816 is thought by some scholars to have been the result of depression, resulting from Beethoven's realisation that he would never marry. Beethoven quarrelled, often bitterly, with his relatives and others, and frequently behaved badly with other people. He moved often from dwelling to dwelling, and had strange personal habits such as wearing filthy clothing while washing compulsively. He often had financial troubles.

It is common for listeners to perceive an echo of Beethoven's life in his music, which often depicts struggle followed by triumph. This description is often applied to Beethoven's creation of masterpieces in the face of his severe personal difficulties.

He was often in poor health, and in 1826 his health took a drastic turn for the worse. Beethoven died in around 1827 of liver disease.

❑❑❑

M.F. Hussain

(1915–2011)

Painter

"I only give expression to the instincts from my soul."

Maqbool Fida Hussain, popularly known as M.F. Hussain, was a well known Indian artist. Famous for his stunning paintings of Indian women, and his habit of getting into controversies, he was also a multi-faceted person, having made movies, and served in India's Parliament.

Hussain was born on September 17, 1915 in Pandharpur, Maharashtra. He lost his mother when he was one and a half year old. After his mother's death, his father remarried and moved to Indore, where Hussain started his studies.

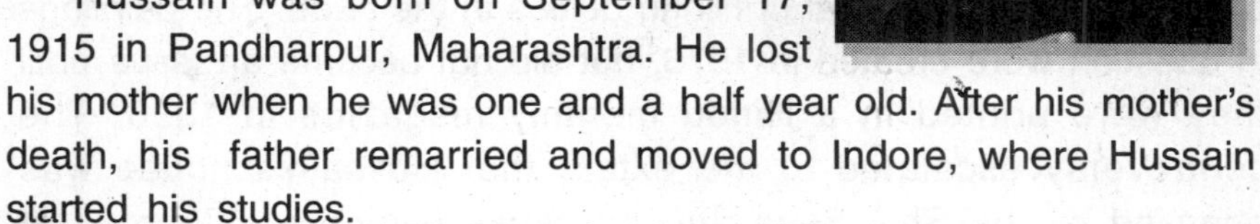

In 1935, he moved to Mumbai (then Bombay) and was admitted to the Sir J. J. School of Art. He started off by painting cinema hoardings. He became well-known as an artist in the late 1940s.

In 1947, Hussain joined the Progressive Artists Group, founded by Francis Newton Souza. This was a clique of young artists who wished to break with the nationalist traditions established by the Bengal school of art and to encourage an Indian avant-garde, engaged at an international level. In 1952, his first solo exhibition was held at Zurich and over the next few years, his work was widely seen in Europe and USA. He went on to become one of the highest paid painters in India. His paintings have fetched millions of dollars at the auction.

In 1966, M.F. Hussain was awarded the prestigious Padmashree prize by the Government of India. He has also been awarded the Padma Bhushan. In the following year, he made his first film, *Through the Eyes of a Painter*. It was shown at the Berlin Film Festival and won a 'Golden Bear'.

Hussain went on to become the highest paid painter in India. His single canvases fetched up to 2 million dollars at a Christie's Auction. In recognition of his distinction, he was appointed to a term in the Rajya Sabha, the Upper House of India's Parliament.

He also worked (produced and directed) on few movies, including *Gaja Gamini* (with his muse, Madhuri Dixit who was the subject of a series of his paintings which he signed 'Fida') and *Meenaxi: A Tale of Three Cities* (with Tabu). His autobiography is being made into a movie tentatively titled, *The Making of the Painter* starring Shreyas Talpade as the young Hussain.

In the 1990s, some of Hussain's works became controversial because of their portrayal of Hindu deities in the nude. The paintings in question were created in 1970, but did not become an issue until they were printed in a Hindu monthly magazine in 1996. The controversy escalated to the extent that Hussain's house was attacked by the Shiv Sena and art works destroyed. Charges of "promoting enmity between different groups ... by painting Hindu Goddesses — Durga and Saraswati — in an uncharitable manner hurting the sentiments of Hindus", had been dismissed by the Delhi High Court in 2004. However, in February 2006, Hussain was charged with hurting sentiments of people because of his nude portraits of

Hindu Gods and Goddesses. A series of cases were brought against him and a court case resulted in issuing a non-bailable warrant against him after he failed to respond to summons. There were also reportedly death threats.

The artist left the country stating that "matters are so legally complicated that I have been advised not to return home." Living in Dubai and London, he continued to stay away from India, but expressed a strong desire to return, despite fears that he may be arrested in connection with these cases. A Supreme Court order suspended an arrest warrant for Hussain. The law ministry examined half-a-dozen works by him and told the government that prosecutors would have a strong case against him if they sued him for deliberately hurting religious feelings.

In February 2010 the Indian Picasso was offered, Qatar Citizenship, which he accepted. He surrendered his Indian passport at mission in Doha on March 8, 2010. He died on June 9, 2011. He was burried at Brookwood Cemetery in Working Surrey, South of London.

❑❑❑

(Dr.) M.S. Swaminathan

(1925-2023)

Agricultural Scientist

"The scientific community is very clear that this is not going to disrupt science or the morale of scientists."

Mankombu Sambasivan Swaminathan, widely known as M. S. Swaminathan, was born on August 7, 1925, in Kumbakonam, Tamil Nadu, India. Raised in a family that valued education and social service, he was deeply influenced by his father, a surgeon and a strong advocate for social reforms. Although he initially aspired to join the Indian Civil Services, the devastating Bengal Famine of 1943 changed his path. Witnessing the widespread hunger and suffering, he decided to dedicate his life to agricultural science and food security in India.

Swaminathan pursued agricultural sciences at the University of Madras and later specialised in genetics and plant breeding at the Indian Agricultural Research Institute (IARI) in New Delhi. He furthered his studies at the University of Cambridge and the University of Wisconsin-Madison, where he deepened his understanding of plant genetics. Armed with this knowledge, he returned to India, determined to transform the country's agricultural landscape.

By the 1960s, India was grappling with severe food shortages and a rapidly growing population. Famine was a major concern, and the country was heavily dependent on food imports. At this critical moment, Swaminathan, in collaboration with Norman Borlaug, introduced high-yielding varieties (HYVs) of wheat and rice to India. By integrating these crops with modern agricultural techniques, fertilisers, irrigation, and pest control, Swaminathan played a crucial role in the Green Revolution, which drastically increased food production. This transformation helped India achieve self-sufficiency in food grains and significantly reduced hunger.

Swaminathan's impact extended beyond scientific research. As the Director of the Indian Agricultural Research Institute (IARI) and later as the Director General of the Indian Council of Agricultural Research (ICAR), he played a key role in shaping agricultural policies that strengthened food security in India. His groundbreaking work earned him India's highest civilian honours, including the Padma Shri (1967), Padma Bhushan (1972), and Padma Vibhushan (1989).

His contributions were recognised on the global stage as well. Swaminathan served as the Director General of the International Rice Research Institute (IRRI) in the Philippines and worked closely with organisations like the United Nations and the Food and Agriculture Organisation (FAO). He strongly advocated for sustainable agriculture and biodiversity conservation, warning against the dangers of over-reliance on chemical fertilisers and pesticides.

In 1988, he established the M. S. Swaminathan Research Foundation (MSSRF), focusing on rural development, climate-resilient farming, and empowering small-scale farmers, especially women. He promoted the idea of an "Evergreen Revolution," which aimed to increase food production while preserving ecological balance.

Swaminathan received numerous international accolades, including the World Food Prize (1987) and the Ramon Magsaysay Award (1971), further cementing his reputation as one of the world's most influential agricultural scientists.

On September 28, 2023, M. S. Swaminathan passed away at the age of 98 in Chennai, India. His death marked the end of an era, but his contributions to Indian and global agriculture continue to influence policies and scientific advancements. His vision for sustainable food production and rural empowerment remains a guiding force for future generations.

By 2025, his legacy endures through the countless lives he impacted. His pioneering work in the Green Revolution not only saved millions from starvation but also laid the foundation for sustainable and climate-resilient farming. M. S. Swaminathan's dedication to science and humanity ensures that his dream of a hunger-free and ecologically balanced world continues to inspire the next generation of agricultural leaders.

❑❑❑

(Pt.) Madan Mohan Malaviya

(1861–1946)

Scholar and Political Leader

"I am a Hindu by faith and I mean no disrespect to any other religion."

An eminent Congressman, Malaviya was the president of the Indian National Congress during 1909 and in 1918. He represented the whole of India with Mahatma Gandhi in the First Round Table Conference in 1931.

Sir Madan Mohan Malaviya popularised the famous slogan, "Satyameva Jayate" (Truth alone will win). Malaviya founded The Banaras Hindu University, which remains as a premier institution of learning in India today.

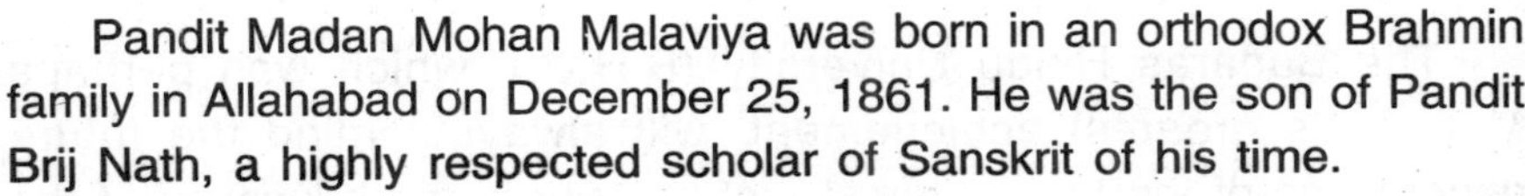

Pandit Madan Mohan Malaviya was born in an orthodox Brahmin family in Allahabad on December 25, 1861. He was the son of Pandit Brij Nath, a highly respected scholar of Sanskrit of his time.

Madan Mohan was first educated traditionally at two Sanskrit *pathshalas* and later sent to an English school. Even during his college days, as a student of the Muir Central College, Allahabad, he took keen interest in public activities. Religion and education were, however, of special interest and he dedicated himself to these till the end of his life.

After graduation in 1884, he joined the Government High School at Allahabad as an assistant master. Being in government service did not prevent him from participating in political movements and he soon joined the fold of the Indian National Congress.

His very first appearance on the Congress platform at its Calcutta session created a lasting impression and gave him a place in the political life of the country. By his earnest and untiring work, Pandit Madan Mohan Malaviya rapidly gained ascendancy in the Congress organisation. He was one of the very few individuals who were honoured by the Congress by being elected as its president three times, the first at the Lahore session (1909), the second time at Delhi (1918) and the third at Calcutta (now Kolkata) (1933).

His zeal for public work made him realise the necessity of starting newspapers, particularly in Hindi, for the education of the public. He started the *Abhyudaya* as a Hindi weekly in 1907 and made it a daily in 1915. He began the *Leader,* an English daily, on 24 October 1909. Both the *Abhyudaya* and the *Leader* rendered valuable service to the cause of national freedom for nearly half a century.

Malaviya took a keen interest in the industrial development of the country and was therefore appointed a member of the Indian Industrial Commission in 1916. He supported the demand for the grant of full Dominion Status to India put forward by Pandit Motilal Nehru.

The Banaras Hindu University (B.H.U.), which was perhaps Malaviya's greatest achievement, will always remind the future generations of the keen interest that he took in the education of the mind and the spirit. It was his deep love for Hindu culture and the spiritual ideas embodied in Hindu religious books that gave birth to the idea of establishing the Banaras Hindu University. The importance that he attached to the economic development of the country made him combine the teaching of science and technology with that of religion.

In 1928, he joined Lala Lajpat Rai, Jawaharlal Nehru and many others in protesting against the Simon Commission, which had been set up by the British to consider India's future.

With Mahatma Gandhi, he represented India at the First Round Table Conference in 1931.

Malaviya passed away in November 12, 1946. But his spirit still lives and there are many who bear the torch that he lit. Many more stand ready to shoulder the mantle of his responsibility.

Madonna

(1958)

Singer and Actress

"When I'm hungry, I eat.
When I'm thirsty, I drink.
When I feel like saying something, I say it."

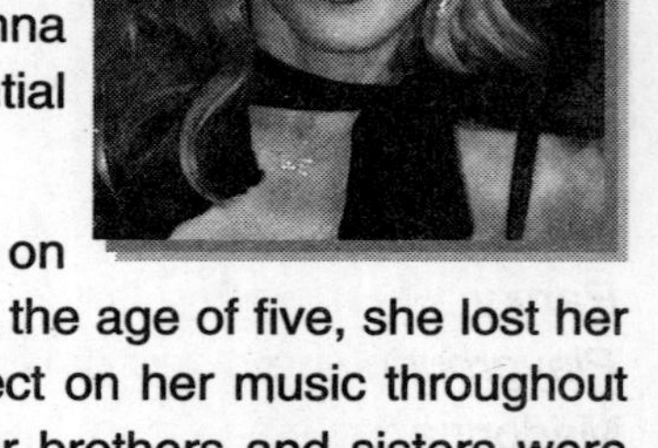

Madonna is one of the most successful artists in the history of popular music. No other female singer in music has been as successful over such a long time. Also an actress, author, activist, diva, pop cultural and fashion icon, many consider, Madonna to be one of the most iconic and influential figures of the late 20th century.

Madonna Louise Ciccone was born on August 16, 1958, in Bay City, Michigan. At the age of five, she lost her mother to breast cancer. This had an effect on her music throughout her life. After the death of her mother, her brothers and sisters were sent to live with various relatives.

When Madonna was twelve, she entered a local Catholic high school. It was there that she learnt a great deal from classes such as, tap, jazz dancing, Baton twirling and Gymnastics. After completing her schooling, she attended the University of Michigan, on a dance scholarship, where the ballet school owner, 'Chris Flynn', taught her.

Later, she arrived in New York and won a scholarship at the "Alvin Ailey Dance Theater", where she spent two years working hard at her classes while holding part-time jobs at various fast food restaurants for some extra money.

She started auditioning for theatric and musical parts. One of the auditions ended up taking her to Paris where she was backing a lead singer, Patrick Hernandez. Hernandez's management realised that Madonna had talent but refused to pay her more when she requested it, so she moved back to New York.

She joined her friend's band as a drummer but quitted soon and set out to start her own band, with her as the lead singer. She finally got a record deal with Gotham Records for $100 a week with Steve Bray as her drummer and song writer. She, eventually got a deal with *Sire Records* for $5000 and released her first single *Everybody*, which sold about 250,000 copies and was number three on the dance charts. Madonna's first album entitled *Madonna* was released in 1983 and won her millions of fans and invitations to be in movies. Her career had begun. She had many accomplishments in the year 1985 for her various albums.

On August 16, 1985, Madonna and Sean Penn were married. However, Madonna officially divorced Sean Penn on January 10, 1989 on the terms of irreconcilable differences.

In the early 1990s, Madonna gave out hit songs: *Vogue*, *Hanky Panky*, *Justify My Love, Rescue Me*, and *This Used to be My Playground* (from the soundtrack, *A League of their Own*). In 1990, Madonna co-starred in the movie, *Dick Tracy*. She also began her *Blonde Ambition*. In 1991, she starred in the film, *Truth or Dare* and had a greatest hit album entitled, *The Immaculate Collection* come out.

In 1992, Madonna signed a deal with her record company, Sire. The deal guaranteed the release of all Madonna's albums, films, and books on her own 'Maverick Production Company'. Madonna published her first book, *Sex* which sold out within hours. Her album,

Erotica, was an overall disappointment. In 1996, she played the starring role in the film *Evita* for which she won the Golden Globe Award for Best Actress.

In December 2000, she married Guy Ritchie, a British film director. In 2002, Madonna starred in Ritchie's film, *Swept Away* and sang the theme song for Bond movie, *James Bond 007: Die Another Day*. In 2003, Madonna released her hit album, *American Life*. Guinness World Records listed her as the world's most successful female recording artist of all time.

In September 2009, Madonna released *Celebration*, her third greatest hits album, and closing release with Warner Bros. In June, *Forbes* Magazine named her as the third-most-powerful celebrity of the year. Madonna appeared at the 2009 MTV Video Music Awards on September 13, 2009, to pay tribute to Michael Jackson with a speech.

Her third live album *Sticky & Sweet* was released in April 2010. In February 2011 her song a "Revolver", reauxed by David Guetta won an award at her 53rd Annual Grammy Award for "Best Remix Recording." In 2012, she was crowned the "Greatest Woman In Music" by VH1. *Forbes* magazine named Madonna the fifth most powerful and the highest earning celebrity of 2013 with net earnings of $125 million between June 2012–13.

In November 2016, Madonna, who actively supported Hillary Clinton during the 2016 U.S. presidential election, performed an impromptu acoustic concert at Washington Square Park in support of Clinton's campaign. In February 2017, Madonna adopted four-year-old twin sisters from Malawi named Esther and Stella.

Madona received the Grammy Lifetime Achievement Award at the 65th Annual Grammy Awards held in February 2023. This award honours her remarkable contributions to the music industry and her lasting impact on popular culture.

Mahendra Singh Dhoni

(1981)

Cricketer

"Cricket is a very cruel game, the moment you relax is when you are in trouble."

Padma Shri Mahendra Singh Dhoni is an Indian cricketer and the former captain of the Indian national cricket team. He made his One Day International (ODI) debut in December 2004 against Bangladesh, and a year later played his first Test, this time against Sri Lanka.

Under his captaincy, India won the 2007 ICC World Twenty20, CB Series of 2007–08, the Border-Gavaskar Trophy in 2008 and 2010 against Australia and 2011 World Cup. He also captained Chennai Super Kings to victory in 2011 IPL and in the Champions League. Under Dhoni's captaincy India became the first team after a gap of more than 20 years to whitewash Australia in a Test series. Dhoni also led the Indian team to the number one position in ICC rankings in Test cricket for the first time.

Dhoni was born on July 7, 1981 in Ranchi, Bihar (now in Jharkhand) in a Rajput family to Pan Singh and Devaki Devi. His paternal village Lvali is in the Lamgarha block of the Almora District of

Uttarakhand. Dhoni's parents, moved from Uttarakhand to Ranchi where his father worked in junior management positions in MECON. Dhoni has a sister Jayanti and a brother Narendra.

Dhoni studied at DAV Jawahar Vidya Mandir, Shyamali,(now the school is known as JVM, Shyamli, Ranchi) Ranchi, Jharkhand where he initially excelled in badminton and football and was selected at district and club level in these sports. Dhoni was a goalkeeper for his football team and was sent to play cricket for a local cricket club by his football coach. Though he had not played cricket, Dhoni impressed with his wicket-keeping skills and became the regular wicketkeeper at the Commando cricket club (1995–1998). Based on his performance at club cricket, he was picked for the 1997/98 season Vinoo Mankad Trophy Under-16 Championship and he performed well. Dhoni focused on cricket after his 10th standard.

Dhoni made his Ranji Trophy debut for Bihar in the 1999–2000 season as an eighteen year old. He made a half century in his debut match scoring 68 in the second innings against Assam cricket team. The future captain was discovered via the BCCI's small-town talent-spotting initiative TRDW. Dhoni was discovered by TRDO PC Podar, captain of Bengal in the 1960s, when he saw Dhoni play for Jharkhand at a match in Jamshedpur in 2003, and sent a report to the National Cricket Academy. Dhoni tends to play mostly from the back foot with a pronounced bottom hand grip.

In his fifth ODI match in 2005 – Dhoni scored 148 against Pakistan, then the highest score by an Indian wicketkeeper. Later in the year, he broke his own record for the highest score in the second innings in ODI matches as he scored 183 against Sri Lanka.

He led India to the ICC World Twenty 20 trophy in South Africa with a victory over arch rivals Pakistan in an intensely fought final on 24 September 2007, and became the second Indian captain to have won a World Cup in any form of cricket, after Kapil Dev.

In 2013, under his captaincy, India became the first team in more than 40 years to whitewash Australia in a Test series. Dhoni became the first captain to win all the ICC trophies, he achieved this feat when India defeated England in champions trophy in England in June 2013.

In 2016, a biopic *M.S. Dhoni: The Untold Story* was made on him.

Dhoni's final game as Indian captain was on 10 January, 2017 in a warmup match between England and India during the limited-overs led of England Tour of India. Dhoni stated he will still fulfill his duties as captains in various domestic teams. He has been the recipient of many awards, including the ICC ODI Player of the Year award in 2008 and 2009 (the first player to win the award twice), the Rajiv Gandhi Khel Ratna award (now Major Dhyanchand Khel Ratna award) in 2007, Padma Shri, India's fourth highest civilian honour, in 2009 and Padma Bhushan, India's third highest civilian honour, in 2018. The Indian Territorial Army conferred the honorary rank of Lieutenant Colonel to Dhoni on 1 November, 2011. He is the second Indian cricketer after Kapil Dev to receive this honour.

Dhoni announced his retirement from international cricket on 15 August, 2020. In September 2021, Dhoni was named as the Mentor of India for the 2021 ICC Men's T20 World Cup.

MS Dhoni continued to lead Chennai Super Kings (CSK) in the Indian Premier League (IPL). He guided CSK to their fifth IPL title in 2023, equaling Mumbai Indians' record. Despite stepping down as full-time captain, he remained a mentor and key player.

Max Verstappen

(1997)

Formula One Racer

"I always try to get the best result out of it, I'm not there to just sit second or sit third. I'm a winner, and I want to win every single race, and I will always go for it."

Max Emilian Verstappen, born on September 30, 1997, in Hasselt, Belgium, is a distinguished racing driver who competes under the Dutch flag in Formula One for Red Bull Racing. Renowned for his exceptional talent and aggressive driving style, Verstappen has secured four consecutive Formula One World Drivers' Championship titles from 2021 to 2024, amassing 63 Grand Prix victories across ten seasons.

Born into a family deeply rooted in motorsports, Max's father, Jos Verstappen, is a former Formula One driver who competed for teams such as Benetton, Simtek, and Arrows. His mother, Sophie Kumpen, was a successful kart racer, competing against future F1 drivers and establishing herself as one of the top kart drivers globally during her time. This rich racing heritage provided Max with a solid foundation and early exposure to the world of competitive racing.

Verstappen's racing career commenced in karting, where he quickly showcased his prodigious talent. By 2010, he had won the Flemish Minimax championship, and in 2013, he clinched the European KF and KZ championships, along with the World KZ championship, marking him as a rising star in motorsports. His seamless transition from karting to single-seater racing further demonstrated his adaptability and skill.

In 2014, at just 16 years old, Verstappen competed in the FIA European Formula 3 Championship with Van Amersfoort Racing, finishing third overall. His remarkable performance caught the attention of several Formula One teams, leading to his signing with Scuderia Toro Rosso for the 2015 season. Making his debut at 17 years and 166 days old, Verstappen became the youngest driver to start a Formula One Race.

Verstappen's inaugural season in Formula One was marked by impressive performances, including a fourth-place finish at the Hungarian Grand Prix. His aggressive driving style and fearless overtakes earned him recognition and respect within the racing community. In May 2016, after just four races into the season, Red Bull Racing promoted Verstappen to their senior team, replacing Daniil Kvyat. He made an immediate impact by winning the Spanish Grand Prix, becoming the youngest driver to win a Formula One Race at 18 years and 228 days old.

Over the subsequent seasons, Verstappen continued to mature as a driver, consistently delivering strong performances and podium finishes. His relentless pursuit of excellence culminated in 2021 when he secured his first World Drivers' Championship title in a dramatic and controversial finale at the Abu Dhabi Grand Prix, edging out seven-time champion Lewis Hamilton. This victory marked a significant milestone, making him the first Dutch driver to win the championship.

Building on his success, Verstappen dominated the 2022 and 2023 seasons, securing back-to-back championships with Red Bull Racing. His exceptional driving skills, combined with the team's strategic prowess, solidified his status as one of the sport's elite drivers. In 2024, Verstappen clinched his fourth consecutive title, joining an exclusive group of drivers who have achieved such a feat, including legends like Michael Schumacher and Lewis Hamilton.

Verstappen's driving style is characterised by his aggressive overtakes, precise car control, and unwavering determination. These attributes have endeared him to fans worldwide and have contributed to his numerous accolades and records in the sport. As of the end of the 2024 season, he has amassed 63 Grand Prix victories and 112 podium finishes, reflecting his consistent excellence on the track.

Off the track, Verstappen maintains a relatively private personal life. He has been in a relationship with Kelly Piquet, daughter of three-time Formula One World Champion Nelson Piquet, since 2020. The couple has been seen together at various racing events, and their relationship has garnered media attention due to their prominent family backgrounds in motorsports.

Verstappen's influence extends beyond his on-track achievements. His success has significantly boosted the popularity of Formula One in the Netherlands, leading to the return of the Dutch Grand Prix at Zandvoort in 2021 after a 36-year absence. The event has since become a highlight on the F1 calendar, with Dutch fans, known as the "Orange Army," fervently supporting their national hero.

In addition to his racing commitments, Verstappen has engaged in various philanthropic endeavours, supporting initiatives that promote road safety and youth engagement in motorsports. His contributions to the sport and society have earned him recognition beyond the racing community, solidifying his status as a global sports icon.

Verstappen's career trajectory reflects a blend of innate talent, rigorous training, and a supportive environment that nurtured his passion from an early age. As he continues to break records and set new benchmarks, the racing world eagerly anticipates the next chapters in his already illustrious career.

Mao Tse Tung

(1893–1976)

Political Leader

"Politics is war without bloodshed while war is politics with bloodshed."

Mao Tse Tung was a Chinese Marxist military and political leader, who led the Chinese Communist Party (CCP) to victory against the Kuomintang (KMT) in the Chinese Civil War, leading to the establishment of the People's Republic of China on October 1, 1949 in Beijing.

The eldest child of a relatively prosperous peasant family, Mao was born on December 26, 1893, in a village called Shaoshan in Xiangtan County, Hunan province, and thus spoke Xiang rather than Mandarin as his first language. His ancestors had migrated from Jiangxi province during the Ming Dynasty, married indigenous women, and had settled there as farmers.

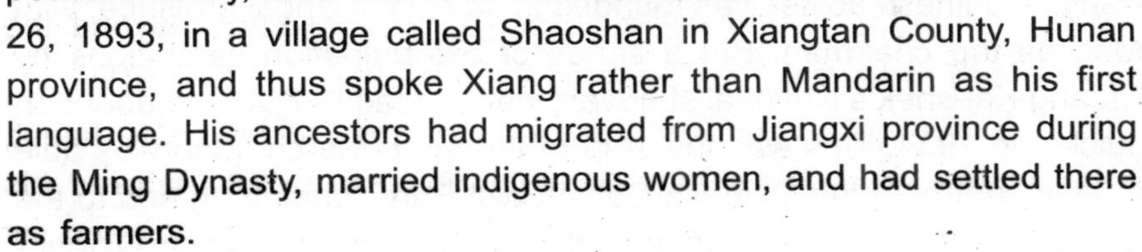

Mao lived with his mother's family in a neighbouring village until he was eight. He then returned to Shaoshan to begin his education. When he was 10, he ran away from school. Following his expulsion from at least three other schools, his father refused to continue to pay for his education.

At the age of 14, Mao entered an arranged marriage with an eighteen year old cousin called Luo. Although he never lived with her and she died in 1910, Mao was allowed to resume his schooling. When he was 16, he against his father's wishes left Shaoshan and enrolled himself in a nearby higher primary school. It was during this period that his political consciousness began to develop.

Mao Tse Tung studied traditional Confucian classics. His mother was devoutly Buddhist. He served briefly in the republican army. Mao then spent six months studying in the provincial library.

He graduated from Hunan First Normal School. He went to Peking, and worked as a library assistant at the Peking University. At the university, Mao Tse Tung made contacts with intellectual radicals who later were high in the Chinese Communist Party. In 1919, Mao returned to Hunan. Here, he engaged in political activity. He organised groups, and published a political review.

In 1920, Mao Tse Tung married Yang K'ai-hui, the daughter of one of his teachers at the provincial normal school in Changsha and an active communist. Yang K'ai-hui was later executed by the Chinese Nationalists in 1930. He later married Ho Tzu-chen, but divorced her in 1937. Then, he married Chiang Ch'ing.

Mao Tse Tung was a founding member of the Chinese Communist Party. A Chinese soviet was founded in Juichin, Kiangsi province, with Mao as the chairman. But a series of extermination campaigns by Chiang Kai-shek's Nationalist government forced the CCP to abandon Juichin in 1934. This was the start of the Long March. Mao was able to gain control of the Chinese Communist Party, putting an end to the Russian direction. The Communist forces reached Shensi, October 1935, after a march of 10,000 km.

The Japanese invasion during the World War II, forced the CCP and the Kuomintang to form a united front. Mao Tse Tung rose in stature as a national leader. Under him, the Chinese Communist Party membership rose from 40,000 members in 1937 to 1,200,000 members in 1945. After the end of the World War II, the united front split and civil war erupted. The Chinese Communist Party came to power and Chiang's government was forced to flee to Taiwan.

When the United States rebuffed Mao Tse Tung, China developed a close alliance with the USSR. During the early 1950s, Mao served as the chairman of the Communist Party, chief of state, and chairman of the military commission.

During the Cultural Revolution, his sayings, printed in a little red book, and buttons bearing his image were distributed.

Mao died at the age of 82, on September 9, 1976 at 10 minutes past midnight in Beijing. He had been in poor health for several years and had declined visibly for some months prior to his death. His body lay in this state at the Great Hall of the People.

A memorial service was held in Tiananmen Square on September 18, 1976. There was a three-minute silence observed during this service. His body was later placed into the Mausoleum of Mao Zedong, although he wished to be cremated and had been one of the first high-ranking officials to sign the "Proposal that all Central Leaders be Cremated after Death" in November 1956.

❑❑❑

Mark Zuckerberg

(1984)
Co-founder of 'Facebook'

"By giving people the power to share, we're making the world more transparent."

Mark Elliot Zuckerberg is an American computer programmer and internet entrepreneur. He is best known as the most prominent of five co-founders of the social networking website, 'Facebook'.

Mark Zuckerberg co-founded Facebook out of his college dorm room. He left Harvard after his sophomore year to concentrate on the site, the user base of which has grown to more than 250 million people, making Zuckerberg a billionaire.

Mark Elliot Zuckerberg was born on May 14, 1984, in White Plains, New York, into a comfortable, well-educated family, and raised in the nearby village of Dobbs Ferry. His father, Edward Zuckerberg, ran a dental practice attached to the family's home. His mother, Karen, worked as a psychiatrist.

Mark developed an interest in computers at an early age; when he was about 12, he used Atari BASIC to create a messaging program he named "Zucknet." His father used the program in his dental office, so that the receptionist could inform him of a new patient without yelling across the room. The family also used Zucknet to communicate within the house. Together with his friends, he also created computer games just for fun. To keep up with Mark's burgeoning interest in computers, his parents hired private computer tutor David Newman to come to the house once a week and work with Mark. He began taking graduate courses at nearby Mercy College around this same time.

Mark later studied at Phillips Exeter Academy, an exclusive preparatory school in New Hampshire. There he showed talent in fencing, becoming the captain of the school's team. He also excelled in literature, earning a diploma in classics. Yet mark remained fascinated by computers, and continued to work on developing new programs. While still in high school, he created an early version of the music software Pandora, which he called Synapse. Several companies—including AOL and Microsoft—expressed an interest in buying the software, and hiring the teenager before graduation. He declined the offers.

After graduating from Exeter in 2002, mark enrolled at Harvard University. By his sophomore year at the ivy league institution, he had developed a reputation as the go-to software developer on campus. It was at that time that he built a program called CourseMatch, which helped students choose their classes based on the course selections of other users. He also invented Facemash, which compared the pictures of two students on campus and allowed users to vote on which one was more attractive. The program became wildly popular, but was later shut down by the school administration after it was deemed inappropriate.

Based on the buzz of his previous projects, three of his fellow students—Divya Narendra, and twins Cameron and Tyler Winklevoss—sought him out to work on an idea for a social networking site they called Harvard Connection. This site was designed to use information from Harvard's student networks in order to create a dating site for the Harvard elite. Mark agreed to help with the project, but soon dropped out to work on his own social networking site with friends Dustin Moskovitz, Chris Hughes and Eduardo Saverin.

Mark and his friends created a site that allowed users to create their own profiles, upload photos, and communicate with other users. The group ran the site—first called The Facebook—out of a dorm room at Harvard until June 2004. After his sophomore year, mark dropped out of college to devote himself to Facebook full time, moving the company to Palo Alto, California. By the end of 2004, Facebook had 1 million users.

In 2005, Mark enterprise received a huge boost from the venture capital firm Accel Partners. Accel invested $12.7 million into the network, which at the time was open only to ivy league students. Zuckerberg's company then granted access to other colleges, high school and international schools, pushing the site's membership to more than 5.5 million users by December 2005. The site then began attracting the interest of other companies, who wanted to advertise with the popular social hub. Not wanting to sell out, Zuckerberg turned down offers from companies such as Yahoo! and MTV Networks. Instead, he focused on expanding the site, opening up his project to outside developers and adding more features.

Mark faced yet another personal challenge when the 2009 book *The Accidental Billionaires*, by writer Ben Mezrich, hit stores. Mezrich was heavily criticized for his re-telling of Zuckerberg's story, which used invented scenes, re-imagined dialogue and fictional characters. Regardless of how true-to-life the story was, Mezrich managed to sell the rights of the tale to screenwriter Aaron Sorkin, and the critically acclaimed film *The Social Network* received eight Academy Award nominations. Mark objected strongly to the film's narrative, and later told a reporter at *The New Yorker* that many of the details in the film were inaccurate.

Yet Mark and Facebook continued to succeed, in spite of the criticism. *Time* magazine named him Person of the Year in 2010, and *Vanity Fair* placed him at the top of their New Establishment list.

Forbes also ranked Zuckerberg at No. 35—beating out Apple CEO Steve Jobs—on its "400" list, estimating his net worth to be $6.9 billion.

Since amassing his sizeable fortune, mark has used his millions to fund a variety of philanthropic causes. The most notable examples came in 2010. In September of that year, he donated $100 million to save the failing Newark Public Schools system in New Jersey. Then, in December 2010, Mark signed the "Giving Pledge", promising to donate at least 50 percent of his wealth to charity over the course of his lifetime. Other Giving Pledge members include Bill Gates, Warren Buffett and George Lucas.

Mark made two major life changes in May 2012. Facebook had its initial public offering, which raised $16 billion.

On May 19, 2012—a day after the IPO—Mark wed his longtime girlfriend, Priscilla Chan. About 100 people gathered at the couple's Palo Alto, California home.

In May 2013, Facebook made the *Fortune* 500 list for the first time—making Mark Zuckerberg, at the age of 28, the youngest CEO on the list.

Mark Zuckerberg focused on advancing Meta's AI and Metaverse Technologies. In 2023, he launched Meta's Llama AI models, boosting competition in generative AI. Under his leadership, Threads became a major rival to X (formerly Twitter). By 2024, Meta expanded into AI-powered virtual assistants and augmented reality. In 2025, he continues driving AI innovation, reshaping social media and digital interaction globally.

As of February 2025, according to the Bloomberg Billionaires Index, Mark Zuckerberg ranks as the second-richest person globally, with an estimated net worth of $252 billion.

❑❑❑

Marlon Brando

(1924–2004)

Actor

"Never confuse the size of your paycheck with the size of your talent."

Marlon Brando was an Oscar winning American actor whose performances in *A Streetcar Named Desire* (1947), *On the Waterfront* (1954) and *The Godfather* (1972) earned him plaudits as one of the greatest actors of all time.

Born on April 3, 1924, Brando's nickname was "Bud." His mother, Dorothy, was active in Nebraska theatre, and was the woman who got Henry Fonda to try his luck at the thespian life. Brando's home life was unhappy. His father was an alcoholic and an adulterer, and his mother turned to the bottle herself in response. Though young Marlon felt abandoned by Dorothy, she did manage to instill in him a love for music, nature, and the theatre.

The rebellious young Brando was sent to, and soon expelled from, the Shattuck Military Academy. He travelled to the New York City, and despite his initial lack of interest in acting, the theatre soon proved to be his calling. When he enrolled in the New School's Dramatic Workshop, his famed teacher, Stella Adler introduced him to Stanislavsky's *Method*, an approach that values emotional honesty and verisimilitude in performance above traditional stagecraft. At the Actors Studio, Method mentor Lee Strasberg also nurtured Brando's monumental talent, preparing the powerhouse actor for his breakthrough role as Stanley Kowalski in Tennessee Williams *A Streetcar Named Desire* (playing some performances with a broken nose after sparring with understudy Jack Palance). Hollywood was impressed, and soon Brando, together with most of the original cast, re-created his role in the film version of *Streetcar* (1951) to a wide acclaim.

From his star turn in *Streetcar*, Brando went on to *The Wild One* in 1954, earning his first Oscar nomination and counterculture celebrity. Brando's explosive emotional intensity was stifled by the big screen, and he was displeased with his Oscar winning portrayal of Terry Malloy in Elia Kazan's *On The Waterfront* (1954), even though it sealed his reputation as an American icon. Says Brando of his famous *I could've been a contender* scene: "People spoke about that, 'Oh, my God, what a wonderful scene, Marlon, blah blah blah blah.' It wasn't wonderful. Everybody feels a sense of loss about something. That was what touched people. It wasn't the scene itself. There are some scenes, some parts that are actor-proof." During *On The Waterfront*, Brando made forays into improvisation, a technique he embraced for the rest of his career.

During the 1960's, Marlon Brando's career slowed down as his political activity revived. He spent time with Bobby Seale of the *Black Panthers* while researching *Burn!* (1969) and took up the Native American cause. In rejecting his Oscar for *The Godfather* (1972), Brando cited Hollywood's indifference to the plight of the native Americans as his reason for not accepting the Oscar, which he called "a door prize." Brando describes his controversial role in Bernardo

Bertolucci's *Last Tango In Paris* (1973) as "the first time, I have felt a total violation of my innermost soul," and after his tortured performance in this masterpiece, he distanced himself from his art. Since then, he had primarily appeared in character and cameo roles, notably in *Apocalypse Now* (1979), *The Freshman* (1990), and *Don Juan DeMarco* (1995). After penning his autobiography, *Songs My Mother Taught Me*, Brando appeared in *The Island of Dr. Moreau* (1996), *The Brave* (1997), *Free Money* (1998), and *The Score* (2001), which teamed him with fellow method actors like Robert De Niro and Edward Norton.

The actor was as famous for his off-screen antics as his on-screen performances. He could be intensely private, and yet he earned realms of publicity for his eccentric behaviour and sometimes, outlandish salary demands.

On *The Score* (2001), Marlon refused to be on the set at the same time as director Frank Oz. He received $4 million for 10 minutes of acting in *Superman* (1978), and sent a woman who called herself Sacheen Littlefeather to decline his Oscar for *The Godfather* (1972).

Marlon Brando died on July 2, 2004.

Martin Luther King Jr.

(1929–1968)

Political Activist

"The ultimate measure of a man is not where he stands in moments of comfort and convenience, but where he stands at times of challenge and controversy."

Martin Luther King, Jr., was an American political activist and the most famous leader of the American civil rights movement. He was considered a peacemaker throughout the world for his promotion of non-violence and equal treatment for different races.

He was awarded the 1964 Nobel Peace Prize for his efforts. He was posthumously awarded the Presidential Medal of Freedom by Jimmy Carter in 1977; the Congressional Gold Medal in 2004, and in 1986, *Martin Luther King Day* was established in his honour. He gave his most influential and well-known speech, "I Have a Dream" at Lincoln Memorial in Washington, DC on August 28, 1963. The speech was attended by more than 250,000 people.

Martin Luther was born on January 15, 1929 in Atlanta, Georgia (on 501 Auburn Avenue) to the Martin Luther King, Sr. and Alberta Williams King. He had a brother, Alfred, and a sister, Christine. Both his father and grandfather were ministers. His mother was a school teacher. She taught him how to read before he went to school. As a child, Martin was so smart that he skipped both the ninth and twelfth grades. At the age of fifteen, he applied to Morehouse College in Atlanta where he earned his Bachelor of Arts degree in Sociology. Later, he graduated as valedictorian from Crozer Theological Seminary in Chester, Pennsylvania with a Bachelor of Divinity degree in 1951. Martin received a Ph.D. in Systematic theology from the Boston University in 1955. On June 18, 1953, Martin Luther King married Coretta Scott. After graduating from college and getting married, Dr. King became a minister and moved to Alabama in 1954.

King experienced racism early in life. He was a true social reformer and decided to do something for the betterment of the people and to make the world a better and fairer place to live in. During the 1950's, Dr. King became active in the movement for civil rights and racial equality. He participated in the Montgomery, Alabama, Bus Boycott and many other peaceful demonstrations that protested the unfair treatment of the African-Americans. The Montgomery Bus Boycott lasted for 382 days. The situation became so tense that King's house was bombed. He was arrested during this campaign. At that time, he was only 27 years old. He was arrested thirty times for his participation in the civil rights activities.

Dr. King helped organise a march in 1965 that was over 50 miles long and would proceed to Montgomery. Its intention was to draw attention to the voting rights of the Blacks. The police responded by spraying pepper spray and beating the marchers. The events were televised and the day became known as 'Bloody Sunday'. Five days later, they arrived in Montgomery where Martin Luther King, Jr. held a rally in front of the capital building. Over twenty thousand people participated in the rally.

He began to shift the focus from civil rights to economic reforms in the period between 1966 and 1967. He began to talk about the nation's wealth compared to the poverty of the Blacks. In 1967, he started planning a Poor People's Campaign to pressurise the nation's lawmakers for economic reforms. He sent the Blacks into White neighbourhoods to protest economic injustice. Sadly, many of these protests ended with violence despite his non-violence movements.

On April 4, 1968, King was shot by James Earl Ray while standing on the balcony of the Lorraine Motel in Memphis, Tennessee. Friends inside the motel room heard the shots and ran to the balcony to find King shot in the throat. He was pronounced dead at St. Joseph's Hospital at 7:05 p.m. The assassination led to a nationwide wave of riots in more than 60 cities. A crowd of 300,000 attended his funeral that took place five days later. He was only 39 at the time of his death. Dr. King was turning his attention to a nationwide campaign to help the poor at the time of his assassination.

Maulana Abul Kalam Azad

(1888–1958)

Freedom Fighter

"I am proud of being an Indian. I am part of the indivisible unity that is Indian nationality."

Maulana Abul Kalam Azad was an Indian poet, writer, journalist and scholar who became an important political leader of the Indian independence movement. In his youth, he adopted the pen name, 'Azad' and was popularly addressed simply as Maulana Azad.

Abul Kalam Azad was born in the year 1888 in Mecca, in modern-day Saudi Arabia, into a family of prosperous and learned Muslim scholars, or *maulanas*. His forefathers hailed from Herat, in Afghanistan,. and his lineage could be traced back to Babar's days. Abul Kalam's father's name was Maulana Khairuddin, and his mother was the daughter of Sheikh Mohammad Zaher Watri.

In 1890, his father moved to Kolkata (formarly known as Calcutta). Educated according to the traditional curriculum, the young Kalam learnt Arabic and Persian at first and then philosophy, geometry, and algebra. He was taught at home, first by his father, and later by appointed teachers who were eminent in their respective fields. Sensing that English was fast becoming the international language, Abul Kalam taught himself to read, write and speak the language. As he adapted to the changing opportunities of his time, he also adopted the pen name, "Azad" to signify his freedom from the traditional Muslim ways of his ancestors.

The freedom of his mind turned him naturally towards the great enterprise of the day, the struggle for independence. Azad was introduced to the freedom struggle by revolutionary Shyam Sunder Chakravarthy. Most revolutionaries in Bengal were Hindus, and many were greatly surprised by his willingness to join the freedom struggle alongwith them, while others were skeptical of his intentions. Azad also discovered that the revolutionary activities were mostly restricted to Bengal and Bihar. Creating his own niche within the movement, he helped to set up secret revolutionary centres all over North India and in Bombay (now Mumbai).

Most revolutionaries of the day were anti-Muslim, because they felt that the British Government was using the Muslim community against India's freedom struggle. Azad tried to convince his colleagues that indifference and hostility towards the Muslims would only make the path to freedom more difficult. Abul Kalam Azad began the publication of a journal called *Al Hilal* (The Crescent), in June 1912, to increase the revolutionary recruits amongst the Muslims. The energy of his efforts paid off, and *Al Hilal's* circulation passed 25,000 within two years, before the heavy hand of the British Government used the Press Act and then the Defence of India Regulations Act in 1916, to shut the journal down.

Undeterred, Azad continued his struggle, both for the independence of India and his vision of an undivided nation in which people of all faiths would live harmoniously. From his earlier revolutionary ways, he now turned to Gandhiji's popular Civil

Disobedience Movement and joined the Indian National Congress in January 1920. He presided over the special session of the Congress Party in September 1923 and at the age of 35, was the youngest man to be elected as the President of the Congress.

He was arrested in 1930, for violation of the salt laws as part of Gandhiji's Salt Satyagraha. He was put in Meerut jail for a year and a half. As the British policies of 'divide and rule' gained roots in the nation's social psyche, Azad remained the staunchest opponent of the partition of India. Partition, he asserted, was against the grain of our nation's culture, equal to "divorce before marriage"! He supported a confederation of autonomous provinces with their own constitutions but common defence and economy, an arrangement suggested in the British Cabinet Mission Plan of May 1946. Despite his exhortations to fellow Muslims in the pre-Independent India, he was unable to avert partition, which shattered his dream of a unified nation. He was unflinching in his opposition to it until the last, and is remembered best for this.

Following independence, Azad served as the Minister of Education in Jawaharlal Nehru's cabinet from 1947 to 1958. He died in August 1958. In 1992, the government of India posthumously awarded her patriotic son, the highest civilian honour - 'the Bharat Ratna'.

❑❑❑

Meryl Streep

(1949)

Actress

"The great gift of human beings is that we have the power of empathy."

Meryl Streep is a double Academy Award winning American actress who has performed in movies, television and theatre. She is one of the most respected and talented actresses of her generation.

Streep was born as Mary Louise Streep in Summit, New Jersey, USA in 1949. Her father, Harry Streep, Jr., was a pharmaceutical executive and her mother, Mary, was a commercial artist of Irish, Swiss, and English descent. Streep was raised in New Jersey. She received her BA in Drama at Vassar College and earned a MFA from the Yale University.

In her first feature film, *Julia* (1977), she had a small but pivotal role during a flashback scene. *The Deer Hunter* (1978) was her second feature film and it earned Streep her first Academy Award nomination, in the category of 'Best Supporting Actress'. The following year, she won an Academy Award for her role opposite Dustin Hoffman in *Kramer vs. Kramer* (Best Supporting Actress, 1979). In 1982, she won again, for *Sophie's Choice* (Best Actress, 1982).

In 1978, she won her first Emmy Award, for 'Outstanding Supporting Actress' in a Mini-series or TV movie, *Holocaust*. A year later, she appeared in her only Woody Allen film, *Manhattan*.

Streep was engaged to *The Deer Hunter* co-star, John Cazale until his death from bone cancer on March 12, 1978. In September 1978, she married sculptor Don Gummer. They have four children: Henry, Mamie, Grace, and Louisa.

In the 1990s, she took a greater variety of roles, including a strung-out B-film actress in a screen adaptation of Carrie Fisher's novel, *Postcards from the Edge*, a farcical role in *Death Becomes Her* alongside Goldie Hawn and Bruce Willis. Streep also appeared in the movie version of Isabel Allende's, *The House of the Spirits*, Clint Eastwood's screen adaptation of *The Bridges of Madison County*, *The River Wild*, *She-Devil*, *Marvin's Room*, *One True Thing* and *Music of the Heart*, in a role which required her to learn to play the violin.

In 2002, she co-starred with Nicolas Cage in Spike Jonze's quirky *Adaptation*, as real-life author Susan Orlean. Within a few months, she appeared in the HBO adaptation of Tony Kushner's six-hour play *Angels in America*, in which she had four roles. She received her second Emmy Award for this film, which reunited her with director Mike Nichols, who directed her in *Silkwood*, *Heartburn* and *Postcards from the Edge*.

In the New York City, she appeared in the 1976 Broadway theatre production of Tennessee Williams' *27 Wagons Full of Cotton*, for which she received a Tony Award nomination for the Best Featured Actress in á play. Her other early Broadway credits include Anton Chekhov's *The Cherry Orchard* and the Bertolt Brecht-Kurt Weill musical *Happy End*. She received Drama Desk Award nominations for both the productions. Once Streep's film career flourished, she took a long break from stage acting. In July 2001, Streep returned to the stage for the first time in more than twenty years, playing Arkadina in the Public Theatre's revival of Anton Chekhov's *The Seagull.*

Meryl Streep has received a number of awards, including a *star* on the *Hollywood Walk of Fame*. Her release in 2006 are *Prime*, Robert Altman's *A Prairie Home Companion* and *The Devil Wears Prada*. In 2007, were released *Evening*, *Redention*, *Lions of Lambs* and *Mamma Mia*. In 2008, she was nominated for a Grammy Award for her work in *Mamma Mia*. In 2009, she starred in *Julie & Julia*, and romantic comedy *It's Complicated*.

Streep holds the record for the most Academy Award nominations of any actor, having been nominated 21 times since her first nomination in 1979 for *The Deer Hunter* (12 for Best Actress and 3 for Best Supporting Actress). Meryl Streep is the most nominated performer for a Golden Globe Award (she has 23 nominations). She has been cast as Margaret Thatcher in *The Iron Lady.* In 2010 she was elected to the American Academy of Arts and Letters. In 2013, Streep joined the motion picture adaptation of *The Giver* with Jeff Bridges and *The Good House* along with Robert De Niro.

In 2017, Streep was awarded the Golden Globe Cecil B. DeMille Award.

Meryl Streep received the Princess of Asturias Award for the Arts (2023) and starred in *Only Murders in the Building,* earning critical acclaim. She secured a Golden Globe nomination (2024) and remained active in philanthropy. By 205, she remains a legendary figure in Hollywood.

❑❑❑

Michael Faraday

(1791–1867)

Scientist

"Nothing is too wonderful to be true if it be consistent with the laws of nature."

Michael Faraday was a British scientist known for his brilliant discoveries of electro-magnetic induction, electro-magnetic rotations, the magneto-optical effect, diamagnetism, field theory and much more. Many famous historians regard him as the most influential and exemplary experimentalist in the history of science. The incredible scope and profundity of Faraday's work spanned a time of 60 years. He is considered as one of the top figures of the 19th century for his remarkable contribution in the field of electricity.

Faraday was born in Newington Butts, London on 22 September, 1791 as the third-child in a poor family, where his father James was a blacksmith. Due to the poor family background young Faraday could not enjoy the niceties of a big school and had to largely educate himself. He developed a great love for reading after he became apprenticed to a local bookbinder and bookseller. After studying the work of great scientists and authors he developed an interest in science, particularly in electricity. It was his early reading and experiments with the idea of force, that enabled him to make imperative discoveries in electricity later in life.

Faraday was always extremely curious and inquisitive. After the end of his apprenticeship (at the age of twenty), he began to attend lectures of different famous chemists in the quest to learn more. During this time he also applied for a job to Humphry Davy, his chemistry lecturer who later appointed him as Chemical Assistant at the Royal Institution in 1813. Few years later in 1821, Faraday married Sarah Barnard.

During the time when he was hired as an assistant to Professor Davy, Faraday discovered two new chlorides of carbon, conducted experiments on the diffusion of gases, investigated the alloys of steel, and produced several new kinds of glass intended for optical purposes. After Davy retired in 1827, Faraday replaced him as lecturer of chemistry at the Royal Institution and published all his research work related to condensation of gases, optical deceptions and the isolation of benzene from gas oils.

His early work centred on chemistry. He made a special study of Chlorine and new chlorides of carbon. Faraday was a great practical inventor and one of the most useful pieces of chemistry equipment he developed was an early form of the Bunsen burner. By mixing air with gas before lighting, Faraday found an easily accessible form of higher temperature. His model of the Bunsen burner was developed, and is still used in laboratories around the world.

Faraday is best recognized for his contributions to electricity and magnetism. In 1821 after being inspired by the work of Danish physicist and chemist, Hans Christian, he began experimenting with electromagnetism and by signifying the conversion of electrical energy into motive force, devised the electric motor. For the next few years he continued conducting experiments from his initial electromagnetic discovery.

In 1831 Faraday discovered the induction of electric currents and constructed the first electric dynamo. In 1839 he conducted several experiments to determine the fundamental nature of electricity and established that electrostatic force consists of a field of curved lines of force and conceived a specific inductive capacity. This led to the development of his theories on light and gravitational systems. His other prominent discoveries include: the process of diamagnetism, the Faraday Effect, Faraday cage and many more.

During the later years of his life he made several other achievements: received a Doctor of Civil Law degree in 1832 by the University of Oxford, elected as a foreign member of the Royal Swedish Academy of Sciences in 1838 and the French Academy of Sciences in 1844.

He refused to help the British government's request that he might develop chemical weapons for the Crimean war.

In the early 1840s, Faraday's health began to deteriorate and he did less research. He died on 25 August 1867 at Hampton Court, where he had been given official lodgings in recognition of his contribution to science.

Michael Jackson

(1958–2009)

Musician

"The greatest education in the world is watching the masters at work."

Michael Jackson, also known as 'The King of Pop', was an American musician and entertainer whose successful music career and controversial personal life have been at the forefront of pop culture for the last quarter-century.

Jackson was born in Gary, Indiana on August 29, 1958. His extraordinary musical career started at the age of five as the lead singer of the Jackson Five, alongwith four of his brothers. These early days saw the Jacksons play the local clubs and bars near their hometown. They were soon discovered by another artist and got to audition for Motown in 1968.

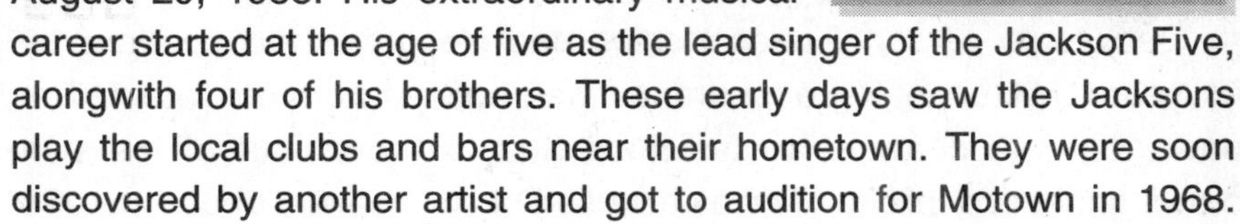

Immediately after their signing, the Jacksons moved to California and the hits started rolling in. *ABC* and *I'll be there* were among the No.1 hits in the US and they went on to record 14 albums.

In 1976, The Jackson Five became 'The Jacksons' and they signed a deal with *Epic* with whom they went on to record a further six albums up until 1984. In 1977, Michael Jackson teamed up with Quincy Jones who produced his first solo album, *Off The Wall*, which became a huge success around the world and realised four No.1 singles in the US.

But it was in 1982 that Jackson was to find true stardom as a solo artist with the release of *Thriller*. Selling 50 million copies worldwide and producing fewer than seven No.1 singles, *Thriller* is the world's largest selling album of all time. In conjunction with this, working with the best film directors and producers, Jackson used the state of the art video technology and special effects to create a 14-minute film to accompany the title track of the album. The *Thriller* led to Jackson winning eight Grammy awards.

An album, *Bad* and a world tour followed in 1987 and in 1991, Jackson signed to Sony and released his fourth solo album, *Dangerous*. In 1994, Jackson married the daughter of Elvis Presley, Lisa Marie Presley. The marriage lasted only 19 months and they divorced in 1996.

Following the release of his fifth album, *History*, Jackson married for a second time to a nurse, Debbie Rowe. Their first child, Prince Michael Joseph Jackson Jr. was born in 1997 and daughter, Paris Michael Katherine Jackson was born the following year in 1998. His third child was from a surrogate mother.

Jackson's personal relationships and life generated controversy for years. His changing appearance was noticed from the late 1970s onwards, with changes to his nose and to the colour of his skin drawing media publicity. He was accused of child sexual abuse in 1993 though no charges were brought, and in 2005 he was tried and acquitted when the jury ruled him not guilty on all charges.

In March 2006, he, who at the time resided in Bahrain, closed down the house on his Neverland ranch. He also paid overdue staff costs after threats of legal action. On November 15, 2006, Michael

Jackson was presented with the Chopard Diamond Award at the World Music Awards. It marked his second public appearance at an awards show since the trial of 2005. Jackson also performed at the show.

Jackson and Sony bought Famous Music LLC from Viacom in 2007. This deal gave him the rights to songs by Eminem, Shakira and Beck, among others. The 25th anniversary of *Thriller* was marked by the release of *Thriller 25*, which sold over three million copies worldwide. In November, Jackson transferred Neverland Ranch's title to Sycamore Valley Ranch Company LLC. This deal cleared Jackson's debt, and he reportedly even gained an extra $35 million from the venture. At the time of his death, Jackson still owned a stake in Neverland/Sycamore Valley, but it is unknown how large that stake was.

In March 2009, Jackson announced in a press conference at London's O_2 arena that he would perform there in major comeback concerts titled *This Is It*. While preparing for this concert tour in 2009, Jackson died at the age of 50 after suffering from cardiac arrest. He reportedly had been administered drugs and his death was ruled a homicide by the Los Angeles County coroner.

Columbia Pictures made a feature documentary concert-film from the rehearsal and pre-recorded footage. *Michael Jackson's This Is It* became the highest grossing documentary or concert movie ever (more than $252 million worldwide). As a result of Jackson's death, he became the biggest selling albums artist of 2009 in the United States with over 8.2 million in album sales.

Michelangelo

(1475–1564)

Painter, Sculptor and Poet

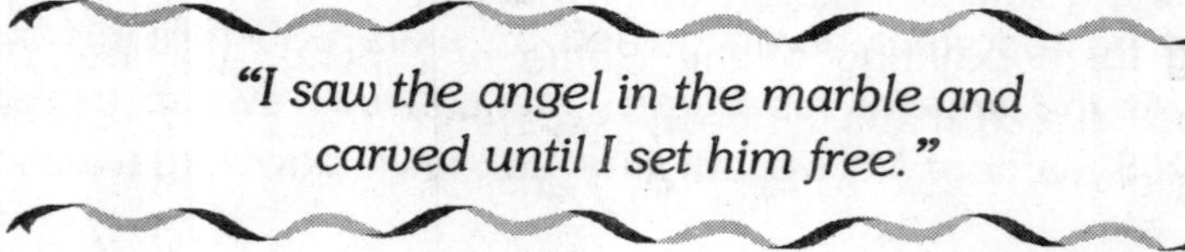

"I saw the angel in the marble and carved until I set him free."

Michelangelo is a famous painter, sculptor, architect and poet of the Renaissance.

He was born on March 6, 1475 in the village, Caprese in Florentine territories to Ludovico di Leonardo di Buonarotto Simoni and Francesca Neri. His mother was too ill to take care of him and so, he was put in a family of stone cutters with a wet nurse. Michelangelo's mother died when he was only six. His father sent him to learn letters where he befriended Francesco Granacci, who was learning to paint with Ghirlandaio's.

At the age of thirteen, he became an apprentice in the workshop of Ghirlandaio and a year later studied at the sculpture school in the Medici gardens. He was invited to the house of the Medici's where he met the future popes of the Medici family. At that time, he used to study bodies at the church of the Santo Spirito. He made the *Wooden Crucifix*, the *Battle of the Centaurs* and the *Madonna of the Stairs.*

The architect of the balance of power in Italy died in 1492. His death had grave repercussions on Italian politics, but he left a precious legacy in the city of Florence. Florence became fractioned and unstable after the death of Lorenzo, the Magnificent and Michelangelo moved to Rome. There he sculptured the *Bacchus* and following the Pieta for Saint Peter's. Michelangelo signed this work in a burst of rage but it remained the only one he signed.

When Florence was once again a republic in 1501, Michelangelo moved there and sculptured the giant David. After this, he made a drawing for a painting of the *Battle of Cascina*, for the Palazzo Vecchio. He also made in these years the *Bruges Madonna* and the painting of the *Tondo* of the Holy Family.

In 1505, Pope Julius commissioned Michelangelo to make his tomb as a sculptural project. However, in 1508, Pope Julius, told him to delay work on the pope's tomb, and paint the *Sistine Chapel ceiling 2* . Michelangelo tried to turn down the commission, but of no use. He wrote in fact a sonnet explaining that painting is not his art (sculpture is). On the vault of the ceiling, he painted scenes from *Genesis* while on the sides are seated prophets and sibyls between the ancestors of Christ.

When Michelangelo returned to work on the Julius tomb, it was demanded that it would be scaled down in magnitude. The main sculpture of this tomb is the *Moses* (c. 1515) in the church of San Pietro in Vincoli. From about this time, the statues of the *Dying Slave* and the *Bound Slave,* remain unfinished.

He moved to Florence and as an architect, Michelangelo in 1519, designed the facade of the San Lorenzo church in Florence and the Laurentian Library. In 1526, Florence was a republic again and with war with Rome. He was helping design the fortifications of the city. He fled to Venice. With the return of the Medici to power, he was allowed back to the city.

In 1535, Michelangelo began to work on the *Last Judgment* which he was commissioned to do by pope Clement VII. The nudity of the painted figures gave rise to criticism on Michelangelo met Vittoria Colonna in 1538. She was a poetess and an educated woman. They became close friends and Michelangelo wrote her some of his best poems. In 1538–39, he planed the buildings of the Campidoglio on the Capitoline Hill. His plan was carried out late and finished only in the 17th century.

During the last years of Michelangelo's life, he made many studies and drawings of the *Crucifixion* and the *Lament* over the *Dead Christ*. In these years, he also sculptured the *Florentine Pieta*, for his own tomb. When he was unsatisfied with the pieta, he broke parts of it with a hammer. He also made the *Rondanini Pieta*. The fresco of *The Last Judgment* on the altar wall of the Sistine Chapel was commissioned by Pope Paul III, and Michelangelo laboured on the project from 1534 to October 1541. Around 1530, he designed the *Laurentian Library* in Florence, attached to the church of San Lorenzo.

Michelangelo died on February 18, 1564, after a slow fever. He was buried in Rome but his nephew, Lionardo Buonarroti, carried the corpse to Florence where Michelangelo wanted to be buried, and was buried in the Santa Croce church.

❑❑❑

Mike Tyson

(1966)

Boxer

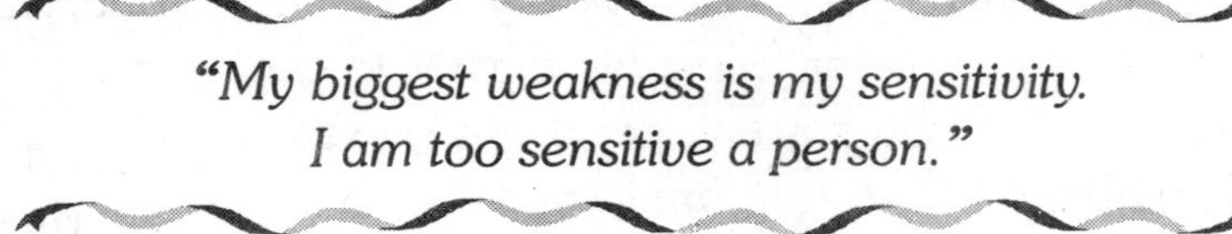

"My biggest weakness is my sensitivity. I am too sensitive a person."

Mike Tyson is one of the most famous boxers in prizefighting history for his actions both inside the ring and outside. His speed, power and angry aggression earned him the World Boxing Council heavyweight title in 1986, making him the youngest champion ever.

Mike Tyson was born in Brooklyn, New York, on June 30, 1966. His parents were Lorna Smith Tyson and Jimmy Kirkpatrick. When he was young, he was always getting into trouble with the police until he joined a boxing gym. His great physical specimen weighing 200 lbs at the age of 13, he could bench press more than his own weight. Tyson was later removed from school by Cus. Cus adopted Tyson later on and began training him. Unfortunately, Cus died in 1985 during Tyson's early professional career. Mike Tyson won his first professional fight on March 6, 1985 by the first round knock out. He continued through out his early career with thunderous early knock-outs.

On November 22, 1986, Tyson was given his first title shot, fighting Trevor Berbick for the WBC heavyweight title. Tyson won the fight and became the champion of the world due to a second round knock out, at 20 years and 4 months. He broke all previous records and became the youngest heavyweight champion ever.

By 1990, Tyson seemed to have lost direction and his personal life and training habits were in disarray. In a fight on February 11, he faced outsider James "Buster" Douglas in Tokyo.

On paper, it looked like an easy victory for Tyson, but Douglas was at an emotional peak after losing his mother to cancer three weeks prior to the fight. Tyson couldn't get past Douglas' speedy jabs and later lost the fight in the 10th round by knock-out.

In 1991, Tyson was arrested on charges of assault and a year later, he went on trial. He was convicted on February 10, 1992. He was given 6 years sentence but was released after serving for 3 years. Tyson did not fight again until 1995.

After starting back his boxing, he was greatly progressing until 1997, when he came across Evander Holyfield. It was the $100 million rematch, 8 months previously they had fought but this was the big one. They began fighting at a good pace however suddenly, with 40 seconds left in the 3rd round, the fight took an unexpected turn.

Holyfield got Tyson in a clinch, and Tyson rolled his head above Holyfield's shoulder. He bit Holyfield's right ear, severing it. Holyfield pushed Tyson away and started hopping up and down in pain, spinning around in a circle holding his ear. The referee gave Tyson a warning however, again when they got into another clinch with Tyson doing the same again.

Tyson was fined $3 million for his ear-biting stunt and banned for a short while from boxing. He began to decline by 1999. Finally, Tyson retired in 2006, with a good record.

Over his career, it's said that Tyson made over $400 Million. But somehow now he is in debt. Money was Tyson's God he said, which was one of the reasons he continued to box after he felt he couldn't be bothered with it.

On June 12, 2011, Tyson was inducted to the International Boxing Hall of Fame. In August 2011, CBS aired an episode of the same name, featuring Mike Tyson.

After debuting a one-man show in Las Vegas, Tyson teamed up with director Spike Lee and brought the show to Broadway in August 2012.

In October 2012, Tyson launched the Mike Tyson Cares Foundation. The mission of the Mike Tyson Cares Foundation is to "give kids a fighting chance" by providing innovative centers that provide for the comprehensive needs of kids from broken homes.

In August 2013, Tyson teamed up with Acquinity Interactive CEO Garry Jonas to form Iron Mike Productions, a boxing promotions company, formerly known as Acquinity Sports.

In March 2015, Tyson appeared on the track "Iconic" on Madonna's album *Rebel Heart.* Tyson says some lines at the beginning of the song.

In January 2017, Tyson launched his Youtube channel with Shots Studios, a comedy video and comedy music production company with young digital stars like Lele Pons and Rudy Mancuso. Tyson's channel includes parody music videos, comedy sketches and training footage.

In May 2017, Tyson published his second book, *Iron Ambition,* which details his time with trainer and surrogate father Cus D'Amato.

In 2020, Bill Caplan of The Ring magazine listed Tyson as number 17 of the 20 greatest heavyweights of all time. In 2020, CBS Sports boxing experts Brian Campbell and Brent Brookhouse ranked the top 10 heavyweights of the last 50 years and Tyson was ranked number 7.

❑❑❑

Milkha Singh

(1935-2021)

Athlete

"A man's primary responsibility is to his family, and once that's taken care of, he should help the less fortunate."

Milkha Singh is a Sikh athlete, who represented India in the 1960 Summer Olympics in Rome and the 1964 Summer Olympics in Tokyo. He is nicknamed as 'The Flying Sikh'. He is one of the greatest athletes India has ever produced.

Milkha Singh was born in the Western Punjab of undivided India on October 8, 1935. He lost his parents in the partition of India and the chaos that ensued. In 1947, he reached India from Pakistan in the cross border trains carrying refugees. Within a decade of his second 'life', he was making a name for himself on the international athletics circuit. Two Asian Games, three Olympics and two Commonwealth Games, he left his mark far and wide.

In the 1958, Asiad at Tokyo, Milkha not only won his pet event, the 400 metres, he also beat the favourite in the 200 metres, the Pakistani Abdul Khaliq and was the toast of Asian sporting circles.

The same year at the Commonwealth Games (then known as the Empire Games), he won his favourite event in 46.6 seconds, beating the South African Malcolm Spence, a name that would come back to haunt him two years later. He was peaking perfectly for the Rome Olympics as his name spread far and wide, making him one of the most famous Indians of his time.

He entered Rome as one of the favourites for a medal, after an outstanding season on the tracks of Europe. Facing him was the greatest array of quarter-milers ever assembled.

Milkha drew the fifth lane in the final after the heats had seen the Olympic record equalled by the American Otis Davis. The Indian star had beaten all the top quarter-milers in the world in the run up to Rome, except Davis. The experts predicted at least a silver medal for Milkha who would later admit that even he had gold on his mind; such was his form at the time. But unluckily he lost. Milkha Singh went out of India and took part in several competitions in order to divert his mind from the defeat.

He returned to India wondering how he would face his supporters. He need not have worried. Back home, he was received as a hero. Though his mistake rankled for years, gradually Milkha regained his confidence and composure. He was soon back to his winning ways, claiming gold in the 400 metres in the 1962 Jakarta Asian Games.

Milkha Singh can be described as one of the most extraordinary athletes of his times. He was a genius and a genius is never trained. Without any formal training, without any financial reward and without any emotional support, he took on the greatest athletes of his time and proved himself as good if not better.

Milkha's national records (200 and 400 metres) have been broken after many decades. But nothing can diminish his towering stature. Married to former international player, Nirmal, he has one son and three daughters. His son, Chiranjeev Milkha Singh, is a top golfer and represented India in the Beijing Asian Games in 1990.

He was awarded the prestigious Padmashree by the then President of India in 1958, when he won the gold medal in the British and Commonwealth Games.

All medals and trophies won by Milkha Singh, including the running shoes with which he broke the world record, blazers and uniforms have been donated by him to the National Sports Museum at the Jawaharlal Nehru Stadium, New Delhi.

Singh and his daughter, Sonia Sanwalka, co-wrote his autobiography, titled *The Race of My Life*. The book inspired *Bhaag Milkha Bhaag*, a 2013 biographical film of Singh's life. Singh sold the movie rights for one rupee stating that a share of the profits would be given to the Milkha Singh Charitable Trust. The Trust was founded in 2003 with the aim of assisting poor and needy sportspeople.

In September 2017, Singh's wax statue - created by sculptors of Madame Tussauds in London - was unveiled at Chandigarh. It depicts Singh in running posture during his victorious run at the 1958 Commonwealth Games. The statue is placed at Madame Tussauds museum in New Delhi, India. After winning the Olympic Gold in 2021 in Japan Neeraj Chopra dedicated his victory to Milkha Singh.

Milkha Singh died of COVID-19 complications on 18 June, 2021 at the age 91.

❑❑❑

Mirza Ghalib

(1797–1869)

Urdu Poet

"Ask not what separation has done to me
You see your composure when I come before you."

Mirza Asadullah Beg Khan — known to posterity as Ghalib, a 'nom de plume' he adopted in the tradition of all classical Urdu poets.

He was born in the city of Agra, of parents with Turkish aristocratic ancestry on December 27, 1797. As to the precise date, Imtiyaz Ali Arshi has conjectured, on the basis of Ghalib's horoscope, that the poet might have been born a month later, in January 1798.

In Delhi, Ghalib lived a life of comfort, though he did not find immediate or great success. He wrote first in a style at once detached, obscure, and pedantic, but soon thereafter, he adopted the fastidious, personal, complexly moral idiom which we now know as his mature style.

The course of his life from 1821 onwards is easier to trace. His interest began to shift decisively away from Urdu poetry to Persian during the 1820's, and he soon abandoned writing in Urdu almost altogether, except whenever a new edition of his works was forthcoming and he was inclined to make changes, deletions, or additions to his already existing opus. This remained the pattern of his work until 1847, the year in which he gained direct access to the Mughal court.

Ghalib was never really a part of the court except in its very last years, and even then with ambivalence on both sides. There was no love lost between Ghalib himself and Zauq, the king's tutor in the writing of poetry; and if their mutual dislike was not often openly expressed, it was a matter of prudence only. There is reason to believe that Bahadur Shah Zafar, the last Mughal emperor, was himself a poet of considerable merit, and did not much care for Ghalib's style of poetry or life. There is also reason to believe that Ghalib not only regarded his own necessary subservient conduct in relation to the emperor as humiliating but he also considered the Mughal court as a redundant institution. Nor was he well-known for admiring the king's verses.

However, after Zauq's death, Ghalib did gain an appointment as the emperor's advisor on matters of versification. He was also appointed, by the royal order, to write the official history of the Mughal dynasty, a project which was to be titled, "Partavistan" and to fill two volumes.

The only favouarble result of his connection with the court between 1847 and 1857 was that he resumed writing in Urdu with a frequency not experienced since the early 1820's. Many of these new poems are not panegyrics, or occasional verses to celebrate this or that. He did, however, wrote many ghazals which were of the same excellence and temper as his early great work.

In its material dimensions, Ghalib's life never really took root and remained always curiously unfinished. In a society where almost everybody seems to have a house of his own, Ghalib never had one and always rented one or accepted the use of one from a patron. He never had books of his own, usually reading borrowed ones. He had no children; the ones he had, died in infancy, and he later adopted the two children of Arif, his wife's nephew who died young in 1852.

In Kolkata, Ghalib saw cleanliness, good city planning, and prosperity. He was fascinated by the quality of the Western mind which was rational and could conceive of constitutional government, republicanism, and skepticism. The Western mind was attractive, particularly to one who, although fully imbued with his feudal and Muslim background, was also attracted by wider intelligence like the one that Western scientific thought offered: good rationalism promised to be good government.

The years between 1857 and 1869 were neither happy nor very eventful ones for Ghalib. During the revolt itself, he remained pretty much confined to his house, undoubtedly frightened by the wholesale massacres in the city. Many of his friends were hanged, deprived of their fortunes, exiled from the city, or detained in jails. By October 1858, he had completed his diary of the Revolt, the "Dast-Ambooh", published it, and presented copies of it to the British authorities, mainly with the purpose of proving that he had not supported the insurrections. Although his life and immediate possessions were spared, little value was attached to his writings. Ghalib was flatly told that he was still suspected of having had loyalties towards the Mughal emperor. During the ensuing years, his main source of income continued to be the stipend he got from the Nawab of Rampur.

Mohandas K. Gandhi

(1869–1948)

Freedom Fighter

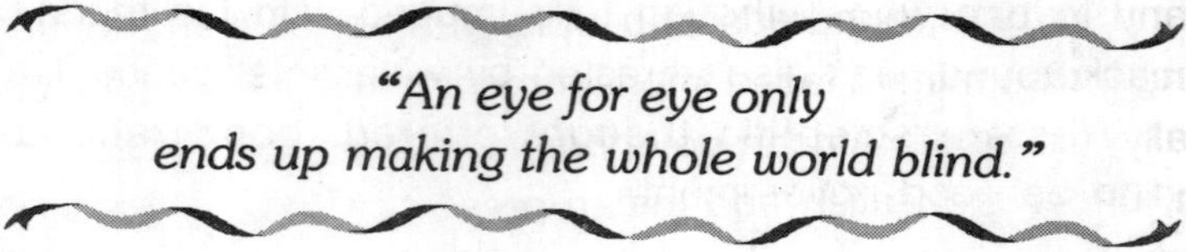

"An eye for eye only ends up making the whole world blind."

Mohandas Karamchand Gandhi, also known as Mahatma Gandhi, was an Indian nationalist leader, who established India's freedom through a non-violent revolution.

M. K. Gandhi was born on October 2, 1869, in the town of Porbander in the state of Gujarat. He did his schooling in nearby Rajkot, where his father served as a *Diwan* to the local ruler. Gandhi went to London, to study law, after his university degree. There he met English socialists and Fabians such as George Bernard Shaw, whose ideas contributed greatly to the shaping of his personality and politics. He returned to India in 1891, and then accepted a job at an Indian law firm in South Africa.

There he witnessed, how the non-Whites are ill-treated by the Whites. He was thrown out of a train compartment and was barred from hotels. Many a times, he was even beaten up badly. Facing all the injustices, he became more assertive, and began educating the fellow Indians in South Africa of their rights. In 1894, he opposed a bill that would deprive Indians of their right to vote, and rapidly became a proficient political activist. While unable to stop the bill, he succeeded in attracting widespread attention to his cause.

Gandhi developed the *satyagraha* ('devotion to truth'), a new non-violent way to redress wrongs. The campaign lasted for over seven years, and in 1913, hundreds of people went to jail - and thousands of striking Indian miners faced imprisonment and injury - for the cause. Eventually, the South African government, agreed to a compromising solution, under the British and Indian pressure, and thus peace was restored.

In 1914, he returned to India. Then in 1919, the British plans to intern people suspected of sedition prompted him to announce a new *satyagraha*. The result shook the subcontinent, and indirectly led to the Amritsar Massacre, in which nearly 400 Indians were killed by the British forces. Mahatma Gandhi dominated Indian politics, by the year 1920. He transformed the Indian National Congress, and his programme of peaceful non co-operation with the British included boycott of British goods and institutions, leading to arrests of thousands of *satyagrahis* - all cheerfully lining up for prison, for defying the British laws.

However, in March 1922, he was sent to jail for six years', but was released after two years. By then, the political landscape of India had changed completely. The Congress Party had split and Hindu-Muslim unity had disintegrated.

For some years, Mahatma Gandhi's political influence was minimal, until the Calcutta Congress in December 1928, where he demanded a dominion status for India, and threatened a nation-wide campaign for complete independence. In 1931, the Round Table Conference took place in London. Gandhiji attended it as the sole representative of the Indian National Congress, but resigned from the party in 1934, in protest at its use of non-violence as a political expedient.

The new Labour Government in Britain from 1945 brought negotiations, and these culminated in the Mountbatten Plan of June 1947, and the formation of the two new dominions of India and Pakistan in mid-August.

However, the country was divided and killings and riots between the Hindus and Muslims took place all over the country. Mahatma Gandhi's appeals for peace were ignored, and so he began fasting. This stopped the riots in Calcutta (now Kolkata) in September, and in Delhi in January 1948 - but only days later, he was shot dead in Delhi on January 30, 1948, by Nathuram Godse, a young fanatic.

❑❑❑

Michael Jordan

(1963)

Basketball Player

"I can accept failure, everyone fails at something. But I can't accept not trying."

Michael Jeffrey Jordan, born on February 17, 1963, in Brooklyn, New York, is widely regarded as one of the greatest basketball players in history. He was the fourth of five children born to James and Deloris Jordan. When Michael was still young, the Jordan family relocated to Wilmington, North Carolina, where he spent most of his formative years. His father worked as a maintenance supervisor, and his mother was a bank teller. Both parents played a key role in shaping Michael's work ethic and character, emphasizing discipline, focus, and the value of hard work.

Growing up, Jordan was passionate about sports and played baseball, football, and basketball. His competitive spirit emerged early, and he constantly sought to improve his abilities. He attended Emsley A. Laney High School in Wilmington, where, as a sophomore, he was cut from the varsity basketball team due to his then-average height of 5 feet 10 inches. This setback became a defining moment for Jordan. Rather than giving up, he used the disappointment as fuel for growth. Over the next year, he trained relentlessly, improved his game, and had a significant growth spurt, reaching 6 feet 3 inches. By his junior year, he had secured a place on the varsity team and quickly became one of the school's standout players.

Jordan's high school success earned him a basketball scholarship to the University of North Carolina at Chapel Hill in 1981. Under coach Dean Smith, he made an immediate impact. As a freshman, he scored the game-winning basket in the 1982 NCAA Championship final against Georgetown, marking the first major highlight of his basketball career. His poise under pressure was evident, and he was soon recognized as one of the best college players in the country, winning the College Player of the Year title in his sophomore and junior years. After three seasons at UNC, Jordan declared for the 1984 NBA Draft.

Selected third overall by the Chicago Bulls in 1984, Jordan quickly established himself as a transformative talent. His first season was marked by explosive scoring, dynamic athleticism, and a charismatic presence. He averaged over 28 points per game and earned the NBA Rookie of the Year Award. He soon became a fan favourite and helped rejuvenate a struggling Bulls franchise. Throughout the late 1980s and early 1990s, Jordan's talent blossomed. He led the league in scoring for ten seasons and dazzled with his gravity-defying dunks, clutch performances, and unrelenting drive to win.

The peak of Jordan's basketball career came in the 1990s when he led the Chicago Bulls to six NBA championships (1991-1993 and 1996-1998). Along the way, he collected five NBA Most Valuable Player (MVP) Awards and six NBA Finals MVPs. His leadership, scoring prowess, and defensive intensity made him a complete player. His mid-air acrobatics and late-game heroics captured the imagination of fans worldwide. Jordan wasn't just a basketball star; he became a global cultural icon, transcending sports.

In 1993, at the height of his career, Jordan shocked the sports world by retiring from basketball following the murder of his father. Driven by a desire to fulfil his father's dream, he pursued a brief career in professional baseball, signing a minor league contract with the Chicago White Sox and playing for the Birmingham Barons. Though he struggled to make an impact on the diamond, his dedication and humility earned respect.

In 1995, Jordan returned to the NBA with the famous words "I'm back." His comeback was met with immense anticipation. After a partial season, he led the Bulls to three consecutive NBA titles from 1996 to 1998, completing a second three-peat and cementing his status as the greatest basketball player of his era. He retired again in 1999 but returned to play two more seasons with the Washington Wizards from 2001 to 2003 before retiring for good.

Off the court, Jordan's personal life drew attention. He married Juanita Vanoy in 1989, and they had three children-Jeffrey, Marcus, and Jasmine. The couple divorced in 2006. In 2013, he married Yvette Prieto, a Cuban-American model. In 2014, they welcomed twin daughters, Victoria and Ysabel. Jordan has always kept his family life relatively private but remains involved in their lives and supports their endeavours.

Jordan's business acumen has been as impressive as his athletic career. In 1984, he partnered with Nike to launch the Air Jordan brand, a line of athletic footwear that revolutionized the industry. Air Jordans became a cultural phenomenon and remain one of the most successful sportswear lines in history. In 2010, he became the majority owner and chairman of the Charlotte Hornets, making him the first former NBA player to own a team. His leadership has focused on team development and community engagement.

In addition to business, Jordan has made significant philanthropic contributions. He has donated millions to causes including disaster relief, education, and racial equity. In 2016, he pledged $2 million to improve police-community relations and supports underprivileged youth through the Jordan Brand's WINGS initiative, which offers scholarships and mentorship programs.

Michael Jordan's legacy is more than just statistics and championships. He changed the way basketball is played and viewed, inspired generations of athletes, and became a symbol of excellence, resilience, and ambition. His life story-from being cut in high school to becoming a global icon—remains a testament to determination and greatness, continuing to inspire people far beyond the basketball court.

❑❑❑

Mother Teresa

(1910–1997)

Social Worker

"No nation can rise to the height of glory unless your women are side by side with you; we are victims of evil customs."

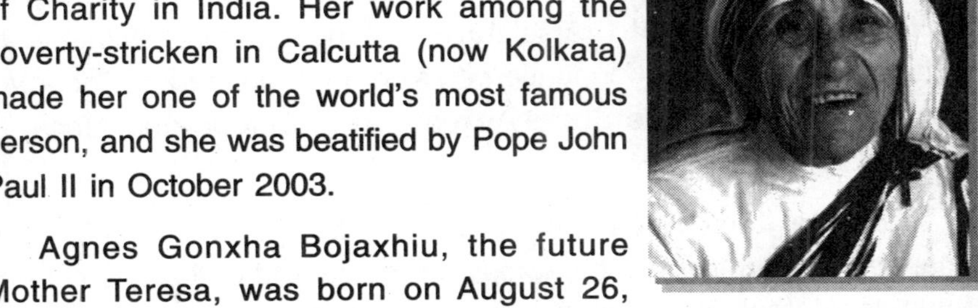

Mother Teresa was an Albanian Roman Catholic nun who founded the Missionaries of Charity in India. Her work among the poverty-stricken in Calcutta (now Kolkata) made her one of the world's most famous person, and she was beatified by Pope John Paul II in October 2003.

Agnes Gonxha Bojaxhiu, the future Mother Teresa, was born on August 26, 1910, in Skopje, Macedonia. Her father, a well-respected local businessman, died when she was eight years old, leaving her mother, a devoutly religious woman, to open an embroidery and cloth business to support the family. After spending her adolescence deeply involved in parish activities, Agnes left home in September 1928, for the Loreto Convent in Rathfarnam (Dublin), Ireland, where she was admitted as a postulant on October 12 and received the name of Teresa, after her patroness, St. Therese of Lisieux.

She was sent by the Loreto order to India and arrived in Calcutta (now Kolkata) on January 6, 1929. Upon her arrival, she joined the Loreto novitiate in Darjeeling. She made her final profession as a Loreto nun on May 24, 1937, and hereafter, was called, Mother Teresa. While living in Calcutta (now Kolkata) during the 1930s and 40's, she taught in St. Mary's Bengali Medium School.

On September 10, 1946, on a train journey from Calcutta (now Kolkata) to Darjeeling, Mother Teresa received what she termed the "call within a call," which was to give rise to the Missionaries of Charity family of sisters, brothers, fathers, and co-workers.

The content of this inspiration is revealed in the aim and mission she would give to her new institute: "to quench the infinite thirst of Jesus on the cross for love and souls" by "labouring at the salvation and sanctification of the poorest of the poor."

Throughout the 1950s and early 1960s, Mother Teresa expanded the work of the Missionaries of Charity both within Calcutta (now Kolkata) and throughout India. On February 1, 1965, Pope Paul VI granted the 'Decree of Praise' to the Congregation, raising it to pontifical right. The first foundation outside India opened in Cocorote, Venezuela, in 1965. The Society expanded to Europe and Africa, in 1968.

From the late 1960s until 1980, the Missionaries of Charity expanded both in their reach across the globe and in their number of members. Mother Teresa opened houses in Australia, the Middle East, and North America, and the first novitiate outside Calcutta (now Kolkata), in London. In 1979, she was awarded the Nobel Peace Prize. By that same year, there were 158 Missionaries of Charity foundations.

The Missionaries of Charity reached the Communist countries in 1979 with a house in Zagreb, Croatia, and in 1980, with a house in East Berlin, and continued to expand through the 1980s and 1990s with houses in almost all Communist nations, including 15 foundations in the former Soviet Union. Despite repeated efforts, however, Mother Teresa was never able to open a foundation in China.

On the Christmas eve of 1985, Mother Teresa opened the 'Gift of Love' in New York, her first house for AIDS patients. In the coming years, this home would be followed by others, in the United States and elsewhere, devoted specifically for those with AIDS.

From the late 1980s through the 1990s, despite increasing health problems, Mother Teresa travelled across the world for the profession of novices, opening of new houses, and service to the poor and disaster-stricken. New communities were founded in South Africa, Albania, Cuba, and war-torn Iraq. By 1997, the sisters numbered nearly 4,000 members, and were established in almost 600 foundations in 123 countries of the world.

She returned to Calcutta (now Kolkata) in July 1997. On September 5, Mother Teresa died at the Motherhouse. Her body was transferred to St. Thomas's Church, next to the Loreto Convent where she had first arrived nearly 69 years earlier. Hundreds of thousands of people from all classes and all religions, from India and abroad, paid their respects. She received a state funeral on September 13, and her body was taken in procession–on a gun carriage that had also borne the bodies of Mahatma Gandhi and Pandit Jawaharlal Nehru–through the streets of Calcutta (now Kolkata).

❑❑❑

Mukesh Ambani

(1957)

Industrial Tycoon

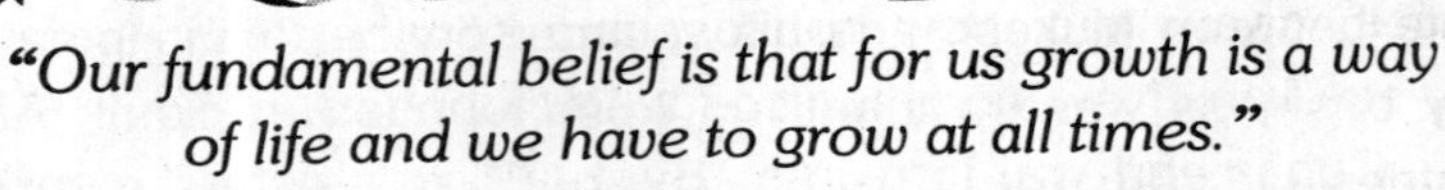

Mukesh Dhirubhai Ambani was born on April 19, 1957, in Aden, Yemen, to Dhirubhai Ambani and Kokilaben Ambani. His father, Dhirubhai, was an ambitious businessman who later founded Reliance Industries, one of India's largest conglomerates. In 1958, the Ambani family moved back to India, settling in Mumbai, where Dhirubhai started a small textile trading business.

Mukesh Ambani grew up in a middle-class household but was exposed to entrepreneurship from an early age. He studied chemical engineering at the Institute of Chemical Technology (formerly UDCT) in Mumbai. Later, he enrolled in an MBA program at Stanford University but left in 1981 to assist his father in expanding Reliance Industries. This decision proved to be a turning point in his life and the future of Indian business.

Under Dhirubhai's leadership, Reliance had already established itself in textiles, but Mukesh played a key role in transforming it into a diversified giant, entering petrochemicals, telecommunications, and retail. In the 1980s and 1990s, he spearheaded Reliance's expansion into oil refining and petrochemicals, laying the foundation for the company's global dominance. His vision led to the creation of Reliance's massive Jamnagar Refinery, which remains one of the largest oil refineries in the world.

In 2002, Dhirubhai Ambani passed away, leaving a leadership dispute between Mukesh and his younger brother, Anil Ambani. The family business was split, with Mukesh taking control of Reliance Industries Limited (RIL), including its oil, gas, and petrochemicals businesses, while Anil took over Reliance Communications, Power, and Financial Services. Over the years, Mukesh's Reliance outperformed Anil's businesses, cementing his status as India's most powerful industrialist.

Mukesh Ambani married Nita Ambani in 1985. Nita, a former teacher and philanthropist, has been actively involved in Reliance Foundation, working in education, healthcare, and rural development. Together, they have three children: Akash, Isha, and Anant Ambani.

One of Mukesh's most groundbreaking achievements was the launch of Reliance Jio in 2016, which revolutionised India's telecom industry. Jio introduced affordable 4G services, leading to a digital revolution and making India one of the largest mobile data consumers in the world. This move disrupted traditional telecom players and redefined internet accessibility in the country.

Reliance Industries has also diversified into retail, green energy, and media. Under Mukesh's leadership, Reliance Retail became India's largest retailer, while Reliance Jio expanded into 5G technology. In 2024, Reliance merged its entertainment division with Disney India in an $8.5 billion deal, further strengthening its hold in the media industry.

As of 2025, Mukesh Ambani remains Asia's richest person, with a net worth exceeding $119.5 billion. He continues to shape the future of India's digital and energy landscape, aiming for a sustainable and tech-driven economy. His journey from a young entrepreneur to a global business leader is a testament to his vision, resilience, and strategic acumen.

Munshi Premchand

(1880–1936)

Writer

"Beauty doesn't need ornaments. Softness can't bear the weight of ornaments."

Munshi Premchand was one of the greatest literary figures of modern Hindi literature. His stories vividly portrayed the social scenario of those times. Premchand wrote on the realistic issues of the day-communalism, corruption, zamindari, debt, poverty, colonialism, etc. He avoided the use of highly Sanskritised Hindi and instead used the dialect of the common people.

Premchand's real name was Dhanpat Rai Srivastava. He was born on July 31, 1880 in Lamahi near Varanasi where his father, Munshi Ajaayab Lal was a clerk in the post office. Premchand lost his mother when he was just seven years old. His father married again. Premchand was very close to his elder sister. His early education was in a *madarasa* under a *Maulavi*, where he learnt Urdu. When he was studying in the ninth class he was married, much against his wishes. He was only fifteen years old at that time.

Premchand lost his father, when he was sixteen years old. Premchand was left responsible for his stepmother and stepsiblings. He earned five rupees a month tutoring a lawyer's child. Premchand passed his matriculation exam with great effort and took up a teaching position, with a monthly salary of eighteen rupees. While working, he studied privately and passed his Intermediate and BA examinations. Later, Premchand worked as the deputy sub-inspector of schools in what was then the United Provinces.

In 1910, he was hauled up by the District Magistrate in Jamirpur for his anthology of short stories, *Soz-e-Watan* (Dirge of the Nation), which was labelled seditious. His book, *Soz-e-Watan* was banned by the then British government, which burnt all of the copies. Initially, Premchand wrote in Urdu under the name of 'Nawabrai'. However, when his novel, *Soz-e-Watan* was confiscated by the British, he started writing under the pseudonym, 'Premchand'.

Before Premchand, Hindi literature consisted mainly of fantasy or religious works. He brought realism to Hindi literature. He wrote over 300 stories, a dozen novels and two plays. The stories have been compiled and published as *Maạnsarovar*. His famous creations are: *Panch Parameshvar*, *Idgah*, *Shatranj Ke Khiladi*, *Poos Ki Raat*, *Bade Ghar Ki Beti*, *Kafan*, *Udhar Ki Ghadi*, *Namak Ka Daroga*, *Gaban*, *Godaan*, and *Nirmala*.

Premchand was a great social reformer. He married a child widow named Shivarani Devi. She wrote a book on him, *Premchand Gharmein* after his death. In 1921, he answered Gandhiji's call and resigned from his job. He worked to generate patriotism and nationalistic sentiments in the general populace. When the editor of the journal, *Maryaada* was jailed in the freedom movement, Premchand worked for a time as the editor of that journal. Afterwards, he worked as the Principal in a school in the Kashi Vidyapeeth.

The main characteristic of Premchand's writings is his interesting storytelling and use of simple language. His writings have been translated not only into all Indian languages, but also Russian, Chinese, and many other foreign languages.

Besides being a great novelist, Premchand was also a social reformer and thinker. His greatness lies in the fact that his writings embody social purpose and social criticism rather than mere entertainment. Literature according to him is a powerful means of educating public opinion. He believed in social evolution and his ideal was equal opportunities for all. Premchand died in 1936 and has since been studied both in India and abroad as one of the greatest writers of the century.

Naomi Campbell

(1970)

Supermodel, Actress

"I make a lot of money, but I don't want to talk about that. I work very hard and I'm worth every cent."

Naomi Campbell is an English supermodel and actress. She has been a prominent fashion model on the runway and in print advertising since the late 1980s.

Campbell was born on May 22, 1970 in Streatham, South London. She is of mixed race, mostly Afro-Jamaican heritage, though her father is also partially of Jamaican-Chinese descent. She went to a comprehensive school in Streatham and attended the London Academy For Performing Arts. A graduate of the Italia Conti Academy stage school, Campbell's first appearance to a wider public was in February 1978 when she was cast as a pupil to appear in a music video with Jamaican reggae superstar, Bob Marley for his song, Is This Love?

Aged 15 and while still a student of the Italia Conti Stage School, Campbell was spotted by Beth Boldt, former head of Synchro models agency, window-shopping in Covent Garden. In April 1986, she appeared on the cover of 'Elle', when a black model had to cancel out of the appearance, and was replaced by Campbell. By August 1988, she had appeared on the cover of the French Vogue as that publication's first black cover girl, and she completed campaigns for Ralph Lauren and Francois Nars.

Her modelling career started as a catwalk model, but she was quickly picked up for various high-profile advertising campaigns for 'Lee Jeans' and Olympus Corporation, which brought her to the American market. The highpoint of her career was in the early 1990's, when she was part of the two major supermodelling powerhouses, the Big Six and the Trinity, (with Linda Evangelista and Christy Turlington).

She has walked the catwalk for many fashion designers, including Gianni Versace and Valentino. Naomi did tumble over on the catwalk at Vivienne Westwood's Anglomania fashion show in 1994. She was the first black model to appear on the cover of *Time* magazine, *Vogue Nippon* and the French and British *Vogue* magazines. She has also appeared on the covers of Harper's *Bazaar* and *ELLE* magazine. Naomi posed nude for *Playboy* magazine, and for a series of lesbian-erotic photos with Madonna in the latter's book, *Sex*.

Campbell has appeared in music videos for artists such as Michael Jackson, Jay-Z, Macy Gray, Prince, Usher and also Madonna's music video, *Erotica*, with Ingrid Casares on October 12, 1992.

Campbell has also tried her hand at singing. Her album, *Baby Woman* sold over one million copies worldwide (but mostly in Japan), and she was featured on 'Vanilla Ice's single' *Cool as Ice*. In 1995, her collaboration with Toshinobu Kubota, *La La La Love Song*, became a number one hit in Japan.

She "co-wrote" the best-selling novel *Swan* in 1996, and followed it up with a photography book entitled *Naomi*. But when questioned about her use of a ghost writer for *Swan*, Campbell admitted that she wrote almost none of the book: "I just did not have time to sit down and write a book". In 2009, Campbell gained a lot of media attention after she dubbed the fashion industry as racist.

Her charity worn began with a facus on the children and people of Africa, including working with Nelson Mandela, since 1997. In 2005, Campbell founded the charity We Love Brazil, which aims to raise awareness and funds to fight poverty in Brazil.That same year, Campbell founded the charity Fashion for Relief, which has organised fund-raising fashion shows to benefit victims of Hurricane Katrina in 2005, the India terrorist attacks in 2009, the Haiti earthquake in 2010, and the Japan earthquake in 2011. In 2012 Fashion for Relief teamed up with YOOX China and leading global and Chinese fashion designers to design Chinese-themed T-shirts to help fund Fashion for Relief international and the various international charities it works with. Fashion for Relief has raised over £4.5 million.

In March 2013, Campbell graced the inaugural cover of *Numero* Russia.

In June 2018, Campbell received the Fashion Icon award by the Council of Fashion Designers of America. In 2019, she received the first beauty contract of her career, with NARS Cosmetics. On January 12, 2021, Campbell was appointed as a tourism ambassador by the Kenyan Ministry of Tourism and Wildlife. In March 2021, she was named as the face of the relaunch advertising campaign for streetwear brand Hood by Air.

In 2023, she co-produced the documentary *Invisible Beauty,* highlighting diversity in fashion. She also launched her own fashion line, collaborating with top designers. In 2024, the Victoria & Albert Museum in London honoured her career with the exhibition "Naomi : In Fashion."

❑❑❑

Napoleon Bonaparte

(1769–1821)

Dictator

"Respect the burden."

Napoleon Bonaparte was the Emperor of France from 1804 to 1815. Because of his interest in and subsequent exploration of Egypt, he is often known as the "Father of Egyptology."

He was born as *Napoleone di Buonaparte* in the town of Ajaccio on Corsica, France, on August 15, 1769, only one year after the island was transferred to France by the Republic of Genoa. He later adopted the more French-sounding name *Napoleon Bonaparte*.

Napoleon commanded troops that quelled a royalist Parisian uprising in 1795 and as a reward was given the army of the interior to lead. Soonafter, he was made the commander in chief of the army of Italy.

He married Josephine de Beauharnais in 1796, before going off to lead the poorly equipped army based in Italy. The Italian campaign was a success over the Austrians. With victory across Italy, and his signature on the 'Truce of Leoben', his popularity across much of Europe was sealed.

He set his sights on British domination and planned to attack at Egypt, then India. While he won a number of triumphs along the way, his fleet was destroyed by Nelson at Abu Qir in 1798.

The Ottomans then declared war on France, but were defeated by Napoleon in Egypt. Back in France, the government was in crisis. Napoleon secretly left Egypt for Paris, where he conspired to stage a coup d'etat and was named first consul on November 9, 1799. His rule saw the centralisation of government, the creation of the Bank of France, reinstatement of Roman Catholicism as the state religion and law reform with the Code Napoleon.

Over the next two years, he would defeat the Austrians at Marengo, and sign the Treaty of Luneville (1801) and Amiens (1802), which established French power on the continent. In 1802, the constitution of France was altered so Napoleon could be consul for life.

Soon after, Britain declared war on France and sent support to Napoleon's enemies to aid in his murder. In 1804, he had proclaimed himself the emperor of the France. Within the year, he claimed kingship of Italy and annexed Genoa, enraging Britain, Austria, Russia and Sweden who allied against him.

Notable battles followed, including a victory at Austerlitz over the Russians and Austrians (1805) and a cruel defeat again at the hands of Nelson at Trafalgar (1805). However, Napoleon gained much territory elsewhere, including annexation of Prussian lands which ostensibly gave him control of Europe. The Holy Roman Empire was dissolved, Holland and Westphalia created, and over the next five years, Napoleon's relatives and loyalists were installed as leaders (in Holland, Westphalia, Italy, Naples, Spain and Sweden).

In 1810, he had his childless marriage annulled and re-married in the hopes of getting an heir. Napoleon II was born a year later.

The Peninsular War of 1808–1814 saw the beginning of Napoleon's decline. Costly defeats, an empire that was unexpectedly difficult to control and growing unrest with his iron will, all contributed. His invasion of Russia cost him further. His Grande Armee of 500,000 men would be virtually destroyed during 1812 and Napoleon returned to Paris in December with fewer allies then he started with.

The Allies defeated him in battle over the course of the next two years, and finally, on March 31, 1814, Paris fell. Napoleon abdicated to Elba. There he learnt that the French, and especially the army, were unhappy with the treatment of the restored Bourbon leadership. He took this opportunity to march on Paris and reinstate himself for his fateful '100 Days'. The Battle of Waterloo ended his brief reign. He surrendered to Britain, hoping for leniency, and instead was exiled to St. Helena where he died on May 5, 1821.

❑❑❑

Narendra Modi

(1950)

Politician

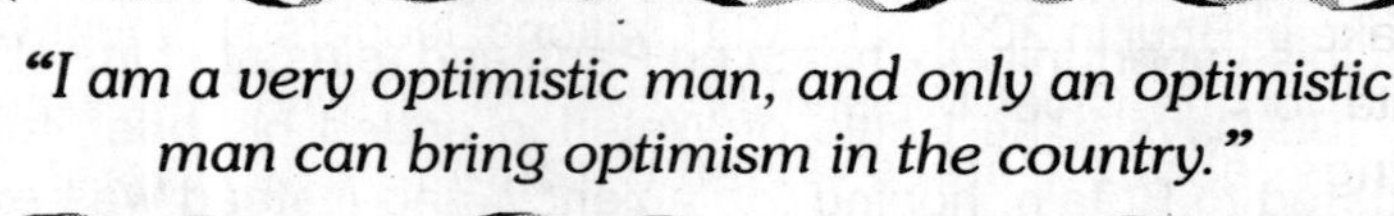

"I am a very optimistic man, and only an optimistic man can bring optimism in the country."

Narendra Damodardas Modi is an Indian politician who is the 14th and current Prime Minister of India. He was the Chief Minister of Gujarat from 2001 to 2014, and is the Member of Parliament from Varanasi.

Narendra Modi was born on 17 September 1950 to a family of grocers in Vadnagar, Mehsana district, Bombay State (present-day Gujarat). He was the third of six children born to Damodardas Mulchand Modi and Hiraben Modi. Modi's family belonged to the Modh-Ghanchi-Teli (oil-presser) community, which is categorised as an Other Backward Class by the Indian government.

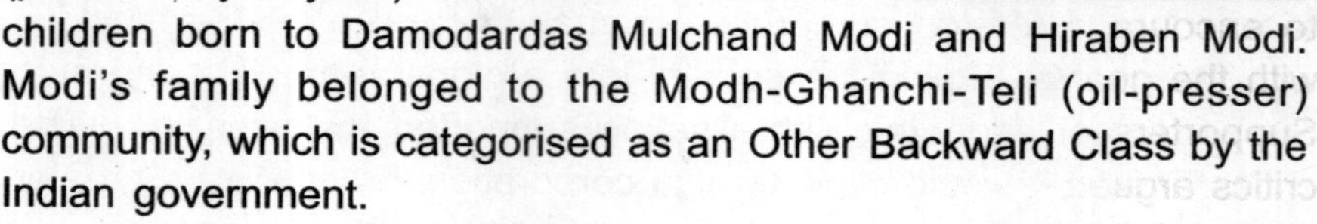

Modi helped his father sell tea as a child, and later ran his own stall. He was introduced to the RSS at the age of eight, beginning a long association with the organisation. He left home after graduating from school, partly because of an arranged marriage which he rejected. Modi traveled around India for two years, and visited a number of religious centres. He returned to Gujarat and moved to Ahmedabad in 1969 or 1970. In 1971 he became a full-time worker for the RSS. During the state of emergency imposed across the country in 1975, he was forced to go into hiding. The RSS assigned him to the BJP in 1985, and he held several positions within the party hierarchy until 2001, rising to the rank of general secretary.

In 2001, Keshubhai Patel's health was failing and the BJP lost a few state assembly seats in by-elections. Allegations of abuse of power, corruption and poor administration were made, and Patel's standing had been damaged by his administration's handling of the earthquake in Bhuj in 2001. The BJP national leadership sought a new candidate for the Chief Ministership, and Modi, who had expressed misgivings about Patel's administration, was chosen as a replacement.

His administration has been considered complicit in the 2002 Gujarat riots, or otherwise criticised for its handling of it, although a court found no evidence to prosecute Modi. His policies as Chief Minister, credited with encouraging economic growth, have received praise. His administration has been criticised for failing to significantly improve health, poverty, and education indices in the state.

Modi led the BJP in the 2014 general election, which gave the party a majority in the Lok Sabha, the first time a single party had achieved this since 1984.

In September 2014, Modi introduced the 'Make in India' initiative to encourage foreign companies to manufacture products in India, with the goal of turning the country into a global manufacturing hub. Supporters of economic liberalisation supported the initiative, while critics argued it would allow foreign corporations to capture a greater share of the Indian market.

On 25 June 2015, Modi launched a programme intended to develop 100 smart cities.

In his first cabinet decision, Modi set up a team to investigate black money. On 9 November 2016, the government demonetised ₹ 500 and ₹ 1000 banknotes, with the stated intention of curbing corruption, black money, the use of counterfeit currency, and terrorism.

Modi was named the Best Chief Minister in a 2007 nationwide survey by *India Today.* In 2016, a wax statue of Modi was unveiled at Madame Tussaud Wax Museum in London.

In October 2018, Modi received United Nations's highest environmental award, the 'Champions of the Earth', for policy leadership by "pioneering work in championing" the International Solar Alliance and "new areas of levels of cooperation on environmental action". On 24 October, 2018, he was conferred with the Seoul Peace Prize for 2018 for his contribution to international cooperation and fostering global economic growth.

He was awarded the Global Goalkeeper Award on 24 September, 2019 in New York City by the Bill & Melinda Gates Foundation in recognition for the Swachh Bharat Mission and "the progress India has made in providing safe sanitation under his leadership".

In 2020, Modi was among eight world leaders awarded the parodic Ig Nobel Prize in Medical Education. On 21 December, 2020, President Donald Trump awarded Modi with the Legion of Merit for elevating the India-United States relations.

On 24 February, 2021, the largest cricket stadium in the world at Ahmedabad was renamed Narendra Modi Stadium by the Gujarat Cricket Association.

He launched PM SHRI Scheme (2022) to modernise schools and inaugurated India's new Parliament building (2023). In 2025, he expanded nuclear energy projects, strengthened U.S.-India trade, and boosted rural development through Svamitva Yojana. His leadership continues shaping India's growth across multiple sectors.

Neil Armstrong

(1930–2012)

Astronaut

"Mystery creates wonder and wonder is the basis of man's desire to understand."

Neil Armstrong is popularly known as the first man to walk on the Moon. He was a former American test pilot and US astronaut.

He was born on August 5, 1930 in Wapakoneta, Ohio, USA. Neil Armstrong was interested in aviation from a young age. At 15, he worked in various jobs in order to pay for his flying lessons. At 16, he got his student pilot's licence before he was legally old enough to drive a car and before he graduated from Blume High School, in Wapakoneta, in 1947.

Immediately after high school, Neil Armstrong received a scholarship from the US Navy. He enrolled at Purdue University in West Lafayette, Indiana and began his studies of aeronautical engineering, but in 1949, the Navy called him to active duty.

In 1950, Neil Armstrong was sent to Korea and served as a naval pilot during the Korean War. He flew 78 combat missions from the USS

Essex in a Grumman F9F-2 Panther. He received three medals: the Air Medal and two Gold Stars for his military service during the Korean War. After the war, he left the Navy and returned to Purdue in 1952 and graduated with a Bachelor of Science degree in Aeronautical Engineering.

In 1955, he joined NACA (National Advisory Committee for Aeronautics - now known as NASA), as a research pilot at the NACA Lewis Research Centre in Cleveland, Ohio. Later that year, he transferred to the NACA High Speed Flight Station (now NASA's Dryden Flight Research Centre), at Edwards Air Force Base in California where he worked as a test pilot for many experimental high speed aircraft including the X-15. From 1960 to 1962, he was a pilot involved in the X-20 Dyna-Soar orbital glider programme.

In 1962, while serving as a test pilot, Neil Armstrong was selected by NASA to join the second group of NASA's astronaut trainees (one of nine NASA astronauts). He moved to El Lago, Texas, near Houston's Manned Spacecraft Centre to begin his astronaut training and underwent four years of intensive training for the Apollo programme. His first assignment was as backup command pilot for the Gemini 5 mission in 1965.

In 1966, Neil Armstrong was assigned as command pilot for the Gemini 8. Gemini 8 mission was launched on March 16, 1966 and achieved the first docking of two orbiting spacecraft. His first space flight was nearly a disaster. He was in the first US emergency in space with his partner, David Scott when their spacecraft spun wildly out of control. Then they returned to Earth safely.

He was the backup command pilot for the Gemini 11 mission in 1966 and the commander of the backup crew for the Apollo 8 lunar orbital mission in 1968, using Apollo Spacecraft.

In 1968, Neil Armstrong was chosen to be a member of the Apollo 11 mission, the first manned lunar landing. The Apollo 11 crews were: Neil Armstrong, Michael Collins and Edwin 'Buzz' Aldrin.

Apollo 11 was launched on July 16, 1969, from Cape Kennedy, Florida by a Saturn V rocket. Four days later, it went into orbit around the Moon. The lunar module Eagle separated from the Command Module with Armstrong and Aldrin aboard and descended to the surface of the Moon. Michael Collins remained in the Command Module in orbit.

During the Moon landing, Armstrong took manual control of the Lunar Module Eagle and piloted it away from a rocky area and made a safe landing on the moon. His first words from the Moon were: *"Houston, Tranquility Base here. The Eagle has landed"*.

Neil Armstrong was the first person to walk on the Moon on July 20, 1969. His first words after stepping on the moon were, *"That's one small step for a man, one giant leap for mankind"*. This event was televised to Earth and seen by millions! The Apollo 11 crew returned safely to Earth on July 24, 1969.

From 1969 to 1971, Neil Armstrong held the position of Deputy Association Administrator for Aeronautics, NASA Headquarters Office of Advanced Research and Technology.

He resigned from NASA in 1971, and became a professor of aerospace engineering at the University of Cincinnati, where he was involved in both teaching and research until 1979. During the years 1982–1992, Armstrong was chairman of Computing Technologies for Aviation Inc., Charlottesville, Virginia.

In 1986, he was appointed as vice chairman of the presidential commission that investigated the Challenger Space Shuttle disaster.

From 1989 until he retired in 2002, Neil Armstrong served as chairman of AIL Technologies (Deer Park, New York), an electronics and avionics manufacturer.

Since 1994, he began refusing any requests for autographs, after he found that his signed items were selling for large amounts of money and that many forgeries are in circulation. Often items reached prices of US$1,000 on auction sites like eBay. Signed photographs of the *Apollo 11* crew could sell for $5,000. Any requests sent to him received a form letter in reply saying that he has stopped signing.

In 2005, Armstrong said that a human voyage to Mars will be easier than the lunar challenge of the 1960s: "I suspect that even though the various questions are difficult and many, they are not as difficult and many as those we faced when we started the Apollo (space program) in 1961." Armstrong also recalled his initial concerns about the *Apollo 11* mission. He had believed there was only a 50 percent chance of landing on the Moon. "I was elated, ecstatic and extremely surprised that we were successful," he said.

In May 2005, Neil Armstrong became involved in an unusual legal battle with his barber of 20 years, Marx Sizemore of Lebanon, Ohio. After cutting Armstrong's hair, Sizemore sold some of it to a collector for $3,000 without his knowledge or consent. Armstrong threatened legal action unless the barber returned the hair or donated the proceeds to a charity of Armstrong's choosing. Sizemore, unable to get the hair back, decided to donate the proceeds to the charity that Armstrong chose.

Armstrong received many honours and awards, including the Presidential Medal of Freedom and the Congressional Space Medal of Honour. His authorized biography, *First Man : The Life of Neil A Armstrong*, was published in 2005. In a 2010 Space Foundation Survey, he was ranked as the number one most popular space hero.

Armstrong died in Cincinnati, Ohio, on August 25, 2012, at the age of 82, after complications from coronary artery bypass surgery.

❑❑❑

Nelson Rolihlahla Mandela

(1918–2013)

Statesman and Leader

"I learned that courage was not the absence of fear, but the triumph over it. The brave man is not he who does not feel afraid, but he who conquers that fear."

Nelson Mandela was the first black President of South Africa. He was a legendary figure in the history of the African National Congress, or ANC. He was arrested for sabotage and conspiracy to overthrow the government which led to his imprisonment for almost 30 years. Mandela was imprisoned for opposing South Africa's white minority government and its policy of racial separation, known as *apartheid*. He became a martyr and worldwide symbol of resistance to racism.

He was born on July 18, 1918, into the royal family of the Thembu in the Transkei region of South Africa. His father Henry Mandela was the principal Councillor to the Acting Paramount Chief of Thembuland. After the death of his father, the young Rolihlahla became the Paramount Chiefs' ward to be groomed to assume the high office. After receiving a primary education at a local mission school, he was sent to Healdtown, a Wesleyan secondary school where he matriculated. Mandela enrolled at the University College of Fort Hare for the Bachelor of Arts Degree where he was elected onto the Student's Representative Council. He was suspended from college for joining in a protest boycott. He went to Johannesburg where he completed his BA by correspondence, took articles of clerkship and commenced study for his LLB. He entered politics in earnest while studying in Johannesburg by joining the African National Congress in 1942.

In September 1944, Mandela established the Youth League of the African National Congress (ANCYL), and was engaged in resistance against the ruling National Party's *apartheid* policies after 1948. He went on trial for treason in 1956–1961 and was acquitted in 1961. After the banning of the ANC in 1960, he argued for the setting up of a military wing within the ANC. In June 1961, the ANC executive considered his proposal on the use of violent tactics and agreed that those members who wished to involve themselves in Mandela's campaign would not be stopped from doing so by the ANC.

Mandela was arrested in 1962 and sentenced to imprisonment with hard labour. He was convicted of plotting to overthrow the government. His statement from the dock in the Rivonia Trial ended with these words: '*I have fought against white domination, and I have fought against black domination. I have cherished the ideal of a democratic and free society in which all persons live together in harmony and with equal opportunities. It is an ideal which I hope to live for and to achieve. But if needs be, it is an ideal for which I am prepared to die.*'

On June 12, 1964, eight of the accused, including Mandela, were sentenced to life imprisonment. From 1964 to 1982, he was incarcerated at Robben Island Prison, off Cape Town: thereafter, he was sent to Pollsmoor Prison, nearby on the mainland.

During his years in prison, Nelson Mandela's reputation grew steadily. He was widely accepted as the most significant Black leader in South Africa and became a potent symbol of resistance as the *anti-apartheid movement* gathered strength. While in prison, Mandela flatly rejected offers made by his jailers for remission of sentence in exchange for accepting the *Bantustan policy* by recognising the independence of the Transkei and agreeing to settle there. Again in the eighties, Mandela rejected an offer of release on condition that he had to renounce violence. "Prisoners cannot enter into contracts. Only free men can negotiate", he said. He consistently refused to compromise his political position to obtain his freedom.

Mandela has been married three times: to the former Evelyn Mase from 1944 to 1957, to Winifred Madikizela (known as Winnie) from 1958 to 1996, and to Graca Machel in 1998, who is his present wife. Mandela's wife, Winnie became a powerful figure in her own right while Mandela was imprisoned; however, her entanglement in a series of scandals led to the couple's estrangement in 1992, her dismissal from his cabinet in 1995, and their official divorce in 1996.

In December 1997, Mandela stepped down as leader of the ANC, in favour of the South African Vice-President Thabo Mbeki. In June 1999, he formally retired as President of South Africa, and was succeeded by Mbeki following the election that month.

His life has been an inspiration, in South Africa and throughout the world, to all who are oppressed and deprived, to all who are opposed to oppression and deprivation. Mandela had honorary degrees from more than 50 international universities and was Chancellor of the University of the North. He won the Nobel Peace Prize in 1993. In 2009, UN General Assembly announced that Mandela's birthday, July 18, is to be known as 'Mandela Day' marking his contribution to world freedom.

He died on December 5, 2013.

❑❑❑

Nicolaus Copernicus

(1473–1543)

Astronomer

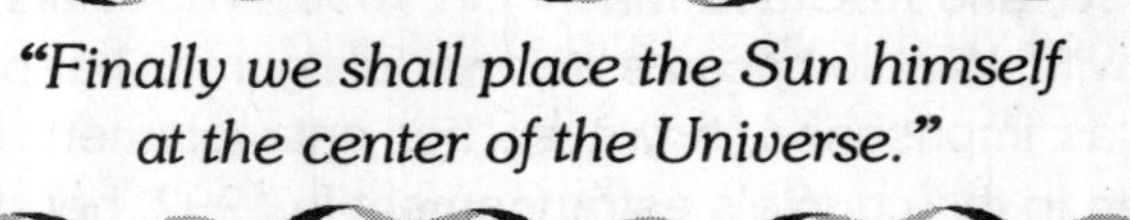

"Finally we shall place the Sun himself at the center of the Universe."

Copernicus was a Polish astronomer, best known for his theory that the Sun and not the Earth is at the centre of the universe.

Also known as the founder of modern astronomy, Copernicus was the first person to devise a comprehensive heliocentric cosmology, which displaced the Earth from the center of the universe. Copernicus' heliocentric theory acted as the catalyst for the scientific revolution of the 16th and 17th centuries, which is sometimes known as the Copernican revolution. His work forever changed the place of man in the cosmos; no longer could man legitimately think his importance greater than his fellow creatures. Besides an astronomer he was also a great mathematician, physician, quadrilingual polyglot, classical scholar, translator and artist.

Copernicus was born on 19 February 1473 in Thorn (modern day Torun) in Poland. His father was a merchant and local official. When

Copernicus was 10, his father died, and his uncle, a priest, ensured that Copernicus received a good education. In 1491, he went to Krakow Academy, now the Jagiellonian University, and in 1496 travelled to Italy to study law. While a student at the University of Bologna he stayed with a mathematics professor, Domenico Maria de Novara, who encouraged his interests in geography and astronomy.

During his time in Italy, Copernicus visited Rome and studied at the universities of Padua and Ferrara, before returning to Poland in 1503. For the next seven years he worked as a private secretary to his uncle, then the bishop of Ermland.

The bishop died in 1512 and Copernicus moved to Frauenberg, where he had long held a position as a canon, an administrative appointment in the church. This gave him more time to devote to astronomy. Although he did not seek fame, it is clear that he was by then well known as an astronomer. In 1514, when the Catholic church was seeking to improve the calendar, one of the experts to whom the pope appealed was Nicolaus Copernicus.

From 1513, the foundation of his great work was laid down at Frauenburg, where he began work on his heliocentric theory. His theory was a concise description of the world's heliocentric mechanism, without mathematical apparatus, and varyied in some important aspects of gèometric construction from De revolutionibus; but it was already based on the same assumptions regarding Earth's triple motions.

He wrote a manuscript explaining his new theory which was read by many astronomers, and rumours of Copernicus' claim that the earth revolves about the sun spread all through Europe. His theory attracted many mathematicians and various astronomers who came to Copernicus to learn more about his new theory. Even though Copernicus finished writing his book, *De revolutionibus orbium coelestium*, about a decade earlier, in 1530, he postponed its publication fearing the reactions his ground-breaking theory might stir up.

However, he finally published his book in May 1543. His book is considered to serve the beginning of modern astronomy and the defining epiphany that began the scientific revolution. Its central theory was that the Earth rotates daily on its axis and revolves yearly around the sun. He also argued that the planets circled the Sun. This challenged the long held view that the Earth was stationary at the centre of the universe with all the planets, the Moon and the Sun rotating around it.

Ironically, Copernicus had dedicated *De revolutionibus orbium coelestium* to Pope Paul III. If his tribute to the pope was an attempt to cull the Catholic Church's softer reception, it was to no avail. The Church ultimately banned *De revolutionibus* posthumously, and the book remained on the list of forbidden reading material for nearly three centuries thereafter.

Suffering the aftermath of a recent stroke, Copernicus is said to have been clutching the book when he died in his bed on May 24, 1543 in Frauenburg, Poland.

Copernicus became a symbol of the brave scientist standing alone, defending his theories against the common beliefs of his time.

❑❑❑

Neeraj Chopra

(1997)

Javelin Thrower

"You have to give your best and never give up on your dreams. Success is not only winning medals but to work consistently for it."

Neeraj Chopra, born on December 24, 1997, in Khandra village, Panipat district, Haryana, India, has emerged as a beacon of excellence in the world of athletics, particularly in the javelin throw. Hailing from a humble farming family, his father, Satish Kumar, is a farmer, and his mother, Saroj Devi, is a homemaker. Neeraj has two sisters, Sangeeta and Sarita.

During his childhood, Neeraj faced challenges due to his weight, which led him to pursue physical activities to improve his fitness. At the age of 11, weighing around 80 kilograms, he joined a gym in Panipat. It was during this period that he discovered his passion for javelin throw at the Shivaji Stadium in Panipat.

Neeraj's dedication to the sport became evident as he trained rigorously, leading to his first major international achievement in 2016.

At the IAAF World U20 Championships in Bydgoszcz, Poland, he clinched the gold medal with a throw of 86.48 meters, setting a world junior record. This remarkable feat marked him as a rising star in athletics.

In 2018, Neeraj continued his impressive trajectory by winning gold medals at both the Commonwealth Games in Gold Coast, Australia, and the Asian Games in Jakarta, Indonesia. His throw of 88.06 meters at the Asian Games not only secured the gold but also set a new national record.

The pinnacle of Neeraj's career came at the Tokyo 2020 Olympics, held in 2021 due to the COVID-19 pandemic. He made history by winning the gold medal in the men's javelin throw with a distance of 87.58 meters, becoming the first Indian to secure an Olympic gold in athletics since independence. This monumental achievement elevated him to national hero status and inspired countless aspiring athletes in India.

Neeraj's success continued as he secured a silver medal at the World Athletics Championships in Eugene, Oregon, in 2022, with a throw of 88.13 meters. He further cemented his legacy by winning the gold medal at the 2023 World Athletics Championships in Budapest, Hungary, with a throw of 88.17 meters, becoming the first Indian to achieve this honour.

Neeraj Chopra achieved a new personal best in the javelin throw, crossing the 90-meter mark for the first time with a throw of 90.23 meters at the Doha Diamond League on May 16, 2025. He also set a new national record with this throw.

Throughout his career, Neeraj has been recognised with numerous accolades, including the prestigious Padma Shri and the Vishisht Seva Medal, reflecting his contributions to sports and his service in the Indian Army, where he holds the rank of Subedar Major.

On the personal front, Neeraj Chopra married former tennis player and coach Himani Mor in January 2025, marking a new chapter in his life.

Neeraj's journey from a village in Haryana to the global stage exemplifies dedication, resilience, and the pursuit of excellence. His achievements have not only brought glory to India but have also inspired a generation to dream big and strive for greatness in the realm of sports.

❑❑❑

Oprah Winfrey

(1954)

Talk Show Host and Actress

"I trust that everything happens for a reason, even when we're not wise enough to see it."

She is a multiple-Emmy Award winning host of 'The Oprah Winfrey Show', the highest rated talk show in television history. She is also an influential book critic, an Academy Award-nominated actress, and a magazine publisher. According to *Forbes* magazine, she was the richest African American of the 20th century.

Born in Kosciusko, Mississippi, in 1954 Oprah Winfrey was reared by her grandmother on a farm where she "began her broadcasting career" by learning to read aloud and perform recitations at the age of three. From the age of 6 to 13, she lived in Milwaukee with her mother. After suffering abuse, she ran away and was sent to a juvenile detention home at the age of 13, only to be denied admission because all the beds were filled. As a last resort, she was sent to Nashville to live under her father's strict discipline. Vernon Winfrey saw to it that his daughter met a midnight curfew, and he required her to read a book and write a book report each week.

Oprah Winfrey's broadcasting career began at the age of 17, when she worked at a local radio station while attending Tennessee State University. After two years, she signed on with WTVF-TV in Nashville as a reporter/anchor. She attended Tennessee State University, where she majored in Speech Communications and Performing Arts.

In 1976, she moved to Baltimore to join WJZ-TV news as a co-anchor, and in 1978 discovered her talent for hosting talk shows when she became the co-host of WJZ-TV's 'People Are Talking,' while continuing to serve as anchor and news reporter.

In January 1984, Oprah Winfrey came to Chicago to host WLS-TV's 'AM Chicago,' a faltering local talk show. In less than a year, she turned 'AM Chicago' into the hottest show in town. The format was soon expanded to one hour, and in September 1985 it was renamed, 'The Oprah Winfrey Show.'

Telecasted nationally since September 8, 1986, 'The Oprah Winfrey Show' became the number one talk show in national syndication in less than a year. In June 1987, in its first year of eligibility, 'The Oprah Winfrey Show' received three Daytime Emmy Awards in the categories of Outstanding Host, Outstanding Talk/ Service Programme and Outstanding Direction.

In June 1988, 'The Oprah Winfrey Show' received its second consecutive Daytime Emmy Award as Outstanding Talk/Service Programme, and she herself received the International Radio and Television Society's 'Broadcaster of the Year' Award.

Before America fell in love with Oprah Winfrey, the talk show host, she captured the nation's attention with her poignant portrayal of Sofia in Steven Spielberg's 1985 adaptation of Alice Walker's novel, *The Colour urple*. Winfrey's performance earned her nominations for an Oscar and Golden Globe Award in the category of Best Supporting Actress. Critics again lauded her performance in *Native Son*.

Her love of acting and her desire to bring quality entertainment projects into production prompted her to form her own production company, HARPO Productions, Inc., in 1986.

In October, 1988, HARPO Productions, Inc. acquired ownership and all production responsibilities for 'The Oprah Winfrey Show'from Capitol Cities/ABC, making Oprah Winfrey the first woman in history to own and produce her own talk show.

The following year, HARPO produced its first television miniseries, *The Women of Brewster Place*, with Oprah Winfrey as star and Executive Producer. It has been followed by the TV movies, *There Are No Children Here* (1993), and *Before Women Had Wings* (1997), which she both produced and acted. In 1998, she starred in the feature film *Beloved*, from the book by the Nobel Prize-winning American author, Toni Morrison.

In 1991, she initiated a campaign to establish a national database of convicted child abusers, and testified before a U.S. Senate Judiciary Committee on behalf of a National Child Protection Act. President Clinton signed the 'Oprah Bill' in 1993.

Oprah Winfrey was named one of the '100 most influential people' of the 20th Century by the *Time* magazine, and in 1998 received a *Lifetime Achievement Award* from the *National Academy of Television Arts and Sciences*. Her on-air book club, Oprah Book Club selections, became instant bestsellers, and in 1999, she was presented with the *National Book Foundation's 50th anniversary gold medal* for her service to books and authors.

Winfrey was called "arguably the world's most powerful woman" by CNN and Time.com, "arguably the most influential woman in the world" by the *American Spectator*, "one of the 100 people who most influenced the 20th Century" and "one of the most influential people" of 2004, 2005, 2006, 2007, 2008 and 2009 by *Time*. *Forbes* named ner the world's most powerful celebrity in 2005, 2007, 2008 and 2010. According to *Forbes*, she was worth over $ 2.7 billion in September 2010.

The series finale of *The Oprah Winfrey Show* aired on May 25, 2011. In a list compiled by the British magazine *New Statesman* in September 2010, she was voted 38th in the list of "The World's 50 Most Influential Figures 2010". As of 2012, Winfrey had also given over 400 scholarships to Morehouse College in Atlanta, Georgia. In 2013, Winfrey donated $12 million to the Smithsonian's National Museum of African American History and Culture.

She was awarded the Presidential Medal of Freedom by President Barack Obama in 2013 and honorary doctorate degree from Duke and Harvard.

Winfrey was elected as a member of the American Academy of Arts and Sciences in 2021.

In October 2022, she co-executive produced the docuseries *The Hair Tales*, exploring Black women's hair narratives. In 2024, she launched *The Oprah Podcast*, featuring discussions with authors and public figures. In January 2025, she revisited Eckhart Tolle's *A New Earth* for her book club, aiming to introduce its teachings to a new generation.

❑❑❑

Orville & Wilbur Wright

(1871–1948 & 1867–1912)

Inventors

"I confess that in 1901, I said to my brother; Orville that man would not fly for fifty years."

The Wright brothers, Orville and Wilbur are Americans generally credited with making the first controlled, powered, heavier-than-air human flight on December 17, 1903. After two years, they developed their flying machine into the world's first practical fixed-wing aircraft, along with many other aviation milestones.

Wilbur and Orville Wright were two of the four children of Milton and Susan Wright. Wilbur was born in Indiana in 1867, whilst his younger brother Orville was born four years later in Ohio. It was inevitable that they would be born in different places, as their father was a bishop whose job dictated that he move house often. All the children were encouraged to learn at home, no matter what the topic. As the house in Ohio had not one but two libraries, they had no excuse not to.

The boys' fascination with aeronautics was kindled in 1878, when their father returned home with a toy helicopter powered by a rubber band. Immediately, they began designing flying machines of their own, but soon became disheartened when they failed to fly for a sustained period of time.

When Wilbur was aged nineteen, he was struck in the face by accident while playing a game. Subsequently, he suffered from heart palpitations, and for the next four years was forced to convalesce. At the same time, he looked after his sick mother who was dying from tuberculosis. Being house bound in such a negative atmosphere took its toll on him, and in essence, he became depressed.

In 1889, the year of their mother's death, the Wright brothers started up a printing business together, producing the weekly, *West Side News*. Three years later, they opened a bicycle shop, a good time to do so as a bicycle craze had the nation gripped. Using their naturally inventive mends, they began to design their own bicycles, and used any money made from the venture to fund more aeronautically orientated experiments.

Shrugging off their pessimism of earlier years, Orville and Wilbur Wright became convinced that the possibility of powered, sustained, controlled flight of an airplane was more than mere fantasy. By 1900, they had built a machine that they believed would fly. A year later, they attempted to do so but failed.

Undeterred, a wind tunnel was built in order to work out the correct lift data required for such an aircraft. While experimenting in the wind tunnel, they discovered that longer, narrower wings were more effective. Combined with their earlier discovery concerning roll, pitch, and yaw, which effectively controlled the aircraft, they had arrived at a winning combination.

On December 17, 1903 Orville took off in 'The Flyer' and controlled it in the air for twelve seconds. Interesting alterations were made and by 1905, in which thirty-minute flights had been achieved. Twelve months later, they had received their patent for the 'Wright

Flying Machine'. They subsequently signed contracts to build planes in Europe and for the US army.

Two years after the death of Wilbur Wright from typhoid in 1912, matters concerning the invention of the airplane became somewhat ugly. The Smithsonian Institution claimed that one of their men had beaten the Wright Brothers to the invention of the airplane. It wasn't until 1942, six years before the death of Orville Wright that they retracted the claim. Happily though, soon after his death a rebuilt 'Flyer III' was put on display in Ohio, his hometown.

❑❑❑

Osho

(1931–1990)

Spiritual Teacher

"I don't want anybody to stand between the individual and existence. No prayer, no priest – you alone are enough to face the sunrise."

Rajneesh Chandra Mohan Jain, better known as Bhagwan Shree Rajneesh and later as Osho, was an Indian spiritual teacher. He was a fully enlightened master who lived during the twentieth century. He was also a man of extraordinary intelligence, erudition, charisma, and powers of communication.

Bhagwan Shree Rajneesh was born on December 11, 1931 in Kuchwara, a small town in Raisen District of Madhya Pradesh. His parent's religion was Jainism. They chose to send him to his maternal grandparents until he was seven years old.

When Osho joined his first school, he was able to discuss with and convince his teacher, who was very strict with children. Osho explains that, if the child receives respect, he is more obedient to his parents. If the parents ignore the child's individuality, the child would in turn ignore them.

After Osho was seven, he went back to his parents. He explains that he received a similar kind of respect from his paternal grandfather who was staying with them. He was able to be very open with his grandfather.

He never subscribed to any religious faith during his lifetime. He received *samadhi* on March 21, 1953, at the age of 21. Rajneesh obtained a masters degree in philosophy from the University of Saugar. He taught philosophy at the University of Jabalpur for nine years and concurrently worked as a religious leader. In 1966, he left his teaching post and gave his full attention to teaching his *sannyasins* (disciples), while pursuing a speaking career. He had an apartment in Bombay (now Mumbai) where he often met individuals and small groups, acting as spiritual teacher, guide and friend.

However, Osho was a controversial spiritual teacher whose disciples at the beginning of the twenty-first century include thousands of Americans, Europeans, and Asians. The spiritual movement is centred at the Osho Commune International in Pune, at 17 Koregaon Park, where it was first established in the early 1970s.

He was a professor of philosophy, a lover of literature, and the author of an extraordinary library of books that explain the Hindu and Buddhist scriptures in matter-of-fact, crystal-clear English. In the 1980s, he and his followers built a 65,000-acre city from a scratch in the Oregon wilderness.

Osho was accused of crimes and eventually deported from the United States for violations of immigration law. He has left us a great legacy in the form of his books.

He explains that this was a major influence on his growth because his grandmother gave him the utmost freedom and respect, and also made other people including her husband to do the same. So, Osho was left reckless and carefree without education or restrictions.

Osho's synthesis of spirituality with personal-growth and psychology attracted significant numbers of Westerners, many in midlife transition. He developed unique meditations, many involving intense, emotionally cleansing activity preceding stillness. Before his death, he shifted his emphasis to meditative therapies encouraging the individuals' responsibility for their own personal and spiritual growth.

Meditation remains central to the movement, and Osho meditations have been taught in schools, corporations, and other venues. Osho's philosophical approach blends Western and Eastern traditions, with special emphasis on Zen Buddhism. His teaching themes include dropping the ego and its conditioned beliefs and integrating the material and the spiritual. In 1989, he took the name Osho, which means dissolving into the totality of existence, or merging with all life.

Osho died in Pune on January 19, 1990. Various rumours spread that he had been poisoned with thallium by the CIA, had been exposed to damaging doses of radiation by the US authorities, or had a heart failure. It is obvious that he did not experience thallium poisoning, because he died with a full beard and only male-pattern baldness on the top of his head. A person suffering from thallium poisoning suffers a dramatic loss of hair with a week of exposure. His death certificate lists heart failure as the cause of his death.

Now there are Osho centres in more than fifty nations. Osho Meditation Resort in Pune began as the *Shree Rajneesh Ashram* and continues as the movement's heart, housing a multiversity offering myriad courses on spiritual growth, healing, creative arts, and intimate relationships. There are also meditation workshops and programmes emphasising meditative aspects of sports.

Otto Von Bismarck

(1815–1898)

Iron Man of Germany

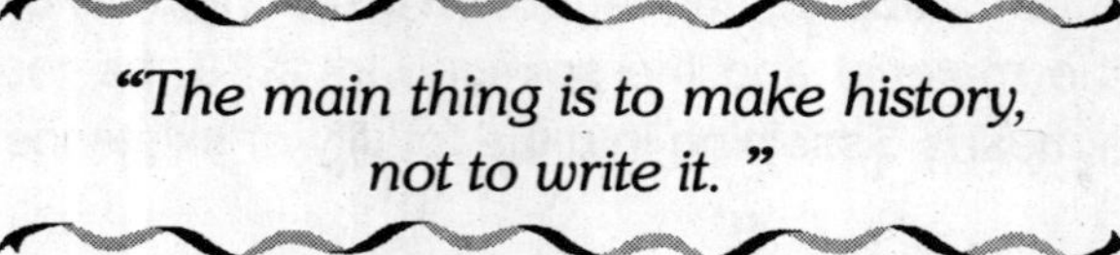

"The main thing is to make history, not to write it."

Known as a strong statesman and a great leader, Otto Von Bismarck paved the way for the rise of the modern German state. As Iron Chancellor, he instituted a social-welfare system while crushing the social-democracy movement. Remembered by some as a moderate, he's seen by others as a ruthless conservative who set the stage for fascism.

Born on April 1, 1815 in Schonhausen to noble parents, Bismarck went on to study law at Gottingen and Berlin. He gained his Bar status in 1835 and then became a lieutenant of the "Life Guards." After serving as a lieutenant, he took up residence of his families estate in Schonhausen and there he gained an interest in governmental affairs. In 1847, he was elected to the Prussian Diet.

Bismarck was a firm believer of wars to accomplish things. He once remarked that things should be settled by "blood and iron". This he certainly carried out in practice. Otto Von Bismarck achieved a unified

Germany by waging wars. He took Schleswig and Holstein (German provinces) from Denmark. With a peace treaty signed on October 30, 1864 in Vienna, these are still part of Germany today. How Bismarck dealt with Austria shows his commitment to maintaining boundries based on political and territorial lines. Prussia was pressuring Austria about the northern provinces of Hannover, Hesse-Kassel, Nassau and Frankfurt. In 1866, at the Battle of Koniggratz, the Austrians were soundly trounced and the "Nothern Confederation" was formed.

This Northern Confederation proved to be a catalyst in finally uniting all of Germany. The Northern Confederation, in particular Bismarck, provoked France into war and in 1870, the Franco-Prussian war broke out. The southern states of Germany believed that France was the aggressor and so joined the Northern Confederation, serving France a resounding defeat. This brought both the southern and northern German states together, resulting in a modern German state, excluding Austria.

A hero to his people, having been instrumental in the creation of the what was then the German empire, Bismarck was named the Chancellor. Using his authority and his diplomatic mettle, he made important and progressive decisions at home and worked to keep peace abroad.

Bismarck was very careful of his nation's place in Europe. He saw Germany's central location geographically, as a potentially fatal position. He had a surprising vision. Bismarck believed that if war erupted throughout Europe, Germany would be caught in the middle of maurding armies and be destroyed which was very close to what happened in World War I. Thus, Bismarck spent much time trying to maintain peace and creating alliances among the major powers of Europe. Unfortunately, many of these alliances made would create the powder keg which would start the First world war.

Internally, Bismarck continued to fight political liberalism. Some of the methods to do so resulted in very democratic and humanitarian laws, such as "guaranteeing accident and health insurance as well as old-age pensions." At the same time, he was having serious trouble with the Social Democrats and the Catholic Centre Party. He was called the "Iron Chancellor". He engaged in a "Kulter Kampf" or a culture war on the Catholics, which proved unsuccessfull. He outlawed the Social Democrats, which also proved fruitless.

In 1890, the Social Democrats made significant gains in the elections and Kaiser Willhelm II insisted that Bismarck resign his post as Chancellor. Otto Von Bismarck left his political career, organised his notes, memoirs and writings and died on July 30, 1898.

His life is a portrait of a successful politician who valued his goals over ideals. As seemingly perspicacious as he was during his life time, his fairlure was his shortsightedness. All of his planning did not prevent Germany being at the centre of the two most devastating wars this world had ever seen. Although being an idealist is no sure preventative to folly, the Bible does teach us to work for heavenly riches and a heavenly kingdom, not an earthly one.

❑❑❑

Pablo Picasso

(1881–1973)

Painter and Sculptor

"Nature does many things the way I do, but she hides them."

Pablo Picasso was a Spanish painter and sculptor. It has been estimated that Picasso produced about 13,500 paintings or designs, 100,000 prints or engravings, 34,000 book illustrations and 300 sculptures or ceramics.

Picasso was born on October 25, 1881 in Malaga, Spain, as the son of an art and drawing teacher. He was a brilliant student. He passed the entrance examination for the Barcelona School of Fine Arts at the age of 14 in just one day and was allowed to skip the first two classes.

According to one of many legends about the artist's life, his father, recognising the extraordinary talent of his son, gave him his brushes and palette and vowed to paint never again in his life.

During his lifetime, the artist went through different periods of characteristic painting styles. *The Blue Period of Picasso* lasted from about 1900 to 1904. It is characterised by the use of different shades of blue underlining the melancholic style of his subjects - people from the grim side of life with thin, half-starved bodies. His painting style during these years is masterly and convinces even those who reject his later modern style.

During *Picasso's Rose Period* from about 1905 to 1906, his style moved away from the *Blue Period* to a friendly pink tone with subjects taken from the world of circus.

In 1937, the artist created his landmark painting *Guernica*, a protest against the barbaric air raid against a Basque village during the Spanish Civil War. Picasso's *Guernica* is a huge mural on canvas in black, white and gray which was created for the Spanish Pavilion of the *Paris World's Fair* in 1937. In *Guernica*, Picasso used symbolic forms - that are repeatedly found in his works following *Guernica* - like a dying horse or a weeping woman.

Guernica was exhibited at the museum of Modern Art in New York until 1981. It was transferred to the Prado Museum in Madrid/Spain in 1981 and was later moved to the Queen Sofia Centre of Art, Madrid in 1992. Picasso had disallowed the return of *Guernica* to Spain until the end of the rule of Fascism by General Franco.

During his early years in Paris, he lived with Fernande Olivier for seven years. During World War I, from 1914 to 1918, Picasso worked in Rome where he met his first wife, Olga Koklova, a Russian ballet dancer. In 1927, he met Marie Therese Walther, a seventeen year old girl and began a relationship with her. In 1936, another woman, Dora Maar, a photographer, stepped into his life. In 1943, he encountered a young female painter, Francoise Gilot.

In 1947, she gave birth to Claude, and in 1949 to Paloma, Picasso's third and fourth child. The artist's last companion was Jacqueline Roque. He met her in 1953 and married her in 1961.

Pablo Picasso had created a total of more than 20,000 art objects during his lifetime - enough to keep the art market for his works in continuous movement.

Picasso prints are a wide hunting ground for art afficionados. Prices vary widely, depending on edition size, whether a print is signed and numbered, on age and on the attraction of the subject. In 1999, an aquatint called *La Femme au Tambourin,* signed in pencil and numbered 30/30 was sold for US$376,500 at Christie's in New York. But you can also buy an original Picasso print for a few hundred dollars from a large and unsigned edition or an edition that was made by a skilled printmaker after Picasso. These prints were often produced after drawings of the great master and with the approval or at least his knowledge. Some have his signatures on the plate, some have no signature at all. Such prints are by no means of any minor artistic value. They may not be the first choice from an investment value aspect. But they are a great way for art lovers who want to own an original piece of art by Picasso without having to spend a fortune.

In 1965, Pablo Picasso had to undergo a prostrate operation. After a period of rest, he concentrated on drawings and a series of 347 etchings. In spite of his health problems, he created a number of paintings during his last years. On April 8, 1973 he died at the ripe age of 91.

❑❑❑

Paul McCartney

(1942)

Musician

"In the end, the love you take is equal to the love you make."

Paul McCartney's work with the Beatles in the 1960s helped lift popular music from its origins in the entertainment business and transform it into a creative, highly commercial art form. He is also one of the most popular solo performers of all time in terms of both sales of his recordings and attendance at his concerts.

Paul McCartney was born on June 18, 1942, in Liverpool, England, to Mary and James McCartney. His mother was a maternity nurse, and his father a cotton salesman and jazz pianist with a local band. The young McCartney was raised in a traditional working-class family, much the same as his future fellow Beatles Ringo Starr and George Harrison. Tragically, when McCartney was only 14 years old, his mother died of complications after a mastectomy.

Encouraged by his father to try out multiple musical instruments, Paul McCartney began his lifelong love affair with music at an early age. Though he took formal music lessons as a boy, the future star preferred to learn by ear, teaching himself the Spanish guitar, trumpet and piano. In 1957, the teenaged musician met John Lennon at a church festival where both young men were performing. Sensing an early affinity, McCartney joined Lennon's band, the Quarrymen. The two quickly became the group's songwriters, ushering it through many name changes and a few personnel changes as well.

By 1960, the group had settled on a new moniker, the Beatles, and George Harrison, Stuart Sutcliffe and Pete Best rounded out the group. The soon-to-be legendary "mod squad" started out in the 1960s in Hamburg, Germany, spending two years playing various nightclubs there. Sutcliffe soon left the band, leaving McCartney to pick up the slack as the group's bass player. While in Hamburg, the Beatles recorded their first tracks, garnering the attention of Brian Epstein, who quickly signed on as the band's manager. It wasn't long before the Beatles headed back to their home country and began working their way into the popular consciousness there. And Best's replacement by drummer Ringo Starr only helped the group gain steam.

The impact that the Beatles would ultimately have on '60s popular culture is hard to overstate. "Beatlemania" soon gripped the world, and when the group made their debut in America, the media dubbed the period of musical crossover between the two nations the "British Invasion." Little could they know at the time, this era would truly have a lasting impact on rock 'n' roll.

During a decade full of political and social strife, the Beatles expressed the broader hopes of their contemporaries for peace, love and rock 'n' roll. McCartney in particular would write more hits for the band than any other member. Songs like "Yesterday," "Hey Jude," "Let It Be," "Yellow Submarine" and "Hello, Goodbye" would provide the soundtrack for a generation.

From 1962 to '70, the group released 12 hit studio albums, touring almost constantly, before disbanding.

The Beatles disbanded in 1970, breaking fans' hearts worldwide. However, McCartney had no intention of dropping out of the public eye. He was the first of the Beatles to release a solo album (*McCartney*, 1970), and though critics' reactions were mixed, the album was a hit with the public. Encouraged, McCartney went on to form Wings, a band that would remain popular throughout the '70s, winning two Grammy Awards and churning out multiple hit singles.

In 1969, McCartney married Linda Eastman, an American photographer who would serve as her husband's muse for the next 30 years. The family had four children: Heather (Linda's daughter from a previous marriage), Mary, Stella and James.

The 1980s proved a trying time for McCartney. An arrest for marijuana possession in Japan in 1980 was followed shortly by the devastating assassination of his longtime partner and friend, John Lennon. In the wake of Lennon's death, McCartney stopped touring until 1989. He continued to play and record new music, however, collaborating with the likes of Stevie Wonder and Michael Jackson. In the '90s, McCartney worked with former bandmates Harrison and Starr on *The Beatles Anthology* documentary series.

Tragedy struck in 1998, when McCartney's wife of 29 years, Linda McCartney, died after a long battle with cancer. Four years later, the musician married Heather Mills, a former model and anti-landmine activist. They welcomed a daughter, Beatrice, in 2003. Amid much press scrutiny and intense animosity, McCartney and Mills parted ways in 2006. He married for the third time, to New York businesswoman Nancy Shevell, in October 2011, in London.

In 2012, McCartney released *Kisses on the Bottom*, which featured renditions of some of his favorite songs from childhood, including classics like "It's Only a Paper Moon" and "My Valentine." McCartney made headlines later that year, after performing with fellow rocker Bruce Springsteen at London's Hyde Park. The two legendary rock musicians even performed two Beatles hits together: "I Saw Her Standing There" and "Twist and Shout."

More recently, McCartney signed on to headline the 2013 Bonnaroo Music & Arts Festival, a four-day event held annually in Manchester, Tennessee.

In 2014, McCartney wrote and performed "Hope for the Future", the ending song for the video game *Destiny.*

On 15 February 2015, McCartney appeared and performed with Paul Simon for the *Saturday Night Live 40th Anniversary Special.* McCartney and Simon performed the first verse of "I've Just Seen a Face" on acoustic guitars, and McCartney later performed "Maybe I'm Amazed".

On 10 June 2016, McCartney released the career-spanning collection *Pure McCartney.*

McCartney appeared in the adventure film *Pirates of the Caribbean: Dead Men Tell No Tales,* which was released in 2017.

In 2023, he co-produced the final Beatles single, "Now and Then," utilising AI technology to incorporate John Lennon's vocals. In February 2025, McCartney performed a surprise concert at New York's Bowery Ballroom, followed by a memorable "Abbey Road" medley during Saturday Night Live's 50th Anniversary Special.

Pandit Jasraj

(1930-2020)

Musician

"We are now in the dawn of new ways of making music with technology, but it is important to realize that we are part of a continuum, and have deep ties to earlier musical forms."

Pandit Jasraj was born on January 28, 1930, in Hisar, Haryana, into a family deeply rooted in Indian classical music. His father, Pandit Motiram, was a well-respected musician of the Mewati Gharana, but he passed away when Jasraj was just four years old. This early loss left a lasting impact on him and shaped his musical journey. Raised in a musical household, Jasraj initially trained as a tabla player under his elder brother, Pandit Maniram, but later discovered his true calling in vocal music. His shift from percussion to vocal training was driven by a deep desire to express music more freely, and this decision led him to become one of the greatest Hindustani classical vocalists of all time.

Throughout his career, Pandit Jasraj developed a distinctive and emotive singing style that set him apart. While adhering to the traditions of the Mewati Gharana, he infused his performances with deep spirituality and devotion, making his renditions unique and emotionally moving. He was known for his Bhakti (devotional) approach, which brought him closer to audiences beyond classical music purists. His exploration of Haveli Sangeet, a form of temple music, further enriched his musical expression and contributed to the preservation and popularisation of this sacred tradition.

Pandit Jasraj's performances were marked by their lyrical beauty, long and flowing phrases, and intricate ornamentations. He had an extraordinary ability to sustain notes with remarkable clarity and depth, mesmerising listeners with his powerful yet soulful voice. His concerts, whether in India or abroad, attracted large audiences who were captivated by his ability to blend technical mastery with emotional intensity. He performed at some of the world's most prestigious venues, including the Lincoln Center in New York, the Royal Albert Hall in London, and the Sydney Opera House, spreading the essence of Hindustani classical music across continents.

Over the decades, Pandit Jasraj received numerous accolades in recognition of his contributions to Indian classical music. He was honoured with the Padma Shri in 1975, the Padma Bhushan in 1990, and the Padma Vibhushan in 2000, which is India's second-highest civilian award. He also received the Sangeet Natak Akademi Award in 1987 and the Maharashtra Bhushan Award in 2012, among many others. Despite these prestigious awards, he remained deeply humble, believing that his music was a divine gift meant to be shared with the world.

Apart from being a performer, Pandit Jasraj was also a dedicated teacher. He trained numerous disciples, many of whom became accomplished musicians in their own right. His teaching style emphasised not only technical precision but also the spiritual and emotional depth of music. His disciples, including Sanjeev Abhyankar and Rattan Mohan Sharma, have carried forward his legacy, ensuring that his contributions continue to inspire future generations.

In his personal life, Pandit Jasraj was married to Madhura Shantaram, the daughter of legendary filmmaker V. Shantaram. Their marriage was a blend of two artistic worlds-music and cinema. Madhura played a key role in managing his career and promoting his work, while their daughter, Durga Jasraj, became a television producer focused on bringing Indian classical music to a wider audience.

Pandit Jasraj continued performing well into his later years, remaining a revered figure in the world of classical music. Even in his final years, his voice retained its magical quality, and his presence on stage remained as powerful as ever. On August 17, 2020, he passed away at the age of 90 in New Jersey, USA. His passing marked the end of an era, but his music remains eternal. His influence on Hindustani classical music is immeasurable, and his recordings continue to inspire and educate aspiring musicians.

❑❑❑

Pelé

(1940-2022)

Football Player

"Enthusiasm is every thing.
It must be taut and vibrating like a guitar string."

Edson Arantes do Nascimento, famously known as Pelé, was born on October 23, 1940, in Três Corações, Brazil. Raised in a humble family, he was introduced to football by his father, Dondinho, a former professional player whose career was cut short due to injury. From a young age, Pelé displayed extraordinary footballing talent. His family could not afford a proper football, so he often played with a sock stuffed with newspapers. His skills quickly gained attention, and by the age of 15, he was signed by Santos FC, beginning his journey to becoming one of the greatest footballers of all time.

At just 16 years old, Pelé made his debut for the Brazilian national team in 1957, scoring in his first match. A year later, he became a global sensation at the 1958 FIFA World Cup in Sweden. At just 17, he scored a hat-trick in the semifinals and two goals in the final against Sweden, leading Brazil to their first World Cup title. His extraordinary dribbling, vision, and finishing ability captivated the world, and he became a national hero overnight.

Pel'és dominance in football continued, and despite being injured in the 1962 World Cup, Brazil won their second consecutive title. However, in 1966, Pelé suffered from harsh tackles and poor officiating, leading to Brazil's early exit. Determined to reclaim Brazil's glory, he returned for the 1970 FIFA World Cup, leading one of the greatest teams in history to victory. With an unforgettable performance in the final against Italy, Pelé won his third World Cup, an achievement no other player has matched. His leadership, passing, and goal-scoring ability made him the undisputed king of football.

At club level, Pelé spent nearly two decades at Santos FC, scoring over 1,000 goals and winning multiple domestic and international titles, including the Copa Libertadores and Intercontinental Cup. In 1975, he moved to the New York Cosmos, helping popularise football in the United States. He retired from professional football in 1977, leaving behind an unmatched legacy.

Pel'és personal life was as eventful as his football career. He married three times and had several children. His first marriage was to Rosemeri dos Reis Cholbi, with whom he had three children. After their divorce, he married Assíria Lemos Seixas, a psychologist, and had twins. In 2016, he married Marcia Aoki, a Japanese-Brazilian entrepreneur.

Even after retirement, Pelé remained an ambassador for football and humanitarian causes. He was honoured with numerous awards, including FIFA's Player of the Century (2000), a UNESCO Goodwill Ambassadorship, and an honorary knighthood from Queen Elizabeth II. His influence extended beyond sports, advocating for social causes and inspiring millions worldwide.

In September 2021, Pelé was diagnosed with colon cancer, and despite multiple treatments, his health declined. He passed away on December 29, 2022, at the age of 82, in São Paulo. His death marked the end of an era, and Brazil declared three days of national mourning. FIFA later renamed its Best Men's Player Award in his honour, ensuring his legacy would live on forever. Pelé remains an eternal symbol of football greatness, inspiring generations to come.

❑❑❑

Prabhas

(1979)

Actor

"Everything else is irrelevant after the bliss of giving a perfect shot."

Prabhas, born as Venkata Satyanarayana Prabhas Raju Uppalapati on October 23, 1979, in Madras (now Chennai), Tamil Nadu, India, is a prominent figure in Indian cinema, particularly in Telugu films. He is the youngest of three children to film producer Uppalapati Surya Narayana Raju and Siva Kumari. His family hails from Mogalthur, near Bhimavaram in the West Godavari district of Andhra Pradesh. Prabhas's uncle, Krishnam Raju, was a renowned actor in Telugu cinema, which influenced his early exposure to the film industry.

Despite his family's involvement in cinema, Prabhas initially had no intention of becoming an actor. He completed his schooling at Don Bosco Matriculation Higher Secondary School in Chennai and DNR School in Bhimavaram. He later pursued a Bachelor of Technology (B.Tech) degree from Sri Chaitanya College in Hyderabad. It was during his college years that Prabhas developed an interest in acting, leading him to enrol at the Satyanand Film Institute in Visakhapatnam to hone his craft.

Prabhas made his acting debut in 2002 with the Telugu film "Eeswar," portraying the titular character. Although the film received mixed reviews, it marked the beginning of his journey in the Telugu film industry. His breakthrough came in 2004 with "Varsham," an action-romance film where he played Venkat, a passionate lover caught in a tumultuous relationship. The film was a commercial success and established Prabhas as a promising actor in Tollywood.

Following the success of "Varsham," Prabhas starred in several notable films. In 2005, he played the lead role in "Chatrapathi," directed by S.S. Rajamouli. His portrayal of a refugee turned saviour garnered critical acclaim and solidified his status as a leading actor. Subsequent films like "Bujjigadu" (2008), "Billa" (2009), "Darling" (2010), and "Mr. Perfect" (2011) showcased his versatility across various genres, from action to romance. In 2013, Prabhas starred in "Mirchi," a family drama that was both a critical and commercial success, earning him the Nandi Award for Best Actor.

A defining moment in Prabhas's career came with the "Baahubali" series, directed by S.S. Rajamouli. He dedicated nearly five years to this magnum opus, portraying dual roles as Amarendra Baahubali and his son Mahendra Baahubali. "Baahubali: The Beginning" (2015) and its sequel, "Baahubali 2: The Conclusion" (2017), were monumental successes, with the latter becoming the highest-grossing Indian film at the time. The films received international acclaim, and Prabhas's performance was lauded for its depth and intensity. His commitment to the project, including undergoing rigorous physical training and performing challenging stunts, earned him widespread recognition and a massive fan following.

Post-"Baahubali," Prabhas continued to expand his repertoire. In 2019, he starred in "Saaho," an action thriller that marked his entry into Hindi cinema. Despite mixed reviews, the film was noted for its high-octane action sequences and showcased Prabhas's dedication to performing his stunts. He further ventured into science fiction with "Kalki 2898 AD," exploring new genres and narratives. His upcoming projects include "Salaar," directed by Prashanth Neel, which has generated significant anticipation among fans and critics alike.

Throughout his career, Prabhas has received numerous accolades. He has been nominated for seven Filmfare Awards and has won several, including the Nandi Award and the SIIMA Award. His portrayal in "Mirchi" earned him the Nandi Award for Best Actor, recognising his ability to balance commercial appeal with critical acclaim. In 2017, he became the first South Indian actor to have a wax statue at Madame Tussauds, reflecting his immense popularity and contribution to Indian cinema.

Despite his towering presence on screen, Prabhas is known for his humility and reclusive nature. He maintains a low-profile personal life, rarely making public appearances outside of film promotions. As of 2024, Prabhas is unmarried and has kept his personal relationships away from the limelight. His dedication to his craft and his ability to transform into diverse characters have endeared him to audiences worldwide.

Prabhas's journey from a reluctant entrant into the film industry to becoming a pan-Indian superstar is a testament to his hard work, versatility, and commitment. He has successfully transcended regional boundaries, appealing to a global audience and setting new benchmarks in Indian cinema. His evolution as an actor continues to inspire many, and his future projects are eagerly awaited by fans and critics alike.

❑❑❑

Pierre and Marie Curie

(1859–1906 & 1867–1934)

Inventors

"Be less curious about people and more curious about ideas."

Pierre and Marie Curie are best known for their pioneering work in the study of radioactivity, which led to their discovery in 1898 of the elements radium and polonium.

Born in Poland in 1867, Marie Sklodowska had no real opportunity for an education after high school. She saved her hard-earned money to help pay for her older sister's medical studies in Paris. She then followed her to France in 1891, studying at the Sorbonne. In 1894, Marie Sklodowska met the French chemist, Pierre Curie (1859–1906), and they were married a year later. Although Pierre had already made a name for himself, their collaboration proved far more fruitful than his solo career.

They spent much of their careers studying radioactivity (a term coined by Marie), examining the particles and energy produced as radioactive atoms decayed, and in the process learned about the building blocks of matter. They established that the heavy element thorium was radioactive and discovered two new elements: polonium and radium. They refined techniques for extracting radium from ores.

The sudden death of Pierre Curie on April 19, 1906 was a bitter blow to Marie Curie. On May 13, 1906, she was appointed to the professorship that had been left vacant on her husband's death. She was the first woman to teach in the Sorbonne. In 1908, she became titular professor, and in 1910, her fundamental treatise on radioactivity was published.

Curie throughout her life actively promoted the use of radium to alleviate suffering and during World War I, assisted by her daughter, Irene, she personally devoted herself to this remedial work. She retained her enthusiasm for science throughout her life and did much to establish a radioactivity laboratory in her native city. In 1929, President Hoover of the United States presented her with a gift of $ 50,000, donated by American friends of science, to purchase radium for use in the laboratory in Warsaw.

Marie was held in high esteem and admiration by scientists throughout the world. She was a member of the Conseil du Physique Solvay from 1911 until 1922. She had also been a member of the Committee of Intellectual Co-operation of the League of Nations. Her work is recorded in numerous papers in scientific journals and she is the author of Recherches sur les Substances Radioactives (1904), L'Isotopie et les Elements Isotopes and the classic Traite' de Radioactivite (1910).

Her death near Sallanches in 1934 was from aplastic anemia, almost certainly due to massive exposure to radiation—much of her work had been carried out in a shed with no safety measures being taken, as the damaging effects of hard radiation were not yet known.

Marie Curie was initially buried at the cemetery in Sceaux where Pierre lay, but in 1995, their ashes were transferred to the Pantheon to honour their works. Her eldest daughter, Irene Joliot-Curie, won a Nobel Prize for Chemistry in 1935.

The importance of Madam Curie's work is reflected in the numerous awards bestowed on her. She received many honorary science, medicine and law degrees and honorary memberships of learned societies throughout the world. Together with her husband, she was awarded half of the Nobel Prize for Physics in 1903, for their study into the spontaneous radiation discovered by Becquerel, who was awarded the other half of the prize.

In 1911, she received a second Nobel Prize, this time in Chemistry, in recognition of her work in radioactivity. She is one of only two people who has been awarded a Nobel Prize in two different fields, the other being Linus Pauling.

Till date, Madam Curie remains the only woman to win two Nobel prizes. She also received, jointly with her husband, the Davy Medal of the Royal Society in 1903 and in 1921, President Harding of the United States, on behalf of the women of America, presented her with one gram of radium in recognition of her service to science.

P.T. Usha

(1964)

Athlete

"When you compete with better athletes, you also get better."

Pilavullakandi Thekkeparambil Usha, affectionately known as P.T. Usha, was born on June 27, 1964, in the village of Koothali near Perambra in Kerala's Kozhikode district. Growing up in the coastal town of Payyoli, she faced economic hardships and health challenges during her childhood. Despite these obstacles, Usha displayed a natural affinity for athletics from a young age, often racing against boys in her village and showcasing remarkable speed.

In 1976, the Kerala State Government inaugurated a sports division for women in Kannur, and Usha was among the inaugural batch of 40 girls selected. It was here that she caught the attention of O.M. Nambiar, a dedicated athletics coach, during a prize distribution ceremony in 1977. Impressed by her lean physique and brisk walking style, Nambiar saw immense potential in her and took her under his mentorship. This partnership would become the cornerstone of Usha's illustrious career.

Usha's ascent in athletics was swift. In 1978, at the inter-state meet for juniors in Kollam, she clinched six medals, including four golds in events like the 100 meters, 200 meters, 60 meters hurdles, and high jump. Her prowess continued at the 1979 National Games and the 1980 National Inter-State Meet, where she set multiple meet records. Her first international appearance came in 1980 at the Qaid-e-Azam Invitational Meet in Karachi, Pakistan, where she secured four gold medals, signaling her arrival on the international stage.

The 1982 Asian Games in New Delhi marked a significant milestone in Usha's career. She earned silver medals in both the 100 meters and 200 meters, clocking times of 11.95 seconds and 25.32 seconds, respectively. This performance solidified her status as India's premier female sprinter. The following year, at the Asian Championships in Kuwait City, she clinched gold in the 400 meters, setting a new national record with a time of 53.6 seconds.

Usha's most memorable performance came during the 1984 Los Angeles Olympics. Transitioning to the 400 meters hurdles, she showcased exceptional talent. After setting a Commonwealth record of 55.94 seconds in the semi-finals, she narrowly missed an Olympic bronze, finishing fourth with a time of 55.42 seconds, just 1/100th of a second behind the third-place finisher. This agonisingly close finish remains one of the most poignant moments in Indian athletics history.

Undeterred, Usha's dominance continued. At the 1985 Asian Championships in Jakarta, she achieved an unprecedented feat by winning five gold medals in the 100 meters, 200 meters, 400 meters, 400 meters hurdles, and the 4x400 meters relay, along with a bronze in the 4x100 meters relay. Her remarkable performance earned her the titles of "Golden Girl" and "Payyoli Express." She replicated this success at the 1986 Asian Games in Seoul, securing four gold medals and one silver, setting new Games records in the process.

Throughout her career, Usha amassed an impressive collection of accolades. She won 33 international medals, including 13 golds in

Asian Games and Asian Championships. Her dominance in the Asian Track and Field events from 1983 to 1989 was unparalleled, as she garnered 13 gold medals during this period. Her contributions to Indian sports were recognised with the Arjuna Award in 1984 and the Padma Shri in 1985.

Beyond her athletic achievements, Usha's personal life has been marked by dedication and resilience. In 1991, she married V. Srinivasan, an officer in the Central Industrial Security Force. The couple was blessed with a son, Ujjwal, in 1992. Balancing family life with her sporting commitments, Usha continued to inspire countless aspiring athletes across the nation.

After retiring from competitive athletics in 2000, Usha channeled her passion for the sport into nurturing young talent. She established the Usha School of Athletics in 2002 in Kerala, aiming to provide world-class training facilities to budding athletes, especially those from underprivileged backgrounds. Her commitment to fostering new talent has significantly contributed to the growth of athletics in India.

Usha's contributions have extended beyond the track and field. In July 2022, she was nominated as a Member of Parliament to the Rajya Sabha, the upper house of India's Parliament, by the President of India. Her nomination recognised her invaluable contributions to sports and her role as a mentor to future generations. Further cementing her legacy, in December 2022, Usha was elected unopposed as the President of the Indian Olympic Association, becoming the first woman to hold this prestigious position.

Throughout her journey, Usha has been the recipient of numerous honours. She was conferred honorary doctorates by several institutions, including Kannur University in 2000, IIT Kanpur in 2017, and the University of Calicut in 2018. In 2019, the International Association of Athletics Federations (IAAF) honoured her with the Veteran Pin Award, acknowledging her longstanding contributions to athletics.

❑❑❑

Pope John Paul II

(1920–2005)

Spiritual Leader

"Freedom consists not in doing what we like, but in having the right to do what we ought."

Pope Saint John Paul II born Karol Józef Wojty was Pope from 1978 to 2005. He is called by some Catholics Saint John Paul the Great.

He was the second longest-serving pope in modern history after Pope Pius IX, who served for nearly 32 years from 1846 to 1878. Born in Poland, John Paul II was the first non-Italian pope since the Dutch Pope Adrian VI, who served from 1522 to 1523. John Paul II's cause for canonisation commenced in 2005 one month after his death with the traditional five-year waiting period waived.

Born Karol Józef Wojtyla on May 18, 1920, in Wadowice, Poland, Pope John Paul II's early life was marked by great loss. His mother died when he was 9 years old, and his older brother Edmund died when he was 12. Growing up, John Paul was athletic and enjoyed skiing and swimming. He went to Krakow's Jagiellonian University in 1938 where he showed an interest in theater and poetry. The school was closed the next year by Nazi troops during the German occupation of Poland. Wanting to become a priest, John Paul began studying at a secret seminary run by the archbishop of Krakow. After World War II ended, he finished his religious studies at a Krakow seminary and was ordained in 1946.

John Paul spent two years in Rome where he finished his doctorate in theology. He returned to his native Poland in 1948 and served in several parishes in and around Krakow. John Paul became the bishop of Ombi in 1958 and then the archbishop of Krakow six years later. Considered one of the Catholic Church's leading thinkers, he participated in the Second Vatican Council-sometimes called Vatican II. The council began reviewing church doctrine in 1962, holding several sessions over the course of the next few years. As a member of the council, John Paul helped the church to examine its position in the world. Well regarded for his contributions to the church, John Paul was made a cardinal in 1967 by Pope Paul VI.

In 1978, John Paul made history by becoming the first non-Italian pope in more than four hundred years. As the leader of the Catholic Church, he traveled the world, visiting more than 100 countries to spread his message of faith and peace. But he was close to home when he faced the greatest threat to his life. In 1981, an assassin shot John Paul twice in St. Peter's Square in Vatican City. Fortunately, he was able to recover from his injuries and later forgave his attacker.

A vocal advocate for human rights, John Paul often spoke out about suffering in the world. He held strong positions on many topics, including his opposition to capital punishment. A charismatic figure, John Paul used his influence to bring about political change and is credited with the fall of communism in his native Poland. He was not without critics, however. Some have stated that he could be harsh with those who disagreed with him and that he would not compromise his hard-line stance on certain issues, such as contraception.

John Paul II died on April 2, 2005, at the age of 84, at his Vatican City residence. More than 3 million people waited in line to say goodbye to their beloved religious leader at St. Peter's Basilica before his funeral on April 8.

On 19 December 2009, John Paul II was proclaimed Venerable by his successor Pope Benedict XVI and was beatified on 1 May 2011 (Divine Mercy Sunday) after the Congregation for the Causes of Saints attributed one miracle to his intercession, the healing of a French nun from Parkinson's disease.

On July 5, 2013, waving the usual five-year waiting period, the Vatican announced that the Roman Catholic Church would declare Pope John Paul II a saint, and that the canonization ceremony would likely take place within the next 16 months. The Vatican also stated that Pope John XXIII, who headed the Catholic Church from 1958 until his death in 1963 and convened the Vatican II council, would also be declared a saint.

❑❑❑

Prince William

(1982)

Royal Prince of Wales

"Being a small boy it's very daunting seeing the Queen around and not really quite knowing what to talk about."

Prince William of Wales is the grandson of Queen Elizabeth II, and second in the line of succession to the British throne.

He is the elder son of Prince Charles and the late Diana, Princess of Wales. Prince William was born Prince William Arthur Philip Louis Windsor on June 21, 1982, in London, England. His official title is "His Royal Highness Prince William of Wales."

Prince William attended Mrs. Mynor's Nursery school in West London (1985-87), Wetherby School in Kensington, London (1987-90), and Ludgrove School in Wokingham (1990-95). In 1995, at the urging of his grandfather, the Duke of Edinburgh, Prince William (nicknamed "Wills") entered Eton College, one of England's most prestigious secondary schools. A serious student with excellent grades, he also excelled in sports at Eton, particularly swimming. With his father and brother, he enjoys outdoor sports including riding, skiing, shooting and fishing.

As he is directly in line to the British throne after his father, Charles, he spends a good deal of time at Windsor Castle with Queen Elizabeth, who is very concerned with his upbringing and career development.

Affected by both his parents' divorce in 1996 and his mother's tragic death in 1997, the tall and handsome young William publicly stated his dislike for the press, and expressed discomfort with the growing attention he received from love-struck adolescent girls. William gives the impression of being a well-mannered, responsible and mature young man who shows a strong sense of duty and loyalty to the royal family, fully aware of the role he is to play in the future as the King of England.

Upon his graduation from Eton, William took a break from his studies to visit South America and Africa. He then attended Scotland's St Andrew's University, where he received a degree in geography in 2005. Following in the footsteps of his younger brother, Prince Harry, William joined the Royal Military Academy Sandhurst as a military cadet and received his commission as a second lieutenant in the Household Cavalry in December 2006. In 2008, he was appointed to be a Royal Knight Companion of the Most Noble Order of the Garter. He is now training to be a search and rescue pilot with the Royal Air Force.

Along with his military career, William supports numerous charities, including serving as patron to Centrepoint, an organization for homeless youth, and the Tusk Trust, which is dedicated to the preservation of African wildlife.

In 2007, William and his brother Harry hosted a special concert to celebrate their late mother and raise funds for charities that Princess Diana supported as well as charities supported by themselves.

As the future king of England, William's personal life has been the subject of much media attention. He had been romantically linked to Kate Middleton; the couple met while attending St. Andrew's University.

In November 2010 it was announced that Prince William was engaged to his long-term girlfriend, Kate Middleton. The couple met during their time at St Andrews University in Fife, Scotland, and have been together since. Their wedding was scheduled for 29 April 2011, which would have been the thirtieth anniversary of the marriage of his parents.

On 29 April 2011, all eyes were on Prince William when he married Kate Middleton at Westminster Abbey. Just a few hours prior to his nuptials, William was made the Duke of Cambridge, Earl of Strathern and Baron Carrickfergus.

The Royal wedding was made a public holiday and around 300 million people watched William get married and enjoy his first kiss with Kate on the balcony outside Buckingham Palace.

Since then, the couple reportedly spent two weeks honeymooning in the Seychelles after William had been at work as an RAF pilot. After their honeymoon, William was sent to the Falklands for ten weeks for RAF training and due to the remote location, his new wife couldn't join him.

The couple have moved into an apartment at Kensington Palace which is where they will stay when they are in London. They claim their home is their rented cottage in Anglesey.

On 22 July 2013, the Duke and Duchess of Cambridge became the proud parents of a baby boy. Their son, the Prince of Cambridge, is third in line to the throne.

He became father of a girl child named princess Charlotte on May 2, 2015.

Following Queen Elizabeth II's passing in September 2022, he was named Prince of Wales. In 2023, he co-founded the Earthshot Prize, promoting environmental solutions.

Queen Elizabeth II

(1926)

Queen of England

"Grief is the price we pay for love."

Queen Elizabeth II was born Princess Elizabeth Alexandra Mary on April 21, 1926, in London, to Prince Albert, Duke of York who later became King George VI, and Elizabeth Bowes-Lyon. She married Philip Mountbatten, Duke of Edinburgh in 1947, became queen on February 6, 1952, and was crowned on June 2, 1953. During her reign, she has tried to make the British monarchy more modern and sensitive to the public.

Being third in line to the throne, it seemed unlikely that Princess Elizabeth would ever be Queen. However, shortly after the death of King George V, the new King - her uncle Edward VIII - dramatically abdicated so he could marry Wallis Simpson, an American divorcee. Princess Elizabeth's father then became King George VI and she became heir to the throne.

Princess Elizabeth and her younger sister Princess Margaret were educated at home. During the Blitz in 1940, they were moved to

Windsor Castle and stayed there for most of the Second World War. In 1945, Princess Elizabeth joined the war effort, training as a driver in the Women's Auxiliary Territorial Service (WATS).

In November 1947, she married a distant cousin, Philip Mountbatten, who was then created His Royal Highness The Prince Philip, Duke of Edinburgh. The wedding - which took place during the austere post-War years - was described by Winston Churchill as a 'flash of colour'. The Princess used ration coupons to buy the material for her dress.

The couple had four children. Prince Charles, The Prince of Wales, was born in 1948 and his sister Princess Anne, was born two years later. After the coronation, Prince Andrew, The Duke of York was born in 1960 and Prince Edward, The Earl of Wessex arrived in 1962. They were the first children to be born to a reigning monarch since Queen Victoria.

George VI died on 6 February 1952 while Princess Elizabeth and Prince Philip were touring Kenya and she immediately became Queen. After months of preparation, Queen Elizabeth II was crowned at Westminster Abbey on 2 June 1953. For the first time, the ceremony and the huge public celebrations were broadcast on TV across the UK, the Commonwealth and the rest of the world.

The Queen began her political duties which included opening Parliament and receiving her prime ministers. Throughout the 1950s, the Queen and Prince Philip cut young and glamorous figures as they extensively toured the UK and the Commonwealth.

During the 1960s, the Queen made historic visits to West Berlin at the height of the Cold War, and welcomed Emperor Hirohito of Japan on a state visit to Britain. Against a backdrop of political and social unrest, she celebrated her Silver Jubilee in 1977. It was a huge success and tens of thousands of street parties were thrown by the public across the country.

Five years later, the UK was at war over the Falkland Islands during which Prince Andrew served with the Royal Navy as a helicopter pilot. The 1980s also saw the birth of her first grandchildren, Peter and Zara Phillips, the son and daughter of Anne, Princess Royal and Captain Mark Phillips.

Disaster struck in 1992 when a devastating fire broke out in Windsor Castle. The same year the respective marriages of Prince Charles, Prince Andrew and Princess Anne disintegrated. The Queen deemed this her 'annus horribilis' (horrible year). In 1996 the marriage of Prince Charles and Diana, Princess of Wales was dissolved. Tragedy was to follow in 1997, when Diana was killed in a car accident. The Queen broadcast live to the nation in tribute to the Princess of Wales.

And 2002 was another year of personal sadness for the Queen, as both her sister Princess Margaret and the Queen Mother died, casting a shadow over the Golden Jubilee celebrations a few months later.

During a period of great change in Britain, the Queen successfully carried her political duties as head of state, her role as head of the Commonwealth, the ceremonial responsibilities of the sovereign and a large annual programme of visits in the UK, as well as many foreign tours.

The Queen also introduced numerous reforms to the monarchy. In 1992, she offered to start paying income and capital gains tax. She opened her official residencies to the public - including Buckingham Palace and Windsor Castle - in order to finance their maintenance.

The Queen introduced more informal engagements and visits, and the 'walkabout' - the meeting and greeting of large numbers of the public.

In 2017 she became the first British monarch to commemorate a Sapphire Jubilee.

She continued fulfilling royal duties until her passing on September 8, 2022, at age 96, after a historic 70-year reign. She was the longest-serving British monarch and celebrated her Platinum Jubilee (June 2022), marking 70 years on the throne. Her passing led to the ascension of King Charles III, and the UK observed national mourning in her honour.

❑❑❑

Rashmika Mandanna

(1996)

Actress

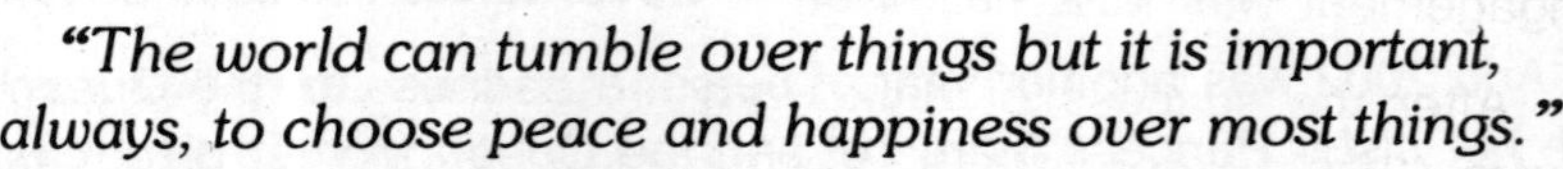

"The world can tumble over things but it is important, always, to choose peace and happiness over most things."

Rashmika Mandanna was born on April 5, 1996, in Virajpet, a town in the Kodagu district of Karnataka, India. She was raised in a middle-class family and developed a keen interest in acting and modelling from a young age. She completed her schooling at Coorg Public School and later pursued a bachelor's degree in Psychology, Journalism, and English Literature at M.S. Ramaiah College of Arts, Science, and Commerce in Bengaluru. During her college years, she actively participated in cultural events and modelling competitions, which eventually led her to the entertainment industry.

Rashmika's journey into the film industry began when she won the Clean & Clear Fresh Face contest in 2014. This recognition helped her gain popularity in the modelling world, and she soon became the brand ambassador for Clean & Clear. She participated in several fashion shows and appeared in advertisements, which opened doors for her entry into cinema. In 2016, she participated in La Mode

Bangalore's Top Model Hunt, where she was one of the finalists. These achievements helped her gain a foothold in the Kannada film industry.

Her acting debut came in 2016 with the Kannada film *Kirik Party*, in which she played the female lead opposite Rakshit Shetty. The film was a massive hit and became one of the highest-grossing Kannada films of the year. Her portrayal of Saanvi, a college student, was widely appreciated, and she quickly gained a large fan following. During the making of *Kirik Party*, she developed a close relationship with co-star Rakshit Shetty, and the two got engaged in 2017. However, their engagement was later called off in 2018 due to personal reasons.

After the success of *Kirik Party*, Rashmika appeared in *Anjani Putra* (2017) opposite Puneeth Rajkumar and *Chamak* (2017) opposite Ganesh. Both films performed well at the box office, further cementing her place in the Kannada film industry. She then made her Telugu debut in 2018 with *Chalo*, co-starring Naga Shaurya. The film received positive reviews, and her performance was well received. However, it was *Geetha Govindam* (2018), where she starred opposite Vijay Deverakonda, that turned her into a household name. The romantic comedy was a massive hit, and her role as Geetha, an independent and strong-willed woman, won her critical acclaim. The film's success established her as one of the leading actresses in Telugu cinema.

Following *Geetha Govindam*, Rashmika starred in *Devadas* (2018) alongside Nagarjuna and Nani, further expanding her fan base. In 2019, she appeared in *Dear Comrade*, once again opposite Vijay Deverakonda. Though the film received mixed reviews, her performance as a student leader with strong convictions was widely praised. She continued her success streak with *Sarileru Neekevvaru* (2020) opposite Mahesh Babu, which became one of the highest-grossing Telugu films of the year.

Rashmika then made her Tamil debut with *Sulthan* (2021) opposite Karthi. The film received moderate success, but her performance was appreciated. However, her biggest breakthrough came with *Pushpa: The Rise* (2021), where she played the role of Srivalli opposite Allu Arjun. The film became a pan-Indian blockbuster, and her character, especially the song *Saami Saami*, became immensely popular. This film catapulted her to national stardom, making her one of the most sought-after actresses in Indian cinema.

After the success of *Pushpa: The Rise*, Rashmika made her Bollywood debut with *Goodbye* (2022) alongside Amitabh Bachchan. She followed it with *Mission Majnu* (2023), where she starred opposite Sidharth Malhotra. She then appeared in *Animal* (2023), sharing screen space with Ranbir Kapoor. These films helped her establish a presence in Bollywood, and despite being new to the industry, she received praise for her performances.

Rashmika continued to work on multiple projects across different languages. She reprised her role as Srivalli in *Pushpa: The Rule*, one of the most highly anticipated Indian films. Additionally, she signed several Telugu, Tamil, and Hindi films, ensuring her pan-Indian appeal. Her ability to adapt to different film industries and connect with audiences has made her one of the most bankable actresses in India.

Apart from her acting career, Rashmika is actively involved in philanthropic activities. She supports animal welfare and mental health awareness initiatives and frequently uses her social media platforms to promote positive messages. She has also been recognised as one of the most influential celebrities on social media, with millions of followers.

Rashmika has won numerous accolades for her performances, including Filmfare Awards South and SIIMA Awards. She is often referred to as the "National Crush of India" due to her charming screen presence and wide fan base. Her dedication to her craft, coupled with her humility and charisma, has made her a favourite among audiences.

❑❑❑

R.K. Laxman

(1927–2015)

Cartoonist

"Crows are very intelligent creatures and that is my art, not cartooning. I love my crows. I draw them whenever I find time."

Rasipuram Krishnaswamy Iyer Laxman was an Indian cartoonist, illustrator and humorist. He is widely regarded as India's greatest-ever cartoonist and is best known for his creation, *The Common Man*.

Laxman was born in 1927 in a well-to-do Kannada family in Mysore. His father was a headmaster in a school. Laxman was the youngest among six brothers. His elder brother, R.K. Narayan, was one of India's best known English-language novelists. Laxman graduated from the University of Mysore. In his autobiography, he says that he hasn't collected his degree yet from the Mysore University, where it must be gathering the dust of time.

Laxman's earliest work was for newspapers and magazines such as *Swarajya* and *Blitz*. While still at the Maharaja's College, Mysore, he began to illustrate his elder brother, R. K. Narayan's stories in *The Hindu*, and he drew political cartoons for the local newspapers. He held a summer job at the Gemini Studios, Madras (now Chennai). His first full-time job was as a political cartoonist for the *Free Press Journal*. He later joined, *The Times of India*, beginning a career that has spanned for over fifty years.

Laxman is best known for his daily one panel comic, 'pocket cartoon' series, *You Said It*, which features *The Common Man*, and chronicles the state of Indian life. The strip began in 1951.

Among his other works, he is known for his distinctive illustrations in several books, most notably for the *Malgudi* stories written by his elder brother R.K. Narayan. He also created a popular mascot for the Asian Paints group called *Gattu*. Laxman has also penned a few novels. His cartoons have appeared in Hindi films such as *Mr. and Mrs. 55*.

R. K. Laxman was a resident of both Mumbai and Pune. In September 2003, he suffered a stroke, which left him paralysed on his left side. He has partly recovered from its effects.

Among his works include, *The Eloquent Brush*: *A Selection of Cartoons from Nehru to Rajiv, 50 Years of Independence through the eyes of R.K.Laxman, The Best of Laxman series, Hotel Riviera, The Messenger, Servants of India, The Tunnel of Time* (autobiography), etc. His autobiography *Lakshmanrekha* is published in Marathi.

Eager to find contradictions that make life unpredictable he embellished his canvas with a keen sense of humour and an ability to take a whimsical, cock-eyed look at anything under the sun. He was a gifted storyteller who pulled the reader on an enchanting, comical journey down the corridors of time.

Laxman was not merely a cartoonist, but also a profound thinker, a social reformer, a political scientist, and so on. Besides provoking laughter, his cartoons have a mystic appeal to a section of the public.

The Government of India awarded him the prestigious Padma Bhushan. The University of Marathawada conferred an honorary

Doctor of Literature degree on him. He had won several awards in his lifetime, including Asia's top journalism award and the Ramon Magsaysay Award in 1984. Laxman had also won B. D. Goenka Award by *Indian Express*, and the Durga Ratan Gold Medal by *Hindustan Times*.

He won the CNN IBN TV 18 Lifetime Achievement Award for Journalism in January 2008. In October 2012 Laxman celebrated his 91st birthday in Pune.

He died on January 26, 2015 in Pune.

Rabindranath Tagore

(1861–1941)
Nobel Laureate

"Every child comes with the message that God is not yet discouraged of man."

Rabindranath Tagore was the first Asian Nobel laureate who won Nobel Prize for his collection of poems, *Gitanjali*, in 1913. He was also awarded knighthood by the British king, George V. Two songs from his *Rabindrasangit* canon are now the national anthems of India and Bangladesh: *the Jana Gana Mana* and *the Amar Shonar Bangla*.

Tagore was born on May 7, 1861 in a wealthy Brahmin family in Calcutta (now Kolkata). He was the ninth son of Debendranath and Sarada Devi. His grandfather, Dwarkanath Tagore was a rich landlord and social reformer. Rabindranath Tagore had his initial education in Oriental Seminary School. But he did not like the conventional education and started studying at home under several teachers. After undergoing his *upanayan* (coming-of-age) rite at the age of eleven, Tagore and his father left Calcutta (now Kolkata) in 1873 to tour India for several months, visiting his father's Shantiniketan estate and Amritsar before reaching the Himalayan hill station of Dalhousie.

There, Tagore read biographies, studied history, astronomy, modern science, and Sanskrit, and examined the classical poetry of Kalidasa.

In 1874, Tagore's poem, *Abhilaasha* (Desire) was published anonymously in a magazine called *Tattobodhini*. Rabindranath's first book of poems, *Kabi Kahini* (tale of a poet) was published in 1878. In the same year, Tagore sailed to England with his elder brother, Satyandranath to study law. But he returned to India in 1880 and began his career as poet and writer. In 1883, Rabindranath Tagore married Mrinalini Devi Raichaudhuri, with whom he had two sons and three daughters.

In 1884, he wrote a collection of poems, *Kori-o-Kamal* (Sharp and Flats). He also wrote dramas - *Raja-o-Rani* (King and Queen) and *Visarjan* (Sacrifice). In 1890, Rabindranath Tagore moved to Shilaidaha (now in Bangladesh) to look after the family estate. Between 1893 and 1900, Tagore wrote seven volumes of poetry, which included *Sonar Tari* (The Golden Boat) and *Khanika*.

In 1901, Rabindranath Tagore became the editor of the magazine, *Bangadarshan*. He established *Bolpur Bramhacharyaashram* at Shantiniketan, a school based on the pattern of old Indian *ashrama*. In 1902, his wife Mrinalini died. Tagore composed *Smaran*, a collection of poems, dedicated to his wife.

In 1905, Lord Curzon decided to divide Bengal into two parts. Rabindranath Tagore strongly protested against this decision. Tagore attended many protest meetings. He introduced the *Rakhibandhan* ceremony, symbolising the underlying unity of undivided Bengal.

In 1909, Rabindranath Tagore started writing *Gitanjali*. In 1912, Tagore went to Europe for the second time. On the journey to London, he translated some of his poems/songs from *Gitanjali* to English. He met William Rothenstein, a noted British painter, in London. Rothensein was impressed by the poems, made copies and gave to Yeats and other English poets. Yeats was enthralled. He later wrote the introduction to *Gitanjali* when it was published in September 1912 in a limited edition by the *India Society* in London. Rabindranath Tagore was awarded, the Nobel Prize for Literature in 1913 for *Gitanjali*.

In 1919, following the Jallianwala Bagh massacre, Tagore renounced his knighthood. He was a supporter of Gandhiji but he stayed out of politics. He was opposed to nationalism and militarism as a matter of principle, and instead promoted spiritual values and the creation of a new world culture founded in multi-culturalism, diversity and tolerance. Unable to gain ideological support to his views, he retired into relative solitude.

In 1921, Rabindranath Tagore established the Viswabharati University. He gave all his money from the Nobel Prize and the royalty money from his books to this university. Tagore was not only a creative genius, he was quite knowledgeable of Western culture, especially Western poetry and science too.

In 1940, the Oxford University arranged a special ceremony in Shantiniketan and awarded Rabindranath Tagore with Doctorate of Literature. Gurudev Rabindranath Tagore passed away on August 7, 1941 in his ancestral home in Calcutta (now Kolkata).

❑❑❑

Rihanna

(1988)

Pop Singer

"Making music is like shopping for me. Every song is like a new pair of shoes."

This is a popular pop singer who is measured equally in R&B (rhythm -and-blue) genre as well and she rose to stardom in the initial years of the 21st century, due to her distinctive voice. Besides, she also remains in popular thoughts due to her stunning appearance splashed in vogue. She has another name as Robyn Rihanna Fenty, who came into this world on February 20, 1988, at St. Michael parish, Barbados.

She was born to a Barbadian father and Guyanese mother. As a child in Barbodas, she fondly listened to Caribbean music and was inclined to American hip-hop and found great fascination in the R&B music section too. She took to singing at an early age and her passion won her high school talent show where she sang Mariah Carey song. She started a girl group with two friends, which influenced Evan Rogers who has produced music records in America. He let Fenty record a demo which opened the doors of an audition with rapper

Jay-Z who spearheaded Jam record label and he took her on board. For passion cum professional purpose, she used her middle name, Rihanna.

She rose to quick international fame when her song "Pon de Replay" was released and was largely considered dancehall-inflected. The success garnered by the song helped to drive sales later when her full-length recording was released with the title, "Music of the Sun" in 2005 with an amalgamation of R&B ballads with dance pops of Caribbean-style, decorated with her melodious lilt from Barbados. She soon pushed the album "A Girl Like Me" in 2006, which featured the "S.O.S" with an Up-tempo club tilt. The song was considered to be inspired by a sample of Soft Cell's 1981 new wave hit "Tainted Love" and triggered Rihanna's first work to top the Billboard singles chart.

In 2007, with the album "Good Girl Gone Bad", it is said that she attempted to transform her youthful image and she garnered collaboration from Justin Timberlake and Timbaland. Besides, she forsook tropical rhythms which earlier influenced her initial two albums alongside R&B which unveiled her as a different role model altogether, rebellious and independent for girls. She also appeared in different hairstyles i.e., spiky asymmetrical, which got popular soon. The album was a hit favourite and sales comprised of several million copies around the world while its song "Umbrella" where an introductory rap from Jay-Z was the highlight, turned out to be the mega-hit of the year and got her crown glory of Grammy Award.

She grabbed the newspaper headlines in early 2009 when she was beaten by fellow R&B star Chris Brown who was her boyfriend too and they part ways thereafter while he faced the conviction for assault. Later that year, her album "Rated R" was released which had lyrics co-written by her and its rough production and a class of lyrics which was a type of revenge. Even though her sales sank but her "Rude Boy" was considered a major hit. In 2010, she gave the album "Loud" and its "S&M" proved to be a Billboard hit which was her 10th in number and was regarded as sexually-oriented but which made her the youngest artist to achieve this milestone at the tender age of 23.

Away from musical career, she gave acting performance in some movies too, such as "Battleship" (2012) and "This Is The End" (2013). She also lent voice to the main characters in "Home" (2015) which is an animated adventure. She later made her appearance in Ocean's 8(2018) as a hacker, which is a reboot of the Ocean's Eleven franchise, from the early 2000s, driven by females. In 2019, she was a star in the musical "Guava Island" alongside Donald Glover, which premiered at the Coachella Valley Festival before Amazon conducted its streaming.

In the early 2010s, she promoted a wide range of cosmetic collections but in 2017 she launched her brand, Fenty Beauty. Her fans, as was expected, turned in in a large number to accept the wide product range, say about 40 different shades. In 2019, reports made rounds that Rihanna would partner with LVMH Moët Hennessy-Louis Vuitton to float a fashion line Fenty. In this way, she became the primary woman of African origin to lead a fashion house at LVMH, which was ranked among the top company in the world dealing in luxury products. A few months later, in that year, Fenty's first collection was released.

In May 2022, she expanded her Fenty Beauty brand into eight African countries, increasing its global presence. In February 2025, she publicly supported her partner, A$AP Rocky, during his legal proceedings, expressing gratitude following his acquittal.

Rajinikanth

(1950)
Actor

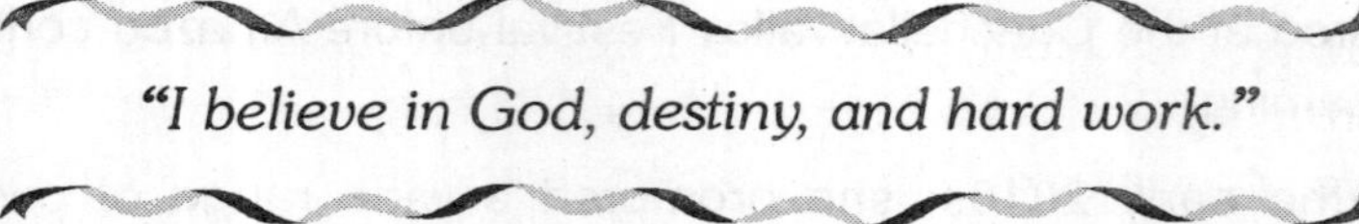

"I believe in God, destiny, and hard work."

Rajinikanth, born as Shivaji Rao Gaekwad on December 12, 1950, in Bangalore, Karnataka, India, is a legendary figure in Indian cinema, particularly in Tamil films. He was the youngest of four siblings in a Marathi family; his father, Ramoji Rao Gaekwad, was a police constable, and his mother was a homemaker. Tragically, he lost his mother at the tender age of nine, a loss that profoundly affected his early years.

Rajinikanth's early life was marked by financial hardships. He attended the Acharya Paathshala in Basavanagudi and later the Vivekananda Balaka Sangha. Before entering the film industry, he undertook various jobs to make ends meet, including working as a coolie and a carpenter. Eventually, he secured a position as a bus conductor with the Bangalore Transport Service. His unique style and charisma were evident even then, making him a popular figure among passengers.

In 1973, Rajinikanth decided to pursue his passion for acting and enrolled at the Madras Film Institute. His decision was met with resistance from his family due to their financial situation, but his unwavering determination led him forward. At the institute, he caught the attention of the renowned director K. Balachander, who became his mentor and offered him a role in the Tamil film "Apoorva Raagangal" in 1975. This film marked Rajinikanth's debut in cinema, where he played a minor role, but it was enough to showcase his potential.

Following his debut, Rajinikanth appeared in a series of films, often portraying antagonistic characters. His unique mannerisms and distinctive style quickly set him apart, leading to a significant fan following. Films like "Moondru Mudichu" (1976), "16 Vayathinile" (1977), and "Aval Appadithan" (1978) showcased his versatility and acting prowess. By the late 1970s, he transitioned to lead roles, with movies like "Bhuvana Oru Kelvikkuri" (1977) and "Mullum Malarum" (1978) cementing his status as a leading actor in Tamil cinema.

The 1980s were a defining period for Rajinikanth. He delivered a string of successful films, including "Billa" (1980), a remake of the Hindi film "Don," where he played a double role. This film's success established him as a bankable star. Other notable films from this era include "Thillu Mullu" (1981), a comedy that showcased his versatility, and "Moondru Mugam" (1982), where he portrayed three distinct characters. His collaboration with director S. P. Muthuraman resulted in several box-office hits, further solidifying his superstar status.

In 1981, Rajinikanth married Latha Rangachari, a graduate of Ethiraj College for Women, in a traditional ceremony in Tirupati, Andhra Pradesh. Latha later founded and managed The Ashram, a school in Chennai. The couple has two daughters: Aishwarya Rajinikanth, born in 1982, and Soundarya Rajinikanth, born in 1984. Aishwarya is a director and playback singer, married to actor Dhanush, while Soundarya is a graphic designer, producer, and director.

Rajinikanth's appeal wasn't confined to Tamil cinema. He made his Bollywood debut with "Andha Kanoon" (1983), sharing screen space with Amitabh Bachchan and Hema Malini. He continued to act in Hindi films like "Geraftaar" (1985) and "Hum" (1991), expanding his pan-Indian appeal. Despite his success in Hindi cinema, his primary focus remained on Tamil films, where his fan base was unparalleled.

The 1990s saw Rajinikanth reaching unprecedented heights. Films like "Annamalai" (1992), "Baashha" (1995), and "Padayappa" (1999) were monumental successes, with "Baashha" in particular elevating him to demigod status among fans. His portrayal of Manikkam, an auto-driver with a mysterious past, became iconic, and the film's dialogues are still celebrated today.

In 2000, Rajinikanth was honoured with the Padma Bhushan, India's third-highest civilian award, recognizing his contributions to Indian cinema. Despite a brief hiatus, he returned with "Chandramukhi" (2005), which ran for over 800 days in theatres, setting a record in Tamil cinema. His subsequent films, "Sivaji" (2007) and "Enthiran" (2010), were among the highest-grossing Indian films of their time, with "Enthiran" showcasing advanced visual effects and Rajinikanth in dual roles.

Rajinikanth's influence extends beyond cinema. His humility, philanthropy, and spiritual pursuits have endeared him to millions. He has undertaken pilgrimages to the Himalayas and is known for his simple lifestyle, often shunning the luxuries associated with stardom. His philanthropic efforts include contributions to various social causes, though he prefers to keep these activities low-key.

❑❑❑

Richard Branson

(1950)

Business Magnate, Investor, and Author

"From my very first day as an entrepreneur, I've felt the only mission worth pursuing in business is to make people's lives better."

Richard Branson is an entrepreneur and businessman, who founded the Virgin group of more than 400 companies. The Virgin group grew from a small record shop he founded in 1972, to become a major multinational company including interests in transport, media, and entertainment. Richard Branson is also a flamboyant character and has taken part in a number of gruelling adventure challenges, such as sailing across the Atlantic and taking part in around the world hot air balloon journeys.

Richard Branson was born in Blackheath, London on 18 July, 1950. His father was a barrister. Branson attended Scaitcliffe School and later Stowe school. Suffering from dyslexia, Branson did not excel at studies; he was more interested in extracurricular activities, such as football and cricket. At the age of 15, he had started to try his first business ventures, which included trying to grow trees and another raising budgerigars. He is the author of 'Losing my Virginity', which is an autobiography that features his story from rags to riches.

In 1997, Branson founded the Virgin Rail Group to bid for passenger rail franchises during the privatisation of British Rail. In 2004, he founded spaceflight corporation Virgin Galactic, based at Mojave Air and Space Port in California, noted for the SpaceShipTwo suborbital spaceplane designed for space tourism.

In March 2000, Branson was knighted at Buckingham Palace for "services to entrepreneurship". For his work in retail, music and transport (with interests in land, air, sea and space travel), his taste for adventure and for his humanitarian work, he has become a prominent global figure.

In 2006, the airline was merged with SN Brussels Airlines forming Brussels Airlines. He has also developed a Virgin Cola and a Virgin Vodka brand, which has not been a very successful enterprise.

Branson has served as a Commissioner on the Broadband Commission for Digital Development, a UN initiative which promotes universal access to broadband services. In 2011, he served on the Global Commission on Drug Policy with former political and cultural leaders of Latin America and elsewhere, "in a bid to boost the effort to achieve more humane and rational drug laws."

In September 2014, Branson announced his investment in drone company 3D Robotics stating, "It's amazing to see what a little flying object with a GoPro attached can do. Before they came along the alternative was an expensive helicopter and crew. I'm really excited about the potential 3D Robotics sees in drones. They can do a lot of good in the world, and I hope this affordable technology will give many more people the chance to see our beautiful planet from such a powerful perspective."

In November 2015, Branson announced the addition of Moskito Island to the Virgin Limited Edition portfolio. This resort, The Branson Estate on Moskito Island, offers 11 bedrooms for 22 guests.

On 11 July, 2021, Branson travelled as a passenger onboard Virgin Galactic Unity 22 at the edge of space, a suborbital test flight for his spaceflight company Virgin Galactic. The mission lasted approximately one hour, reaching a peak altitude of 53.5 miles. At 71, Branson was the third oldest person to fly to space and the first billionaire to do so.

His extra ordinary chracteristics brought Branson so many awards and honors. He was knighted by Charles, Prince of Wales on 30 March, 2020. His long list of awards and honors include: Doctor of Technology from Loughborough University (1993), the Tony Jannus Award for his accomplishments in commercial air transportation (2000), United Nations Correspondents Association Citizen of the World Award for his support for environhmental and humanitarian Causes (2007), German Media Prize (2011), ISTA Prize for his pioneering achievements in the development of suborbital transport systems with "Virgin Galactic" (2011), National Academy of Recording Arts and Sciences. Presidents Merit Award for his contributions to the music industry (2012), 2014 Business for Peace Award (2014), the International Crisis Group Chairman's Award (2015) and others.

He expanded Virgin's aerospace and finance sectors. In 2023, Virgin Orbit launched the UK's first space mission. In 2024, he sold Virgin Money UK for £724 million. By 2025, he backed Toforest Johnson's legal case and invested in Tyypo, a dyslexia-assisting app.

Ram Charan

(1985)

Actor

"The sky takes on shades of orange during sunrise and sunset, the colour that gives you hope that the sun will set only to rise again."

Ram Charan, born on March 27, 1985, in Chennai, Tamil Nadu, is a prominent figure in Indian cinema, particularly in the Telugu film industry. He hails from a distinguished lineage; his father is the legendary actor Chiranjeevi, and his mother, Surekha, is the daughter of the renowned comedian Allu Ramalingaiah. This illustrious background paved the way for Ram Charan's entry into the world of cinema.

Growing up in a family deeply rooted in the film industry, Ram Charan was exposed to the nuances of acting and filmmaking from an early age. He completed his schooling at Padma Seshadri Bala Bhavan School in Chennai and later attended Lawrence School in Lovedale. His educational journey continued at The Hyderabad Public School in Begumpet and St. Mary's College in Hyderabad. Despite his academic pursuits, the allure of cinema remained strong, leading him to enrol in a specialised acting course in Mumbai to hone his craft.

Ram Charan made his acting debut in 2007 with the film "Chirutha," directed by Puri Jagannadh. In this action-packed drama, he portrayed the character Charan, a young man seeking vengeance for his father's death. The film garnered positive reviews, and his performance earned him the Filmfare Award for Best Male Debut - South, marking a promising start to his career.

However, it was his second film, "Magadheera" (2009), that catapulted him to stardom. Directed by S.S. Rajamouli, this reincarnation-themed movie showcased Ram Charan in dual roles: Kala Bhairava, a valiant warrior from the 17th century, and Harsha, a modern-day bike racer. The film's compelling narrative, combined with his stellar performance, led to massive box office success. "Magadheera" became one of the highest-grossing Telugu films at the time and earned him the Filmfare Award for Best Actor - Telugu.

In 2013, Ram Charan ventured into Bollywood with the film "Zanjeer," a remake of the 1973 classic. He played the role of ACP Vijay Khanna, originally portrayed by Amitabh Bachchan. Despite the high expectations, the film received mixed reviews and did not perform well at the box office. Undeterred, he continued to focus on Telugu cinema, delivering notable performances in films like "Yevadu" (2014) and "Govindudu Andarivadele" (2014), both of which were commercially successful.

A significant milestone in his career came with the 2018 film "Rangasthalam," directed by Sukumar. Set in a rural backdrop, he portrayed Chitti Babu, a hearing-impaired villager. His authentic depiction of the character resonated with audiences and critics alike, earning him widespread acclaim and his second Filmfare Award for Best Actor - Telugu. The film's success further solidified his position as a versatile actor capable of taking on diverse roles.

Beyond acting, Ram Charan has ventured into film production. In 2016, he established the Konidela Production Company, under which he produced his father's comeback film, "Khaidi No. 150" (2017). The movie was a commercial success, reaffirming his acumen not just as an actor but also as a producer.

In his personal life, Ram Charan married Upasana Kamineni on June 14, 2012. Upasana is the Vice-Chairman of Apollo Foundation and the Chief Editor of B Positive magazine. The couple's union is often highlighted in the media, reflecting a blend of cinema and corporate worlds. Their relationship has been marked by mutual respect and support, with both actively participating in philanthropic activities.

Ram Charan's contributions to cinema have been recognised with several awards and accolades. He has received multiple Filmfare Awards and Nandi Awards, underscoring his talent and dedication to the craft. His ability to adapt to various genres and deliver compelling performances has made him one of the most sought-after actors in the Telugu film industry.

In addition to his film career, he has ventured into entrepreneurship. He owns the Hyderabad Polo and Riding Club, reflecting his passion for horse riding and equestrian sports. Furthermore, he was a co-owner of the regional airline service TruJet, showcasing his diverse business interests.

Ram Charan's journey in the film industry exemplifies a blend of legacy and individual talent. While his lineage provided him with a platform, it is his dedication, versatility, and relentless pursuit of excellence that have carved his niche in Indian cinema. As he continues to take on challenging roles and explore new avenues in filmmaking, his contributions are poised to leave an indelible mark on the industry.

❑❑❑

Ratan Tata

(1937-2024)

Industrial Tycoon

"The future potential is enormous and the country's destiny is in our hands."

Ratan Naval Tata was born on December 28, 1937 in an old Parsi family of Bombay (present-day Mumbai). He was the first child of Soonoo and Naval Hormusji Tata. After his parents separated in mid 1940s, he and his younger brother were raised by their grandmother Lady Navajbai.

He was schooled in Mumbai's Campion School and received a Bachelor's Degree in Architecture and Structural Engineering from Cornell University, USA in 1962. Ratan Tata had a short period with Jones and Emmons in Los Angeles, California. After returning to India in late 1962, he joined the Tata Group in December and was sent to Jamshedpur to work at Tata Steel.

In 1971, Ratan Tata was appointed the Director-in-Charge of the National Radio & Electronics Company Limited (NELCO), a company that was in dire financial difficulty. Under his leadership from 1972-75 the company recovered its losses but owing to the state of emergency declared in 1975, which led to an economic recession, the venture did not survive and was closed down in 1977. Then Ratan Tata was entrusted with Empress Mills, a textile mill controlled by the Tatas. In spite of the progress the mill made, it was closed down in 1986. Owing to unavoidable reasons.

In 1981, Ratan Tata was selected Chairman of Tata Industries. He was assigned the task of transforming the company into a Group policy think-tank and an advertiser of new ventures in high technology businesses.

In 1991, he took over the Chairmanship from JRD Tata, which today has the largest market capitalization of any business house on the Indian stock market. Under him, Tata Consultancy Services went public and Tata Motors was listed on the New York Stock Exchange. In 1998, Tata Motors introduced Ratan's brainchild, the Tata Indica—the first truly Indian car.

On January 31st 2007, under Ratan Tata's chairmanship, Tata Sons successfully acquired Corus Group, an Anglo-Dutch steel and aluminium producer. With the acquisition, Ratan Tata became a celebrated personality in Indian corporate business culture.

Ratan Tata was honoured with the highest Indian civilian award, the Padma Bhushan, on 26th January 2000. In March 2006, Tata was honoured by Cornell University as the 26th Robert S. Hatfield Fellow in Economic Education.

He has received many honorary doctorates including one from the London School of Economics. In January 2008, he was awarded the Padma Vibhushan by the Indian government and in 2009 he was appointed an honorary Knight Commander of the British Empire and honoured with Legend in Leadership award from Yale in 2010.

Ratan Tata launched his dream car Tata Nano on March 23, 2009. He was the chairman of the Tata group from 1991-2012. He stepped down voluntarily on 28 December 2012.

In October 2021, Ratan Tata witnessed a historic deal when the Tata Group won the bid to purchase national carrier Air India, the airline founded by JRD Tata in 1932. Air India's return to the Tata fold happened after 68 years of being a government company. The Jawaharlal Nehru government had taken over Air India through nationalisation in 1953. Back then, the government had paid ₹ 2.8 crore to Tata Group and took over a 100 per cent stake in the venture.

He was awarded Honorary Doctor of Law by York University, Canada in 2014 and Commander of the Legion of Honour by Government of France in 2016, Honorary Doctorate by Swansea University in 2018.

In 2022, he was awarded an Honorary Doctorate of Literature by HSNC University. The following year, King Charles III appointed him as an Honorary Officer of the Order of Australia. In August 2023, the Maharashtra government conferred upon him the Udyog Ratna Award The esteemed Indian industrialist and former chairman of the Tata Group, passed away on October 9, 2024, at the age of 86.

❑❑❑

(Pt.) Ravi Shankar

(1920–2012)

Musician and Composer

"Pop changes week to week, month to month. But great music is like literature."

Ravi Shankar was an Indian musician and composer best known for his success in popularizing the sitar. He also served as director of All-India Radio and toured India and the United States, winning three Grammy Awards and collaborating with many notable American musicians, including George Harrison and Philip Glass.

Born on April 7, 1920, in Varanasi (also known as Benares), Ravi Shankar came into the world as a Brahmin. Shankar lived in Varanasi until the age of 10, when he accompanied his brother, Uday Shankar, to Paris. Uday was a member of a dance troupe called the Compagnie de Danse et Musique Hindou (Company of Hindu Dance and Music), and the young Shankar spent his adolescence hearing the rhythms and watching the traditional dances of his culture.

At the same time, Shankar was absorbing the musical traditions of the West and attending Parisian schools. This mixture of Indian and

Western influences would be apparent in his later compositions, and would help him cultivate the respect and appreciation from Westerners that he sought for Indian music.

At a music conference in 1934, Shankar met guru and multi-instrumentalist Allaudin Khan, who became his mentor and musical guide for many years. Just two years later, Khan became the soloist for Uday's dance troupe. Shankar went to Maihar, to study sitar under Khan in 1938. Just one year after he began studying under Khan, Shankar began giving recitals.

Ten years after meeting Khan and six years after beginning his music studies, Shankar's sitar training ended. Thereafter, he went to Mumbai, where he worked for the Indian People's Theater Association, composing music for ballets until 1946. He went on to become music director of the New Delhi radio station All India Radio, a position he held until 1956. During his time at AIR, Shankar composed pieces for orchestra that mixed sitar and other Indian instruments with classical Western instrumentation. Also during this period, he began performing and writing music with violinist Yehudi Menuhin, with whom he would later record three songs: "West Meets East" (1967), "West Meets East, Vol. 2" (1968) and "Improvisations: East Meets West" (1977). All the while, the name Ravi Shankar was becoming more and more recognized internationally.

In 1954, Shankar gave a recital in the Soviet Union. In 1956, he debuted in the United States and Western Europe. Also helping his star rise was the score he wrote for famous Indian film director Satyajit Ray's *The Apu Trilogy*. The first of these films, *Pather Panchali*, won the Grand Prix—now known as the Golden Palm or Palme d'Or—at the Cannes Film Festival in 1955. The prize is been awarded to the best film of the festival.

Already an ambassador of Indian music to the Western world, Shankar embraced this role even more fully in the 1960s. That decade saw Shankar's performance at the Monterey Pop Festival, as well as his set at Woodstock in 1969. Additionally, in 1965, George

Harrison began studying sitar with Shankar, and even played the instrument on the Beatles' track "Norwegian Wood."

Shankar's partnership with Harrison proved to be even more significant years later. In 1971, Bangladesh became a hotbed of armed conflict between Indian and Muslim Pakistani forces. Along with the issues of violence, the country was inundated with ferocious flooding. Seeing the famine and hardship faced by the country's civilians, Shankar and Harrison organized the Concert for Bangladesh. Proceeds from the show went to the aid organization UNICEF to help Bangladeshi refugees. Additionally, the album made for the benefit by the performing artists won the 1971 Grammy Award for album of the year.

From the 1970s to the early 21st century, Shankar's fame, recognition and achievement continued to grow steadily. In 1982, his score for Richard Attenborough's film *Gandhi* earned him an Oscar nomination. In 1987, Shankar experimented with adding electronic music to his traditional sound, sparking music's New Age movement.

All the while, he continued to compose orchestral music blending Western and Indian instrumentation, including a collaboration with Phillip Glass: the 1990 album *Passages*.

Shankar won many awards and honors throughout his career, including 14 honorary degrees, two Grammy Awards, and a membership to the American Academy of Arts and Letters.

Shankar died on December 11, 2012, in San Diego, California, at the age of 92. He was survived by two daughters who are also musicians, sitar player Anoushka Shankar and Grammy Award-winning singer-songwriter Norah Jones.

Known fondly today as the "godfather of world music," Shankar is remembered for using his wealth of talent to infuse Indian culture into the world's forever-growing music scene, and is largely credited with building a large following for Eastern music in the West.

❑❑❑

Rudyard Kipling

(1865–1936)

Writer and Poet

"We have forty million reasons for failure, but not a single excuse."

Rudyard Kipling was a great English Writer. He is best known for his poems and stories set in India during the period of British imperial rule. He wrote *The Jungle Book* and "Gunga Din." Eventually becoming the highest paid writer in the world, Kipling was recipient of the Nobel Prize for Literature in 1907.

Rudyard Kipling was born in Bombay, on 30 December 1865. His father was an artist and teacher. In 1870, Kipling was taken back to England to stay with a foster family in Southsea and then to go to boarding school in Devon. In 1882, he returned to India and worked as a journalist, writing poetry and fiction in his spare time. Books such as 'Plain Tales from the Hills' (1888) gained success in England, and in 1889 Kipling went to live in London.

In 1892, Kipling married Caroline Balestier, the sister of an American friend, and the couple moved to Vermont in the United States, where her family lived. Their two daughters were born there and Kipling wrote 'The Jungle Book' in 1894. In 1896, a quarrel with his wife's brother prompted Kipling to move back to England and he settled with his own family in Sussex. His son John was born in 1897.

By now Kipling had become an immensely popular writer and poet for children and adults. His books included 'Stalky and Co.' (1899), 'Kim' (1901) and 'Puck of Pook's Hill' (1906). The 'Just So Stories' (1902) were originally written for his daughter Josephine, who died of pneumonia aged six.

In the winter of 1899, Carrie, who was homesick, decided that the whole family needed to travel back to New York to see her mother. But the journey across the Atlantic was brutal, and New York was frigid. Both Kipling and young Josephine arrived in the States gravely, ill with pneumonia. For days, the world kept careful watch on the state of Kipling's health as newspapers reported on his condition. *The New York Times* reported a front-page story on his health.

Kipling did recover, but his beloved Josephine did not. The family waited until Kipling was strong enough to hear the news, and even then, Carrie could not bear to break it to him, asking his publisher, Frank Doubleday, to do so. To those who knew him, it was clear that Kipling never recovered from her death. He vowed never to return to America.

Kipling turned down many honours in his lifetime, including a knighthood and the poet laureateship, but in 1907, he accepted the Nobel Prize for Literature, the first English author to be so honoured.

In 1902, Kipling bought a 17th century house called Bateman's in East Sussex where he lived for the rest of his life. He also travelled extensively, including repeated trips to South Africa in the winter months.

As much of Europe braced for war with Germany, Kipling proved to be an ardent supporter of the fight. In 1915, he even traveled to France to report on the war from the trenches. He also encouraged his son John to enlist. Since Josephine's death, Kipling and his boy had grown tremendously close. It was for John that Kipling wrote one of his famous poems, "If."

Wanting to help his son enlist, Kipling drove John to several different military recruiters. But plagued with the same eyesight problems his father had, John was repeatedly turned down. Finally, Kipling made use of his connections and managed to get John enlisted with the Irish Guard as a second lieutenant.

In October of 1915, the Kiplings received word that John had gone missing in France. The news devastated the couple. Kipling, perhaps feeling guilty about his push to make his son a soldier, set off for France to find John. But nothing ever came of the search, and John's body was never recovered. A distraught and drained Kipling returned to England to once again mourn the loss of another child.

While the last two decades continued to see Kipling write, he never again returned to the bright, cheery children's tales he had once so delighted in crafting. Health issues eventually caught up to both Kipling and Carrie, the result of age, but also of grief.

Over his last few years, Kipling suffered from a painful ulcer, which eventually took his life on January 18, 1936. Kipling's ashes were buried in Westminster Abbey in Poets' Corner next to the graves of Thomas Hardy and Charles Dickens.

Ruskin Bond

(1934)

Poet and Writer

"To return to my own trees, I went among them often, acknowledging their presence with a touch of my hand against their trunks."

Ruskin Bond is known internationally as one of India's most prolific writers in English for children, young adults, and adults. He was awarded the Padma Shri in 1999 for contribution to children's literature.

Ruskin Bond was born in Kasauli, Himachal Pradesh in 1934. He grew up in Jamnagar (Gujarat), Mussoorie, Dehradun, and Shimla. When he was 10, his father passed away in 1944 during the World War II, not to the war but to the malaria, and he was raised by his mother. He has two half-brothers from his mother's remarriage after his father's death.

For a while, he attended Hampton Court School, which is still in existence on Mussoorie's Mall Road, once the town's major promenade. He completed his schooling at Bishop Cotton School in Shimla, from where he graduated in 1952. Given his childhood in various hill stations, most of his writings revolve around the foothills of the Himalayas, especially the greater Doon Val

As a young man, Ruskin Bond spent four years in the Channel Islands and London, having moved there with his family, as was common for many Anglo-Indian and domiciled British families to have done in the years after 1947. Bond, to the surprise of his family, returned to India alone in 1956, and since then, he has never left the country since.

He has lived in Mussoorie since 1962. A lifelong bachelor, he moved to Landour by himself, but over the decades, an extended foster family has grown around him. Among blood relatives, Bond has a sister, who lived in England but now too may have returned to India.

At the time, Ruskin Bond moved there, Mussoorie and Landour were losing population given the decline of the boarding schools of the area and the gradual departure of the once-dominant expatriate classes, primarily British and American missionaries.

Bond initially moved to Landour for the "peace and quiet". Things are rather different now in Mussoorie, which is often described as "Delhi's Chandni Chowk on a Hillside", though the Landour Cantonment where Bond lives is much calmer. Earlier he lived in Mussoorie proper, in Maplewood Cottage just below Wynberg-Allen School, until 1976.

Ruskin was seventeen when his first novel, *The Room on the Roof*, came out. The book won the *John Llewellyn Rhys Prize* in 1957. *Vagrants In The Valley* was also written in his teens and picked up from where *The Room On The Roof* left off.

In 1992, Ruskin Bond received the 'Sahitya Academy Award' for English writing in India for, *Our Trees Still Grow In Dehra*.

In 1994, his much acclaimed collection of his non-fiction writing; *Rain In The Mountains, Delhi Is Not Far* and *The Best Of Ruskin Bond*, were also published.

In 1997, Bond's autobiography, *Scenes from a Writer's Life*, was published. He has written over three hundred short stories, essays and novels, including *Vagrants in The Valley*, *The Blue Umbrella*, *Funny Side Up*, *A Flight of Pigeons* and more than 30 books for children. He has also published two volumes of autobiography. *Scenes from a Writer's Life* describes his formative years growing up in Anglo-India; *The Lamp is Lit* is a collection of essays and episodes from his journal.

Ruskin Bond was awarded Padma Shri in 1999. His interest in the paranormal led him to write popular titles like, *Ghost Stories from the 'Raj'*, *A Season of Ghosts*, *A Face in the dark and other hauntings*.

His novel, *The Flight of Pigeons*, has been adapted into the film *Junoon*. *The Room on the Roof* has been adapted into a BBC-produced TV series. Several stories have been incorporated in the school curriculum in India, including "The Night Train at Deoli", "Time Stops at Shamli" and *Our Trees Still Grow in Dehra*. In 2007, the Bollywood director Vishal Bhardwaj made a film based on his popular novel for children, *The Blue Umbrella*. The movie won the National Award for Best Children's film.

Ruskin Bond made his maiden foray on the big screen with a cameo in Vishal Bhardwaj's film *7 Khoon Maaf* (2010) based on short story Susanna's Seven Husbands. He was conferred with Lifetime Achievement Award by Delhi government for his contribution in Literature, especially in Child Literature. He was awarded Padma Bhushan in 2014.

In May 2024, he was honoured with the Sahitya Akademi Fellowship, India's highest literary accolade. Later that year, in November 2024, he received the Ramnath Goenka Sahithya Samman Lifetime Achievement Award for his outstanding contributions to literature. In January 2025, Bond was awarded the Golden Book Award for his memoir, "The Hill of Enchantment: The Story of My Life."

He now lives with his adopted family in Mussoorie.

❑❑❑

Sachin Tendulkar

(1973)

Cricketer

"I have never thought where I will go, or forced any targets on myself."

Sachin was born on April 24, 1973, in Bombay (now Mumbai) into a middle-class Rajapur Saraswat Brahmin family. Tendulkar was named after his family's favourite music director Sachin Dev Burman. His late father, Ramesh Tendulkar was a Marathi novelist. He was encouraged to play cricket by his elder brother.

He attended Sharadashram Vidyamandir School where he began his cricketing career under the guidance of his coach and mentor, Ramakant Achrekar.

In 1988-89, he scored 100 not-outs in his first first-class match for Bombay against Gujarat. At the age of 15, he was the then youngest cricketer to score a century on his first-class debut.

Sachin Tendulkar is the only player to score a century while making his Ranji Trophy, Duleep Trophy and Irani Trophy debut.

John Wright, who later became the coach of India, took the catch that prevented Tendulkar from becoming the youngest centurion in Test cricket. His maiden Test century came in next tour, to England in

August 1990, at Old Trafford. Tendulkar further enhanced his development into a world-class batsman during the 1991-1992 tour of Australia that included an unbeaten 148 in Sydney and a brilliant century on the fast and bouncy track at Perth.

Tendulkar's performance through the years, 1994-1999, coincided with his physical peak, at the age of 20 through 25. He went on to make 82 runs off 49 balls. His first ODI century came on September 9, 1994, against Australia in Sri Lanka at Colombo. It had taken Tendulkar 79 ODIs to score a century.

A chronic back problem flared up when Pakistan toured India in 1999, with India losing the historic Test at Chepauk. Worse was to come as Tendulkar's father, Professor Ramesh Tendulkar, died in the middle of the 1999 Cricket World Cup. He flew back to India to attend the final rituals of his father, missing the match against Zimbabwe. However, soon he returned back to the World cup scoring a century (unbeaten 140 off 126 balls) against Kenya in Bristol. He then led India on a tour of Australia, where the visitors were beaten by the newly-crowned World Champions. He resigned, and Sourav Ganguly took over as captain in 2000. India's tour to Australia in 2003-2004 saw him making his mark in the last Test of the series, with a double century in Sydney. 'Tennis elbow' then took its toll on him, leaving him out of the side for the first two Tests when Australia toured India in 2004.

On December 10, 2005, at the Feroz Shah Kotla, he delighted his fans with a record-breaking 35th Test century, against Sri Lanka. On November 25, 2007 he broke Allan Borders record of 11, 174 runs in Test match in New Delhi against Pakistan.

Tendulkar passed 30,000 runs in international cricket on 20 November 2009. On 5 December 2012, he became first batsman in history to cross the 34,000 run aggregate in all formats of the game put together. At 36 years and 306 days, he became the first ever player to score a double-century in the history of ODIs. Two years later he became the first player to score 100 international centuries.

Tendulkar has been honoured with the Padma Vibhushan award, India's second highest civilian award, and the Rajiv Gandhi Khel

Ratna award, India's highest sporting honour. He was also the first sportsperson and the first one without aviation background to be awarded the honorary rank of Group Captain by the Indian Air Force.

In April 2012, Tendulkar accepted the Rajya Sabha nomination proposed by the President of India and became the first active sportsperson and cricketer to have been nominated.

Sachin Tendulkar retired from cricket on 16 November, 2013 after playing his 200th test match against the West Indies at Wankhede Stadium, Mumbai. He was given a never before farewell by the cricket world and his fans and awarded 'Bharat Ratna' by the Government of India.

In 2013, Indian Postal Service released a stamp of Tendulkar and he became the second Indian after Mother Teresa to have such stamp released in their lifetime. In 2017, he was awarded the Asian Fellowship Award at the 7th Asian Awards.

In 2019, he was inducted into the ICC Cricket Hall of Fame. In 2020, he was awarded the Laureus World Sports Award for Best Sporting Moment (2000-2020). In 2019, he was awarded the most effective Swachhta Ambassador by India Today Group's fifth edition of Safaigiri awards.

In October 2023, he was appointed as the Global Ambassador for the ICC Men's Cricket World Cup 2023, enhancing the tournament's global appeal. In February 2025, the Board of Control for Cricket in India (BCCI) honoured him with the Col. C.K. Nayudu Lifetime Achievement Award at the BCCI Naman Awards 2025, recognising his unparalleled contributions to Indian cricket.

Sachin's Journey of Records—• His double century is the first in 41 years of ODIs, including 60-overs-a-side matches. • Highest run-getter in ODIs, with 18,426 runs from 463 matches. • Highest scorer in Tests, 15,921 runs from 200 matches. • Most Test centuries (51).

❑❑❑

Subhash Ghai

(1945)

Director

"Film making is a democratic art.
Like we have different faces, we have
different sensibilities, which come across in our films."

Cinema and films are the mirrors of society and sum up real emotions through real-life characters and thereby entertain the masses and provide a relaxing distraction. In the case of India, our Bollywood or Hindi film industry is regarded as the branch of our culture which has given way to other streams such as Tollywood and Bhojpuri cinema based on specific language, dialect and tradition exclusive to regions.

Subhash Ghai was born in Nagpur, India and was the son of a dentist. He did his graduation from FTII (Film & Television Institute of India) Pune and shifted to Mumbai to try luck in films as an actor but later took to screenplay writing and luck favoured him with the movie *Kalicharan* in 1976 which gathered big success and made him an indispensable asset to various other blockbusters that followed. For his outstanding contribution in films, many media establishments have crafted unique titles for him such as "showman" and "dream merchant" and he has won various awards too. His superb movie "Karma" which is an anti-terrorism motion picture has bagged him a national award in 1986. Besides, his other movies "Pardes" and "Taal" broadened the audience strength and went on to be included in Hollywood top twenty at the box-office for numerous weeks. He then produced the movie "Iqbal" in 2001 which added another feather in his cap with a national award in 2007.

He then set up a film and media institute in Mumbai, replete with state of art infrastructure. In 1978, he created "Mukta Films" after his wife's name, a film producing company and the movie "Karz" was made under its banner.

Mukta Films turned a Private Limited company in 1982 with its new name Mukta Arts which made the blockbuster film "Hero" and the tradition of giving hit films was started since then.

In fact, Mukta Arts is the first film industry corporate in India which is proactive in the field of film production, distribution, exhibition and education and training.

Also, during the past few decades, Mr. Ghai has paved way for many young artists and talent such as Jackie Shroff, Mahima Choudhry etc. and has introduced many technicians and craftsmen and his contribution is immense to the Hindi film industry.

Mr. Ghai was asked to be the jury member to judge the final round of talent for the International EMMY Awards and he remained on the position for several years.

Further, he founded Whistling Woods International and is its Chairman which is the largest Institute for Film, Television, Animation & Media Arts in Asia and is widely regarded for prolific academic staff and smooth functioning and imparts quality education and training to the coming generation of filmmakers. His vision is to get India a unique place in the world of entertainment. The Hollywood Reporter regards Whistling Woods International as One of The Ten Best Film Schools in The World.

National Award - United Nations Council of Indian Youth (1986); Filmfare Award for Best Director Saudagar(1992); Diploma of Honour - American Biographical Institute (1995); Certificate of Commendation - United States Senate (1996); Filmfare Award for Best Screenplay - Pardes (1997); Winner of the IIFA Lifetime Achievement Award (2015); Director of Mumbai Film Festival; International Panel member at the Cannes Film Festival, 2004 on anti-piracy; Honored by the United States Senate in October 1996 for his achievements; State Honor award from Haryana government for his life achievements; National award for 'Iqbal' - Best Film on Social issues (2006)

Awarded the Karamveer Chakra Award, awarded by the ICONGO (International Conglomerate of NGOs), a United Nations body. IIFA : International Indian Film Academy - Outstanding contribution to Indian cinema 2015; Cinema Tourism Award : Thailand - Pioneer of Cinema Tourism; WCRC - The Pride of India Awards : The Most Responsible Leader (education & empowerment); Lifetime Achievement Award : DIORAMA International Film Festival.

In August 2022, he received the Lifetime Achievement Award at the 67th Filmfare Awards, honouring his extensive contributions to Indian cinema. In December 2024, Ghai was hospitalised due to respiratory issues but later assured fans of his recovery. By February 2025, he was developing "Aitraaz 2," considering Taapsee Pannu for the lead role.

Sardar Vallabhbhai Patel

(1875–1950)

Political and Social Leader

"I cannot speak anything but the truth.
I cannot turn back on my duty,
just to please some one."

Vallabhbhai Jhaverbhai Patel, popularly referred to as Sardar Patel, was an Indian statesman, an important leader of the Indian National Congress and the Deputy Prime Minister of India in the first cabinet of Independent India.

Vallabhbhai Patel, the iron-man of India was born on October 13, 1875 in a small village, Karamsadh of Bombay (now Mumbai) region. His father, Jhaverbhai Patel was a simple farmer and mother, Laad Bai was a housewife.

From his childhood itself, Patel was a very hard-working individual. He used to help his father in farming and studied in a school at Petlad. He passed his high-school examination in 1896. Throughout school, he was a very wise and intelligent student. Inspite of poor financial conditions, his father decided to send him to college but Vallabhbhai refused. Around three years, he stayed at home, worked hard and prepared for the District Leader's examination, hence passing with very good percentage.

Sardar Patel did not like to work for anyone, especially the Britishers. He was a person of independent nature. He began his own practice of law in a place called Godhara. Soon the practice flourished. He saved money, and made financial arrangement for the entire family. He got married to Jhaberaba and in 1904, he got a baby daughter, Maniben. In 1905, his son, Dahya was born. Vallabhbhai sent his elder brother to England for higher studies in law.

In 1908, Vitthalbhai returned as barrister and started practising in Bombay (now Mumbai). In 1909, his wife became seriously ill and was taken to Bombay (now Mumbai) for treatment. When his wife died he was arguing for an important case in the court. He received the news and stunned, but continued with the argument. He admitted his children in St. Mary's school Bombay (now Mumbai), and left for England. Then he became a barrister and retuned to India in 1913.

He started his practice in Ahmedabad and soon became aware of the local life, activities and people's problems. He became an extremely popular person and got elected in the Municipal Corporation in 1917. Around 1915, he came across Mahatma Gandhi. The Swadeshi Movement was at its peak at the time. Gandhiji gave a lecture at a place in Ahmedabad where Patel heard him and was very impressed. He started actively participating in the freedom movement. The British government's atrocities were increasing. The government declared to confiscate all the lands of farmers. He forced the British government to amend the rules, and brought together the farmers encouraging them to rebel against the tyrannical rule of the British. This is how he got the title of 'Sardar' and thus, became famous.

The British government considered him as a threat and his lectures were considered anti-government. Sardar Patel was imprisoned several times. In 1942, he took part in the Quit India Movement under the leadership of Mahatma Gandhi. He was arrested along with other leaders and was sent to Ahmednagar jail. Inspite of the British Rule, rulers of the small kingdoms were spending a lot of public money, and were having a nice time. Sardar Vallabhbhai opposed this.

With great wisdom and political foresight, he consolidated the small kingdoms. The public was with him. He tackled the Nizam of Hyderabad and the Nawab of Junagarh who initially did not want to join India. There were a lot of problems connected with the reunion of the numerous states into India. Sardar Patel's untiring efforts towards the unity of the country brought success. Due to the achievement of this massive task, Sardar Vallabhbhai Patel got the title of 'Iron Man'. He is one of the prestigious leaders of the world who became immortal by uniting a scattered nation without any bloodshed.

His enthusiasm to work for the independent nation got a big jolt when Gandhiji was murdered. Patel was very attached to Mahatma Gandhi and considered him, his elder brother and teacher. He was encouraged by the Mahatma in all his work. Gandhiji's death left him broken. On December 15, 1950, Sardar Patel died of a cardiac arrest. The news of his death spread all over the world. The entire nation plunged into deep sorrow, and everyday life came to a standstill. A grateful nation paid a tearful homage to its beloved leader. In 1991, he was honoured with the highest civilian award of 'Bharat Ratna'.

The Statue of Unity, the world's tallest statue, located on the Narmada River in the Kevadiya colony, in the state of Gujarat, was dedicated to him by the Prime Minister Narendra Modi on 31 October, 2018 which is approximately 182 metres (597 ft) in height.

Samantha Ruth Prabhu

(1987)

Actress and Model

"There's a thin line between catering to the masses and making a fool of yourself; I try to walk that line."

Samantha Ruth Prabhu, born on April 28, 1987, in Chennai, Tamil Nadu, India, is a renowned Indian actress and model who has made significant contributions to the Telugu and Tamil film industries. She was born to Joseph Prabhu, a Telugu-speaking father, and Ninette, a Malayali mother from Alappuzha, Kerala. Raised in a modest household in Pallavaram, Chennai, Samantha is the youngest of three siblings, with two elder brothers, Jonathan and David.

Samantha completed her schooling at Holy Angels Anglo Indian Higher Secondary School in Chennai. She pursued a degree in commerce at Stella Maris College, Chennai, where she excelled academically. To support herself financially during her college years, she ventured into modelling, which eventually opened doors to the film industry.

In 2010, Samantha made her acting debut with the Telugu film "Ye Maaya Chesave," directed by Gautham Vasudev Menon. Her portrayal of Jessie Thekkekuttu received critical acclaim, earning her the Filmfare Award for Best Female Debut - South and a Nandi Award. The same year, she appeared in the Tamil film "Vinnaithaandi Varuvaayaa" in a cameo role, marking her entry into Tamil cinema.

Following her debut, Samantha's career witnessed a meteoric rise. She starred in several successful films, including "Dookudu" (2011), "Eega" (2012), and "Neethaane En Ponvasantham" (2012). Her performances in these films garnered her numerous accolades, including Filmfare Awards for Best Actress in both Telugu and Tamil categories.

In 2017, Samantha married Naga Chaitanya, a prominent actor and son of Telugu superstar Nagarjuna Akkineni. The couple's wedding was a grand affair, celebrated both in Hindu and Christian traditions, reflecting their diverse cultural backgrounds. However, in October 2021, they announced their separation, ending their four-year marriage.

Samantha's versatility as an actress is evident from her diverse filmography. She has portrayed a wide range of characters, from the girl-next-door to intense dramatic roles. Notable films like "Theri" (2016), "Mersal" (2017), and "Rangasthalam" (2018) showcased her acting prowess and solidified her position as one of the leading actresses in South Indian cinema.

In 2021, Samantha ventured into the digital space with the second season of the Hindi web series "The Family Man," where she played the role of Rajalekshmi Sekharan (Raji), a rebel operative. Her performance received widespread critical acclaim, earning her the Filmfare OTT Award for Best Actress in a Drama Series.

Beyond her acting career, Samantha is known for her philanthropic efforts. She founded Pratyusha Support, an NGO aimed at providing medical support to women and children in need. Her commitment to social causes has earned her recognition and respect beyond the film fraternity.

In 2022, Samantha was diagnosed with myositis, an autoimmune condition affecting the muscles. Despite facing health challenges, including severe symptoms like "crippling spasms," fatigue, and light sensitivity, she demonstrated remarkable resilience. During the filming of "Citadel: Honey Bunny," an Amazon Studios production, Samantha persevered through complex action sequences, showcasing her dedication to her craft. Post-filming, she took a year off to focus on her health, exploring alternative medicine treatments. Her journey has been inspirational, highlighting her strength and determination.

Samantha's contributions to cinema have been recognised with several awards and accolades. She has received four Filmfare Awards South, two Nandi Awards, and a Tamil Nadu State Film Award, among others. Her ability to adapt to various genres and deliver compelling performances has made her one of the most sought-after actresses in the Telugu and Tamil film industries.

In addition to her film career, Samantha has ventured into entrepreneurship. She launched a health-centric podcast and a wellness startup, aiming to inspire others through her journey and advocacy. Her determination and resilience have reinforced her status as a significant role model, a responsibility she takes seriously.

Samantha's journey in the entertainment industry exemplifies resilience, versatility, and an unwavering commitment to her craft. From her humble beginnings to becoming one of South India's highest-paid actresses, she has navigated personal and professional challenges with grace. Her story continues to inspire many, reflecting her passion for acting and dedication to making a positive impact in society.

❑❑❑

Shahrukh Khan

(1965)

Actor

"Cinema in India is like brushing your teeth in the morning. You can't escape it."

Shahrukh Khan is one of the most coveted Bollywood actors today, having won all the awards the Indian entertainment industry can offer. Apart from movies, he has done many TV commercials of big brands.

Shahrukh Khan, son of Late Mir Taj Mohammad and Late Fatima Begum, was born on November 2, 1965. He did his schooling from St. Columba's school and had a Masters Degree in Mass Communication from Jamia Milia Islamia, Delhi.

Shahrukh Khan married before he got his break in Bollywood. SRK's devotion towards his wife, Gauri has been lauded. Shahrukh began his career as an actor with *Fauji* (1988), a television serial which gave him instant success. After a couple of TV serials, he joined the big league and gave a smashing hit, *Deewana* (1992) with the late Divya Bharati. After that, he gave a series of hit films both as a hero and a villain.

In 1993, he shot to stardom with two successive villain roles as a paranoid lover in *Baazigar* and *Darr*. In 1995, Shahrukh got another hit, *Dilwale Dulhania Le Jayenge* which elevated him as one of the most successful actor in Hindi cinema. After *DDLJ*, he got a series of hit movies which include *Pardes* (1997), *Yes Boss* (1997), *Dil To Pagal Hai* (1997), *Dil se* (1998), *Kuch Kuch Hota Hai* (1998), *Hey Ram* (2000), *Josh* (2000), *Har Dil Jo Pyar Karega* (2000), *Mohabbatein* (2000), etc.

Shahrukh as one of the ascendants to the Magadha throne in Santosh Sivan's *Ashoka* (2001) gave a wonderful performance as a romantic, ruthless warrior. Karan Johar's *Kabhi Khushi Kabhi Gham* was another movie in the same year in which he was unable to take full advantage of the character. In 2002, he excelled in *Devdas*, which was India's official entry to the 2002 Oscar.

He started a production company *Dreamz Unlimited* with co-star Juhi Chawla and director, Aziz Mirza. In 2004, another of his production houses, *Red Chillies Entertainment*, produced the hit film, *Main Hoon Na* and co-produced *Kaal* in 2005 with Karan Johar as director.

Shahrukh also produced and acted in *Paheli*, which was India's official entry to the 2005 Oscar. A noted British filmmaker, Nasreen Munni has produced a two-part documentary on Shahrukh, *The Inner and Outer World of Shahrukh Khan*. In his personal life, he is very simple and frank. He strongly believes in Hindu-Muslim peace and unity, as many other Bollywood actors. Shahrukh was awarded the Padmashree in 2005.

SRK has a superb drive to top in anything he does and says. He also took over the hot seat of the 'Big B' in the popular show *Kaun Banega Crorepati-III* of the Star Plus in 2007. His award winning performance same year was in *Chak De India*.

His film *Om Shanti Om* is a hit film for 2007. This film is also produced by him. He anchored a TV show *Kya Aap Panchvi Pas Se*

Tez Hain in 2008. In 2008, Newsweek named him one of the 50 most powerful people in the world.

He also starred in *Rab Ne Bana Di Jodi* (2008), *Billu* (2009) and *My Name is Khan* (2010). He won Filmfare Award for Best Actor for *My Name Is Khan* and *Jab Tak Hai Jaan*. His much talked about film is science fiction *Ra One*.

Khan's only release in 2012 was Yash Chopra's last romantic drama *Jab Tak Hai Jaan* and would eventually become Chopra's venture.

For his contributions to film, the Government of India honoured him with the Padma Shri, and the Government of France awarded him both the *Ordre des Arts et des Lettres* and *the Legion d'honneur.*

As of 2015, Khan is co-chairman of the motion picture production company Red Chillies Entertainment and its subsidiaries, and is the co-owner of the Indian Premier League cricket team Kolkata Knight Riders.

Khan is one of the most decorated Bollywood actors. He has received 15 Filmfare Awards from 30 nominations and special awards, including eight for Best Actor.

In 2018, Khan was honoured by the World Economic Forum with their annual Crystal Award for his leadership in championing children's and women's rights in India.

2019 : La Trobe University started a PhD scholarship in Khan's honour for an aspiring female researcher from India.

2019 : Honoured for his contribution to the world's film industry at Joy Forum 2019 in Riyadh by The Saudi General Authority for Entertainment.

In 2023, he headlined three major films: "Pathaan", "Jawan", and "Dunki", all achieving significant box office success. His performance in "Jawan" earned him the Best Actor award at the 2024 IIFA Awards. Additionally, in August 2024, Khan was honoured with the Pardo Lifetime Achievement Award at the Locarno Film Festival.

❑❑❑

Sigmund Freud

(1856–1939)

Psychologist

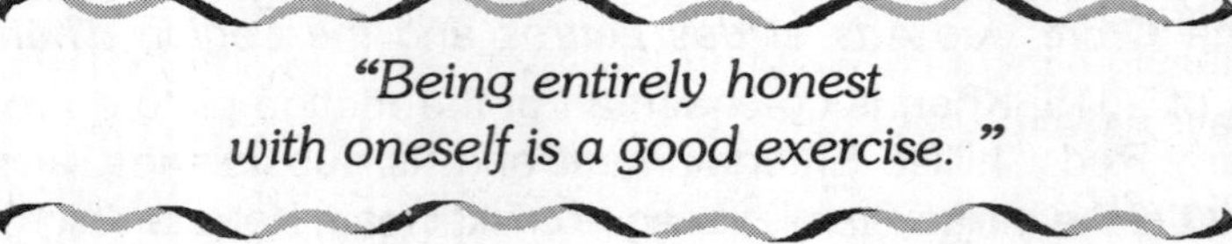

"Being entirely honest with oneself is a good exercise."

Sigmund Freud was an Austrian neurologist and the founder of the psychoanalytic school of psychology. Freud is best known for his theories of sexual desire, repression, dreams, and the unconscious mind.

Sigmund Schlomo Freud was born on May 6, 1856, in Freiberg (now Príbor, Czech Republic). His mother, Amalia, was actually the third wife of Jacob Freud and some twenty years younger than her husband. Sigismund was the first child of their marriage, and seven more children were to follow. Jacob's earlier marriages had produced two sons who were almost of the same age as Amalia. The household was Jewish and Jacob earnt a fairly modest living as a merchant in wool. In 1859, the family moved initially to Leipzig and then, a few months thereafter, settled permanently in Vienna.

Although Sigmund's early aspiration had been for a career in law, he later decided to pursue a course in medicine and entered the Vienna University in 1873. It seems that he became deeply involved, from 1876, in researches into the central nervous system to the extent that he neglected to closely pursue the range of courses that would have allowed him to promptly qualify as a doctor. Another source of delay was a compulsory one year of military service. As a result, it was only in the year, 1881 that he was awarded a degree in medicine under the name, 'Sigmund Freud' (following an adaptation in his personal name of 1877).

Immediately, subsequent to this graduation, several years were spent in Vienna working as a practical psychologist and a lecturer in psychology. In 1886, he established a private practice in Vienna specialising in nervous disorders. He also got married to Martha Bernays in that year.

Sigmund Freud worked in association with another Viennese hypnotherapist named Josef Breuer in the preparation and publication of a learnt paper (1893) that was later developed into their publication Studies on Hysteria (Cathartic Method) (1895). However, his interest gradually moved away from the investigation of neurological- physiological causes of mental disorders towards the investigation of more purely psychological causes of such disorders and in 1896, he coined the term, 'Psychoanalysis' to refer to the investigation of the psychological causes of mental disorders.

In 1899, *The Interpretation of Dreams*, the book that Sigmund regarded as his most important work was published. Although the orthodox medical profession in Vienna tended to look upon his work with deep suspicion, he was appointed as a professor in Vienna in 1902, very largely as the result of the gratitude of an highly influential patient.

By 1908, a group of psychologists interested in Freud's methods formed themselves into the Viennese Association of Psychoanalysis.

Psychoanalysis increasingly gained an international acceptance as a method of psychological investigation. Delegates from five countries attended a Freudian psychology congress in Salzburg in

1908. In 1909, Freud was invited, along with Alfred Adler and Carl Gustav Jung to lecture at the Clark University in the United States. In 1910, an International Psychoanalytical Association was founded.

Adler and Jung were associated with Freud in the Psychoanalytic movement for a time but in Adler's case there was a parting of the ways in 1911 and in Jung's case in 1913.

In 1923, Freud was diagnosed as having cancer of the jaw. Nevertheless, during the next sixteen years, he remained productive in Psychoanalysis but also in a broadening of his interests into associated philosophical and cultural matters. Freud's subsequently received many international awards and recognitions of his work.

Other international developments were, however, less welcome - such as, Austria was threatened with being absorbed into Hitler's Greater German Reich and effectively taken over by Hitler in mid-March 1938. Although Freud seems to have been personally irreligious, he and his family were very open to being classed, by the Nazis, as Jews and as such, saw the practical necessity of evading Hitler's encroachments on their liberties by emigrating from Austria. In the event, the family relocated to London. Freud was at this time in his early eighties and only survived until September 1939.

❑❑❑

Silvio Berlusconi

(1936-2023)

Entrepreneur, Politician and Media Tycoon

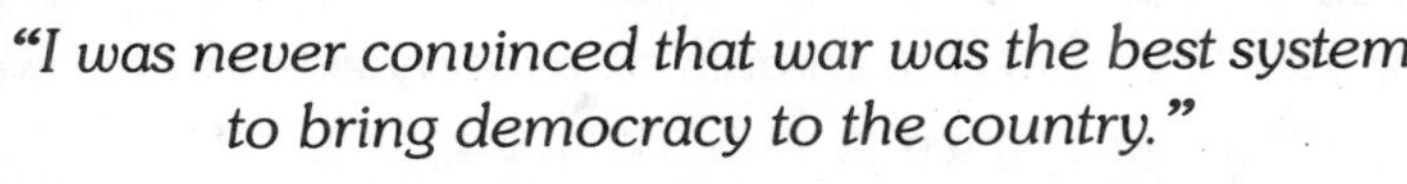

"I was never convinced that war was the best system to bring democracy to the country."

Silvio Berlusconi was born in Milan, Italy, on September 29, 1936. He sold vacuum cleaners and sang on cruise ships before making a fortune in real estate.

Berlusconi launched a cable channel, Telemilano, in 1974. Although Italian television was heavily regulated, Berlusconi then started a commercial network. He introduced Italy to many foreign TV shows and to *veline*, showgirls who would strip or dance during game shows and news programs.

In 1993, Berlusconi founded a political party, Forza Italia (Go Italy). He became prime minister in 1994, but the coalition that brought him to power fell apart seven months later. However, Berlusconi was still a popular political figure, especially with people who hoped that his business acumen would help Italy's economy. With promises of tax cuts and job growth, he took over as prime minister again in 2001, staying in power until 2006.

With his renamed political party, Popolo della Libertà (People of Freedom), Berlusconi became prime minister for a third time in 2008. He resigned in 2011, after witnessing Italy's debt burdens surge during the eurozone crisis.

Berlusconi promoted many of the *veline* from his television programs to government positions. In 2007, Berlusconi told Mara Carfagna, a *velina* he had brought into politics, "If I weren't already married, I would marry you right now." Hearing this public declaration, Berlusconi's wife, Veronica Lario, published a letter demanding an apology. After Berlusconi attended an aspiring *velina*'s 18th birthday party in 2009, Lario opted to end the marriage.

Another Berlusconi scandal was the revelation about his "bunga bunga" sex parties. At these parties, women—often wearing costumes—danced and disrobed for Berlusconi and his guests. Berlusconi has stated that the gatherings were nothing more than dinner parties.

Accusations of criminal misbehavior had followed Berlusconi since his first days in office. He was charged with embezzlement, tax fraud and bribery. Being in power helped Berlusconi avoid some charges—he passed one law that granted the prime minister immunity while in office (the law was later struck down). Berlusconi was also able to fight other accusations until the statute of limitations ran out.

However, Berlusconi was convicted multiple times. In October 2012, Berlusconi was sentenced to four years for tax fraud. And in June 2013, Berlusconi was sentenced to seven years for paying an underage woman, Karima "Ruby" el Mahroug, for sex. El Mahrough was 17 when she attended several of Berlusconi's "bunga bunga" parties in 2010. Berlusconi was also convicted of abusing the power of his office (while prime minister).

Berlusconi tried to get el Mahrough out of jail by telling police that she was related to Egypt's Hosni Mubarak). Along with this conviction, Berlusconi was barred from public office.

With his broadcast success and long political career, Berlusconi changed the worlds of media and politics in Italy. His wealth—in 2013, *Forbes* magazine estimated Berlusconi and his family's fortune at $6.2 billion

In 2009, *Forbes* ranked him 12th in the List of The World's Most Powerful People due to his domination initalian politics.

In 2018, Forbes magazine ranked him as the 190th richest man in the world with a net worth of US $8.0 billion.

In June 2023, he passed away at 86 due to complications from chronic myelomonocytic leukemia. His state funeral was held at Milan Cathedral. Posthumously, in September 2024, a proposal to rename Milan's Malpensa Airport after him sparked controversy and was met with appeals. Additionally, in October 2024, Italy's Supreme Court overturned acquittals in the "Bunga Bunga" case, mandating retrials.

Sir Donald George Bradman

(1908–2001)

Cricketer

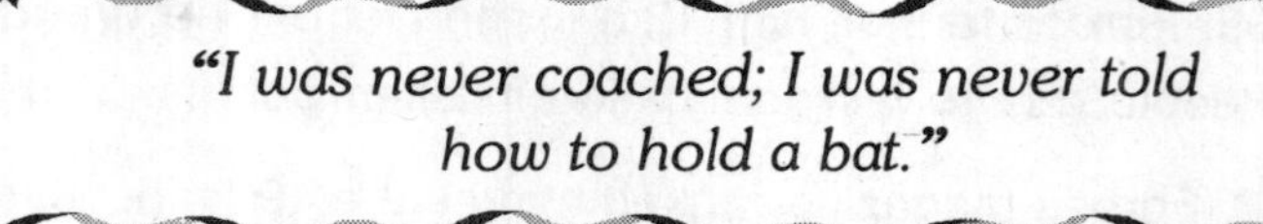

"I was never coached; I was never told how to hold a bat."

Sir Donald George Bradman, often called The Don, was an Australian cricketer who is universally regarded as the greatest batsman of all time.His Test batting average of 99.94 is by some measures the greatest statistical performance of all time in any major sport.

Donald Bradman was born in Cootamundra, New South Wales, on August 27, 1908. He was the youngest child in the family. In 1911, his family moved to Browral because of his mother's ill health.

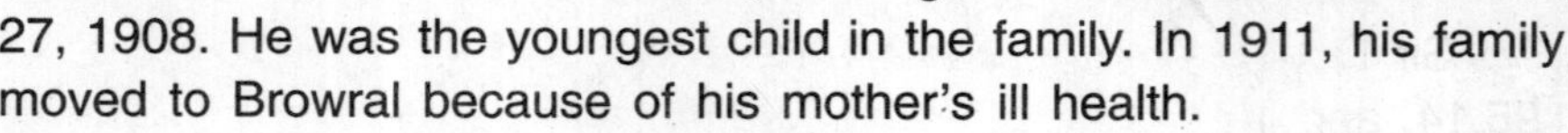

He learnt cricket from his maternal uncles, George and Richard Whatman. Bradman developed his batting by throwing a golf ball against a tank stand and playing it with a stump, and his fielding by throwing a golf ball at the bottom rail of a fence.

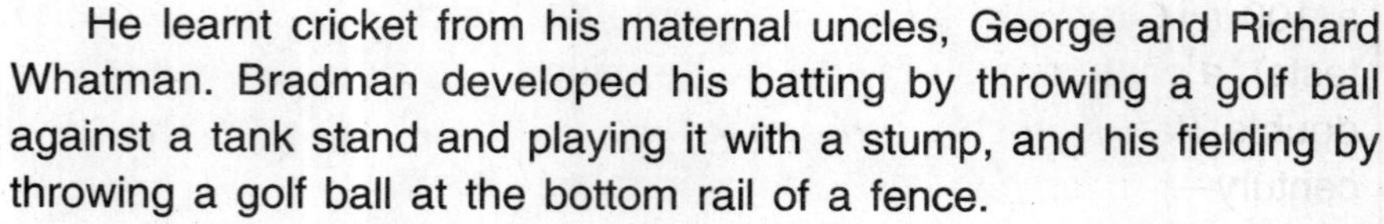

As a teenager, Bradman played Saturday afternoon cricket in the country and quickly proceeded to amass huge scores. In 1926, the New South Wales Cricket Association, which was incidentally looking for bowlers, asked Bradman to play in trial games. While making modest scores, he nonetheless attracted the eye of the selectors as a player of the future.

After a series of big scores at the beginning of the 1928–1929 season, he was chosen to play for Australia against Perry Chapman's English side. While performing poorly in the first test and being dropped to 12th man for the second, he scored two centuries in the remaining rubbers to establish his place in the Australian team.

In his initial tour of England in 1930, Sir Donald Bradman established himself as a figure of international stature. He scored 2,960 runs on tour at an average of 98.66. In test matches, he scored 974 runs at an average of 139.14, including scores of 131, 254, 334, and 452.

On both the 1930 and 1938 tours of England, Bradman scored 1,000 runs before the end of May. He became the only player to achieve such a distinction. In the 1938–1939 season, he scored six centuries in a row, equalling C. B. Fry's record. Only the bodyline bowling, where the ball is pitched short and aimed in the general direction of the head, employed by Douglas Jardine's 1932–1933 English side curbed Bradman. His average fell to 56.57, which would still be the envy of most batsmen. Such was the hostility generated by the bodyline bowling that diplomatic exchanges occurred between Australia and England.

Sir Donald George Bradman's average in first class cricket was 95.14, and in test cricket, it was 99.94, being only four runs short of a 100 average. He scored 117 centuries in first class cricket (29 in tests), a century every third time he batted. His centuries included 31 double (ten in tests), five triple (two in tests), and one quadruple century—his famous 452 got out against Queensland in 1930.

In 1936, Bradman was appointed captain of Australian cricket team to oppose Gubby Allen's touring English side. He continued captaining Australian cricket team until 1948, notwithstanding a five year absence from cricket caused by World War II. Bradman was a most successful captain. In the 24 tests while he was the captain, Australia won 15, lost three, and drew six. The team which toured England in 1948 had the distinction of never losing a game.

George Bradman was selected as one of the five Wisden Cricketers of the Year in 1931. He was awarded a knighthood in 1949, and a Companion of the Order of Australia (Australia's highest civil honour) in 1979. In 1996, he was inducted into the Australian Cricket Hall of Fame as one of the ten inaugural members. He maintained contact with the game as a selector and administrator, having two stints as chairman of the Australian Cricket Board, 1960 to 1963 and 1969 to 1972.

His most important decision as chairman was to cancel the visit of a South African team in 1971–1972 because of the expected bitterness and violence associated with opposition to South Africa's apartheid politics. From 1965 to 1973, Bradman served as president of the South Australian Cricket Association.

The late 1980s and 1990s saw a spate of biographical material on Bradman. In 1988, he released his book, *The Bradman Albums*, and two biographies of him, *Charles Williams Bradman: An Australian Hero*, and Roland Perry's book, *The Don*, were published in 1996.

Sir Donald George Bradman died at the ripe age of 92 on February 25, 2001. Clearly time does not diminish Bradman's status as a hero in his native Australia, or anywhere else where cricket is appreciated.

❑❑❑

Sir Winston Churchill

(1874–1965)
Political Leader

"A pessimist sees the difficulty in every opportunity; an optimist sees the opportunity in every difficulty."

Sir Winston Churchill was best known for his stubbornness yet courageous leadership as Prime Minister of Great Britain, when he led the British people from the brink of defeat during World War II.

He was born on November 30, 1874, to the aristocrat, Lord Randolph Churchill. He was eldest among his siblings. After his graduation from the Royal Military College in Sandhurst, he was commissioned in the Forth Hussars, in February 1895. During the Boer War, he was captured as a war correspondent. Churchill became a National Hero after his escape. Ten months later, he was elected as a member of the Conservative Party. He joined the Liberal Party in 1904, where he became the president of the Board of Trade.

In 1910, Sir Winston Churchill became the Home Secretary, where he worked with David Lloyd George. But he left the Home Office and became the first Lord of the Admiralty in 1911. His career was almost destroyed as a result of the unsuccessful Gallipoli campaign during the First World War. He was forced to resign from the Admiralty. However, he returned to the government as the Minister of Munitions in1917.

In this year, he joined the coalition party in which he was a member until it collapsed in 1922 when for two years, he was out of parliament.

In 1924, Churchill returned to the conservative government and was given the job of Chancellor of the Exchequer. During the depression, he was denied the cabinet office for ten years. His backing and support for King Edward VIII, during his abdication were frowned upon by the national government.

However, in September 1939, when Nazi Germany declared war on Poland, the public supported him in his views. Once again, Neville Chamberlain appointed him the First Lord of the Admiralty on September 3, 1939.

Churchill succeeded Chamberlain in 1940, as Prime Minister and during World War II, he successfully secured military aid and moral support from the United States. He travelled endlessly during the war, establishing close ties with leaders of other nations and co-ordinated a military strategy which subsequently ensured Hitler's defeat.

His efforts got noticed and was appreciated all over the world for his tireless efforts. However, during the 1945 election, he was defeated by the Labour Party who ruled until 1951. Sir Winston Churchill regained his power in 1951 and lead Britain once again until April 5, 1955 when ill health forced him to resign. He spent much of his latter years writing (*The History of the English-Speaking People*) and painting. In recognition of these historical studies, Churchill received the Nobel Prize for Literature in 1953 and in 1963, the US Congress conferred on him the honorary American citizenship.

Churchill died of a stroke, at the age of 90 in 1965. His death ked the end of an era in British History. He was given a state funeral and was buried in St. Martin's Churchyard, Bladon, in Oxfordshire.

Sir Winston Churchill was a prolific historical writer, although much of his work was dedicated to justifying his past actions and his place in history. Some of his famous works include, *The World Crisis* (4 vols., 1923–1929), *My Early Life* (1930), *Marlborough* (4 vols., 1933–1938), *The Second World War* (6 vols., 1948–1953), and *A History of the English-Speaking Peoples* (4 vols., 1956–1958). He received the Nobel Prize for Literature and a knighthood in 1953.

S.S. Rajamouli

(1973)

Film Director

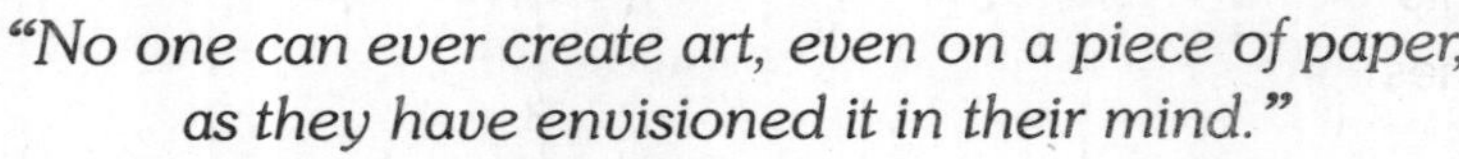

"No one can ever create art, even on a piece of paper, as they have envisioned it in their mind."

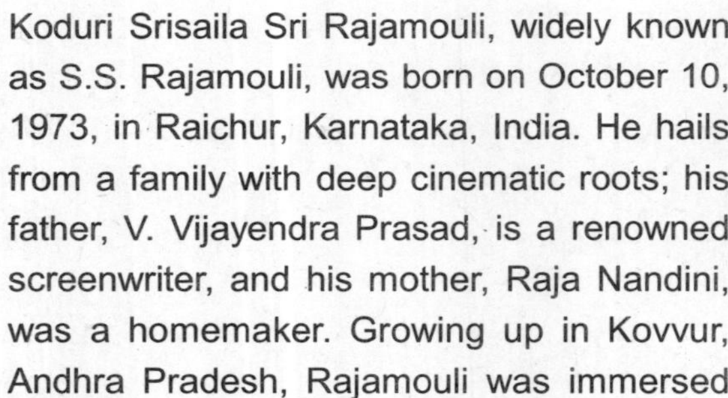

Koduri Srisaila Sri Rajamouli, widely known as S.S. Rajamouli, was born on October 10, 1973, in Raichur, Karnataka, India. He hails from a family with deep cinematic roots; his father, V. Vijayendra Prasad, is a renowned screenwriter, and his mother, Raja Nandini, was a homemaker. Growing up in Kovvur, Andhra Pradesh, Rajamouli was immersed in storytelling and cinema from an early age, which significantly influenced his career path.

Rajamouli began his career in the entertainment industry as an assistant to veteran director K. Raghavendra Rao. He initially worked on the Telugu television series "Shanti Nivasam," which provided him with valuable experience and insights into direction and storytelling.

In 2001, Rajamouli made his directorial debut with the Telugu film "Student No.1", starring Jr. NTR. The film was a commercial success, marking the beginning of a series of successful collaborations between the director and the actor. He followed this with "Simhadri" in 2003, another hit that solidified his reputation for delivering engaging mass entertainers.

Rajamouli's penchant for blending mythology with contemporary storytelling became evident with "Yamadonga" (2007), a socio-fantasy film that was both a critical and commercial success. However, it was "Magadheera" (2009) that catapulted him to unprecedented fame. This reincarnation-themed epic set new benchmarks in Telugu cinema for its grand visuals and compelling narrative, becoming one of the highest-grossing Telugu films at the time.

In 2012, Rajamouli directed "Eega", a fantasy film where the protagonist is reincarnated as a housefly seeking vengeance. The film's unique storyline and innovative visual effects garnered international attention, earning awards such as the Most Original Film at the 8th Toronto After Dark Film Festival.

Rajamouli's vision reached its zenith with the "Baahubali" series. "Baahubali : The Beginning" (2015) and its sequel, "Baahubali 2 : The Conclusion" (2017), were monumental in scale and ambition. These films not only broke box office records but also showcased Indian cinema's potential on the global stage. "Baahubali 2" became the highest-grossing Indian film at the time, with Rajamouli receiving accolades for his direction and storytelling.

In 2022, Rajamouli directed "RRR", a period action drama set in the 1920s, focusing on two Indian revolutionaries. The film received critical acclaim and achieved significant international success, further cementing Rajamouli's status as a master storyteller. "RRR" won several international awards, including a Golden Globe for Best Original Song for "Naatu Naatu".

On the personal front, Rajamouli married Rama Rajamouli in 2001. Rama has been an integral part of his filmmaking journey, working as a costume designer on many of his projects. Rajamouli adopted Rama's son from her previous marriage, Karthikeya, and the couple also has an adopted daughter, Mayookha. Karthikeya has followed in his stepfather's footsteps, involving himself in film production and related ventures.

Throughout his illustrious career, Rajamouli has been the recipient of numerous awards and honours. He has won several National Film Awards and Filmfare Awards for his contributions to Indian cinema. In 2016, the Government of India honoured him with the Padma Shri, the country's fourth-highest civilian award, recognising his significant contributions to the arts.

Rajamouli's filmmaking style is characterised by grandiose visuals, intricate storytelling, and a deep connection to Indian mythology and history. His ability to blend traditional narratives with cutting-edge technology has set new standards in Indian cinema, inspiring a generation of filmmakers. His films often explore themes of heroism, sacrifice, and the eternal battle between good and evil, resonating with audiences across cultural and linguistic barriers.

❑❑❑

Stephen Hawking

(1942-2018)

Physicist and Cosmologist

"The Greatest enemy of knowledge is not ignorance, it is the illusion of knowledge. "

Stephen William Hawking is an English theoretical physicist, cosmologist, author and Director of Research at the Centre for Theoretical Cosmology within the University of Cambridge. Among his significant scientific works have been a collaboration with Roger Penrose on gravitational singularities theorems in the framework of general relativity, and the theoretical prediction that black holes emit radiation, often called Hawking radiation. Hawking was the first to set forth a cosmology explained by a union of the general theory of relativity and quantum mechanics. He is a vocal supporter of the many-worlds interpretation of quantum mechanics.

He is an Honorary Fellow of the Royal Society of Arts, a lifetime member of the Pontifical Academy of Sciences, and a recipient of the Presidential Medal of Freedom, the highest civilian award in the United States. Hawking was the Lucasian Professor of Mathematics at the University of Cambridge between 1979 and 2009.

Stephen Hawking was born on January 8, 1942, in Oxford, England. His parents' house was in north London, but during the second world war, Oxford was considered a safer place. When he was eight, his family moved to St. Albans, a town about 20 miles north of London. At the age of eleven, Stephen went to St. Albans School and then on to University College, Oxford; his father's old college. Stephen wanted to study Mathematics, although his father would have preferred medicine. Mathematics was not available at University College, so he pursued Physics instead. After three years and not very much work, he was awarded a first class honours degree in Natural Science.

Stephen then went on to Cambridge to do research in Cosmology, there being no one working in that area in Oxford at the time. His supervisor was Denis Sciama, although he had hoped to get Fred Hoyle who was working in Cambridge. At age 21, while studying cosmology at the University of Cambridge, he was diagnosed with Amyotrophic Lateral Sclerosis. Despite his debilitating illness, he has done ground-breaking work in physics and cosmology, and his several books have helped to make science accessible to everyone. After gaining his Ph.D. he became first a Research Fellow and later on a Professorial Fellow at Gonville and Caius College. After leaving the Institute of Astronomy in 1973, Stephen came to the Department of Applied Mathematics and Theoretical Physics in 1979, and held the post of Lucasian Professor of Mathematics from 1979 until 2009. The chair was founded in 1663 with money left in the will of the Reverend Henry Lucas who had been the Member of Parliament for the University. It was first held by Isaac Barrow and then in 1669 by Isaac Newton. Stephen is still an active part of Cambridge University and retains an office at the Department for Applied Maths and Theoretical Physics. His title is now Director of Research at the Centre for Theoretical Cosmology.

Stephen Hawking has worked on the basic laws which govern the universe. With Roger Penrose he showed that Einstein's General

Theory of Relativity implied space and time would have a beginning in the Big Bang and an end in black holes. These results indicated that it was necessary to unify General Relativity with Quantum Theory, the other great Scientific development of the first half of the 20th Century. One consequence of such a unification that he discovered was that black holes should not be completely black, but rather should emit radiation and eventually evaporate and disappear. Another conjecture is that the universe has no edge or boundary in imaginary time. This would imply that the way the universe began was completely determined by the laws of science.

His many publications include The Large Scale Structure of Spacetime with G F R Ellis, General Relativity: An Einstein Centenary Survey, with W Israel, and 300 Years of Gravity, with W Israel. Stephen Hawking has three popular books published; his best seller A Brief History of Time, Black Holes and Baby Universes and Other Essays, The Universe in a Nutshell, and most recently in 2010, The Grand Design.

Professor Hawking has twelve honorary degrees. He was awarded the CBE in 1982, and was made a Companion of Honour in 1989. He is the recipient of many awards, medals and prizes, is a Fellow of The Royal Society and a Member of the US National Academy of Sciences.

On 20 July 2015, Hawking helped launch Break through Initiatives, an effort to search for extraterrestrial life. Hawking created Stephen Hawking: Expedition New Earth, a documentary on space colonisation, as a 2017 episode of Tomorrow's World.

In August 2015, Hawking said that not all information is lost when something enters a black hole and there might be a possibility to retrieve information from a black hole according to his theory. In July 2017, Hawking was awarded an Honorary Doctorate from Imperial College London. Hawking's final paper - A smooth exit from eternal inflation? - was posthumously published in the Journal of High Energy Physics on 27 April, 2018.

Hawking died at his home in Cambridge on 14 March, 2018, at the age of 76.

Steve Jobs

(1955–2011)

Co-founder of Apple Inc.

"The ones who are crazy enough to think that they can change the world, are the ones who do."

Steven Paul 'Steve' Jobs was an American entrepreneur, marketer, and inventor, who was the co-founder, chairman, and CEO of Apple Inc. Through Apple, he is widely recognized as a charismatic pioneer of the personal computer revolution and for his influential career in the computer and consumer electronics fields, transforming "one industry after another, from computers and smartphones to music and movies".

Steve Jobs was born in San Francisco, California, on February 24, 1955, to two University of Wisconsin graduate students who gave him up for adoption. As an infant, Steven was adopted by Clara and Paul Jobs and named Steven Paul Jobs. Clara worked as an accountant and Paul was a Coast Guard veteran and machinist. The family lived in Mountain View within California's Silicon Valley. As a boy, Jobs and his father would work on electronics in the family garage. Paul would show his son how to take apart and reconstruct electronics, a hobby which instilled confidence, tenacity and mechanical prowess in young Jobs.

While Jobs has always been an intelligent and innovative thinker, his youth was riddled with frustrations over formal schooling. A prankster in elementary school, Jobs's fourth-grade teacher needed to bribe him to study. Jobs tested so well, however, that administrators wanted to skip him ahead to high school—a proposal that his parents declined.

Not long after Jobs did enroll at Homestead High School (1971), he was introduced to his future partner, Steve Wozniak, through a friend of Wozniak. Wozniak was attending the University of Michigan at the time.

After high school, Jobs enrolled at Reed College in Portland, Oregon. Lacking direction, he dropped out of college after six months and spent the next 18 months dropping in on creative classes.

In 1974, Jobs took a position as a video game designer with Atari. Several months later he left Atari to find spiritual enlightenment in India, traveling the continent and experimenting. Smart but directionless, Jobs experimented with different pursuits before starting Apple Computers. In 1976, when Jobs was just 21, he and Wozniak started Apple Computers. The duo started in the Jobs family garage, and the rest, they say, is history.

But after a power struggle with the board of directors in 1985, Jobs left Apple and founded NeXT, a computer platform development company specializing in the higher-education and business markets. In 1986, he acquired the computer graphics division of Lucas film, which was spun off as Pixar. He was credited in *Toy Story* (1995) as an executive producer. In 1996, after Apple had failed to deliver its operating system,Copland, Gil Amelio turned to NeXT Computer, and the NeXTSTEP platform became the foundation for the Mac OS X. Jobs returned to Apple as an advisor, and took control of the company as an interim CEO. Jobs brought Apple from near bankruptcy to profitability by 1998. As the new CEO of the company, Jobs oversaw the development of the iMac, iTunes, iPod, iPhone, and iPad, and on the services side, the company's Apple Retail Stores, iTunes Store and the App Store. The success of these products and services provided several years of stable financial returns, and propelled Apple to become the world's most valuable publicly traded company in 2011.

The reinvigoration of the company is regarded by many commentators as one of the greatest turnarounds in business history.

Apple's revolutionary products, which include the iPod, iPhone and iPad, are now seen as dictating the evolution of modern technology.

Jobs also co-founded and served as chief executive of Pixar Animation Studios; he became a member of the board of directors of The Walt Disney Company in 2006, when Disney acquired Pixar. Jobs was among the first to see the commercial potential of Xerox PARC's mouse-driven graphical user interface, which led to the creation of the Apple Lisa and, one year later, the Macintosh. He also played a role in introducing the LaserWriter, one of the first widely available laser printers, to the market.

In 2003, Jobs was diagnosed with a pancreas neuroendocrine tumor. Though it was initially treated, he reported a hormone imbalance, underwent a liver transplant in 2009, and appeared progressively thinner as his health declined. On medical leave for most of 2011, Jobs resigned in August that year, and was elected Chairman of the Board. He died of respiratory arrest related to his tumor on October 5, 2011.

In the 1980s, Jobs found his birth mother, Joanne Schieble Simpson, who told him he had a biological sister, Mona Simpson. They met for the first time in 1985, and became close friends. The siblings kept their relationship secret until 1986, when Mona introduced him at a party for her first book.

After deciding to search for their biological father, Mona found him (Jandali) managing a coffee shop. Without knowing who his son had become, Jandali told Mona that he had previously managed a popular restaurant in the Silicon Valley, mentioning that "even Steve Jobs used to eat there. Yeah, he was a great tipper."

Jobs received a number of honors and public recognition for his influence in the technology and music industries. He has been referred to as "legendary", a "futurist" or simply "visionary", and has been described as the "Father of the Digital Revolution", a "master of innovation", "the master evangelist of the digital age" and a "design perfectionist". ❑❑❑

Subhash Chandra Bose

(1897–1945)

Freedom Fighter

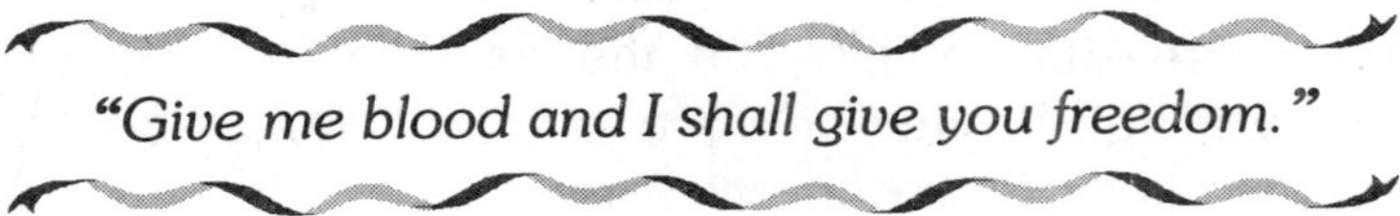

"Give me blood and I shall give you freedom."

Subhash Chandra Bose was one of the most influential and charismatic leader of pre-Independent India. His life was full of mystery and adventure and indeed, his death has been a major issue, and creates controversy from time to time.

Subhash Chandra Bose was born on January 23, 1897. His father was Rai Bahadur Janakinath Bose, a prominent lawyer of Cuttack, Orissa. His mother was Prabhavati Bose, a remarkable example of Indian womanhood. Later, the world came to know him as Netaji. After completing his early studies at the European Protestant Collegiate School in Cuttack, he came to Calcutta (presently, Kolkata) to study at the Presidency College in 1913. Upon completing his graduation, he left India for England to appear at the Indian Civil Service Examination.

Subhash Chandra Bose felt that young militant groups could be molded into a military arm of the freedom movement and used to further the cause. Gandhiji opposed this ideology because it directly conflicted with his policy of Ahimsa (non-violence). The British Government in India perceived Subhash as a potential source of danger and had arrested him without any charge on October 25, 1924. He was sent to Alipore Jail, Caluatta (now Kolkata), and on January 25, 1925 transferred to Mandalay, Burma (now Myanmar). He was released from Mandalay in May, 1927 due to his ill health. Upon return to Calcutta (now Kolkata), Subhash was elected president of the Bengal Congress Committee on October 27, 1927.

Subhash was one of the few politicians who sought and worked towards Hindu-Muslim unity on the basis of respect of each community's rights. He, being a man of ideals, believed in independence from the social evil of religious discord.

In January 1930, Subhash Chandra Bose was arrested while leading a procession condemning imprisonment of revolutionaries. He was offered bail on condition that he signs a bond to refrain from all political activities which, he refused. As a result, he was sentenced to a year's imprisonment.

On his release from jail, Subhash was sworn in as 'Mayor of the Calcutta Corporation'. In 1931, the split between Gandhiji and Subhash crystallised. Although the two never saw eye to eye on their view of freedom and the movement itself, Subhash felt that Gandhiji had done a great disservice to the movement by agreeing to take part in the 'Second Round Table Conference'. He viewed freedom as an absolute necessity, unlike the freedom which Gandhiji was "negotiating" with the British. Subhash was arrested again while returning from Bombay to Calcutta (Mumbai to Kolkata), and imprisoned in several jails outside West Bengal in fear of an uprising. His health once again deteriorated and the medical facilities diagnosed him with tuberculosis. It was recommended that he be sent to Switzerland for treatment.

Realising that his avenues abroad were greater with the restrictions of the British, Subhash Chandra Bose set sail for Europe on February 23, 1933. He stayed in various parts of Europe from March 1933 to 1936 making contacts with Indian revolutionaries and European socialists supporting India's Struggle for Independence. Subhash met Mussolini in Italy and made Vienna his headquarters. He was opposed to the racial theory of Nazism but appreciated its organisational strength and discipline. On March 27, 1936, he sailed for Bombay (Mumbai), but was escorted to jail immediately after disembarkation.

After lying low for a year, he was able to work actively. He attended the 'All India Congress Committee Session' in Calcutta (Kolkata), the first one he attended after a lapse of nearly six years. Time had healed the tensions between Subhash and Gandhiji. Now, Gandhiji supported Subhash in his efforts to become the president of the next Congress session, 1938.

He went to England for a month in 1938 and rallied for the Indian freedom cause amongst Indian students and British labour leaders sympathetic towards India's cause. It was a bold move since he was constantly under the British surveillance. Upon his return to India in February 1938, Subhash Chandra Bose was elected president of the Indian National Congress.

Despite opposition from the Congress, Subhash Chandra Bose was a favourite amongst the majority as he was re-elected for a second term in March 1939. Bose was believed to have died in a plane crash over Taiwan, while flying to Tokyo on August 18, 1945. However, his body was never recovered, and theories concerning his possible survival abound.

The Ministry of Railways of India renamed one of the oldest running trains of India, Kalka Mail as Netaji Express from 23 January, 2021. In 2021, the Government of India declared 23 January as Parakram Divas to commemorate the birth anniversary of Subhash Chandra Bose.

❑❑❑

Sunil Gavaskar

(1949)

Cricketer

"Pete Sampras, Tiger Woods, Sachin Tendulkar are three sportspersons who are colossuses in their respective sport, and wonderful role models, too."

Sunil Gavaskar nicknamed 'Sunny', is a cricket player who played during the 1970s and 1980s for Bombay (now Mumbai) and India. He is considered one of the greatest opening batsmen in the history of the sport.

He was born to a middle class family in Bombay (now Mumbai) on July 10, 1949. Cricket fascinated him ever since he was a little boy. He used to have daily cricket matches with his mother in the small gallery of their middle-class apartment. During his childhood, Gavaskar scored centuries after centuries, so much that his father who gave him ₹ 10 for every century had a tough time to keep the household budget from getting derailed.

Gavaskar learnt his cricket in Bomaby (now Mumbai) which is regarded as the nursery of cricket in India. He was fascinated by his uncle, Madhav Mantri, a former Test cricketer. Gavaskar's favourite heroes were the classy Rohan Kanhai, the stylist ML Jaisimha who came on the field with a handkerchief around his neck and Viswanath.

From a young 21-year-old, who toured West Indies and amassed runs, Gavaskar's hunger for runs never diminished. By the time he retired, he was the first man to reach the figure of 10,000 runs in the history of the game. Many batsmen in Test history have scored runs but the consistency of Gavaskar was in its own class. Without wearing helmet or other equipments, Sunny blasted the deadly pace battery of West Indies for almost fifteen years.

He made a spectacular Test debut in 1971 scoring 774 runs in his first Test series against the West Indies helping India to become one of the few teams to defeat the West Indies at their home ground in the Caribbean. Gavaskar went on to average a mammoth 70.20 runs per innings in the West Indies throughout his career - a feat no batsman in his era was able to surpass consistently. From then until his retirement in 1987, he was a mainstay of the Indian batting line-up.

In 1983, Sunil Gavaskar broke one of the oldest and most prestigious records in the game: Donald Bradman's total of 29 Test centuries. Gavaskar was the holder of the record for the most number of Test centuries (34) until 2005 when his countryman, Sachin Tendulkar broke that record.

Gavaskar was the only player to score centuries in each innings, three times (Ricky Ponting equalled this record against South Africa in 2006). He was also the first batsman to reach 10,000 Test runs and held the record for the most number of runs until it was broken by Allan Border. Along with Hannan Sarkar, Gavaskar holds the dubious distinction of being the only Test cricketer to be dismissed with the first delivery of the Test match on three occasions.

Despite the ignominious 36 in 60 overs in a One Day International match, Gavaskar acclimatised himself to the limited overs' cricket and ended with more than 3,000 runs at a handsome average of 35. His choice of ball is legendary as he left any ball outside the off-stump. He rarely fell victim to this temptation. His keen eyesight and selection of ball was the chief reason behind his stupendous success.

Sir Len Hutton had said, "If Gavaskar had been born a British or Australian, the critics would have bracketted him at par with Bradman".

He was a national icon and captain of the Indian cricket team on several occasions in the late '70s and early '80s. He had several successes as captain, especially a 2-0 victory over Pakistan in 1979-80 and a victory in the World Championship of Cricket held in Australia in early 1985.

Gavaskar was also a fine slip fielder and his safe catching in the slips helped him become the first Indian (excluding wicket-keepers) to take over a hundred catches in Test matches. The only wicket claimed by him is of Zaheer Abbas in 1983-84.

Sunil Gavaskar was named 'Wisden Cricketer of the Year' in 1980 and has also been awarded the Padma Bhushan. In December 1994, he was appointed the Sheriff of Bombay (now Mumbai), an honorary for a year. After retirement, he has been a popular, sometimes, controversial commentator, both on TV and in print. He has written four books on cricket – *Sunny days* (autobiography), *Idols*, *Runs n' Ruins* and *One day wonders*. He also served as an adviser to the Indian cricket team during the home series against Australia in 2004.

In 2012, Gavaskar was awarded the Col. CK Nayudu Lifetime Achievement Award for Cricket in India.

On 28 March 2014, Supreme Court of India, appointed Gavaskar as the Interim BCCI President primarily to oversee 7th Season of Indian Premier League.

On 15 October 2017, Gavaskar inaugurated a cricket field in Louisville in the state of Kentucky in United States, thus making it the first international sporting facility named after an Indian sportsperson. The "Sunil M. Gavaskar Cricket Field", serves as the home ground for the Louisville Cricket Club, which is part of the 42-team MidWest Cricket League.

❑❑❑

Sunil Bharti Mittal

(1957)

Telecom Entrepreneur

"Everything begins with a small step, but you have to dream big to take a leap."

Sunil Bharti Mittal is India's "Mr. Mobile". As founder, Chairman and Managing Director of Bharti Group, India's largest GSM-based mobile phone service provider, he is responsible for the boom in mobile phone usage and can be labelled as the most ambitious telecom entrepreneur in India. He is a pioneer, a dreamer and also an achiever.

Sunil Mittal was born on October 23, 1957 in Rajasthan, India. He is a graduate from Punjab University, India and an alumnus of Harvard Business School, USA. He started his career at a young age of 18. From making bicycle parts as a teenager, he has come a long way. Sunil got together with his friend and started a small bicycle business with borrowed capital in the1970s. But by 1979, he realized that this business would remain small. So he moved out of Ludhiana, spent a few years in Mumbai and in 1981, was running an import and distribution operation out of New Delhi and Mumbai.

Sunil Mittal got interested in push button phones while on a trip to Taiwan, and in 1982, introduced the phones to India, replacing the old fashioned, bulky rotary phones that were in use in the country then. Bharti Telecom Limited (BTL) was incorporated and entered into a technical tie up with Siemens AG of Germany for manufacture of electronic push button phones. By the early 1990s, Mittal was making fax machines, cordless phones and other telecom gear.

The turning point came in 1992 when the Indian government was awarding licenses for mobile phone services for the first time. One of the conditions for the Delhi cellular license was that the bidder have some experience as a telecom operator. Mittal clinched a deal with the French telecom group Vivendi. Two years later, Sunil secured rights to serve New Delhi. In 1995, Bharti Cellular Limited (BCL) was formed to offer cellular services under the brand name AirTel. Within a few years Bharti became the first telecom company to cross the 2-million mobile subscriber mark. In 2001, the company entered into a joint venture with Singapore Telecom International for a $650-million submarine cable project, the countries first ever undersea cable link connecting Chennai in India and Singapore. Today, Sunil Mittal heads a successful empire focused on different areas of business through independent Joint Venture companies with market capitalization of approximately $2 billion, and still growing.

Apart from his role at Bharti, Sunil has also been a member of the Prime Minister's Council on Trade and Industry. He has also been the Vice President of Confederation of Indian Industry (CII) and served on several boards including the Board of Standard Chartered PLC, the International Advisory Board of the Center for the Advanced Study of India (CASI); University of Pennsylvania, Harvard Business School India Advisory Board, International Business Council of the World Economic Forum, Global GSM Association, Indo-British Partnership (IBP), Singapore-India Partnership Foundation, the Indian Institute of Management, Lucknow, and the Indian Institute of Technology, Mumbai.

Sunil Bharti Mittal has to his credit the breaking up of the 100 year old monopoly of state run companies to operate telecom services in India. He was chosen as one of the top entrepreneurs in the world for the year 2000 and amongst 'Stars Of Asia', by 'Business Week', he received IT Man of the Year Award 2002 from Dataquest and CEO Of the Year, 2002 Award (World HRD Congress).

His other awards include the Asia Businessman of the Year, 2006—Fortune magazine, Asia Pacific CEO of the Year—Frost and Sullivan 2006, Best Asian Telecom CEO—Telecom Asia 2005; Entrepreneur of the Year—Ernst & Young 2004; India's Best People CEO—Hewitt Associates 2004; Business Leader of the Year—Economic Times 2005.

The Government of India in 2007 conferred on Sunil one of the highest civilian awards, the Padma Bhushan. He has also been conferred the degree of Doctor of Science (Honoris Causa) by the G.B. Pant University of Agriculture & Technology, and is an Honorary Fellow of The Institution of Electronics and Telecommunication Engineers (IETE) of India. Leading internatioal business school INSEAD honoured him with its Business Leader for the World Award, 2011.

Bharti Airtel clocked revenues of over USD 14.75 billion in FY2016. He is listed as the 8th Richest person in India by Forbes with a Net worth of $7 Billion.

In 2017, Mittal announced "war on roaming" by scrapping charges for outgoing and incoming calls within India as well as international roaming charges. Global Mobile Industry Honours Sunil Bharti Mittal for his contributions to the Global Mobile Industry as Chairman of the GSMA Board, 2019.

In August 2024, he acquired a 24.5% stake in BT Group from Altice, becoming its largest shareholder. This strategic investment underscores India's expanding global economic influence. Additionally, in 2024, Mittal was honoured with an Honorary Knighthood (KBE) by King Charles III for his contributions to UK-India business relations.

Swami Vivekananda

(1863–1902)

Spiritual Leader

"You cannot believe in God until you believe in yourself."

Swami Vivekananda was one of the most famous and influential spiritual leaders of the Vedanta philosophy. He was the chief disciple of Ramakrishna Paramahamsa and was the founder of the Ramakrishna Math and Ramakrishna Mission. Many consider him an icon for his fearless courage, his positive exhortations to the youth, his broad outlook on social problems, and countless lectures and discourses on Vedanta philosophy.

Narendranath Datta (Vivekananda) was born into a prominent Calcutta (now Kolkata) family on January 12, 1863. His father was a well-known lawyer and his mother was a cultured and aristocratic woman. As a child, he was uncontrollably boisterous and high spirited. As a boy, he was an excellent athlete and superlative student. He read everything ravenously and retained everything he read. Never content to believe what he was told, he always demanded incontrovertible proof or experiential certainty before he would believe anything.

Vivekananda was deeply religious and this same integrity coloured his quest for God. He went from one religious man to another and asked them if they had seen God. Finally, he met Sri Ramakrishna who was the only one to tell him that yes, he had seen God and could show him, too. Thus began the discipleship of this highly educated and cultured boy to the mostly illiterate rustic temple priest saint.

After five years of training, his teacher died. Before, Sri Ramakrishna had named Narendranath, the leader of all of his disciples, young Narendra took the monastic name, Swami Vivekananda and founded a monastery where he and his brother disciples could carry on their spiritual practices. Following Indian monastic tradition, he and the other monastics divided their time between the monastery and travelling as itinerant monks. Swami Vivekananda spent many years travelling through all parts of the Indian subcontinent.

In May of 1893, a group of his disciples sent the Swami to the United States to attend the Parliament of World Religions that was being conducted in conjunction with the World's Fair in Chicago. His speeches at the Parliament so impressed listeners that Swami Vivekananda was invited to speak all around Chicago, and then all through the eastern United States. Everywhere he went, he insipired people with his master's message: Each soul is divine and the goal of life is for each of us to realise that divinity for ourselves.

After four years of strenous teaching, the Swami returned to India to win the accolades of the entire country. In India, Swamiji's message was a fiercely patriotic one. Because in his travels throughout India, he had felt such impotent compassion for the poor and uneducated, that when he returned to India, he exhorted his brother monks to serve the poor and the needy, to serve God as he manifests in man. He said, "In addition to realising your own inherent divinity, you must see that same divinity in others and serve them." Thus, was born the

Ramakrishna Mission, the purpose of which is to help to alleviate the sufferrings of the poor on the Indian subcontinent.

His books on the four *Yogas* (*Raja Yoga, Karma Yoga, Bhakti Yoga, Jnana Yoga*) are very influential and still seen as fundamental texts for anyone interested in the Hindu practice of Yoga. His letters are of great literary and spiritual value. He was also a very good singer and a poet. He had composed many songs including his favourite Goddess, Kali the Mother. He used humour for his teachings and was also an excellent cook. His language is very free flowing. His own Bengali writings stand testimony to the fact that he believed that words - spoken or written should be for making things easier to understand rather than show off the speaker or writer's knowledge.

In a fitting irony, the Swami, whose main teaching was done in the United States, died at the monastery, he founded in the village of Belur which is on the Ganges, just north of Kolkata on July 4, 1902 at the age of 39. In the ten years in which he preached Strength, Freedom, Manliness, and that every soul is Divine, he touched the hearts and minds, and changed the lives of many thousands of men and women around the world.

❑❑❑

Thomas Alva Edison

(1847–1931)

Inventor

"What you are will show in what you do."

Thomas Alva Edison was an American inventor and businessman who developed many important devices. The most famous of his inventions was an incandescent light bulb. Besides the light bulb, Edison developed the phonograph and the "kinetoscope," a small box for viewing moving films.

Edison was born on February 11, 1847 in Milan, Ohio and was the seventh and last child of Samuel and Nancy Edison. Edison had very little formal education as a child, attending school only for a few months.

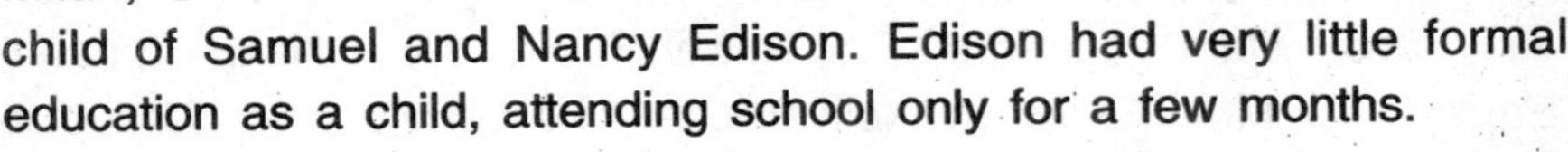

He moved to New York City in 1869. Edison continued to work on inventions related to the telegraph, and developed his first successful invention, an improved 'stocksticker' called the "Universal Stock Printer". For his invention of 'stock sticker', he was paid $40,000. This gave Edison the money, he needed to set up his first small laboratory and manufacturing facility in Newark, New Jersey in 1871. In 1876,

Edison sold all his Newark manufacturing concerns and moved his family and staff of assistants to the small village of Menlo Park, twenty-five miles southwest of New York City. He established a new facility containing all the equipment necessary to work on any invention.

The first public demonstration of the Edison's incandescent lighting system was in December 1879, when the Menlo Park laboratory complex was electrically lighted. Edison spent the next several years creating the electric industry. In September 1882, the first commercial power station, located on Pearl Street in lower Manhattan, went into operation providing light and power to customers in a one square mile area. The electric age had begun. His various electric companies continued to grow until in 1889, when they were brought together to form the 'Edison General Electric'. Despite the use of Edison in the company title, Thomas Alava Edison never controlled this company. The tremendous amount of capital needed to develop the incandescent lighting industry had necessitated the involvement of investment bankers such as J. P. Morgan. When 'Edison General Electric' merged with its leading competitor, 'Thompson-Houston' in 1892, Edison was dropped from the name, and the company became simply 'General Electric'.

This period of success was marred by the death of Edison's wife Mary in 1884. His involvement in the business end of the electric industry had caused Edison to spend less time in Menlo Park. After Mary's death, Edison lived in New York City with his three children. A year later, while vacationing at a friend's house in New England, Edison met Mina Miller and fell in love. The couple was married in February 1886 and moved to West Orange, New Jersey where he had purchased an estate, Glenmont, for his bride. Thomas Alva Edison lived here with Mina until his death.

The new laboratory complex consisting of five buildings opened in November 1887. A three-storey main laboratory building contained a power plant, machine shops, stock rooms, experimental rooms and a large library. Four smaller one-storey buildings built perpendicular to the main building contained a physics lab, chemistry lab, metallurgy lab, pattern shop, and a chemical storage.

The large size of the laboratory not only allowed Edison to work on any sort of project, but also allowed him to work on as many as ten or twenty projects at a time. Facilities were added to the laboratory or modified to meet Edison's changing needs as he continued to work in this complex. Over the years, factories to manufacture Edison inventions were built around the laboratory. The entire laboratory and factory complex eventually covered more than twenty acres and employed 10,000 people at its peak during World War I.

The last experimental work of Thomas Alva Edison's life was done at the request of Edison's good friends, Henry Ford who asked Edison to find an alternative source of rubber for use in automobile tyres. The natural rubber used for tyres up to that time came from the rubber tree, which does not grow in the United States.

He purchased a home known as "Glenmont" in 1886 as a wedding gift for Mina in Llewellyn Park in West Orange, New Jersey. The remains of Edison and his wife, Mina, are now buried there. The 13.5 acre property is maintained by the National Park Service as the Edison National Historic Site.

Thomas Alva Edison died on October 18, 1931, in New Jersey at the age of 84. His final words to his wife, Mina were "It is very beautiful over there." Mina died in 1947. Edison's last breath is purportedly contained in a test tube at the Henry Ford Museum.

Tiger Woods

(1975)

Golfer

"I get to play golf for a living.
What more can you ask for -
getting paid for doing what you love."

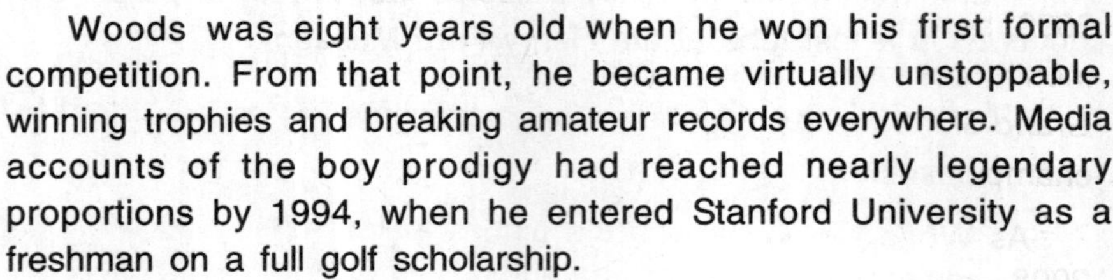

Eldrick "Tiger" Woods is considered one of the greatest golfers of all time. In 2005, at the age of 29, he reached the milestone of nine major golf championships at such a young age. He also holds the PGA Tour record for most consecutive tournament cuts made with 142.

Tiger Woods was born as Eldrick Woods on December 30, 1975, in Cypress, California. He is the only child of Earl and Kultida Woods.

Woods was eight years old when he won his first formal competition. From that point, he became virtually unstoppable, winning trophies and breaking amateur records everywhere. Media accounts of the boy prodigy had reached nearly legendary proportions by 1994, when he entered Stanford University as a freshman on a full golf scholarship.

During Tiger Woods first year of college, he won the 'US Amateur' title and qualified to play in the Masters tournament in Augusta,

Georgia, in the spring of 1995. Although he played as an amateur—not for prize money—Woods's reputation preceded him. By 1996, he had won three 'US Amateur' titles, one after another, an amazing accomplishment in itself. He was only twenty years old, and in August 1996, Woods decided to quit college in order to play professional golf. It soon became evident that he was destined for success. *Sports Illustrated* named him as the 1996 "Sportsman of the Year," and by January 1997, he had already won three professional tournaments. He was a media sensation.

In April of 1997, only eight months into Woods's professional career, he played in the prestigious 'Masters tournament' held at Georgia's Augusta National Golf Club. The 'Masters title' is perhaps, the greatest honour in the world of golf.

In 1999, Woods achieved the greatest moment in his career when he won the 'PGA Championship' by one shot. In November 1999 he shot the best total in the World Cup, helping to lead the United States to victory in the tournament. He was also named the 'PGA Tour Player of the Year' for the second time on November 30, 1999, earning more than $6.6 million in prize money during the season.

On January 9, 2000, he won the 'Mercedes Championship'. It was his fifth consecutive victory and, at the time, golf's longest winning streak in forty-six years. On February 7, 2000, he extended that streak by winning the 'Pebble Beach National Pro-Am'. On June 18, 2000, he won the 'US Open', his third major championship. The next month, on July 23, Woods won the 'British Open', thus winning the *Grand Slam*. He became the youngest player to win all the four major championships.

As World No. 1, he was the highest-paid professional athlete in 2008, having earned an estimated $110 million from winnings and endorsements. He has won 15 professional major golf championships, the second highest of any male player, and 82 PGA Tour events. He is the youngest player to achieve the career Grand Slam. Woods has won 18 World Golf Championships, and has won at least one of those events each of the 11 years they have been in existence.

He has been awarded PGA Player of the Year a record 11 times, the Byron Nelson Award for lowest adjusted scoring average a record eight times, and has the record of leading the money list in 10 different seasons.

At the last major of the year, the 2018 PGA Championship, Woods finished second, two shots behind the winner Brooks Koepka.

Woods returned to the winner's circle for the 80th time in his PGA Tour career on September 23, 2018, when he won the season-ending Tour Championship at East Lake Golf Club for the second time and that tournament for the third time. On April 14, 2019, Woods won the Masters, which was his first major championship win in eleven years and his 15th major overall. He finished 13 under par to win by one stroke over Dustin Johnson, Xander Schauffele and Brooks Koepka. Woods played in his first 2020 PGA Tour event at the Zozo Championship in October 2019, which was the first-ever PGA Tour event played in Japan. The win was Woods's 82nd on Tour, tying him with Sam Snead for the most victories all time on the PGA Tour.

In May 2019, Woods was awarded the Presidential Medal of Freedom by Donald Trump, the fourth golfer to receive the honor.

In 2023, he participated in the Masters Tournament, making the cut but later withdrawing due to a foot injury. Despite limited play, Woods secured the Player Impact Program (PIP) award in 2024, earning $10 million for his influence on the sport. In February 2025, he announced plans to return at the Genesis Invitational, marking a significant comeback.

❑❑❑

Tom Cruise

(1962)

Actor

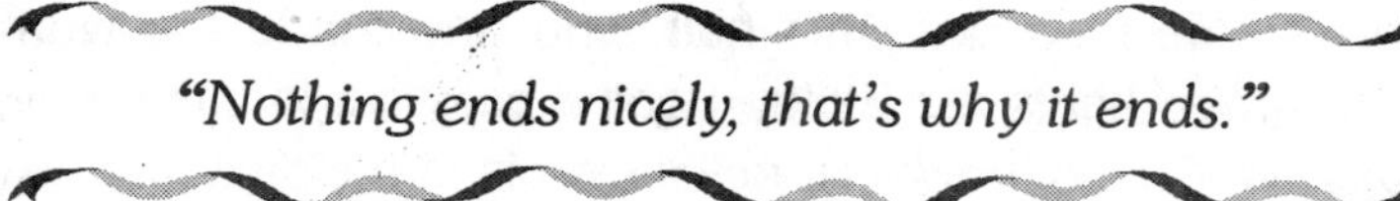

"Nothing ends nicely, that's why it ends."

Tom Cruise is an 'Academy Award'-nominated, 'Golden Globe Award'-winning American actor and film producer. He is the only actor to have six consecutive $100 million plus blockbusters on his resume.

Born on July 3, 1962, his name has become synonymous with All-American testosterone-driven entertainment movies. Tom Cruise spent the 1980s as one of Hollywood's brightest shining Golden Boys. With black hair, blue eyes, and unabashed cockiness, Cruise rode high on such hits as *Top Gun* and *Rain Man*. By the mid-90s, he was indisputably the most powerful movie star of his generation, only bested by the relatively grizzled, Harrison Ford as the world box-office champ, and by the end of the millennium, he had surpassed even Ford, becoming Hollywood's most bankable star with five consecutive films grossing in excess of $100 million prior to the release of the hotly anticipated *Eyes Wide Shut* (1999), Stanley Kubrick's directorial swan song. Cruise had managed this feat without developing an insufferable movie star ego, perhaph his greatest accomplishment of all.

Tom Cruise gained celebrity in the superior teen sex satire, *Risky Business* (1983) as an anxious, affluent, suburban teen poised precariously on the brink of young adulthood, creating a resonant protagonist for young Reagan-era audiences.

Cruise performed well in a more naturalistic mode in *All the Right Moves* (1983), a sober high school football drama which pitted him against hot-headed coach, Craig T Nelson that fared modestly at the box office. He next grew his hair long and made the wrong move donning green tights for Ridley Scott's colossal fantasy flop, *Legend* (1985). Tom Cruise, however, solidified his star status and established his onscreen persona with one of the signature hits of the 80s, *Top Gun* (1986).

Not content to be a matinee idol, Cruise crafted his career carefully, teaming with talented directors and co-stars for *The Color of Money* (1986) and *Rain Man* (1988). The former, Martin Scorsese's sharply made, nicely textured sequel to 1961's *The Hustler*, cast him as a talented but arrogant small-time pool hotshot, a younger, greener version of Paul Newman's Fast Eddie Felsen. They made an eclectic pair— Cruise's boisterous 'All-American boy' versus Newman's seasoned 'con man', and though the old stud picked up the 'Best Actor Oscar', he was clearly passing the mantle to the new stud, and not just on the screen. The time spent talking with the politically-active Newman had a profound consciousness-raising effect on Cruise who would later choose Oliver Stone's extremely anti-war, *Born on the Fourth of July* (1989) to counter his contribution to the jingoistic, *Top Gun*. He broadened his serious dramatic credentials in his work with director, Barry Levinson on *Rain Man*, playing another self-centred hotshot, whose relationship with his autistic brother (Dustin Hoffman) changes his life. Hoffman shone as the idiot savant and took home the Oscar, but Cruise was equally important to the Oscar-winning Best Picture equation.

For Stone's, *Born on the Fourth of July*, he did not have to share the spotlight (with anybody but the man at the helm who snared the Best Director Oscar for his efforts) and earned his first *Best Actor Oscar* nomination for a hard-hitting portrayal of paraplegic, anti-war activist, Ron Kovic. Cruise then stumbled a bit with his next two projects—*Days of Thunder* and *Far and Away* (1992). He returned to box office clover after that critical and commercial disappointment, successfully confronting an iconic Jack Nicholson in Rob Reiner's highly popular court-martial drama, *A Few Good Men* (1992).

Cruise was all but omnipresent in the media as he aggressively promoted his feature producing debut, the post-Cold War espionage movie *Mission: Impossible* (1996). Nonetheless, despite international location shooting, high-tech stunts, computer-generated visual effects and last-minute re-writes by a stellar assortment of scripters (including his buddy Towne again), *Mission: Impossible* came in on time and under budget at approximately $67 million. The sweetly offbeat romantic comedy, *Jerry Maguire* (1996), in which he played the eponymous, shallow, back-stabbing sports agent, provided a sort of mid-career breakthrough for Cruise. He worked with Kubrick on *Eyes Wide Shut*, starring opposite Kidman for the first time since *Far and Away*.

Following the arduous shoot with Kubrick and the mixed critical and box-office reaction to *Eyes Wide Shut*, Tom took on a pivotal role in Paul Thomas Anderson's ensemble drama *Magnolia* (1999). He segued back to leading parts in more high profile mainstream work reprising his role as Ethan Hunt in the big-budget, special effects laden *M:I-2* (*Mission: Impossible* 2) released in 2000, directed by John Woo. Steven Spielberg's, *Minority Report* scored a direct hit at the box office, and Cruise could next be seen gearing up for his role in Edward Zwick's, *The Last Samurai*. In crime-thriller *Collateral* (2004) he was seen as a cool and calculating sociopathic hitman. Since 2005, Cruise and Paula Wagner have been in charge of the United Artists film studio, with Cruise as producer. He is also known for his controversial support of and adherence to the Church of Scientology.

In the 2010s, he has starred in the action comedy *Knight and Day* (2010), the thriller *Jack Reacher* (2012), the post-apocalyptic science fiction film *Oblivion* (2013), and the military science fiction film *Edge of Tomorrow* (2014). In 2012, Cruise was Hollywood's highest-paid actor. 16 of his films grossed over $100 million domestically; 22 have grossed in excess of $200 million worldwide.

Cruise starred in the 2017 reboot of Boris Karloff's 1932 horror movie *The Mummy*. . In 2018, Cruise again reprised Ethan Hunt, in the sixth film in his franchise, *Mission: Impossible - Fallout.* The film grossed over $791 million at the box office. It is Cruise's biggest commercial success to date.

In May 2020, it was reported that Cruise would be starring and producing a movie shot in outer space. Doug Liman would be directing, writing, and co-producing. Both will fly to the International Space Station as part of a future Axiom Space mission in a SpaceX Dragon 2 spacecraft.

In May 2021, Cruise protested against the Hollywood Foreign Press Association (HFPA) by returning all three of his Golden Globe Awards in light of controversy surrounding the HFPA, particularly its lack of diversity, specifically no black members, and ethical questions related to financial benefits to some of its members.

In 2022, he starred in and produced "Top Gun : Maverick", which premiered at the Cannes Film Festival, earning him an Honorary Palme d'Or. The film grossed over $1 billion, becoming his highest-grossing movie. In 2023, he reprised his role as Ethan Hunt in "Mission : Impossible - Dead Reckoning Part One". In December 2024, the U.S. Navy awarded him the Distinguished Public Service Award for his contributions to naval aviation through his work on the "Top Gun" films.

❑❑❑

Tyeb Mehta

(1925–2009)

Artist and Filmmaker

"Age does not hamper creativity."

Tyeb Mehta is a well-known Indian artist. A multifaceted personality, he was a brilliant filmmaker and a world famous painter. He holds the record for the highest price for which an Indian painting has ever been auctioned. In December 2005, Tyeb Mehta's painting, *Gesture* was sold for 31 million Indian rupees at the *Osian's* auction.

Mehta was born on July 26, 1925 in Kapadvanj, Gujarat. He initially worked as a film editor in a cinema laboratory. However, his interest in painting took him to Sir J. J. School of Art, Bombay (now Mumbai), where he studied painting from 1947 to 1952. In J. J. School of Art, Tyeb came in contact with Akbar Padamsee and was a close associate of the painters in the Progressive Artists' Group.

In 1954, Tyeb Mehta visited London and Paris for four months, then returned to India to concentrate on painting and sculpture. He took part in numerous group exhibitions and organised his first solo exhibition of drawings, paintings and sculptures at the Jehangir Art Gallery, Bomaby (now Mumbai), in 1959. He lived and worked in London from 1959 to 1965.

He returned to India in 1965 and lived in Delhi till 1968. In 1968, Tyeb visited the US on a Rockefeller Fellowship. He also dabbled in films.

In 1970, Tyeb won the Filmfare Critic's Award for his first and only film, the experimental, *Koodal* on the life of the common man. Made for the Films Division of India, *Koodal* was included in Satyajit Ray's essay collection, *Our Films Their Films*. Financial problems disallowed more features, but what he could not capture in moving form, he froze on his canvas. In the 1980s, he worked as an Artist in Residence in Shantiniketan.

Tyeb Mehta has participated in several international shows like *Ten Contemporary Indian Painters* at Trenton in the US in 1965; *Deuxieme Biennial Internationale de Menton*, 1974; *Festival Internationale de la Peinture, Cagnes- -Sur-Mer, France* 1974; *Modern Indian Paintings* at Hirschhom Museum, Washington 1982, and *Seven Indian Painters* at Gallerie Le Monde de U art, Paris 1994.

Mehta's large body of work spanning over six decades has established him as one of the greatest names of modern Indian art. His paintings raise unanswered and unanswerable questions about the human condition.

Tyeb Mehta was awarded the 'Kalidas Samman' by the Madhya Pradesh Government in 1988. His art developed distinctive nuances. In Mumbai, he was strongly influenced by the Progressive Artists' Group, a consortium formed by FN Souza, seeking to voice the trials of post-Independent India. Mehta said, "When you are young, you try to understand the world. As you grow old, you try to understand yourself. Your work then becomes the essence of these efforts."

The search for new idioms continued. With charcoal, paint and clay, he interpreted mythological figures such as those of Goddess Durga, Kali and the demon Mahishasura.

After successive heart attacks and three throat operations, Mehta slowed down further, but refused to give up. He said, "Age does not hamper creativity. Youth has this advantage. You are relaxed. There's all the time in the world to work. Now I don't have much time left. The day I feel I'm not at my best, I'll stop painting."

Tyeb Mehta was awarded the Padma Bhushan in 2007. In 2008 one of his paintings sold for $2 million. The noted painter breathed his last on July 2, 2009, but for the admirers of his art, he will live forever.

❑❑❑

Ustad Bismillah Khan

(1916–2006)
Musician

"Music has no caste. I have received love and affection all over the world. The government has given me all the four highest civilian awards in the past five decades."

Ustad Bismillah Khan, the most outstanding and world-famous *shehnai* player, has attained astonishing mastery over the instrument. He was the third classical musician to be awarded the Bharat Ratna, the highest civilian honour in India. He also had the distinction of being one of the few people to be awarded all the top four civilian awards.

Bismillah Khan was born on March 21, 1916 at Bhirung Raut Ki Gali, in Dumraon as the second son of Paigambar Khan and Mitthan. He was named as Qamaruddin to rhyme with Shamsuddin, their first son. His grandfather, Rasool Baksh Khan uttered "Bismillah" after looking at the newborn, and thus he was named Bismillah Khan.

His ancestors were court musicians in the princely states of Bhojpur, now in the state of Bihar. His father was a *shehnai* player in the court of Maharaja Keshav Prasad Singh of Dumraon Estate, now in state of Bihar.

Despite his fame, Khan's lifestyle retained its old world Varanasi charm. His chief mode of transport was the cycle rickshaw. A man of tenderness, he believed in remaining private, and that musicians are supposed to be heard and not seen.

He was a pious Shi'a Muslim and also, like many Indian musicians regardless of creed, a devotee of Mother Saraswati. He often played at various temples and on the banks of the river, Ganga in Varanasi, besides playing outside the famous Vishwanath temple in Varanasi. He received his training under his uncle, the late Ali Baksh 'Vilayatu', a *shehnai* player attached to the Varanasi's Vishwanath Temple.

Khan was perhaps single handedly responsible for making the *shehnai* a famous classical instrument. He brought the *shehnai* to the centre stage of Indian music with his concert in the *Calcutta All India Music Conference* in 1937. He was credited with having almost monopoly over the instrument as he and the shehnai are almost synonyms.

Khan is one of the finest musicians in the post-independent Indian Classical music and one of the best examples of Hindu-Muslim unity in India.

His concept of music was very beautiful and his vision, superb. He once said, "Even if the world ends, the music will still survive" and he often said, "Music has no caste".

He has played in Bangladesh, Afghanistan, Europe, Iran, Iraq, Canada, West Africa, USA, USSR, Japan, Hong Kong and almost every capital city across the world.

Khan had the rare honour of performing at Delhi's Red Fort on the eve of India's Independence in 1947. He also performed *Raga Kafi* from the Red Fort on the eve of India's first Republic Day ceremony, on January 26, 1950. His recital had almost become a cultural part of the Independence Day Celebrations telecast on Doordarshan every year on 15th of August. After the Prime Minister's speech from the Lal Qila (Red Fort) in old Delhi, Doordarshan broadcasts live performance by the *shehnai* maestro. And this tradition had been going on since the days of Pandit Nehru.

Bismillah Khan had honorary doctorates from the Banaras Hindu University, and the Visva Bharati University, Shantiniketan.

Khan had a brief association with movies. He played the *shehnai* for Dr. Rajkumar's role of Appanna in the movie *Sanaadi Appanna*. He acted in *Jalsaghar*, a movie by Satyajit Ray and provided the sound of *shehnai* in *Goonj Uthi Shehnai*. Noted director Goutam Ghose directed, *Sange Meel Se Mulaqat*, a documentary about the life of Khan.

On August 17, 2006, Ustad Bismillah Khan was taken ill and admitted to the Heritage Hospital, Varanasi for treatment. He died after four days on August 21, 2006, due to a cardiac arrest. He was ninety years old, and is survived by five sons, three daughters and a large number of grandchildren and great-grandchildren.

The Government of India declared one day of national mourning on his death. His body was buried at Fatemain burial ground of old Varanasi under a *neem* tree with '21-gun salute' from Indian Army.

V.S. Naipaul

(1932-2018)

Writer

"I am the kind of writer that people think other people are reading."

V. S. Naipaul was a master of English prose style who he is known for his penetrating analyses of alienation and exile. In fiction and essays, his writing style is marked by virtuosity and psychological insight.

The British writer was born on August 17, 1932 in Trinidad as Vidiadhar Surajprasad Naipaul. His grandfather worked in a sugarcane plantation and his father was a journalist and writer.

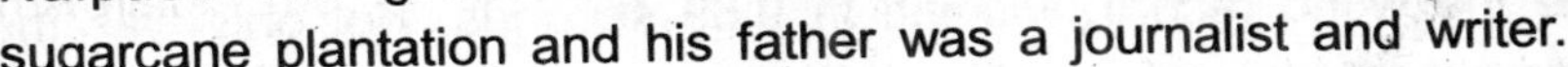

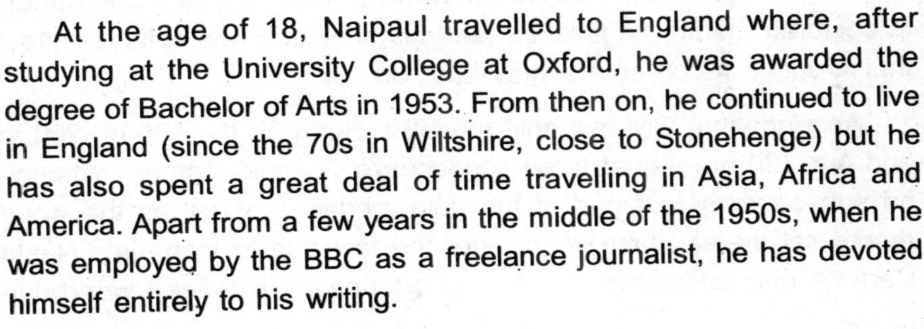

At the age of 18, Naipaul travelled to England where, after studying at the University College at Oxford, he was awarded the degree of Bachelor of Arts in 1953. From then on, he continued to live in England (since the 70s in Wiltshire, close to Stonehenge) but he has also spent a great deal of time travelling in Asia, Africa and America. Apart from a few years in the middle of the 1950s, when he was employed by the BBC as a freelance journalist, he has devoted himself entirely to his writing.

At the age of 15, he took his first shot at success on the world stage at the 2002 World Junior Championships in Kingston, Jamaica, where he won the 200-meter dash, making him the youngest world-junior gold medalist ever. Bolt's feats impressed the athletics world, and he received the International Association of Athletics Foundation's Rising Star Award that year and soon was given the apt nickname "Lightning Bolt."

Bolt was chosen for the Jamaican Olympic squad, despite a nagging hamstring injury, for the 2004 Athens Olympics. He was eliminated in the first round of the 200-meter, though, again hampered by injury.

Bolt made a serious change in 2005, replacing long-time coach Pablo McNeil with Glenn Mills. He then reached the world Top 5 rankings in 2005 and 2006. Unfortunately, injuries continued to plague the sprinter, preventing him from completing a full professional season.

The year 2007 proved to be a breakthrough one for Bolt, as he broke the national 200-meter record held for over 30 years by Donald Quarrie, and earned two silver medals at the World Championship in Osaka, Japan. These medals boosted Bolt's desire to run, and he took a more serious stance toward his career.

Bolt decided that he would run the 100-meter and 200-meter events at the Beijing Summer Olympics. In the 100-meter final, Bolt broke the world record, winning in 9.69 seconds. Not only was the record set without a favorable wind, but he also visibly slowed down to celebrate before he finished (and his shoelace was untied), an act that aroused much controversy later on.

An eight-time Olympic gold medalist, Bolt won the 100 m, 200 m and 4 × 100 m relay at three consecutive Olympic Games, although he subsequently lost one of the gold medals (as well as the world record set therein) nine years after the fact due to teammate Nesta Carter's disqualification for doping offences. He gained worldwide popularity for his double sprint victory at the 2008 Beijing Olympics in world record times. Bolt is the only sprinter to win Olympic 100 m and 200 m titles at three consecutive olympics (2008, 2012 and 2016), a feat referred to as the "triple double."

An eleven-time World Champion, he won consecutive World Championship 100 m, 200 m and 4 × 100 metres relay gold medals from 2009 to 2015, with the exception of a 100 m false start in 2011. He is the most successful athlete of the World Championships and was the first athlete to win three titles in both the 100 m and 200 m at the competition.

Bolt improved upon his first 100 m world record of 9.69 with 9.58 seconds in 2009 - the biggest improvement since the start of electronic timing. He has twice broken the 200 metres world record, setting 19.30 in 2008 and 19.19 in 2009. He has helped Jamaica to three 4 × 100 metres relay world records, with the current record being 36.84 seconds set in 2012. Bolt's most successful event is the 200 m, with three Olympic and four World titles. The 2008 Olympics was his international debut over 100 m; he had earlier won numerous 200 m medals (including 2007 World Championship silver) and holds the world under-20 and world under-18 records for the event.

His achievements as a sprinter have earned him the media nickname "Lightning Bolt", and his awards include the IAAF World Athlete of the Year, Track & Field Athlete of the Year, and Laureus World Sportsman of the Year (four times). Bolt retired from athletics after the 2017 World Championships.

❑❑❑

Verghese Kurien

(1921–2012)

Father of White Revolution

"The backward sections of society in India have been exploited and ill-treated for many years. Therefore, there is a need to make up for it."

Dr. Verghese Kurien is called the "father of the white revolution" in India. He is credited with architecting 'Operation Flood' — the largest dairy development program in the world. Verghese Kurien, set up the Anand model of cooperative dairy development, engineered the White Revolution in India, and made India the largest milk producer in the world.

Verghese Kurien was born on November 26, 1921 in Calicut, a seaport now known as Kozhikode, in the state of Kerala in southwestern India.

Dr. Kurien graduated with Physics from Loyola College, Madras (now Chennai) in 1940 and then did B.E.(Mech) from the Madras University. After passing out of the university, he joined the Tata Steel Technical Institute, Jamshedpur from where he graduated in 1946. He then went to USA on a government scholarship to do his Master

Naipaul's works consist mainly of novels and short stories, but also include some that are documentaries. He is to a very high degree a cosmopolitan writer, a fact that he himself considers to stem from his lack of roots. He is unhappy about the cultural and spiritual poverty of Trinidad, and feels alienated from India. In England, he is incapable of relating to and identifying with the traditional values of what was once a colonial power.

The events in his earliest books take place in the West Indies. A few years after the publication of his first work, *The Mystic Masseur* (1957), came what is considered by many to be one of his most outstanding novels, *A House for Mr. Biswas* (1961), in which the protagonist is modelled on the author's father.

After the enormous success of *A House for Mr. Biswas,* Naipaul extended the geographical and social perspective of his writing to describe with increasing pessimism the deleterious impact of colonialism and emerging nationalism on the third world, for instance, in *Guerrillas* (1975) and *A Bend in the River* (1979), the latter a portrayal of Africa that has been compared to Conrad's *Heart of Darkness*.

In his travel books and his documentary works, he presents his impressions of the country of his ancestors, India, as in *India : a Million Mutinies Now* (1990), and also critical assessments of Muslim fundamentalism in non-Arab countries such as Indonesia, Iran, Malaysia and Pakistan in *Among the Believers* (1981) and *Beyond Belief* (1998).

The novels *The Enigma of Arrival* (1987) and *A Way in the World* (1994) are to a great extent autobiographical. In *The Enigma of Arrival* he describes how a landed estate in southern England and its proprietor, with a colonial background and afflicted by a degenerative disease, gradually decline before finally perishing. *A Way in the World*, which is a cross between fiction, memoirs and history, consists of nine independent but thematically linked narratives in which Caribbean and Indian traditions are blended with the culture encountered by the author when he moved to England at the young age of 18.

V. S. Naipaul has been awarded a number of literary prizes, among them the salient being the *Booker Prize* in 1971 and the *T. S. Eliot Award* for Creative Writing in 1986. He is an honorary doctor of St. Andrew's College and Columbia university and of the universities of Cambridge, London and Oxford. In 1990, Naipaul was knighted by Queen Elizabeth. In 1993, he won the David Cohen Prize and was awarded the Noble Prize in Literature in 2001. In 2008, *The Times* ranked Naipaul seventh on their list of the 50 greatest British writers since 1945. His new release was *The Masque of Africa: Glimpses of African Belief* in 2011.

Naipaul died at his home in London on 11 August, 2018. Before dying he read and discussed Lord Tennyson's poem Crossing the Bar with those at his bedside. His funeral took place at Kensal Green Cemetery.

❑❑❑

Usain Bolt

(1986)

Olympian Sprinter

"As long as I'm in great shape, nobody beats me, for sure."

Usain Bolt, the Jamaican sprinter, is arguably the fastest man in the world, winning three gold medals at the 2008 Olympic Games in Beijing, China, and becoming the first man in Olympic history to win both the 100-meter and 200-meter races in record times. Bolt won his fourth Olympic gold medal in the men's 100-meter race at the 2012 Summer Olympic Games in London. He set three world records in a single Olympic Games competition.

Bolt was born in Jamaica on August 21, 1986. Both a standout cricket player and a sprinter early on, Bolt's natural speed was noticed by coaches at school, and he began to focus solely on sprinting under the tutelage of Pablo McNeil, a former Olympic sprint athlete. As early as age 14, Bolt was wowing fans of sprinting with his lightning speed, and he won his first high school championships medal in 2001, taking the silver in the 200-meter race.

of Science in Mechanical Engineering from the Michigan State University.

When he came back to India, he was posted as a Dairy Engineer at the government creamery, Anand, in May 1949.

Through his Anand model, Kurien provided great promise. He made a point that development policies could flow from such models, and if lessons could be generalised, the country could transform itself from a deficit to a surplus state. Dairy technology had earlier revolved round processing cow's milk, and not buffalo milk. But considering millions of farmers owned buffaloes, Kurien showed how buffalo milk could be used for making milk powder, baby food and condensed milk. He established brands which became household names.

As a man, he is considered self-centred, authoritarian, even offensive, but a thorough professional. As head of the National Dairy Development Board, he was the boss. He was a rank outsider with a sophisticated lifestyle who did not speak the language of the locals. Yet the farmers regarded him as their "Dudhwallah", the "milk man" who built a model institution of economic democracy.

Around the same time, the infant cooperative dairy, Kaira District Cooperative Milk Producers' Union Limited (KDCMPUL), — now famous as AMUL — was fighting a battle with the Polson Dairy which was privately owned. Young Kurien, fed up with being at the government creamery which held no challenge, volunteered to help Shri Tribhuvandas Patel, the chairman of KDCMPUL, to set up a processing plant. This marked the birth of AMUL and the rest is history.

Kurien has since then built this organisation into one of the largest and most successful institutions in India. The Amul pattern of cooperatives had been so successful, that in 1965, the then Prime Minister of India, Shri Lal Bahadur Shastri, created the National Dairy Development Board (NDDB) to replicate the programme on a nationwide basis citing Kurien's "extraordinary and dynamic leadership" upon naming him the chairman.

Dr. Verghese Kurien also set up GCMMF (Gujarat Cooperative Milk Marketing Federation) in 1973 to sell the products produced by the dairies. Today GCMMF sells AMUL brand products not only in India but also overseas.

Kurien plays a key role in many other organisations, ranging from chairing the Viksit Bharat Foundation, a body set up by the President of India to chairman of the Institute of Rural Management's Board of Governors in India.

He was an official Indian delegate to the International Dairy congresses held in Rome in 1956 and Copenhagen in 1962. He is a member of both the Dairy Science and the Dairy Education committees of the Government of India. As a nominee of the Industrial Finance Corporation of India, he serves as a Director of Tensile Steel in Baroda and of Air Control and Refrigeration in Ahmedabad, and is a member of the Gujarat State Electricity Board.

For his contribution to the dairy industry, Kurien has received top awards not only in India but also overseas. He was awarded the prestigious Padmashree (1965), Padmabhushan (1966), and the Krishi Ratna Award (1986), by the President of India. Dr. Verghese Kurien has also received the Ramon Magsaysay Award for Community Leadership (1963), Wateler Peace Prize Award of Carnegie Foundation (1986), World Food Prize Award (1989), International Person of the Year (1993) by the World Dairy Expo, Madison, Wisconsin, USA and Padma Vibhushan (1999).

Verghese Kurien died on 9 September 2012 after a brief spell of illness in Nadiad, near Anand in Gujarat. He was 90.

Vincent Van Gogh

(1853–1890)

Artist

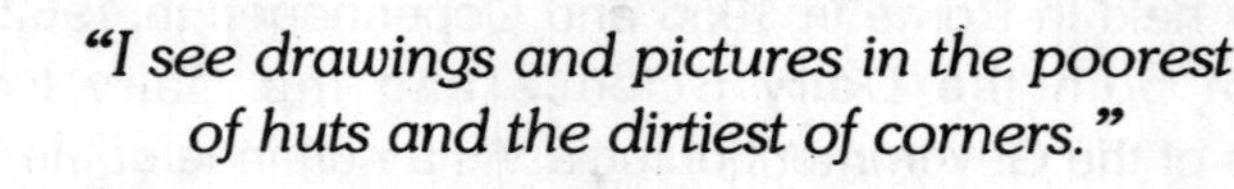

"I see drawings and pictures in the poorest of huts and the dirtiest of corners."

Vincent van Gogh was a post-impressionist painter whose work, notable for its beauty, emotion and color, highly influenced 20th century art. He struggled with mental illness, and remained poor and virtually unknown throughout his life.

Vincent Willem van Gogh was born on March 30, 1853, in Zundert, Netherlands. His father, named Theodorus van Gogh, was a Protestant minister. Vincent Van Gogh was given the name of his elder brother, who had died at birth a year before Van Gogh was born. He had two junior brothers and three sisters, and was strongly attached to his brother Theo.

Young Van Gogh was brought up in a religious and strict atmosphere. He had a very uncontrollable temper, was highly emotional, and lacked self-confidence. From the age of 7 to 11 he was taught at home by a governess. Then from the age of 11 to 15 he was sent to boarding schools in the Netherlands. His first art teacher was

Constantijn Huysmans, a professional artist, who taught the young Van Gogh basic drawing and composition. From 1869-1873 Van Gogh worked for an established art dealer, Goupil & Cie, in the Hague. Then he worked in London and Paris until 1876, when he was fired for showing resentment to the customers. Van Gogh went to England as a minister's assistant. Then he studied theology at the University of Amsterdam for one year, but gave up. He tried to follow his father's profession and became a preacher in Belgium, but was dismissed after a year.

He studied at the Royal Academy of Art in Brussels for six months in 1880 and 1881. In the summer of 1881 Van Gogh fell in love with his widowed cousin, Kee Vos, but was cruelly rejected by her. He became upset and resentful. This led to a violent quarrel with his father on Christmas, and he moved in with an alcoholic prostitute for a year. In 1884 Van Gogh had a romance with a neighbor's daughter, who shared his interest in art, but their marriage was opposed by both families. This and the death of his father in March of 1885 caused depression. At that time Van Gogh made his first major work, "The Potato Eaters". In September of 1885 he was accused of making one of his sitters, a young peasant girl, pregnant and was ostracized by the local Church. He moved to Antwerp, where he studied color theory and painting at the Antwerpen School of Arts, and matriculated in January of 1886. While he was away, his mother and sister moved. They left behind almost all of his paintings, of which 70 were bought by a junk dealer and some were burned.

From March 1886 to February 1888, Van Gogh lived in Paris. There he met the Impressionists: Claude Monet, Auguste Renoir, Edgar Degas, Alfred Sisley, Paul Signac, Georges Seurat, and brothers Lucien and Camille Pissarro. The Impressionist's use of light and color inspired Van Gogh on updating his own palette. During the Paris years, his color scheme became brighter and lighter. His use of complementary colors in proximity produced remarkable decorative effects. Van Gogh also adopted some ideas of pointillism, but developed his own technique with stronger brush-strokes, sharp composition, and his own color scheme using complementary colors. He created about 200 oil paintings during his two years in Paris.

In February of 1888 Van Gogh moved to Arles with a plan to found an art colony. His friend Paul Gauguin joined in October. Van Gogh presented him several paintings of sunflowers, but their cooperation lasted only for two months. Their arguments about art and life were exacerbated by drinking and rivalry for prostitutes. Van Gogh's mental state was alternating between fits of depression and lucidity. At times, his madness led to aggressive actions. In December of 1888 he attacked Paul Gauguin with an open razor, was stopped, but eventually cut part of his ear off and gave it to a prostitute. Paul Gauguin sent a note to his brother Theo and left forever. Theo immediately came to help. Van Gogh was sent to the state mental hospital of St. Paul in Saint Remy de Provence. There he lived for a year and made some of his best works: "Starry Night", "Vincent's Bedroom", and several paintings of Irises.

Van Gogh was released in May of 1890 and moved to live in Auvers-sur-Oise under supervision of Dr. Gachet. His health improved enough to give him energy for the most intensive work marathon. In just two months there he painted ninety excellent works. This included portraits of Dr. Gachet, landscapes, still-lives, and "Wheat Field with Crows". In a state of depression he went out into the wheat field and shot himself in the chest on July 27, 1890. Fatally wounded, Van Gogh died two days later in the arms of his brother Theo. He was laid to rest at the cemetery of Auvers-sur-Oise.

Theo, who was suffering from syphilis and weakened by his brother's death, died six months later in a Dutch asylum. He was buried in Utrecht, but in 1914 Theo's wife, Johanna, who was a dedicated supporter of van Gogh's works, had Theo's body reburied in the Auvers cemetery next to Vincent.

Johanna then collected as many of van Gogh's paintings as she could, but discovered that many of them had been destroyed or lost, van Gogh's own mother having thrown away crates full of his art. On March 17, 1901, 71 of van Gogh's paintings were displayed at a show in Paris, and his fame subsequently grew enormously. His mother lived long enough to see her son hailed as an artist and a genius.

Today, Vincent van Gogh is considered the greatest Dutch painter after Rembrandt. He completed more than 2,100 works, consisting of 860 oil paintings and more than 1,300 watercolors, drawings and sketches. Several of his paintings rank among the most expensive in the world; "Irises" sold for a record $53.9 million, and his "Portrait of Dr. Gachet" sold for $82.5 million.

After more than 100 years since van Gogh's death, more of his artwork was released. A painting of a landscape entitled "Sunset at Montmajour" was discovered and unveiled by the Van Gogh Museum in Amsterdam in September 2013. Before coming under the possession of the Van Gogh Museum, a Norwegian industrialist owned the painting and stored it away in his attic, having thought that it wasn't authentic. The painting is believed to have been created by van Gogh in 1888—around the same time that his artwork "Sunflowers" was made—just two years before his death.

Van Gogh's disobedience drove his creativity towards new horizons. Although categorized as a Post-impressionist, Van Gogh pioneered the style of Expressionism and had a very important influence on 20th century art. He influenced many artists and art movements, such as Henri Matisse and the French Fauves, Ernest Ludwig Kirchner and German Expressionists, as well as Francis Bacon and other artists. Van Gogh has been the topic of several biographical films. He was played most memorably by Kirk Douglas in Lust for Life (1956) and by Tim Roth inVincent & Theo (1990). The highly popular song "Vincent" by Don McLean was a tribute to Van Gogh.

❑❑❑

Viswanathan Anand

(1969)

Chess Player

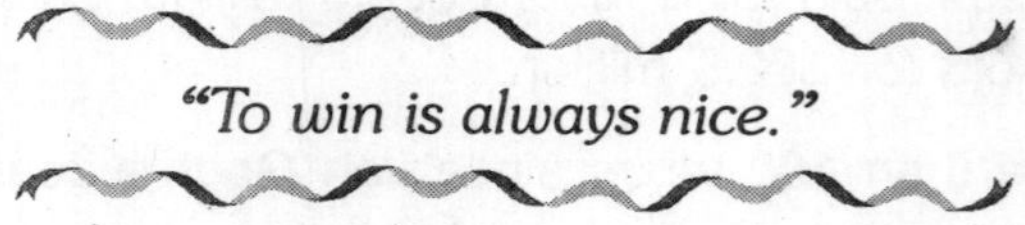

Viswanathan Anand is the first Asian to win the 'World Chess Championship' title. He won the title on December 24, 2000, defeating Spain's Alexei Shirov youngest at Teheran.

Born in Madras (now Chennai), in December 1969, he started playing chess at the age of 6. He learnt chess from his mother, Susheela. His parents encouraged him and used to take him to the Tal Chess Club. Young Anand had an exceptional memory power and an ability to grasp things fast which made him excel in Chess.

He has won many titles even at a young age. He was the youngest Asian to win the 'International Master's' title at the age of fifteen. At sixteen, he became the National Champion; at eighteen India's first Grandmaster. He played games at blitz speed, earning him the nickname "Lightning Kid" ("Blitz chess" is known in India as "Lightning chess").

In 1987, Anand became the first Asian to win the World Junior Chess Championship. In 1992, he won the formidable Reggio Emilia Tournament. He beat Kasparov in the rapid chess tournament in September 1996 and Karpov in June 1997 in Hamburg Rapid Chess. Anand outplayed the most popular chess software programme, Fritz in July 1999.

He has also received many awards, such as the Arjuna Award for Outstanding Indian Sportsman in 1985, Padmashree, National Citizens Award and Soviet Land Nehru Award in 1987, Rajiv Gandhi Khel Ratna Award (India's highest sporting honour), in the year 1991-1992, and Chess Oscar in 1997, 1998, 2003, 2004, 2007 and 2008. In 2007 he was awarded the Padma Vibhushan.

Viswanathan Anand has also won the British Chess Federation 'Book of the Year' Award, in 1998 for his book, *My Best Games of Chess*. It has been released both in English and German. He has also won Padma Bhushan, in 2000. Anand received the "Jameo de Oro", one of Spain's highest civilian award given to a foreigner.

His wife Aruna supports him in his preparations for the tournaments. This genius, although he has achieved so much, still remains simple in character. Anand, known as the "One man Indian Chess revolution", keenly promotes the game, through innovative methods in the country, where the game first originated. It is his ambition to be able to take chess to the grass roots level.

In conjunction with NIIT, his global sponsor, is all set to make chess available to every nook and corner of the country. Anand regularly collaborates with young Indian chess players to help make existing talent reach higher.

Viswanathan Anand shares his time between India and Spain. Being fluent in Spanish, the little town of Collado Mediano near Madrid has adopted him as their "Hijo Predelicto" or famous son.

Anand was Crowned World Champion of Chess on September 30, 2007 as he won the tournament in Mexico City which brought together eight of the games best players. He replaced Vladimir Kramnik of Russia as November 1, Champion in 2008. With this win, he became the first player in chess history to have won the World Championship in three different formats : Knockout, Tournament and Match. He successfully defended his title in the World Chess Championship 2010 against Veselin Topalov and in the World Chess Championship 2012 against Boris Gelfand.

In the World Chess Championship 2013 he lost to challenger Magnus Carlsen and he lost again to Carlsen in the World Chess Championship 2014.

Anand competed in the 4th Sinquefield Cup, the third leg of the 2016 Grand Chess Tour. This specific tournament was held in the Chess Club and Scholastic Center of Saint Louis in St. Louis, Missouri, from August 4 to 17, 2016.

From 28 May to 7 June, 2018 he competed in the sixth edition of Norway Chess, placing fourth with 4½/8 (+2 – 1 = 5). In January 2019, he competed in the 81st Tata Steel Masters tournament held in Wijk aan Zee. There he scored 7.5/13 which netted him a third-place finish. He placed third in the 2019 Gashimov Memorial tournament. Vishwanathan Anand finishes second in Croatia Grand Chess Tour 2021.

In 2022, he was elected as the Deputy President of FIDE, marking a significant administrative role. In 2024, Anand clinched his 10th Leon Masters title, showcasing his enduring competitive prowess.

❑❑❑

Vladimir Ilyich Lenin

(1870–1924)

Political Leader

Vladimir Ilyich Lenin was one of the leading political figures and revolutionary thinkers of the 20th century. He masterminded the Bolshevik take-over of power in Russia in 1917. He was the main leader of the October Revolution and the first head of the then Soviet Russia. He posthumously gave name to the Marxist-Leninist ideology, but by the death of the communist system in 1991, his legacy was largely discredited.

Lenin was born on April 22, 1870 in the city of Simbirsk on the Volga River. He was the son of Ilya Nikolaevich Ulyanov, a Russian civil service official who worked for progressive democracy and free universal education in Russia, and his liberal wife, Maria Alexandrovna Ulyanova.

Like "Stalin" for Dzhugashvili, "Lenin" is one of several pseudonyms used by Mr. Ulyanov. Just as "Stalin" is said to be from the Russian root word, "stal," meaning 'steel,' "Lenin" is based on the

Russian root word, "Lena," meaning the name of a peaceful Siberian river that Lenin discovered during one of his exiles.

Lenin grew up in provincial Russia, in a well educated family. He excelled at school and went on to study law. At university, he was exposed to radical thinking, and his views were also influenced by the execution of his elder brother, a member of a revolutionary group. Expelled from university for his radical policies, Lenin managed to complete his law degree as an external student in 1891.

Lenin took his first overseas trip in 1895. He visited Switzerland, where he came in contact with Plekhanov's "Emancipation of Labour" group, Berlin, and Paris. Shortly after his return to St. Petersburg, he formed the "League of Struggle for the Emancipation of the Working Class," or "League of Struggle" in short. The first pamphlets and brochures were distributed and in December, Lenin was arrested for the first time and exiled to Siberia for three years.

He continued to publish articles, reviews and translations in 1897 while still in exile. He also worked on his exhaustive "Development of Capitalism in Russia," which was completed in 1899. It was also during this exile that Lenin met and married Nadezhda Konstantinovna Krupskaya in 1898. It was with her that Lenin translated Volume One of *Industrial Democracy* by Sydney and Beatrice Webb. In 1900, his exile came to an end.

After his Siberian exile, Lenin - the pseudonym, he adopted in 1901 - spent most of the subsequent decade and a half in Western Europe, where he emerged as a prominent figure in the international revolutionary movement, and became the leader of the 'Bolshevik' faction of the Russian Social Democratic Worker's Party.

In 1917, exhausted by the First World War, Russia was ripe for change. Assisted by the Germans, who hoped that he would undermine the Russian war effort, Lenin returned home and started working against the provisional government that had replaced the tsarist regime. He eventually led what was soon to be known as the October Revolution, but was effectively a coup d'etat.

Almost three years of civil war followed. The Red Army emerged victorious, and the Bolsheviks assumed total control of the country. During this period of revolution, war and famine, Lenin demonstrated a chilling disregard for the sufferings of his fellow countrymen. In his merciless destruction of any opposition, he was instrumental in creating the conditions for Stalin's dictatorship.

Lenin was ruthless but also pragmatic. When his efforts to transform the Russian economy to a socialist model stalled, he introduced the New Economic Policy, where a measure of private enterprise was still permitted. This policy continued for several years beyond his death.

In 1918, Vladimir Ilyich Lenin survived an assassination attempt. His long term health was affected, and in 1922, he suffered a stroke from which he never really recovered. In his declining years, he was worried about the bureaucratisation of the regime, and also expressed concern over the increasing role of Stalin. Finally, he died on January 21, 1924.

On a personal level, Lenin was a modest man and disapproved of adulation. But after his death, he became the subject of a personality cult of grotesque proportions which lasted until the final years of the Soviet system. His embalmed corpse remains in a mausoleum on Moscow's Red Square. Once a place of communist worship, it has now become a symbol of a political ideology and system which ultimately failed miserably.

❑❑❑

Vladimir Putin

(1952)

Political Leader

"The path towards a free society has not been simple. There are tragic and glorious pages in our history."

Vladimir Vladimirovich Putin is the President of Russia, a position he has held since 7 May 2012.

Vladimir Vladimirovich Putin was born on October 7, 1952 in St. Petersburg, then known as Leningrad. He was raised as an only child; his two brothers died young, one shortly after birth, and the other of diphtheria during World War II. In his youth, he was often called 'Putka'. His father, Vladimir Spiridonovich Putin, was a factory foreman and died in August 1999 while his mother, Maria Ivanovna Putina, died six months earlier. Vladimir Putin is married to Lyudmila (1958), and has two daughters: Katya and Masha.

Putin has good command of English and German and he is fond of sports, especially wrestling. He has been going in for *sambo* (a Russian style of self-defence) and *judo,* since the age of 11. He won the *sambo* championships of St. Petersburg many times.

In 1970, Vladimir graduated from preparatory school and enrolled in the Leningrad University. There, he majored in studies of civil law, while also continuing his practice of martial arts. After he graduated, he was recruited by the KGB, the Soviet Union's intelligence organisation. He was sent to Moscow, where he studied espionage and foreign intelligence. There, he learnt the German language and was awarded a 'black belt' in *judo*.

In 1985, Putin was sent to Eastern Germany to live in Dresden under a fake name. He was given a false job at a German-Soviet friendship society, which had been set up by the KGB. It is believed that he was spying on NATO's member nations and recruiting new agents during this time. During his time in Germany, he was able to get an idea of Western cultures and ideas that changed his perspective of the world.

In 1990, the Soviet Union collapsed under the leadership of Mikhail Gorbachev. Putin returned to Russia after the KGB withdrew from reunited Germany and was highly decorated for his intelligence efforts. He was also given an administrative position at the Leningrad University, although he continued conducting intelligence gathering operations.

Putin was eventually hired as an assistant to his old professor of law, Anatoly Sobchak, who had become the chairman of the city council. When Sobchak was elected mayor of the newly-renamed St. Petersburg in 1991, Vladimir was given the position of deputy mayor. During his tenure as the deputy mayor, he helped direct foreign investors in the expansion of the city's economy and infrastructure.

In 1996, Sobchak lost his reelection campaign and left the mayoral office, along with Putin. Despite allegations and charges of corruption against Sobchak, Putin's career was not tainted. In 1997, he was given a position in the Kremlin as deputy to Pavel Borodin, the man in charge of the government's property department.

Putin put his time in the Kremlin to good use, making powerful friends and impressing his superiors. In 1998, he was appointed head of the Federal Security Service, the replacement for the KGB, by President Boris Yeltsin. In 1999, he was named the Prime Minister by Yeltsin after numerous failures by other individuals appointed to that same office.

In the elections of March 2000, Putin won by a good margin, becoming Russia's youngest leader since Josef Stalin in 1922.

Due to constitutionally mandated term limits, Putin was ineligible to run for a third consecutive Presidential term. After the victory of his successor, Dmitry Medvedev, in the 2008 presidential elections, he was then nominated by the latter to be Russia's Prime Minister; Putin took the post on May 8, 2008 and again became the President on May 7, 2012.

In the 2018 election he was re-elected for a six-year term.

In April 2021, following a referendum, he signed into law constitutional amendments including one that would allow him to run for re-election twice more, potentially extending his presidency to 2036.

He was honoured Order of Jose Marti, the Cuba's highest decoration in 2014, Order "For contribution to the development of cooperation" (2017) by Turkmenistan, Order of Manas (2017) by Kyrgyzstan, Order of Friendship (2018) by China, Order of Nazarbayev (2019) by Kazakshtan.

He secured a fifth presidential term (2024) with 88.48% of the vote. He intensified military operations in Ukraine, controlling 20% of its territory by 2025. In September 2024, he warned of nuclear retaliation against Western threats. Marking 25 years in power, Putin emphasised Russia's resilience in his 2024 New Year's address, reinforcing his influence on global politics.

❑❑❑

Voltaire

(1694–1778)

Poet and Philosopher

"Man is free at the moment he wishes to be."

The French poet, dramatist, historian, and philosopher, Voltaire was an outspoken and aggressive enemy of every injustice, especially of religious intolerance. His works are an outstanding embodiment of the principles of the French Enlightenment.

The son of a notary, he was born in 1694 in Paris and was educated at the Jesuit College Louis-le-Grand. Because of insults to the regent, Philippe II d'Orleans, wrongly ascribed to him, Voltaire was sent to the Bastille (1717) for 11 months. There he rewrote his first tragedy, *Oedipe* (1718), and began an epic poem on Henry IV, the Henriade. It was at this time that he began to call himself Voltaire. *Oedipe* won him fame and a pension from the regent. Voltaire acquired an independent fortune through speculation; he was often noted for his generosity but also displayed a shrewd business acumen throughout his life and became a millionaire.

While in England, he wrote the first of his historical works, a history of Charles XII of Sweden, which remains a classic in biography. Returning to France in 1729, he produced several tragedies, salient were among them *Brutus* (1730) and *Zaire* (1732). In 1733, he met Mme Du Chatelet, whose intellectual interests, especially in science, accorded with his own. They took up residence together at Cirey, in Lorraine, under the Marquis Du Chatelet's tolerant eye. The connection with Emilie Du Chatelet lasted until her death in 1749.

At Cirey, Voltaire worked on physics and chemistry experiments and began his long correspondence with Crown Prince Frederick of Prussia (later Frederick II). In addition, he wrote *Elements de la philosophie de Newton* (1736), which was partially responsible for bringing awareness of Newtonian physics to the Continent; a burlesque treatment of the Joan of Arc legends, *La Pucelle* (1755); and the dramas, *Mahomet* (1742), *Merope* (1743), and *Semiramis* (1748). Through the influence of Mme de Pompadour, Voltaire was made royal historiographer, a gentleman of the king's bedchamber, and a member of the French Academy.

Voltaire first visited Berlin in 1743, and after Mme Du Châtelet's death, he accepted Frederick II's invitation to live at his court. His relations with Frederick, a man whose unbending nature matched his own, were generally stormy. His interference in the quarrel between Maupertuis and Konig led to renewed coldness on the part of Frederick, and in 1753, Voltaire hastily left Prussia. At a distance, the two men later became reconciled, and their correspondence was resumed. Unwelcome in France, Voltaire settled in Geneva, where he acquired the property "Les Delices". He also acquired another house near Lausanne. The Genevese authorities soon objected to Voltaire's holding private theatrical performances at his home and still more to the article, *Geneve* written for Diderot's Encyclopedie, on Voltaire's instigation, by Alembert. The article, which declared that the Calvinist pastors of Geneva had seen the light and ceased to believe in organised religion, stirred up a violent controversy.

Voltaire purchased an estate, Ferney, just over the French border, where he lived until shortly before his death. He conducted an extensive correspondence with most of the outstanding men and women of his time; and received hosts of visitors who came to pay homage to the "patriarch of Ferney". He employed himself in seeking justice for victims of religious or political persecution and in campaigning against the practice of torture; contributed to the Encyclopédie; and managed his estate, taking an active interest in improving the condition of his tenants.

Voltaire also edited the works of Corneille, wrote commentaries on Racine, and turned out a stream of anonymous novels and pamphlets in which he attacked the established institutions of his time with unremitting virulence. Ironically, it is one of these disavowed works, *Candide* (1759), that is most widely read today. It is the masterpiece among his "philosophical romances," which also include the inimitable short tale *Jeannot et Colin* (1764), perhaps, the quintessence of Voltaire's style. In *Candide*, Voltaire attacked the philosophical optimism made fashionable by Leibniz.

In 1778, his 84th year, he attended the first performance of his tragedy, *Irene*, in Paris. His journey and his reception were a triumph and apotheosis, but the emotion was too much for him and he died in Paris soon afterward. In order to obtain Christian burial, he had signed a partial retraction of his writings. This was considered insufficient by the church, but he refused to sign a more general retraction. To a friend he gave the following written declaration: "I die adoring God, loving my friends, not hating my enemies, and detesting persecution." An abbot secretly conveyed Voltaire's corpse to an abbey in Champagne, where he was buried. His remains were brought back to Paris in 1791 and buried in the Pantheon.

❑❑❑

Walt Disney

(1901–1966)

Entertainer

"I always like to look on the optimistic side of life, but I am realistic enough to know that life is a complex matter."

Walter Elias Disney was an American film producer, director, screenwriter, voice actor, animator, and philanthropist. He was the father and creator of children's one of the most favourite cartoon character, "Mickey Mouse" and founder of the most fascinating amusement park (world) for children, the "Disney Land". He was truly the greatest entertainer ever born.

Walt Disney was a true dreamer, a person who could take the imagination and put it into reality. He transformed the entertainment industry, and pioneered the fields of animation, finding new ways to teach, and educate. Much more than just the creator of Mickey Mouse, Walt Disney shaped the twentieth century by bringing joy to millions of people —young and old.

Walt Disney was born on December 5, 1901 in Chicago Illinois. His father, Elias Disney, was an Irish-Canadian. His mother, Flora Call

Disney, was of German-American descent. Walt was one of the five children, four boys and a girl.

When he was only 5 years old, his family moved to Marceline, Missouri, which is commonly believed to be his inspiration for Mainstreet USA in Disneyland. Walt lived most of his childhood here. While living in this farming community, he developed a love of animals that would later become the motivation behind his cartoon characters.

Walt began to love, and appreciate nature and wildlife, as well as family and community, which were a large part of agrarian living. During his school years, he loved to entertain his friends with comedy skits. Though his father could be quite stern, and often there was little money, Walt was encouraged by his mother, and elder brother, Roy to pursue his talents.

He pursued his art career, by studying art and photography by going to McKinley High School in Chicago. Disney was the cartoonist for the school newspaper. His cartoons were very patriotic and political, focusing on World War I. He dropped out of high school at the age of 16 so that he could join the army. But the army didn't take him because he was too young. Instead, Walt joined the Red Cross and was sent overseas to France, where he spent a year driving an ambulance and chauffeuring Red Cross officials. It was covered from top to bottom with his imaginative Disney characters.

Walt began to pursue a career in commercial art once he returned from France. He started a small company called Laugh-O-Grams, which eventually fell bankrupt. Even though the company ended, Walt did not give up. With his suitcase, and twenty dollars, he headed to Hollywood to start afresh.

After making a success of his *Alice Comedies*, Walt became a recognised Hollywood figure. On July 13, 1925, he married one of his first employees, Lillian Bounds, in Lewiston, Idaho. Later on, they were blessed with two daughters, Diane and Sharon .

In 1932, the production entitled *Flowers and Trees* (the first colour cartoon) won Walt the first of his studio's Academy Awards. In 1937, he released *The Old Mill*, the first short subject to utilise the multi-plane camera technique.

On December 21, 1937, *Snow White and the Seven Dwarfs*, the first full-length animated musical feature, was premiered at the Carthay Theater in Los Angeles. The film produced at the unheard cost of $1,499,000 during the depths of the Depression, is still considered one of the great feats and imperishable monuments of the motion picture industry. During the next five years, Walt Disney Studios completed other full-length animated classics such as *Pinocchio*, *Fantasia*, *Dumbo*, and *Bambi*.

Walt Disney's dream of a clean, and organised amusement park, came true, as Disneyland Park opened in 1955. Walt also became a television pioneer, and began television production in 1954. He was among the first to present full-colour programming with his *Wonderful World of Color* in 1961. Walt Disney died of lung cancer on 15 December, 1966 in Burbank, California.

Walt is a legend; a folk hero of the 20th century. His worldwide popularity was based upon the ideals which his name represents: imagination, optimism, creation, and self-made success in the American tradition. He brought us closer to the future, while telling us of the past, and it is certain, that there will never be such as great a man, as Walt Disney.

❑❑❑

Warren Buffett

(1930)

Business Tycoon and Investor

"Without passion, you don't have energy. Without energy, you have nothing."

American businessman and investor Warren Buffett was born on August 30,1930, in Omaha, Nebraska. Investing by age 11, Buffett was running a small business at 13. Buffett later started the firm Buffett Partnership in Omaha, with huge success.

Buffett's father Howard worked as stockbroker and served as U.S. Congressman. His mother, Leila Stahl Buffett, was a homemaker. Buffett was the second of three children and the only boy.

Buffett demonstrated a knack for financial and business matters early on in his childhood. The young boy was a mathematical prodigy, and was able to add large columns of numbers in his head—a talent he still occasionally shows off to friends and business associates.

Warren often visited his father's stockbrokerage shop as a child. At 11 years old he made his first investment; he bought three shares of Cities Service Preferred at $38 per share. The stock quickly dropped to only $27, but Buffett held on tenaciously until they reached $40. He sold his shares at a small profit, but regretted the decision when Cities Service shot up to nearly $200 a share. He later cited this experience as an early lesson in patience in investing.

By the age of 13, Buffett was running his own businesses as a paperboy and selling his own horseracing tip sheet. That same year, he filed his first tax return, claiming his bike as a $35 tax deduction.

In 1942, Buffett's father was elected to the U.S. House of Representatives, and his family moved to Fredricksburg, Virginia, to be closer to the congressman's new post. Buffett attended Woodrow Wilson High School in Washington, D.C., where he continued plotting new ways to make money. During his high school tenure, he and a friend purchased a used pinball machine for $25. They installed it in a Washington, D.C. barbershop and, within a few months, the profits of the machine allowed Buffett and his friend to buy other machines. Buffett owned three machines in three different locations before he sold the business to a War Veteran for $1,200.

Buffett enrolled at the University of Pennsylvania at the age of 16 to study business. He stayed two years, moved to the University of Nebraska to finish up his degree, and emerged from college at age 20 with nearly $10,000 from his childhood businesses.

Buffett attended Columbia University for his advanced degree and in 1956, shortly after graduation, he formed the firm Buffett Partnership in his hometown of Omaha. His investment successes, particularly in buying undervalued companies whose stocks shortly began to rise, made him extremely rich and gained him the sobriquet, "Oracle of Omaha." Other notable career successes include helping rescue Salomon Brothers from corporate raiders (1987) and taking charge of the New York City house (1992) in the wake of an insider trading scandal.

In 1986, Buffett bought a used Falcon aircraft for $850,000. As he had become increasingly recognizable, it was no longer comfortable for him to fly commercially. The idea of the luxury was hard for him to adjust to, but he loved the jet immensely. The passion for jets eventually, in part, led him to purchase Executive Jet in the 90's.

The most profound and upsetting events in Buffett's life took place. When at forty-five, Susan Buffett left her husband - in form. Although she remained married to Warren, the humanitarian / singer secured an apartment in San Francisco and, insisting she wanted to live on her own, moved there. Warren was absolutely devastated; throughout his life. The two remained close, speaking every day, taking their annual two-week New York trip, and meeting the kids at their California Beach house for Christmas get-togethers. The transition was hard for the businessman, but he eventually grew somewhat accustomed to the new arrangement.

In June 2006, Buffett made an announcement that he would be giving his entire fortune away to charity (est. $62 billion), committing 85 percent of it to the Bill and Melinda Gates Foundation. This donation became the largest act of charitable giving in United States history.

In 2023, he began reducing Berkshire Hathaway's stake in Apple Inc., selling over half by June 2024, to accumulate cash for potential market disruptions. In late 2024, he invested $1.24 billion in Constellation Brands, known for Mexican beers like Corona and Modelo, while significantly reducing holdings in Bank of America and Citigroup.

As of February 2025, Warren Buffett's net worth is estimated at $150.4 billion, positioning him among the world's wealthiest individuals.

❑❑❑

Will Smith

(1968)

Actor, Producer and Rapper

"Money and success don't change people; they merely amplify what is already there."

Willard Carroll "Will" Smith, Jr. is an American actor, producer, and rapper. He has enjoyed success in television, film and music.

Smith was born on September 25, 1968 and raised in West Philadelphia. He has also lived in Germantown in Northwest Philadelphia. His mother, Caroline (née Bright), was a school administrator who worked for the Philadelphia school board, and his father, Willard Christopher Smith, Sr., was a refrigeration engineer. He was raised Baptist. His parents separated when he was thirteen, but did not actually divorce until around 2000.

Smith started as the MC of the hip-hop duo DJ Jazzy Jeff & The Fresh Prince, with his childhood friend Jeffrey "DJ Jazzy Jeff" Townes as turntablist and producer, as well as Ready Rock C (Clarence Holmes) as the human beat box. The trio was known for performing humorous, radio-friendly songs, most notably "Parents

Just Don't Understand" and "Summertime". They gained critical acclaim and won the first Grammy award in the Rap category (1988).

In the late 1980s, Smith achieved modest fame as a rapper under the name The Fresh Prince. In 1990, his popularity increased dramatically when he starred in the popular television series *The Fresh Prince of Bel-Air*. The show ran for nearly six years (1990–1996) on NBC. In the mid-1990s, Smith moved from television to film, and ultimately starred in numerous blockbuster films. He is the only actor to have eight consecutive films gross over $100 million in the domestic box office, and 11 consecutive films gross over $150 million internationally and the only one to have eight consecutive films in which he starred open at #1 spot in the domestic box office tally.

Smith's first major roles were in the drama *Six Degrees of Separation* (1993) and the action film *Bad Boys* (1995).

In 1996, Smith starred as part of an ensemble cast in Roland Emmerich's *Independence Day*. The film was a massive blockbuster, becoming the second highest grossing film in history at the time and establishing Smith as a prime box office draw. He later struck gold again in the summer of 1997 alongside Tommy Lee Jones in the summer hit *Men in Black* playing Agent J. In 1998, Smith starred with Gene Hackman in *Enemy of the State*.

He received Best Actor Oscar nominations for *Ali* and *The Pursuit of Happyness*.

Smith has been married twice. His first marriage in 1992 lasted only three years but produced a son, Willard Smith III, who is also known as Trey. He has been married to actress Jada Pinkett Smith since 1997. The couple has a son, Jaden, who was born in 1998 and a daughter, Willow, born in 2000.

He is a fan of chess and video games and is known to take his mother on vacation every year, usually to the Canyon Ranch spa in Tucson, Arizona.

In 2005, Smith was entered into the Guinness Book of World Records for attending three premieres in a 24-hour time span.

Smith and his son Jaden played father and son in two productions: the 2006 biographical drama *The Pursuit of Happyness*, and the science fiction film *After Earth*, which was released on May 31, 2013.

Smith portrayed The Genie (originally voiced by Robin Williams) in the live-action adaptation of Disney's Aladdin, directed by Guy Ritchie. He also participated in the soundtracks by recording singles: "Arabian Nights (2019)", "Friend Like Me" and "Prince Ali". The film was released on May 24, 2019. Aladdin grossed over $1 billion worldwide to become Smith's highest-grossing film, surpassing Independence Day.

Smith voiced Lance Sterling, a spy who teams up with the nerdy inventor who creates his gadgets (Holland). The film was released on December 25, 2019. In 2020, he reteamed with Martin Lawrence for the third film in their franchise, Bad Boys for Life.

In 2019, Smith invested $46 million in esports organization Gen. G with Smith's Dreamers Fund, which he co-founded with Keisuke Honda.

He won the Best Actor Oscar for "King Richard" but faced backlash for slapping Chris Rock. In 2023, he announced sequels for "I Am Legend" and "Hancock". By 2024, he returned to music, releasing new singles. In February 2025, he made his first major awards appearance at the Grammys, marking his comeback to Hollywood events.

William Shakespeare

(1564–1616)

Poet and Playwright

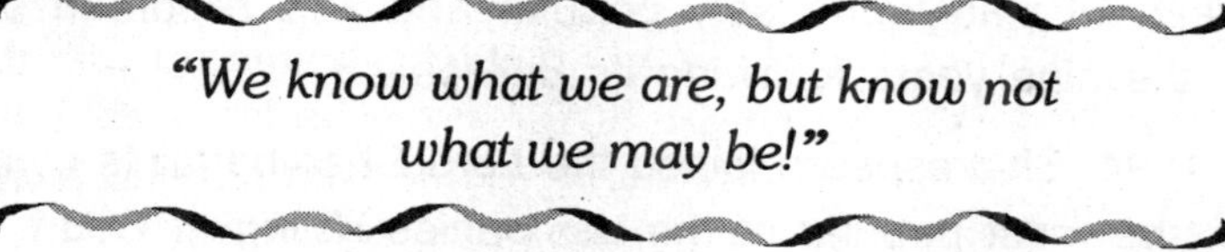

William Shakespeare was one of the greatest English poets and playwrights of all times. He was a truly versatile writer. Though he was not much educated formally, yet his plays are very popular even after 400 years and are part of the educational curriculum throughout the world.

William Shakespeare is believed to be born on April 23, 1564, and baptised on April 26, 1564 in Stratford-on-Avon. The son of John Shakespeare and Mary Arden, he was probably educated at the King Edward IV Grammar School in Stratford, where he learned Latin and a little Greek and read the Roman dramatists. At eighteen, he married Anne Hathaway, a woman seven or eight years his senior. Together they raised two daughters: Susanna, who was born in 1583, and Judith whose twin brother died in boyhood, born in 1585.

Little is known about Shakespeare's activities with certainty between 1585 and 1592. Robert Greene's *A Groatsworth of*

Wit alludes to him as an actor and playwright. Shakespeare shortly after 1585 went to London to begin his apprenticeship as an actor. Due to the plague, the London theaters were often closed between June 1592 and April 1594. During that period, Shakespeare probably had some income from his patron, Henry Wriothesley, earl of Southampton, to whom he dedicated his first two poems, *Venus and Adonis* (1593) and *The Rape of Lucrece* (1594). The fomer was a long narrative poem depicting the rejection of Venus by Adonis, his death, and the consequent disappearance of beauty from the world. Despite conservative objections to the poem's glorification of sensuality, it was immensely popular and was reprinted six times during the nine years following its publication.

In 1594, Shakespeare joined the Lord Chamberlain's company of actors, the most popular of the companies acting at Court. In 1599 Shakespeare joined a group of Chamberlain's Men that would form a syndicate to build and operate a new playhouse: the Globe, which became the most famous theater of its time. With his share of the income from the Globe, Shakespeare was able to purchase New Place, his home in Stratford.

Shakespeare wrote more than 30 plays. These are usually divided into four categories: histories, comedies, tragedies, and romances. His earliest plays were primarily comedies and histories such as *Henry VI* and *The Comedy of Errors*, but in 1596, Shakespeare wrote *Romeo and Juliet*, his second tragedy, and over the next dozen years he would return to the form, writing the plays for which he is now best known: *Julius Caesar*, *Hamlet*, *Othello*, *King Lear*, *Macbeth*, and *Antony and Cleopatra*. In his final years, Shakespeare turned to the romantic with *Cymbeline*, *A Winter's Tale*, and *The Tempest*.

Only eighteen of Shakespeare's plays were published separately in quarto editions during his lifetime; a complete collection of his works did not appear until the publication of the First Folio in 1623, several years after his death. Nonetheless, his contemporaries recognized

Shakespeare's achievements. Francis Meres cited "honey-tongued" Shakespeare for his plays and poems in 1598, and the Chamberlain's Men rose to become the leading dramatic company in London, installed as members of the royal household in 1603.

While Shakespeare was regarded as the foremost dramatist of his time, evidence indicates that both he and his contemporaries looked to poetry, not playwriting, for enduring fame. Shakespeare's sonnets were composed between 1593 and 1601, though not published until 1609. That edition, *The Sonnets of Shakespeare*, consists of 154 sonnets, all written in the form of three quatrains and a couplet that is now recognized as Shakespearean. The sonnets fall into two groups: sonnets 1-126, addressed to a beloved friend, a handsome and noble young man, and sonnets 127-152, to a malignant but fascinating "Dark Lady". Nearly all of Shakespeare's sonnets examine the inevitable decay of time, and the immortalization of beauty and love in poetry.

In his poems and plays, Shakespeare invented thousands of words, often combining or contorting Latin, French and native roots.

Sometime after 1612, Shakespeare retired from the stage and returned to his home in Stratford. He drew up his will in January of 1616, which included his famous bequest to his wife of his "second best bed." He died on April 23, 1616, and was buried two days later at Stratford Church.

Today, his plays are highly popular and constantly studied and reinterpreted in performances with diverse cultural and political contexts. The genius of Shakespeare's characters and plots are that they present real human beings in a wide range of emotions and conflicts that transcend their origins in Elizabethan England.

William Wordsworth

(1770–1850)

Poet

"That best portion of a man's life, his little, nameless, unremembered acts of kindness and love."

William Wordsworth was one of the most influential of England's Romantic poets. He is known for writing *Lyrical Ballads* (1798) with Samuel Taylor Coleridge, considered by many to have launched the English Romantic movement. Wordsworth's literary credits also include "Tintern Abbey," and his poetry is perhaps most original in its vision of the relation between man and the natural world—a vision that culminated in the metaphor of nature as emblematic of the mind of God.

William Wordsworth was born on 7 April 1770 at Cockermouth in Cumbria. His father was a lawyer. Both Wordsworth's parents died before he was 15, and he and his four siblings were left in the care of different relatives. As a young man, Wordsworth developed a love of nature, a theme reflected in many of his poems.

While studying at Cambridge University, Wordsworth spent a summer holiday on a walking tour in Switzerland and France. He became an enthusiast for the ideals of the French Revolution. He began to write poetry while he was at school, but none was published until 1793.

In 1795, Wordsworth received a legacy from a close relative and he and his sister Dorothy went to live in Dorset. Two years later they moved again, this time to Somerset, to live near the poet Samuel Taylor Coleridge, who was an admirer of Wordsworth's work. They collaborated on 'Lyrical Ballads', published in 1798. This collection of poems, mostly by Wordsworth but with Coleridge contributing 'The Rime of the Ancient Mariner', is generally taken to mark the beginning of the Romantic movement in English poetry. The poems were greeted with hostility by most critics.

In 1799, after a visit to Germany with Coleridge, Wordsworth and Dorothy settled at Dove Cottage in Grasmere in the Lake District. Coleridge lived nearby with his family. Wordsworth's most famous poem, 'I Wandered Lonely as a Cloud' was written at Dove Cottage in 1804.

In 1802, Wordsworth married a childhood friend, Mary Hutchinson. The next few years were personally difficult for Wordsworth. Two of his children died, his brother was drowned at sea and Dorothy suffered a mental breakdown. His political views underwent a transformation around the turn of the century, and he became increasingly conservative, disillusioned by events in France culminating in Napoleon Bonaparte taking power.

In 1813, Wordsworth moved from Grasmere tc nearby Ambelside. He continued to write poetry. After 1835, he wrote little more. In 1842, he was given a government pension and the following year became poet laureate.

Wordsworth's literary career began with Descriptive Sketches (1793) and reached an early climax before the turn of the century, with Lyrical Ballads. His powers peaked with Poems in Two Volumes (1807), and his reputation continued to grow; even his harshest reviewers recognized his popularity and the originality.

The important later works were well under way. His success with shorter forms made him the more eager to succeed with longer, specifically with a long, three-part "philosophical poem, containing views of Man, Nature, and Society, . . having for its principal subject the sensations and opinions of a poet living in retirement." The 17,000 lines which were eventually published made up only a part of this mammoth project. The second section, *The Excursion*, was completed (pub. 1814), as was the first book of the first part, *The Recluse*. During his lifetime he refused to print *The Prelude*, which he had completed by 1805, because he thought it was unprecedented for a poet to talk as much about himself — unless he could put it in its proper setting, which was as an introduction to the complete three-part *Recluse*.

Inspiration gradually failed him for this project, and he spent much of his later life revising *The Prelude*. Critics quarrel about which version is better, the 1805 or the 1850, but agree that in either case it is the most successful blank verse epic since *Paradise Lost*.

Wordsworth died on 23 April 1850 and was buried in Grasmere churchyard. His great autobiographical poem, 'The Prelude', which he had worked on since 1798, was published after his death.

❑❑❑

Xavier de Maistre

(1763–1852)

Writer, Painter & Miltaryman

"Imagination, realm of enchantment !
Which the most beneficent of beings bestowed
upon man to console him for reality
I must quit you now."

Xavier de Maistre of Savoy (then part of the Kingdom of Piedmont-Sardinia), lived largely as a military man, but is known as a French writer. The younger brother of noted philosopher and counter-revolutionary Joseph de Maistre, Xavier was born to an aristocratic family at Chambéry in October 1763. He served when young in the army of Piedmont-Sardinia, and in 1790 wrote his fantasy, *Voyage autour de ma chambre* ("Voyage Around My Room", published 1794), when he was under arrest in Turin as the consequence of a duel.

Xavier shared the political sympathies of his brother Joseph, and after a French revolutionary army annexed Savoy to France in 1792, he left the service, and eventually took a commission in the Russian army. He served under Alexander Suvorov in his victorious Austro-Russian campaign and accompanied the marshal to Russia in 1796. By then, Suvorov's patron Catherine II of Russia had died, and the new monarch Paul I dismissed the victorious general (partly on account of the massacre of 20,000 Poles after he conquered Warsaw). Xavier de Maistre shared the disgrace of his general, and supported himself for some time in St. Petersburg by miniature painting, particularly landscapes.

In 1803, Joseph de Maistre was appointed as Piedmont-Sardinia's ambassador to the court of Alexander I, Tsar of Russia. On his brother's arrival in St. Petersburg, Xavier de Maistre was introduced to the Minister of the Navy, and was appointed to several posts including director of the Library, and of the Museum of Admiralty. He also joined active service, and was wounded in the Caucasus, attaining the rank of major-general. In 1812 he married a Russian lady, related to the Tsars, Mrs. Zagriatsky. He remained in Russia even after the overthrow of Napoleon and the consequent restoration of the Piedmontese dynasty.

His *Voyage autour de ma chambre* (1794), a parody set in the tradition of the grand travel narrative, is an autobiographical account of how a young official, imprisoned in his room for six weeks, looks at the furniture, engravings, etc., as if they were scenes from a voyage in a strange land. He praises this voyage because it does not cost anything, for this reason it is strongly recommended to the poor, the infirm, and the lazy. His room is a long square, and the perimeter is thirty-six paces. "When I travel through my room," he writes, "I rarely follow a straight line: I go from the table towards a picture hanging in a corner; from there, I set out obliquely towards the door; but even though, when I begin, it really is my intention to go there, if I happen to meet my armchair en route, I don't think twice about it, and settle down in it without further ado." Later, proceeding North, he encounters his bed, and in this way he lightheartedly continues his "Voyage". This work is remarkable for its play with the reader's imagination, along the lines of Laurence Sterne, whom Xavier admired. Xavier did not think much of *Voyage*, but his brother Joseph had it published.

Most of his other works are of modest dimensions; these include *Le Lépreux de la Cité d'Aoste* ("The Leper from Aoste," 1811), a touching humane story in a simple style, involving a dialogue between a leper who reminisces with a soldier about his lost youth and his sequestered life in a tower with a view of the Alps; *Les Prisonniers du Caucase*, ("The Prisoners of the Caucasus," 1825) a powerful sketch of Russian character, *La Jeune Sibérienne*, ("The Young Siberian," 1825), and *Expédition Nocturne Autour de ma Chambre* ("Night Voyage Around My Room," 1825), a sequel to *Voyage Autour de ma Chambre*.

In 1839, after the publication of a French edition of *La Jeune Siebérienne* (1825) Maistre went on a long journey to Paris and Savoy. He was surprised to find himself well known in literary circles. Alphonse de Lamartine dedicated a poem to him (*Retour*, 1826) praising his genius: "the future sons will say [...] it is your heart, which through your mellifluous writings you have passed to us". He met Charles Augustin Sainte-Beuve, who has left some pleasant reminiscences of him.

For a time, he lived at Naples, but eventually he returned to St. Petersburg and died there in 1852

❑❑❑

Xavier Samuel

(1983)

Actor

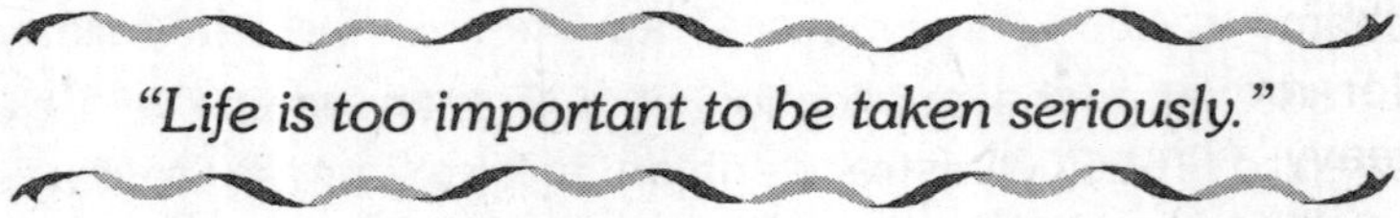

"Life is too important to be taken seriously."

Xavier Samuel is an Australian actor. He has appeared in leading roles in the feature films *September*, *Further We Search*, *Newcastle*, *The Loved Ones* and *A Few Best Men*, and played Riley Biers in *The Twilight Saga: Eclipse*.

Samuel was born in 1983 in Hamilton, Victoria, the son of Maree and Clifford Samuel. He grew up in Adelaide, South Australia and graduated from Rostrevor College in 2001. Xavier has a younger brother, Benedict Samuel, who is a writer, producer and actor. He also has an older sister Bridget Samuel who is a stage manager.

Despite completing his senior secondary years at Rostrevor College, Samuel undertook final year drama at Christian Brothers College under the tutelage of Amanda Portus. During the same year, he played the part of Tom Snout (the wall) in Rostrevor College's production of Shakespeare's *A Midsummer Night's Dream* as well as playing the part of Belvile in CBC's production of Aphra Behn's *The Rover (The Banished Cavaliers)*.

Samuel attended Flinders University Drama Centre in 2005, where he studied under renowned acting teacher Professor Julie Holledge. He played Hamlet in the graduate production.

Samuel made his debut on an Australian TV show named *McLeod's Daughters* in 2003. He starred in the Australian horror movie Road Train as Marcus, and also acted in the Australian movie *Drowning with Elephant Princess* star Miles Szanto, directed by Craig Boreham. In 2009, he was cast as Brent in the Australian horror/thriller movie *The Loved Ones* in the lead role opposite Robin McLeavy. Although it received several award nominations, the film was a financial failure.

In early 2010, Samuel was cast as Riley Biers in *The Twilight Saga: Eclipse*. The film gave Samuel his first blockbuster film worldwide. Samuel received his first award nomination and win at the 2011 MTV Movie Awards.

Samuel appeared in the 2011 film *Anonymous*. He plays a lead role in *A Few Best Men* (2011/2012). He was cast in 3D feature *Bait*, released in September 2012 and short film *Sanctuary*, which was also released in 2012.

In 2013, he played Ian in Adore/Two Mothers alongside Robin Wright and Naomi Watts. In 2016, Samuel plays the titular character in Cris Jones' The Death and Life of Otto Bloom, with Rachel Ward and her daughter, Matilda Brown. The film is set to open the Melbourne International Film Festival.

Starring alongside Hugo Weaving yet again, Samuel played the role of Simon Heywood in the Australian TV series, Seven Types of Ambiguity in 2017. The series was based on Seven Types of Ambiguity, a 2003 novel by Australian writer Elliot Perlman. Samuel played Kit Parker in the Amazon thriller series, Tell Me Your Secrets in 2021.

❑❑❑

Srinivasa Ramanujan

(1887-1920)

Indian Mathematician

"An equation for me has no meaning unless it expresses a thought of God."

Srinivasa Ramanujan was born on December 22, 1887, in Erode, Tamil Nadu, India. He belonged to a Brahmin Iyengar family and was the son of K. Srinivasa Iyengar, a clerk at a sari shop, and Komalatammal, a housewife. When he was just a year old, his family moved to Kumbakonam, where he spent most of his childhood. From a young age, Ramanujan showed an exceptional talent for mathematics, often surprising his teachers with his ability to solve complex problems without formal training.

At the age of ten, he secured the highest marks in his school exams and demonstrated a deep understanding of numbers. He was introduced to advanced mathematics through a book titled A *Synopsis of Elementary Results in Pure and Applied Mathematics* by G.S. Carr, which contained thousands of theorems but very few proofs. Ramanujan began working on these problems independently, rediscovering many established results and formulating new mathematical theories on his own.

Despite his brilliance, Ramanujan struggled in school due to his obsession with mathematics. While he excelled in numbers, he neglected other subjects, which ultimately led to his failure in college. He first attended Government Arts College in Kumbakonam but lost his scholarship due to poor performance in subjects other than mathematics. He later attempted to study at Pachaiyappa's College in Madras but failed to pass his exams. His academic failures left him without a formal degree, making it difficult for him to find a stable job.

In 1912, Ramanujan took a clerical job at the Madras Port Trust to support himself. During this time, he continued his mathematical research, filling notebooks with original theorems and equations. His work caught the attention of prominent mathematicians in India, who recognised his extraordinary talent. Encouraged by his mentors, he wrote to British mathematician G.H. Hardy at the University of Cambridge in 1913, sending a letter that contained over a hundred mathematical theorems. Hardy was initially skeptical but soon realised that Ramanujan was a mathematical genius, producing results that were groundbreaking and highly original.

Hardy invited Ramanujan to Cambridge in 1914, and despite initial hesitation due to his deeply religious beliefs, Ramanujan agreed to travel to England. At Cambridge, he worked closely with Hardy and John Littlewood, collaborating on several mathematical problems. Hardy described Ramanujan as one of the most brilliant mathematicians of the 20th century, comparing his talent to that of legendary figures like Euler and Jacobi.

During his time at Cambridge, Ramanujan made significant contributions to number theory, continued fractions, infinite series, and mathematical analysis. His work on partitions, the Ramanujan prime, and modular forms became the foundation for many modern mathematical discoveries. His most famous contribution was the formulation of the *Ramanujan theta function*, which later played a crucial role in the development of string theory and quantum physics.

In 1916, Ramanujan earned a Bachelor of Science degree (later renamed Ph.D.) from Cambridge for his dissertation on highly composite numbers. In 1918, he became a Fellow of the Royal Society, making him one of the youngest members ever to receive this honour. He was also the first Indian to be elected a Fellow of Trinity College, Cambridge.

However, his time in England took a toll on his health. The harsh weather, dietary restrictions, and rigorous work schedule led to a decline in his physical condition. By 1919, he was diagnosed with severe health issues, possibly tuberculosis or a liver infection. Due to his worsening health, he returned to India in 1919, hoping to recover in his homeland.

Unfortunately, his health continued to deteriorate, and on April 26, 1920, at the age of 32, Ramanujan passed away in Kumbakonam. Despite his short life, he left behind an incredible legacy, with over 3,900 mathematical results recorded in his notebooks. Many of his theorems were later proven correct and have since influenced various fields, including physics, computer science, and cryptography.

Ramanujan's legacy continues to inspire mathematicians around the world. His notebooks, filled with groundbreaking discoveries, remain a valuable source of research. In 2012, the National Mathematics Day was declared in India on his birth anniversary, December 22, to honour his contributions. His life was also depicted in the 2015 film *The Man Who Knew Infinity*, starring Dev Patel as Ramanujan and Jeremy Irons as G.H. Hardy.

❑❑❑

Yehudi Menuhin

(1916–1999)

Violinist and Conductor

"The violinist is that peculiarly human phenomenon distilled to a rare potency – half tiger, half poet."

Yehudi Menuhin was an American violinist and conductor who spent most of his performing career in the United Kingdom, and eventually became a British citizen.

Yehudi was born on April 22, 1916 in New York of Russian-Jewish parents. He made his violin debut at the age of seven with the San Francisco Symphony in Lalo's Symphonie Espagnole, and a recital in New York followed a year later. By the time he was eleven, he had made his historic debuts in Paris and Carnegie Hall. At twelve, he played in Berlin and at thirteen in London, launching himself at an early age on a lifelong career that was to take him all over the world, playing with leading conductors and orchestras. In addition to his fame as an exceptional musician, he has been equally recognised as a committed humanitarian.

Yehudi Menuhin performed for allied soldiers during World War II, and went with the composer Benjamin Britten to perform for the inmates of Bergen-Belsen concentration camp, after its liberation in April 1945. He went back to Germany in 1947 to perform music under the conductor, Wilhelm Furtwängler as an act of reconciliation, becoming the first Jewish musician to go back to Germany after the Holocaust.

After building early success on richly romantic and tonally opulent performances, he experienced considerable physical and artistic difficulties caused by overwork during World War II and unfocussed early training. Careful practise and study combined with meditation and yoga helped him overcome many of these problems, and he continued to perform to an advanced age, becoming known for profound interpretations of an austere quality.

On his first visit to India in 1952, at the invitation of Prime Minister Pandit Nehru, he met Ravi Shankar and developed a deep admiration for both Shankar and Indian music. Subsequently, they gave many concerts together and made numerous recordings. Later on, he was also awarded the Nehru Peace Prize for 'International Understanding'.

In 1963, Yehudi achieved one of his greatest ambitions by setting up a boarding school in England, the Yehudi Menuhin School. Intended for promising young musicians, it was based on the concept of the Central School of Moscow, where the students receive both their scholastic and musical education under one roof.

In 1977, he founded the International Menuhin Music Academy for young graduate string players in Gstaad, Switzerland. The Academy became the site of the Menuhin Music Festival, of which he was the artistic director for 40 years. For his contribution, he was awarded the Swiss citizenship.

In recognition of the many concerts he gave for the Allied Forces during the Second World War, flying over from America whenever he could find space in a military plane, Yehudi Menuhin was awarded numerous honours. The list of honours has continued to increase over the years and to date includes, among many others, the Legion d'Honneur from France; the Great Order of Merit, Germany's highest honour; the Ordre Leopold and the Ordre de la Couronne from Belgium; from England the Royal Philharmonic Society's Gold Medal and from Spain the Gran Cruz de la Orden del Merito Civil and the Premio Principe de Asturias de la Concordia. Queen Elizabeth II bestowed a knighthood on him in 1965 and gave him the Order of Merit in 1987, followed by a life peerage in 1993.

He is an Honorary Doctor of over 30 universities in different countries, including those of Oxford, Cambridge, St Andrew's and the Sorbonne, as well as being a Freeman of the cities of Edinburgh, Bath, Reims and Warsaw and holding the Gold Medals of the cities of Paris, New York and Jerusalem. He was also the first Westerner to be made an Honorary Professor of the Beijing Conservatoire in recognition of his concerts in China and for his endeavours to help many young Chinese violinists continue their studies in the West.

After his death on March 12, 1999, the Royal Academy of Music acquired the *Yehudi Menuhin Archive*, one of the most valuable and comprehensive collections ever assembled by an individual musician.

❑❑❑

Zakir Hussain

(1951-2024)

Tabla Player

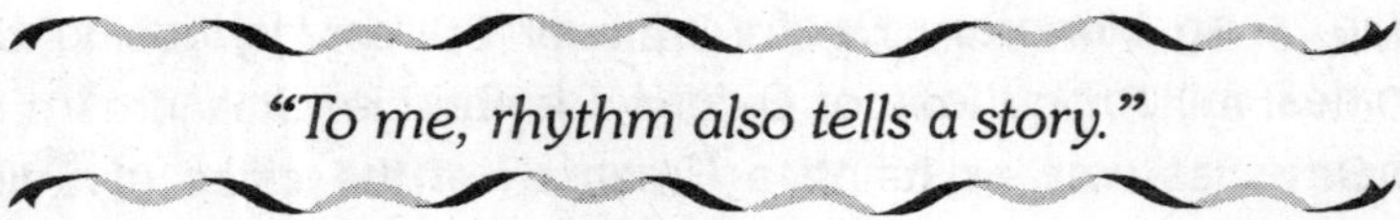

"To me, rhythm also tells a story."

Considered as the chief architect of the contemporary world of music movement, Zakir Hussain was the youngest percussionist to be ever awarded the title of Padmashree. He was a classical *tabla* virtuoso, and the most famous *tabla* player.

Ustad Zakir Hussain was born on March 9, 1951. His father, Ustad Allarakha was himself an established *tabla* player. Zakir Hussain did his schooling from St. Michael's High School in Mahim, and completed his graduation from St Xaviers, Mumbai.

A child prodigy, Zakir was touring by the age of twelve, and came to United States in 1970, embarking on an international career which includes no fewer than 150 concert dates a year.

Zakir has worked with many western and Indian artists, and has produced many works for fusion, perhaps most notably with *The Beatles*. In 1971, he recorded with an American psychedelic band called *Shanti*. He has also worked with John McLaughlin in *Shakti* in

1975, with L. Shankar in the *Diga Rhythm Band*, and with Mickey Hart on his *Rolling Thunder* album.

In 1987, his first solo release, *Making Music,* was acclaimed as "one of the most inspired East-West fusion albums ever recorded." In 1990, he was awarded the *Indo-American Award*. In April, 1991, he was presented with the *Sangeet Natak Akademi Award* by the President of India.

In 1992, *Planet Drum*, an album co-created and produced by Zakir and Mickey Hart, was awarded a *Grammy* for *Best World Music Album*, the *Downbeat Critics Poll* for *Best World Beat Album*, and the *NARM Indie Best Seller Award* for *World Music Recording*. *Planet Drum*, with Zakir as music director. In Summer'99, *Shakti* re-grouped for an international tour.

In 1992, Zakir founded live concert performances by masters of the classical music of India. The *label* presents Zakir's own world percussion ensemble, *The Rhythm Experience*, both *North and South Indian classical* recordings, *Best of Shakti*, and a *Masters of Percussion* series. He recorded and performed with artists as diverse as George Harrison, Ali Akbar Khan, Ravi Shankar, Aashish Khan, Vasant Rai, Imrat Khan, Joe Henderson, Van Morrison, Jack Bruce, Tito Puente, Pharoah Sanders, Billy Cobham, the Hong Kong Symphony and the New Orleans Symphony.

Zakir was a founding member of Bill Laswell's 'World Music Supergroup' Tabla Beat Science.

He starred in the Merchant Ivory Film, *Heat and Dust*, in which he also performed the score. He composed soundtracks for several movies, most notably *In Custody* and *The Mystic Masseur* by Ismail Merchant, and has played *tabla* on the soundtracks of Francis Coppola's *Apocalypse Now*, Bernardo Bertolucci's *Little Buddha*, and many other films.

Zakir composed, performed and acted as Indian music advisor for *Vaanaprastham*, which screened at the *Cannes Film Festival* in 1999.

Zakir Hussain was awarded the title of Padma Bhushan by the Indian government in 2002 for his contributions to the field of Indian music.

On February 8, 2009 for 51st Grammy Awards, Zakir Hussain won the Grammy in the Contemporary World Music Album category for his collaborative album "Global Drum Project" along with Mickey Hart, Sikiru Adepoju & Giovanni Hidalgo.

In 2016, Zakir Hussain was amongst many legendary Jazz, World and Fusion musicians invited by President Obama to the International Jazz Day 2016 All-Star Global Concert at the White House.

Nasreen Munni Kabir compiled 15 interview sessions (each lasting about 2 hours) from 2016-2017 into the book Zakir Hussain: A Life in Music, which was published in 2018. This book takes the reader through Zakir's life from his youth, his years of intense training, and growth to fame as a renowned musician.

On 18 January, 2017, San Francisco Jazz Center gave Hussain a Lifetime Achievement Award. In 2019, Sangeet Natak Academy, India's National Academy of Music, Dance & Drama, honoured Ustaad Zakir Hussain with the Academy Fellow award, also known as the Academy Ratna, for the year 2018.

Zakir's Discographies:

The Melody of Rhythm (2009) by Bela Fleck, Zakir Hussain, Edgar Meyer. Mysterium Tremendum (2012) by Mickey Hart Band.

In 2022, he was honoured with the Kyoto Prize in Arts and Philosophy. The following year, he received India's Padma Vibhushan award. In February 2024, Hussain made history by winning three Grammy Awards in one night, a first for an Indian musician. Tragically, he passed away in December 2024 due to idiopathic pulmonary fibrosis.

❑❑❑

Zubin Mehta

(1936)

Musician

"Although I am flexible and ready to take advice, I can't carry an umbrella of thoughts over my head that would distract me and affect my music making."

Zubin Mehta is one of the world's greatest conductors.

Zubin was born in a Parsee musical family in Bomaby (now Mumbai) in 1936. After studying medicine for two semesters, he concentrated on music and attended the Vienna Academy where he trained as a conductor under Hans Swarowsky. He won the Liverpool International Conducting Competition and was also a prize-winner at the Koussevitzky Competition in Tanglewood. His first public concert was given for the victims of political turmoil, the Communist suppression in Hungary and the Revolution of 1956.

His musical career has been a long series of 'firsts.' He was the youngest man to conduct the Vienna Philharmonic and the Berlin Philharmonic, the youngest to become music director of a major American orchestra, the first music director of the Israel Philharmonic. His debut in London, on the night of Sir Thomas Beecham's death, was the first time any person from the former dominion of India had appeared with a major British orchestra.

Zubin Mehta made his debut as an opera conductor with *Tosca* in Montreal in 1964. In 1978, he became the music director of the *New York Philharmonic* commencing a tenure lasting 13 years during which he conducted over 1,000 concerts.

In 1994, Mr. Mehta and members of the Sarajevo Symphony Orchestra and Chorus performed *Mozart's Requiem* amid the ruins of Sarajevo's National Library. It was broadcast to twenty-six countries worldwide with the aim of raising money for the UN Refugee Fund. Maestro Mehta also conducted the now legendary *Three Tenors Concerts* in Rome and Los Angeles. In the same year, he brought the *Israel Philharmonic Orchestra* to his birthplace, India.

Zubin Mehta's list of awards and honours is extensive and includes the "Nikisch-Ring" – the Vienna Philharmonic's ring of honour. He is an honorary citizen of both Florence and Tel Aviv and was made an honorary member of the *Vienna State Opera* in 1997. In 1999, Zubin was awarded the "Lifetime Achievement Peace and Tolerance Award" of the United Nations which was presented to him by Lea Rabin.

On his 60th birthday, a grand finale took place in Los Angeles. Both the Los Angeles and the Israel Philharmonic Orchestras performed together. Later in 1996, Zubin performed at the Salzburg Festival, toured Japan with both the *Florence Opera* and the *Vienna Philharmonic*, and performed in Italy, Israel, Vienna, Munich and New York.

Zubin Mehta has conducted over 1,600 performances on five continents with the *Bavarian State Orchestra*. Since 1985, he has been chief conductor of *Teatro del Maggio Musicale Fiorentino* in Florence. Since 1986, he has also acted as music adviser and chief conductor of the Maggio Musicale Fiorentino, the summer festival in Florence, Italy.

Additionally, from 1998 until 2006, Mehta was Music Director of the *Bavarian State Opera* in Munich.

Mehta conducted the Vienna New Year's Concert in the years 1990, 1995, 1998 and 2007.

Indian government honoured Mehta in 1966 with the Padma Bhushan and in 2001 with the Padma Vibhushan. In 2006 he as one of the recipients of that year's Kennedy Center Honors and in 2007, he was the recipient of the Second Annual Bridgebuilder Award at Loyola Marymount University. In 2007 he received the prestigious Dan David Prize. On October 2, 2011 he received the Echo Klassik in Berlin, for his life's work.

On 6 September 2013, President of India, Pranab Mukherjee awarded him the Tagore Award 2013 for his outstanding contribution towards cultural harmony. Mehta is a permanent resident of the United States, but retains his Indian citizenship. In 2016, Zubin Mehta has been appointed as Honorary Conductor of the Teatro San Carlo, Naples.

In September 2019, President of Slovenia Borut Pahor conferred the Golden Order of Merit on Zubin Mehta for his contribution to music and the inspiring effort to connect people and nations with this form of art.

In November 2020, the World Jewish Congress presented Mehta with their fifth Teddy Kollek Award for the Advancement of Jewish Culture.

In September 2022, he was appointed an Honorary Companion of the Order of Australia for his eminent service to the Australia-India relationship and contributions to classical music. In January 2024, Mehta received the Golden Medal of Honour from the city of Munich, recognising his extraordinary cultural achievements. He also led the Symphony Orchestra of India during their Autumn 2024 season.

❑❑❑

Some More Important Personalities

Cristiano Ronaldo

(1985)

Footballer

"Talent isn't everything. You can have it from the cradle, but it is necessary to learn the trade to be the best."

When the diagnosis of a critical heart problem was made for a 15-year-old boy and surgery was prescribed, people around pity him thinking of a little scope for him ahead in life but nature had other brighter plans. When thinking about the game of football, hugely popular in Europe, America and elsewhere and about the luminaries of the game on global landscape, Christiano Ronaldo is the name that comes to mind trailing other legends like Pele, Maradona, Messi, Michael Beckam etc.

Christiano Ronaldo, his full name Christiano Ronaldo dos Santos Aveiro was born on February 5, 1985, in Funchal, Madeira, Portugal and achieved a great milestone in the football arena on a world-scale.

His father Jone Dinis Aveiro did a humble job as an equipment manager for a local club and as he was a great fan of famous movie star Ronald Reagan who later became President by the time Ronaldo was born, Christiano's name got an addition of this name.

The football field was set for him and his passion-driven chase for football was kicked off earlier when he entered the field for clube Desportiro Nacional of Madeira and later joined hands with Sporting Clube de Portugal which was also known as Sporting Lisbon.

Clearly, after playing so many games, he finally made his debut in 2002 when he was selected for Sporting's first team. He was a formidable athlete with a height of 6 feet 1 inch and was initially a right-winger but was groomed to be a forward who led apposite attacks on the opposite goalposts.

Following a glorious season with Sporting, he got into the limelight and he soon signed a contract with English powerhouse Manchester United in 2003. He astonished everyone there and was hailed among the best forwards in the game.

In 2007-08, he won the "Golden Shoe" award as Europe's promising scorer after scoring 42 league and cup goals. United won the Champion's League title in May 2008 in which Ronaldo's efforts stood out and he was given FIFA World Player of the Year honour for his stellar performance in the season.

Later he joined hands with Spain's Real Madrid for an amount of £80 million ($131 million) as a transfer fee. In this new team as well, his high-decibel scoring performance remained unchanged and he kicked in 40 goals which is a record in La Liga history during 2010-2011. In 2014, he helped Madrid to a Champions League title by registering 52 goals in 43 games and this feat got him another Ballon d'Or award which is another name to FIFA World Player of the Year.

On the home field, in 2003, Ronaldo joined Portugal's national team and played against Kazakhstan and in the 2006 World Cup, when Portugal finished at fourth place, he was a key player. He was appointed a full-time captain of Portugal's national team in 2008. In 2012, his classy performance led Portugal to the semi-finals of the European Championship but they were eliminated by rival Spain in match which had a penalty kick decider.

In 2016, Portugal was established with the European Championship win which was the country's first international tournament title while in 2018 World Cup, he scored four goals in four games as Portugal reached the knockout round but was defeated by Uruguay.

Ronaldo gathered great limelight off the field too and his immense popularity got him high income from endorsements too in sports history and in November 2016, he got a "lifetime contract" from sportswear Nike, and he is third to receive this honour, after Michael Jordon and LeBron James.

Further, he floated his brand of products, "CR7" containing shoes, underwear and fragrances. His market reading ability got him into hot waters too in June 2007 as prosecutors filed a lawsuit accusing him of defrauding Spanish government of €14.7 million by concealing his income from image rights in Spain from 2011 to 2014. Besides, he was also accused of underestimating the income he made from sale and licensing of his image rights and other tax obligations, but Ronaldo trashed such charges.

However, in June 2018, he made accepted to a two-year prison sentence and agreed to pay €18.8 million to the Spanish government, as final case settlement.

In 2018, he joined Juventus, winning two Serie A titles and the Italian Cup. In 2021, he returned to Manchester United, becoming their top scorer before moving to Al Nassr in 2022. He surpassed 900 career goals, aiming for 1,000 before retirement. Internationally, Ronaldo reached 135 goals in 217 appearances for Portugal, maintaining his status as the top international scorer. Remarkably, he has scored in 24 consecutive years, highlighting his enduring excellence.

❑❑❑

Dwayne Douglas Johnson

(1972)

Actor and Wrestler

"Success isn't overnight. It's when every day you get a little better than the day before. It all adds up."

Dwayne Douglas Johnson, also known as The Rock, was born on May 2, 1972 in Hayward, California. He is the son of Ata Johnson and professional wrestler Rocky Johnson. His father, from Amherst, Nova Scotia, Canada, is black, and his mother is of Samoan background (her own father was Peter Fanene Maivia, also a professional wrestler). A man with an inspiring story - from being a WWE wrestler to a Hollywood superstar, he was declared by Forbes as the highest paid actor in the world in 2016. Dwayne Johnson is a Canadian-American actor, producer and a professional athlete, who first established himself as a mainstream third-generation wrestler at the World Wrestling Federation before attaining fame in the film industry.

Dwayne Johnson got married to Dany Garcia in 1997, and the two have a daughter named Simone Alexandra. After a decade-long relationship, they split amicably in 2007. Johnson then got into a romantic relationship with Lauren Hashian, the daughter of Boston drummer, Sib Hashian. They were married on August 18, 2019, in Hawaii. The couple have two daughters: Jasmine (born December 17, 2015) and Tiana (born April 17, 2018).

Johnson left WWE in 2004 and returned in 2011 as a part-time performer until 2013, making sporadic appearances until retiring in 2019. A 10-time world champion, including the promotion's first of African-American descent, he is also a two-time Intercontinental Champion, a five-time Tag Team Champion, the 2000 Royal Rumble winner, and WWE's sixth Triple Crown champion. Johnson headlined the most-bought professional wrestling pay-per-view (Wrestle- Mania XXVIII) and was featured among the most watched episodes of WWE's flagship television series (Raw and SmackDown).

Dwayne Johnson made an entry into mainstream cinema with the film *Beyond the Mat* in 1999. He made a brief appearance as The Scorpion King in *The Mummy Returns* (2001). As this movie was successful, he was cast in his first leading role as Mathayus in the 2002 release *The Scorpion King,* which revolved around Mathayus and his rise to emerge as the Scorpion King. He was touted as the biggest star to hit the big theatre screen since Arnold Schwarzenegger. In 2001, he won the Teen Choice Award for the Choice Movie Villain category for his role as The Scorpion King in *The Mummy Returns.*

Johnson proved that he is more than just an action hero, by trying his hand with comedy roles in movies like *Be Cool* (2005), *The Game Plan,* a 2007 flick alongside John Travolta and Uma Thurman, and *Tooth Fairy* (2010). For his performance in *The Game Plan,* he was nominated in the Favorite Movie Actor Award category at the 2008 Nickelodeon Kid`s Choice Awards. He returned to an action movie with 2010 *Faster* alongside Billy Bob Thornton. As he was busy with film projects between 2004 and 2009, he made only part-time appearances in the wrestling arena.

The year 2011 got millions of fans what they long wished for as Johnson and Vin Diesel appeared together in the fifth instalment of The Fast and Furious film series titled *Fast Five.* Johnson portrayed the role of a Diplomatic Security Service agent Luke Hobbs. The film got the biggest ever opening for a Fast & Furious movie and also for any Dwayne Johnson film. The actor continued his successful association with the Fast & Furious franchise by starring in its consecutive installments like Fast & Furious 6 in 2013 and Fast & Furious 7 in 2015. He then starred in the American disaster film *San Andreas* that released in 2015, revolving around a rescue-chopper pilot and his ex-wife who try to track down their daughter just after a massive earthquake. The 2016 action comedy film *Central Intelligence* featured Johnson and Kevin Hart in lead roles as two old high school friends who come together to save the world from a terrorist after one of them joins the CIA. His other release in the year was a voice role in *Moana* for the character of Maui. The following year, Johnson reprised his role as agent Luke Hobbs in *Fate of the Furious,* the eighth installment in the Fast and the Furious series, which is directed by F. Gary Gray. His 2018 release includes *Skyscraper,* an action thriller directed by Rawson Marshall Thurber. His 2019 releases include *Fighting with My Family, Fast & Furious: Hobbs & Shaw and Jumanji: The Next Level.*

In 2000, Johnson published his autobiography, titled The Rock Says..., which he co-wrote with Joe Layden. It debuted at No. 1 on The New York Times Best Seller list and remained on the list for several weeks. In 2013, Johnson hosted and produced the TNT reality competition series The Hero. In 2014, he hosted another TNT reality series entitled Wake Up Call. In 2019, Johnson started hosting an NBC competition series called The Titan Games.

His extraordinary characteristics brought Johnson so many awards and honours which includes. NCAAF National Championship (1991); Teen Choice Awards (2001); Kids Choice Awards (2013); People's Choice Awards (2016, 2017); NAACP Image Awards (2017); Hollywood Walk of Fame (2017); Golden Raspberry Awards (2018); MTV Movie & TV Awards (2019) and others.

In 2022, he starred in the DC Extended Universe film "Black Adam", portraying the titular anti-hero.

Donald Trump

(1946)

Politician

"What separates the winners from the losers is how a person reacts to each new twist of fate."

Donald John Trump was born on 14th June, 1946, in New York, U.S. and went on to become 45th President of the USA with tenure from 2017 through 2021. He was a real-estate businessman who sold his name as a brand with a license to several hotels, casinos, golf courses, resorts and even to residential areas in the city of New York as well as across the world.

From the 1980s he also pushed his name forth to numerous retail ventures which includes branded lines of clothing, cologne, food and furniture. Besides, a university is set up by his name (Trump University) which operated from 2005 to 2015 and it conducted seminars in real-estate education. In the beginning of this century, he oversaw a private conglomerate Trump Organization which consisted of 500 companies indulged in a wide array of businesses such as hotels and resorts, residential properties, merchandise and also in the entertainment field with TV programs included.

As a president, he was the third in American history (following Andrew Johnson in 1868 and Bill Clinton in 1998) to face impeachment by the U.S. House of Representatives and the only President to be impeached for a couple of times - once for the abuse of power and obstructing Congress in Ukraine scandal investigation in 2019 and then in 2021 on the charge of "incitement of insurrection" related to the storming of the United States Capitol by his supporters who went violent when a joint session of Congress was taking place to count electoral college votes from the 2020 presidential election. Trump faced defeat in the 2020 election and former vice president Joe Biden won the election by 306 electoral votes to 232. Besides, his popular vote also plummeted by seven million votes.

His father's name was Fredrick Christ Trump who got successful in real estate business while his mother's name was Mary MacLeod. He was the fourth child of a total of five and his elder sister, Maryanne Trump Barry was a U.S. district court judge from 1983 to 1999 and then served as a judge on the U.S Court of Appeals for the Third Circuit and remained there until she retired in 2011. Her elder brother Fredrick Jr became an airline pilot in the 1960s but died early at the age of 43 due to alcoholism.

In the late 1920s, Fred Trump had constructed hundreds of single-family houses and rowhouses in the Queens and Brooklyn boroughs of the city of New York and from the late 1940s, he made thousands of apartment units, mostly in Brooklyn by making use of federal loan guarantees which were in place for push forth the affordable housing construction.

As for their son, from 1959 till 64, Donald Trump attended New York Military Academy and from 1964 to 66, he went to Fordham University in the Bronx and then was enrolled in Wharton School of Finance and Commerce which was controlled by University of Pennsylvania and studied there till 1968 and he did his graduation in economics with a bachelor's degree. On completing his graduation, he joined his father's business full time and helped in the management of rental housing which was valued at somewhere between 10,000 and 22,000 units. In 1974, he was made president of a conglomeration of corporations and partnerships owned by Trump, which he later renamed as Trump Organization.

In 1990, when the U.S. economy was in recession, scores of his businesses suffered and he found it difficult to pay on his $5 billion debt, while he guaranteed $900 million. Trump had to surrender his airline and it was taken over by US Airways in 1992, under a restructuring agreement.

Under the agreement, this was also a clause that Trump would need to limit his expenses and would need to have $450,000 as a personal budget in a year. Trump has also gathered acclaim for a lot of books based on entrepreneurship highlighting his business career, such as Trump: The Art of the Deal (1987), Trump: The Art of the Comeback (1997), Why We Want You to Be Rich (2006), Trump 101: The Way to Success (2006), and Trump Never Give Up: How I Turned My Biggest Challenges into Success (2008).

In June 2015, the declaration was made about Trump being a candidate in the U.S. presidential election of 2016. He pledged to "make America great again" and he also promised to create millions of new jobs, to punish those American companies who gave jobs in other countries, to repeal legislative achievement of Obama, the Affordable Act (ACA), to replenish the U.S. coal industry, to reduce the power of lobbyists in Washington D.C. ("drain the swamp"), to pull the country out of 2015 Paris Agreement on Climate Change, to put new tariffs on countries that indulged in trade practices which were unfair to U.S., to construct a wall along the U.S. border with Mexico to halt illegal immigration from Latin America and to put a ban on immigration by Muslims.

Trump lost the 2020 presidential election to Joe Biden but refused to concede. He falsely claimed that there was widespread electoral fraud and attempted to overturn the results by pressuring government officials, mounting scores of unsuccessful legal challenges, and obstructing the presidential transition. On January 6, 2021, Trump urged his supporters to march to the Capitol, which thousands of them then attacked, resulting in multiple deaths and interrupting the electoral vote count.

Trump is the only federal officeholder in American history to have been impeached twice. After he pressured Ukraine to investigate Biden in 2019, the House of Representatives impeached him for abuse of power and obstruction of Congress in December. The Senate acquitted him of both charges in February 2020. On January 13, 2021, the House of Representatives impeached Trump a second time, for incitement of insurrection.

The Senate acquitted him on February 13, after he had already left office. Scholars and historians generally rank Trump as one of the worst presidents in American history.

He made a political comeback, winning the 2024 U.S. presidential election, defeating Kamala Harris with 312 electoral votes. His victory was driven by key wins in Georgia, Pennsylvania, and Wisconsin, along with increased support from Black and Latino voters. The Republican Party regained control of the Senate and maintained its House majority, securing a full government trifecta. His return to the White House was met with mixed reactions globally. Domestically, his administration focused on immigration reforms, economic policies, and foreign relations, setting the stage for a highly debated second term in office.

❑❑❑

Elon Musk

(1971)

Entrepreneur and Business Magnate

"When I was in college, I wanted to be involved in things that would change the world."

When a 12-year-old boy ended designing a computer game and sold it to a magazine that centred around computer technology, it was evident that nature had planned something incredible for him. When we feel respite following quick and successful funds reliably transfer through Paypal, we implicitly get thankful to Elon Musk for he cofounded this framework and went on launch SpaceX, which makes launch vehicles and spacecraft. Further in the field, he becomes CEO of Tesla, which manufactures e-vehicles.

As for his childhood, he was born in Pretoria, South Africa, to a South African father while his mother belonged to Canada. He got fascinated to computers at an early age and designed games and developed specific programs with it. He got weary of racial discrimination that prevailed in South Africa and he left the country after getting a Canadian passport while the riches and brighter prospects that dotted the United States also enticed to him dearly.

Musk enrolled in Queen's University in Kingston, Ontario and later got admission in the course of physics and economics in the University of Pennsylvania and he got a bachelor's degree. He then decided to take up physics in graduate school but within 2 days, his mind changed as he realized the abundance in potential hidden in the internet framework.

In 1995, he established the company Zipa2, which offered maps and business directories to newspapers that flourished online. In 1999, Zipa2 was sold to computer manufacturer Compaq for $307 million and he was goaded to open Xcom that was a company to offer financial services online and it later bloomed to become Paypal, which still facilitates online money transfers. In 2002, eBay purchased PayPal against the payment of $1.5 billion.

A belief strongly cherished by Mr Musk since early childhood was about enabling human existence across planets but huge costs of rockets and launching services always troubled him. The very idea enabled him to set up Space Exploration Technologies SpaceX, with which he sought to design affordable rockets.

The company started designing rockets and its first one was Falcon1 which was launched in 2006 and the Falcon9 was unveiled for the launch in 2010. The effort was to bring down the prices of rockets. Later in 2018, Falcon Heavy gathered acclaim that is made to carry 53000 kg to any orbit, which is double the weight that its competitor Delta IV Heavy, owned by Boeing Company can carry. Recently SpaceX has announced the recent addition to Falcon9 and the Falcon Heavy, i.e., Super- Heavy-Starship system which is designed to lift 100,000 kg to a low Earth orbit. Their ultimate objective is to build stations on the moon and Mars and to offer transportation services to these planets from various cities of Earth.

Further, SpaceX also made Dragon spacecraft, which takes supplies to International Space Station (ISS) and up to 7 astronauts can travel to space while inside Dragon and just last year in 2020, it carried astronauts Dong Hurley and Robert Behuken to ISS. The most amazing aspect about Mr Musk's observation is that he tends to design a reusable rocket that could cut costs associated with spaceflight. Mr Musk volunteered to be in the team of engineers who designed Falcon rockets and Dragon.

For a clean environment, the idea of electric vehicles has always allured him and this made him stand in the line of biggest financers for Tesla Motors (which got shortened to Tesla later), a company that manufactures electric cars and was founded by Martin Eberhard and Marc Tarpennin. The company unveiled its first car, the Roadster, which cover a wide distance of 394 kilometres after a single charge.

In 2010, the company raised about $262 million by initial offering. After two years, Tesla put forth the Model S Sedan which garnered acclaim from automotive critics for its design and performance. Later in 2015, with the launch of the Model X Luxury SUV, the company gathered more appreciation while the Model 3 is the cheaper vehicle as compared to others and its production took off in 2018.

Mr Musk, in 2013, put forth the idea of Hyperloop, a pneumatic tube containing a pod to carry 28 people to cover 350 miles between Los Angeles and San Francisco in just 35 minutes when it would be at speed of 760 miles per hour, which equals the speed of sound.

In October 2022, he acquired Twitter for $44 billion, rebranding it as X. In 2023, he founded xAI, an artificial intelligence startup, and constructed two mega-data centers in Memphis and Atlanta to support its development. By 2024, Musk's net worth reached $393 billion, making him the world's richest person. In January 2025, he was appointed to lead the Department of Government Efficiency (DOGE) under President Donald Trump, aiming to streamline federal operations.

Hillary Clinton

(1947)

Politician, Diplomat, Lawyer and Writer

"Women are the largest untapped reservoir of talent in the world."

Hillary Clinton, in full Hillary Rodham Clinton, was born on October 26, 1947, in Chicago, Illinois, U.S. She is a popular name in American mainstream polity and society. She is a lawyer and a politician who remained as a U.S. senator (from 2001 till 09) and occupied the seat of Secretary of State (2009-13) when Barack Obama was the president. When her husband (Bill Clinton) was the 42nd president of the United States, she served as first lady (1993-2001). Then, in 2016, she was the Democratic Party's nominee for president and this was the first time that a woman aspired to be the president of a major party in the United States.

During the peace that prevailed soon after World War II, she was born and was the eldest child of Hugh and Dorothy Rodham. She spent her childhood in a Chicago suburb named Park Ridge, Illinois and her father was a textile dealer and her family basked under a considerable income drawn from the business. Her parents stressed hard work and Hillary was sent to a prestigious school which resulted in her academic excellence.

While in school, she led a zestful life and developed a leaning towards Republican Party ideology gradually and even campaigned for Barry Goldwater who was a Republican presidential candidate in 1964. She managed the chair for the local chapter of the Young Republicans. Later in life, some events, such as the assassinations of Malcolm X, Robert F Kennedy and Martin Luther King Jr, forced her to part ways with the Republican stream and she turned towards the Democratic Party. She volunteered in the presidential campaign of antiwar candidate Eugene McCarthy.

Later in 1969, she got enrolment in Yale Law School where she got influenced by Marian Wright Edelma, who was a Yale alumna and was a lawyer and an advocate for children's rights. Hillary developed strong bonding with family law and issues that victimized children.

At Yale, Hillary met Bill Clinton but they opted for different pathways after completing graduation in 1973. Where he came back to his native state Arkansas but she continued to work with Edelman in Massachusetts raising money for the Children's Defense Fund. In 1974, she took part in the Watergate inquiry which would have resulted in the possible impeachment of President Richard M Nixon. At the end of her assignment which witnessed Nixon's resignation in August 1974, she decided to move to Arkansas and became a lecturer at the School of Law, under the University of Arkansas. She married Bill Clinton on October 11, 1975, and then joined a prestigious Rose Law Firm in Little Rock, Arkansas and she became the partner of this firm later.

Later is 1978, Bill was elected governor of Arkansas and their daughter (only child) Chelsea Victoria was born in 1980.

During Bill's tenure as governor, Hillary's work was mainly focused on issues concerning children as well as those facing grave problems in life, but she also managed successful law practice.

She was obliged to be on the boards of numerous high-end corporations and featured in the nation's 100 most influential lawyers list twice from 1988 to 1991 by the National Law Journal. She also chaired the Arkansas Education Standards Committee and laid the foundation of the Arkansas Advocates for Children and Families. In 1983, she bagged the Arkansas Woman of The Year title and also got the recognition of Young Mother of the Year in 1984.

When Bill ran for president in 1992, Hillary was actively involved in the campaign, from greeting voters to addressing a huge public gathering and also advised her husband on several critical issues. Her name became a household word following a popular TV news program "60 Minutes" where she appeared with Bill.

In December 2008, Obama picked up Clinton as her secretary of state and she got easy approval by the Senate in January 2009. In the capacity of secretary of state, her tenure was widely acclaimed for refining foreign relations with other countries. She quit her post in 2013 and John Kerry came in her place. In 2015, reports made rounds that she used a private email address and a secret server when she was secretary of state and this raised security concerns and also put the government's transparency in question, compelling the FBI to investigate the matter.

Clinton served as Chancellor of Queen's University Belfast starting in 2020 and in 2023, she joined Columbia University as a professor and fellow in global affairs. In 2024, she co-produced the Broadway musical "Suffs", highlighting the women's suffrage movement. In January 2025, President Joe Biden awarded her the Presidential Medal of Freedom for her service.

Jack Ma

(1964)

Business Magnate, Investor and Philanthropist

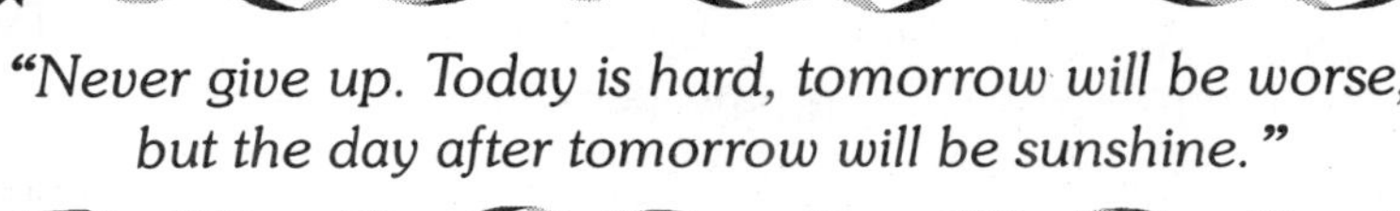

"Never give up. Today is hard, tomorrow will be worse, but the day after tomorrow will be sunshine."

When the brand Alibaba.com stuns us, it's equally stunning to note that the brain behind it, Jack Ma is from China, the country that calls for equality but Jack's unequalled talent and determination have left others far behind and he is a world-famous entrepreneur. He headed Alibaba Group which managed numerous websites from China that are widely popular, such as business-to-business marketplace Alibaba.com and the shopping site Taobao.com.

Born on September 10, 1964, in Hangzhou, Zhejiang province of China as Ma Yun, he developed a great interest in the English language and earned a good sum in teenage as a guide for foreign tourists to Hangzhou. He appeared for the Hangzhou Teachers College but was not successful in the entrance exam as mathematics was his weak area. However, he got success in the third try in 1984 and 1988, he got a bachelor's degree in English. The next five years he spent in teaching English at the Hangzhou Institute of Electronics and Engineering which is now called Hangzhou Dianzi University. In 1994, he laid the foundation of his company the Haibo Translation Agency, which served with English translations and interpretation.

That was in 1995 when he toured the United States while his expenses were covered by Hangzhou city government, that his eyes widened to see promising Internet framework and how his country managed without any website. On his return, he set up China Pages, which served Chinese businesses by creating a website and it became the first internet company in China. After two years, he abandoned the company as he faced a tough time from communications company Hangzhou Telecom and it had floated a rival company "Chinesepage".

Now during the period from 1998 to 1999, Ma headed an internet company in Beijing that was supported by the Ministry of Foreign Trade and Economic Cooperation. He soon realized that if he remained with the government, he would not be able to utilize the opportunities that the internet was pushing forth. Consequently, he asked his crew to return to Hangzhou with him and he set up Alibaba Group which started a website that made deals between small businesses easy and swift.

He was pretty certain about the growth potential hidden in the Internet market meant for small-business-to-small-business rather than the Internet market serving to business-to-consumer. Now to become a certified and authentic seller on Alibaba.com, a membership fee was charged from small businesses and for businesses who wished to sell beyond China, the greater amount of fee was charged from them. To garner trust in online sales, Alipay was created in 2003 to become a third party in transactions. As was expected, Alibaba registered a massive growth in a short time and in 2005, Yahoo!!, a prominent internet portal from America which bought its 40% stake and in 2007, Alibaba.com was able to raise $1.7 billion dollars through its IPO (initial public offering) in Hong Kong.

In 2003, Mr. Jack set up a new company, Taobao which in Chinese means searching for treasure and was the consumer-to-consumer online marketplace. During that time, eBay, an American company enjoyed an 80% market share, which was associated with Chinese company EachNet but Jack considered a weak point when users were charged a fee against every transaction. As such, no charging fee was taken by Taobao and earned money through online advertising and by serving additionally to users. As a result, Taobao gained ground and occupied 67% of the market share and eBay had to grant majority ownership for its operations in China to TOM group, which was a media company for the Chinese language and a subsidiary was created in form of TOM EachNet. In 2011, a declaration was made from Mr. Jack about the split of Taobao and three companies were created: Taobao Marketplace, Taobao Mall and eTao, a search engine encouraging shopping.

At Taobao Marketplace, it facilitated in buying and selling of goods, while Taobao Mall is a shopping portal online. By the time it was 2014, New York Stock Exchange got listed with the Alibaba Group IPO and it raised $21.8 billion. Such is considered to be the largest IPO in United States and got the company its market value of $168 billion, which is a record in IPO history that any internet company could make.

Mr. Jack managed the creation of the Ant Group, which was the parent group of Alipay and other financial services. In 2020, Ant was prepared for an IPO but it was put on hold, as the Chinese government emphasized upon its restructuring.

❑❑❑

Justin Bieber

(1994)

Pop Singer

"I'm not a fighter by nature, but, if I believe in something, I stand up for it"

Justin Drew Bieber, the pop singer with global fame and flamboyance, was born on March 1, 1994, in London, Ontario, Canada. He is a youth icon and is worshipped by millions around the world. He records pop songs that widely appeal to the masses while his fresh-face appearance mesmerizes all and sundry.

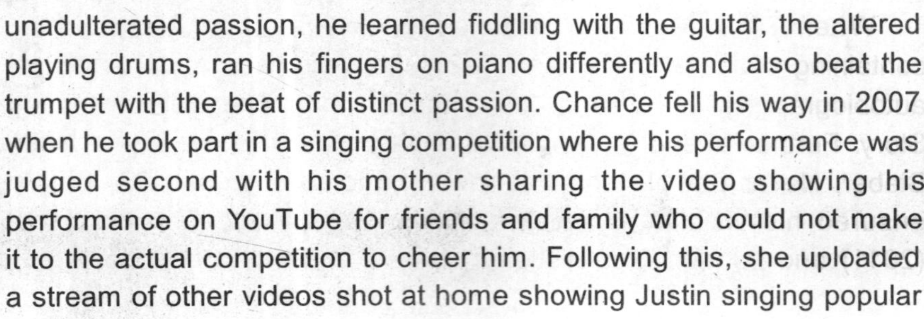

During childhood, a strong bond he felt towards musical instruments and with unadulterated passion, he learned fiddling with the guitar, the altered playing drums, ran his fingers on piano differently and also beat the trumpet with the beat of distinct passion. Chance fell his way in 2007 when he took part in a singing competition where his performance was judged second with his mother sharing the video showing his performance on YouTube for friends and family who could not make it to the actual competition to cheer him. Following this, she uploaded a stream of other videos shot at home showing Justin singing popular rhythm-and-blues (R&B) songs while she took to the acoustic guitar which got them massive recognition beyond the limited audience, they first targeted. Luck turned out for Justice when Scott Braun (music promoter and talent agent) saw Justin's videos when latter was just 13 years old and invited him to record demos at their Atlanta studio. At the spot, Justin confronted R&B singer Usher and there was organized an unofficial audition with him. Now, judging his passion for vocal talent and real zeal, Usher facilitated a recording contract with Justin in the closing months of 2008.

In May following year, Bieber pulled up the curtain from his first puppy-love song titled "One Time" and after six months he presented the seven-track EP My World, which was originally a pop that was heavily influenced by R&B. Gradually, his audience base widened dramatically as appreciation poured in from every quarter of society and he became a heartthrob among young girls while over a million copies of his recordings were sold. He released his full-length album "My World 2.0" in 2010 which went on to feature in Billboard album chart.

In the album, the song "Baby" has garnered immense acclaim wherein rapper Ludacris has been in a guest appearance and this song went on to take place in the top 5 of Billboard's singles chart while other songs ended by getting a place in the top 40. On YouTube, the official video of Baby amassed more than 500 million views. Besides, social media is said to have played a major role in boosting his popularity such as Twitter and then he has appeared frequently in numerous TV shows as well.

When 2010 set in, his album "My World Acoustic" went public containing a different version of his songs while he also published an autobiographical book titled Justin Bieber: First Step 2 Forever: My Story. Further ahead, a film documentary was also made as Justin Bieber: Never Say Never, replete with concert footage in 3D. Bieber ensured his visibility in albums "Never Say Never: The Remixes" (2011) and "Under The Mistletoe" based upon a Christman theme which went on to become a popular favourite and hit the No. 1 spot in the United States and Canada. In the following year, he worked hard on "Belief" (2012), followed by "Believe Acoustic" in 2013 and also introduced a more cultivated beat sound with the hit "Boyfriend" which smacked of suave R&B of Justin Timberlake.

As Justin grew more mature and signs of manliness became prominent on his face, reports started to make rounds about his romantic relationship with Selena Gomez while some other names also floated in the public domain. Then, his altercations with law enforcement on certain occasions also turned the media spotlight on him. In 2015, he released the album "Purpose" which got him admiration from a vast audience comprising even adults. In the same year, he contributed vocals to Jack U's electro-pop hit "Where Are U Now" which won him Grammy Award. There was a series of collaborations with other musicians which ended in the creation of numerous popular songs. In 2018, he married model Hailey Baldwin and such a relationship goaded his studio album "Changes" released in the year 2020.

In January 2023, he sold his music catalog rights up to 2021 for over $200 million. In August 2024, Justin and his wife, Hailey Bieber, welcomed their first child, Jack Blues. By February 2025, concerns arose regarding Justin's well-being after displaying unusual behaviour at Hailey's skincare event, leading to public speculation about his health.

Jennifer Lynn Lopez

(1969)

Singer, Actress and Dancer

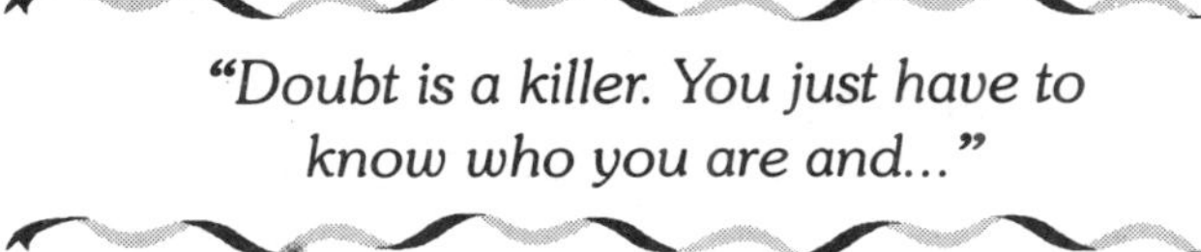

"Doubt is a killer. You just have to know who you are and..."

Jennifer Lynn Lopez is an American actress, singer, dancer, producer and fashion designer. She became the first Latina to get $1 million for a movie role. She is also an accomplished musician. She is one of the most successful ladies in Hollywood. Her music career has also been on the top level.

Jennifer Lynn Lopez was born on July 24, 1969 in The Bronx, New York City, New York to Lupe López & David López. The two were brought to the continental United States during their childhoods and, eventually, met while living in New York City.

Lopez's first feature film was the critically acclaimed Mi Familia, or My Family, in 1995. She also appeared in Money Train (1995), opposite Wesley Snipes and Woody Harrelson, and in Jack (1996), directed by Francis Ford Coppola and starring Robin Williams.

Lopez's first big break came in 1997 when she was chosen to play the title role in Selena, a biopic of the Tejano pop singer Selena Quintillana-Perez, who was killed by a fan in 1995. Lopez earned widespread praise for her performance, including a Golden Globe nomination. Lopez's first professional job came in 1989 when she spent five months touring Europe with the musical revue show Golden Musicals of Broadway.

Lopez's most high-profile job as a professional dancer was as a Fly Girl on the sketch comedy television series In Living Color, which starred comedians. She appeared in some other television series, before debuting in Hollywood with the film 'My Family' in 1995. The film enjoyed reasonable commercial and critical success. Lopez starred opposite George Clooney in the crime caper Out of Sight (1998). In 1999, she made her debut in music with the album, On the 6, from which the song "If You Had My Love" became a huge success. Her second big hit came in 2000 with the single "Waiting for Tonight" and the same year, she starred in two films The Cell and Enough.

In 2007, she starred with her husband, Marc Anthony, in the biographical film El Cantante which was a huge critical success.

She returned as judge on the reality show American Idol for its thirteenth season. In 2014, released her eighth studio album, A.K.A.

In 2019, she was seen in the film Hustlers. Her performance in the movie was highly appreciated and she was nominated for Best Supporting Actress at the Golden Globe Awards, Screen Actors Guild Awards, Critics' Choice Movie Awards and Independent Spirit Awards.

In 2020, she co-headlined the Super Bowl LIV halftime show alongside Shakira. She also released two songs "Pa' Ti" and Lonely" in collaboration with Colombian singer Maluma.

In January 2021, Lopez launched her skincare line, JLo Beauty. Despite all the popularity and success, Lopez had a bad experience in romance. She married and then split for several times. She first married to dancer Ojani Noa on February 22, 1997 but divorced him on January 1, 1998; and in 1999 she dated musician P. Diddy, but both split in 2001. After that she met Cris Judd, a dancer and choreographer, while filming the music video for her single "Love Don't Cost a Thing".

They married on September 29, 2001 in a small ceremony with about 170 guests at a home in a Los Angeles suburb, but she formally split from Judd on January 26, 2003. In 2004, Lopez secretly married Anthony but they finalized their divorce in 2014. She had an on-off relationship with her former backup dancer Casper Smart from October 2011 to August 2016. She dated New York Yankees baseball player Alex Rodriguez from February 2017 to early 2021. They became engaged in March 2019 but postponed their wedding twice due to the pandemic.

In 2010, Lopez was honored by the World Music Awards with the Legend Award for her contribution to the arts. In 2014, she became the first female recipient of the Billboard Icon Award. Billboard magazine ranked her as the ninth greatest dance club artist of all time in 2016. In 2017, she was awarded the Telemundo Star Award. In 2018, Lopez received the Michael Jackson Video Vanguard Award at the 2018 MTV Video Music Awards.

In 2022, she married Ben Affleck, but they divorced in 2025. Professionally, she released the album "This Is Me... Now" in 2023 and starred in the film "Kiss of the Spider Woman", which premiered at the 2025 Sundance Film Festival to standing ovations. Additionally, Lopez was honoured with the Legend & Groundbreaker Award at the 2025 Palm Springs International Film Festival.

❑❑❑

Kader Khan

(1937-2018)

Actor

"I ran alone in the race of my life and stood second. No man should be number one because the place is the least at the height."

Born in Kabul on 22 October, 1937, his family migrated to Mumbai and could manage a dwelling in slums only, owing to their precarious financial condition. Besides, our country too, was passing through tough times, during 40s. Family to remain without food for days as his father didn't have any proper job or source of living.

Being so much driven by circumstances, young Kader once suspended the idea of attending school on regular basis, but his Mother insisted that he should find passion in studies and inculcated that knowledge is the vaccine to eliminate poverty and hunger. Such words uttered by his Mom resonated so deeply in his heart and mind that he became a die-hard seeker of education and went along the academic path with incredible zeal and diligence only to bag the degree of graduate and then post graduate too, in civil engineering.

While in college, he took to writing and put down several thousand words, while engrossed in deep imagination and such words were so arranged in a proper order comprising characters and situations that glimpses of interesting stories could be found in them. He started writing dramas for college get together and later, one of his plays, "The Local Train" won the All India Best Play Award, alongside best writer, best director and best actor award too and a cash prize of ₹ 1500 too, which was too much for him at that time in life.

This event marked a turning point in his career as a writer, thereby paving way for Kader Khan to move ahead towards screen and great fame in years to come. This was also because that the judges of the play were a handful of luminaries of Indian cinema, such as Mrs. Kamini Kaushal, famous actress, Mr. Ramesh Behel of Rose Movies, eminent filmmaker Mr. Rajinder Singh Bedi and Mr. Narinder Bedi. In those days, Mr. Narinder Bedi was working on a film "Jawani Diwani" that starred Randhir Kapoor, Jaya Bhadhuri and R.D. Burman and Kader Khan was asked to write dialogues for it, again for the amount of ₹ 1500.

This movie was widely liked by masses and then, a word about Kader Khan spread across the spectrum of Indian cinema that a prolific writer has emerged who writes creatively and whose dialogues bear essence and a type of hidden message and guidance for the society. As a result, scores of other movies were lined up before him, awaiting the stroke of brightness to be ushered from his mind through his pen.

There was a special reason as to why he emerged so successful as a dialogue writer, as he has always said in interviews, that every time he would sit to write, that was the common man, his circumstances filled with too many restraints and social compulsions, and the injustice he bears because of this, combinely keep running in Kader Saheb's mind. In fact, it won't be wrong to claim that his pen used to convey the voice of poor and common Indians and how they have been exploited by a nexus of criminals and police and those in power as well as with money power.

Other than a gifted writer, showcasing reality of life, he was also the acting genius and has acted in over 300 Hindi movies thereby adding a distinct aspect in every film through his powerful performance, utter dialogue delivery and bodacious screen presence. His tryst with bollywood started with the movie *Daag,* that had superstar of that time Rajesh Khanna in lead role while Kader's role was of supporting actor of an advocate. Then, in many other movies such as *Dil Diwana, Mukaddar Ka Sikandar* and *Mr. Natwarlal,* he performed brief roles but such movies had dialogues and screenplay being contributed by him. He also worked in movies: *Masterji, Ghar Sansar, Sherni, Khoon Bhari Maang, Vardi, Sone Pe Suhaga, Dharam Adhikari* and so many other in the row.

Later, as the year 1988 turned on, scripts were written to adjust him in pivotal roles and in key situations in plots, like in the movies: *Jaisi Karni Waisi Bharni, Biwi Ho To Aisi, Ghar Ho To Aisa* and so forth, where there used to be a clear message and a lesson to middle class audience in India and around the world, that family bonding is more important and that greed and cunningness only brings downlfall.

Later, his mettle was also tested in comedy genre and in light hearted funny roles and Almighty's gift of performing art glowed much brighter in such categories too, like in *Aaj Ka Daur, Himmatwala,* etc, that were followed by other flicks with his hit comedy roles such as *Kishan Kanhayya, Sikka,* ....and this trend continued till 90s and later in the next century as well. He passed away in 2018.

He was honored with so many awards including Sahitya Shiromany Award (2013) for his work and contributions to Hindi Film Industry and Cinema. He won Filmfare Awards thrice (in 1982 for *Meri Awaaz Suno,* in 1991 for *Baap Numbri Beta Dus Numbri* and in 1993 for *Angaar)*. He was posthumously awarded Padma Shri on January 26, 2019.

❑❑❑

Kylie Jenner

(1997)

Socialite, Model, and Businesswoman

"I always try to do my best to inspire people to be good and do the right thing."

Kylie Jenner was born in 1997 in California. Jenner grew up in the spotlight among her famous siblings in the reality series, Keeping Up With The Kardashians. She's harnessed her family's fame to launch her own business ventures including a successful cosmetics line, Kylie Cosmetics, and earned millions from sales of her signature Kylie Lip Kit. Additionally, she's amassed a mega social media following and in 2015 was named one of Time magazine's Most Influential Teens.

According to Forbes, in 2019, Jenner's net worth was estimated at US $1 billion, making her, at age 21, the world's youngest self-made billionaire as of March 2019, though the notion of Jenner being self-made is a subject of controversy, owing to her privileged background. In May 2020, however, Forbes released a statement accusing Jenner of forging tax documents so she would appear as a billionaire. The publication also accused her of fabricating revenue figures for Kylie Cosmetics.

At the early age of 10, Kylie started her career in 2007 with the TV reality show KUWTK (Keeping Up With The Kardashians) in which shows the personal and professional history of the family. After this series, Kylie appeared in numerous shows like Kourtney and Kim Take Miami, Kourtney and Khloé Take The Hamptons, Kourtney and Kim Take New York, and Khloé & Lamar as a multiple guest appearance.

In 2015, Kylie admitted about getting a Lip Augmentation where she enhanced her lip from lip fillers which gained her publicity. Jenner also stated after this that "I'm not here to try & encourage people/ young girls to look like me or to think this is the way they should look." Later in the same year, Kylie announced that she Is going to launch her first lipstick line under the name of "Kylie Lip Kit". In February 2016, Jenner Cosmetic company was renamed "Kylie Cosmetics".

Further in May Jenner made her musical debut rapping in the song "Beautiful Day" with her best friend of that time Jordyn Wood. Again next month she starred in another song "Come and See Me" which was PartyNextDoor's music video.

After the success of "Kylie Cosmetic" Jenner placed 59th position on the Forbes Celebrity 100 in the year 2017 and was among the list of 100 highest-paid celebrities. Kylie Cosmetics launched another cosmetic line called "Kris Cosmetic" in collaboration with Kris Jenner, Kylie's mother on mothers day. Also, Kylie collaborated with her half-sister Kim Kardashian and launched KKW x Kylie Cosmetic. Later in the same month, she launched the Kylie Cosmetic mobile app.

Kim Kardashian's KKW Beauty teamed up with Kylie to launch a new fragrance which became Kylie's first introduction into fragrance and was launched in April 2019. After this in May 2019, Jenner founded her own Skincare brand called 'Kylie skin'.

In June 2019, Kylie Cosmetic launched their third collaboration with Kylie's half-sister Khloé Kardashian called Kylie Cosmetic x Koko Kollection. Kylie has done many tv shows and debuted with Keeping

Up With the Kardashians. Since then she has given many shows. Based on Kylie Jenner's life show "Life of Kylie" made in 2017. She has also done many cameo roles and also was part of a cameo in the 2020 series Justin Bieber: Seasons.

Kylie Jenner has also some music videos in her bags with some of the famous stars in Hollywood. She has done music like "Stimulated, Dope'd Up, and Feel Me" with her ex-boyfriend Tyga. After that, Kylie made music with Travis Scott in the year 2018 named "Stop Trying To Be God".

Kylie did a cameo in Arian Grande and Justin Bieber's song named "Stuck With U", she also did a cameo in Cardi B and Megan Thee Stallion's "Wap" music video.

In April 2017, Jenner was first seen with Travis Scott at Coachella. On February 1, 2018, she gave birth to their daughter, Stormi Webster. Jenner appeared in the music video for "Stop Trying to Be God", from Scott's third studio album Astroworld. They broke up in September 2019, but quarantined together during the COVID-19 pandemic for the sake of their daughter.

Kylie Jenner has won many popular awards in her career, she has won the Teen Choice Awards for Choice TV Reality Star Female in the year 2013, the Capricho Awards and WWD Beauty Inc. Awards (2016), the Capricho Awards for International Fashionista and WWD Beauty Inc. Awards for Newsmaker of the Year (2017), the Streamy Awards for Best Collaboration (2019) and the Fragrance Foundation Awards for Fragrance of the Year Popular in the year 2020. Along with these popular awards she has been nominated for several other popular awards throughout her career.

In 2020, she sold a majority stake in Kylie Cosmetics to Coty Inc. In 2021, she launched Kylie Swim and Kylie Baby. By 2024, she introduced her fashion brand Khy and a canned cocktail line called Sprinter. On the personal front, Jenner welcomed her second child in 2022 and began a relationship with actor Timothée Chalamet in 2023.

❑❑❑

Robert Downey Jr.

(1965)

Actor and Producer

"Maybe the goal really should be a life that values honor, duty, good work, friends and family."

Robert Downey Jr. is an American actor known for roles in a wide variety of films, including *Iron Man, The Avengers, Sherlock Holmes* and *Chaplin.* Downey was born on April 4, 1965 in Manhattan, New York, the son of writer, director and filmographer Robert Downey Sr. and actress Elsie Downey.

He married with actress and singer Deborah Falconer on May 29, 1992, after a 42-day courtship. Their son, Indio Falconer Downey, was born in September 1993. Downey and Falconer finalized their divorce on April 26, 2004.

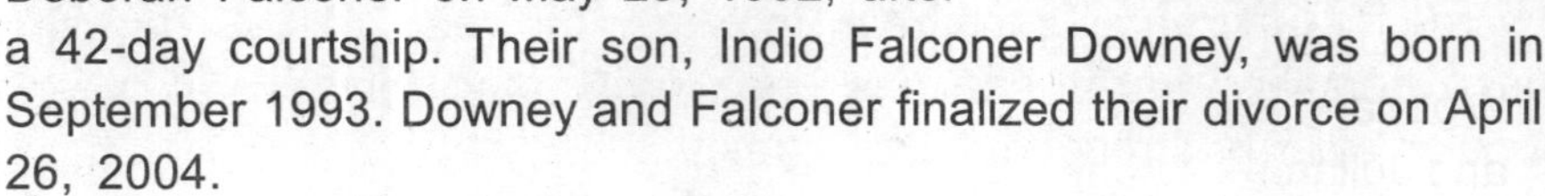

In 2003, Downey met producer Susan Levin, an Executive Vice President of Production at Joel Silver's film company, Silver Pictures on the set of Gothika. Though Susan twice turned down his amorous advances, she and Downey did quietly strike up a romance during production. Despite Susan's worries that the romance would not last after the completion of shooting because "he's an actor; I have a real job", the couple's relationship continued after production wrapped on

Gothika, and Downey proposed to Susan on the night before her thirtieth birthday. In August 2005, the couple were married, in a Jewish ceremony, at Amagansett, New York.

His career has been characterized by critical and popular success in his youth, followed by a period of substance abuse and legal troubles, before a resurgence of commercial success later in his career. In 2008, Downey was named by Time magazine among the 100 most influential people in the world, and from 2013 to 2015, he was listed by Forbes as Hollywood's highest-paid actor.

Downey began building upon theater roles, including in the short-lived off-Broadway musical American Passion at the Joyce Theater in 1983, produced by Norman Lear. In 1985, he was part of the new, younger cast hired for Saturday Night Live. That same year, he played James Spader's character's sidekick in Tuff Turf and then a bully in John Hughes's Weird Science. He was considered for the role of Duckie in John Hughes's film Pretty in Pink (1986), but his first lead role was with Molly Ringwald in The Pick-up Artist (1987). In 1987, Downey played Julian Wells, in the film version of the Bret Easton Ellis novel Less Than Zero. His performance in Zero drove Downey into films with bigger budgets and names, such as Chances Are (1989) with Cybill Shepherd and Ryan O'Neal, Air America (1990) with Mel Gibson, and Soapdish (1991) with Sally Field, Kevin Kline, and Whoopi Goldberg.

In 1993, he appeared in the films Heart and Souls with Alfre Woodard and Kyra Sedgwick and Short Cuts with Matthew Modine and Julianne Moore, along with a documentary that he wrote about the 1992 presidential campaigns titled The Last Party (1993). He starred in the 1994 films, Only You with Marisa Tomei, and Natural Born Killers with Woody Harrelson. Steady work followed, but much of it went unnoticed until Downey's appearance in 1992 as the title character in Richard Attenborough's Chaplin biopic, which earned him numerous plaudits and an Academy Award nomination for best actor.

By this time, Downey had developed a substance-abuse problem, and, his frequent skirmishes with the law and his public struggle with drug addiction often overshadowed his on-screen successes. He reached a low point in 1999, when he was sentenced to three years in prison for having violated parole from an earlier arrest.

In 2000, after being granted an early release, Downey was cast in a recurring role on the television series Ally McBeal, and he won a Golden Globe Award for his work on the show. In 2003 Downey thrust himself into his work, appearing in 13 feature films over the next five years, including The Singing Detective (2003), Good Night, and Good Luck. (2005), A Scanner Darkly (2006), and Zodiac (2007).

In 2008 Downey won acclaim for his roles in two summer blockbusters—*Iron Man* and the satiric comedy Tropic Thunder. For the latter role Downey received an Academy Award nomination for best supporting actor.

Having emerged, somewhat surprisingly, as one of Hollywood's most-bankable stars, Downey was cast as an anxious father-to-be in the road-trip comedy Due Date (2010).

He took a supporting role in Iron Man director Jon Favreau's pet project, Chef (2014), before playing a lawyer defending his father (Robert Duvall), who is accused of vehicular homicide, in The Judge (2014). He reprised the role of Tony Stark in the Iron Man sequels (2010 and 2013), The Avengers (2012) and its sequels (2015, 2018, and 2019), Captain America: Civil War (2016), and Spider-Man: Homecoming (2017). In 2020 Downey starred in the family comedy Dolittle, which was based on the character created by Hugh Lofting.

In 2023, he portrayed Lewis Strauss in "Oppenheimer", earning an Academy Award for Best Supporting Actor. In 2024, he was cast as Doctor Doom in the upcoming Marvel films "Avengers: Doomsday" and "Avengers: Secret Wars", marking his return to the Marvel Cinematic Universe. Additionally, Downey Jr. made his Broadway debut in "McNeal" and hosted the series "Downey's Dream Cars".

❑❑❑

Raja Ram Mohan Roy

(1772–1833)

Indian Reformer

"To abuse and insult, is inconsistent with reason and justice"

After hundreds of years of women oppression and social backwardness nature turned kind on them and blessed the household of Ramakanta Roy with a son. Ramakanta was a wealthy brahmin and orthodox person who performed his religious duties strictly. At the age of 14, he wanted to become a monk, but his mother Tarini Devi stood in vehement opposition and he dropped the thought.

Ram Mohan Roy was born on May 22, 1772, in Radhanagar village, Hoogli, Bengal, India and left this world on September 27, 1833, in Bristol, Gloucestershire, England. He was a prominent religious, social and educational reformer in India and put challenges before the traditional Hindu culture and also underlined ways leading to progress for Indian society under British rule. He is commonly referred to as the "Father of Modern India".

His was a prosperous Brahman family in Bengal when it was ruled by the British. He is said to have developed liberal views about religion at an early age. At a young age, he undertook wide travels outside Bengal and also gained mastery over several languages, such as Sanskrit, Persian, Arabic and English other than Bengali and Hindi.

He relied upon moneylending and also managed his limited estates and traded in the bonds held by the British East India Company. In 1805, through his employment with John Digby, who was a lower company official, he came in contact with western culture and literature. In the following decade, he served British East India Company as Digby's assistant.

Roy carried out a deep study in religion and in 1803, he denounced what he saw as superstition prevailed in Indian society and its religious divisions. As an antidote to such issues, he supported monotheistic Hinduism where there should be a reason to guide towards the "Absolute Originator who is the first principle of all religions."

In 1815, he founded Atmiya-Sabha, a Friendly Society to propagate the doctrines of monotheistic Hinduism but such effort was short-lived. He showed interest in Christianity and also picked up Hebrew and Greek languages to be comfortable with Old and New Testaments. In 1820, he took excerpts from four Gospels and published Christ's ethical teachings with the title "Precepts Of Jesus", the Guide to Peace and Happiness.

In 1823, the Britishers muzzled Calcutta (Kolkata) press and as Roy founded a couple of India's earliest weekly newspapers, he rose in protest and emphasized freedom of speech and religion as natural and basic rights. This protest was a turning point in his life, as this was through his newspapers, treatises and books that he always registered his strong disapproval for the widespread superstition that prevailed in Indian society and the caste system with strong attacks on sati custom too, where widows were supposed to be burned in the burning pyre of their husbands. Now, this was through his writing that

British East India Governing Council was encouraged to take strong action on the issue and Sati practice was abolished in 1829.

In 1822 Roy established the Anglo-Hindu School and Vedanta College was set up just four years later intending to teach Hindu monotheistic doctrines. In 1823, the Bengal government advised more traditional Sanskrit colleges but Roy disliked the idea thinking that such classical Indian literature would be insufficient for youth to be prepared for modern life. He favoured modern studies with an updated curriculum from the west. Besides, he also opposed the obsolete British legal and revenue administration in India.

In the year 1828, he laid the foundation of Brahmo Samaj (Society of Brahma) which was a Hindu reformist sect that was inclusive of Unitarian and Christian elements representing liberal values in its psychology. Needless to state but the Brahmo Samaj played a dominant role in Indian society and went on to become a prime Hindu movement for reforms, in the coming decades of the 19th century.

In 1829, Roy went to England and represented the titular King of Delhi unofficially. The king bestowed upon him the title "Raja" but the British did not recognize it. Roy received a warm welcome in England, Unitarians were especially happy to see him there and King William IV also was very pleased. Roy passed away in Bristol in 1833, while he was taken care of by Unitarian friends and his funeral took place.

Roy had a broader social vision alongside modernity in thought and this makes him a valuable figure in Indian history. He put relentless efforts for social reforms and to counter western assault on Indian culture, he also revived interest in the Vedanta School in terms of ethical principles. He published many textbooks and treatises by which he sought to popularize the Bengali language. Besides, he also applied the fundamental social and political ideas of the French and American revolutions to the Indian socio-political setup.

❑❑❑

Virat Kohli

(1988)

Cricketer

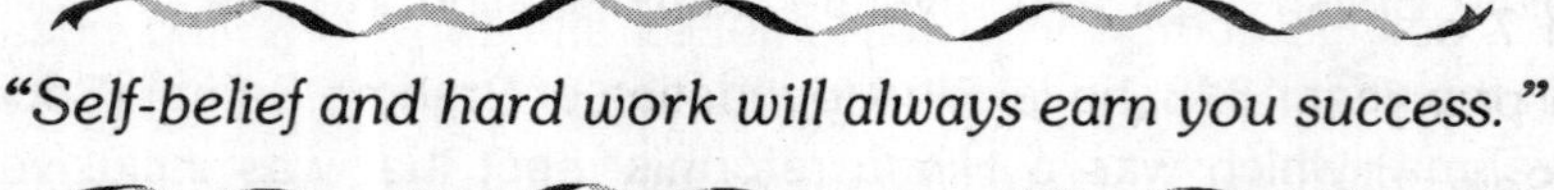

"Self-belief and hard work will always earn you success."

That was in early 2008 that a spirited teenager attracted everyone's attention when India took the winning run in the Under-19 World Cup at Kuala Lampur resulting in his quick rise to fame. As a result, he rose through the ladder of success, one with gelled hair but with a furious attitude (both on the field as well as off the field).

In August 2008, he became a part of the senior team (matured Men in Blue) in Sri Lanka and as no reliable batsman was there to shoulder opening responsibility, a chance fell by Virat's way. Grabbing the occasion, he put up a brilliant performance and levered India's ODI series win. But still, the tremendous pair of Tendulkar and Sehwag eclipsed his luck.

Aged 20 and breathing his cricketing passion, he kept the momentum of great performance going for Delhi by leading from the front and his style and technique truly reflected his class. Kohli was sent to Australia in 2009, to participate in the Emerging Players tournament where his performance stained with exuberance batted to mirror his stature. Interestingly, he added another dimension to the game which was of "big-match temperament" as he laced a hundred with effortless fluency in the final against South Africa and thus registered a clinical victory.

The wunderkind managed to lay hands upon man-of-the-match champagne as he sealed the tournament in style by putting 398 runs from 7 outings comprising two centuries and two fifties and became face prominent enough in selectors' minds.

Selectors were not left with any option but to let Kohli in the Indian squad and he also repaid their beliefs by becoming a literal run machine and in 2009 he scored his maiden ODI century when Sri Lanka posted a big score on the board and India chased it down impressively.

Further, in the 2011 World Cup final, when India suffered early blows in form of wickets, he built India's defence with help from Gautam Gambhir and prepared the groundwork for MS Dhoni's fine knock of 91 which led India to victory on that memorable evening in Mumbai.

He is a talented cricketer, who has devoted himself to fitness through which he picks up the length early and moves backwards or forward in the most abrupt manner which holds the key to putting up a great performance in real terms. He reads the line early too and as an outcome, his reaction is swift too.

When our regular captain MS Dhoni ailed from an injury, Kohli's name appeared as stand-in captain for the first Test to be played at Adelaide in the Border-Gavaskar trophy.

He continued his emphatic run-scoring in the World T20, hitting the ball around and running like a man with a spirit in him and ridiculous ease. Indeed, it troubles the heart that he fell short of making it to the "Player of the tournament" occasion for the second successive Twenty20 World Cup; which is a distinction he would have gladly mingled with.

During the 2016 edition of the Indian Premier League, he went on to pile up 973 runs, which is still a record in the tournament history, resulting Royal Challengers Bangalore (RCB) franchise managed to a runners-up finish.

India toured South Africa in early 2018, which was a major testing occasion overseas since Australia tour 2014 and everyone was keen to find Virat's approach against the new ball. He was shielded from the new ball by a stoic Vijay and promising Pujara until now. But then, owing to thirst for runs and to migrate from "good" to "great", Virat Kohli had to clear the mist about his uneasiness with the new ball as well as about his overall capability.

In 2019, during the ODI World Cup, he captained India and became the fastest player to reach 20,000 international runs, though the team exited in the semifinals. In 2022, Kohli stepped down from India's Test captaincy. Despite a challenging period, he achieved his 50th ODI century in 2023, becoming the second player after Sachin Tendulkar to do so. In 2024, he announced his retirement from T20 internationals after leading India to a World Cup victory.

❑❑❑

2506